"Scott Kellum's look at the book of Act
contribution of the Greek to understan
does an excellent job of interacting with .... and with the voices of commentators about it with an eye to cultural context, the meaning of words, and its resultant
theology. For those who love to dig into the text, this is a solid resource."

—Darrell L. Bock, executive director of cultural engagement and senior research
professor of New Testament studies, Dallas Theological Seminary

"Kellum's exegetical guide to Acts is an extraordinary resource. I have heard seminary
alumni many times bemoan the fact that they did not keep up with their Greek after
graduating. This book was the aid they needed to help them do so, but they can still
profit much from consulting it now. The Greek of Acts may be less inviting since it
is more literary, less vernacular, and colored with Semitisms, but Kellum is an adept
guide who clears the way for a fresh grasp of what Luke actually writes. I cannot see
persons seriously studying, preaching, or teaching Acts without this companion by
their side."

—David E. Garland, professor of Christian Scriptures, George W. Truett Theological
Seminary, Baylor University

"Dr. Kellum powerfully examines a powerful book. This commentary is both precise
and practical. If a preacher's aim is to get it right and make it stick, this is a very useful
tool."

—Andrew P. Hopper, lead pastor, Mercy Hill Church, Greensboro, NC

"Most students in graduate theological education learn Greek by reading the letters of
John or Paul. When they reach the Greek of Acts, they find themselves grammatically
lost. This helpful commentary by Scott Kellum will serve as a helpful introduction into
the Lukan writings."

—Osvaldo Padilla, professor of divinity, Beeson Divinity School, Samford University

"Teachers, preachers, and students of the Greek text of Acts who aim to faithfully
proclaim Jesus's continuing work in the book of Acts notoriously face several interpretive challenges, one of which is understanding the Greek text of Acts! Scott Kellum's
EGGNT volume is now the go-to resource for negotiating the complex details of the
text of Acts. Combining clarity with concise and careful analysis of the grammatical,
syntactical, and interpretive options, Kellum has provided an excellent guide to the
riches of God's Word. Highly recommended."

—Alan J. Thompson, lecturer in New Testament, Sydney Missionary and Bible
College, Australia

The Exegetical Guide to the Greek New Testament

Volumes Available

Matthew	Charles L. Quarles
Mark	Joel F. Williams
Luke	Alan J. Thompson
John	Murray J. Harris
Acts	L. Scott Kellum
Romans	John D. Harvey
2 Corinthians	Colin G. Kruse
Ephesians	Benjamin L. Merkle
Philippians	Joseph H. Hellerman
Colossians, Philemon	Murray J. Harris
Hebrews	Dana M. Harris
James	Chris A. Vlachos
1 Peter	Greg W. Forbes

Forthcoming Volumes

1 Corinthians	Jay E. Smith
Galatians	David A. Croteau
1–2 Thessalonians	David W. Chapman
1–2 Timothy, Titus	Ray Van Neste
2 Peter, Jude	Terry L. Wilder
1–3 John	Robert L. Plummer
Revelation	Alexander Stewart

EXEGETICAL
GUIDE TO THE
GREEK
NEW
TESTAMENT

ACTS

L. Scott Kellum

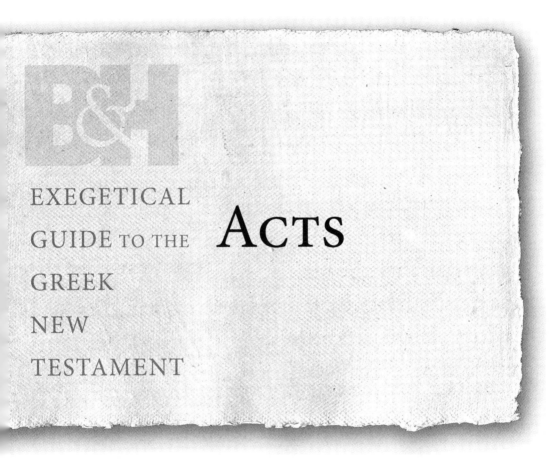

EXEGETICAL
GUIDE TO THE ACTS
GREEK
NEW
TESTAMENT

Andreas J. Köstenberger
Robert W. Yarbrough
GENERAL EDITORS

ACADEMIC
Nashville, Tennessee

Exegetical Guide to the Greek New Testament: Acts

Copyright © 2020 by L. Scott Kellum

Published by B&H Academic

Nashville, Tennessee

All rights reserved.

ISBN: 978–1–4336–7604–8

Dewey Decimal Classification: 226.6

Subject Heading: BIBLE. N.T. ACTS—STUDY AND
TEACHING / BIBLE. N.T. ACTS—CRITICISM

The Greek text of Acts is from *The Greek New Testament*, Fifth Revised Edition,
edited by Barbara Aland, Kurt Aland, Johannes Karavidopoulos, Carlo M. Martini,
and Bruce M. Metzger in cooperation with the Institute for New Testament Textual
Research, Munster/Westphalia, © 2014 Deutsche Bibelgescllschaft, Stuttgart. Used
by permission.

Printed in the United States of America

1 2 3 4 5 6 7 8 9 10 VP 25 24 23 22 21 20

For Roy Lee Groner, my father-in-law,
who went to be with the risen Christ
as I was working on Acts 26:8,
"Why do any of you consider it incredible
that God raises the dead?"

I'll spend the rest of my life
trying to be half the man of God you were, Pops.

Contents

ACTS

Acknowledgments

This work has been a great privilege to produce. There are quite a number to whom I owe thanks. I want to thank Andreas Köstenberger for offering me the opportunity to contribute to this series. I have found the other volumes tremendously helpful in my own ministry; my prayer is that this one is as well. I have loved the series since Murray Harris first began it many years ago. I am humbled to participate in it.

I want to thank Dr. Harris for reimagining the commentary genre. This work would not exist without his ingenuity. Thanks also to the general editors, Andreas Köstenberger and Robert Yarbrough, for their support in producing this commentary. The Southeastern Baptist Theological Seminary's board of trustees was very gracious in granting me a sabbatical to complete this work; without it, I would not have finished. Thank you, gentlemen. I want to publicly thank Chris Thompson and the team at B&H for their support during the death of my father-in-law while the work was in progress. Finally, graduate students never get enough credit. Thanks to Jimmy Roh, Bradley Johnson, and Levi Baker for their help.

My precious bride, Cathy, gets the bulk of my thanks. She has labored with me, comforted, and encouraged along the way. I am forever grateful for her and our children.

My prayer is that this work will inspire many others to dig into the treasure that is the book of Acts; to preach its contents with anointing and boldness; and to take the gospel to the ends of the earth.

Publisher's Preface

It is with great excitement that we publish this volume of the Exegetical Guide to the Greek New Testament series. When the founding editor, Dr. Murray J. Harris, came to us seeking a new publishing partner, we gratefully accepted the offer. With the help of the coeditor, Andreas J. Köstenberger, we spent several years working together to acquire all of the authors we needed to complete the series. By God's grace we succeeded and contracted the last author in 2011. Originally working with another publishing house, Murray's efforts spanned more than twenty years. As God would have it, shortly after the final author was contracted, Murray decided God wanted him to withdraw as coeditor of the series. God made clear to him that he must devote his full attention to taking care of his wife, who faces the daily challenges caused by multiple sclerosis.

Over the course of many years, God has used Murray to teach his students how to properly exegete the Scriptures. He is an exceptional scholar and professor. But even more importantly, Murray is a man dedicated to serving Christ. His greatest joy is to respond in faithful obedience when his Master calls. "There can be no higher and more ennobling privilege than to have the Lord of the universe as one's Owner and Master and to be his accredited representative on earth."[1] Murray has once again heeded the call of his Master.

It is our privilege to dedicate the Exegetical Guide to the Greek New Testament series to Dr. Murray J. Harris. We pray that our readers will continue the work he started.

B&H Academic

---

1. Murray J. Harris, *Slave of Christ: A New Testament Metaphor for Total Devotion to Christ* (Downers Grove, IL: InterVarsity Press, 1999), 155.

General Introduction to the EGGNT Series

Studying the New Testament in the original Greek has become easier in recent years. Beginning students will work their way through an introductory grammar or other text, but then what? Grappling with difficult verb forms, rare vocabulary, and grammatical irregularities remains a formidable task for those who would advance beyond the initial stages of learning Greek to master the interpretive process. Intermediate grammars and grammatical analyses can help, but such tools, for all their value, still often operate at a distance from the Greek text itself, and analyses are often too brief to be genuinely helpful.

The Exegetical Guide to the Greek New Testament (EGGNT) aims to close the gap between the Greek text and the available tools. Each EGGNT volume aims to provide all the necessary information for understanding the Greek text and, in addition, includes homiletical helps and suggestions for further study. The EGGNT is not a full-scale commentary. Nevertheless, these guides will make interpreting a given New Testament book easier, in particular for those who are hard-pressed for time and yet want to preach or teach with accuracy and authority.

In terms of layout, each volume begins with a brief introduction to the particular book (including such matters as authorship, date, etc.), a basic outline, and a list of recommended commentaries. At the end of each volume, you will find a comprehensive exegetical outline of the book. The body of each volume is devoted to paragraph-by-paragraph exegesis of the text. The treatment of each paragraph includes:

1. The Greek text of the passage, phrase by phrase, from the fifth edition of the United Bible Societies' *Greek New Testament* (UBS[5]).

2. A structural analysis of the passage. Typically, verbal discussion of the structure of a given unit is followed by a diagram, whereby the verbal discussion serves to explain the diagram and the diagram serves to provide a visual aid illumining the structural discussion. While there is no one correct or standard way to diagram Greek sentences, the following format is typically followed in EGGNT volumes:

a. The original Greek word order is maintained.

b. When Greek words are omitted, this is indicated by ellipses (. . .).

c. The diagramming method, moving from left to right, is predicated on the following. In clauses with a finite verb, the default order is typically verb-subject-object. In verbless clauses or clauses with nonfinite verb forms, the default order is typically subject-(verb)-object. Departures from these default orders are understood to be pragmatically motivated (e.g., contrast, emphasis, etc.).

d. Indents are used to indicate subordination (e.g., in the case of dependent clauses).

e. Retaining original word order, modifiers are centered above or below the word they modify (e.g., a prepositional phrase in relation to the verb).

f. Where a given sentence or clause spans multiple lines of text, drawn lines are used, such as where a relative pronoun introduces a relative clause (often shifting emphasis).

g. Underline is used to indicate imperatives; dotted underline is used to indicate repetition (the same word or cognate used multiple times in a given unit); the symbol ⁞ may be used where an article is separated from a noun or participle by interjected material (such as a prepositional phrase).

h. In shorter letters diagrams are normally provided for every unit; in longer letters and Revelation, ellipses may be used to show less detail in diagramming (keeping larger blocks together on the same line) in order to focus primarily on the larger structure of a given unit; in the Gospels and Acts, detailed diagrams will usually not be provided, though less detailed diagrams may be used to illustrate important or more complex structural aspects of a given passage.

3. A discussion of each phrase of the passage with discussion of relevant vocabulary, significant textual variants, and detailed grammatical analysis, including parsing. When more than one solution is given for a particular exegetical issue, the author's own preference is indicated by an asterisk (*). When no preference is expressed, the options are judged to be evenly balanced, or it is assumed that the text is intentionally ambiguous. When a particular verb form may be parsed in more than one way, only the parsing appropriate in the specific context is supplied; but where there is difference of opinion among grammarians or commentators, both possibilities are given and the matter is discussed.

4. Various translations of significant words or phrases.

5. A list of suggested topics for further study with bibliography for each topic. An asterisk (*) in one of the "For Further Study" bibliographies draws attention to a discussion of the particular topic that is recommended as a useful introduction to the issues involved.

6. Homiletical suggestions designed to help the preacher or teacher move from the Greek text to a sermon outline that reflects careful exegesis. The first

suggestion for a particular paragraph of the text is always more exegetical than homiletical and consists of an outline of the entire paragraph. These detailed outlines of each paragraph build on the general outline proposed for the whole book and, if placed side by side, form a comprehensive exegetical outline of the book. All outlines are intended to serve as a basis for sermon preparation and should be adapted to the needs of a particular audience.[1]

The EGGNT volumes will serve a variety of readers. Those reading the Greek text for the first time may be content with the assistance with vocabulary, parsing, and translation. Readers with some experience in Greek may want to skip or skim these sections and focus attention on the discussions of grammar. More advanced students may choose to pursue the topics and references to technical works under "For Further Study," while pastors may be more interested in the movement from grammatical analysis to sermon outline. Teachers may appreciate having a resource that frees them to focus on exegetical details and theological matters.

The editors are pleased to present you with the individual installments of the EGGNT. We are grateful for each of the contributors who has labored long and hard over each phrase in the Greek New Testament. Together we share the conviction that "all Scripture is inspired by God and is profitable for teaching, for rebuking, for correcting, for training in righteousness" (2 Tim 3:16 CSB) and echo Paul's words to Timothy: "Be diligent to present yourself to God as one approved, a worker who doesn't need to be ashamed, correctly teaching the word of truth" (2 Tim 2:15).

Thanks to Michael Naylor, who served as assistant editor for this volume.

Andreas J. Köstenberger
Robert W. Yarbrough

---

1. As a Bible publisher, B&H Publishing follows the "Colorado Springs Guidelines for Translation of Gender-Related Language in Scripture." As an academic book publisher, B&H Academic asks that authors conform their manuscripts (including EGGNT exegetical outlines in English) to the B&H Academic style guide, which affirms the use of singular "he/his/him" as generic examples encompassing both genders. However, in their discussion of the Greek text, EGGNT authors have the freedom to analyze the text and reach their own conclusions regarding whether specific Greek words are gender specific or gender inclusive.

Abbreviations

For abbreviations used in discussion of text-critical matters, the reader should refer to the abbreviations listed in the Introduction to the United Bible Societies' *Greek New Testament*.

*	indicates the reading of the original hand of a manuscript as opposed to subsequent correctors of the manuscript, *or*
	indicates the writer's own preference when more than one solution is given for a particular exegetical problem, *or*
	in the "For Further Study" bibliographies, indicates a discussion of the particular topic that is recommended as a useful introduction to the issues involved
§, §§	paragraph, paragraphs

Books of the Old Testament

Gen	Genesis	Song	Song of Songs (Canticles)
Exod	Exodus	Isa	Isaiah
Lev	Leviticus	Jer	Jeremiah
Num	Numbers	Lam	Lamentations
Deut	Deuteronomy	Ezek	Ezekiel
Josh	Joshua	Dan	Daniel
Judg	Judges	Hos	Hosea
Ruth	Ruth	Joel	Joel
1–2 Sam	1–2 Samuel	Amos	Amos
1–2 Kgs	1–2 Kings	Obad	Obadiah
1–2 Chr	1–2 Chronicles	Jonah	Jonah
Ezra	Ezra	Mic	Micah
Neh	Nehemiah	Nah	Nahum
Esth	Esther	Hab	Habakkuk
Job	Job	Zeph	Zephaniah
Ps(s)	Psalm(s)	Hag	Haggai
Prov	Proverbs	Zech	Zechariah
Eccl	Ecclesiastes	Mal	Malachi

Books of the New Testament

Matt	Matthew	1–2 Thess	1–2 Thessalonians
Mark	Mark	1–2 Tim	1–2 Timothy
Luke	Luke	Titus	Titus
John	John	Phlm	Philemon
Acts	Acts	Heb	Hebrews
Rom	Romans	Jas	James
1–2 Cor	1–2 Corinthians	1–2 Pet	1–2 Peter
Gal	Galatians	1–3 John	1–3 John
Eph	Ephesians	Jude	Jude
Phil	Philippians	Rev	Revelation
Col	Colossians		

Dead Sea Scrolls

1QpHab	*Pesher Habakkuk*
1QS	*Rule of the Community*
4Q175	*Testimonia* (AKA 4QTest)
CD	*Damascus Document*

Josephus

| *Ant.* | *Antiquities of the Jews* |
| *J.W.* | *The Jewish War* |

General Abbreviations

ABD	*The Anchor Bible Dictionary*, 6 vols., ed. D. N. Freedman (New York: Doubleday, 1992)
abs.	absolute(ly)
acc(s).	accusative(s)
act.	active(s) (voice)
adj(s).	adjective(s), adjectival(ly)
adv(s).	adverb(s), adverbial(ly)
advers.	adversative
anar.	anarthrous
aor.	aorist
apod.	apodosis
appos.	apposition, appositive, appositional
Aram.	Aramaic, Aramaism
art.	(definite) article, articular
attend. circum.	attendant circumstance
attrib.	attributive

AUSS	*Andrews University Seminary Studies*
BAFCS	*The Book of Acts in Its First Century Setting*, 5 vols., ed. Bruce W. Winter (Grand Rapids: Eerdmans, 1993–1996)
Barrett	C. K. Barrett, *The Acts of the Apostles*, 2 vols., ICC (London: T&T Clark, 1994–1998)
BASHH	C. J. Hemer, *The Book of Acts in the Setting of Hellenistic History*, ed. C. H. Gempf, WUNT 49 (Tübingen: J. C. B. Mohr [Paul Siebeck], 1989)
BBR	*Bulletin for Biblical Research*
BDAG	*Greek-English Lexicon of the New Testament and Other Early Christian Literature*, rev. and ed. F. W. Danker (Chicago/London: University of Chicago, 2000), based on W. Bauer's *Griechisch-deutsches Wörterbuch* (6th ed.) and on previous English ed. by W. F. Arndt, F. W. Gingrich, and F. W. Danker. References to BDAG are by page number and quadrant on the page, *a* indicating the upper half and *b* the lower half of the left-hand column, and c and *d* the upper and lower halves of the right-hand column. With the use of dark type, biblical references are now clearly visible within each subsection.
BDF	F. Blass and A. Debrunner, *A Greek Grammar of the New Testament and Other Early Christian Literature*, tr. and rev. R. W. Funk (Chicago: University of Chicago Press, 1961)
Beale and Carson	G. K. Beale and D. A. Carson, eds., *Commentary on the New Testament Use of the Old Testament* (Grand Rapids: Baker/Nottingham: Apollos, 2007)
Beginnings	K. Lake, *The Beginnings of Christianity: Part 1: The Acts of the Apostles,* ed. F. J. Foakes-Jackson and K. Lake, 5 vols. (London: MacMillan, 1933)
BHGNT	Baylor Handbook on the Greek New Testament
Bib	*Biblica*
BibInt	*Biblical Interpretation*
BSac	*Bibliotheca Sacra*
byz.	The Byzantine Text Type (the Majority Text)
c.	circa (Lat.), about
CBQ	*Catholic Biblical Quarterly*
CCC	A. J. Köstenberger, L. S. Kellum, and C. L. Quarles, *The Cradle, the Cross, and the Crown,* 2nd ed. (Nashville: B&H Academic, 2016)
CEB	Common English Bible (2010, 2011)
cf.	*confer* (Lat.), compare
CGk.	Classical Greek
ch(s).	chapter(s)

CIL	*Corpus Inscriptionum Latinarum*
colloq.	colloquial(ism)
comp.	comparative, compare(d), comparing, comparison
compl(s).	complementary, complement(s)
ConcorJ	*Concordia Journal*
cond.	condition(al)
conj.	conjunctive, conjunction
consec.	consecutive
contr.	contrast
cop.	copula; copulative
CSB	Christian Standard Bible (2017)
cstr.	construction, construe(d)
dat(s).	dative(s)
decl.	declension, decline
def.	definite(ly); definition
delib.	deliberative
descr.	description, descriptive
dimin.	diminutive
dir.	direct
*DJG*²	*Dictionary of Jesus and the Gospels*, ed. J. B. Green, S. McKnight, J. K. Brown, and N. Perrin, 2nd ed. (Leicester, UK: InterVarsity Press, 2013)
DLNT	*Dictionary of the Later New Testament and Its Developments*, ed. R. P. Martin and P. H. Davids (Leicester, UK: InterVarsity Press, 1997)
DNTB	*Dictionary of New Testament Background*, ed. C. A. Evans and S. E. Porter (Leicester, UK: InterVarsity Press, 2000)
DPL	*Dictionary of Paul and His Letters*, ed. G. F. Hawthorne, R. P. Martin, and D. G. Reid (Leicester, UK: InterVarsity Press, 1993)
DSD	*Dead Sea Discoveries*
Eccl. Hist.	*Ecclesiastical History* (Eusebius)
ed(s).	edited, edition(s), editor(s)
e.g.	*exempli gratia* (Lat.), for example
encl.	enclitic
Eng.	English
epex.	epexegetic, epexegetical
esp.	especially

ESV	English Standard Version (2001)
et al.	*et alii* (Lat.), and others
etym.	etymology, etymologically
EVV	English versions of the Bible
ExpTim	*Expository Times*
fem.	feminine
f(f).	and the following (verse[s] or page[s])
fig.	figurative(ly)
freq.	frequently
fut.	future
gen(s).	genitive(s)
Gk.	Greek
Haenchen	E. Haenchen, *The Acts of the Apostles,* tr. B. Noble and G. Shinn, H. Anderson, rev. R. McL. Wilson (Philadelphia: Westminster, 1971)
Harris	M. J. Harris, *Prepositions and Theology in the Greek New Testament* (Grand Rapids: Zondervan, 2012)
HCSB	Holman Christian Standard Bible (1999)
Heb.	Hebrew, Hebraism, Hebraic
Hengel Ἰουδαία	"Ἰουδαία in the Geographical List of Acts 2:9–11 and Syria as 'Greater Judea,'" *BBR* 10 (2000): 161–180
HGk.	Hellenistic Greek
	ibidem (Lat.), in the same place
Holmes	Michael W. Holmes, *The Apostolic Fathers: Greek Texts and English Translations*, updated ed. (Grand Rapids: Baker, 1999)
i.e.	*id est* (Lat.), that is
impers.	impersonal
impf.	imperfect (tense)
impv.	imperative(s) (mood), imperatival(ly)
incl.	including, inclusive
indecl.	indeclinable
indef.	indefinite
indic.	indicative (mood)
indir.	indirect
inf(s).	infinitive(s)
instr.	instrument, instrumental(ly)
interr.	interrogative

intrans.	intransitive
iter.	iterative
JBL	*Journal of Biblical Literature*
JETS	*Journal of the Evangelical Theological Society*
JSJ	*Journal for the Study of Judaism in the Persian, Hellenistic, and Roman Period*
JSNT	*Journal for the Study of the New Testament*
JTC	*Journal for Theology and the Church*
JTS	*Journal of Theological Studies*
Jub.	*Book of Jubilees*
Keener	C. S. Keener, *Acts: An Exegetical Commentary*, 4 vols. (Grand Rapids: Baker Academic, 2012–2015)
KJV	King James Version (= "Authorized Version"; 1611)
KMP	A. J. Köstenberger, B. Merkle, R. L. Plummer, *Going Deeper with New Testament Greek: An Intermediate Study of the Grammar and Syntax of the New Testament* (Nashville: B&H Academic, 2016)
Levinsohn	S. Levinsohn, *Discourse Features of New Testament Greek: A Coursebook on the Information Structure of New Testament Greek,* 2nd ed. (Dallas: SIL, 2000)
lit.	literal(ly)
LN	J. P. Louw and E. A. Nida, eds., *Introduction and Domains*, vol. 1 of *Greek-English Lexicon of the New Testament Based on Semantic Domains* (New York: United Bible Societies, 1988)
LNTS	Library of New Testament Studies
locat.	locative, locatival(ly)
LXX	Septuagint (= Greek Old Testament)
m	Mishnah
masc.	masculine
mat.	material
Metzger	B. M. Metzger, *A Textual Commentary on the Greek New Testament* (Stuttgart: Deutsche Bibelgesellschaft/New York: United Bible Societies, 1994). The original edition of 1971 is based on UBS.[3]
mg.	margin
mid.	middle
Midr.	Midrash
MIT	The Idiomatic Translation of the New Testament (2012)

MM	J. H. Moulton and G. Milligan, *The Vocabulary of the Greek Testament Illustrated from the Papyri and Other Non-Literary Sources* (Grand Rapids: Eerdmans, 1972, repr. of 1930 ed.)
mng(s).	meaning(s)
Moulton	J. H. Moulton, *Prolegomena*, vol. 1 of *A Grammar of New Testament Greek*, ed. J. H. Moulton (Edinburgh: T&T Clark, 1908)
ms(s).	manuscript(s)
MT	Masoretic text
NASB	New American Standard Bible (1995)
neg.	negative, negation, negated
Neot	*Neotestamentica*
NET	New English Translation Bible (2005)
neut.	neuter
New Docs	Horsley, G. H. R., *New Documents Illustrating Early Christianity: A Review of the Greek Inscriptions and Papyri* (Grand Rapids: Eerdmans, 1987)
NICNT	Bruce, F. F., *The Book of the Acts*, rev. ed., New International Commentary on the New Testament (Grand Rapids: Eerdmans, 1988)
NIDNTTE	Silva, M. ed., *New International Dictionary of New Testament Theology and Exegesis* (Grand Rapids: Zondervan, 2014)
NIV	New International Version (2011)
NJB	New Jerusalem Bible (1985)
NKJV	New King James Version (1982)
NLT	New Living Translation of the Bible (1996)
nom(s).	nominative(s)
NovT	*Novum Testamentum*
NRSV	New Revised Standard Version (1990)
NT	New Testament
NTS	*New Testament Studies*
NTTS	New Testament Tools and Studies
obj(s).	object(s), objective
opt.	optative
orig.	origin, original(ly)
OT	Old Testament
p(p).	page(s)
part.	partitive
pass.	passive

periph.	periphrastic
pers.	person(al)
pf.	perfect (tense)
pl(s).	plural(s)
plpf.	pluperfect (tense)
Polhill	J. B. Polhill, *Acts*, New American Commentary, vol. 26 (Nashville: Broadman, 1992)
poss.	possessive, possession
pred.	predicate, predicative
pref.	prefix
prep.	preposition(al)
pres.	present
prog.	progressive
pron(s).	pronoun(s), pronominal
prot.	protasis
PRSt	*Perspectives in Religious Studies*
ptc(s).	participle(s), participial(ly)
purp.	purpose
R	A. T. Robertson, *A Grammar of the Greek New Testament in the Light of Historical Research,* 4th ed. (Nashville: Broadman, 1934)
RB	*Revue Biblique*
rdg(s).	(textual) reading(s)
ref.	reference(s), referring
refl.	reflexive
rel.	relative
rep.	represents; represented
rev.	revised, reviser, revision
Rhoads	J. H. Rhoads, "Josephus Misdated the Census of Quirinius," *JETS* 54 (2011): 65–87.
Robertson, *Pictures*	A. T. Robertson, *Pictures in the New Testament*, 6 vols. (Nashville: Broadman, 1930–33)
RSV	Revised Standard Version (1952)
RTR	*The Reformed Theological Review*
Runge	S. Runge, *Discourse Grammar of the Greek New Testament: A Practical Introduction for Teaching and Exegesis* (Peabody, MA: Hendrickson, 2010)
Sanh.	Mishna *Sanhedrin*

SE	*Studia Evangelica*
Sem.	Semitic, Semitism
sg.	singular
sim.	similar(ly), similarity
SNTSMS	Society for New Testament Studies Monograph Series
SR	*Studies in Religion*
ST	*Studia Theologica*
str.	structure
Str-B	H. L. Strack and P. Billerbeck, *Kommentar zum Neuen Testament aus Talmud und Midrasch,* 6 vols. (Beck: Munich, 1922–1961)
subj(s).	subject(s), subjective
subjunc(s).	subjunctive(s)
subord.	subordinate, subordination
subst.	substantive, substantival(ly)
superl.	superlative
SW	A. N. Sherwin-White, *Roman Society and Roman Law in the New Testament: The Sarum Lectures 1960–1961* (Oxford: Oxford University Press, 1963)
T	N. Turner, *Syntax*, vol. 3 of *A Grammar of New Testament Greek*, ed. J. H. Moulton (Edinburgh: T&T Clark, 1963)
TBT	*Theologische Bücherei*
TDNT	*Theological Dictionary of the New Testament*, 10 vols., ed. G. Kittel and G. Friedrich, tr. G. W. Bromiley (Grand Rapids: Eerdmans, 1964–74)
temp.	temporal(ly)
Thompson	Alan Thompson, *Luke*, Exegetical Guide to the Greek New Testament (Nashville: B&H Academic, 2016)
Thrall	M. E. Thrall, *Greek Particles in the New Testament* (Leiden: Brill, 1962)
TNIV	Today's New International Version, New Testament (2001)
TR	Textus Receptus (Lat., Received Text)
tr.	translate(d), translator, translation(s)
trans.	transitive
Turner, *Insights*	N. Turner, *Grammatical Insights into the New Testament* (Edinburgh: T&T Clark, 1965)
Turner, *Style*	N. Turner, *Style*, vol. 4 of *A Grammar of New Testament Greek*, ed. J. H. Moulton (Edinburgh: T&T Clark, 1976)
Tyn	*Tyndale Bulletin*

UBS/UBS[5]	*The Greek New Testament*, ed. B. Aland, K. Aland, J. Karavidopoulos, C. M. Martini, and B. M. Metzger, 5th rev. ed. (Stuttgart: Deutsche Bibelgesellschaft/ New York: United Bible Societies, 2014); 1st ed. 1966 (= UBS[1]); 2nd ed. 1968 (= UBS[2]); 3rd ed. 1975 (=UBS[3]); 4th ed. 1993 (=UBS[4])
v(v).	verse(s)
var(s).	variant (form or reading)
vb(s).	verb(s)
voc(s).	vocative(s), vocatival
vol(s).	volume(s)
Vulg.	Vulgate (= Bible in Latin)
Wallace	D. B. Wallace, *Greek Grammar beyond the Basics. An Exegetical Syntax of the New Testament* (Grand Rapids: Zondervan, 1996)
Wis	*Wisdom of Solomon*
WUNT	Wissenschaftliche Untersuchungen zum Alten und Neuen Testament
Z	M. Zerwick, *Biblical Greek Illustrated by Examples*, tr. J. Smith (Rome: Pontifical Biblical Institute, 1963)
ZG	M. Zerwick and M. Grosvenor, *A Grammatical Analysis of the Greek New Testament,* 5th rev. ed. (Rome: Pontifical Biblical Institute, 1996)
ZNW	*Zeitschrift für die neutestamentliche Wissenschaft und die Kunde der älteren Kirche*

ACTS

Introduction

AUTHORSHIP

The traditional view is that Luke, a companion of Paul, wrote both the Gospel of Luke and the book of Acts. If so, Paul referred to this Luke three times in the NT (Col 4:14; 2 Tim 4:11; Phlm 24), and Luke obliquely referred to himself repeatedly in the book of Acts in the "we passages." Whoever this Luke was, the preface to the Gospel, to go no further, displays a refined use of the Gk. language that points to an author who was well educated (see H. J. Cadbury, *The Style and Literary Method of Luke* [Cambridge, MA: Harvard University Press, 1920]). It is apparent the author was male (self-references are in the masc. gender), that he had access to a variety of sources about the life of Jesus and the early church, that he was not an eyewitness of Jesus's ministry, and that he had the opportunity to investigate the story of Jesus and the apostles at length.

The strongest internal evidence for Lukan authorship is the so-called we passages in Acts (places where the narrative shifts to a first-person-plural reference, 16:10–17; 20:5–15; 21:1–18; 27:1–28:16). The most natural understanding of these references is that they suggest the author was traveling with Paul, a view attested as early as Irenaeus (c. 130–200; see *Against Heresies* 3.1.2).

Not all would agree, though. C. J. Hemer lists three alternative views (see BASHH 312–13). First, many see the "we passages" as reflecting a source composed by the author himself, a travel diary of sorts. Although this is possible, the theory is impossible to prove and may be based on the (now largely discarded) assumption that all sources must be written. Second, some argue the "we passages" are from a travel diary written by someone other than the author. Yet if these sections are from someone else's diary, Luke has stamped his unique style on all but the first-person-plural pronouns. It does not seem likely that such would escape his notice. Third, many suggest that these sections are merely literary devices. If this is true, the writer would be so subtle as to confuse (if not mislead) part of his audience.

When eliminating those named in the "we sections" (assuming the author did not use a third person reference to himself alongside a first-person reference) and cross-referencing those named by Paul's letters composed at the time we may reduce the candidates to just a few. Of these, Luke, the beloved physician of Col 4:14, is the most viable option (see D. A. Carson and D. Moo, *An Introduction to the New Testament,* 2nd ed. [Grand Rapids: Zondervan, 2005], 204–5). Combining this with the universal opinion of the early church that Luke, Paul's companion, wrote Acts and the Gospel of Luke makes the claim compelling. Most scholars today who reject Lukan authorship do so on the contention that Luke's theology and historical detail differ substantially from Paul's. Many are willing to see a "Luke" as the author of the Gospel but one who was not a disciple of Paul and who wrote after the year 70.

DATE

Scholars have proposed three basic positions on the date of Acts: (1) a date prior to 70 (see, e.g., Bock 27, who prefers a date just before AD 70); (2) a date between 70 and 100 (see, e.g., Keener 1:400. For Keener, a late date for Mark, synoptic solutions, and a date during the lifetime of an eyewitness necessitate this date.); (3) a date in the second century (see, e.g., M. C. Parsons, *Acts,* Paideia Commentary on the New Testament [Grand Rapids: Baker, 2008], 3, 17).

I am convinced that an early date is the best option for the following five reasons.

1. The presentation of the Roman Empire is downright disturbing for a date after Nero. It has long been noted that Luke's presentation on the Empire is rather even-handed, if not neutral/friendly. The church never forgot that Nero was the first to raise the sword against her (AD 64–68). After that the church in the Empire (rightly) took the position of skepticism about the intentions of those holding the imperium while trying to maintain the position of good citizen. The implication in Acts (expecting justice and/or exoneration from Caesar; see Acts 25:11, 26:32) is hard to explain after Nero.

Witherington rightly notes that the climate of the Flavians (AD 69–96) treated eulogies of the victims of the emperors as a capital crime (Witherington 62). He goes on to suggest the state of the text of Acts (see below) was due to them persecuting and burning Luke's work for eulogizing Peter, Paul, and Jesus, who had been executed. He does so defending a date in the 70s for Acts. I find Witherington's argument compelling for a date in the early 60s rather than the 70s. Why would Luke write such a book in such a climate? In such a climate, would Luke be so neutral about Rome? Would he have been tempted to be over-the-top positive?

2. Acts makes no mention of Paul's letters. It is unthinkable that a late document dealing so extensively with Paul would not make reference to Paul's epistolary production. For example, the *Acts of Paul* (c. AD 160 apocryphal Acts) pictures Paul as a letter writer and includes a letter to the Corinthians (with allusions to 1 Corinthians) that is labeled "3 Corinthians." Clearly the author(s) are well aware of the Pauline corpus. In contrast, the book of Acts makes no mention that Paul ever wrote a letter. This phenomenon is far more likely early than late.

3. Luke mentions no events after c. AD 62. This includes the deaths of James the Just, Peter, and Paul. In matters of world history, the following go unmentioned: the great fire of Rome and subsequent persecution (AD 64); the death of Nero (AD 68); the year of the four emperors (68–69); the installment of emperors Vespasian (69) and Titus (79); the falls of Jerusalem (70) and Masada (73); the eruption of Vesuvius (79; it

killed Drusilla, wife of Felix—see Acts 24:24). The provinces were restructured under Vespasian in AD 72; Acts reflects the earlier terminology (BASHH 381), without any clarification. Although these lie outside of the narrative chronology, one could easily expect a clarification or side note on any of these issues.

4. Hemer noted an air of immediacy about the book (BASHH 365). The events recorded do not seem to be records of long-ago events. For example, one would expect a sailing narrative to be "reduced and schematized," as Hemer puts it, if the events had been resting in the author's mind for some time. This is not what we see in Acts 27. Furthermore, the earlier scenes (some nearly thirty years before the events at the end of the book) do show such refinement. It would make sense that the latter, less polished scenes were more recent (BASHH 366). Witherington (61) rightly notes that Acts does not appear to be looking at a bygone age.

5. The ending of Acts is rather abrupt. Some have suggested Luke has finished his literary purposes to show the gospel getting to Rome. This is undoubtedly true, but completion of the literary purpose does not explain ending at the point he does. Why not tell us what happened to Paul? His death would not dilute the completion. The gospel is unhindered by the death of saints (see Acts 7:60; 12:2). Further ministry would not diminish it either. It seems better to explain the ending by setting the date of composition during this imprisonment. Thus, I find an early date the most compelling (c. AD 62–63).

PROVENANCE

If the evidence for the date has been rightly evaluated, the only option for the provenance of the book is the city of Rome. If Luke had caught up in time with Paul so that the apostle was awaiting trial in Rome at the time of writing, and if the "we sections" are an indication of personal involvement, then Luke was with Paul when he wrote the book.

PURPOSE AND AUDIENCE

The purpose of Acts is not directly stated in the book. The preface (1:1–5) addresses the former book (Luke) about what Jesus began to do. The implication is that this book is about what Jesus continues to do. If the preface to Luke applies to Acts as well—and given the brevity of Acts' preface, this is most likely the case—then Luke set out to write an orderly account and to provide assurance and an apology or defense of the Christian faith.

The contents of the book demonstrate an emphasis that the gospel goes to the ends of the earth (represented by Rome) at the command and empowerment of Christ. The narrative revolves around showing the early expansion of the church from a local sect to a worldwide movement as empowered by God. Each expansion is brought about by the leading of the Holy Spirit rather than by the disciples' own initiative. In this theological emphasis, the book manifests the same focus on God's plan (including promise and fulfillment) that is prominent in Luke's Gospel. This also answers the question of why a sequel to Luke's Gospel was needed in the first place. The Gospel is "about all that Jesus began to do and teach" (Acts 1:1), and Acts narrates the continuation of that which was begun in the Gospel. The story of Jesus is not complete until the gospel has moved from the Jewish capital to "the end of the earth"—all the way to Rome (Acts 1:8) and beyond.

The literary structure of the book thus points to a historical apologetic that explains God's plan of extending the gospel to the Gentiles while including believing Jews as well. While it can be surmised that Luke's target audience included non-Aramaic speakers who were familiar with the OT, the apologetic presented is wide-ranging, including the evangelism of Diaspora Jews as well as the edification of Gentile Christians who worship the Jewish Messiah whom the Jews had rejected. Luke's purpose was to write an accurate historical narrative designed to edify his Christian readers and help them evangelize unbelievers. On other matters such as genre, sources, historical reliability, and theological themes, see my essay on Acts in CCC.

NOTES TO THE READER OF ACTS IN GREEK

I had several conversations with students and laymen about the book of Acts as I was working on this commentary. Many of them had the expectation that Luke's prose was very classical in style and literary art. This has to be classified as somewhat of an evangelical urban myth (true of the prologue but not throughout the book). Oddly enough, the academy has criticized Luke in the opposite direction. These criticisms range from "vulgarisms" (de Zwann, *Beginnings* 3.33) to "solecisms" (Haenchen 682) to, at certain places, being "untranslatable" (Barrett 1.240, 521). This, too, in my opinion, is inaccurate. The difficulties are pointed out in the commentary and a solution offered. Most come in reported speeches that may suggest Luke is being faithful to his sources. So, then, the truth is somewhere between these two poles.

The reader of Acts in Gk. should expect the narrative to follow an expression of Gk. fairly standard in the literary work of the day. Luke is an example of Koinē Gk. (or HGk.) in the literary spectrum. The style spans a period from c. 330 BC to the sixth century AD. It is the result of a sort of standardization of Gk. as the result of Alexander's conquest (D. Aune, *The Westminster Dictionary of New Testament & Early Christian Literature & Rhetoric* [Philadelphia: Westminster John Knox, 2010], 207). In the first century AD an archaicizing movement began among Gk. speakers who sought to write in a style of the great writers of Greece, known as Atticism (for the Attic Gk. dialect). These writers preferred a simple, straightforward manner of expression imitating the prose and poetry of Attic writers (450–330 BC; Aune, *Christian Literature & Rhetoric*, 68). Koinē and Asianic Gk. especially tended toward more literary flourishes (Aune, 66). To judge Luke's style by the canons of the Atticists is anachronistic. Luke predates much of the Atticist movement and is clearly no Atticist in his expression (D. L. Mealand, "Hellenistic Historians and the Style of Acts," *ZNW* 82 [1991]: 42). Nor does he fit within the more florid Asianic style. So how would we describe his style?

D. L. Mealand made a noteworthy assessment of Luke's language in Acts and compared it to works of the HGk. historians like Polybius. His conclusion is worth repeating:

Acts may well at times use words and phrases condemned by the Atticists. But in doing so Acts is in the main in agreement with Polybius or his successors. There is also often some classical precedent for the usages we find in Acts. This last point must not be overstated. The aim of the Atticists was to be selective even in their following of Attic usage. Acts to a large extent ante-dates the establishment of that trend. But it is not thereby to be relegated to comparison with works of no literary standing. Rather it is in the broad mainstream of Hellenistic history writing in the instance examined (Mealand, "Hellenistic Historians," 65).

This assessment would place Luke's style somewhere along the literary Koinē spectrum. But readers should also be prepared for distinctive elements that make it somewhat unusual in places. For example, the reader of Acts in Gk. should also note that Luke had the ability to write in various styles. Nearly a century ago, Plummer noted about the author of Luke's Gospel: "He can be as Hebraistic as the LXX, and as free from Hebraisms as Plutarch. And, in the main, whether intentionally or not, he is Hebraistic in describing Hebrew society, and Greek in describing Greek society" (A. Plummer, *A Critical and Exegetical Commentary on the Gospel According to St. Luke*, 5th ed. [Edinburgh: T&T Clark, 1922], xlix). I find the pattern continues in the book of Acts.

Luke often wrote in a style reminiscent of the LXX in both narrative and speech. We particularly find the latter in Palestinian settings. For example, Jesus's use of the future ἔσεσθέ μου μάρτυρες "you will be my witnesses" at 1:8 is a Semitism expressing a command. Luke's tr. of Jesus's words gave them the appropriate Jewish flavor reflective of the event. These are rather common in Acts.

His narrative also has a LXX flavor. That is, he wrote in a "biblical style" as expressed in the Bible he knew: the LXX. He used the common ἐγένετο δέ (see 4:5) mng. "and it came to pass" throughout the narrative. He also used other words and phrases that are suggestive of the LXX. Some of these are ἰδού ("behold," see 1:10), pleonastic verbs and ptcs. (see 4:19), ὃν τρόπον ("in the way that," see 7:28), and ἀνοίξας τὸ στόμα ("having opened his mouth," see 8:35). In larger structures, Satterthwaite has noted that Luke employs conventions similar to OT narrative techniques (suggesting similar items in classical writers, BAFCS 1:360–67). These are: simple juxtaposition of scenes to make a point, analogical patterning (structural similarities between scenes), and agreement in narration and dialogue (suggesting truth and falsehood of speakers). I believe that Luke was writing in what he considered sacred writing (whether conscious or not).

Luke could also write in a way to add flavors appropriate to other settings. For example, Luke was apparently well aware of classical forensics and employed varying degrees of competence depending on the speaker (Keener 1.141). Paul's testimony before Agrippa (26:1–32) shows classical forms, a carefully crafted plan, and a host of rhetorical features (for a longer list of such forms, see Witherington 45). This is totally appropriate of Paul before the elite of Gk. society.

On the other hand, the speech by Tertullus (a Jewish prosecutor) before Felix (24:1–9) begins with a well-crafted *capitio benevolentiae*. But in the progress of the charges, it fizzles out rhetorically (see comments there). It comes across as pandering. Not only is it historically likely, but Luke has revealed his ability to demonstrate it in writing. In doing so, he highlights the trumped-up nature of the charges.

That is not to say that the entirety of the work should be considered a work of rhetoric. Luke, as a historian, worked more in the style of a straightforward Polybius rather than the rhetorical flourishes of a Livy (Witherington 43). He could, however, employ rhetorical conventions when appropriate.

Many in scholarship have suggested that the book of Acts is an unrevised document (see Barrett 2.897; Witherington 165). There are certainly, as Bruce called them, some awkward cstrs. in the book (F. F. Bruce, *The Acts of the Apostles: The Greek Text with Introduction and Commentary.* 3rd ed. [Grand Rapids: Eerdmans, 1990], 67). Some of these are, in my opinion, intentional. Some are likely due to being faithful to sources. Others, to be sure, are head-scratchers. There are not many of the latter category, but the reader of Gk. Acts should be prepared to have to work through the grammar closely on occasion.

Four other characteristics of Luke's narrative should be noted by the reader of Acts in Gk. The first two are observations by Haenchen (103–5). Luke enlivens bare facts with narrative scenes. That is, he paints the picture rather than simply stating the outcome. Thus, carefully reading the narrative for subtle clues is warranted.

Second, Luke condenses the chronology. That is, he may condense a long period of time in a single scene. Since Acts covers a period of thirty years or so, this is to be expected (and part of historiography of the time). The best example is chapter 9. When we compare the narrative to Paul's autobiographical statements, we see that Luke has compressed his narrative to only Paul in Damascus. He leaves out a visit to the Nabatean kingdom (Gal 1:17, note even Paul compresses the reference).

Third, Luke has very few theologizing or moralizing comments (BAFCS 1.360; Witherington 29). For example, he neither condemns nor excuses the rift between Paul and Barnabas over John Mark (Acts 15:39). For that matter, he has no comment on John Mark's defection. In the main, he leaves the reader to infer these matters. The reader should note well where he made such a comment (see, e.g., 5:17; 10:2; 13:45; 17:5).

Fourth, Witherington (29) notes that Luke portrays his characters in a straightforward manner. Non-Christians and Christians alike are portrayed in both negative and positive lights. For Witherington, Luke has a commitment to objectivity along the lines of Gk. historiography.

Regarding vocabulary, Acts demonstrates the vocabulary of one well-read in Gk. literature. While he is not strictly an Atticist (as noted above) his language is strongly peppered with a series of Atticisms. So what does this tell us of the man? Primarily that his language and vocabulary are that of the educated. H. J. Cadbury, responding to W. K. Hobart, demonstrated that Luke's terminology was not strictly medical (Hobart's thesis) but consistent with other works in HGk. (see, e.g., H. J. Cadbury, "Lexical Notes on Luke-Acts: II. Recent Arguments for Medical Language," *JBL*

[1926]: 190–209). Hawkins noted the rate of "non-classical" language in the book of Acts was the least in the NT, less than one-sixth (J. C. Hawkins, *Horae Synopticae: Contributions to the Study of the Synoptic Problem*, 2nd rev. ed. [Oxford: Clarendon, 1909], 207). Some of these classical words may appear for effect. For example, in Paul's Areopagus address (17:29) the attic χρυσῷ ἢ ἀργύρῳ appears rather than the more common diminutive form χρυσιῷ ἢ ἀργύριῳ (in HGk. the diminutive form was standard in certain terms; see K. Elliott, "An Eclectic Textual Study of the Book of Acts," in *The Book of Acts as Church History: Text, Textual Traditions and Ancient Interpretations*, ed. M. Tilly and T. Nicklas, [New York: De Gruyter, 2003], 15–16). Elliott suggests an inconsistent atticizing replacement by later scribes. I feel that since the replacement is late and not made elsewhere with these words, it is more likely Luke is intentionally being more literary by using a nondiminutive form in the Areopagus. It is exactly the sort of subtlety that would demonstrate that Paul was no babbler (see 17:18).

The reader of Acts in Gk. should also take care to note how Luke employed rhetorical underlining. Like the Gospel of Luke, the book of Acts frequently avoids the frequency of the historical pres. found in HGk. Hawkins's *Horae Synopticae* noted "the extreme rarity of the historical present in the narrative" (four times, two more possible) of the Gospel (*Horae Synopticae*, 24). I find something similar in Acts. There are 364 pres. indics. in Acts. Of these, only twenty-two are historical pres. and only five are not words of speaking (see Levinsohn 201; he went on to note when the historical pres. does appear, it seems to be highlighting something following as an important development in the narrative—boundary markers and highlighting).

So why is this important for the reader of Acts in Gk? This observation should lead us to 1) mark the uses of the historical pres. when we find them in Acts, and 2) seek to understand how Luke replaces the highlighting features that are used in the other Gospels (Mark and John most notably).

The first is rather easy (there are only twenty-two in Acts). When it occurs in words of speaking, it marks the statement that follows as the next development in the discourse. For example, λέγει at Acts 12:8 introduces the angel's instruction to Peter to get dressed and follow him out of the prison. The use of the historical pres. leaving the prison is the next important step. The two nonspeech historical pres. (Acts 10:11, 27) point forward to significant events (i.e., Peter's vision and the interrogation by Jewish brothers).

The second question is also important. What does Luke use instead of the historical pres. to mark such development? Runge's work in synoptic comparison is helpful. Comparing Mark's expansive use of the historical pres. to Matthew and Luke, he states, "Mark regularly uses the HP to signal the next development in the discourse, chunking the text in ways comparable to the use of δέ by Matthew and Luke" (S. Runge, "The Exegetical Significance of Synoptic Differences from the Standpoint of Discourse Grammar," *JETS* 58 [2015]: 330). In other words, Luke preferred another developmental marker (i.e., δέ) to the historical pres. The use in Acts is a reflection of the same style.

Understanding δέ as a marker of development (the next important thing in the discourse) views the conjunction as a matter of function rather than lexigraphically (see Levinsohn 69–93; Runge 28–36). While the context may allow different translations, the pragmatic function is developmental. This distinction is the most prominent in intersentence conjs. (i.e., linking clauses). While the developmental aspect remains in paired cstrs. (like the famous μὲν . . . δέ cstr.) they are generally lower level. In more recent studies it has been noted that τέ *solitarium* (i.e., not a τέ . . . καί or τέ . . . τέ cstr.; mostly found in Acts in the NT) is not a more literary form of δέ but adds distinct material characterized by sameness. "They may refer to different aspects of the same event, the same occasion, or the same pragmatic unit" (Levinsohn 107). The reader of Acts who comes upon an intersentence δέ should understand it as introducing the next important matter in the narrative (context will tell in either lower or higher levels of discourse). This is generally not pointed out in the commentary for the sheer number of them.

In Hawkins's comparison between the historical pres. of Mark and the other Gospels (*Horae Synopticae,* 143–48), Luke substituted other constituents for δέ as well. When tracking down the texts Hawkins indicated, we find, along with δέ, ἰδού/ καὶ ἰδού, a pleonastic ptc. (e.g., λέγων) ἐγένετο δέ. Luke uses these same forms in Acts as well. Some, like ἐγένετο δέ (see commentary at 4:5), are boundary markers. Others mark some form of highlighting (like ἰδού). The reader of Acts in Gk. should note these as highlighting markers as well as their function in the text.

Of special note is Luke's use of the impf. tense. He employed the impf. 766 times in Luke-Acts, 408 times in Acts alone. In contrast, Matthew, Mark, and John employ the tense 882 times together. Luke's rate is rather impressive and, at times, puzzling. Levinsohn notes the impf. in narrative is aspectual in its force, portraying action as incomplete. However, when it is not obvious that this fits the context, it is likely backgrounding the information (Levinsohn 175). Most of Luke's impfs. can be classified progressive and are left unmarked in the commentary. When other classifications make sense (i.e., "ingressive," "tendential," "habitual") these are employed. In many of these, the reader may look for a backgrounded interpretation.

THE SO-CALLED WESTERN TEXT OF ACTS

One of the more interesting phenomena in NT studies is the Western text of Acts. The primary witness for the Western text is Codex Bezae (Bezae Cantabrigiensis, catalogued as D or 05), produced c. AD 400 (ABD 1:1070). It is the only Gk. ms. that consistently contains the so-called Western readings (S. E. Porter, "Developments in the Text of Acts before the Major Codices," in Tilly and Nicklas, *Book of Acts as Church History* 32). However, the rdgs. appear in quite a number of other Gk. mss. (although not consistently), in the margins (apparatus) of the Harklean Syriac, in Old Latin versions, and in parts of Irenaeus, Cyprian, and Augustine (Barrett 1.21). The origins (of at least some) of these rdgs. seem to date from the second century (see Irenaeus). However, the rdgs. in Irenaeus are not the same as Bezae (more of a paraphrase), nor do the other witnesses of the type agree with one another or Bezae identically (Barrett 1.27).

The so-called Western text is longer than the eclectic text. In Codex Bezae, the text is incomplete (missing 8:29–10; 22:10–20; 22:29–end) but has around 800 more words than the eclectic text. The most interesting of these are in the form of historical notes (some with the ring of truth). For example, in the Western text of Acts 19:9, Paul rented the hall of Tyrannus ἀπο ὥρας πέμπτης ἕως δεκάτης, "from the fifth hour until the tenth" (i.e., 11 a.m. to 4 p.m.). This was the heat of the day, when work normally stopped and people slept (Bruce, NICNT, 366, "more people would be asleep at 1 p.m. than at 1 a.m."). The hall would be easily available at that time.

Other rdgs. seem to be theologically motivated. One of the most famous regards the apostolic decree of Acts 15. Tuckett notes, "the 'Western' text consistently omits the reference to things 'strangled' from the four items forbidden to Gentiles in the Decree, and also adds a version of the Golden Rule" (C. Tuckett, "How Early is the 'Western' Text of Acts?," Tilly & Nicklas, *Book of Acts as Church History*, 84). The change seems to change the ritual implications to solely ethical ones. Phenomena like this have led to several works on the theological *Tendenz* of the text (see, e.g., E. J. Epp, *The Theological Tendency of Codex Bezae Cantabrigensis in Acts* [Cambridge: Cambridge University Press, 1966]).

Others have also seen literary "improvement," elaboration, smoothness, fullness, and emphasis in the Western rdgs. (J. H. Ropes, *The Text of Acts*, vol. 3 of *The Beginnings of Christianity, Part 1: The Acts of the Apostles* [Eugene, OR: Wipf and Stock, 2002], cxxvii–cxxix). All this is important for the understanding of scribal tendencies, the state of the text in the earliest centuries, and even canon consciousness. The Western rdgs. hold promise for telling us a great deal about earliest Christianity.

For our purposes, these very interesting rdgs. and subsequent questions are not germane to the exegetical task. These variants will be addressed in the commentary only in the case of a so-called Western rdg. being original (this is certainly possible) and affecting the mng. of the text. I agree with the majority that the Western text is a later expansion of Acts. For the preacher and teacher of Acts, then, the task of exegesis must not be sidetracked. I try to stick to this task in the commentary ahead and not be distracted by these very interesting questions. Only where the establishment of the text is concerned will the Western text be addressed.

I would also warn the preacher/teacher to proclaim the text and not the historical possibilities represented by the Western rdgs. When we do so, we informally emend the text as much as any Western scribe who sought to improve it. Even if the timing of Paul's use of Tyrannus's lecture hall is representative of the culture of the time, it is not in the text.

OUTLINE

VII. To the Ends of the Earth: On to Rome (19:21–28:31)

The outline is an adaptation of the one used in our *The Cradle, the Cross, and the Crown*. When one surveys the various outlines in the literature for the book of Acts, as expected, a number of different outlines appear. In my opinion, the book of Acts is broadly outlined in Acts 1:8, ". . . you will be my witnesses in Jerusalem, in all Judea and Samaria, and to the end of the earth." In the narrative of the book, each step is at the divine directive. Persecution, divine appointments, communication after fasting, visions, and prophetic warnings precede or permeate the movement into different sociopolitical, ethnic, and geographic regions. Acts has a chronological and geographical outline in presenting the expansion of the gospel as God's plan. I have attempted to keep the geography and progress in mind in the outline divisions.

I have further tried to provide a homiletical outline that would not only cover the broad sections, but some in more limited scope. It is my desire to facilitate thought and prayer for the preacher/teacher of the text. It is my hope that such reflection expands or elaborates on the text as well as nourishes the preacher of the text. Take them or leave them, run with them or run from them. If they get the herald praying and thinking, I feel I have succeeded.

In the commentary itself, I have tried to follow the guidelines provided by the publisher. In a few places (due to Luke's sequence) I have not been able to follow the Gk. word order to adequately explain the text. I have tried to note a NT hapax where possible, CGk. cstrs., and other matters of interest. The commentary is not exhaustive in these matters due to space constraints. I have avoided matters of textual criticism for the most part. I have especially not interacted with the Western text of Acts other than a few places (as stated above). I comment on textual criticism only where I either disagree with the UBS[5] committee or other factors demand a comment. I have declined to provide diagrams of passages due to the limitation of space as well. I have tried to keep in mind the movements of speeches and point them out in the commentary.

I have also tried to produce a readable guide for the exegete. Common Lukan cstrs. are cross-referenced with "see . . ." Cross-references to other portions of Scripture are provided when particularly helpful. Although, again, it is not comprehensive.

For terminology issues I have tried to limit myself to the language of A. Köstenberger, B. Merkle, and R. Plummer's recent offering, *Going Deeper with New Testament Greek: An Intermediate Study of the Grammar and Syntax of the New Testament* (Nashville: B&H, 2016). I have also quite often transposed the terminology of previous grammarians and commentators to be consistent. In a few places I found it helpful to stray beyond this terminology.

RECOMMENDED COMMENTARIES

This commentary features consistent references to the following eight commentaries. These are written (or tr.) in Eng. and based on the Gk. text of Acts.

Barrett, C. K. *Acts of the Apostles.* 2 vols. ICC. New York: T&T Clark, 1974.

Bruce, F. F. *The Acts of the Apostles: The Greek Text with Introduction and Commentary.* 3rd ed. Grand Rapids: Eerdmans, 1990.

Bock, D. L. *Acts.* BECNT. Grand Rapids: Baker, 2007.

Haenchen, E. *The Acts of the Apostles.* Translated by B. Noble and G. Shinn, H. Anderson. Revised by R. McL. Wilson. Philadelphia: Westminster, 1971.

Johnson, L. T. *The Acts of the Apostles.* Sacra Pagina 5. Collegeville, MN: Liturgical, 1992.

Keener, C. S. *Acts: An Exegetical Commentary.* 4 vols. Grand Rapids: Baker Academic, 2012–2015.

Schnabel, E. *Acts.* Zondervan Exegetical Commentary on the New Testament 5. Grand Rapids: Zondervan, 2012.

Witherington III, B. *The Acts of the Apostles: A Socio-Rhetorical Commentary.* Grand Rapids: Eerdmans, 1998.

Also frequently cited are M. Culy and M. C. Parsons, *Acts: A Handbook on the Greek Text* (Waco: Baylor, 2003); C. L. Rogers, Jr. and C. L. Rogers III, *The New Linguistic and Exegetical Key to the Greek New Testament* (Grand Rapids: Zondervan, 1998); and A. T. Robertson, *Pictures in the New Testament,* vol. 3, *The Acts of the Apostles* (New York: Smith, 1930). In a few places I referenced F. F. Bruce, *The Book of the Acts*, rev. ed., NICNT (Grand Rapids: Eerdmans, 1988).

Barrett's two-volume International Critical Commentary has earned its reputation as a standard in the field, as well as the late F. F. Bruce's 3rd ed. of his Gk. commentary on Acts.

Bock's BECNT offering on Luke was particularly helpful in theological implications of the text.

Johnson's *Sacra Pagina* volume is very helpful for classics, rhetoric, and historical matters as well as exegetical insight. Haenchen's is helpful to get a view of Continental scholarship. While I do not agree with many of his higher-critical stances, I found his willingness to disagree with established Continental opinion refreshing. His explication of the text, notwithstanding these disagreements, was excellent and informative. His ability to succinctly deal with matters of philology and grammar is impressive. Witherington's familiarity with the issues around classical literature and rhetoric are invaluable when dealing with Acts. Matters glossed over in other commentaries often find a valuable treatment in Witherington.

Keener's is a four-volume juggernaut dealing with almost every conceivable issue in the book of Acts. While he does not consistently refer directly to the Gk. text, his detail is invaluable to the exegete of Acts. Finally, Schnabel's commentary deals with both the Gk. text directly and is particularly concerned with the theological texture of the book. All are highly recommended.

I. Foundations for the Church and Her Mission (1:1–2:47)

The introductory section of the book of Acts is presented in three movements. In the first movement, Luke describes the preliminary steps (1:1–14): a review of Jesus's ministry and instructions for the disciples in the immediate present (1:1–5), followed by the ascension (1:6–14). These recapitulate the last passages of Luke (see Luke 24:50–53), marking the transition to Acts. Staying in Jerusalem is the fulfillment of both Luke 24:49 and Acts 1:8.

The second movement is the replacement of Judas (1:15–26). This new information shows how the disciples handled the difficult issue of Judas's apostasy and highlights many of Luke's important themes in the book of Acts (e.g., fulfillment of Scripture and God's sovereignty).

The third movement contains the events at Pentecost (2:1–47). This includes not only the initial filling of the Spirit but also the first major evangelistic speech in the book of Acts. Many of the theological themes that highlight the book are presented in this ch. Thus, the first two chs. provide not only historical background but somewhat of a theological introduction to the book (Keener 1.647).

A. PRELIMINARY STEPS (1:1–14)

1. Review of Jesus's Ministry and Instructions (1:1–5)

The first portion sets up the book by both looking backward to the Gospel of Luke and forward to at least the narrative at hand.

1:1–2 Μέν is a forward-looking device in Koinē Gk., expecting a related clause to follow (Runge 74). Bruce (*Acts of the Apostles*, 97) rightly suggests this is an example of anacoluthon, pointing to an unexpressed thought. Barrett agrees and suggests the unexpressed item is a ref. to the contents of the present book (citing 1:8, 1:65) connecting the two vols. A series of linguistic clues will suggest this is the correct understanding.

First, the two works are explicitly connected. All agree that πρῶτον λόγον refers to the Gospel of Luke. It does not imply more than two vols. (although the use of the superl. in CGk would; ZG 349; Z §151; cf. T 56). The distinction between the adj. "first," πρῶτος, and "former," πρότερος (πρότερος, -α, -ον) was blurring in the Koinē period. Πρῶτος had mostly superseded πρότερος (Keener 1.651). It does, however, closely connect the two. It was typical to employ λόγος when referring to a work that used more than one roll of papyrus (Bruce, *Acts of the Apostles*, 97). Ἐποιησάμην (1st sg. aor. mid. indic. of ποιέω) is an example of Luke's CGk. influence. There, ποιέω often appeared in the mid. with a verbal noun (see T 56; ZG 349; Z §227) perhaps attracted to the pers. involvement in the verbal idea. This explicit connection is also made through the address to Theophilus (Θεόφιλε voc. sg. masc. of Θεόφιλος, -ου, ὁ). This is likely a ref. and dedication to Luke's patron (the same man addressed at Luke 1:3) who would have provided room, board, and writing mats while the book was being produced (CCC 316).

Second, the former treatise is described as what ἤρξατο ὁ Ἰησοῦς ποιεῖν τε καὶ διδάσκειν. The use of ἤρξατο (3rd pl. aor. mid. indic. of ἄρχομαι, "begin") with two compl. infs. (ποιεῖν and διδάσκειν [both pres. act. inf.]) suggests contrast to the present work. It is more likely that the base mng. of ἤρξατο is intended rather than a meaningless Sem. pleonasm (Bruce, *Acts of the Apostles*, 97; Keener 1.651–52). Thus, it implies that the content of Acts is the continuation of Jesus's works. Its appearance with τε forms a closer connection than καί alone, and the joined words have a "logical affinity" (T 339). The description of the gospel as περὶ πάντων that Jesus did is clearly hyperbole yet indicates a comprehensive treatment (Keener 1.653).

A third matter that points to the present work as a continuation of the former is the case of the rel. pron. ὧν. Normally, one would expect it to be in the acc. case (as the obj. of ἤρξατο). Many note that it is not uncommon in Gk. for a rel. pron. to be attracted to the case of its antecedent (see, e.g., BDF §294 [153b–54]). It is likely that the subord. clause takes a highly prominent place in the argument. Altogether then, if the former treatise is about what Jesus *began,* the present one is about what Jesus *continues.*

Luke notes the extent of Jesus's incarnational ministry through the prep. phrase ἄχρι ἧς ἡμέρας . . . ἀνελήμφθη (3rd sg. aor. pass. indic. of ἀναλαμβάνω) ref. to the ascension. Only Luke narrates it in the Gospels, at the end of Jesus's ministry in the flesh. Acts picks it up at the beginning of the apostolic ministry and beyond. The placement of the rel. pron. (ἧς) in the same phrase as its antecedent (ἡμέρας, acc. sg. fem. of ἡμέρα, -ης, ἡ) is unusual and prominent. It is rightly understood as "until the *very* day" (BHGNT 3). The adv. temp. ptc. ἐντειλάμενος (nom. sg. masc. of aor. mid. ptc. of ἐντέλλομαι, "command") is best understood as a ref. to Luke 24:49 (so Bruce, *Acts of the Apostles*, 99; Bock 53; Haenchen 139; Keener 1.661). The more disputed question is what does the prep. phrase διὰ πνεύματος ἁγίου reference? Since it falls outside the rel. clause phrase that follows (οὓς ἐξελέξατο, "whom he chose") it is unlikely to be modifying ἐξελέξατο (3rd sg. aor. mid. indic. of ἐκλέγομαι, "chose") but rather ἐντειλάμενος (so Bock 55; Barrett 1.69; contra Haenchen 139). If so, the continuity between the Spirit speaking through Jesus and the promise of the Spirit to speak through the apostles is hard to miss (Keener 1.661).

1:3 A second rel. pron. clause (with οἷς), modifying ἀποστόλοις in v. 2, describes the forty days between the crucifixion and the ascension. Ἑαυτόν ("himself") and ζῶντα (acc. sg. masc. of pres. act. ptc. of ζάω) are in a double-acc. cstr. with παρέστησεν (3rd sg. aor. act. indic. of παρίστημι, "present"). Μετά with an aor. inf. παθεῖν (aor. act. inf. of πάσχω) and an acc. subj. of the inf. αὐτόν is a temp. cstr. mng. "after he suffered." (A sim. pres. temp. cstr. in Luke's writings uses ἐν and a pres. inf.; see, e.g., Luke 2:43). The effects of the presentation are described by the nature of the proofs Jesus gave. Τεκμηρίοις (dat. pl. neut. of τεκμήριον, -ου, τό, "proof") is a NT hapax signifying a decisive proof (BDAG 994a). This is apparently repeatedly done over the forty days (ἐν πολλοῖς τεκμηρίοις, "by many proofs," functions as an instr. clause). The substance of the presentation is contained in two adv. ptcs. The first, ὀπτανόμενος (nom. sg. masc. of pres. mid. ptc. of ὀπτάνομαι, "appear"), speaks of Jesus's appearances. The second, λέγων (nom. sg. masc. of pres. act. ptc. of λέγω), in conjunction with the prep. phrase (nominalized by the acc. neut. pl. τά), describes the theme of Jesus's discourses during that time: the kingdom of God.

1:4 Συναλιζόμενος (nom. sg. masc. of pres. mid. ptc. of συναλίζω, "gather"; temp.; NT hapax) could also mean "eating with" (a cognate with ἅλας, "salt"). If the latter, the setting is a meal (so Barrett 1.71; Bock 56; Haenchen 141). In favor of a meal, 10:41 does ref. post-resurrection meals and may echo 1:4 (BDAG 964b). The major objection to the normal mng. "gathering" is the singular. However, the use of the singular agrees with the finite vb. it modifies and explains the usage (BHGNT 5). Thus, the objection to the singular is not particularly weighty. At a minimum, either legitimate interpretation implies a gathering (Keener 1.675). That the group is described in v. 6 as οἱ συνελθόντες, "the ones who gathered," would suggest the normal reading. The command is expressed in indir. discourse (employing infs. as vbs.: μὴ χωρίζεσθαι [pres. pass. inf. of χωρίζω, "do not depart"] and περιμένειν [pres. act. inf. of περιμένω, "wait"]). Πατρός is a subj. gen. Ἣν ἠκούσατέ μου is another ref. to Luke 24:49. The indir. discourse transitions to dir. discourse (ZG 35; note the indic. ἠκούσατε). Luke thus continues the overlap with Luke 24.

1:5 At v. 5, there is an allusion to Luke 3:16 where John notes the same contrast between his baptism (ὕδατι, locat. dat.; the absence of the corresponding καὶ πυρί suggests that Luke 3 is not hendiadys—i.e., not Holy Spirit/fire but Holy Spirit *or* fire—judgment). The second use of μέν in this passage is followed by the contrasting δέ. The promise is to be baptized (βαπτισθήσεσθε, 2nd pl. fut. pass. indic. of βαπτίζω). The placement of ἁγίῳ after the vb. serves to continue the contrast between John's and Jesus's baptisms (BHGNT 6). Οὐ μετὰ πολλὰς ταύτας ἡμέρας is an example of litotes (ZG 350, = "in a few days"; the figure emphasizes the brevity, in about ten days; see 14:28). The time ref. locates the fulfillment of John's prophecy in Luke 3:16 (one of Luke's special interests) and is faith-building among his disciples. Thus, the story begun in Luke (of all that Jesus *began* to do and teach) is continued in the present story on many levels. Due to the eschatological transition being made, there should be no thought of a static baptism in the Spirit after conversion in the present age.

FOR FURTHER STUDY

1. Lukan Prologues (1:1–5)

Alexander, L. *The Preface to Luke's Gospel: Literary Convention and Social Context in Luke 1.1–4 and Acts 1.1.* SNTSMS 78. Cambridge: Cambridge University Press, 1993.
Keener, 1.649–62.
Lake, K. "The Preface of Acts and the Composition of Acts." In *Beginnings* 5, 1–6.
Robbins, V. K. "Prefaces in Greco-Roman Biography and Luke-Acts." *PRSt* 6 (1979): 94–108.

2. The Unity of Luke-Acts

Bird, M. F. "The Unity of Luke-Acts in Recent Discussion." *JSNT* 29 (2007): 425–48.
Green, J. B. "Luke-Acts or Luke and Acts? A Reaffirmation of Narrative Unity." In *Reading Acts Today: Essays in Honour of Loveday C. A. Alexander.* Edited by S. Walton, T. E. Phillips, L. K. Pietersen, and F. S. Spencer. London: T&T Clark, 2011.
Gregory, A. *The Reception of Luke and Acts in the Period before Irenaeus: Looking for Luke in the Second Century.* WUNT 2/169. Tübingen: Mohr Siebeck, 2003.
Keener, 1.550–74
Rowe, C. K. "History, Hermeneutics and the Unity of Luke-Acts." *JSNT* 28 (2005): 131–57.
Marshall, I. H. "Acts and the 'Former Treatise.'" In BAFCS 1, 163–82.

3. The Genre of Acts

Alexander, L. *Acts in Its Ancient Literary Context: A Classicist Looks at the Acts of the Apostles.* LNTS 298. London: T&T Clark, 2005.
———. "Acts and Ancient Intellectual Biography." In BAFCS 1, 31–64.
Keener, 1.51–147.
Palmer, D. W. "Acts and the Ancient Historical Monograph." In BAFCS 1, 1–30.
Parsons, M. C., and R. I. Pervo. *Rethinking the Unity of Luke and Acts.* Minneapolis: Fortress, 1993.

HOMILETICAL SUGGESTIONS

Jesus's Ministries (1:1–5)

1. Jesus's former ministry (vv. 1–2)
2. Jesus's validating ministry (v. 3)
3. Jesus's promise of continuing ministry (vv. 4–5)

2. The Ascension of Jesus (1:6–14)

Acts 1:6–14 frames an important outlook regarding the kingdom. The disciples (connecting "Spirit" to the realization of the second exodus, as in texts like Joel 2:28–29) ask about the time of the restoration. Jesus's response ("not now"), the mission of the disciples ("witness"), and the note that Jesus will visibly return together set the program in Acts in its salvation-historical location. He will gather Israel and the nations at his return, but first the worldwide proclamation of the gospel must take place. This time line is also suggested in the Olivet discourse (Luke 21:5–36). Luke artfully stitches together the account to focus on the present mission and its empowerment. In this way, he sets the theme of the book within the story line of the Scripture.

1:6 Μὲν οὖν points both forward and backward. The context is closely related to the previous through the use of οὖν. The μέν points to the answer to the disciples' questions in v. 7 (where the corresponding δέ is found). The use together is rather frequent in Acts (1:18; 2:41; 5:41; 8:4, 25; 9:31; 11:19; 12:5; 13:4; 14:3; 15:3, 30; 16:5; 17:12, 17, 30; 19:32, 38; 23:18, 22, 31; 25:4, 11; 26:4, 9; and 28:5). Levinsohn notes that μέν continues to anticipate a sentence but also "downgrades the importance of the sentence containing μέν" (Levinsohn 170; see also Bruce, *Acts of the Apostles*, 102). The subj. is a subst. ptc. (συνελθόντες [nom. pl. masc. of aor. act. ptc. of συνέρχομαι; see 1:4] mng. "the ones having gathered," contra Barrett 1.75 and most EVV). Ἠρώτων (3rd pl. impf. act. indic. of ἐρωτάω) is an inceptive impf., "they began asking." The employment of εἰ ("if") in a cstr. with a dir. question is not CGk. but a Heb. found in the LXX (rendering *hă* and *'im*—BDF §440[3]; R 916; Turner, *Style,* 54). The question itself seems reasonable enough as Jesus has taught for forty days regarding the kingdom. The use of the prep. with the dat. (ἐν τῷ χρόνῳ τούτῳ) indicates a point in time, this time, now. This is reinforced by the tense of ἀποκαθιστάνεις (2nd sg. pres. act. indic. of ἀποκαθιστάνω, "you are restoring"). The gist of the question implies the hope of an immediate eschatological realization of the second exodus promised in the OT (see, e.g., Isa 2:2–4).

1:7 Jesus's answer (highlighted by δέ, see above) is in two parts. The first part (v. 7) has been interpreted as a renouncement of any hope of an immediate *parousia* (Haenchen 143). As Bock points out, though, the question of when the end comes is avoided, not denied (Bock 62). Instead, the neg. gen. pl. ὑμῶν (poss.) makes the knowledge beyond the apostles' privilege: "yours is not to know." The phrase χρόνους ἢ καιρούς ("times or seasons") is inclusive and ambiguous. Both words describe a single concept (called "hendiadys") and encompass the whole of the restoration process (however short or long). The precise timing resides (ἔθετο, 3rd sg. aor. act. indic. of τίθημι, "place") in God's own (τῇ ἰδίᾳ) sovereign authority.

1:8 Jesus clarifies their mission and its prerequisite. Ἀλλά creates a strong contrast to the previous statement. Instead of that which is out of their control, Jesus announces an empowerment and a ministry. The empowerment is introduced by a gen. abs. phrase (ἐπελθόντος τοῦ ἁγίου πνεύματος ἐφ᾽ ὑμᾶς) unusually after the vb. it modifies (λήμψεσθε, 2nd pl. fut. pass. indic. of λαμβάνω; predictive fut., KMP 270). In this position, ἐπελθόντος (gen. sg. masc. of aor. act. ptc. of ἐπέρχομαι) is not merely a temp. ptc. but also unpacks the mng. of receiving power (Runge 262). The sequence implied by the aor. tense is more logical than strictly chronological, but the sense is "after the Holy Spirit comes upon you" rather than "when" (see RSV, NASB, CSB). So then, the implication is a state of empowerment because of the indwelling.

The second fut. in the statement (ἔσεσθε, 2nd pl. fut. mid. indic. of εἰμί) is as much prophetic as it is impv. (as the previous fut., βαπτισθήσεσθε, in v. 5). The fut. used as an impv. is likely the result of Sem. influence. Clearly Christ is commanding the disciples, and the use of the fut. form marks the seriousness of the command (Wallace 570). This fits the pattern of the rest of the book, where the gospel is continually moving out into new areas and new people groups, always under the direction of the sovereign Lord. The rest of the book of Acts follows this basic geographic pattern as the narrative moves forward. Thus, there is a prophetic element as well, demonstrating Luke's interest in fulfilled prophecy. Those who see a broad outline of the book expressed here are correct (see, e.g., Haenchen 141).

The list begins with ἐν . . . Ἰερουσαλήμ, which is not their home but where they were. It continues (in a τε . . . καί . . . καί cstr., in this case connecting sim. entities, possibly tr. as "and" [see BDAG 993c]). Next, the adj. πάσῃ with the following art. τῇ closely connects Ἰουδαίᾳ and Σαμαρείᾳ (dat. sg. fem. of Σαμάρεια, -ας, ἡ), "all Judea and Samaria."

The phrase ἕως ἐσχάτου τῆς γῆς has created a good bit of discussion over the years (see Bock 66–67). In Eng. idiom, the plural "ends of the earth" (as in some EVV) suggests a global target. However, the Gk. is singular (ἐσχάτου "end") and suggests to some a more specific destination in mind (Schnabel 79, rejecting the idea, notes that Rome, Spain, and Ethiopia have been suggested). However, the phrase is used throughout the Gk. OT and normally has the mng. of "the entire inhabited world" (Keener 1.708. See, esp., Isa 49:6, εἰς φῶς ἐθνῶν τοῦ εἶναί σε εἰς σωτηρίαν ἕως ἐσχάτου τῆς γῆς—"so that you would be the light of the nations for salvation to the end of the earth"; see also Isa 8:9; 45:22; 48:20; and 62:11). Barrett sees a possible ref. to Rome (so also Johnson 27). Rightly and more significantly, he notes the inclusion here is related to Luke's eschatology (Barrett 1.81). Worldwide proclamation is the present mission of Jesus's followers. Nothing in the text, however, demands that the *parousia* is "a necessarily distant event" (Keener 1.686). The gift of the Spirit, then, comes with both an obligation to the church and an eschatological promise.

The ascension is narrated only here and Luke 24:51 (see also Luke 9:51). The event, however, is not isolated to Luke. Jesus referred to it at John 20:17, and it is mentioned at Eph 4:8–10; 1 Tim 3:16; and 1 Pet 3:22 (phrases that state he rose to the right hand of the Father also suggest the ascension). It is most sim. to the Elijah ascension, although it differs from any other ascent, either pagan or Jewish (Haenchen 149).

Thus, claims of a wholesale Lukan composition based on imitation are difficult to sustain. The account itself does not necessarily describe an ancient cosmology (contra Keener 1.723). Instead, it describes Jesus's rising out of their sight, making the disciples both eyewitnesses (Haenchen 149) and, in a sense, successors (Keener 1.713–15), although in this case, the disciples are the vehicle of Jesus's continued works through the Holy Spirit that he shares with them (Bock 67).

1:9 Καὶ ταῦτα εἰπών is the normal temp. ptc. (εἰπών, nom. sg. masc. of aor. act. ptc. of λέγω) used in sequencing events, "after speaking these things." The second is also a temp. ptc.: a gen. abs. βλεπόντων (masc. gen. pl. of pres. act. ptc. of βλέπω) αὐτῶν, mng. "as they were watching." Both ptcs. set the stage for the ascension. The close connection (by virtue of καί) of ἐπήρθη (3rd sg. aor. pass. indic. of ἐπαίρω, "lift up") to νεφέλη ὑπέλαβεν (3rd sg. aor. act. indic. of ὑπολαμβάνω) mng. "a cloud received," describes not only the motion but also the extent of it. They watched until they could see him no more (ἀπὸ τῶν ὀφθαλμῶν αὐτῶν, lit., "from their eyes").

1:10 The introductory adv. ὡς is temp. and fairly common in Luke-Acts (BDAG 1105d; BDF §455), mng. "while" or "when." Ἀτενίζοντες ἦσαν is a periph. impf. (nom. pl. masc. of pres. act. ptc. of ἀτενίζω, "gaze" and 3rd pl. impf. indic. of εἰμί; see Wallace 648). The use of the periph. cstr. rather than a simple impf. emphasizes the ongoing nature of actions. Here it describes a prolonged gaze into the sky (the sg. οὐρανόν most likely should not be translated "heaven"). Καὶ ἰδού ("And, behold!") is commonly understood as an imitation of the LXX (i.e., a "biblical style," Barrett 1.82; Turner, *Style,* 53). It shows the startling nature of the appearance of the angels who appear stereotypically as two men dressed in "white clothing" (ἐσθήσεσιν λευκαῖς [fem. dat. pls. of ἐσθής, -ῆτος, ἡ, "clothing," and λευκός, -ή, -όν, "bright, white").

1:11 The angels addressed the disciples as "men of Galilee" in the voc. pl. masc. (ἄνδρες Γαλιλαῖοι). The question asked is clearly rhetorical. "Why do you stand (ἑστήκατε, 2nd pl. pf. act. indic. of ἵστημι) staring into the sky?" The force of the question is impv., "Do not stand there looking up!" Instead, they are assured that Jesus will come back. The phrase ὃν τρόπον is normally used to denote equivalent activity (see 7:28; 15:11; and 27:25), i.e., "in the same way." Thus, the expectation is a visible, bodily, return from the sky (i.e., not another birth, or merely an appearance on earth).

1:12–14 "Then they returned to Jerusalem" is in obedience to the command of Jesus in 1:4. Σαββάτου ἔχον ὁδόν (lit. "having a Sabbath's journey," likely idiomatic, Barrett 1.85–86) describes the proximity to Jerusalem and is best tr. "about a Sabbath day's journey" (i.e., about a half mile; ZG 351). In Jerusalem, they return to the upper room (ὑπερῷον [acc. sg. neut. of ὑπερῷον, -ου, τό], likely the ἀνάγαιον, -ου, τό, "upstairs room" of Luke 22:12). The gen. rel. pron. οὗ functions as an adv. "where" (BDAG 733a). Ἦσαν καταμένοντες (nom. pl. masc. of pres. act. ptc of καταμένω; periph. impf. "residing") suggests that the room had been used by the disciples during the forty days (Schnabel 82). Ὁμοθυμαδόν indicates a united attitude (ZG 351, see the var. at 2:1 and 2:47). Here it is in ref. to prayer (τῇ προσευχῇ a locat. of sphere). Luke lists all living apostles as well as Mary and the brothers of the Lord. It is likely James is already converted (see 1 Cor 15:7). In listing the apostles, Luke brings to mind the defection of Judas to those familiar with the Gospel of Luke.

FOR FURTHER STUDY

4. Luke's Eschatology

Conzelmann, H. *The Theology of St. Luke.* Translated by G. Buswell, 95–136. New York:
  Harper, 1960.
Keener, 1.518–19; 685–88.
Schellenberg, R. S. *DJG*[2], 237–38.

5. The Ends of the Earth (1:8)

Ellis, E. "'The End of the Earth' (Acts 1:8)." *BBR* 1 (1991): 123–32.
Schnabel, E. J. *Early Christian Mission.* Vol. 1, *Jesus and the Twelve*, 373–76. Downers
  Grove, IL: InterVarsity, 2004.
Thornton, T. C. G. "To the End of the Earth: Acts 1.8." *ExpTim* 89 (1977–78): 374–75.

HOMILETICAL SUGGESTIONS

The Promise and the Obligation (1:8)

1. Power is promised.
   a. Given to more than just the apostles
   b. The power of the Holy Spirit is internal and external
2. The power is for an obligation.
   a. To be his witnesses
   b. Unto the ends of the earth

B. THE REPLACEMENT OF JUDAS (1:15–26)

1:15 Ἐν ταῖς ἡμέραις ταύταις, "in those days," is fronted for emphasis and refers to the time period between the ascension and Pentecost. The ptc. ἀναστάς (nom. sg. masc. of aor. act. ptc. of ἀνίστημι, "stand up"; temp.) is common in the LXX but virtually unique to Luke (only at Rom 15:12 outside of Luke-Acts). It is common for Luke to use it to mark a new section (see, e.g., 1:15; Barrett 1.282). Εἶπεν (3rd sg. aor. act. indic. of λέγω) oddly precedes a parenthetical aside. It may be more evidence of a LXX-like style in that numbers are often given in parenthetical statements (R 434). It is made even more curious by employing τε (instead of δέ). The use of τε is striking in Acts (151 times, sixty-four times in the rest of the NT). It is more of an additive than δέ, esp. used alone, yet retaining a degree of development (Levinsohn 107–9). The gathering is called ὄχλος ὀνομάτων, lit. "a crowd of names," i.e., people (Bock 81). The number of disciples in the room described as ὡσεὶ ἑκατὸν εἴκοσι ("around 120") is prominent, although scholars cannot agree as to why. Some have suggested that since 120 was the number of citizens required to have a local Sanhedrin, the choice of the apostles as a council is implied, but this is unconvincing (Schnabel 95), as is ten times the number of apostles (Bruce, *Acts of the Apostles,* 108). It is best to suggest that the number merely reflects Luke's interest in the historical details (much like the 3,000 of the next ch.). All that is implied is a rather large community of believers (Bock 81).

1:16 The Gospel of Luke does not record the fate of Judas (the last ref. to Judas is the betrayal at 22:48). Peter gives Luke's orig. readers the final fate of Judas through a speech. Ultimately it is an appeal to replace Judas. Peter's contention that Scripture had (ἔδει, 3rd sg. impf. act. indic. of δεῖ) to be fulfilled, strikes a familiar note in Lukan theology regarding the plan of God. While no specific Scripture is cited until 1:20, Peter refers to several OT texts as he describes Judas's fate. It is possible that contextual texts lie in the background (e.g., Ps 41:9 [40:10 LXX]; so Barrett 1.96–97). However, given Luke's interest in fulfilled prophecy, it is unlikely the ref. is so opaque (see Beale and Carson 529b). The statements are described as the words of the Holy Spirit διὰ στόματος Δαυίδ ("through the mouth of David"). Thus, it is a ref. to the Psalter. Since the ref. at 1:20 will cite two specific passages from the Psalms, it is likely that those citations are what Peter had in mind.

Here in v. 16, Peter describes the treachery and demise of Judas. He addresses the crowd as ἄνδρες ἀδελφοί. The first noun functions as an adj. here (T 185). Most EVV simply translate it "brothers" to avoid redundancy (note the exceptions of NIV and NKJV). Peter first notes that the events surrounding Judas were predicted long ago, yet Judas is implicated for treachery. Γενομένου (gen. sg. masc. of aor. mid. ptc. of γίνομαι; attrib.) with ὁδηγοῦ (gen. sg. masc. of ὁδηγός, -οῦ, ὁ, "guide" [inferring betrayal]) modifying Ἰούδα, the obj. of the prep. περί. Τοῖς συλλαβοῦσιν (dat. pl. masc. of aor. act. ptc. of συλλαμβάνω, "seize, arrest") is a dat. of advantage (for the soldiers).

1:17 Ὅτι presents the grounds for the assertion that Judas fulfilled Scripture: only a member of the Twelve could betray Christ (κατηριθμημένος, nom. sg. masc. of pf. pass. ptc. of καταριθμέω; periph. plpf. [with ἦν] mng. "he had been counted"). It was not uncommon to use the term "lot" (κλῆρος, -ου, ὁ) when referring to ministry, recalling the Levites' "allotment" (cf. Num 18:21–26; 26:55; Johnson 35). It is technically a marked pebble (BDAG 548c) to be blindly drawn from a group of sim. but unmarked pebbles, occasionally used in divination (see, e.g., Lev 16:9). In 1:26 they will cast lots (κλήρους) to determine God's will in Judas's replacement.

1:18–19 These two vv. are best understood to be a comment by Luke himself. Three items from 1:19 support this proposition. First, Peter's hearers have no need to be informed for "it is known to all Jerusalem" (γνωστὸν [nom. sg. neut. of γνωστός, -ή, -όν, "known"] ἐγένετο πᾶσιν τοῖς κατοικοῦσιν [dat. pl. masc. of pres. act. ptc. of κατοικέω] Ἰερουσαλήμ). Second, "in their own language" (τῇ ἰδίᾳ διαλέκτῳ [dat. sg. fem. of διάλεκτος, -ου, -ή, "language"]) is a distinction not appropriate to Peter's audience. And, third, the tr. of the Aram. Ἀκελδαμάχ (indecl.) as "field of blood" (χωρίον [acc. sg. neut. of χωρίον, -ου, τό, "field"; subj. of the inf.] αἵματος [neut. gen. sg., content or attrib.]) is yet another item unnecessary to Peter's audience, but necessary to Luke's (Bruce, *Acts of the Apostles*, 110).

The account of Judas's death in 1:18 (on μὲν οὖν, see 1:6) raises a series of questions regarding the event as reported in Matt 27:3–5. Although there are differences, harmonizing the accounts does not require unlikely stretches of the imagination (Keener 1.761–65). The first question is, who bought the field, Judas or the high priests? In the first clause, ἐκτήσατο (3rd sg. aor. mid. indic. of κτάομαι, "acquire") is likely an example of a causative use of the mid. voice (Wallace 425). Robertson defines the causative: "in one sense this idiom is due to the fact that what one does through another he does himself" (R 801). The debate as to whether the vb. is act. or deponent (see BHGNT 16) is rather irrelevant since both act. and mid. may express a causative idea; it is not really a function of the voice but the notion and use of the vb. in its context (R 808). If so, Judas set forth the activity of buying a field (χωρίον, acc. sg. neut., dir. obj.) by throwing the bribe (lit. "out of the wage of his crime"; ἐκ μισθοῦ τῆς ἀδικίας [ἀδικία, -ας, ἡ]) in the temple (Matt 27:5). Although some have suggested Judas died in the field, nothing in the text demands such an idea (Bock 84).

The next question is the manner of Judas's death. The adj. πρηνής (nom. sg. masc. of πρηνής, -ές) is sometimes translated as "swollen" (Bruce, *Acts of the Apostles*, 109), assuming that it is etym. related to πίμπρημι (a medical term mng. "burn with fever" or "swell up" BDAG 814a). This is etym. unlikely (BDAG 863b), although some ancients certainly thought so (Bruce, *Acts of the Apostles*, 109; see, e.g., Papias's quote in Holmes 582–85). Instead, the pred. adj. cstr. πρηνὴς γενόμενος (nom. sg. masc. of aor. mid. ptc. of γίνομαι; temp.) is best tr. "falling headlong" as in most EVV. The ptc. logically precedes and is background information to the main vb. ἐλάκησεν (3rd sg. aor. act. indic. of λακάω, "burst apart"). Bruce (*Acts of the Apostles*, 110) notes an accompanying sound is assumed with λακάω. Ἐξεχύθη (3rd sg. aor. pass. indic. of ἐκχέω, "pour out") referred to the intestines (σπλάγχνα, nom. neut. pl. of σπλάγχνον, -ου, τό, "entrails"; neut. pl. often takes a singular vb.) of Judas as a result of the rupture. Again, it takes no hermeneutical gymnastics to harmonize Matthew's hanging with Luke's description, given the violent nature of hanging (contra Johnson 37). Yet we do not have the exact details. What we do know is that Luke's choice to describe the gruesome details suggests he saw it as evidence of dying under God's displeasure (Schnabel 99).

FOR FURTHER STUDY

6. The Death of Judas (1:18–19)

Lake, K. "The Death of Judas." In *Beginnings* 5, 22–29.

Novick, T. "Succeeding Judas: Exegesis in Acts 1:15–26." *JBL* 129 (2010): 795–99.

Oropeza, B. J. "Judas' Death and Final Destiny in the Gospels and Earliest Christian Writings." *Neot* 44 (2010): 342–61.

Upton, J. "The Potter's Field and the Death of Judas." *ConcorJ* 8 (1982): 213–19.

Van de Water, R. "The Punishment of the Wicked Priest and the Death of Judas." *DSD* 10 (2003): 395–419.

HOMILETICAL SUGGESTIONS

Central Truths for the Church and Her Ministry (1:1–14)

1. The church's ministry is founded on the accomplishments of Christ (vv. 1–5)
2. The church's ministry is a Spirit-empowered witness to the world (vv. 6–14)

Waiting on God (1:12–14)

1. Waiting is done in obedience (vv. 4, 12)
2. Waiting is done resting on the promises of God (v. 5)
3. Waiting is done in faith and prayer (vv. 13–14)

1:20 Luke returns to Peter's speech with a standard quotation formula employing γέγραπται (3rd sg. pf. pass. indic. of γράφω). The citation, however, is a conflation of two psalms (69:25; 109:8 [LXX 68:25; 108:8]). The use of Psalm 69 is not unusual in connection with the death of Christ and related contexts (see, e.g., John 2:17; 15:2; Rom 11:9–10; 15:3; Eph 4:8; and Acts 2:33). At the very least, the early Christians saw it as typological of the death of Christ. Its use here related to Judas is probably based on that assumption (Beale and Carson 530). The second citation is connected to the first through the pron. αὐτοῦ (a contemporary hermeneutical technique known as *gezera shewa*—"an equivalent regulation" [Bock 86]). The opt. of the LXX reading is replaced by the slightly more prominent 3rd sg. aor. act. impv. λαβέτω (from λαμβάνω, "take"; see Bock 86). It is given in a pred. adj. cstr. with ἔπαυλις (nom. sg. fem. of ἔπαυλις, -εως, ἡ, "residence") as the subj. Γενηθήτω (3rd sg. aor. pass. impv. of γίνομαι), "let it become," is completed by the nom. sg. masc. pred. adj. ἔρημος (ἔρημος, -ον, "deserted"). The first citation is completed with ἔστω (3rd sg. pres. impv. of εἰμί), "let there be," and neg. (μή) subst. ptc. κατοικῶν (nom. sg. masc. of pres. act. ptc. of κατοικέω). The "empty residence" is not Judas's office but his field, supposing it either had a home on it or the orig. intent was residential (Bock 86). The second citation (Ps 109:8) is not explicitly cited elsewhere. It is best to understand that Peter made an analogy in the face of God's judgment rather than a promise-fulfillment pattern.

1:21 The combination of δεῖ οὖν suggests a cause-and-effect relationship from the Scripture citations that is best described as obedience to the word. Δεῖ (3rd sg. pres.

act. indic. of δεῖ, "necessary") is a specialized vb. (impers., appearing only in the 3rd sg.) and is used freq. by Luke (22 times in Acts; 18 in Luke). It requires a compl. inf. to complete its mng., which occurs at the end of v. 22. The ptc. συνελθόντων (gen. pl. masc. of aor. act. ptc. of συνέρχομαι) is completed by the dat. ἡμῖν functioning as the obj. of the ptc. (words with the συν– pref. often take a dat. dir. obj. [BHGNT 18]). The adj. phrase then modifies ἀνδρῶν. The gen. is best understood as a part. gen. that describes the first characteristic of qualified candidates to replace Judas: they were men who accompanied the apostles. This criterion is further expanded to include the extent of their presence. It is the whole time (ἐν παντὶ χρόνῳ—in the attrib. position παντί should be translated "whole") of Jesus's arrival (εἰσῆλθεν) and his departure (ἐξῆλθεν). The prep. ἐφ' possibly is suggesting association (a rare usage) or it may be used with the two vbs. as an idiomatic expression denoting "to go about with" (LN 83.9). The rel. pron. ᾧ is another dat. of attraction (see 1:2 above); as such it highlights the present clause.

1:22 Why the temp. ptc. ἀρξάμενος (nom. sg. masc. of aor. mid. ptc. of ἄρχω) appears in the nom. is debated. Some have suggested it is attracted to the nom. ὁ κύριος Ἰησοῦς (see, e.g., BHGNT 18), as it is the subj. of the two vbs. However, since it appears elsewhere without such an apparent attraction (e.g., 10:37), Zerwick is likely correct to call it a nom. abs. (ZG 352). The use of the adv. ptc. further defines the time frame. It is from the baptism of John (for this mng., see T 155; i.e., his public announcement rather than his birth, taking Ἰωάννου as a subj. gen.) to Christ's ascension (i.e., his public departure rather than his death). The last qualification is that they were to be eyewitnesses of his resurrection. Σὺν ἡμῖν indicates that the current apostles met these criteria as well. Γενέσθαι (aor. mid. inf. of γίνομαι) completes the verbal idea begun with δεῖ in v. 21 with the masc. acc. obj. ἕνα (εἷς, μία, ἕν, "one") followed by the partitive gen. τούτων, i.e., to become one of the Twelve.

1:23 Ἔστησαν (3rd pl. aor. act. indic. of ἵστημι, "put forward") suggests a democratic process among the 120 (those addressed at the beginning of the speech at v. 15, Barrett 1.102). This process is repeated in Acts 6:5. They nominated two men, assuming only these met the stated criteria. Joseph is described with καλούμενον (acc. sg. masc of pres. pass. ptc. of καλέω) that is compl. by Βαρσαββᾶν (not to be confused with Joseph Barnabas in ch. 4). The name indicates either being born on the Sabbath (i.e., "Son of the Sabbath") or a late son to an older father (i.e., "Son of grey hair" [Schnabel 101]). He is also "nicknamed" (ἐπεκλήθη, 3rd sg. aor. pass. indic. from ἐπικαλέω) the Latin Ἰοῦστος (nom. sg. masc. of Ἰοῦστος, -ου, ὁ), mng. "the just." This may have been chosen for its sim. to Ἰωσήφ (Bruce, *Acts of the Apostles*, 112). The other candidate was Μαθθίαν (masc. sg. acc. of Μαθθίας, -ου, ὁ, "Matthias").

1:24–25 The choice between the two men is made in two stages: prayer and the casting of lots. Προσευξάμενοι nom. pl. masc. of aor. mid. ptc. of προσεύχομαι; attend. circum. With εἶπαν (3rd pl. aor. act. indic. of λέγω), it is best tr. "they prayed and said." The address is typical of the grammatical difficulties in Acts. It is clear what is meant, but the exact grammatical cstr. of σὺ κύριε καρδιογνῶστα πάντων is debated. There could be two or possibly three interpretations:

1. While κύριε (voc. sg. masc. of κύριος, -ου, ὁ) is clearly voc., σὺ . . . καρδιογνῶστα (voc. sg. masc. of καρδιογνώστης, -ου, ὁ, "knower of hearts") might be a nom. subj. phrase ("Lord, you who know the heart . . . show"). If so, the pron. is emphatic. "Knower of all hearts" is in appos. to σύ. See KJV, RSV, NASB, ESV, MIT, NKJV. They function as the subj. of ἀνάδειξον (2nd sg. aor. act. impv. of ἀναδείκνυμι, "clearly show").

2. All the forms might be voc. If so, it is an extended description of the Lord in an address (Wallace 71). Most EVV that take this route promote it to a finite sentence: "Lord . . . you know . . ." See NLT, NRSV, TNIV, NET, NJB.

3. It is remotely possible that it is a pred. adj. cstr. with an assumed being vb.: "You, Lord, [are] the one who knows every heart." In all three, the upshot is that the mitigated appeal to the Lord's omniscience is foundational to the following request.

Like 1:2 above, the rel. pron. (ὅν) appears with the antecedent (ἕνα) in its own clause ἀνάδειξον ὅν . . . ἕνα, with a similar emphasis: "show which one . . ." Ἐξελέξω (2nd sg. aor. mid. indic. of ἐκλέγομαι) must belong to another clause, for it is completed by λαβεῖν in the next verse, mng. "you chose from these two to receive . . ." (BHGNT 21).

The ministry one of these men is to take is available through the apostasy of Judas. Thus, the reason he is to be replaced is not his death but his rejection of Christ (Bruce, *Acts of the Apostles*, 112). Luke, in presenting Peter's words, makes a play on the word τόπος. Judas left his *place* of this ministry (explained with an epex. καί that defines the ministry as ἀποστολῆς [gen. sg. fem. of ἀποστολή, -ῆς, ἡ, apostleship], Barrett 1.103) in order to go to his own *place* (εἰς τὸν τόπον τὸν ἴδιον). Πορευθῆναι (aor. pass. inf. of πορεύομαι, "go") might suggest a ref. to the place where Judas died (Keener 1.773) or another "office" (Barrett 1.104). However, since he died under God's displeasure (see 1:18–19), and "his own place" is in contrast to the destination of the other apostles (Bock 89), a more eternal destination is surely in mind (Schnabel 102). One should recall Jesus's condemnation of Judas as well (John 19:11, etc.).

1:26 The process of choosing was done by lots (κλήρους, acc. pl. masc. of κλῆρος, -ου, ὁ), an acceptable practice in the OT (see, e.g., Prov 16:33), but never used again in the NT. The phrasing concerning the lots is a bit unusual if one were to take ἔδωκαν (3rd pl. aor. act. indic. of δίδωμι, "give") as the action of the Twelve in casting the lot (as Barrett 1.104–5; BHGNT 21–22). It is better to take the verb's ref. to the assigning of lots to Matthias and Joseph by the Eleven making the dat. pron. αὐτοῖς a simple indir. obj. Thus, the description that the lot "fell" (ἔπεσεν, 3rd sg. aor. act. indic. of πίπτω) describes the normal process of a marked pebble falling out of a jar or bag. The result is considered the Lord's providential act, and thus Matthias is added (συγκατεψηφίσθη, 3rd sg. aor. pass. indic. of συγκαταψηφίζομαι) to the Eleven. With the number restored to Twelve, the foundation of the church (Eph 2:20) is back to full strength.

Nothing in the text suggests that the selection of Matthias was premature or illegitimate. It immediately raises the question of the nature of Paul's apostleship (as well as a few others in Scripture, e.g., Barnabas, Acts 14:14; James, 1 Cor 15:7; and Andronicus and Junia, Rom 16:7). First, the Twelve are clearly reflective of the twelve tribes of Israel as the church becomes the reconstructed new covenant people of God (Matt

19:28; Luke 22:30; Rev 21:12–14). In this sense, they are a finite completed group. Second, Paul is considered to be equal to this group although one of special circumstances (1 Cor 15:7–8). It is notable that the enumeration of the twelve tribes as the sons of Abraham is less than linear as well (incl. two half tribes of the sons of Joseph). Third, Paul also belonged to a group of itinerate missionaries to whom a less specific use of the term "apostle" is applied (see, e.g., 1 Cor 9:1–6). So, then, neither Paul nor Matthias are invalidated as apostles in the full sense in the book of Acts.

FOR FURTHER STUDY

7. Apostleship and the Twelve

Barnett, P. W., *DPL*, 45–51.
Barrett, C. K. *The Signs of an Apostle.* Philadelphia: Fortress, 1972.
Brown, S. "Apostleship in the New Testament as an Historical and Theological Problem." *NTS* 30 (1984): 474–80.
Clark, A. C. "Apostleship: Evidence from the New Testament and Early Christian Literature." *VoxEv* 19 (1989): 49–82.
Kirk, J. A. "Apostleship Since Rengstorf: Towards a Synthesis." *NTS* 21 (1984): 249–64.
Kruse, C. *DLNT*, 76–82.
Lake, K. "The Twelve and the Apostles." In *Beginnings* 5, 37–58.
NIDNTTE, 1.365–76.
Rengstorf, K. H. *TDNT*, 1.398–447.

HOMILETICAL SUGGESTIONS

The Betrayal of Jesus, the Sovereignty of God, and the Culpability of Judas (1:15–26)

1. Recognize God's foreknowledge regarding betrayal (vv. 15–17)
2. Recognize God's judgment on Judas (vv. 18–19)
3. Recognize God's selection of Matthias (vv. 20–26)

C. PENTECOST: THE CHURCH IS BORN (2:1–47)

1. The Event: The Exalted Jesus Sends the Spirit (2:1–4)

The first v. moves from the upper room to another day, indicating a literary transition. It provides the setting for the significant event that follows.

2:1 Luke, following the LXX as his custom (Bruce, *Acts of the Apostles*, 113; Turner, *Style* 47; Z §387), presents a temporal orienter by employing ἐν and a subst. inf., συμπληροῦσθαι (pres. pass. inf. of συμπληρόω, "fulfill"). This usually indicates a rather significant shift in the narrative. The phrase suggests the day of Pentecost had arrived (i.e., contemporaneous time, BHGNT 23; Wallace 595, contra ZG 352). Pentecost (πεντηκοστῆς gen. sg. fem. of πεντηκοστή, -ῆς, ἡ, gen. of identification, BHGNT 23) is a subst. adj. mng. "fiftieth," (i.e., the fiftieth day, hence the fem. form, after Passover). It is best rendered "when the day of Pentecost had arrived."

In some circles Pentecost had taken on more meaning. In later Judaism, it was connected with the giving of the Law. In this perspective, there is a comp./contrast between Jesus/Moses and Spirit/Law (Witherington 131). As tempting as this is, the known Jewish traditions regarding the giving of the Law all postdate the NT (Barrett 1.111). Likewise, identifying the feast with a covenant renewal (specifically God's covenant with Noah, Jub. 6:16–17) is unlikely (contra Schnabel 113). Any connection here is too tenuous to strongly defend. The giving of the Spirit alone is enough to indicate eschatological implications (as Peter notes below).

Πάντες is the nom. pl. subj. of ἦσαν (3rd pl. impf. indic. of εἰμί). The prep. phrase ἐπὶ τὸ αὐτό is an idiomatic phrase common in the LXX (55 times), mng. "together" or "come together." In the NT, it is used ten times, seven by Luke, all with the mng. "together." Because ὁμοῦ (adv., "together") is also used in the same phrase, we are forced to use the lit. "in the same place." The redundancy probably led to the *byz.* var. ὁμοθυμαδόν (adv., "with one accord").

2:2 Καὶ ἐγένετο (3rd sg. aor. mid. indic. of γίνομαι) is not to be confused with the LXX rendering of the Heb. *waw*-consec. (Barrett 1.113, see 4:5). Here, the introduction with καί (see 4:5), appearing with the pred. nom. ἦχος (nom. sg. neut. of ἦχος, -ου, ὁ, "noise"), and modified by an adv. (ἄφνω, "suddenly") is best tr. "there came" (KJV, NASB, NRSV). Ὥσπερ (adv., "like") suggests Luke is describing the sound rather than a physical wind (Keener 1.799—the same can be said of πῦρ below). The sound is described in spectacular terms. It is, first, modified by an attrib. ptc. φερομένης (gen. sg. fem. of pres. pass. ptc. of φέρω). Normally "bring," it may be used to signify movement; in terms of wind (πνοῆς, gen. sg. fem. of πνοή, -ῆ , ἡ) it describes a driving wind. Second, the wind is violent (βίαιος, gen. sg. fem. of βίαιος, -α, -ον). Culy and Parsons note the gen. phrase cannot be a gen. abs. (the subj. has not really changed); but rather the noun is a gen. of production ("the sound made by . . ."; BHGNT 24). On οὗ see 1:13. The sound filled (ἐπλήρωσεν 3rd sg. aor. act. indic. of πληρόω) an unspecified house (οἶκον). Ἦσαν καθήμενοι (nom. pl. masc. of pres. mid. ptc. of κάθημαι) is a periph. impf. mng. "they were sitting."

2:3 The second part of the event is visible, as indicated by ὤφθησαν (3rd pl. indic. aor. pass. of ὁράω, in the pass. "they appeared," e.g., KJV, RSV, NASB; see BDAG 719d). The antecedent of αὐτοῖς is the 120. What they saw were divided (διαμεριζόμεναι nom. pl. fem. of pres. pass. ptc. of διαμερίζω; attrib.) tongues. It is a bit vague as to exactly what these were. Like the wind, the tongues are comp. (adv., ὡσεί) to flames, not identified as them. Πυρός (gen. sg. neut. of πῦρ, -ος, τό, "fire") is likely a gen. of description. Ἐκάθισεν (3rd sg. aor. act. indic. of καθίζω, "sit") represents a switch in grammatical number from 3rd pl. to 3rd sg. and is distributive of γλῶσσαι (nom. pl. fem. of γλῶσσα, -ης, ἡ, "tongues"). One of the tongues sat on each of the disciples. The symbolism of flickering tongues of flame is normally connected to the divine (Johnson 42). It is likely that γλῶσσαι points forward to the speech phenomenon below as a divine enablement.

2:4 Πάντες is the subj. of ἐπλήσθησαν (3rd pl. aor. pass. indic. of πίμπλημι, "filled"). If we identify the subj. as the 120, "all" might be important to the application of Joel 2 below. The gen. sg. neut. πνεύματος ἁγίου ("Holy Spirit") suggests the content of the filling (often used with vbs. of filling [ZG 353]; Wallace 52, "gen. of content"), thus, "with the Holy Spirit" rather than "by the Spirit" is better. Since "filled" is used in a variety of ways describing a person's inner life (BDAG 813d), it likely indicates the source of the utterances as well. Because it is the fulfillment of 1:5, it is both filling and baptism. It is unwarranted to assume subsequent fillings in Christians (see, e.g., 4:8) suggest loss of the Spirit. Those are better understood as specific empowerments (Barrett 1.115). Ἤρξαντο (3rd pl. aor. mid. indic. of ἄρχομαι) with λαλεῖν (pres. act. inf. of λαλέω, compl.) emphasizes the beginning of the action (BDAG 140a). Ἑτέραις γλώσσαις (dat. pl. fem. of γλῶσσα, -ης, ἡ) is a dat. of manner, mng. "with other tongues" (KJV, NASB, CEB; i.e., "other languages"). The adv. by implicit contr. clearly indicates the ref. to be to known human languages (see 2:8–11).

In the second clause, the subord. conj. καθώς ("as") puts the speaking under the constraint of the Spirit (Johnson 42). The nature of ἐδίδου (3rd sg. impf. act. indic. of δίδωμι) in this context is causatory (BHGNT 25). As an iter. impf., it suggests discreet events of speaking and not speaking over each other. Although the use of the inf. as a dir. obj. is rare (KMP 370), ἀποφθέγγεσθαι (pres. mid. inf. of ἀποφθέγγομαι, six times LXX, three times Acts) is employed in this way and should be tr. as a noun, "utterance." Ἀποφθέγγομαι is a "weighty or oracular utterance" (Bruce, *Acts of the Apostles*, 115) closely connected to prophecy (whether true or false). The choice here previews the citation of Joel 2 as Peter identifies the utterances as the fulfillment of "they shall prophesy."

2. The Evidence of the Spirit's Coming: Foreign Languages (2:5–13)

2:5 The use of δέ is striking. Previously, only lower levels of development have been indicated (1:5, 7). The present use marks it as the major development in the story so far. Levinsohn goes so far as to say that all of 1:1–2:4 is preamble to this event (Levinsohn 178). Luke also slows down the narrative time with the use of long elements. The first is a periph. impf. ἦσαν . . . κατοικοῦντες (nom. pl. masc. of pres. act. ptc. of κατοικέω), mng. "they were dwelling." Ἰουδαῖοι ("Jews") refers to Diaspora Jews in Jerusalem

(Bock 100). The second elongated expression is ἄνδρες εὐλαβεῖς (nom. pl. masc. of εὐλαβής, -ές), "devout men," modified by the prep. phrase ἀπὸ παντὸς ἔθνους ("from every nation"), and the nominalized (by the art. τῶν) prep. phrase ὑπὸ τὸν οὐρανόν, "under heaven."

2:6 Γενομένης (gen. sg. fem. of aor. mid. ptc. of γίνομαι; gen. abs., temp.) The subj. of the ptc. is τῆς φωνῆς ταύτης and should be tr. "when this sound occurred" (NASB). The sound gathered (συνῆλθεν, 3rd sg. aor. pass. indic. of συνέρχομαι) a crowd (πλῆθος nom. sg. neut. of πλῆθος, -ους, τό, "multitude"). Once gathered, their response was confusion (συνεχύθη, 3rd sg aor. indic. pass. of συγχέω), perhaps "amazed" (BDAG 953d; but cf. v. 7). Εἷς ἕκαστος (nom. sg. masc. subst. adj., "each one") is the subj. of the vb. ἤκουον (3rd pl. impf. act. indic. of ἀκούω, iter., "hear"). Τῇ ἰδίᾳ διαλέκτῳ (fem. sg. dat. of διάλεκτος, -ου, ἡ, dat. of manner, ZG 353) "in their own languages" removes all doubt that they heard known languages (Schnabel 117). The vb. takes a double-gen. obj.-compl. cstr. (because ἀκούω takes a gen. dir. obj., BDF §173[1]) λαλούντων (gen. pl. masc. of pres. act. ptc. of λαλέω; compl.) and the obj. αὐτῶν.

2:7 Ἐξίσταντο (3rd pl. impf. mid. indic. of ἐξίστημι, "amaze") and ἐθαύμαζον (3rd pl. impf. act. indic. of θαυμάζω, "marvel") are both progressive impfs. Because these near synonyms are joined by καί, there is a stacking effect that has led many EVV to translate them as "utterly amazed" (NIV, TNIV) or "completely baffled" (NET). Λέγοντες (nom. pl. masc. of pres. act. indic. of λέγω, attend. circum.) introduces dir. speech, describing a two-step reason for their confusion. The first is expressed in a pred. nom. cstr. The neg. adv. οὐχ expects a positive reply (on ἰδού, see 1:6). The subj. is οὗτοι (see Wallace 44–45, on the pecking order of pred. noms.). Λαλοῦντες is the nom. pl. masc. of pres. act. ptc. of λαλέω. Γαλιλαῖοι is the compl. Keener notes that "Galilean" was the opposite of "cosmopolitan" (Keener 1.835). They were not expected to be so multilingual.

2:8 The second reason is that, given the first, the crowd was hearing in their own dialects. Ἡμεῖς, a redundant pron., is an emphatic cstr. Ἀκούομεν (1st pl. pres. act. indic. of ἀκούω) ἕκαστος (appos. to the subj.) together has a distributive force, "we each hear." Τῇ ἰδίᾳ διαλέκτῳ (dat. sg. fem. of διάλεκτος, -ου, ἡ; "manner") may refer to regional dialects (BDAG 232b-c) but is more likely "language" given the list below. It means "in our native language" (BHGNT 29) in combination with ἐν ᾗ ἐγεννήθημεν (1st pl. aor. pass. indic. of γεννάω, lit. "in that which we were born").

2:9–11 The majority of these two verses is commonly called "the list of nations." It is important to investigate more closely if for no other reason than its sheer length marks it as important. It is tempting to see Luke alluding to a reversal of the Tower of Babel (closely connected to the Table of Nations in Genesis 10 and 11). However, the sim. is not very close to Genesis 10. The list most closely resembles Diaspora lists in other works (Barrett 1.122).

Grammatically, the list is a complicated nom. abs. cstr. (relating to the vb. ἀκούομεν in v. 11; BHGNT 28). The list starts in the east using nom. pl. masc. subst. adjs. (Πάρθοι of Πάρθος, -ου, ὁ, "Parthians;" Μῆδοι of Μῆδος, -ου, ὁ, "Medes;" and Ἐλαμῖται of Ἐλαμίτης, -ου, ὁ, "Elamites") and circles to the west then south using nouns under the control of a subst. ptc. (κατοικοῦντες. nom. pl. masc. of pres. act. ptc. of κατοικέω) that takes the objs. Μεσοποταμίαν (acc. sg. fem. of Μεσοποταμία, -ας, ἡ, "Mesopotamia"),

Πόντον (acc. sg. masc. of Πόντος, -ου, ὁ, "Pontus"), Ἀσίαν (acc. sg. fem. of Ἀσία, -ας, ἡ, "Asia"), Αἴγυπτον (acc. sg. fem. of Αἴγυπτος, -ου, ἡ, "Egypt"), and τὰ μέρη (acc. pl. neut. of μέρος, -ους, τό + the part. gen. Λιβύης [gen. sg. fem. of Λιβύη, -ης, ἡ] + the phrase τῆς κατὰ Κυρήνην [acc. sg. fem. of Κυρήνη, -ης, ἡ, obj. of prep.] is best tr. "the portion of Libya that is under the control of Cyrene"). The nom. abs. continue (moving the list east again) with Ῥωμαῖοι (nom. pl. masc. of Ῥωμαῖος, -α, -ον modified by ἐπιδημοῦντες [nom. pl. masc. of pres. act. ptc. of ἐπιδημέω], mng. "the visiting Romans"), Κρῆτες (nom. pl. masc. of Κρής, -ητός, ὁ, "Cretes"), and Ἄραβες (nom. pl. masc. of Ἄραψ, -βος, ὁ, "Arabs," ref. to the Nabatean Kingdom).

Twice in the list certain nouns are modified with a τε . . . καί cstr. ("both–and"). The cstr. is used twenty-eight times in Acts, joining opposite, unlike, or unrelated words (e.g., men and women; Jews and Gentiles; customs and disputes; proselytes and Jews). The use here likely gives more information regarding the head noun. Τε καί joins Ἰουδαίαν (acc. sg. fem. of Ἰουδαία, -ας, ἡ, "Judea") and Καππαδοκίαν (acc. sg. fem. of Καππαδοκία, -ας, ἡ, "Cappadocia") to Mesopotamia. It is best tr. ". . . Mesopotamia (incl. Judea and Cappadocia)."

The second appearance clearly has this understanding of τε . . . καί. Asia is further described by Phrygia (Φρυγίαν, acc. sg. fem. of Φρυγία, -ας, ἡ) and Pamphylia (Παμφυλίαν, acc. sg. fem. of Παμφυλία, -ας, ἡ), using the cstr. Luke uses Ἀσία to describe both the province and the coastal cities in Acts. Since Phrygia was in the province of Asia, the latter is ref. here (BAFCS 1.302). So then, "the ones dwelling . . . in Asia (incl. Phrygia and Pamphylia)" seems the best translation.

The inclusion of Judea (given Jerusalem is in Judea and the language would be known by the speakers) is difficult. The grammatical connection to Mesopotamia is the best clue to solve the issue. Bruce plausibly suggests that Ἰουδαία indicates the widest extent of the nation (i.e., to the Euphrates—Bruce, *Book of Acts*, 56). Hengel also ably defends the view that the ref. is to "greater Judea" i.e., Syria (a suggestion also made by Jerome). Thus, the region on both sides of the Euphrates in Mesopotamia is described. If so, the way Syria is included as "greater Judea" leads the observant reader to see the ideal Israel as promised by God (Gen 15:18) and only briefly achieved by David (1 Chr 18:3). The language further lends itself to a messianic expectation of the restoration of Israel (Hengel "'Ἰουδαία" 179).

Those seeking a subtle ref. to a deeper mng. in the list have often looked to things like zodiac lists, the Table of Nations, or the tower of Babel (Keener 1.837–44). However, it is more likely an allusion to the Isaianic new exodus (Isa 11:10–13), for the passage describes Diaspora Jews returning to Jerusalem observing an eschatological event. The Isaiah passage also features a list of the countries of the Diaspora returning to Jerusalem. A comp. of the list from the LXX of Isa 11:11 to Acts 2:9–11 is striking. That list includes Assyria, Egypt, Babylon, Ethiopia, the Elamites, the rising of the sun, and Arabia. While not exactly the same list (even after updating to the first-century geography), the parallels are conspicuous.

Ἀκούομεν (1st pl. pres. act. indic. of ἀκούω, "hear") takes an obj.-compl. double obj. λαλούντων (gen. pl. masc. of pres. act. ptc. of λαλέω) as a compl. and αὐτῶν (gen. pl. masc.) as its dir. obj. (see 2:6). Ταῖς ἡμετέραις γλώσσαις (dats. of manner) indicates how they were speaking ("with our languages"). The content of their speaking is rendered as a subst. adj. (μεγαλεῖα, acc. pl. neut. of μεγαλεῖος, -α, -ον) functioning as the obj. of the ptc., mng. "the great things of God."

2:12 The crowd, having identified the phenomenon, struggles to understand it. The two impf. vbs. ἐξίσταντο (3rd pl. impf. indic. act. of ἐξίστημι, "be amazed") and διηπόρουν (3rd pl. impf. indic. act. of διαπορέω, "perplexed") are stacked synonyms (a doublet, BHGNT 29; much like the vb. at 2:7, "completely at a loss," ZG 353) to indicate complete bewilderment. Λέγοντες (nom. pl. masc. of pres. act. ptc., of λέγω; attend. circum.) introduces dir. speech. The clause τί θέλει (3rd sg. pres. act. indic. of θέλω, "want") τοῦτο εἶναι (pres. inf. of εἰμί) is an idiomatic phrase mng. "what can this mean?" (BDAG 448c, cf. 17:18).

2:13 The speaker of the previous phrase (ἄλλος) is contrasted with the subj. of v. 13 (ἕτεροι). The distinction inherent in ἕτεροι seems to be that this group was more cruel toward Galileans. Διαχλευάζοντες is nom. pl. masc. pres. act. ptc of διαχλευάζω, "mocking"; manner (an intensive form, Johnson 44). Ἔλεγον (3rd sg. impf. act. indic. of λέγω) suggests a repeated charge. Ὅτι introduces dir. speech. Their assessment is given in a periph. pf. cstr. (μεμεστωμένοι, masc. nom. of pl. pf. pass. ptc. of μεστόω and εἰσίν; mng."they have been filled.") with γλεύκους (gen. sg. neut. of γλεῦκος, -ου, τό, NT hapax), referring to wine still fermenting, so "new" or "sweet" wine. This was an insult hurled by hecklers (Keener 1.861). In a mocking context, "cheap wine" (Barrett 1.125) seems to fit best.

FOR FURTHER STUDY

8. Speaking in Tongues (2:6–11)

Behm, J. *TDNT*, 1.719–27.
Davids, P. H. *DLNT*, 1177–79.
Johnson, L. T. *ABD*, 6:596–600.
NIDNTTE, 1:588–91.

9. The List of Nations (2:8–11)

Hengel, M. "Ἰουδαία in the Geographical List of Acts 2:9–11 and Syria as 'Greater Judea,'" *BBR* 10 (2000): 161–80.
*Keener, 1.835–51.

HOMILETICAL SUGGESTIONS

The Birth of the Church (2:1–13)

1. The gift of the indwelling Spirit (vv. 1–4)
2. The response of the unbelieving world (vv. 5–13)
   a. Bewilderment (vv. 5–12)
   b. Belittlement (v. 13)

3. The Explanation: Peter's Message (2:14–40)

Peter's response to the crowd marks the next movement in the section. In 2:14–21, Peter identifies the phenomenon: it is the promised outpouring of the Holy Spirit. In 2:22–35 Peter declares Christ to be Lord in three movements. He declares the resurrection of Jesus (2:22–24). Then he provides scriptural support for the resurrection of the Messiah (2:25–32). Finally he summarizes in 2:33–35, connecting resurrection and the pouring out of the Spirit. Acts 2:36 concludes with the ultimate point: Jesus (both Lord and Messiah) is the Lord whom Joel announced, upon whom humans should call in repentance and faith.

a. Peter Identifies the Event (2:14–21)

Peter cites Joel 2:28–32 (LXX 3:1–5) as the prophetic grounds for the event. That the prophecy goes from the pouring out of the Spirit to the "day of the Lord" leads to questions on how Pentecost fulfills the prophecy. There is no reason to suggest that Luke has misappropriated and distorted the text in Joel to fit to the Pentecost event.

There are some changes made as Peter cites Joel. In Acts 2:17, Joel's μετὰ ταῦτα ("after these things") is changed to ἐν ταῖς ἐσχάταις ἡμέραις ("in the last days"). This makes the implication of Joel explicit and is explanatory (Bock 112). Quite a number of rabbis interpreted the setting of the prophecy as "the world to come" (i.e., the messianic age, see Str-B 2.615–16). In the same v., λέγει ὁ θεός ("God says") is also added. It likely is not intended as an adaptation but reminds the hearers that God spoke the words. The order of elders and young men is also reversed. In 2:18, Luke adds the activity προφητεύσουσιν ("they will prophesy") to the sons and daughters, which is the implication of the Joel text. In 2:19, Luke adds ἄνω ("above") and κάτω ("below") that is best understood as an emphatic expression. In the same verse, σημεῖα ("signs") is added in parallel to τέρατα (acc. pl. neut. of τέρας, -ατος, τό, "a wonder"). This is likely added to complete the parallel and explain the nature of the wonders (Bock 115; *TDNT* 8.125 also hints at the order as an "assessment"). These alterations are not conceptually foreign to the context in Joel but seem to be clarification and emphasis.

So how should Pentecost be understood in relation to Joel's prophecy? The text in Joel does not present a strict sequence of events that have a one-to-one correspondence with the ministry of Jesus and Pentecost. The sequence of somewhat indefinite plurals (sons, daughters, old/young men, servants, signs/wonders, and all who call) and "in those days" suggests kinds of signs at the inauguration of a new era. The context, environmental signs, and references to the remnants of battle before "the day of the Lord" suggest an eschatological age.

Moreover, it is unlikely that the events are meant to be in a strict sequence. For example, calling on the name of the Lord may occur at any time in the sequence. Likewise, Peter did not suggest dreams and visions have occurred (they do later). Finally, it nowhere suggests the pouring out of the Spirit is a one-time event, but a continuing event characterizing the last days. The text does refer to environmental signs, but it does not have to be restricted to the events at the crucifixion (contra Schnabel 139). Most of Peter's hearers experienced a three-hour "eclipse" and should have associated it with Joel's text. Thus, Peter's explanation does refer to "powers, signs, and wonders" (see 2:21) in Jesus's ministry, but it should be seen as a characteristic of the messianic age rather than a one-to-one correspondence (see Bock 112; Bruce, NICNT, 63). Joel announced a new age accompanied by certain signs and events. Peter affirmed that the age had been inaugurated in the life, death, burial, and resurrection of Jesus Christ that was accompanied by confirmatory wonders and signs that God, through Joel, said would happen.

2:14 Σταθείς is the nom. sg. masc. of aor. pass. ptc. of ἵστημι; temp. (on the use of the pass., see Z §231). Σὺν τοῖς ἕνδεκα ("with the eleven") modifies ἐπῆρεν (3rd sg. aor. act. indic. of ἐπαίρω) with the dir. obj. φωνήν, "he lifted his voice," and expresses manner (BHGNT 32; reflecting Heb. idiom, Bruce, *Acts of the Apostles*, 120). Ἀπεφθέγξατο (3rd sg. aor. mid. indic. of ἀποφθέγγομαι, "declare") suggests a solemn formal utterance (see also 2:4, ZG 353; BDAG 125a adds urgency.). Peter begins with a pair of vocs: ἄνδρες Ἰουδαῖοι ("Jewish men") and κατοικοῦντες (nom. pl. masc. of pres. act. ptc. of κατοικέω; subst.) Ἰερουσαλήμ (dir. obj., see 19:10, mng. location) πάντες (nom. pl. masc.) "all the ones dwelling in Jerusalem," i.e., non-Jewish inhabitants. The phrase employing γνωστὸν ἔστω (3rd sg. pres. act. impv. of εἰμί), "let it be known," is somewhat of a stock phrase signaling the importance of what follows (see 4:10, 13:38, 28:28). This is compounded by the connected ἐνωτίσασθε (2nd pl. aor. mid. impv. of ἐνωτίζομαι, "pay close attention to," Schnabel 135).

2:15 The grounds (γάρ) for this exhortation is that the supposition ὡς . . . ὑπολαμβάνετε (2nd pl. pres. act. indic. of ὑπολαμβάνω, "assume, suppose") is baseless. The contrast provided by the emphatic nom. pron. ὑμεῖς enhances the baselessness of the supposition (BHGNT 33). Peter's appeal to it being "the third hour" (ὥρα τρίτη, fem. nom. sgs., pred. nom.) refers to about 9 a.m. (reckoning from sunrise, Bruce, *Acts of the Apostles*, 120, the standard Judean practice, Keener 1.870). It is far too short a time (after rising) to have gotten drunk off low-alcoholic cheap wine.

2:16 Peter offers a contrasting interpretation with ἀλλά introducing a pred. nom. cstr. with the subst. ptc. εἰρημένον (nom. sg. neut. of pf. pass. ptc. of λέγω) as the pred. nom. The prep. phrase διὰ τοῦ προφήτου Ἰωήλ, "through the prophet Joel," is a common identification. The fulfillment refers to the manifestation of the Holy Spirit and not the languages themselves (Haenchen 178).

2:17 Acts 2:17–21 is a lengthy quotation of Joel 2:28–32 (LXX 3:1–5). Καὶ ἔσται (3rd sg. fut. mid. indic. of εἰμί) . . . ἐκχεῶ (1st sg. fut. act. indic. of ἐκχέω, "pour out") is a Heb. idiom mng. "it will come to pass that . . . I will pour out" (Bruce, *Acts of the Apostles*, 121). Ἀπὸ τοῦ πνεύματός μου is an exact quote of the LXX but presents some theological/syntactical questions. Some suggest ἀπό is designating source, attempting to evade the suggestion that one receives *some* of the Spirit. It is best to understand that it functions like a part. gen. "pointing to the distribution of the Spirit" (Bock 113). The Spirit is poured out on all flesh (πᾶσαν σάρκα), illustrated by gender, age, and social status (Schnabel 136). The sons will prophesy (προφητεύσουσιν, 3rd pl. fut. act. indic. of προφητεύω); the daughters and young men will see (ὄψονται, 3rd pl. fut. mid. indic. of ὁράω) visions (ὁράσεις, acc. pl. fem. of ὅρασις, -εως, ἡ); the elders will dream (ἐνυπνιασθήσονται, 3rd pl. fut. pass. indic. of ἐνυπνιάζομαι) dreams (ἐνυπνίοις, dat. pl. neut. of ἐνύπνιον, -ου, τό; dat. of manner [R 532]).

2:18 Καί γε ("and indeed" ZG 354) is understood by BDAG (190d) as "an intensive even." If so, it lends credence to Culy and Parson's suggestion that δούλους μου/ δούλας μου ("my male and female servants") is a summary of the previously stated people (BHGNT 34). On ἐκχεῶ, see 2:18. Προφητεύσουσιν is 3rd pl. fut. act. indic. of προφητεύω.

2:19 Peter continues the quotation in vv. 19–20 with the second characteristic of the last days: environmental signs. Δώσω (1st sg. fut. act. indic. of δίδωμι) is followed by a compound acc. pl. neut. dir. obj. τέρατα (acc. pl. neut. of τέρας, -ατος, τό, "a wonder") and σημεῖα ("signs"). The description of the signs upon the earth includes "blood and fire" (αἷμα καὶ πῦρ). The final addition (ἀτμίδα [acc. sg. fem. of ἀτμίς, -ίδος, ἡ, acc. of appos., "vapor"] καπνοῦ [gen. sg. masc. of καπνός, -οῦ, ὁ, "smoke"; gen. of mat.]) paints the picture of the smoldering aftermath of a devastating battle.

2:20 Likewise, devastation occurs in the heavens. The first two clauses are parallel cstrs. where the latter assumes the same vb. The sun (ἥλιος, nom. sg. masc. of ἥλιος, -ου, ὁ, subj.) is changed (μεταστραφήσεται, 3rd sg. fut. pass. indic. of μεταστρέφω) to darkness. The moon (σελήνη, nom. sg. fem. of σελήνη, -ης, ἡ) is changed to blood (i.e., red). Πρίν (subordinating conj., "before") ἐλθεῖν (aor. act. inf. of ἔρχομαι, "come"; another of Luke's temp. expressions with an inf.; see 1:3) indicates the changes occur before the day of the Lord (KMP 367). That day is described as "great" and "splendid" (ἐπιφανῆ, acc. sg. fem. of ἐπιφανής, -ές). Presumably God is the agent of these signs and wonders so an eschatological judgment is clearly connected to the day of the Lord inaugurated by the outpouring of the Spirit (Bock 116).

2:21 The use of καὶ ἔσται (3rd sg. fut. mid. indic. of εἰμί) recalls the opening lines at v. 17. Ὅς ἄν and ἐπικαλέσηται (3rd sg. aor. mid. subjunc. of ἐπικαλέω) forms the typical Koinē indef. rel. clause, mng. "everyone who calls. . . ." To "call upon the name" (ὄνομα) is to invoke his name in faith (Barrett 1.139). The Heb. uses the tetragrammaton but Jesus is meant here (see below). It is not uncommon for ref. to YHWH in the OT to be applied to Jesus in the NT (Bruce, *Acts of the Apostles*, 122). Altogether the phrase functions much like a subst. ptc. and is the subj. of the main vb. σωθήσεται (3rd sg. fut. pass. indic. of σῴζω). This implicit invitation will be made explicit below.

b. Peter Proclaims the Resurrection of Jesus (2:22–24)

2:22 Peter elaborated on the thesis that the pouring out of the Spirit is the proof of the last days, judgment to come, and salvation through a complicated sentence on the life, death, and resurrection of Jesus. That the elaboration is significant is highlighted by the solemn address employing two vocs. Ἄνδρες Ἰσραηλῖται (voc. pl. masc. of Ἰσραηλίτης, -ου, ὁ, lit. "Israelite men"). The expression would cover all who were present regardless of nationality but suggests those who have taken on the Mosaic covenant. The call to "hear these words" (ἀκούσατε, 2nd pl. aor. act. impv. of ἀκούω) is also a highlighting device. Jesus is described in a list of accs. of apposition modifying τοῦτον in v. 23. As a result, they together form a complex dir. obj. of ἀνείλατε (2nd pl. aor. act. indic. of ἀναιρέω, "execute") in v. 23. Jesus the Nazorean (Ναζωραῖον, acc. sg. masc. of Ναζωραῖος, -ου, ὁ; most EVV "of Nazareth," the noun in appos. is common in Luke-Acts) is described as "accredited" (ἀποδεδειγμένον, acc. sg. masc. of pf. pass.

ptc. of ἀποδείκνυμι) by God. "Powers," "wonders," and "signs" (Δυνάμεσιν, τέρασιν [dat. pl. fem. of τέρας, -ατος, τό], and σημείοις) are all dat. of means describing Jesus's public approval by God (likely referencing Joel's environmental signs). The rel. pron. οἷς is a dat. of attraction (see 1:1). Peter made it explicit by the prep. phrase ἐν μέσῳ ὑμῶν ("in your midst") and noted that the audience was aware of this.

2:23 The demonstrative pron. τοῦτον is resumptive (Ἰησοῦν is the antecedent). A series of dats. of means (τῇ ὡρισμένῃ [dat. sg. fem. of pf. pass. ptc. of ὁρίζω, "predeter-mine"; attrib.], βουλῇ ["plan"] καὶ προγνώσει [dat. sg. fem. of πρόγνωσις, -εως, ἡ, "fore-knowledge]) suggests the death of Jesus was God's plan (a major theme in Luke-Acts), but it does not hold the Judeans in Jerusalem guiltless, nor the Romans (see 4:24–27, contra Haenchen 180; Bruce, *Acts ot the Apostles*, 123 notes that ἀνόμων [gen. pl. masc. of ἄνομος, -ον, "lawless"] may refer to the Romans; see also Keener 1.942; ZG 354). Ἔκδοτον (acc. sg. masc. of ἔκδοτος, -ον, subst. adj., "given up") agrees with τοῦτον. Προσπήξαντες (nom. pl. masc. of aor. act. ptc. of προσπήγνυμι, "crucify") is a ptc. of means.

2:24 While many EVV start a new unit here, it is unlikely for the rel. pron. ὅν (referring to Jesus—the antecedent is τοῦτον . . . ἔκδοτον) introduces a dependent clause. Luke will not separate Jesus's death from the resurrection. Ὅν θεὸς ἀνέστησεν (3rd sg. aor. act. indic. of ἀνίστημι, "raise") identifies God as the agent of the resurrection. Λύσας (nom. sg. masc. of aor. act. ptc. of λύω; means) τὰς ὠδῖνας (acc. pl. fem. of ὠδίν, -ῖνος, ἡ, "birth pains") τοῦ θανάτου vividly describes the event employing a phrase from the Psalter (see LXX Ps 17:5, 6 [EV 18:5, 6] and 114:3 [EV 116:3]; Johnson 51). The phrase presents death as a painful traumatic experience that is destroyed by raising Christ from the dead (Keener 1.943). Καθότι ("because") introduces the reason for this and presents Christ as the one with inherent power over death. Κρατεῖσθαι (pres. pass. inf. of κρατέω) should be tr. "restrain" (BDAG 565a). The antecedent for αὐτόν is most likely ὅν (Christ) as the one restrained by death. That death is not able (οὐκ . . . δυνατόν, a pred. adj.) to subdue him is the reason God raised him. Robertson notes this is the first public proclamation of the resurrection of Christ (while still verifiable; Robertson, *Pictures,* 29).

c. Scriptural Support for the Resurrection of the Messiah (2:25–32)

2:25 Peter's use of εἰς αὐτόν ("about him," KMP 402) introduces a citation of the LXX of Ps 16:8–11/LXX 15:8–11. He interpreted the citation as a ref. to Christ. Προορώμην is the 1st sg. impf. mid. indic. of προοράω. The mid. suggests the sense of "to see before me" (BHGNT 38). Σαλευθῶ is the 1st sg. aor. subjunc. pass. of σαλεύω, "be shaken," NT hapax. The Heb. behind the ἵνα phrase suggests a strong confidence in God (Barrett 1.145). It is more likely a result clause in concord with the Heb. mng. than a purp. clause (contra Barrett 1.145; see Schnabel 144).

2:26 The result of the presence of God and confidence is gladness (ηὐφράνθη, 3rd sg. aor. pass. indic. of εὐφραίνω) and joy (ἠγαλλιάσατο, 3rd sg. aor. mid. indic. of ἀγαλλιάω, only rarely act. [BDAG 4b]). The phrase ἔτι δὲ καί points forward (followed by three fut. vbs. through v. 27) and underscores the third result, that Peter identified as the resurrection. The speaker's confidence is expressed as "dwelling in hope," employing the first fut. vb., κατασκηνώσει (3rd sg. fut. act. indic. of κατασκηνόω, "dwell").

2:27 The grounds for the hope (causal ὅτι) is that God will not leave (ἐγκαταλείψεις, 2nd sg. fut. act. indic. of ἐγκαταλείπω) his soul in Hades or allow (lit., "give" [δώσεις, 2nd sg. fut. indic. act. of δίδωμι]) decay (διαφθοράν, acc. sg. fem. of διαφθορά, -ᾶς, ἡ).

The last ref. has caused some difficulty. The assumption is that the psalmist spoke of his own life, mainly on the basis of the MT that reads "pit" instead of "decay" (which fits as a parallel to Sheol/Hades in the psalm's previous clause). Thus, some suggest the phrase "to see the pit" is a Heb. idiom that merely means not to die prematurely (Haenchen 181, BHGNT 39). The application to Jesus, then, is problematic.

At least two matters challenge that conclusion. First, the difference between the LXX and the MT may be due to the sim. between "pit" (šáḥaṭ) and "decay" (šiḥēt). It is not at all certain that the orig. is "pit." In an unpointed text (as the exemplar for the LXX) both words are rendered the same (šḥt). Furthermore, since "pit" may have the connotation of decay, the difference may be minimal (Beale and Carson 538).

Second, the psalm was interpreted as messianic and rather literally by some Jews. For example, *Midr. Tehillim* on Ps 16:9 notes "my glory rejoices over King Messiah" (Bruce, *Acts of the Apostles*, 124). Likewise, "decay" is not merely a Gk. phenomenon. According to Str-B 2:618, citing Midr. Ps 16, "My flesh also shall dwell in safety" (Ps 16:9, namely after death. R. Jicchaq [c. 300] said: "This shows that over his flesh rotting and worm had no control.")

A large number of respected evangelical scholars solve the issue by considering the appeal to the text as typology (i.e., representing a pattern that was true in the Messiah). See Bock 123: "The kind of defense God gave to the psalmist is like that which Jesus received"; Keener (Jesus as "par-excellence") 1.945; Robertson, *Pictures,* 30. Certainly, the phenomenon of typology exists in the NT, but as Marshall notes, it is unlikely that typology exists where the pattern (not seeing decay) is not true of the "type" (David) (Beale and Carson 538).

Johnston rightly notes that Peter's interpretation is based on four shared presuppositions regarding the Psalter: 1) David is the author; 2) he was God's anointed; 3) his was an eternal dynasty by the oath of God; and 4) the ref. in the Psalms to the King were either to David or the Messiah (Johnson 54). Peter notes since the ref. cannot refer to him (he did see corruption), David speaks of the promised descendant.

2:28 This v. is a verbatim citation of Ps 16:11 (15:11 LXX). Ἐγνώρισας (2nd sg. aor. act. indic. of γνωρίζω, "make known") takes ὁδοὺς ζωῆς ("ways of life") as its obj. Although the MT is sg. ("way of life"), the pl. suggests a pattern of behavior is understood. Πληρώσεις (2nd sg. fut. act. indic. of πληρόω) takes a gen. obj., εὐφροσύνης (gen. sg. fem. of εὐφροσύνη, -ης, ἡ, "gladness"). The source of gladness is expressed with a prep. phrase μετὰ τοῦ προσώπου σου (lit. "with your face," i.e., association [BHGNT 40]), an idiom mng. "in your presence" (NIV, TNIV).

2:29 A major shift is indicated by the use of the vocs. Ἄνδρες ἀδελφοί highlights what follows. Ἐξόν is an impers. vb. in the nom. sg. neut. of pres. act. ptc. of ἔξεστι, followed by the compl. inf. εἰπεῖν (aor. act. inf. of λέγω). The cstr. is a likely a periph. ptc. (the εἰμί is understood, ZG 355). The following prep. phrase μετὰ παρρησίας functions adv.

Thus, the sentence is often tr. "I may speak confidently about the patriarch David." Ὅτι introduces indir. speech. David has both (καί . . . καί) died (ἐτελεύτησεν, 3rd sg. aor. act. indic. of τελευτάω) and been buried (ἐτάφη, 3rd sg. aor. pass. indic. of θάπτω). The overall effect is that Peter avoids brusque language about David's body (i.e., that it has rotted in his tomb) perhaps because David was one of the seven men thought to have not suffered decay in ancient Judaism (these are listed in Barrett 1.146). Nevertheless, he still makes his point: the psalm could not refer to David, for his tomb (μνῆμα, nom. sg. neut. of μνῆμα, -ατος, τό) is still among them. It would be the evidence that while the psalmist expected life, David was dead (and suffered decay).

2:30–31 Peter offered another interpretation, namely that the text speaks of Christ. These two vv. form a rather complicated sentence with v. 30, forming the background of David's speaking, employing a compound ptc. phrase. Both ὑπάρχων (nom. sg. masc. of pres. act. ptc. of ὑπάρχω) and εἰδώς (nom. sg. masc. of pf. act. ptc. of οἶδα) are causal ptcs. giving the reason for his speaking (in v. 32). He is first a prophet (προφήτης), a proposition widespread in Judaism (Keener 1.952). This fact laid the foundation for a messianic interpretation of the psalm. Second, the bulk of the v. is a paraphrase of Ps 132:11(LXX 131:11—Beale and Carson 539–40; Johnson 52) describing God's promise to David. The dat. ὅρκῳ (dat. sg. masc. of ὅρκος, -ου, ὁ) is likely instr., "by an oath." Ὤμοσεν is the 3rd sg. aor. act. indic. of ὀμνύω, "swear." The inf. καθίσαι (aor. act. inf. of καθίζω) indicates indir. speech, describing the content of the oath. Ἐκ καρποῦ τῆς ὀσφύος (gen. sg. fem. of ὀσφῦς, -ύος, ἡ, "loins") αὐτοῦ modifies an unexpressed noun ("one" or "a son") and functions as the de facto subj. of the inf. (BHGNT 40). Clearly the ref. is to the promise to David in 2 Sam 7:16.

Προϊδών (nom. sg. masc. of aor. act. ptc. of προοράω) could either be attend. circum. or causal (likely the latter: "because he saw beforehand"). In either understanding, it picks up the previous v. as the background for the main vb. (ἐλάλησεν, 3rd sg. aor. act. indic. of λαλέω). Peter suggests he speaks about the resurrection because (causal ὅτι) Christ does fulfill Ps 16:10. The rest of the v. paraphrases the passage, mainly converting the fut.-pointing form of the LXX (ἐγκαταλείψεις and δώσεις . . . ἰδεῖν) to the aor. forms ἐγκατελείφθη (3rd sg. aor. pass. indic. of ἐγκαταλείπω, "abandon") and εἶδεν (3rd sg. aor. act. indic. of ὁράω), indicating fulfillment.

2:32 Τοῦτον τὸν Ἰησοῦν is the dir. obj. (fronted for emphasis; Bruce, *Acts of the Apostles*, 126) of the main vb. It refers back to Χριστοῦ of the previous v. and serves to identify the Messiah as Jesus of Nazareth that God raised (ἀνέστησεν, 3rd sg. aor. act. indic. of ἀνίστημι). In the next clause, οὗ is likely a neut. rel. pron. mng. "of which fact" (Bruce, *Acts of the Apostles*, 126), referring to the resurrection event (not specifically the noun). Both πάντες and ἡμεῖς are "particularly emphatic" (BHGNT 41), highlighting the veracity through a large number of witnesses.

d. The Implications (2:33–36)

2:33 Τῇ δεξιᾷ is a dat. of location (contra Barrett 1.149 and Bruce, *Acts of the Apostles*, 126, who take it as an instr.). The phrase previews the third scriptural support: Ps 110:1. Ὑψωθείς (nom. sg. masc. of aor. pass. ptc. of ὑψόω, "lift up") is a temp. ptc. The voice is a divine pass. demonstrating God's activity in raising Christ (Schnabel

148). It and the next ptc. (λαβών, nom. sg. masc. of aor. act. ptc. of λαμβάνω) are both necessary prior events to the main vb. ἐξέχεεν (3rd sg. aor. act. indic. of ἐκχέω, "pour out"). The expression is the fulfillment of Luke 24:49 and is consistent with the rest of Scripture that involves both the Father and the Son in sending the Spirit (see John 14:26 and 15:26). Τοῦ πνεύματος τοῦ ἁγίου is an epex. gen. explaining that the promise was the Spirit (ZG 355). The vb. is likely an allusion to Joel 2:28 (LXX 3:1, Schnabel 149).

2:34–35 The position of οὐ neg. Δαυίδ, not the vb. (Barrett 1.150). Thus, Δαυίδ is not the subj. of ἀνέβη (3rd sg. aor. act. indic. of ἀναβαίνω) but the compl. of an understood ἦν, "it was not David he raised." The contention is further supported by the citation of Ps 110:1 (LXX 109:1). The intensive use of αὐτός ("it was David himself. . .") further highlights the importance of the citation. David referred to another at the right of God. The implication is that the position implies raising. This echoes Christ's own arguments recorded in Luke 20:43.

2:36 Peter sums up (οὖν, Barrett 1.151) the defense with an appeal. The message is addressed to the whole house of Israel (not just the ones in attendance). The expression γινωσκέτω (3rd sg. pres. act. impv. of γινώσκω) with the nom. sg. subj. phrase πᾶς οἶκος Ἰσραὴλ ("let the house of Israel know," widespread in Judaism as a self-referent, although only here in the NT; Bruce, *Acts of the Apostles*, 128) highlights the importance of the message. The use displays the nationwide significance of this event. The content is that God has made (used in the sense of an appointment, Barrett 1.151) the risen Jesus (τοῦτον τὸν Ἰησοῦν, recalling v. 32) both (καὶ . . . καί) Lord and Christ. Αὐτόν and κύριον . . . χριστόν are in a double-acc. cstr. as the obj./compl. of ἐποίησεν. The compound nature of the latter accs. serves to exalt the position of Christ. Ultimately, Christ is the Lord upon whom we must call. The final note, ὃν ὑμεῖς ἐσταυρώσατε (2nd pl. aor. act. indic. of σταυρόω, "crucify"), is intended to call the hearers to repentance (BHGNT 43). While it was the plan of God all along, their guilt for their part in the matter is not alleviated.

FOR FURTHER STUDY

10. Peter's Use of Ps 16 (15) (2:25–28)

Bierberg, R. P. *Conserva me Domine, Ps 16 (15).* Washington, D. C: The Catholic University of America Press, 1945.

Evans, C. "The Prophetic Setting of the Pentecost Sermon." *ZNW* 74 (1983): 148–50.

Trull, Gregory V. "An Exegesis of Psalm 16:10." *BSac* 161 (2004): 304–21.

———. "Peter's Interpretation of Psalm 16:8–11 in Acts 2:25–32." *BSac* 161 (2004): 432–48.

*———. "Views on Peter's Use of Psalm 16:8–11 in Acts 2:25–32." *BSac* 161 (April 2004): 194–214.

HOMILETICAL SUGGESTIONS

The Foundational Appeal to Israel (2:14–36)

1. The promised Spirit has come (vv. 14–21)
2. The foundation is the resurrection of Jesus (vv. 22–24)
3. The Scriptures promised it (vv. 25–32)
4. You should embrace it (vv. 33–36)

Who Killed Jesus? (2:23)

1. Jewish leaders of Jerusalem (ἀνείλατε)
2. Romans (ἀνόμων)
3. God (βουλῇ καὶ προγνώσει τοῦ θεοῦ)

e. The Response of the Hearers (2:37–40)

2:37 The response of those who heard (ἀκούσαντες, nom. pl. masc. of aor. act. ptc. of ἀκούω; temp.) is a deep conviction (κατενύγησαν, 3rd pl. aor. indic. pass. of κατανύσσομαι, "stab"). The vb., in conjunction with καρδίαν (acc. of ref.), means "cut to the heart" (BDAG 523b). Ποιήσωμεν (1st pl. aor. act. subjunc. of ποιέω, delib. subjunc.) poses a question that assumes the large portion of the crowd is convinced what Peter said was true.

2:38 Peter's response calls for each of his hearers to make an individual commitment to Christ. "Repent" (μετανοήσατε, 2nd pl. aor. act. impv. of μετανοέω) and "be baptized" (βαπτισθήτω, 3rd sg. aor. pass. impv. of βαπτίζω) are strongly connected by the conj. καί.

The two impvs. are modified by two prep. phrases that narrow the understanding of what is commanded. The first, ἐπὶ τῷ ὀνόματι Ἰησοῦ Χριστοῦ, could be understood as "concerning the name of Jesus" or, perhaps, "on the authority of Jesus" (Bruce, *Acts of the Apostles*, 129). The choice of the prep. is influenced by 2:21, where it is found in a compound vb. from the Joel citation. It is most likely a subtle ref. to "calling upon the name of the Lord." The second prep. phrase is a bit more controversial for it became a foundation for the idea of baptismal regeneration (assuming εἰς to signify purp.). There are two more likely interpretations of εἰς ἄφεσιν (acc. sg. fem. of ἄφεσις, -έσεως, ἡ, "forgiveness") that do not convey efficacy in baptism.

1. As Robertson suggests, εἰς may imply the basis or grounds for something (R 592; see also BDAG 291c; BDF §207). If so, "at" or "because" of the forgiveness of sins is proper (see, e.g., Matt 12:41, Luke 11:32). Baptism is then the result of forgiveness, not the cause (Robertson, *Pictures,* 35–36; Wallace's critiques of this view are valid but fall short of a refutation [Wallace 370–71]).

*2. It is possible that εἰς does indicate purp. here (see BDAG 290d). However, it does not necessarily mean baptismal regeneration. Elsewhere (see Luke 24:47 and Acts 5:31) Luke employs the exact same phrase modifying μετάνοια alone. Thus, it is unlikely that the prep. phrase εἰς ἄφεσιν τῶν ἁμαρτιῶν ὑμῶν modifies βαπτισθήτω apart from repentance. Repentance and baptism are the beginning and ending events of the believer's initial steps into the kingdom and the church. Peter presents these as a "single complex act" (BHGNT 44). Harris states something sim.: "repentance and faith are prerequisites for receiving forgiveness and the Spirit (cf. 20:21), baptism seems to be a natural and necessary concomitant of repentance and faith . . ." (Harris 237–38).

Repentance is, at times, a euphemism for salvation (2 Pet 3:9). The word is used nine times in Luke and five in Acts (cf. 3:19; 8:22; 17:30; 26:20); each time the command is to those outside the kingdom. Baptism was considered an outward public sign that the candidate had both repented and been forgiven (Bruce, NICNT, 129). It is the initiatory rite for entering the church and a public profession of faith. Ἕκαστος ὑμῶν (gen. pl. masc., a part. gen.) indicates it was incumbent on the individual to repent and be baptized. Salvation is granted to the individual based on repentance and faith rather than any other qualification (family, nationality, race, etc.). Thus, Peter compactly describes a wholesale change in the individual's private and public life. Baptism means nothing apart from true repentance (Bruce, *Book of the Acts*, 69). The result of calling upon the name of Jesus is the reception of the Holy Spirit. Λήμψεσθε is the 2nd pl. fut. mid. indic. of λαμβάνω. Τοῦ ἁγίου πνεύματος is an obj. gen. (i.e., the gift which is the Holy Spirit). It is a characteristic of the last days, according to Joel.

2:39 The ground for the reception is conveyed in three dats. of advantage: it is for you (ὑμῖν); your children (τέκνοις); and all who are far off (πᾶσιν τοῖς εἰς μακράν). The implication is that the promise in Joel is directly made to Peter's hearers. The final ref. is likely geographical in scope, intending to include Gentiles (Bock 145). In the final clause, προσκαλέσηται (3rd sg. aor. subjunc. mid. of προσκαλέω, "summons") seems to be an allusion to Joel 2:32 (LXX 3:5). Here the privilege of all humanity to call upon the name of the Lord for salvation is counterbalanced by the prior summons of God. Without a doubt, whoever calls upon the name of the Lord shall be saved, but "at the same time it is 'the Lord our God' who calls people into his presence" (Schnabel 166).

2:40 Luke was well aware that Peter said much more on the day of Pentecost than is recorded in Acts 2. He employed an instr. dat. (ἑτέροις τε λόγοις πλείοσιν, "with many other words") to describe the length of his message. He also referred to it as a solemn testimony (διεμαρτύρατο 3rd sg. aor. mid. indic. of διαμαρτύρομαι). The aor. refers to the whole of Peter's words. In contrast, his urging is in the impf. tense (παρεκάλει, 3rd sg. impf. indic. act. of παρακαλέω) that signifies a repeated event (Haenchen 184). Λέγων (nom. sg. masc. of pres. act. ptc. of λέγω) introduces dir. speech. His desire was for their salvation (σώθητε, 2nd pl. aor. pass. impv. of σώζω) that indicates that they stand in danger and must put themselves in the place where they can be rescued (the force of the pass.—salvation is God's work). The phrase τῆς γενεᾶς τῆς σκολιᾶς (gen. sg. fem. of σκολιός, -ά, -όν, "crooked") ταύτης ("this crooked generation") is an allusion to Deut 32:5 (and perhaps Ps 78:8 [77:8 LXX]) to the wilderness generation, making an implicit comp. (Johnson 58). Bruce notes that such a comp. was also made at Qumran to those who rejected the teacher of righteousness (CD 3:7–12; Bruce, *Acts of the Apostles*, 131).

4. The Expansion: The Growth of the Early Church (2:41–47)

2:41 On μὲν οὖν, see 1:6. The response was phenomenal. Luke was careful to avoid confusion and presented the number as about (ὡσεί) 3,000 souls (ψυχαί). This would cover any who received (οἱ . . . ἀποδεξάμενοι, nom. pl. masc. of aor. mid. ptc. of ἀποδέχομαι; subst.) Peter's message. By describing the response thus, Luke also made it clear that they believed/called upon the name of the Lord. These followed through in baptism (ἐβαπτίσθησαν, 3rd pl. aor. indic. pass. of βαπτίζω) that very day. It was likely a very public event at pools near the temple (Schnabel 167–68). Προσετέθησαν (3rd pl. aor. pass. indic. of προστίθημι, "add") indicates that they were added to the 120 disciples. So not only did they receive Christ, the disciples received them.

2:42 Ἦσαν . . . προσκαρτεροῦντες (nom. pl. masc. of pres. act. ptc. of προσκαρτερέω, "continue, pay attention to") is a periphr. impf. emphasizing the continuing aspect of the activity. Προσκαρτερέω takes a dat. as its dir. obj. In this case it is complex. Luke's use of conj. and asyndeton suggest two clusters of activity for the new church. Each cluster has a specific activity, then a general one. In the first set, the specific activity is attention "to the apostles' teaching" (τῇ διδαχῇ [dat. sg. fem. of διδαχή, -ῆς, ἡ] τῶν ἀποστόλων [a subj. gen.]). The phrase indicates the new believers were continually learning. The general activity is expressed as κοινωνία. This is an innate sense of community and partnership in Christ. The second cluster follows the same pattern. The specific activity is "to the breaking of bread" (τῇ κλάσει [dat. sg. fem. of κλάσις, -εως, ἡ] τοῦ ἄρτου [an obj. gen.]). It is likely a ref. to table fellowship, but one cannot dismiss that it might include the Lord's Supper as well (Bock 150; Bruce [*Acts of the Apostles*, 132] notes that the two are often connected). Προσευχαῖς ("to prayers") is also likely a ref. to the general activity of intercession, praise, and supplication. "General" in no way suggests a common or meaningless activity. Holy Spirit–empowered prayer will be the very atmosphere of the young church in the chs. that follow. The word is used some thirty-four times in Luke-Acts (only fifty times more in the entire NT). It is a defining element of the New Testament Church (Bock 151).

2:43 The impf. ἐγίνετο (3rd sg. impf. indic. mid. of γίνομαι) suggests that the fear was a deep, settled response and "no momentary panic" (Bruce, *Acts of the Apostles*, 132). Φόβος is the correct response to the holy God manifesting himself in unusual ways. Several EVV interpret the word as "awe" in one sense or another (cf. NLT, NASB, NIV, NRSV, ESV, TNIV, NET, MIT, NJB). To do so, however, obfuscates the response of the manifestation of the Holy God by making part of the human response the totality of it. The gloss "fear" represents it far better (see comments at 5:11; cf. Barrett 1.166, Bock 151). Τε . . . καί (normally "both . . . and") is comprehensive. Τέρατα (dat. pl. fem. of τέρας, -ατος, τό) καὶ σημεῖα ("wonders and signs," see 2:19) is an unusual order in the Gk. Bible (normally reversed; used only in Acts and Wis 10:16). Here it recalls v. 22 that describes the ministry of Jesus. Since Luke describes these as "through the hands of the apostles," he is connecting their wonders to Jesus's (echoing "began to do" at 1:1). The indication is that only the apostles were being used in this manner.

2:44 Luke specifically unpacks the activity of the young group. They are identified as οἱ πιστεύοντες (nom. pl. masc. of pres. act. ptc. of πιστεύω), because believing is the defining aspect of the Christian. Ἦσαν (3rd pl. impf. indic. of εἰμί) indicates that the unity among disciples was not fleeting. Ἐπὶ τὸ αὐτό (cf. 1:15; 2:1) idiomatically employs the identifying use of the pron. as the obj. of the prep. (mng. "to be together") and here it describes the inner concord among the disciples rather than merely location (Schnabel 181). The outward expression of their unity employs the impf. εἶχον (3rd pl. impf. act. indic. of ἔχω) in a double-acc. cstr. Ἅπαντα ("all things") is a subst. adj. (dir. obj.) that, with the compl. κοινά (acc. pl. neut. of κοινός, -ή, -όν, "common"), indicates a community sharing of property and goods. While such community sharing was known in Judaism (cf. 1QS 1:1; 5:2; Josephus J.W. 2.122, referring to the Essenes; see Barrett 1.168–69), it did not seem to be a common practice. Josephus described the Essenes' surrender of possessions as mandatory upon entering the community. The early church is different; the stress is on the voluntary generosity of the believers among themselves.

2:45 The specifics of this generosity are described in v. 45. Κτήματα (acc. pl. neut. of κτῆμα, -ατος, τό, "possessions") specifically ref. to property, esp. real estate (cf. 5:1, BHGNT 47). Ὑπάρξεις (acc. pl. fem. of ὕπαρξις, -εως, ἡ, also "possessions") refers to the more moveable possessions, i.e., "goods" (BDAG 1029b). Together the ref. is comprehensive. Both were being sold (ἐπίπρασκον, 3rd pl. impf. act. indic. of πιπράσκω) and distributed (διεμέριζον, 3rd pl. impf. act. indic. of διαμερίζω) to those in need. The impfs. suggest ongoing activity (iter. impfs.). The criterion of benefit was having need. Καθότι is used in the sense of "to the degree that" (BDAG 493b) and argues against a sort of "Christian commune" (see comments at Acts 5:1; Schnabel 182).

2:46 The specifics of their fellowship are described in v. 46. Καθ᾽ ἡμέραν is an idiomatic expression mng. "daily" (cf. Luke 11:3). The structure of the sentence backgrounds temple worship and breaking bread to eating in concord and gladness through the use of two attend. circum. ptcs. Προσκαρτεροῦντες (nom. masc. pl. of pres. act. ptc. of προσκαρτερέω, "persisting") describes a state. The translation of the CSB "devoted themselves to meeting" fits nicely. It is followed by an acc. of ref. The mng. of ὁμοθυμαδόν is contested in EVV as either "united" (i.e., "with one mind" NASB) or "in one place" (i.e., "together"). Judgments made regarding the previous use at 1:14 (also modifying προσκαρτερέω) are likely determinative. The option taken here is the former. The second specific is the breaking of bread. Κλῶντες (nom. pl. masc. of pres. act. ptc. of κλάω, "break") is another idiomatic expression, referring to the eating of meals. Κατ᾽ οἶκον is distributive and means "from house to house." Μετελάμβανον is 3rd pl. impf. indic. act. of μεταλαμβάνω, "share." The prep. phrase ἐν ἀγαλλιάσει (fem. dat. sg. of ἀγαλλίασις, -εως, ἡ) functions like a dat. of manner. It suggests a stronger feeling than χαρά, perhaps "great joy." Ἀφελότητι (dat. sg. fem. of ἀφελότης, -ητος, ἡ) modified by the gen. καρδίας is, lit., "simplicity of heart" and describes the inner motives of the disciples. Because it is a biblical hapax and "rare elsewhere" (Barrett 1.170, cf. Bock 154) it is debated whether the idiom means "generosity" (Bruce, *Acts of the Apostles*, 133), "simplicity of heart" (BDAG 155b), or "with sincerity" (see BHGNT 48).

2:47 Following the main vb. in the previous v., two ptcs. describe the result of the Spirit's activity in the new believers. The first is actively done by the believers. Αἰνοῦντες (nom. pl. masc. of pres. act. ptc. of αἰνέω, "praise") takes θεόν as its object.

The second is more of a pass. idea; ἔχοντες (nom. pl. masc. of pl. pres. act. ptc. of ἔχω) takes χάριν πρὸς ὅλον τὸν λαόν as its object. The use of πρός here should be understood in the sense of "in the presence of" or "before" and indicates the people's favor of the new community.

Luke's ultimate summary of the church's early days is short and centered on the actions of God. Προσετίθει (3rd sg. impf. act. indic. of προστίθημι, "add") is a progressive impf. The use of the subst. σῳζομένους (acc. pl. masc. of pres. act. ptc. of σῴζω) links nicely to the promise in Joel (Keener 1.1038). It not only shows the activity of God but also the fulfillment of the promise made in Joel 2. The mng. of ἐπὶ τὸ αὐτό is debated, BDAG (363b) gives the gloss, "to their number." Technically, it means "together" but that sense doesn't work here. Barrett (citing Vazakis) argues convincingly that it is simply an idiomatic phrase that was common in the LXX, the NT, and the apostolic fathers (Barrett 1.173), mng. "in the community/church" (see also Keener 1.1038). Although the difficulty of the phrase has spawned a significant var. rdg. (giving rise to the *byz.* rdg. behind the KJV/NKJV) the difference in mng. is negligible. Barrett is likely correct about the mng. here.

HOMILETICAL SUGGESTIONS

The Promise of Salvation (2:37–47)

1. New covenant believers in Christ are: (vv. 37–38)

   repentant
   believing
   saved
   sealed

2. New covenant believers in Christ should be: (vv. 38–47)

   baptized
   fellowshipping
   fearful
   generous
   praying
   witnessing

II. The Early Church in Jerusalem (3:1–6:7)

A. A MIRACLE AND ITS AFTERMATH (3:1–4:31)

Peter and, to a lesser extent, John are center stage in the early life of the church in Jerusalem. A notable miracle was performed at the temple. The healing of the lame man is notable in that it is the continuation of Jesus's messianic ministry (cf. Isa 35:6, "the lame will leap like a deer"), in his authority (Peter had no intrinsic power at his disposal). The man's status as outcast, invisible, and unclean continue Luke's theme of the gospel for all people. Peter took the opportunity to preach to the crowd that gathered, with two results. First, a large number were converted. Second, it drew the attention of the Sanhedrin. In the latter's inquiry, Peter again declared the gospel. Upon their release, Peter and John returned to the church where, upon prayer, the gathered assembly was again filled with the Holy Spirit. The gospel was taking deep and significant root in Jerusalem.

1. The Miracle (3:1–10)

3:1 The term "ascend" (ἀνέβαινον, 3rd pl. impf. act. indic. of ἀνάβαινω) is appropriate for going to the temple (from any direction; Bruce, *Acts of the Apostles*, 135–36). Sim. usage is found elsewhere in the NT and seems to be inspired by the convention of going to Jerusalem and the mountain of God in the OT expressed as "ascending" (see, e.g., Ps 23:3). The impf. implies that the event happened as they were attempting to enter the temple at the "ninth hour." Ὥραν (acc. sg. fem., obj. of prep.) is modified by προσευχῆς (gen. sg. fem., descriptive gen., "prayer"). This would be about 3:00 p.m., the second of three such hours (Bruce, *Acts of the Apostles*, 136).

3:2–3 The verbal description of the lame man employs a pred. adj. (χωλός, nom. sg. masc. of χωλός, -ή, -όν, "lame") following ὑπάρχων (nom. sg. masc. of pres. act. ptc. of ὑπάρχω). Ἐβαστάζετο is the 3rd sg. impf. pass. indic. of βαστάζω, "carry, bear." Ἐτίθουν is the 3rd. pl. impf. act. indic. of τίθημι. The impfs. here suggest the laying at the temple gate was customary (cf. καθ᾽ ἡμέραν, BHGNT 50; Barrett 1.179). Πρὸς τὴν θύραν has the sense of "at the gate of" (RSV, ESV, NET [NIV "to"]; lit., "door"; but since it is "gate" in 3:10, the latter is the best tr. for both words). It is typical to use a pass. (λεγομένην, acc. sg. fem. of pres. pass. ptc. of λέγω) to name an obj., in this instance "beautiful" (ὡραίαν, acc. sg. fem. of ὡραῖος, -α, -ον). Scholars are not sure of which gate this is; most suggest the eastern gate made of Corinthian bronze (Johnson 65). The articular αἰτεῖν (pres. act. inf. of αἰτέω) in the gen. is a purp. clause: "to beg alms." Εἰσπορευομένων is the gen. pl. masc. of pres. mid. ptc. εἰσπορεύομαι, "enter"; subst. he would not have been permitted to enter the temple (cf. Lev 21:17–18).

The rel. pron. (ὅς) continues the topic of the lame man. Ἰδών (nom. sg. masc. of aor. act. ptc. of ὁράω; temp.) takes a compound double-acc. cstr. with Peter and John as the obj. and μέλλοντας (acc. pl. masc. of pres. act. ptc. of μέλλω) compl. by εἰσιέναι (pres. act. inf. of εἴσειμι, "enter") as the compl. (BHGNT 51). The impf. ἠρώτα (3rd sg. impf. act. indic. of ἐρωτάω) implies repeated action. It might either be for vividness (Bock 161; Haenchen 199) or, more likely, an inceptive impf.: "he began asking" (NASB; Robertson, *Pictures,* 43). There is no distinction with the previous αἰτέω (Barrett 1.181).

3:4 Ἀτενίσας is the nom. sg. masc. of aor. act. ptc. of ἀτενίζω, "look intently at"; temp. That Peter has to command the beggar's attention (βλέψον, 2nd sg. aor. act. impv. of βλέπω, "look") suggests the man would not make eye contact.

3:5 The art. ὁ functions as a pers. pron. and the subj. of the verb. Ἐπεῖχεν (3rd sg. impf. act. indic. of ἐπέχω) is lit. "was holding fast." The obj. of the vb. is an implied ὀφθαλμούς ("eyes") or νοῦν ("attention," Barrett 1.181; Bruce, *Acts of the Apostles*, 137). Given Peter's previous command, βλέψον, the former is more likely but with little difference in mng. EVV typically choose the latter, "paying attention." Προσδοκῶν (nom. sg. masc. of pres. act. ptc. of προσδοκάω, "expect") is a causal ptc. that is completed with the inf. λαβεῖν (aor. act. inf. of λαμβάνω). The beggar goes from "asking" to "expecting" because Peter addressed him.

3:6 Peter's response is marked for emphasis through the use of fronting and a resumptive pron. Lit. Peter says, "Silver and gold does not exist (ὑπάρχει, 3rd sg. pres. act. indic. of ὑπάρχω) to me." The headless (i.e., no antecedent, BHGNT 52) rel. pron. (ὅ) introduces a fronted dir. obj. clause with ἔχω (1st sg. pres. act. indic. of ἔχω). Δίδωμι is the 1st sg. pres. act. indic. of δίδωμι. The resumptive pron. τοῦτο is the dir. obj. Ἐν τῷ ὀνόματι means "by the authority of" (not as in magical usage, but "name" suggests the source of the power is Jesus wielded by an authorized agent [cf. 8:9–11], Schnabel 195). On Ναζωραίου (gen. sg. masc. of Ναζωραῖος, -ου, ὁ) see 2:22. The command περιπάτει (2nd sg. pres. act. impv. of περιπατέω) implies complete healing, a continuous walking (Bock 161).

3:7 Πιάσας (nom. sg. masc. of aor. act. ptc. of πιάζω, "seize"; temp.) is typically found with the acc. of pers. and the gen. of part seized (Barrett 1.183). Here it is αὐτόν and τῆς δεξιᾶς χειρός, ("the right hand") respectively. The grasping was to raise the beggar (ἤγειρεν, 3rd sg. aor. act. indic. of ἐγείρω). The use of παραχρῆμα ("immediately") is virtually unique to Luke-Acts (sixteen times, Schnabel 196). It is likely that it is Luke's preferred term to εὐθύς (used once each in Luke and Acts). The vb. ἐστερεώθησαν (3rd pl. aor. pass. indic. of στερεόω, "strengthen") defines the healing of the man's feet (βάσεις, nom. pl. fem. of βάσις, -εως, ἡ) and ankles (σφυδρά, nom. pl. neut. of σφυδρόν, -οῦ, τό). While quite specific, neither are particularly "medical terminology" (Barrett 1.184).

3:8–9 Ἐξαλλόμενος (nom. sg. masc. of pres. mid. ptc. of ἐξάλλομαι, "leap") is a ptc. of manner modifying both ἔστη (3rd sg. aor. act. indic. of ἵστημι) and περιεπάτει (3rd sg. impf. act. indic. of περιπατέω). The healed beggar's entrance into the temple continued to be rather athletic. Εἰσῆλθεν is followed by a series of pres. ptcs. of manner: περιπατῶν (nom. sg. masc. of pres. act. ptc. of περιπατέω), ἁλλόμενος (nom. sg. masc. of pres. mid. ptc. of ἅλλομαι, "leap"), and αἰνῶν (nom. sg. masc. of pres. act. ptc. of αἰνέω, "praise"). Unlike human healing, there is obviously no need for any physical therapy to strengthen atrophied muscles. In the temple, v. 9, the former beggar is seen (εἶδεν) by all the people (πᾶς ὁ λαός), ostensibly from his activity (περιπατοῦντα and αἰνοῦντα, both acc. sg. masc. pres. act. ptcs.).

3:10 Seeing becomes recognizing (ἐπεγίνωσκον, 3rd pl. impf. act. indic. of ἐπιγινώσκω, "recognize"). The epex. ὅτι clause identifies the recognition. He was the one sitting (καθήμενος nom. sg. masc. of pres. mid. ptc. of κάθημαι; subst.). It functions as the

pred. nom. of ἦν. As such, it functions much like a periph. impf., although not technically so (see Barrett 1.185). Most EVV tr. it habitually, "the one who used to sit . . ."
Πρὸς τὴν ἐλεημοσύνην (fem. acc. sg. of ἐλεημοσύνη, -ης, ἡ, "alms") is a purp. clause
(BDAG 874c). "To beg alms" is the gist of it. The location is indicated by ἐπί followed
by the dat. τῇ ὡραίᾳ πύλῃ (fem. dat. sgs. of ὡραῖος, -α, -ον, "beautiful," and πύλη, -ης, ἡ,
"gate"), "at the beautiful gate." The response of the crowd is described by ἐπλήσθησαν
(3rd pl. aor. pass. indic. of πίμπλημι, "filled") with a compound obj. (πίμπλημι takes
a gen. obj.). The objs., θάμβους (gen. sg. neut. of θάμβος, -ους, τό, "amazement") and
ἔκστασις (gen. sg. fem. of ἔκστασις, -εως, ἡ, "astonishment"), should be taken together.
They describe "someone emotionally impacted" (Bock 163). "Beside themselves"
would be a good colloq. tr. (it has little to do with a "trancelike ecstasy," Schnabel 197;
contra *TDNT* 2.449 ff.). The force of ἐπί is causal (BHGNT 54). The obj. of the prep.
is the subst. ptc. συμβεβηκότι (dat. sg. neut. of pf. act. ptc. of συμβαίνω), mng. "the
thing which happened." Αὐτῷ is a dat. of advantage. This remarkable sight becomes
the magnet to draw a crowd for Peter's speech that follows.

FOR FURTHER STUDY

11. Miracles in Acts

Davids, P. H. *DLNT*, 747–52.
Hamm, D. "Acts 3:1–10: The Healing of the Temple Beggar as Lukan Theology." *Bib* 63
(1986): 305–19.
———. "Acts 3:12–26: Peter's Speech and the Healing of the Man Born Lame." *PRSt* 11
(Fall 1984): 199–217.
NIDNTTE, 4.283–90.
Rengstorf, K. H. *TDNT*, 7.239–43.
*Twelftree, G. *Paul and the Miraculous: A Historical Reconstruction.* Grand Rapids:
Baker, 2013.

HOMILETICAL SUGGESTIONS

The Gospel for All People (3:1–10)

1. God cares for the invisible
2. God cares for the outcast
3. God cares for the unclean
4. God cares for the helpless

2. Peter's Temple Sermon (3:11–26)

Peter's second recorded public appeal to Israel was prompted by the very public miracle performed at the gate. The sermon has two major movements after it is introduced
by v. 11. Each movement is marked by a voc. First, 3:12 introduces the speech with
ἄνδρες Ἰσραηλῖται and provides God's approval of Jesus as Israel's Messiah as the basis

for the miracle. Likewise, Peter's appeal for salvation is introduced at 17–26 by the voc. ἀδελφοί and provides scriptural support and admonition.

3:11 The ptc. κρατοῦντος (gen. sg. masc. of pres. act. ptc. of κρατέω, "seize," in this case, "cling") fronts a gen. abs. phrase. Συνέδραμεν (3rd sg. aor. act. indic. of συντρέχω, "run together") has the collective πᾶς ὁ λαός ("all the people") as its subj. and is rightly tr. as a plural. They ran toward Solomon's portico (cf. John 10:23; Acts 5:12; BASHH 224). Καλουμένη (dat. sg. fem. of pres. pass. ptc. of καλέω) is a typical expression of naming in the NT. Perhaps the most significant linguistic item is the right dislocation of the pl. attrib. adj. ἔκθαμβοι (nom. pl. masc. of ἔκθαμβος, -ον, "amazed"). One would expect it in a typical placement in an attrib. position since it modifies ὁ λαός. Functioning as an appos. of sorts, the Eng. tr. "all the people, utterly amazed" expresses the mng. However, the dislocation to the end of the sentence highlights the state (BHGNT 55).

3:12 Peter began by defining how the crowd should understand the event. Peter's address is introduced in a rather standard form: a temp. ptc. (ἰδών, nom. sg. masc. of aor. act. ptc. of ὁράω) setting the background to the speaking, a vb. of address identifying the speaker (ἀπεκρίνατο, 3rd sg. aor. mid. indic. of ἀποκρίνομαι), and an identification of the audience (πρὸς τὸν λαόν, "to the people"). Regarding the vb., Wallace suggests it may be an indication of "vested interest" since all of the other nineteen uses of the vb. ἀποκρίνομαι in Acts are act. in form (Wallace 421; BHGNT 55). Peter addressed the audience (for ἄνδρες Ἰσραηλῖται, see 2:22).

Peter began with two rhetorical statements introduced with a neut. interr. τί, "Why?," each with the force of "you should not. . ." (BHGNT 55). They should neither marvel (θαυμάζετε, 2nd pl. pres. act. indic. of θαυμάζω) nor assume (ἀτενίζετε, 2nd pl. pres. act. indic. of ἀτενίζω, lit.,"stare at") the healers acted in their own power or righteousness (δυνάμει and εὐσεβείᾳ [dat. sg. fem. of εὐσέβεια, -ας, ἡ, "piety"]). The last clause is rather difficult to tr. It assumes the obj. of ἀτενίζετε (ἡμῖν) as the subj. The adjs. and ptc., πεποιηκόσιν (dat. pl. masc. of pf. act. ptc. of ποιέω) are dats. of means. The ptc. is either an independent verbal ptc. (acting like a vb.) or a rare anar. subst. ptc. (BHGNT 55) likely as the compl. of an understood ἐσμέν. Both uses would expect a nom. case, but the dat. of the ptc. is by attraction to ἡμῖν and both would be tr. in Eng. as "we have made." Τοῦ περιπατεῖν is an inf. of result with αὐτόν as its subj. The combination of the ptc. with the inf. creates a causative cstr. (Schnabel 208).

3:13 Peter introduced the real source of the miracle in v. 16. He first, however, affirmed the status of Jesus and built an accusation against his hearers. Jesus has been glorified by their own ancestral historical God. A series of gen. of poss. (Ἀβραάμ, Ἰσαάκ, Ἰακώβ, τῶν πατέρων ἡμῶν) makes this identification. Their God glorified (ἐδόξασεν, 3rd sg. aor. act. indic. of δοξάζω) Jesus, who is described as God's servant (παῖδα, acc. sg. masc. of παῖς, παιδός, ὁ). Although παῖς could have sonship overtones, it would be the only use of the word with this sense in the NT. It is more likely that it is an allusion to the rather unusual use in Isa 52:13, where both παῖς and δοξάζω refer to God's servant (Schnabel 208). Jesus is further identified by the rel. pron. ὅν. On μέν, see 1:1. It does not correlate to v. 14's δέ (i.e., a μέν . . . δέ cstr., Bruce, *Acts of the Apostles*, 141; identical actions, denial, are described) but points forward to the next clause. The sin of the people is again brought forth in that they not only betrayed Christ (παρεδώκατε, 2nd pl. aor. act. indic. of παραδίδωμι) but also denied (ἠρνήσασθε, 2nd pl. aor. mid. indic. of ἀρνέομαι) that he was their king. Ὑμεῖς is emphatic in position and redundant and in this context accusatory. They did this despite the opportunity Pilate had given for clemency. Κρίναντος (gen. sg. masc. of aor. act. ptc. of κρίνω—gen. abs. for the subj. of the gen. is different from the subj. of the main clause [BHGNT 56]) in the last clause is most likely a concessive ptc. mng. "though," though temp. "when" is also possible (see ESV).

3:14 In contrast to this opportunity (using δέ), they denied Christ, who is described with the subst. adj. τὸν ἅγιον καὶ δίκαιον, "the holy and just one." The art. controls both adjs., so they should be considered one Christological thought (Barrett 1.195). It is likely the ref. to the fourth servant song continues, for there the servant is referred to as δίκαιος (Isa 53:11, Barrett 1.196; see also Isa 52:10 where the Lord's arm is ἅγιος, and then 53:1 when the servant is introduced as the Lord's arm). Who they requested (the force of the mid.; ᾐτήσασθε, 2nd pl. aor. mid. indic. of αἰτέω) instead was a murderer (ἄνδρα φονέα [acc. sg. masc. of φονεύς, -έως, ὁ, "murderer"]). It is a moral estimation in contrast with ἅγιον καὶ δίκαιον (Barrett 1.195–96). The effect was that Peter described the event as a morally indefensible choice by his hearers.

3:15 The accusation is continued with a paradox (using an adversative δέ): they killed (ἀπεκτείνατε, 2nd pl. aor. act. indic. of ἀποκτείνω, causative) the author of life. There is a debate whether ἀρχηγόν (acc. sg. masc. of ἀρχηγός, -οῦ, ὁ) means "author/originator" or "Prince" (BDAG 138d–39a, Bock 171). EVV using the former are ESV, NET, NIV, NLT. Preferring the latter: NAS, NKJV, KJV. Both mngs. are true of Jesus in other contexts so true vs. false is not really at stake. At issue is if the description of Jesus refers to his role in salvation or his inherent nature.

1. Those who support the latter see it as the one leading to life (in which ζωῆς is interpreted as a gen. of direction). Hence, the translation "Prince" (Haenchen 206). In Acts 5:31 the term clearly is a title and means "Prince." If so, the description refers primarily to salvation.

*2. However, both instances of the term in Heb (2:10; 12:2) mean "author/origi-nator." Furthermore, the usage in Acts 5 is clearly a title; in Acts 3:15 it is more descriptive. In this understanding, the gen. ζωῆς is an obj. gen., a more likely classification. If so, the series of contrasts in the context are continued (see Barrett 1.197–98). In that case the description refers primarily to Jesus's inherent character, making the choice of Barabbas totally indefensible on moral grounds.

3. It is possible some double entendre is meant (Bock 171). Bruce notes it is a CGk. word that combines the idea of originator and leader (Bruce, *Acts of the Apostles*, 141).

The author of life is not left dead, for God raised (ἤγειρεν, 3rd sg. aor. act. indic. of ἐγείρω) him. And finally, Peter declared that the disciples were eyewitnesses to all these things.

3:16 Peter turned to the true source of the miracle. Emphasizing the importance of the name of Jesus (stated twice) in this v. produces difficulties for a word-for-word tr. in

Eng. Descriptions like "intolerable clumsy" (Barrett 1.198) and "contorted syntax" (Bock 172) are value judgments that are not helpful. Carefully walking through the sentence's structure is the most helpful procedure. The prep. phrase ἐπὶ τῇ πίστει is fronted for emphasis. Many EVV tr. it as an instr. "by," but it is more naturally understood as causal "upon faith in his name" (BHGNT 57; Harris 138; see NASB). The major question is whose faith? There are three options.

1. Faith of the apostles. In this sense, it is the faith of the apostles who used the name of Jesus. The trouble with this interpretation is that it lends itself to understanding the name of Jesus as a magical phrase. Barrett concludes that the v. itself points to the faith itself, not the name wielded as the agent of the healing (Barrett 1.200). It is more possible that the apostle acted in faith wielding the authority of Jesus. As Keener states, "Peter acted in Jesus's name, as Jesus's agent, carrying out Jesus's own ministry" (Keener 2.1101). In this way, no faith on the part of the beggar is needed.

2. The faithfulness of Jesus. Culy and Parsons suggest the possibility that "name" should be understood as a metonym for "him," referring to Christ (BHGNT 57). In this understanding Jesus is the one who performed the miracle. The first instance of ὀνόματος is a subj. gen. Thus, the sentence should be read "because of the faithfulness of his name, his name [i.e., "he"] strengthened this man" (BHGNT 58). While appealing, it is difficult to find sim. uses of ὄνομα elsewhere in Luke-Acts. Keener also notes that name is a metonym, but for his authority (Keener 2.1101). The combination of (perhaps) overly subtle syntax and unlikely ref. of ὄνομα casts doubt on this position.

*3. The faith of the beggar. While the first position is possible, it is more likely that faith in Jesus (as the one with authority) is the foundation for the miracle—namely, the faith of the beggar. There is no doubt that Peter was wielding the authority of Jesus (cf. 3:6). However, it is the faith in his name that strengthened the man. Furthermore, faith in the name of Christ (expressed in full repentance, 3:19) is what was suggested by Peter in the appeal that follows and suggests a natural parallel with the mng. in 3:16. Bock notes that it is not impossible that the apostles and the beggar are meant but that the one emphasized is the man himself (Bock 172). The faith here, then, is the initial faith of the man.

Next, the dir. obj. of the main vb. (still to come) is a pron. referring to the healed beggar, τοῦτον. Still before the introduction of the main verb, the man is identified by a rel. pron. phrase. The hearers both see (θεωρεῖτε, 2nd pl. pres. act. indic. of θεωρέω) and know (οἴδατε, 2nd pl. pf. act. indic. of οἶδα) the man. Finally, the main vb. "strengthened" (ἐστερέωσεν, 3rd sg. aor. act. indic. of στερεόω) and the subj., a repetition of "his name" (τὸ ὄνομα αὐτοῦ) completes the first sentence.

By fronting the phrase, the role of the man's faith in Christ is emphasized. The nom. πίστις ("faith") is modified by a prep. phrase in the attrib. position that is made into an adj. by the art. While technically faith is the subj. of the vb., clearly it is the obj. of the faith that gave (ἔδωκεν, 3rd sg. aor. act. indic. of δίδωμι) the man wholeness (ὁλοκληρίαν, acc. sg. fem. of ὁλοκληρία, -ας, ἡ, dir. obj., NT hapax). Finally, Peter noted that the man was before them (ἀπέναντι, "against," likely a substitute for πρό, like κατὰ πρόσωπον in v. 13 [Bruce, *Acts of the Apostles*, 142]). The expression is a common LXX expression (ZG 353).

3:17 Καὶ νῦν marks the transition to the meat of the speech. His address to them as "brothers" (ἀδελφοί) was likely as fellow Jews (see Bock 173; contra Haenchen 207). The charge of murdering the Messiah was certain to recall at least the question of level of guilt. Peter's address absolved them of pure unmitigated evil. Οἶδα (1st sg. pf. act. indic. of οἶδα) expresses his confidence that they acted (ἐπράξατε, 2nd pl. aor. act. indic. of πράσσω) in ignorance (ἄγνοιαν, acc. sg. fem. of ἄγνοια, -ας, ἡ). The rulers (ἄρχοντες) are also included (ὥσπερ "just as") in the same category.

3:18 Peter turned to his main point, that the events are the fulfillment of God's plan announced from long ago. A long rel. clause separates the subj. (θεός) and the vb. (ἐπλήρωσεν, 3rd sg. aor act. indic. of πληρόω). Thus, the basic clause is "God fulfilled." Ἄ is best understood as a "headless" rel. clause ("that which") and functions as the dir. obj. of ἐπλήρωσεν (BHGNT 58). The content of the subord. clause is that God had promised beforehand (προκατήγγειλεν, 3rd sg. aor. act. indic. of προκαταγγέλλω, a rare vb. [MM 541d]). The promise is through the prophets (διὰ στόματος, "through the mouth," a LXX expression [Barrett 1.202]), but πάντων is likely hyperbolic, considering the prophets as a unity (Haenchen 208). The mng. of παθεῖν τὸν χριστὸν αὐτοῦ is not really debated, although the syntax of παθεῖν (aor. act. inf. of πάσχω, "suffer") is.

1. Wallace (606–7) sees the inf. as appos. ("namely").
2. Culy and Parsons see it as epex., in tr., not much different than Wallace 607.
*3. However, it is far more likely that it is an example of indir. speech, giving the gist of the message. Οὕτως refers to the manner of the fulfillment and points to the sufferings of Christ.

3:19–21 The structure of 19–20 is clear: two impvs. followed by three purp. clauses, although the structure does not indicate a sequential list (see below). The two impvs. define the wise response to the miracle. They should "repent" (μετανοήσατε, 2nd pl. aor. act. impv. of μετανοέω) and "turn back" (ἐπιστρέψατε, 2nd pl. aor. act. impv. of ἐπιστρέφω). It is difficult to tell if Peter was calling for a corporate or a personal repentance. The nature of the specific sin to be repented (killing their king) and the scope of the results (the return of the Messiah) would suggest he had in mind a corporate repentance. This is in line with the expectation of many of the rabbis that the repentance of Israel would usher in the age to come (Keener 2.1106–8). Οὖν also suggests the grounds for the repentance is in the previous context. They should repent of killing their promised Messiah who suffered as the prophets said: a corporate event.

However, there are striking similarities with the appeal in Acts 2:38. That appeal is undeniably individual (see, e.g., ἕκαστος ὑμῶν, "each of you"). Furthermore, the first purp. clause, the prep. phrase εἰς τὸ ἐξαλειφθῆναι (aor. pass. inf. of ἐξαλείφω, "be erased"), indicates the intent is to have their sins "wiped out." It is unlikely that corporate sin alone or the one sin of rejecting the Messiah is meant. Ultimately pers. and genuine corporate conversion are intimately connected. The latter without the former would be a sham (see Barrett 1.204).

Verse 20 forms the last two of the three purp. clauses. These clauses are distinguished in that they are compounded (joined by καί) and introduced by a different marker, here a subord. conj., ὅπως (with ἄν). So, then, the last two join together and are alike in some way. How they are alike determines how they are to be understood. The second of the two clauses clearly refers to the reign of the returned Jesus. That he is "your appointed (προκεχειρισμένον, masc. sg. acc. of pf. mid. ptc. of προχειρίζομαι; attrib.) Christ" means that he is the one God appointed as Christ, not that he will become Christ at his return (Barrett 1.204–5). The first purp. clause also employs καιροί, "seasons." Since it suggests a period of time, it is tempting to see it as synonymous with the eschatological reign of Christ. However, the plural militates against this understanding (see Barrett 1.205). That would indicate a period of sim. refreshing events rather than a single event. It is likely that this v. is parallel to Acts 2:39, where the promise of the Holy Spirit is given to those who repent (Schnabel 215). If so, what is described is a period of refreshings. "Refreshing" (ἀναψύξεως, gen. sg. fem. of ἀνάψυξις, -εως, ἡ, attrib. gen.) is modified by the prep. phrase ἀπὸ προσώπου τοῦ κυρίου ("from the presence of the Lord"), denoting the source of refreshment, likely mediated through the Holy Spirit.

Δέξασθαι (aor. act. inf. of δέχομαι), "welcome, receive," might seem odd of Christ waiting in heaven, but as BDAG defines it, it can be used "of places receptive to pers." (BDAG 221b). Heaven is an appropriate place for Christ, so he waits until (ἄχρι) the time of restoration. The gen. ἀποκαταστάσεως (gen. sg. fem. of ἀποκατάστασις, -εως, ἡ) describes the kind of time. It is not that he waits until it is over, but that he comes at the restoration time. This is, as stated earlier, according to the word of God through the prophets.

3:22 Vv. 22–23 form a loose citation of Deut 18:15, 18–19. It is a close paraphrase of the passage (suggested by ὅτι). Προφήτην is fronted for emphasis. The first fut. (ἀναστήσει, 3rd sg. fut. act. indic. of ἀνίστημι) is prophetic. The prep. phrase ἐκ τῶν ἀδελφῶν ὑμῶν means a fellow Jew. Ὡς ἐμέ ("like me") suggests an undefined sim. to Moses. The second fut. (ἀκούσεσθε, 2nd pl. fut. mid. indic. of ἀκούω) is impv., mng. "obey." The scope of obedience is absolute, expressed by a distributive κατὰ πάντα ("everything," NLT, NASB, NIV). The prep. phrase is further modified by the indef. rel. pron. cstr. ὅσα ἂν λαλήσῃ (3rd sg. aor. act. subjunc. of λαλέω). The hope for the prophet continued through Judaism (John 1:32; cf. 1 Macc 4:46; Beale and Carson 548; see also 4Q175). Peter identified Jesus as that prophet (see John 6:14; 7:40). The use here, though, is specifically to warn about the dangers of disobeying him (i.e., not believing on him).

3:23 The consequences (ἔσται, 3rd sg. fut. mid. indic. of εἰμί) of disobedience are spelled out by continuing the Deuteronomy 18 citation. The rel. pron. ἥτις is here (as a LXX citation) an indef. rel. pron., "whoever." Ἀκούσῃ (3rd sg. aor. act. subjunc. of ἀκούω), like the previous use, refers to obedience (here the neg. means disobedience). The citation of Deut 18:19 concludes with τοῦ προφήτου ἐκείνου ("that prophet," the gen. obj. of the vb.). The warning in Deuteronomy is replaced by a phrase from Lev 23:29. That context refers to the one who rejects the day of atonement (Beale and Carson 548). The allusion is subtle but clearly intended to suggest the repercussions of failure to turn to Christ. They will be rejected (ἐξολεθρευθήσεται, 3rd sg. fut. pass. indic. of ἐξολεθρεύω, "destroy," NT hapax) from the covenant people.

3:24 Peter then added a summary. The list is specific: from Samuel and his followers (τῶν καθεξῆς, an adv. mng. "subsequent" made a subst. by the art.: "the successors"). However, the correlative adj. (ὅσοι) limits the ref. to the ones who spoke (ἐλάλησαν, 3rd sg. aor. act. indic. of λαλέω) and proclaimed (κατήγγειλαν, 3rd sg. aor. act. indic. of καταγγέλλω). Τὰς ἡμέρας ταύτας refers to Peter's present days of fulfillment.

3:25–26 Peter concludes with an appeal to the crowd. He describes his hearers with a pred. nom., οἱ υἱοί, modified by compound gen. phrases. The first gen. phrase, τῶν προφητῶν, is technically a gen. of relationship. "Sons of the prophets" refers in the books of the Kings to a school of the prophets. The occurrence here is the only use of the plural phrase outside of Kings in the Bible (the sg. is found at Amos 7:14). It is unlikely that Peter was drawing on the Kings refs. here. It is more likely that it is a ref. to being Israelites. Strack and Billerbeck cite Hillel the elder (c. 20 BC), "Let only the Israelites, if they are not prophets, be so, they are sons of prophets" (*j Shabbuth* 19.17a4; *Pesahim* 66a, Str-B 2.627) as evidence of the allusion. In one sense, it prefigures v. 26, in that the heirs of the prophets should hear the message first. The second gen. phrase, τῆς διαθήκης, is a gen. of description (BHGNT 62). It is modified with the subord. clause ἧς διέθετο (3rd sg. aor. mid. indic. of διατίθημι, "ordain"; the common LXX rendering of the Heb. *karat*, "cut"). The classification of the gens. helps to see the implication Peter made. They are not only kinsmen (relationship); they are also participants (descriptive) in God's covenant.

He made it clear that the covenant he pointed to was not Sinai but Abrahamic. Λέγων (nom. sg. masc. of pres. act. ptc. of λέγω; temp.) πρὸς Ἀβραάμ introduces a citation that is a conflation of Gen 12:3; 18:18; and 22:18. It is much closer in wording to 22:18. Only αἱ πατριαί reflects 12:3 alone and agrees with the MT rather than the LXX's φυλαί, "tribes" (Bruce, *Acts of the Apostles*, 146). The reminder of the Abrahamic covenant's blessing (ἐνευλογηθήσονται, 3rd pl. fut. pass. indic. of ἐνευλογέω) to all the families of the earth is a reminder of the universal plan of God. The agent of the blessing is Abraham's seed (ἐν τῷ σπέρματι) (see 3:12). When Peter described the mission of Christ in the next verse with the ptc. of purp. εὐλογοῦντα (masc. sg. acc. of pres. act. ptc. of εὐλογέω, "bless"), he was subtly identifying the ultimate seed as Christ.

Peter explains the fulfillment of the promise to Abraham. "Raising up" as a ptc. (ἀναστήσας, nom. sg. masc. of aor. act. ptc. of ἀνίστημι; temp.) makes it very unlikely he was thinking of the resurrection (although some double entendre is possible). As an aor. adv. ptc. the sequence is before the sending to bless. It is more likely that the whole process until the public ministry of Christ was in mind. Ἀπέστειλεν (3rd sg. aor. act. indic. of ἀποστέλλω) refers to the earthly ministry of Christ. Referring to Christ as τὸν παῖδα αὐτοῦ may be an allusion to Isa 52:13, where the servant is ὁ παῖς μου ("my servant") in the LXX (see 3:13).

Peter noted that Christ was sent to them first. This may simply be sequence; however, it sounds very Pauline (see, e.g., Rom 1:16, Ἰουδαίῳ τε πρῶτον). At the very least it implies a second offer, to Gentiles next (Barrett 1.214).

It had already been noted that εὐλογοῦντα was an adv. ptc. of purp. The blessing is further defined by the prep. phrase ἐν τῷ ἀποστρέφειν (pres. act. inf. of ἀποστρέφω, "turn"). How to interpret this is the last major question of the speech.

Generally, such cstrs. in Luke-Acts are temp. in force. If so, the turning and blessing are at the same time (see BHGNT 63). However, most of the other instances occur in narrative sequencing. Here it is amid an expository/hortatory genre. Most have little question that the phrase is not temp. but instr. ("by turning," Bruce, *Acts of the Apostles*, 146). Thus, the major question is whether ἐν τῷ ἀποστρέφειν is trans. or intrans.

1. If intrans., ἕκαστον is the subj. of the inf. Then it means "each one of you by turning from your sins" (Barrett 1.214). There is little grammatically to suggest an intrans. mng., which are usually mid. in form. Generally, proponents of an intrans. mng. point to the semantic fit of an appeal at the end of Peter's sermon (see, e.g., Bock 181–82).

*2. If trans., ἕκαστον is the dir. obj. The phrase would then mean "The servant turns each of you from your sins." This is the option for most EVV. The complaint that it is not an appeal to the hearers is unfounded. In Luke 1:17, John the Baptist's mission is described as "to turn the hearts of fathers to their children, and the disobedient to the understanding of the righteous. . . ." The implicit appeal there was made explicit by John in his preaching of repentance (Luke 3:3). So too, here there is an implicit appeal to repent "from your wickedness" (ἀπὸ τῶν πονηριῶν ὑμῶν) while acknowledging that it is the intent of Christ.

HOMILETICAL SUGGESTIONS

Receiving God's Achievement in the Glorified Christ (3:11–26)

1. Admit and reject the sins of the past (vv. 12–16)
2. Receive refreshing through repentance (vv. 17–26)

3. The Aftermath: Peter and John's Arrest and Bold Witness (4:1–31)

This section builds off the notable healing of ch. 3. It is in four movements. First, vv. 1–12 feature the ire of the Sanhedrin and the apostles' reply. Peter's answer comes in two parts. First, he straightforwardly answers the question in vv. 8–10. Second, he elaborates on the identity of Jesus and the guilt of his hearers, then offers an implicit appeal in vv. 11–12. The next movement reveals the council's deliberations in vv. 13–18. The council enforces their decision in vv. 19–22. The section ends in a memorable prayer meeting with another manifestation of the Spirit of God in vv. 23–31. Throughout the section the name of Jesus is highlighted, likely building off the appearance at 2:38 and 3:6 where the offer of salvation and healing (using σῴζω at 4:9) is in his name. His name is the subj. of the legal deliberations at 4:10, 17, 18. The disciples' prayer is to continue in his name (4:30). The capstone seems to be the declaration at 4:12: "There is salvation in no one else, for there is no other name under heaven given to people by which we must be saved." This conviction drove the actions of the early church.

4:1–3 The result of the speech was a large number of converts. The temp. gen. abs. phrase λαλούντων (gen. pl. masc. of pres. act. ptc. of λαλέω) . . . αὐτῶν modified by a prep. phrase (πρὸς τὸν λαόν) suggests the incident was not merely a single speech but an extended opportunity (see below). The large crowd and the substance of the teaching drew the attention (ἐπέστησαν, 3rd pl. aor. act. indic. of ἐφίστημι, "confront") of the priestly caste (οἱ ἱερεῖς, ὁ στρατηγὸς [nom. sg. masc. of στρατηγός, -οῦ, ὁ (chief magistrate) of τοῦ ἱεροῦ, and the Σαδδουκαῖοι [nom. pl. masc. of Σαδδουκαῖος, -ου, ὁ, "Sadducee"]). The commander of the temple (ὁ στρατηγός) was likely there because of the disturbance itself, for part of his job was to keep the peace at the temple (Keener 2.1127; see also Str-B 2:628–30). The cause of their confrontation is indicated by the ptc. διαπονούμενοι (nom. pl. masc. of pres. mid. ptc. of διαπονέομαι, "be annoyed"). The cause of their annoyance is indicated by διά followed by compounded infs. governed by the same art. Both τὸ διδάσκειν and καταγγέλλειν are pres. act. infs. suggesting the confrontation was an interruption. The mng. of the phrase ἐν τῷ Ἰησοῦ τὴν ἀνάστασιν τὴν ἐκ νεκρῶν is disputed. There are three possible mngs.:

1. It could suggest "the resurrection that comes by Jesus" (a locat. of sphere).
2. It might be equivalent to a dat. of ref. mng. "the resurrection with ref. to Jesus" (see Turner, *Insights,* 156).
*3. Slightly more likely, it could suggest support for the resurrection by means of the Jesus event (means, Barrett 1.219–20; Bruce, *Acts of the Apostles*, 148). That the substance of the teaching is the resurrection of the dead explains the lack of involvement by the Pharisees, even though some surely were present.

The authorities arrested (ἐπέβαλον, 3rd pl. aor. act. indic. of ἐπιβάλλω, "seize") and imprisoned (ἔθεντο, 3rd pl. aor. idic. act. of τίθημι; with εἰς τήρησιν [acc. sg. fem. of τήρησις, -εως, ἡ, "into prison"]) them because evening was near. The delay is fairly standard practice in antiquity (Keener 2.1133). Since the speech began around 3:00 p.m. and ended at evening (ἑσπέρα fem. nom. sg. of ἑσπέρα, -ας, ἡ), the recorded speech is clearly a summary of Peter's words. This is further indication that the speeches in Acts are condensed from Luke's sources (Keener 2.1133).

4:4 The result of the preaching was that many of the hearers (ἀκουσάντων, gen. pl. masc. of aor. act. ptc of ἀκούω; subst.; part. gen.) believed (ἐπίστευσαν, 3rd pl. aor. act. indic. of πιστεύω). The mng. of the number is disputed (Bock 188). It could mean the total number of believers has been raised to 5,000 (Barrett 1.221), or the church increased by 5,000. Either way it was a large increase of the church. The latter, however, is more likely. Elsewhere Luke mentions the increase of the church without specific numbers (see, e.g., 6:1, 7; 11:21; 14:1). This suggests that Luke is not specifically interested in a running tally but the increase.

HOMILETICAL SUGGESTIONS

Faithful Testimony (4:1–4)

1. Expect discomfort: Peter and John are put in bonds (vv. 1–3)
2. Expect results: the Word of God is unbound (v. 4)

4:5 The events at the temple led to an official inquiry. The use of ἐγένετο δέ followed by a temp. expression (ἐν or a compl. inf.) is common in Luke–Acts (Levinsohn 170–71; see R 1422–23). Translating the Heb. "and it came to pass" (Heb. *wayyĕhī*) is what Bruce calls "Luke's favorite Septuagintalism" (Bruce, *Acts of the Apostles*, 149; see also Turner, *Style*, 57). It is, generally, background information to the following context (Levinsohn 170–71). In this case, it employs the aor. pass. inf. of συνάγω (συναχθῆναι, "gather") to give the context of vv. 6–7. The participants are generically described in the acc. case as required by the inf. Τοὺς ἄρχοντας καὶ τοὺς πρεσβυτέρους καὶ τοὺς γραμματεῖς ("the rulers and the elders and the scribes") represent the components of the Sanhedrin (Bruce, *Acts of the Apostles*, 149).

4:6–7 In addition to Ἅννας, three members of the high-priestly family (ἐκ γένους ἀρχιερατικοῦ) are named (Καϊάφας, Ἰωάννης, and Ἀλέξανδρος), among unnamed others (ὅσοι). They are, curiously, all nom. sg. masc.; one would expect an acc. of appos. (as, in fact, rep. in the *byz*) if they were in the previous sentence. Barrett suggests it to be a solecism (Barrett 1.224). Bruce suggests it is due to the intention to call particular attention to those listed (Bruce, *Acts of the Apostles*, 150). It is more likely that they are the subj. of ἐπυνθάνοντο (3rd pl. impf. mid. indic. of πυνθάνομαι, "inquire, ask") in v. 7 (BHGNT 66). In this view, the irregularity is the inclusion of καί at the beginning of the temp. ptc. phrase στήσαντες (nom. pl. masc. of aor. act. ptc. of ἵστημι) αὐτούς and not before the list of proper nouns in v. 6. Perhaps the list is fronted for emphasis. Ἐν τῷ μέσῳ reflects the fact that the Sanhedrin met in a semicircle to see each other (Barrett 1.224).

The substance of their inquiry is the matter of authority rather than the legitimacy of the miracle. It has two parts: "In what power" (ἐν ποίᾳ δυνάμει) is the question of source (Schnabel 237). Next, ἢ ἐν ποίῳ ὀνόματι (on this use of ὄνομα, see 3:6) is the question of "Who gave you the authority to do this?" Both were already proclaimed by Peter (3:6, 16); this was a question for them to hear for themselves from Peter (Schnabel 237). "You" (ὑμεῖς) is emphatic (Bock 191). In effect, it is a pers. denigration that will be repeated at v. 13 (Bruce 151: "scornfully emphatic").

4:8–9 Πλησθείς (nom. sg. masc. of aor. pass. ptc. of πίμπλημι, "fill") is followed by a gen. of. content, πνεύματος ἁγίου, signifying Peter's empowerment (see comments at 2:4). The event recorded is a fulfillment of Luke 12:12; the source of the defense is the Holy Spirit (Bock 190). Peter addressed (εἶπεν, 3rd sg. aor. act. indic. of λέγω) the rulers of the people and elders (ἄρχοντες τοῦ λαοῦ καὶ πρεσβύτεροι). The address is both frank and respectful (Haenchen 216). Verses 8–9 are technically a first-class cond. sentence with the prot. in v. 8 and the apod. in v. 9. The force, however, is a straightforward assertion. Ἀνακρινόμεθα (1st pl. pres. pass. indic. of ἀνακρίνω, "question, examine") often describes the action of a formal inquiry (Bock 191), here an inquiry into the source of the man's healing. The vb. σέσωται (3rd sg. pf. pass. indic. of σώζω) appears, unusually, at the end of the sentence. It is likely placed there for emphasis (Bock 191) and is likely intentionally loaded with mng. (Haenchen 217). Jesus also brings spiritual salvation.

4:10 Peter's assertion with γνωστόν (acc. sg. neut. of γνωστός, -ή, -όν) ἔστω is solemn and forceful ("Let it be known"; see 2:14). The source is Jesus (ἐν τῷ ὀνόματι) the Nazorean (Ναζωραίου, gen. sg. masc. of Ναζωραῖος, -ου, ὁ, see 2:22). He is identified with two rel. clauses (ὅν). He is the one they crucified (ἐσταυρώσατε, 2nd pl. aor. act. indic. of σταυρόω) and whom (ὅν) God raised (ἤγειρεν, 3rd sg. aor. act. indic. of ἐγείρω). In v. 9, the man's cond. is ἀσθενοῦς ("weak") but now he is ὑγιής (nom. sg. masc. of ὑγιής, -ές; pred. adj., "healthy, sound").

4:11 It was rather standard in ancient courts to accuse one's accusers, but not the judges (Keener 2.1148). Peter boldly turned the table by alluding to Ps 118:22. The identification is presented in a pred. nom. cstr. with the identifying pron. compl. (οὗτος) fronted. He identified Jesus as the rejected (ἐξουθενηθείς, nom. sg. masc. of aor. pass. ptc. of ἐξουθενέω, "disdainfully reject") stone. Peter also identified the leaders of Israel as the builders (οἰκοδόμων, gen. pl. masc. of οἰκοδόμος, -οῦ, ὁ). The term "builder" was used at Qumran to describe religious leaders (CD 4.12; 4:19; see Bruce, *Acts of the Apostles*, 152). The noun only occurs here in the NT (Schnabel 240). Christ became (ὁ γενόμενος, nom. sg. masc. of aor. mid. ptc. of γίνομαι; subst.) the κεφαλὴν γωνίας (gen. sg. fem. of γωνία, -ας, ἡ, "corner"), the cornerstone or keystone. Ἐν τούτῳ might refer to Ἰησοῦ Χριστοῦ (so ESV, NIV). It more likely ref. to τῷ ὀνόματι (so Barrett 1.229).

4:12 Peter picked up on the spiritual rescue implied when he employed σώζω at 4:9. The noun cognate σωτηρία is likely the subj. of ἐστί (3rd sg. pres. indic. of εἰμί). Many EVV employ a dummy subj. "there is" but this is unnecessary. The art. likely indic. that the noun is the subj. of the vb. Thus, "and salvation is in no other. . ." (so NIV). The double-neg. (οὐκ . . . οὐδενί) is emphatic, thus it is difficult to tease out a distinction between ἄλλος and ἕτερος in this context. Furthermore, Robertson correctly notes "the point of ἕτερον is rather that no other name at all than that of Jesus, not that of difference in kind" (R 749). The subst. ptc. δεδομένον (nom. sg. neut. of pf. pass. ptc. of δίδωμι) is unusual but functions like a rel. clause, "that has been given" (Haenchen 217; BDF §412[4]). The use of δεῖ ("must") compl. by the aor. pass. inf. σωθῆναι (from σώζω) has more than a tone of necessity given the danger all humanity (the definite and singular ἡ σωτηρία is the implied subj. of the inf.) is in. In sum, a stronger statement of exclusivity would be difficult to make.

HOMILETICAL SUGGESTIONS

The Saving Name of Jesus (4:5–12)

1. Only the name of Jesus saves the body (vv. 5–10)
   a. Physical healing is possible
   b. Resurrection is the ultimate healing
2. Only the name of Jesus saves the soul (vv. 6–12)

4:13 The council's deliberation and decree began with an observation about the apostles. Two temp. ptc. phrases set up the main vb. (ἐθαύμαζον, see below). They first see (θεωροῦντες, nom. pl. masc. of pres. act. ptc. of θεωρέω) their boldness/confidence (παρρησίαν): the characteristic of Greek philosophers (particularly Cynics, Witherington 195). Πέτρου and Ἰωάννου are both attrib. gens. modifying παρρησίαν (Peter is highlighted by position). They marveled after they recognized (καταλαβόμενοι, nom. pl. masc. of aor. mid. ptc. of καταλαμβάνω) that they were both ἄνθρωποι ἀγράμματοι (nom. pl. masc. of ἀγράμματος, -ον, "unschooled, illiterate") and ἰδιῶται (nom. pl. masc. of ἰδιώτης, -ου, ὁ, "layperson, amateur"). Because this is Luke's comment, the first term means "unschooled," not illiterate (Bock 195; BDAG 15a). The second indicates a layperson in rhetorical contexts; the two together would not necessarily be an insult (Keener 2.1156). As a result, they were marveling (ἐθαύμαζον, 3rd pl. impf. act. indic. of θαυμάζω). The council's response is given in indir. speech. Thus, the tense of εἰσιν (3rd pl. pres. indic. of εἰμί) is retained from the implied dir. speech (Wallace 539). Ἐπεγίνωσκον 3rd pl. impf. act. indic. of ἐπιγινώσκω, "recognize." That they had been with Jesus indicates that they "have received training from outside the official circle. . ." (Bock 196). The connection to Jesus has the effect of "taking up his mantle" of sorts.

4:14 On τε, see 1:15. Ἄνθρωπον (dir. obj.) is fronted for emphasis but is part of a double-acc. cstr. Βλέποντες (nom. pl. masc. of pres. act. ptc. of βλέπω) is best understood as causal, "because they saw." Ἑστῶτα (acc. sg. masc. of pf. act. ptc. of ἵστημι) is the compl. in the previously mentioned double-acc. cstr. (BHGNT 71). Τεθεραπευμένον (acc. sg. masc. of pf. pass. ptc. of θεραπεύω) is attrib. to the fronted ἄνθρωπον. The result of the plain evidence was that the council had nothing they could object to (εἶχον [3rd pl. impf. act. indic. of ἔχω] and the epex. inf. ἀντειπεῖν [aor. act. inf. of ἀντεῖπον, "speak against"]).

4:15 Κελεύσαντες (nom. pl. masc. of aor. act. ptc. of κελεύω, "order"; temp.) takes ἀπελθεῖν (aor. act. inf. of ἀπέρχομαι, "depart") as its compl. Συνέβαλλον (3rd pl. impf. act. indic. of συμβάλλω, a word exclusive to Luke-Acts in the NT) is best understood as an inceptive impf.: "they began to confer" (cf. NASB, NET).

4:16 Λέγοντες (nom. pl. masc. of pres. act. ptc. of λέγω) introduces dir. speech. Ποιήσωμεν is 1st pl. aor. act. subjunc. of ποιέω; delib.: "What will we do?" Ἀνθρώποις τούτοις is associative: "with these men." The bare dat. instead of the more HGk. use of the prep. is part of Luke's literary/CGk. style (as is the word order of the v.). Ὅτι introduces a subst. clause acting as the subj. of an understood ἐστίν (BHGNT 71, cf. NASB "that a notable sign . . . is apparent"). According to BDAG 629d μὲν γὰρ introduces a concessive clause that contrasts within the next v., mng. "for indeed . . . but." Γνωστὸν σημεῖον (nom. sg. neut. forms of γνωστός, -ή, -όν and σημεῖον, -ου, τό) is "a notable sign" (the subj. of γέγονεν [3rd sg. pf. act. indic. of γίνομαι]). Πᾶσιν τοῖς κατοικοῦσιν (dat. pl. fem. of pres. act. ptc. of κατοικέω, " dwell"; subst.) are dats. of advantage modifying φανερόν (nom. sg. neut. of φανερός, -ά, -όν); the pred. adj. of the assumed ἐστίν.

4:17 Although conceding the miracle, the rulers' goals were to stop the movement. It was an act of "political damage control" (Keener 2.1159). Ἵνα μή introduces a negated purp. clause. Ἐπὶ πλεῖον is "yet more" (ZG 361), but in a negated clause it is best "no further" (cf. RSV, ESV). Διανεμηθῇ is the 3rd sg. aor. pass. subjunc. of διανέμω, "spread." Ἀπειλησώμεθα (1st pl. aor. mid. subjunc. of ἀπειλέω) is a hortatory subjunc.; in the mid. it is "let us warn." It takes a form of μή (μηκέτι, "no longer") and an inf. (BDAG 629d–30a); technically, indir. speech (Robertson, *Pictures*, 53). Here it is λαλεῖν (pres. act. inf. of λαλέω). The phrase ἐπὶ τῷ ὀνόματι τούτῳ ("in this name") recalls Peter's words in the healing event (see 3:6).

4:18 The plan was implemented formally. Καλέσαντες is the nom. pl. masc. of aor. act. ptc. of καλέω; temp. Παρήγγειλαν is the 3rd pl. aor. act. indic. of παραγγέλλω, "charge." The adv. καθόλου modifying the negated verb means "not at all" (ZG 361). The alternating infs. of indir. speech give the contents of the order neither to φθέγγεσθαι (pres. mid. inf. of φθέγγομαι, "speak") nor to διδάσκειν (pres. act. inf. of διδάσκω, "teach"). It is likely this refers to public and private instruction that was forbidden (Barrett 1.237). The prep. phrase ἐπὶ τῷ ὀνόματι τοῦ Ἰησοῦ (lit., "upon the name of Jesus," likely means the same as ἐν (Bruce, *Acts of the Apostles*, 155).

4:19–20 The combination of ἀποκριθέντες (nom. pl. masc. of aor. pass. ptc. of ἀποκρίνομαι; pleonastic) and εἶπον (3rd pl. aor. act. indic. of λέγω) is a redundant Heb. (Bruce, *Acts of the Apostles*, 155; Turner, *Style*, 51). It is frequent in the LXX (sixty-nine times; Haenchen 219) and a major part of synoptic style (cf. the fifty times in Luke's Gospel). This ptc. form, however, is uncommon in Acts (six times). Levinsohn suggests it introduces a response that is unexpected but decisive in resolution (Levinsohn 232). That is certainly the case here. The answer is both a commitment to God and a rebuke of the council. The commitment is to obey (ἀκούειν, pres. act. inf. of ἀκούω; compl. to δίκαιον) God rather than the council. The rebuke is seen in the sentence cstr. Rather than a straightforward declaration, Peter and John couch it in terms of a cond. sentence. The prot. defines the demands of the council as disobedience to God, whom they define as τοῦ θεοῦ ὑμῶν ("your God"), suggesting they should obey too. The short apod., κρίνατε (2nd pl. aor. act. impv. of κρίνω) has the effect of a rhetorical question. The affirmative answer should have been obvious to them. In v. 20, Peter and John gave the grounds (γάρ) for their actions in terms of the judgment they made in the matter. The redundant nom. pron. ἡμεῖς is emphatic and is a stinging contrast to the council. Δυνάμεθα (1st pl. aor. mid. indic. of δύναμαι) is completed by λαλεῖν (pres. act. inf. of λέγω). Thus, the double neg. οὐ . . . μή (even though not contiguous) is also emphatic. The rel. clause phrase functions as the dir. obj., rehearsing the evidence they have seen (εἴδαμεν, 1st pl. aor. act. indic. of ὁράω) and heard (ἠκούσαμεν, 1st pl. aor. act. indic. of ἀκούω).

4:21–22 The council threatened (προσαπειλησάμενοι, nom. pl. masc. of aor. mid. ptc. προσαπειλέω; temp.) and released (ἀπέλυσαν, 3rd pl. aor. act. indic. of ἀπολύω) the apostles. The council could not find (εὑρίσκοντες, nom. pl. masc. of pres. act. ptc. εὑρίσκω; causal) a path to penalize them, expressed as πῶς κολάσωνται (3rd pl. aor. mid. subjunc. of κολάζω, delib., [see Bruce, *Acts of the Apostles*, 155]) for fear of the citizenry (διὰ τὸν λαόν), who were glorifying (ἐδόξαζον, 3rd pl. impf. indic. act. δοξάζω) God for the miracle they had seen. Γεγονότι is the dat. sg. neut. of pf. mid. ptc. of γίνομαι; subst., mng. "that which happened." The reason (γάρ) for the crowd's response was the age of the man. Ἐτῶν τεσσεράκοντα πλειόνων is best "more than forty years old" (Barrett 1.239). Culy and Parsons suggest the phrase is a gen. of time: "for the man . . . had been that way over the course of more than forty years!" (BHGNT 74). Since this would be a rare cstr. and the fact that the man had been lame since birth (3:2) produces no change in mng., it is best to understand the more common classifications with Barrett.

HOMILETICAL SUGGESTIONS

Being with Jesus (4:13–22)

1. An unexplainable confidence (v. 13)
2. An undeniable change (vv. 14, 16, 22)
3. An underhanded charge (vv. 15–18)
4. An unexpected commitment (vv. 19–21)

4:23 The response of the church is highlighted to the end of the section. Peter and John, upon release (ἀπολυθέντες, nom. pl. masc. of aor. pass. ptc. of ἀπολύω; temp.), returned (ἦλθον) and reported (ἀπήγγειλαν) what was said (εἶπαν) (all 3rd pl. aor. act. indics.). The major question is the identification of ἰδίους (acc. pl. masc. of ἴδιος, -ία, -ον, subst.; obj. of prep.). Is it their own home/place or their own people? If the latter, what is the makeup of the group? Generally, it is agreed that Luke refers to a group of people (Bock 203; cf. RSV, NLT, NASB, ESV, NET). Much speculation surrounds the makeup of the group. Was it the apostles alone, or with a few of the community; a portion of the church at large; possibly a larger audience (see Schnabel 253; Bock 203)? Most hold it is a ref. to the whole of the church (Keener 2.1165; Schnabel 253–54). It is more important to note that the term indicates a separation from at least the Jewish leadership and identifies the Christians as a new community (Bock 203).

4:24 The hearers (ἀκούσαντες, nom. pl. masc. of aor. act. ptc. of ἀκούω; subst.) respond as a collective whole (see ὁμοθυμαδόν, "together" [see 1:14] and the sg. obj. φωνήν) in prayer as indicated by ἦραν (3rd pl. aor. act. indic. of αἴρω). The address δέσποτα (voc. sg. masc. of δεσπότης, -ου, ὁ, "master") appears frequently in the LXX translating hā' ādôn yhwh, "the Lord GOD" (although only ten times in the NT). It is a term that emphasizes the sovereignty of God. This is underscored by the further description as the Creator (ποιήσας, nom. sg. masc. of aor. act. ptc. of ποιέω; subst.). The phrase seems to be an allusion to Exod 20:11 or Neh 9:6 (see Beale and Carson 552).

4:25 Another OT citation is introduced by a difficult grammatical phrase, although the mng. is clear (Barrett 1.244). It introduces a citation of Psalm 2, noting the inspiration of the Holy Spirit and the Davidic source. However, the wording is confusing. Neither the *byz.* rdg. (that drops "Holy Spirit" and "our father" [preferred by Haenchen 226]) nor the Western rdg. (that radically rephrases it) are likely original (BHGNT 76; Metzger 280–81). The art. ὁ functions like a rel. pron. with v. 24's δέσποτα as its antecedent, thus it still is addressing God (as evidenced by the description παιδός σου, "your servant" [on παῖς referring to Jesus, see 3:12]). Culy and Parsons rightly suggest the following: τοῦ πατρός is a gen. of means, "by our father"; πνεύματος ἁγίου is the obj. of the prep. διά; στόματος is a gen. of means, "by the mouth"; and Δαυίδ is a poss. gen. with παιδός σου in appos. (BHGNT 77). The activity of speaking (εἰπών, nom. sg. masc. of aor. act. ptc. of λέγω) belonged to David. Psalm 2 is then quoted exactly from the LXX (Bruce, *Acts of the Apostles*, 157). The adv. ἱνατί "for what reason" is sometimes expressed separately as ἵνα τί with the same mng. Ἐφρύαξαν (3rd pl. aor. act. indic. of φρυάσσω), often tr. "rage," is used of spirited animals (like horses) or to mean insolent or arrogant people (BDAG 1067a). The action in parallel, ἐμελέτησαν (3rd pl. aor. act. indic. of μελετάω), has κενά (vain things) as its dir. obj. making the mng. rather neg. "conspire vanity" (BDAG 627a). The choice of vbs. characterizes those actions as a doomed rebellion.

4:26 The citation of Ps 2:1 continues. The vbs. demonstrate a progression from thought to action. The kings of the earth (οἱ βασιλεῖς τῆς γῆς) "took their stand" (παρέστησαν, 3rd pl. aor. act. indic. of παρίστημι/παριστάνω, normally "stand beside" but here in the sense of opposition [Barrett 1.246]). The rulers were assembled (συνήχθησαν, 3rd pl. aor. pass. indic. of συνάγω). The prep. phrase ἐπὶ τὸ αὐτό, "at the same place" (BDAG 363c), is normally left untranslated for the redundancy in Eng. Κατά with the gen. obj. is "against" and denotes the obj. of their opposition: the Lord and his Anointed (τοῦ χριστοῦ αὐτοῦ).

4:27–28 Γάρ indicates an inference to be made regarding Ps 2:1. The adv. prep. phrase (ἐπ᾽ ἀληθείας, "truly") does not intensify but suggests what follows is the fulfillment of the OT passage. To further note fulfillment, several items are repeated from the psalm. Herod and Pontius Pilate gathered together (συνήχθησαν, 3rd pl. aor. pass. indic. of συνάγω). Jesus is the holy servant whom God anointed (ἔχρισας, 2nd sg. aor. act. indic. of χρίω). The λαοί of v. 25 is identified as Israel (λαοῖς Ἰσραήλ) who collude with the Gentiles (ἔθνεσιν). The prayer, however, acknowledges the implication of fulfilled prophecy: that God was in complete control (v. 28). Ποιῆσαι is the aor. act. inf. of ποιέω. Προώρισεν is the 3rd sg. aor. act. indic. of προορίζω, "predetermine." Γενέσθαι is the aor. mid. inf. of γίνομαι.

4:29–30 The prayer shifts at v. 29 to supplication. Καὶ τὰ νῦν is unique to Acts in the NT (see 5:38; 20:32; 27:22) and rare in the LXX (three times). It is best understood as a low-level developmental marker. It indicates the main point is upcoming (BHGNT 78). The inclusion of the voc. κύριε further highlights what is coming up. What follows is essentially three interrelated supplications (Schnabel 258). Ἔπιδε (2nd sg. aor. act. impv. of ἐφοράω) is, lit., "look upon" (compound vb. ἐπί + ὁράω), but fig., "concern yourself with" (hence, rightly, "consider," or NASB: "take note of"). The obj. is "their threats" (ἀπειλάς, acc. pl. fem. of ἀπειλή, -ῆς, ἡ), a ref. back to 4:17, where the cognate vb. is used.

The second request is to give (δός, 2nd sg. aor. act. impv. of δίδωμι) all boldness to speak (λαλεῖν, pres. act. inf. of λαλέω; compl.) God's word (τὸν λόγον σου). Here, the ref. is clearly the gospel (Haenchen 227; Keener 2.1172).

The third request features Luke's frequent use of ἐν τῷ + inf. (here a compound use; ἐκτείνειν, pres. act. inf. of ἐκτείνω and γίνεσθαι, pres. mid. inf. of γίνομαι) to represent a temp. phrase (see 4:5). Healing (εἰς ἴασιν [acc. sg. fem. of ἴασις, -εως, ἡ]) is the purp. for God stretching forth his hand. Purpose is also communicated in the second inf.

(γίνεσθαι). Signs and wonders (σημεῖα καὶ τέρατα [acc. pl. neut. of τέρας, -ατος, τό]; subj. of γίνεσθαι) are requested through the authority (the sense of διὰ τοῦ ὀνόματος; see 3:6) of Jesus. That he is called "your holy servant" (τοῦ ἁγίου παιδός σου) is an allusion to the servant songs of Isa (see 3:13).

4:31 The section ends with the results of the prayer. It highlights both God's immediate response and an ongoing response. Their location is indicated by a periph. plpf. pass. cstr. (ἦσαν, 3rd pl. impf. of εἰμί + συνηγμένοι, nom. pl. masc. of pf. pass. ptc. of συνάγω). Immediately after praying (δεηθέντων, gen. pl. masc. of aor. pass. ptc. of δέομαι; gen. abs., temp.), something like Pentecost occurred. Instead of tongues of fire, the place was shaken (ἐσαλεύθη, 3rd sg. aor. pass. indic. of σαλεύω). However, in almost identical phrasing, they were filled (ἐπλήσθησαν, 3rd pl. aor. pass. indic. of πίμπλημι). The physical manifestation and the filling indicated God's blessing on the event. The long-term answer to the prayer is indeed boldness in speaking (ἐλάλουν, 3rd pl. impf. act. indic. of λαλέω) God's word.

FOR FURTHER STUDY

12. The Name of Jesus in Acts

Busch, A. "Presence Deferred: The Name of Jesus and Self-Referential Eschatological Prophecy in Acts 3." *BibInt* 17 (2009): 521–53.

Ziesler, J. A. "The Name of Jesus in the Acts of the Apostles." *JSNT* 4 (1979): 28–41.

HOMILETICAL SUGGESTIONS

The Prayer of the Persecuted (4:29–30)

1. Acknowledge the threat in prayer (v. 29a)
2. Pray for God to grant boldness of speech (v. 29b)
3. Pray for God to continue to use your circumstances as a platform for the gospel (v. 30)

B. TROUBLE WITHIN AND WITHOUT (4:32–6:7)

This section is divided into five parts that swirl around the difficulties for the new community. It begins with a narrative of the exceptional generosity of the church and esp. Barnabas. His example leads to the cautionary tale of Ananias and Sapphira that is told in two parts. First Ananias sins, is confronted, and dies (5:1–6). Then his wife, a coconspirator, also sins and dies under the judgment of God (5:7–11).

The numerical expansion of the church is then connected to a twofold testimony regarding the work of the Spirit and the Christian message. First, signs of healing demonstrated work of the Spirit, some quite unique. Second, the unclean spirits were exorcised, demonstrating the authority associated with Jesus's name.

This led to the almost comical attempt of the Sanhedrin to suppress the preaching of the apostles. In fulfillment of Luke 21:12–17, preaching in the name of Jesus brought the ire of the religious leadership. Ultimately Peter would give another bold testimony to Christ. And, at the advice of Paul's famous mentor, Gamaliel (see Acts 22:3), the formal Jewish hostility abates for a time.

Finally, a conflict between Gk.-speaking widows (Hellenists) and the Aram.-speaking widows (Hebrews) served to introduce Stephen, who will be the subj. through ch. 7. This is traditionally seen as the birth of the office of deacon, as the cognate noun "ministry" (διακονία) is in v. 1 and the vb. "serve" (διακονέω) is used in v. 2.

1. The Sharing of Property in the Early Church: A Good Example (4:32–37)

4:32 The initial sentence is somewhat complicated. It begins with a string of gens. Τοῦ πλήθους ("multitude" nearly unique to Luke in the NT, twenty-four of thirty-one occurrences) is a descriptive gen. modifying καρδία καὶ ψυχή. There is little doubt the entirety of the church is meant (Barrett 1.252). Likewise, the subst. ptc. πιστευσάντων (gen. pl. masc. of aor. act. ptc. of πιστεύω) modifies πλήθους. The basic sentence is a pred. adj. cstr. The heart and soul (καρδία καὶ ψυχή, collective sgs.) of the church was (ἦν, 3rd sg. impf. indic. of εἰμί) lit. "one," μία (nom. sg. fem. of εἷς, μία, ἕν; pred. adj., i.e., "united"). A lit. tr. would be "the heart and soul of the number who believed were united." The expression of their unity was their unusual sharing stated as indir. speech. Τι is likely an acc. of ref. (BHGNT 81). The sense is, "no one was saying (ἔλεγεν, 3rd sg. impf. act. indic. of λέγω) regarding their belongings" (ὑπαρχόντων [gen. pl. masc. of pres. act. ptc. of ὑπάρχω; subst.] and a poss. dat., αὐτῷ). The indir. speech is indicated by an inf. cstr. using εἶναι (pres. inf. of εἰμί). It, too, is a pred. adj. clause using ἴδιον. The sense is "that it was their own." Instead (employing a third pred. adj. clause) everything was held to be common (κοινά nom. pl. neut. of κοινός, -ή, -όν).

4:33–35 Luke summarized the situation in the church. It begins with a fronted dat. of means, δυνάμει μεγάλῃ, "with great power." The activity of the apostles is expressed with a progressive impf., ἀπεδίδουν (3rd pl. impf. act. indic. of ἀποδίδωμι, "give"). The fronted dir. obj. (μαρτύριον) is further defined by a gen. of ref., ἀναστάσεως, "resurrection," followed by a poss. gen. phrase, τοῦ κυρίου Ἰησοῦ. Mirroring the initial clause, the experience of the church was (ἦν, see previous v.) χάρις . . . μεγάλη, "great grace."

Substantiating the previous clause (γάρ), there were (ἦν) none needy (ἐνδεής, nom. sg. masc. of ἐνδεής, -ές, NT hapax) among them. This perhaps alludes to Deut 15:4–7, where God's blessing results in none being needy (also ἐνδεής in LXX). If so, this suggests that the new community is fulfilling its mandates as the people of God (see Beale and Carson 554). The provision is expressed as a pred. nom. clause employing the vb. ὑπῆρχον (3rd pl. impf. act. indic. of ὑπάρχω, "exist") with the subj. ὅσοι and the compl. κτήτορες (κτήτωρ, -ορος, ὁ; NT hapax) "owners." The ptc. πωλοῦντες (nom. pl. masc. of pres. act. ptc. of πωλέω, "sell"; attend. circum.) backgrounds to a compound clause with two impfs., both iter. The first is ἔφερον, 3rd pl. impf. act. indic. of φέρω, "bring." Thus, Luke backgrounds the selling to the act of bringing and delivering the money (τιμάς). Πιπρασκομένων (gen. pl. neut. of pres. pass. ptc. of πιπράσκω; subst., mng. "the things sold") functions as a descriptive gen. noun. The second clause (employing the vb. ἐτίθουν, 3rd pl. impf. act. indic. of τίθημι) is the delivery of the money. In turn (marked for development by δέ), the apostles distributed (διεδίδετο, 3rd sg. impf. act. indic. of διαδίδωμι; iter.) to those who had (εἶχεν, 3rd sg. impf. act. indic. of ἔχω) need.

4:36–37 Barnabas is offered as a prominent example of such generosity. Joseph is called (ἐπικληθείς, nom. sg. masc. of aor. pass. ptc. of ἐπικαλέω; attrib.) "Barnabas." The prep. phrase ἀπὸ τῶν ἀποστόλων is unusual. One would expect ὑπό if agency were meant (as in some late mss.). Some have suggested it means Barnabas was considered one of the Twelve. It is more likely that source is meant so that the nickname came from the apostles but was employed by all. Luke interprets (μεθερμηνευόμενον, nom. sg. neut. of pres. pass. ptc. of μεθερμηνεύω; periph. pres.) it for us as υἱὸς παρακλήσεως. Barrett makes a compelling case that the ref. is built off the Sem. form of prophet, *nebî*, thus the ref. is to a magnificent preacher (Barrett 1.258–59). If so, "son of exhortation" is a better tr. than the popular "son of encouragement." He is further identified as a native (γένει, dat. sg. neut. of γένος, -ους, τό; dat. of ref.) of Cyprus and a Levite.

Barnabas's activity is described in sim. terms to 4:34. The ownership of a field is expressed as a gen. abs. (because the subj., ἀγροῦ, is different than the main vb.) using ὑπάρχοντος (gen. sg. masc. of pres. act. ptc. of ὑπάρχω; gen. abs.) with a poss. dat., αὐτῷ. Like v. 34, he sold the property (πωλήσας, nom. sg. masc. of aor. act. ptc. of πωλέω, "sell"; attend. circum.) and brought (ἤνεγκεν, 3rd sg. aor. act. indic. of φέρω) the money and placed (ἔθηκεν, 3rd sg. aor. act. indic. of τίθημι) it at the apostles' feet.

2. The Sharing of Property in the Early Church: A Bad Example (5:1–11)

5:1–2 Ἀνὴρ δέ τις introduces a new character with a developmental δέ. The dat. ὀνόματι is a dat. of ref., typical with naming conventions. Ananias (and his wife) are in dir. contr. to Barnabas (Bock 221; Bruce, *Acts of the Apostles*, 162). He sold (ἐπώλησεν, 3rd sg. aor. act. indic. of πωλέω) a portion of land. Luke is clear that Sapphira was also complicit through the prep. phrase σὺν Σαπφίρῃ (dat. sg. fem. of Σάπφιρα, -ης, ἡ) τῇ γυναικὶ αὐτοῦ. Ananias reserved (ἐνοσφίσατο, 3rd sg. aor. mid. indic. of νοσφίζω, refl., Schnabel 282) part of the price. The word recalls Achan at Josh 7:1 (Bruce, *Acts of the Apostles*, 162; Haenchen 237; Johnson 88) and represents financial fraud (Bock 221). At Qumran, lying about money to the community earned a year's probation (1QS 6.24). The severity here is due to the obj. of the deceit (the Holy Spirit). The prep. phrase ἀπὸ τῆς τιμῆς functions as a part. gen. Again, Luke is clear on the complicity of Ananias's wife by indicating her knowledge of the matter with a gen. abs. phrase employing συνειδυίης (gen. sg. fem. of pf. act. ptc. of σύνοιδα, "understand"). Μέρος τι ("a certain part") is the dir. obj. of ἐνέγκας (nom. sg. masc. of aor. act. ptc of φέρω, temp.), "having brought a certain part." Ἔθηκεν is the 3rd sg. aor. act. indic. of τίθημι. The phrase παρὰ τοὺς πόδας τῶν ἀποστόλων suggests a public display of the act (Schnabel 283).

5:3 Peter's address to Ananias is expressed as a question using διὰ τί ("why") although it is more of an accusation than a request for information. The vb. ἐπλήρωσεν (3rd sg. aor. act. indic. of πληρόω) is followed by two infs. of result (BHGNT 86; Bock 222; Schnabel 283): ψεύσασθαί (aor. mid. inf. of ψεύδομαι, "lie") and νοσφίσασθαι (aor. mid. inf. of νοσφίζω, "reserve"). The prep. phrase ἀπὸ τῆς τιμῆς τοῦ χωρίου (see 5:2) functions as a part. gen. mng. "the price of the property."

5:4 Ananias's rightful ownership of the property is affirmed by Peter. Μένον (nom. sg. neut. of pres. act. ptc. of μένω; temp.) sets the background for the main vb. Ἔμενεν (3rd sg. impf. act. indic. of μένω) is modified with a dat. of advantage, σοί (in this instance, fronted). The assumed subj. refers to the property. The whole phrase is introduced with the adv. οὐχί that expects a positive answer. Overall, Peter affirmed Ananias's right to personal property. He went on to affirm that the money generated was also Ananias's to control. Πραθέν is the nom. sg. neut. of aor. pass. ptc. of πιπράσκω, "sell." Ὑπῆρχεν is the 3rd sg. impf. act. indic. of ὑπάρχω. Ananias's control is expressed with ἐν τῇ σῇ ἐξουσίᾳ (where σῇ is a poss. dat.), lit., "in your authority," that is, "at your disposal" (cf. RSV, ESV, NET, NIV). The gift, then, was completely voluntary (Barrett 1.267; Bruce, *Acts of the Apostles*, 163). At 5:3 Satan placed it in his mind; at 5:4, in Peter's second accusatory question (τί ὅτι "How is it that?" [Wallace 459–60, s.v. "epex. ὅτι"]), Ananias placed (ἔθου, 2nd sg. aor. mid. indic. of τίθημι) "this matter" (πρᾶγμα, acc. sg. neut. of πρᾶγμα, -ατος, τό; dir. obj. to ἔθου) in his heart. Peter directly stated the sin as lying (ἐψεύσω, 2nd sg. aor. mid. indic. of ψεύδομαι) to God. Because the lie in v. 4 is against the Holy Spirit and in v. 5 made against God, this parallel becomes a classic (and appropriate) proof text for the personhood and divinity of the Holy Spirit (Bruce, *Acts of the Apostles*, 163; Bock 222).

5:5 The unusual combination of ptcs. presents a dramatic sequence regarding Ananias's death by the judgment of God (Barrett 1.268). The pres. ptc. (ἀκούων, nom. sg. masc. of pres. act. ptc. of ἀκούω; temp.) depicts action as continuing at the same time of the main vb. (ἐξέψυξεν, 3rd sg. aor. act. indic. of ἐκψύχω, "expire"). The vb., however, has an aor. ptc. (πεσών nom. sg. masc. of aor. act. ptc. of πίπτω; temp.) that depicts action before the main vb. This combination presents a sequence that suggests the entirety of the ref. takes place as Peter was speaking. While Peter's words were ongoing, Ananias fell and expired. The report generated (ἐγένετο, 3rd sg. aor. mid. indic. of γίνομαι) great fear on "those who heard" (ἀκούοντας, acc. pl. masc. of pres. act. ptc. of ἀκούω; subst.).

5:6 The scene concludes with a brief description of Ananias's burial. The ptc. ἀναστάντες (nom. pl. masc. of aor. act. ptc. of ἀνίστημι) introduces the arrival of νεώτεροι (nom. pl. masc. of νέος, -α, -ον, "young"; comp. adj., subst.). The term does not refer to an office but to a group of younger men who would naturally do such tasks as needed (Haenchen 238). The burial is expressed rather quickly: συνέστειλαν (3rd pl. aor. act. indic. of συστέλλω, "cover"); they carried him out (ἐξενέγκαντες, nom. pl. masc. of aor. act. ptc. of ἐκφέρω; temp.) and buried (ἔθαψαν, 3rd pl. aor. act. indic. of θάπτω) him. The burial practices of the day would be to simply wrap the body and put it in a tomb. It is quite likely this could have been done without his wife having heard about it in the time expressed. However, the act, apart from family involvement, is unusual and suggests recognition that Ananias had been struck down under the judgment of God (Bock 224; Schnabel 285).

5:7 On ἐγένετο δέ, see 4:5. Used with numbers, ὡς suggests the generalization "about" (ZG 364). The phrase ὡρῶν τριῶν is a gen. of time modifying the interval (διάστημα, nom. sg. neut. of διάστημα, -ατος, τό; pred. nom.). The ptc. εἰδυῖα (nom. sg. fem. of pf. act. ptc. of οἶδα; attend. circum.) takes the subst. ptc., γεγονός (acc. sg. neut. of pf. mid. ptc. of γίνομαι) as the dir. obj. mng. "what had happened." Ananias's wife had no clue regarding the events as she entered (εἰσῆλθε, 3rd sg. aor. act. indic. of εἰσέρχομαι).

5:8 Ἀπεκρίθη (3rd sg. aor. pass. indic. of ἀποκρίνομαι) is used as a synonym of λέγω (see Barrett 1.269). Εἰπέ (2nd sg. aor. act. impv. of λέγω, "speak") is formally the apod. of a cond. statement that follows (i.e., a dir. question, BHGNT 88). It creates a serious tone to introduce the question regarding the property. Ἀπέδοσθε (2nd pl. aor. mid. indic. of ἀποδίδωμι) in the mid. means "sold." The pl. implicates both husband and wife. The art. ἡ functions as the fem. pron. subj. of εἶπεν (3rd sg. aor. act. indic. of λέγω). Both instances of τοσούτου ("for so much" RSV, ESV, KJV, NKJV) are gens. of price (Barrett 1.270; Bruce, *Acts of the Apostles*, 165). At this point, there is not an accusatory tone as with Ananias. Sapphira had the opportunity to tell the truth (Schnabel 286; contra Haenchen 239). She, however, answered in the affirmative using ναί, continuing the lie.

5:9 Συνεφωνήθη (3rd sg. aor. indic. pass. of συμφωνέω) is impers. with τί as an interr. pron., "Why was it agreed upon?" Πειράσαι (aor. act. inf. of πειράζω, "test"; compl.) suggests a ref. to Deut 6:16. If so, that the dir. obj. is τὸ πνεῦμα κυρίου has the same trinitarian implications as 5:4. The particle ἰδού introduces a solemn, rather prophetic, pronouncement. By making the feet (πόδες) of the ones who buried (θαψάντων, gen. pl. masc. of aor. act. ptc. of θάπτω) her husband the subj. of the sentence, Peter created a dramatic picture of hearing approaching doom (see Barrett 1.270). Ἐξοίσουσιν is the 3rd pl. fut. act. indic. of ἐκφέρω, "carry out."

5:10 Peter's prophecy immediately comes true. Much like her husband, Sapphira fell (ἔπεσεν, 3rd sg. aor. act. indic. of πίπτω) and expired (ἐξέψυξεν, 3rd sg. aor. act. indic. of ἐκψύχω). Εἰσελθόντες is the nom. pl. masc. of aor. act. ptc. of εἰσέρχομαι; temp Εὗρον (3rd pl. aor. act. indic. of εὑρίσκω) takes αὐτὴν νεκράν as double-acc. dir. obj. compl. It suggests the young men (νεανίσκοι, nom. pl. masc. of νεανίσκος, -ου, ὁ; the same group as v. 6) were not coming to get her specifically. Ἔθαψαν is the 3rd pl. aor. act. indic. of θάπτω, "bury." It is telling that no public mourning is described for either party (see, e.g., 8:2). This, again, suggests the judgment of God (Keener 2.1195).

5:11 Luke closes the section with a summary. Φόβος μέγας ("great fear") is the subj. of ἐγένετο (3rd sg. aor. mid. indic. of γίνομαι). Fear is the normal reaction to the judgment of God in the Scriptures, signifying the reception of the message regarding the holiness God expects (Keener 2.1197). The sentence concludes with a double prep. phrase, upon (ἐφ'/ἐπί) the whole church and all others who heard (ἀκούοντας, acc. pl. masc. of pres. act. ptc. of ἀκούω; subst.).

FOR FURTHER STUDY

13. Ananias and Sapphira (5:1–11)

Harrill, J. A. "Divine Judgment against Ananias and Sapphira (Acts 5:1–11): A Stock Scene of Perjury and Death." *JBL* 130 (2011): 351–69.

Le Donne, A. "The Improper Temple Offering of Ananias and Sapphira." *NTS* 59 (2013): 346–64.

McCabe, D. *How to Kill Things with Words: Ananias and Sapphira under the Prophetic Speech Act of Divine Judgment (Acts 4:32–5:11).* New York: T&T Clark, 2011.

HOMILETICAL SUGGESTIONS

The Pleasing Gift (4:32–5:11)

1. Be generous in giving: Barnabas's giving is a demonstration of Christian charity (4:32–37)
2. Be selfless in giving: Ananias's giving is a demonstration of Christian self-promotion (5:1–6)
3. Be wise in giving: Sapphira's giving is a demonstration of Christian foolishness (vv. 7–11)

3. Further Growth in Numbers and Geographical Extension (5:12–16)

5:12–13 Διὰ . . . τῶν χειρῶν τῶν ἀποστόλων ("through the hands of the apostles") is fronted for emphasis. It describes an intermediate agency, where God is doing the work through them (BHGNT 90). Ἐγίνετο (3rd sg. impf. mid. indic. of γίνομαι) is used as a being vb. with σημεῖα καὶ τέρατα (nom. pl. neut. of τέρας, -ατος, τό) πολλά as a compound subj. The referent for ἐν τῷ λαῷ ("among the people") is debated and is the key identifying the pron. ref. in the passage. Previously in Acts λαός, "people," has been used exclusively of the people of the city. Furthermore, if we take a consistent ref. for λαός throughout this passage, it is likely a ref. to the non-Christian inhabitants in Jerusalem as well (Bock 230). Thus, "they were all together" (ἦσαν, 3rd. pl. impf. indic. of εἰμί) is employing ὁμοθυμαδόν ("together") as a locat., not an expression of unity (see 1:14; BHGNT 90; contra Keener 2.1198). The place of gathering is identified as ἐν τῇ στοᾷ (dat. sg. fem. of στοά, -ᾶς, ἡ, "colonnade"). Σολομῶντος (gen. sg. masc. of Σολομών, -ῶνος, ὁ, "of Solomon") is a gen. of identification. Thus, the passage is a description locating the public ministry of the apostles.

Λοιπῶν (part. gen.) modifies οὐδείς and continues the debate regarding the identity of the referents. Since λαός is introduced in the final clause as a new subj. (with the art. of previous ref.), λοιπῶν cannot refer to the city inhabitants. The impf. prog. ἐτόλμα (3rd sg. impf. act. indic. of τολμάω) is completed by κολλᾶσθαι (pres. pass. inf. of κολλάω, "join"). So "the rest" is likely the believers apart from apostles (Schnabel 291; Bock 231). The question is generally that such timidity doesn't comport with the prayer in ch. 4. However, τολμάω suggests not fear but inappropriate boldness, "no one was daring to join." The city inhabitants, however, did hold the church (αὐτούς) in great honor (ἐμεγάλυνεν, 3rd sg. impf. act. indic. of μεγαλύνω).

5:14 Μᾶλλον δέ supplements the previous information, mng. "now more than ever" (BDAG 613b, RSV, ESV). Πιστεύοντες (nom. sg. masc. of pres. act. ptc. of πιστεύω; subst.) is a rare use of an anar. subst. ptc. (R 1007) and functions as the subj. of προσετίθεντο (3rd pl. impf. act. indic. of προστίθημι, "add"). Κυρίῳ may modify the vb., but more likely πιστεύοντες since it often takes a dat. (Bruce, Acts of the Apostles, 168). Ἀνδρῶν τε καὶ γυναικῶν ("both men and women") are gen. because πλήθη often takes a gen. It might represent "hundreds if not thousands of Jews" (Schnabel 292).

5:15 The consec. ὥστε is difficult to connect to v. 14, but easily connects to v. 13. Thus, bringing the sick to be healed was a function of the people's high regard for the believers (Barrett 1.276). Verse 14 is parenthetical, reinforced by the fact that the subj. of the infs. (normal with consec. ὥστε) is unexpressed, but likely the λαός of v. 13. Ἐκφέρειν (pres. act. inf. of ἐκφέρω, "bring out") and τιθέναι (aor. act. inf. of τίθημι, "place") are compound and complete the consec. cstr. Κλιναρίων (gen. pl. neut. of κλινάριον, -ου, τό, "cots") and κραβάττων (gen. pl. masc. of κράβαττος, -ου, ὁ, "pallets") are near synonyms, two of the four words for a sick bed (Bruce, Acts of the Apostles, 168) and possibly indicated the poor of the masses (Keener 2.1200).

Ἐρχομένου (gen. sg. masc. of pres. mid. ptc. of ἔρχομαι; gen. abs.) in combination with ἐπισκιάσῃ (3rd sg. aor. act. subjunc. of ἐπισκιάζω, "overshadow, cover") depicts the hope of the crowd that Peter, passing by, might cast his shadow on some of them (τινὶ αὐτῶν, i.e., the sick, part. gen.). The text gives no indication of a planned healing event, but shows the high regard of the people.

5:16 Concluding the summary, a crowd was gathering (συνήρχετο, 3rd sg. impf. mid. indic. of συνέρχομαι). Πόλεων is a gen. of source. Πέριξ is a strengthened form of περί and takes Ἰερουσαλήμ as its obj. The mng. is "from the cities *all* around Jerusalem" (cf. BDAG 802d; most EVV make no distinction between πέριξ and περί). Φέροντες (nom. pl. masc. of pres. act. ptc. of φέρω; temp. or manner) is pl. because the neut. sg. subj., πλῆθος, is a collective. The ptc. takes ἀσθενεῖς (acc. pl. masc. of ἀσθενής, -ές, "sick"; subst. adj.) and ὀχλουμένους (acc. pl. masc. of pres. act. ptc. of ὀχλέω, "troubled"; subst., although anar. modified by πνευμάτων ἀκαθάρτων "unclean spirits") as a compound dir. obj., together mng. "the sick and those tormented by unclean spirits" (NRSV; cf. CSB). Οἵτινες is modified by "all" (ἅπαντες) and is the subj. of ἐθεραπεύοντο (3rd pl. impf. pass. indic. of θεραπεύω).

4. Another Attempt to Stop the Movement (5:17–42)

5:17–18 On the ptc. ἀναστάς (nom. sg. masc. of pres. act. ptc. of ἀνίστημι; attend. circum.), see 1:15. Οὖσα (nom. sg. fem. of pres. ptc. of εἰμί; attrib.) modifies αἵρεσις (nom. sg. fem. of αἵρεσις, -έσεως, ἡ, "party"). Σαδδουκαίων is the gen. pl. masc. of Σαδδουκαῖος, -ου, ὁ, "Sadducee"; descriptive gen. Bruce suggests "the so-called" is the best tr. (Bruce, Acts of the Apostles, 170). Their presence brings a rather official (and menacing) tone to their actions (Haenchen 248). The vb. ἐπλήσθησαν (3rd pl. aor. pass. indic. of πίμπλημι) followed by ζήλου (gen. sg. masc. of ζῆλος, -ου, ὁ, "jealousy"; gen. of content) explains the motivation for the arrest in v. 18.

The arrest is presented in a compound sentence. The phrase ἐπέβαλον (3rd pl. aor. act. indic. of ἐπιβάλλω, "cast upon") τὰς χεῖρας ἐπὶ . . . (lit. "cast their hands upon . . .") is euphemistic and descriptive of an arrest (ZG 365). The second vb. (ἔθεντο, 3rd pl. aor. mid. indic. of τίθημι; mid. of special interest) with the prep. phrase ἐν τηρήσει δημοσίᾳ (fem. dat. sgs. of τήρησις, -εως, ἡ, "prison" [see 4:3], and δημόσιος, -ία, ιον, "public"; "in a public prison") completes the act. The jail was perhaps the Jewish state prison in Herod's former palace (BAFCS 3:137; Schnabel 306).

5:19–20 When the angel intervened is described as διὰ νυκτός, "during the night" (NASB, ESV). The release is expressed with two temp. ptcs., ἀνοίξας (nom. sg. masc. of aor. act. ptc. of ἀνοίγω) and ἐξαγαγών (nom. sg. masc. of aor. act. ptc. of ἐξάγω, "lead out"). This cstr. highlights what the angel said (εἶπεν, 3rd sg. aor. act. indic. of λέγω).

The command is twofold: "go" (πορεύεσθε, 2nd pl. pres. act. impv. of πορεύομαι) and "speak" (λαλεῖτε, 2nd pl. pres. act. impv. of λαλέω). The pres. indicates that it was to be an ongoing command. Although the attend. circum. ptc. σταθέντες (nom. pl. masc. of aor. pass. ptc. of ἵστημι) takes on the force of the impv. main verbs (thus, "stand"), the choice of the ptc. backgrounds it to the impv. in its clause. Thus, something like "speak publicly" is the sense (BHGNT 94). On occasion, ῥῆμα, "word," is a synonym for λόγος. The use here, however, coupled with πάντα ref. individual words: "all the words." The command is to be constant and comprehensive. Τῆς ζωῆς ταύτης ("of this life," a gen. of resp., BHGNT 95) modifies ῥήματα, determining the scope of the words. The phrase is equiv. to τῆς σωτηρίας ταύτης ("this salvation") at 13:26 (Bock 249; Haenchen 249; Keener 2.1212).

5:21 Ἀκούσαντες (nom. pl. masc. of aor. act. ptc. of ἀκούω; temp.) has the idea of obedience (hence HCSB, "in obedience to this"). Εἰσῆλθον is the 3rd pl. aor. act. indic. of εἰσέρχομαι, "enter." The prep. phrase ὑπὸ τὸν ὄρθρον (acc. sg. masc. of ὄρθρος, -ου, ὁ, "daybreak") means "around dawn" (i.e., when worshippers came to the temple for the morning prayer, Keener 2.1214), a CGk. cstr. (Bruce, *Acts of the Apostles*, 170). The impf. ἐδίδασκον (3rd pl. impf. act. indic. of διδάσκω, "teach") picks up the progressive aspect of λαλεῖτε in 5:20.

Παραγενόμενος (nom. sg. masc. of aor. mid. ptc. of παραγίνομαι) is sg. although the sentence has a compound subj. (ἀρχιερεύς + οἱ σὺν αὐτῷ, "chief priest" and "those with him") and a plural main vb. (συνεκάλεσαν, 3rd pl. aor. act. indic. of συγκαλέω, "convene"). This is likely emphasizing the high priest (BHGNT 95). Τὸ συνέδριον καὶ πᾶσαν τὴν γερουσίαν (acc. sg. fem. of γερουσία, -ας, ἡ, "council of elders") τῶν υἱῶν Ἰσραὴλ ("the council and all the elders of the sons of Israel"—see Exod 12:21) does not suggest two groups but one (i.e., epex., Bruce, *Acts of the Apostles*, 171). The καί is likely ascensive = "even" (Bock 240). Apparently, the escape was not known to them for they sent (ἀπέστειλαν, 3rd pl. aor. act. indic. of ἀποστέλλω) word to the prison (εἰς τὸ δεσμωτήριον [acc. sg. neut. of δεσμωτήριον, -ου, τό, "prison"]) to bring (ἀχθῆναι, aor. pass. inf. of ἄγω, "lead") the apostles to the council.

5:22 The compliance is straightforward. Ὑπηρέται (nom. pl. masc. of ὑπηρέτης), tr. "officers" in NASB, ESV, NET, and "temple police" in NRSV, is best understood as the assistants to the commander of the temple (see 5:26, στρατηγός). Thus, "temple police" is a good description. Παραγενόμενοι (nom. pl. masc. of aor. mid. ptc. of παραγίνομαι) is temp. Εὗρον is the 3rd pl. aor. act. indic. of εὑρίσκω. They made a return (ἀναστρέψαντες, nom. pl. masc. of aor. act. ptc. of ἀναστρέφω) to report (ἀπήγγειλαν, 3rd pl. aor. act. indic. of ἀπαγγέλλω).

5:23 The report is given in dir. speech indicated by λέγοντες (nom. pl. masc. of pres. act. ptc. of λέγω) and ὅτι (BHGNT 96). Thus, the vbs. are now 1st pl. (εὕρομεν, 1st pl. aor. act. indic. of εὑρίσκω, also repeated at the end). Δεσμωτήριον (see v. 21) and κεκλεισμένον (acc. sg. neut. of pf. pass. ptc. of κλείω, "lock") form an obj. compl. double-acc. cstr. Ἐν πάσῃ ἀσφαλείᾳ (dat. sg. fem. of ἀσφάλεια, -ας, ἡ, "security") is the equivalent of a strengthened adv. "securely" (e.g., NASB "quite securely"). Another obj. (φύλακας, acc. pl. masc. of φύλαξ, -ακος, ὁ, "guards") and compl. (ἑστῶτας, acc. sg. masc. of pf. act. ptc. of ἵστημι) double-acc. structure (assuming εὕρομεν as the vb.) describes the state of the guards. Ἀνοίξαντες (nom. pl. masc. of aor. act. ptc. of ἀνοίγω) is temp.

5:24 Ὡς is temp., "when." Ἤκουσαν is the 3rd pl. aor. act. indic. of ἀκούω. The compound subj. of ἤκουσαν (ὁ στρατηγός and οἱ ἀρχιερεῖς τοῦ ἱεροῦ) is expressed with a τε . . . καί cstr. that is stronger than a simple καί. On τε, see 1:15. The report was very disturbing (διηπόρουν, 3rd pl. impf. act. indic. of διαπορέω, "greatly perplexed"; see 2:12 and 10:17). The use of the opt. γένοιτο (3rd sg. aor. opt. mid. of γίνομαι, potential opt.) with ἄν indicates indefiniteness (Bruce, *Acts of the Apostles*, 171). It is also the apod. of an incomplete 4th class cond. (also, "less probable fut.," Wallace 702). This is an expression of wishful thinking on the part of the officials.

5:25 A report from the temple dashed their hopes. An unnamed man (τις) arrived (παραγενόμενος, nom. sg. masc. of aor. mid. ptc. of παραγίνομαι, "having arrived"; temp.) and reported (ἀπήγγειλεν, 3rd sg. aor. act. indic. of ἀπαγγέλλω) the missing prisoners were preaching in the temple. Ἔθεσθε (2nd pl. aor. mid. indic. of τίθημι) is a mid. of special interest. The preaching activity is described with a compound periph. cstr. Εἰσίν is the 3rd pl. pres. indic. of εἰμί, followed with ἑστῶτες (nom. pl. masc. of pf. act. ptc. of ἵστημι; periph. pf.), and διδάσκοντες is the nom. pl. masc. of pres. act. ptc. of διδάσκω; periph. pres.

5:26 On ὁ στρατηγός, see 4:1. On ὑπηρέταις, see 5:22. Ἀπελθών (nom. sg. masc. of aor. act. ptc. of ἀπέρχομαι) is temp. The impf. ἦγεν (3rd sg. aor. act. impf. of ἄγω) implies the procession back to the Sanhedrin (Bock 241). The negated μετὰ βίας (gen. sg. fem. of βία, -ας, ἡ, "force") connotes a lack of violence (see the adj. at 2:2; RSV, NASB, ESV, "without violence"). Thus, the commander with his guard provides a show of force, but with no intention to use it. Ἐφοβοῦντο is the 3rd pl. impf. pass. indic. of φοβέομαι (the word occurs in both the mid. and the pass. in Acts with no change of mng.). Μὴ λιθασθῶσιν (3rd pl. aor. subjunc. pass. of λιθάζω) is equiv. to a ἵνα μή cstr. (note the *byz.* var.) and means "lest they be stoned" (see Wallace 477; BHGNT 97–98).

5:27–28 Ἀγαγόντες (nom. pl. masc. of aor. act. ptc. of ἄγω) is temp. On "standing (ἔστησαν, 3rd pl. aor. act. indic of ἵστημι) in the midst," see 4:7. The high priest's interrogation is expressed as an aor. indic. (ἐπηρώτησεν, 3rd sg. aor. act. indic. of ἐπερωτάω, "question"; RSV, NASB, NRSV, ESV). Λέγων (nom. sg. masc. of pres. act. ptc. of λέγω) introduces dir. speech. The question of whether οὐ was orig. or not does not change the general mng. of the text but affects whether the sentence is a question (see CSB, KJV, NLT) or a statement (RSV, NASB, NIV, ESV, NET). Παραγγελία (dat. sg. fem. of παραγγελία, -ας, ἡ, "order") παρηγγείλαμεν (1st pl. aor. act. indic. of παραγγελλω) is an emphatic Sem. idiom (the inf. cstr., Bruce, *Acts of the Apostles*, 172; R 531). "Strictly charged" is a good tr. (see RSV, ESV, Haenchen 250). The prohibition is a nearly verbatim ref. to the command in 4:18 and is likewise expressed in indir. speech (BHGNT 98) as μὴ διδάσκειν (pres. act. inf. of διδάσκω) ἐπὶ τῷ ὀνόματι τούτῳ (see 4:18 and 3:6). Καὶ ἰδού is emphatic and introduces a twofold accusation. First, πεπληρώκατε (2nd pl. pf. act. indic. of πληρόω) followed by a dir. obj. (τὴν Ἰερουσαλήμ) and a gen. of content (τῆς διδαχῆς ὑμῶν) indicates the extent of the disobedience. It is citywide. Second, βούλεσθε (2nd pl. pres. mid. indic. of βούλομαι) with the compl. inf. ἐπαγαγεῖν (aor. act. inf. of ἐπάγω, "lay upon") expresses the motive for disobedience: to charge the Sanhedrin with murder.

5:29 The response of the apostles also mirrors the exchange in 4:19. While Ἀποκριθείς (nom. sg. masc. of aor. pass. ptc. of ἀποκρίνομαι; pleonastic [see 4:19], indic. dir. speech) is sg., εἶπαν (3rd pl. aor. act. indic. of λέγω) is pl. This suggests that Peter was speaking for the whole group (Wallace 401–2; BHGNT 99). Πειθαρχεῖν (pres. act. inf. of πειθαρχέω, "obey"; compl.) takes the dat. θεῷ and ἀνθρώποις as "necessary complements" (BDF §100) instead of the normal acc. (cf. 5:32).

5:30 Peter's response affirmed both accusations in reverse order. Ἤγειρεν is the 3rd sg. aor. act. indic. of ἐγείρω. Ὑμεῖς is fronted for emphasis. The vb. διεχειρίσασθε (2nd pl. aor. mid. indic. of διαχειρίζω, "lay violent hands on") is only mid. in the NT and implies handling with malicious intent (BDAG 240a). Κρεμάσαντες is the nom. pl. masc. of aor. mid. ptc. of κρεμάννυμι, "hang," means.

5:31 Peter continued with Jesus's exaltation. The basic cstr. is a complicated double-acc. God exalted (ὕψωσεν, 3rd sg. aor. act. indic. of ὑψόω) this man (τοῦτον) to be "ruler and Savior" (ἀρχηγὸν καὶ σωτῆρα). The mission is defined with an inf. of purp. δοῦναι (aor. act. inf. of δίδωμι). The inf. has two dir. obj. phrases: μετάνοιαν τῷ Ἰσραήλ ("repentance to Israel") and ἄφεσιν ἁμαρτιῶν (obj. gen.; "forgiveness of sins").

5:32 Ἡμεῖς ἐσμεν (1st pl. pres. indic. of εἰμί) is emphatic. Ῥημάτων (obj. gen. completing the pred. nom. μάρτυρες) is technically "words," but in another Sem. idiom, it can mean "thing" or "event" (BDAG 905a–b). Τὸ πνεῦμα τὸ ἅγιον is the subj. of an implied ἐστίν. Most EVV tr. "and so is the Holy Spirit" (NASB, NIV, ESV, etc.). The final rel. pron. (ὅ) phrase notes the gift of the Spirit. Ἔδωκεν is the 3rd sg. aor. act. indic. of δίδωμι. Πειθαρχοῦσιν is the dat. pl. masc. of pres. act. ptc. of πειθαρχέω, "obey"; subst.; dat. of indir. obj. It is a subtle theological point regarding the coming of the new age.

5:33 Ἀκούσαντες is the nom. pl. masc. of aor. act. ptc. of ἀκούω, temp. Διεπρίοντο is the 3rd pl. impf. pass. indic. of διαπρίω; lit., "sawn through"; fig., "infuriated" (BDAG 235b, see also 7:54). There is no sense of "conviction" as the tr. "cut to the quick" (e.g., NASB) is often interpreted by laypeople. This is further indicated by the response: ἐβούλοντο, 3rd pl. impf. mid. indic. of βούλομαι + ἀνελεῖν, pres. act. inf. of ἀναιρέω; compl. to ἐβούλοντο, together mng. "wanting to kill them."

5:34 The purp. of this v. is to introduce Gamaliel to Luke's audience. He is shown as a man with authority, regardless of whether the source is profound respect or by virtue of an office. He is described in terms that could suggest either. He is a νομοδιδάσκαλος (a teacher of the Law of Moses) and τίμιος παντὶ τῷ λαῷ ("man regarded as honorable by all the people"). Ἀναστάς (nom. sg. masc. of aor. act. ptc. of ἀνίστημι) is temp. Ἐκέλευσεν is the 3rd sg. aor. act. indic. of κελεύω, "order." Ποιῆσαι (aor. act. inf. of ποιέω, compl.) in combination with the adv. ἔξω (used intrans.) has the mng. "to be put outside" (BDAG 354b).

5:35 For the address, ἄνδρες Ἰσραηλῖται, see 2:22. Gamaliel gives a mitigated warning employing προσέχετε (2nd pl. pres. act. impv. of προσέχω, "pay attention") regarding their intent. Μέλλετε (2nd pl. pres. act. indic. of μέλλω, "about to take place") is compl. by πράσσειν, pres. act. inf. of πράσσω (NIV, "what you intend to do").

5:36 The grounds for the warning are two historical precedents. The first was Theudas. Πρὸ . . . τούτων τῶν ἡμερῶν is lit. "before these days." Ἀνέστη is the 3rd sg. aor. act. indic. of ἀνίστημι, "arise." The ptc. λέγων (nom. sg. masc. of pres. act. ptc. of λέγω; indir. speech) takes the refl. pron. ἑαυτόν as a dir. obj. indicating a self-made claim. The contents are obscure but summarized with the compl. inf. εἶναί + τινα, mng. "to be someone." The technical subj. of Gamaliel's summary (ἀριθμός, nom. sg. masc. of ἀριθμός, -οῦ, ὁ, "number") is sg. modified by a part. gen. (ἀνδρῶν). Thus, προσεκλίθη (3rd sg. aor. pass. indic. of προσκλίνω, "joined") is a collective sg. Ὡς τετρακοσίων is a standard way of estimating numbers ("about 400," cf. 5:7). As for Theudas, "he was executed" (ἀνῃρέθη, 3rd sg. aor. pass. indic. of ἀναιρέω). The phrase ὅσοι ἐπείθοντο (3rd pl. impf. pass. indic. of πείθω) αὐτῷ employs an idiomatic use of πείθω followed by a dat. to mean "obey" or "follow." It is typically tr. "who followed" (RSV, NASB, ESV, NET, but note HCSB, "partisans") to smooth out the expression in Eng. These followers were scattered (διελύθησαν, 3rd pl. aor. pass. indic. of διαλύω). And the whole affair was ultimately meaningless (lit., "came to nothing"; ἐγένοντο, 3rd pl. aor. mid. indic. of γίνομαι + εἰς οὐδέν).

A Theudas whom we know from Josephus is dated to the governorship of Fadus (44–46, *Ant.* 20.97). This is, however, ten to fifteen years after Gamaliel's speech. At least three interpretations have arisen.

1. Many suggest Luke made a mistake: an anachronism (see Barrett 1.296; Keener 2.1236). Josephus's account of Theudas is followed by the description of Judas of Galilee (*Ant.* 20:102). The sim. has led some (e.g., Haenchen 252) to conclude that Luke is incorrectly using Josephus (his description is of the death of Judas's *sons* shortly after the time of the aforementioned Theudas by Alexander, the successor to Fadus). This posits a date for Acts well beyond Josephus (c. AD 95). Few follow this line of reasoning today, preferring simply to cite Josephus as correct and Luke in error.

2. It is possible that Josephus made the mistake. Under this view, Theudas is misplaced by Josephus under Fadus's governorship. Generally, the thought is that when comp. Luke's accuracy to Josephus's, Luke is to be preferred. Most suggest this as a possibility without a great number of advocates (see, however, Witherington 239, who cites it as one of the two likeliest possibilities).

3. The interpreters might be the ones making the mistake. It is possible that the Theudas mentioned in Acts is a different man than the one in Josephus. While

Gamaliel's summation is brief, there are some differences. For example, in Acts, Theudas gathered an army of 400 men, while Josephus referred to "the majority of the masses." Furthermore, Barrett (1.295) notes that the Western MS D and Eusebius (*Eccl. Hist.* 2.11.1) both describe Theudas's death by suicide. This is in stark contrast to Josephus's account. The name Theudas was more common than normally cited (*New Docs* 4.183–85). In the immediate aftermath of Herod's death, numerous uprisings occurred (Josephus, *Ant.* 17:269). This otherwise unknown Theudas may be one of them.

The position here favors the third option. However, absolute proof in any of the three options is not forthcoming. The literature is rife with rather shallow assertions in all directions. What we can affirm is that two of the three options favor Luke's accuracy. Given this, that Acts 5:36 is a pivot denying Luke's accuracy and, by extension, the inspiration of Scripture, is unwarranted.

FOR FURTHER STUDY

14. Gamaliel, Theudas, and Luke's Accuracy (5:36–37)

Crabbe, Kylie. "Being Found Fighting against God: Luke's Gamaliel and Josephus on Human Responses to Divine Providence." *ZNW* 106 (2015): 21–39.

Longenecker, B. W. "The Wilderness and Revolutionary Ferment in First-Century Palestine: A Response to D R Schwartz and J Marcus." *JSJ* 29 (1998): 322–36.

Rhoads, J. "Josephus Misdated the Census of Quirinius." *JETS* 54 (2011): 65–87.

5:37 The description of Judas of Galilee intentionally parallels the description of Theudas for effect, making the point that these men are exactly alike. Judas arises (ἀνέστη, 3rd sg. aor. act. indic. of ἀνίστημι) in the days of the census (ἀπογραφῆς, gen. sg. fem. of ἀπογραφή, -ῆς, ἡ). Ostensibly it is the same one that brought Joseph and Mary to Bethlehem. He drew (ἀπέστησεν, 3rd sg. aor. act. indic. of ἀφίστημι) followers from the people. But he was destroyed (ἀπώλετο, 3rd sg. aor. mid. indic. of ἀπόλλυμι), and his followers (using the same construction as Theudas's; ἐπείθοντο, 3rd pl. impf. pass. indic. of πείθω + a dat.) were scattered (διεσκορπίσθησαν, 3rd pl. aor. pass. indic. of διασκορπίζω).

5:38–39 Gamaliel drew his conclusion in solemn tones using λέγω (1st sg. pres. act. indic. of λέγω) ὑμῖν. Τὰ νῦν is a pron. use of the art. with a temp. adv., lit. "the now things." It is best understood as an acc. of ref., "regarding the present matters" (see NASB, NIV, ESV; "in the present case," Bruce, *Acts of the Apostles*, 178). He urges them to stay away (ἀπόστητε, 2nd pl. aor. act. impv. of ἀφίστημι) and release (ἄφετε, 2nd pl. aor. act. impv. of ἀφίημι) the apostles. The grounds for these commands are a third-class cond. (uncertain but likely). If it is (ᾖ, 3rd sg. pres. subjunc. of εἰμί) the plans or work of men, it will be destroyed (καταλυθήσεται, 3rd sg. fut. pass. indic. of καταλύω).

In the contrasting statement, the cstr. is switched to a first-class cond. (assumed true for argument's sake) using the indic. ἐστίν in the prot. The switch in cstr. increases the significance of the consequences. It does not suggest Gamaliel's belief in Christianity (Bruce, *Acts of the Apostles*, 178). The apod. is a statement regarding the futility of opposition (Bock 251): δυνήσεσθε (2nd pl. fut. mid. indic. of δύναμαι) followed by the compl. inf. καταλῦσαι (aor. act. inf. of καταλύω). Previously the sense of καταλύω was "destroy"; here it means "to stop." It is likely the play on the semantic domains is intentional.

Μήποτε is either a neg. purp. ("lest," the more common use) or weakened to express a conjecture ("perhaps" or "may . . . be"). Most EVV choose the latter (NASB, ESV, CSB). Given the presence of an impv. (in the previous verse) and the presence of an aor. subjunc. (εὑρεθῆτε, 2nd pl. aor. pass. subjunc. of εὑρίσκω), it is likely the sense is "leave them alone. . .lest you be found as. . ." (see NKJV). In this case, εὑρίσκω functions as a being vb., describing a state. Thus, θεομάχοι (nom. pl. masc. of θεομάχος, -ον, "fighting against God"; subst. adj.) is the compl. in a pred. nom. cstr. "Lest you be found as God-fighters" is the lit. sense. The hearers found the logic impeccable. Ἐπείσθησαν is 3rd pl. aor. pass. indic. of πείθω. Luke certainly intended an implicit fulfillment of this statement in Christianity. However, the statement falls short of how one should judge all religious movements if success is defined by a large number of adherents. Success should be defined by the actual destination of the followers.

5:40 Προσκαλεσάμενοι (nom. pl. masc. of aor. mid. ptc. of προσκαλέομαι; temp.) and δείραντες (nom. pl. masc. of aor. act. ptc. of δέρω; temp.) is best expressed, "having called and beaten." These are backgrounded to παρήγγειλαν (3rd pl. aor. act. indic. of παραγγέλλω, "order"). Μὴ λαλεῖν (pres. act. inf. of λαλέω; compl.) ἐπὶ τῷ ὀνόματι τοῦ Ἰησοῦ (see 4:18 and 3:6) is the substance of the command and brings the narrative right back to the orig. charge (and does not really obey Gamaliel's advice). Ἀπέλυσαν is the 3rd pl. aor. act. indic. of ἀπολύω, "release."

5:41 On μέν, see 1:1. The apostles' (οἱ) departure is in the impf. (ἐπορεύοντο, 3rd pl. impf. mid. indic. of πορεύομαι), suggesting an ongoing attitude of rejoicing (χαίροντες, masc. nom. of pl. pres. act. ptc. of χαίρω; manner). The grounds for the rejoicing was that they were considered worthy (κατηξιώθησαν, 3rd pl. aor. pass. inidc. of καταξιόω) to be dishonored (ἀτιμασθῆναι, aor. pass. inf. of ἀτιμάζω). The juxtaposition of vbs. demonstrates the Christian's high esteem of God's opinion versus the larger culture's.

5:42 On τε, see 1:15. Πᾶσάν . . . ἡμέραν (acc. sg. fem.; acc. of time; "every day") and κατ' οἶκον (distributive; "in each house") are fronted for emphasis. The activity is both public and private. In dir. disobedience to the Sanhedrin, they did not stop (ἐπαύοντο, 3rd pl. impf. mid. indic. of παύω; intrans. mid.) teaching (διδάσκοντες, nom. pl. masc. of pres. act. ptc. of διδάσκω; compl.) and evangelizing (εὐαγγελιζόμενοι, nom. pl. masc. of pres. mid. ptc. of εὐαγγελίζομαι; compl.; the act. voice only occurs in Rev 10:7; 14:6, and a var. at Acts 16:17; it is mid. in all other forms, BDAG 402a). Τὸν χριστὸν Ἰησοῦν may be a double-acc. cstr. (i.e., Jesus as Christ; see, e.g., NASB, NIV). However, it is more likely to be a simple dir. obj. noun phrase "Jesus Christ" (Wallace 184; see KJV).

HOMILETICAL SUGGESTIONS

Worthy to Suffer Dishonor for the Name (5:12–42)

1. Those worthy to suffer participate in God's work (vv. 12–16)

2. Those worthy to suffer draw the anger of God's enemies (vv. 17–20)
3. Those worthy to suffer obey in the face of persecution (vv. 21–33)
4. Those worthy to suffer rejoice in God's deliverance (vv. 34–42)

Poor Advice from a Theologian (5:34–42)

1. Gamaliel misunderstood Christianity (vv. 34–37)
   He comp. it to political insurrections
2. Gamaliel advised to wait (vv. 38–39)
   Some might (and did) wait too long to affirm the movement

5. Serving the Hellenists' Widows: Potential Conflict Avoided (6:1–7)

6:1 Pressure arose internally at the same time (ἐν δὲ ταῖς ἡμέραις ταύταις, denoting a new section [Bruce, *Acts of the Apostles*, 180]) as the disciples were multiplying (πληθυνόντων, gen. pl. masc. of pres. act. ptc. of πληθύνω, "increased"; gen. abs., temp.). The two groups disputing were Ἑλληνιστῶν (gen. pl. masc. of Ἑλληνιστής, -οῦ, ὁ, "Hellenists"; i.e., Gk.-speaking Jews, ZG 368) and Ἑβραίους ("Jews"; i.e., Aram.-speaking Jews, ZG 368). The neglect (παρεθεωροῦντο, 3rd pl. impf. pass. indic. of παραθεωρέω) of the Diaspora converts' widows who had settled in Jerusalem was surely unintentional (Keener 2.1258); they were likely the new believers at Pentecost. The neglect is over a daily (καθημερινῇ, dat. sg. fem. of καθημερινός, -ή, -όν) ministry that likely included meals and other services.

6:2 Προσκαλεσάμενοι (nom. pl. masc. of aor. mid. ptc. of προσκαλέομαι; temp.) takes τὸ πλῆθος τῶν μαθητῶν as a dir. obj. phrase. The gathering is backgrounded to the Twelve's (δώδεκα, only here in Acts [Bruce, *Acts of the Apostles*, 182]) address. Ἀρεστόν (nom. sg. neut. of ἀρεστός, -ή, -όν, "acceptable") is a pred. adj. compl. to ἐστιν. Καταλείψαντας (acc. pl. masc. of aor. act. ptc. of καταλείπω, "leave"; attend. circum.) takes on the force of the inf. διακονεῖν (pres. act. inf. of διακονέω, "serve"; with ἡμᾶς as its acc. subj.). Τὸν λόγον τοῦ θεου likely refers to preaching the gospel.

6:3–4 The apostolic solution is for the congregation to choose (ἐπισκέψασθε, 2nd pl. aor. mid. impv. ἐπισκέπτομαι) seven men. They list three general characteristics, each an adj. form that modifies ἄνδρας. Μαρτυρουμένους (acc. pl. masc. of pres. pass. ptc. of μαρτυρέω; attrib.) in the pass. suggests a good reputation (see Barrett 1.312). The second and third qualifications, πνεύματος καὶ σοφίας, are gen. of contents required by the adj. πλήρεις ("full"). It suggests pious and wise men. Barrett rightly describes it as "showing all the marks of the work of the Holy Spirit" and naturally gifted (Barrett 1.313). Καταστήσομεν is the 1st pl. fut. act. indic. of καθίστημι, "appoint."

The nom. pron. ἡμεῖς is emphatic by redundancy and position. Προσκαρτερήσομεν (1st pl. fut. act. indic. of προσκαρτερέω, "be devoted to"), taking a dat. obj., is frequent in Acts (six times, see 1:14) and rare outside (four times). The apostolic ministry is twofold: prayer (τῇ προσευχῇ) and preaching (τῇ διακονίᾳ τοῦ λόγου). The latter implies both study and proclamation.

6:5 The vb. ἤρεσεν (3rd sg. aor. act. indic. of ἀρέσκω, "please") appearing with the prep. ἐνώπιον is unusual in Gk. (Barrett 1.324). The appearance here is best understood as influence from the LXX (twelve times, see, e.g., 1 Kgs 20:2). Zerwick notes it is "a respectful circumlocution for simple dat." (ZG 368). Although little different in mng., most EVV tr. πλήθους as the dir. obj., ignoring ἐνώπιον. Παντός in the pred. position means "the whole crowd." The democratic nature of the early church is on display as they chose (ἐξελέξαντο, 3rd sg. aor. mid. indic. of ἐκλέγομαι) the men (as instructed). Clearly the introduction of Stephen is the main point for the list, as only he is listed with the qualifications of v. 3 (ἄνδρα πλήρης πίστεως καὶ πνεύματος ἁγίου). This highlights Stephen rather than denying the others had similar qualifications. Of the remaining list, only Philip appears as a character in Acts. They are all Gk. names. Some names, as yet, have not been found in Jerusalem, suggesting at least some were Diaspora Jews (Schnabel 333).

6:6 The rel. pron. οὕς is normally tr. as a pron. starting a new sentence (RSV, NIV, ESV, NET, CSB), although it is formally a subord. clause. The actions taken by the church strongly suggest an official position within the church. The men were publicly presented (ἔστησαν, 3rd pl. aor. act. indic. of ἵστημι); prayed over (προσευξάμενοι, nom. pl. masc. of aor. mid. ptc. of προσεύχομαι; temp.); and set apart by laying on of hands (ἐπέθηκαν, 3rd pl. aor. act. indic. of ἐπιτίθημι).

6:7 The summary signals the end of a major section. The section features three impf. vbs. The first two are progressive. The word's growth (ηὔξανεν, 3rd sg. impf. act. indic. of αὐξάνω [see also 12:24; 19:20]) continues. The phrase suggests the message of Christ was spreading rapidly. The second vb. (ἐπληθύνετο, 3rd sg. impf. pass. indic. of πληθύνω, "multiplied") also implies a continuation of previous activity. The third impf. vb., ὑπήκουον (3rd pl. impf. act. indic. of ὑπακούω, the sg. subj. ὄχλος is a collective), should be seen as inceptive (ZG 369): "began to be obedient." The unusual phrase ὄχλος τῶν ἱερέων (part. gen.) observes the large number of priests in Jerusalem, likely apart from the temple hierarchy (Keener 2.1291; Schnabel 336). These men help validate the Christian message and also identify the opposition of the temple hierarchy as isolated (Keener 1.1292).

FOR FURTHER STUDY

15. Stephen and Deacons (6:1–6)

Blackburn, B. L. *DLNT*, 1123–26.
Bruce, F. F. *Peter, Stephen, James, and John: Studies in Early Non-Pauline Christianity.* Grand Rapids: Eerdmans, 1979.
Kilgallen, J. J. *The Stephen Speech: A Literary and Redactional Study of Acts 7, 2–53.* AnBib 67. Rome: Biblical Institute, 1976.
Lake, K. "The Communism of Acts II. and IV.–VI. and the Appointment of the Seven." In *Beginnings* 5, 140–50.
NIDNTTE, 1:701–5.
Smith, S. "Acts 7: Stephen and the Temple." In *The Fate of the Jerusalem Temple in Luke-Acts: An Intertextual Approach to Jesus's Laments over Jerusalem and Stephen's Speech*, 140–89. LNTS 553. London: Bloomsbury, T&T Clark, 2016.

HOMILETICAL SUGGESTIONS

The Ministry of the Seven (6:1–7)

1. It arose from a church problem (v. 1b)
2. The apostles could not leave their work (v. 2)
3. The church selected seven godly men (vv. 3–6)
4. The results were greater ministry (v. 7)

III. Initial Expansion: Stephen, Samaria, and Saul (6:8–9:31)

This section of acts records the first great movement outside Jerusalem, predicted at 1:8. The church will move from Jerusalem to Judea and Samaria. The conversion of Saul hints at God's preparation for the Gentile mission to come in the next section.

A. SUFFERING: ONE OF THE SERVANTS ARRESTED AND MARTYRED (6:8–8:1A)

The arrest, defense, and death of Stephen is a historically and theologically pivotal point in the narrative of Acts. As the longest speech in Acts, its importance is underlined by its sheer length (Barrett 1.334). Historically it explains the first expansion of the gospel out of Jerusalem: it comes by violence. Theologically it lays the case for an explanation of Israel's hostility against the gospel. They have always resisted the work of the Holy Spirit and tended toward idolatry. The charges against Stephen were a twofold blasphemy charge: 1) he spoke against Moses and God (6:11); and 2) he spoke against the temple (6:13). Stephen directly denied the first charge. In 7:2–38, Stephen addressed the formation of the covenant people and the giving of the law. Moses is clearly considered a prophet, miracle worker, and lawgiver (see, e.g., 7:36). However, the people responded in idolatry (7:39–43). Likewise, Stephen addressed the charge against the temple in 7:44–50. The tabernacle and temple were given by God, but he does not dwell in them (vv. 48–49). At v. 50, Stephen began to charge the present people with the same misdeeds as their ancestors. Given the context, he was likely charging them with making the temple and its institutions into an idol. But at 7:54, the mob interrupted the defense; they would hear no more. The section is divided into three major parts: 6:8–15 contains the formal charges; 7:1–53 is Stephen's defense; and 7:54–8:1a records the death of Stephen and its aftermath.

1. The Charges against Stephen (6:8–15)

6:8 Δέ marks the section as a major new development. The description of Stephen as πλήρης χάριτος καὶ δυνάμεως ("full of grace and power"; gen. of content) defines the source of his works as from God (cf. Keener 2.1296). Ἐποίει is the 3rd sg. impf. act.

indic. of ποιέω. Τέρατα (acc. pl. neut. of τέρας, -ατος, τό) καὶ σημεῖα μεγάλα describes significant miracles. Ἐν τῷ λαῷ consistently describes Israelites in Jerusalem (see 5:12), implying an empowered evangelism.

6:9 Ἀνέστησαν (3rd pl. aor. act. indic. of ἀνίστημι) means to appear for a function or role (BDAG 83b). In this case, it is opposition. Τινες functions as a subj. phrase of the vb. Τῶν (a part. gen.) is the pron. use of the art. It appears they represent at least one Hellenistic synagogue, named (λεγομένης, gen. sg. fem. of pres. pass. ptc. of λέγω) "of the Freedmen" (Λιβερτίνων, gen. pl. masc. of Λιβερτῖνος, -ου, ὁ—a Latin loanword designating a slave [or their descendants] who had been freed, BDAG 594b–95a). The following list, introduced by καί, may represent as many as four other synagogues. Barrett suggests two from the presence of καὶ τῶν ἀπὸ, understanding the art. to be parallel to the one with τινες (Barrett 1.324; cf Haenchen 271; but see BHGNT 111). Most EVV take it as one synagogue. While Barrett is compelling, the exact identification is uncertain, but unnecessary for the interpretation. These all seem to be Diaspora Jews who opposed (συζητοῦντες, nom. pl. masc. of pres. act. ptc. of συζητέω, "dispute, debate, argue"; manner) Stephen. Bruce suggests the possibility, from the presence of Κιλικίας (gen. sg. fem. of Κιλικία, -ας, ἡ, "Cilicia") that this was the synagogue to which Paul belonged (Bruce, *Acts of the Apostles*, 187).

6:10 The impf. verbs are both progressive, indicating an ongoing (losing) debate (Schnabel 346). The parallel language in Luke 21:15 is likely intentional (Barrett 1.369), continuing an emphasis on fulfilled prophecy. The first vb., ἴσχυον (3rd pl. impf. indic. act. of ἰσχύω), is compl. by ἀντιστῆναι (aor. act. inf. of ἀνθίστημι, "resist"). Τῇ σοφίᾳ καὶ τῷ πνεύματι are dats. required by ἀνθίστημι. They are closely connected by καί, suggesting the latter is a demeanor (i.e., "spirit" rather than "Spirit," although the divine source is not in dispute). If so, the rel. pron. (ᾧ) is a dat. of manner rather than instr. Ἐλάλει is the 3rd sg. impf. act. indic. of λαλέω.

6:11 Τότε is not a causal conj. but one of sequence indicating a rapid, if not rabid, response (BHGNT 112). Ὑπέβαλον (3rd pl. aor. act. indic. of ὑποβάλλω) indicates a secret instigation (cf. NASB, NIV, ESV, "secretly. . ."; KJV, "suborned"). Λέγοντας is the acc. pl. masc. of pres. act. ptc. of λέγω; indir. speech. The vb. ἀκηκόαμεν (1st pl. pf. act. indic. of ἀκούω) takes both αὐτοῦ and λαλοῦντος (gen. sg. masc. of pres. act. ptc. of λαλέω) as a double compl. The accusation is ῥήματα βλάσφημα, "blasphemous words" against Moses and God.

6:12 Συνεκίνησαν (3rd pl. aor. act. indic. of συγκινέω, "they stirred up") reveals the results of the testimony. The combination of ἐπιστάντες (nom. pl. masc. of aor. act. ptc. of ἐφίστημι, temp.) "having come near" (i.e., with hostile intentions, BDAG 418d), and συνήρπασαν (3rd pl. aor. act. indic. of συναρπάζω, "seize"), suggests a physical ambush of Stephen. Ἤγαγον is the 3rd pl. aor. act. indic. of ἄγω. Stephen was now before the Sanhedrin.

6:13 The subj. of ἔστησαν (3rd pl. aor. act. indic. of ἵστημι) is the Hellenists (Bock 272) who placed perjurers (μάρτυρας ψευδεῖς, lit. "false witnesses"). Λέγοντας (acc. pl. masc. of pres. act. ptc. of λέγω) introduces dir. speech. The phrase ὁ ἄνθρωπος οὗτος is accusatory and dismissive (Schnabel 349). The negated present vb. παύεται (3rd sg. pres. mid. indic. of παύω, intrans. mid.) suggests "never stopped." Λαλῶν is the nom.

sg. masc. of pres. act. ptc. of λαλέω; compl. Κατὰ τοῦ τόπου τοῦ ἁγίου refers to speaking against the temple.

6:14 Γάρ provides substantiation for the charge, which is an interpretation of Stephen's preaching. Ἀκηκόαμεν (1st pl. pf. act. indic. of ἀκούω) takes two gen. compl.: αὐτοῦ and λέγοντος (gen. sg. masc. of pres. act. ptc. of λέγω). Οὗτος, like v. 13, has undertones of dismissal. On the noun Ναζωραῖος (nom. sg. masc. of Ναζωραῖος, -ου, ὁ, "Nazorean") see 2:22. The charge will contain euphemisms for the temple and the law, likely due to the formality of the setting. They suggest Jesus will destroy (καταλύσει, 3rd sg. fut. act. indic. of καταλύω) the temple (using the same euphemism as v. 13, τὸν τόπον τοῦτον). Secondly, he will change (ἀλλάξει, 3rd sg. fut. act. indic. of ἀλλάσσω) the law, expressed as the customs (ἔθη, acc. pl. neut. of ἔθος, -ους, τό), that Moses delivered (παρέδωκεν, 3rd sg. aor. act. indic. of παραδίδωμι).

6:15 Ἀτενίσαντες (nom. pl. masc. of aor. act. ptc. of ἀτενίζω; temp.) is explained by εἶδον (3rd pl. aor. act. indic. of ὁράω). The sense is "having gazed . . . they saw." The viewers are mentioned directly for the first time in the narrative with a subst. ptc. καθεζόμενοι (nom. pl. masc. of pres. mid. ptc. of καθέζομαι, "sit"). The πρόσωπον ἀγγέλου ("face of an angel") description is unique in the NT. The closest verbal parallel is Esther's description of Xerxes (LXX Esth 5:2), yet that seems distant in context. Moses's transformation coming off Mount Sinai (Exod 34:29–35) would be meaningful to the audience. While perhaps not shining like Moses, something visible and holy is apparent to the members of the Sanhedrin.

Barrett, following critical scholarship, is suspicious of the suggestion it is a formal trial involving the Sanhedrin. In his mind, Luke is rewriting an occurrence of mob violence. Exhibit A is the fact that in all the existing records of formal trials it is never shown that the high priest ever questioned the accused (Barrett 1.340). However, the night interrogation of Jesus clearly demonstrates the interrogation of the accused by the high priest (see Matt 26:62 parallels). The high priest's dir. involvement, then, calls in question not the historicity of the event but the legality of the gathering. Other irregularities may be brought forth as well. First, Luke shows no delay between the ambush and the "trial." Ordinarily such a trial would take some time to convene. Second, Stephen's execution is in violation of Roman law, for the Sanhedrin did not have the authority to enact the death penalty. Third, even if they did, the action of the crowd is not a state execution but the act of a murderous frenzy. All in all, it seems the trial of Stephen was from beginning to end a lynching in which the Sanhedrin was complicit. The event has the appearance of a frustrated and desperate group determined to stop the movement.

FOR FURTHER STUDY

16. Stephen's Trial and Defense (6:8–7:60)

Bammel, E. "Jewish Activity against Christians in Palestine according to Acts." In BAFCS 1, 357–64.

Bruce, F. F. "Stephen's Apologia." In *Scripture: Meaning and Method: Essays Presented to Anthony Tyrrell Hanson for His Seventieth Birthday*, 37–50. Hull, England: Hull University Press, 1987.

Jones, B. C. "The Meaning of the Phrase 'and the Witnesses Laid Down Their Cloaks' in Acts 7:58." *ExpTim* 123 (2011): 113–18.

Kilgallen, J. J. "The Function of Stephen's Speech (Acts 7:2–53)." *Bib* 70 (1989): 173–93.

———. "The Speech of Stephen, Acts 7:2–53." *ExpTim* 115 (2004): 293–97.

Klijn, A. F. J. "Stephen's Speech: Acts 7:2–53." *NTS* 4 (1957): 25–31.

Peterson, B. K. "Stephen's Speech as a Modified Prophetic Rîb Formula." *JETS* 57 (2014): 351–69.

Whitenton, M. "Rewriting Abraham and Joseph: Stephen's Speech (Acts 7:2–16) and Jewish Exegetical Traditions." *NovT* 54 (2012): 149–67.

Wischmeyer, O. "Stephen's Speech before the Sanhedrin against the Background of the Summaries of the History of Israel (Acts 7)." In *History and Identity: How Israel's Later Authors Viewed Its Earlier History*, 341–58. Berlin: de Gruyter, 2006.

2. Stephen's Defense (7:1–53)

Stephen was not on defense but offense (Witherington 260). His speech was, at face value, a history of Israel. He specifically highlights Joseph and Moses as men sent by God that the fathers had rejected (Schnabel 355). The subtle undercurrent moves the topic to Jesus as the most recent example. Along the way, he answered the first charge that he spoke against the law by calling it "living oracles" (7:38). The second charge regarding the temple is answered by citing Scripture (contra Johnson 119). In essence, while God approved and directed its construction, he did not live there (7:48–49). Stephen's charge of law breaking (and he seemed to be about to charge them with idolatry) cut off the speech at the hands of an infuriated mob (7:51–53). Literarily the speech closes the Jerusalem narrative and sets up the movement out of the capitol (Witherington 260).

7:1 The high priest's questioning of Stephen is dir. and simple. Εἶπεν is the 3rd sg. aor. act. indic. of λέγω. Most EVV correctly tr. the question dynamically (e.g., CSB, "Are these things true?"). Formally it is a cond. statement presenting a dir. question (see 1:6) with an idiomatic expression. Οὕτως ἔχει (3rd sg. pres. act. indic. of ἔχω) is used elsewhere in Acts (12:15; 24:9) as an affirmation of truth (Barrett 1.340; BHGNT 114).

a. The Formation of the Covenant People and Giving of the Law (7:2–38)

7:2 Ἔφη (3rd sg. aor. act. indic. of Acts φημί, "say") might be impf. by form but no legitimate syntactical/aspectual reason is compelling for suggesting so. Typical of good rhetoric, Stephen first identifies with his audience with ἄνδρες ἀδελφοὶ καὶ πατέρες (cf. 7:51, where he separates from them). Second, he calls for an audience (ἀκούσατε, 2nd pl. aor. act. impv. of ἀκούω). The defense begins with God's appearance (ὤφθη, 3rd sg. aor. pass. indic. of ὁράω) to Abram, temporally located as "while in Mesopotamia" with the ptc. ὄντι (dat. sg. masc. of pres. ptc. of εἰμί; temp., attrib. dat.). Πρὶν ἤ and the inf. κατοικῆσαι (aor. act. inf. of κατοικέω, "dwell"; temp. [subsequent time], BDAG 863c) also locate him before he dwelled in Haran.

7:3 Stephen closely parallels the LXX of Gen 12:1 and the call of Abram. Εἶπεν is the 3rd sg. aor. act. indic. of λέγω. Abram is to depart (ἔξελθε, 2nd pl. aor. act. impv. of ἐξέρχομαι) his ancestral home and relatives (συγγενείας, gen. fem. sg. of συγγένεια, -ας, ἡ). The use of δεῦρο (dir. adv. "here" with the force of an impv.) does not suggest God is located in Canaan, but that Abram will find him by obedience (Barrett 1.342). The subj. δείξω (1st sg. aor. act. subjunc. of δείκνυμι, "show") with the indef. part. ἄν indicates that the specific land is not yet indicated and that showing is dependent on going. **7:4** The story continues in summary form. As instructed, Abram departed (ἐξελθών, nom. sg. masc. of aor. act. ptc. of ἐξέρχομαι; temp.) and dwelled (κατῴκησεν, 3rd sg. aor. act. indic. of κατοικέω). His father's death is described by the art. inf. ἀποθανεῖν (aor. act. inf. of ἀποθνήσκω, subst.) as obj. of μετά (with πατέρα as the subj. of the inf.). The subj. of μετῴκισεν (3rd sg. aor. act. indic. of μετοικίζω, "resettle") is God (αὐτόν refers to Abram). Κατοικεῖτε is 2nd sg. pres. act. indic. of κατοικέω. **7:5** The gift of the land, however, rather than given (ἔδωκεν, 3rd sg. aor. act. indic. of δίδωμι) was promised (ἐπηγγείλατο, 3rd sg. aor. act. indic. of ἐπαγγέλλομαι) to Abraham's descendants. Δοῦναι is aor. act. inf. of δίδωμι; compl. It is noted that this is before Abraham had children. Normally in Koinē, μή would be expected with the ptc. In CGk. the ptc. could be neg., depending on whether the ptc. was factual (οὐ) or subjective (μή; see BDF §430; 7:5; Z §440). Ὄντος is the gen. sg. neut. of pres. act. ptc. of εἰμί; gen. abs., concessive Αὐτῷ (dat. sg. masc.) is a poss. dat. **7:6** Culy and Parsons suggest that the first clause is causal and anaphoric, i.e., "God spoke (ἐλάλησεν, 3rd sg. aor. act. indic. of λαλέω) this way (οὕτως) because . . ." (BHGNT 117). The statement is clearly indir. speech because αὐτοῦ replaces σοῦ. However, since ὅτι can introduce either dir. or indir. speech, the content of the quote should make the decision. In this case, that is unlikely. Slavery does not suggest the cause of Abraham's lack of property. The vb. ἔσται (3rd sg. fut. mid. indic. of εἰμί) is sg. because σπέρμα is neut. The subj. of δουλώσουσιν (3rd pl. fut. act. indic. of δουλόω, "enslaved") is unexpressed but suggested by γῇ ἀλλοτρίᾳ (dat. sg. fem. of ἀλλότριος, -ία, -ον, "a foreign land"). The outlook was that Egypt mistreated (κακώσουσιν, 3rd pl. fut. act. indic. of κακόω) them for 400 years. The number is calculated by the rabbis to represent the time from Isaac to the exodus. The 430 years stated in Exod 12:40 is from the promise to the exodus (Bruce, *Acts of the Apostles*, 193). **7:7** Again, Stephen cites the LXX (Gen 15:13–14). The basic sentence is τὸ ἔθνος . . . κρινῶ (1st sg. fut. act. indic. of κρίνω) ἐγώ, mng. "I will judge the nation." The fronted dir. obj. (ἔθνος) is modified by a rel. indef. clause, ᾧ ἐὰν δουλεύσουσιν (3rd pl. fut. act. indic. of δουλεύω, see 7:6). The use of ἐάν with a fut. rather than an aor. subjunc. is a postclassical phenomenon (Bruce, *Acts of the Apostles*, 194) that essentially means the same thing. Ὁ θεὸς εἶπεν is Stephen's insertion that transitions to a paraphrase of Exod 3:12. After the exodus, they will come out (ἐξελεύσονται, 3rd pl. fut. mid. indic. of ἐξέρχομαι) and serve (λατρεύσουσιν, 3rd pl. fut. act. indic. of λατρεύω) God in the land. **7:8** The unexpressed subj. of ἔδωκεν (3rd sg. aor. act. indic. of δίδωμι) is God. Διαθήκην is defined with the descriptive gen. περιτομῆς. Οὕτως is based on the grant of the covenant, so he sired (ἐγέννησεν, 3rd sg. aor. act. indic. of γεννάω) *and* circumcised (περιέτεμεν, 3rd sg. aor. act. indic. of περιτέμνω) him. And it continued through the twelve patriarchs.

7:9 Picking up the subj. of the last clause, ζηλώσαντες (nom. pl. masc. of aor. act. ptc. of ζηλόω, "jealous"; causal) gives the reason for Joseph's enslavement. Ἀπέδοντο (3rd pl. aor. mid. indic. of ἀποδίδωμι) in the mid. means "sold." Καί is generally considered to be adversative (see, e.g., BHGNT 119; most EVV). However, the NASB's "yet" may be preferable.

7:10 Καί continues the story of Joseph's deliverance (ἐξείλετο, 3rd sg. aor. mid. indic. of ἐξαιρέω, "deliver") from trouble in Egypt. The subj. of ἔδωκεν (3rd sg. aor. act. indic. of δίδωμι) is to be understood as God who is the giver of grace and wisdom (χάριν καὶ σοφίαν). Likewise, Φαραώ (gen. sg. masc., indecl.) βασιλέως Αἰγύπτου is not the implied subj. of κατέστησεν (3rd sg. aor. act. indic. of καθίστημι, "place") but God is (Bock 287). Although anar., ἡγούμενον (acc. sg. masc. of pres. mid. ptc. of ἡγέομαι) is subst. (i.e., "ruler") in a double-acc. cstr. with αὐτόν. The prep. ἐπ' indicates the obj. of the rule ("over" BDAG 367b). The phrase ὅλον τὸν οἶκον αὐτοῦ ("his whole house") refers to the world known by Joseph.

7:11 The developmental conj. δέ marks a famine (λιμός nom. sg. masc./fem. of λιμός, -οῦ, ὁ and ἡ) as the event that moves the story forward (suggesting the point of the narrative is not Joseph's ascension but the story of Israel). The nom. θλῖψις μεγάλη most likely shares the vb. ἦλθεν (3rd sg. aor. act. indic. of ἔρχομαι) with λιμός (see BHGNT 120 for other options). Bruce (*Acts of the Apostles*,195) proposes the impf. ηὕρισκον (3rd pl. impf. act. indic. of εὑρίσκω) combined with οὐχ suggests "could not find" food (χορτάσματα, acc. pl. neut. of χόρτασμα, -ατος, τό; NT hapax).

7:12 The next δέ marks another important step, the news heard (ἀκούσας, nom. sg. masc. of aor. act. ptc of ἀκούω; temp.) by Jacob. Ὄντα (acc. sg. neut. of pres. ptc. of εἰμί) is indir. speech (Wallace 645) giving the content of what Jacob heard. Εἰς Αἴγυπτον means "in Egypt." Ἐξαπέστειλεν is the 3rd sg. aor. act. indic. of ἐξαποστέλλω, "send off." Πρῶτος, "first," contrasts with δεύτερος in the next verse (Bruce, *Acts of the Apostles*, 195).

7:13 Ἐν τῷ δευτέρῳ assumes "visit" (see NASB, NIV, ESV). Even though Joseph revealed himself (Gen 45:1–4), ἀνεγνωρίσθη (3rd sg. aor. pass. indic. of ἀναγνωρίζω, "cause to be recognized") is likely a divine pass. (contra BHGNT 121, who calls it a permissive pass.). If so, it keeps God as the major agent through the narrative. The pred. adj. φανερόν is placed before the vb. ἐγένετο (3rd sg. aor. mid. indic. of γίνομαι) for emphasis. The note of the revelation of Joseph's family (γένος, gen. sg. neut. of γένος, -ους, τό) to Pharaoh is proleptic (and ominous). The term γένος, possibly mng. "race," is most likely a ref. to family since Pharaoh already knew Joseph's heritage (Gen 41:12; Haenchen 280).

7:14 The move to Egypt is introduced by δέ, marking it as the next important thing. The ptc. ἀποστείλας (acc. sg. masc. of aor. act. ptc. of ἀποστέλλω; temp.) and the vb. μετεκαλέσατο (3rd sg. aor. mid. indic. of μετακαλέω, "summon") summarizes a sequence. The use of ἐν is debated. Quite a few scholars suggest it signifies "amounting to" (Barrett 1.350; Haenchen 280; Bruce 195; BDF §198; BDAG 330a). Culy and

Parsons suggest the mng. "with ref. to" (BHGNT 121). Neither significantly changes the mng., although the former is well attested in the literature.

7:15–16 Καί continues the previous statements. Jacob went down (κατέβη, 3rd sg. aor. act. indic. of καταβαίνω) to Egypt. Ἐτελεύτησεν (3rd sg. aor. act. indic. of τελευτάω, "die") although sg. takes a compound subj. (αὐτός and πατέρες). Stephen identifies with Israel and his accusers by referring to the patriarchs as "our (ἡμῶν) fathers" (Bock 288). Stephen notes they were carried back (μετετέθησαν, 3rd pl. aor. pass. indic. of μετατίθημι) to Shechem. The bodies are placed (ἐτέθησαν, 3rd pl. aor. pass. indic. of τίθημι) in the same tomb (μνήματι, dat. sg. neut. of μνῆμα, -ατος, τό) Abraham had bought (ὠνήσατο, 3rd sg. aor. mid. indic. of ὠνέομαι). The rel. pron. ᾧ is dat. by attraction to μνήματι (see 1:2).

7:17 The mng. of καθώς is disputed. It is likely a temp. ref. mng. "when" (Barrett 1.352; Bock 289; Haenchen 280; BDAG 494a; R 974 [as possible]). Stephen sets the next sequence in reminder of 7:6 (430 years). The time was nearing (ἤγγιζεν, 3rd sg. impf. act. indic. of ἐγγίζω). Ὡμολόγησεν (3rd sg. aor. act. indic. of ὁμολογέω) in this context is "promised, assured." He notes that the people were growing (ηὔξησεν, 3rd sg. aor. act. indic. of αὐξάνω) and multiplied (ἐπληθύνθη, 3rd sg. aor. pass. indic. of πληθύνω).

7:18 Except for the initial ἄχρι οὗ (mng. "when," cf. BDF §381[1]; BHGNT 123) replacing δέ, this verse cites Exod 1:8 LXX verbatim. The change is likely due to the developmental constraint of δέ not fitting the present context. Ἀνέστη is the 3rd sg. aor. act. indic. of ἀνίστημι. The prep. phrase ἐπ᾽ Αἴγυπτον means "over Egypt." A functional aor., ᾔδει (3rd sg. plpf. act. indic. of οἶδα), negated, spelled trouble for the family in Egypt.

7:19 Κατασοφισάμενος (nom. sg. masc. of aor. mid. ptc. of κατασοφίζομαι, "trick"; temp., NT hapax) is used in Exod 1:10. It is usually tr. as a ptc. of attend. circum.: "He dealt deceitfully . . . and . . ." (see also KJV, RSV, NASB, NIV). However, at Exod 1:10, the shrewd proposal by the new pharaoh was the enslavement and harsh treatment of the Hebrews. It is likely repeated here as a summary that precedes the infanticide. Thus, it is more likely a temp. ptc. Γένος (see 7:13) is the obj. of the ptc. and refers to the race that Stephen again identifies with by the pron. ἡμῶν (as in the next phrase). Pharaoh's mistreatment (ἐκάκωσεν, 3rd sg. aor. act. indic. of κακόω) takes πατέρας as dir. obj. Ποιεῖν (pres. act. inf. of ποιέω) is likely not purp., but epex. (Bruce, *Acts of the Apostles*, 197; Rogers and Rogers 260, still involving a sense of purpose). The infants (βρέφη, nom. sg. neut. of βρέφος, -ους, τό) were to be exposed (ἔκθετα, acc. pl. neut. of ἔκθετος, -ον; NT hapax), a euphemism for the practice of leaving newborns in the open to die of predation or exposure to the elements. The ultimate purp. is expressed in the negated prep. phrase of purp. εἰς τὸ μὴ ζωογονεῖσθαι (pres. pass. inf. of ζωογονέω, "keep alive"). The tr. "so that they wouldn't survive" captures the practice of exposure well.

7:20 The prep. phrase Ἐν ᾧ καιρῷ is equiv. to "at this time," that is, the time appointed by God. The description of Moses's birth (ἐγεννήθη, 3rd sg. aor. pass. indic. of γεννάω) echoes Exod 2:2. Thus, the choice of the phrase "was beautiful" (ἀστεῖος, nom. sg. masc. of ἀστεῖος, -α, -ον; pred. adj.) is reflective of his mother's response. The mng. is disputed; BDAG (145b) suggests it means "well-bred," yet that hardly fits the context.

Bruce suggests that in combination with the dat. τῷ θεῷ (an ethical dat.) the phrase is an elative idiom, i.e., "very handsome" (Bruce, *Acts of the Apostles*, 197; ZG 371). This would follow current Jewish teaching of the beauty of the child and agree with Exod 2:2 (See BHGNT 125). Ἀνετράφη is the 3rd sg. aor. pass. indic. of ἀνατρέφω, "bring up, educate."

7:21–22 Stephen summarizes Moses's early life by paraphrasing Exod 2:5. After Moses was exposed (ἐκτεθέντος, gen. sg. masc. of aor. pass. ptc. of ἐκτίθημι; gen. abs.), the vb. ἀνείλατο (3rd sg. aor. mid. indic. of ἀναιρέω) is used (as in Exod 2:5) to describe the actions of Pharaoh's daughter. It might mean "adopted" (see BDAG 64b; Barrett 1.355; Bruce, *Acts of the Apostles*, 197–98). However, the mng. "lifted up" is clear in the LXX and is the likely intent here (BHGNT 127) given that Moses's adoption (ἀνεθρέψατο, 3rd sg. aor. mid. indic. of ἀνατρέφω) as a son (εἰς υἱόν) is clearly stated. Verse 22 concludes with Moses's education (ἐπαιδεύθη, 3rd sg. aor. pass. indic. of παιδεύω) in "all the wisdom of Egypt." The topic is not in the LXX, but Philo treated it at length (Beale and Carson 561). That he was able (δυνατός; pred. adj.) in his words and deeds (ἐν λόγοις καὶ ἔργοις) is not necessarily a contradiction to Exod 4:10. The Exodus ref. may be Moses being humble (Bock 291), or it may be that Moses overcame earlier deficiencies (Bruce, *Acts of the Apostles*, 198).

7:23 The opening clause expresses Moses's age (paraphrasing Exod 2:11). Ὡς is temp., "when." The pass. vb. ἐπληροῦτο (3rd sg. impf. pass. indic. of πληρόω) takes the phrase τεσσερακονταετὴς χρόνος as its subj. Αὐτῷ is a dat. of advantage. It is lit. "When forty years of time was completed to him" (BHGNT 127). "When he was forty years old" (RSV, NRSV) is the best expression of it. It is followed by another idiomatic expression. Ἀνέβη (3rd sg. aor. act. indic. of ἀναβαίνω) ἐπὶ τὴν καρδίαν is best expressed as "it entered his mind" (NET). The vb. is compl. by ἐπισκέψασθαι (aor. mid. inf. of ἐπισκέπτομαι, "visit"; compl.). Τοὺς υἱοὺς Ἰσραήλ is explanatory of ἀδελφοὺς αὐτοῦ.

7:24 Καί continues the previous v. The ptc. ἰδών (nom. sg. masc. of aor. act. ptc. of ὁράω; temp.) sets the stage for Moses's actions. Τινα, "someone," is the obj. of the previous ptc. The following ptc. ἀδικούμενον (nom. sg. masc. of pres. pass. ptc. of ἀδικέω) may either be:

1. an attrib. ptc. (lit. "a being-wronged someone")
2. the compl. in a double-acc. cstr. ("someone being wronged," see BHGNT 127).

The vb. ἠμύνατο (3rd sg. aor. mid. indic. of ἀμύνομαι, "defend") is connected by καί to an idiomatic phrase ἐποίησεν (3rd sg. aor. act. indic. of ποιέω) ἐκδίκησιν (acc. sg. fem. of ἐκδίκησις, -εως, ἡ, "vengeance, punishment"). BDAG 301a suggests "meted justice" for the idiom. Others suggest "take revenge" (Bock 292; BHGNT 128; Bruce, *Acts of the Apostles,* 198; ZG 372). The latter fits better with the story in Exodus. The following dat. (advantage) indicates the one for whom the vengeance is made (in this case καταπονουμένῳ, dat. sg. masc. of pres. pass. ptc. of καταπονέω, "oppress"; subst.). Vengeance is described by another ptc., πατάξας (nom. sg. masc. of aor. act. ptc. of πατάσσω; manner, mng. "by striking down [i.e., killing] the Egyptian" [NASB, ESV, NET]).

7:25 Moses's assumptions are expressed in ἐνόμιζεν (3rd sg. impf. indic. act. of νομίζω, "suppose"). It is compl. by the inf. συνιέναι (pres. act. inf. of συνίημι, "understand"; with ἀδελφούς as the subj. of the inf.). The content (the sense of ὅτι) of the brothers' understanding is a recognition that God was using Moses to rescue them. Δίδωσιν is 3rd sg. pres. act. indic. of δίδωμι. Διὰ χειρὸς αὐτου suggests an appointment to deliver. The term *salvation* (σωτηρίαν) is a common enough word. Yet, it is likely anticipatory of Jesus's work, establishing a parallel between the reaction of Moses's hearers and Stephen's. They, however, did not understand. Συνῆκαν is the 3rd pl. aor. act. indic. of συνίημι, "understand."

7:26 On τε, see 1:15. Restating Exod 2:13, 14 the dat. τῇ . . . ἐπιούσῃ (dat. sg. fem. of pres. act. ptc. of ἔπειμι, "follow"; attrib.) ἡμέρᾳ describes a point in time (Turner 243), i.e., "on the following day" (RSV, NASB). Ὤφθη (3rd sg. aor. pass. indic. of ὁράω, "appeared") is common in Acts (see 2:3) but here suggests a sudden encounter (BHGNT 128; Rogers and Rogers 243). The ptc. μαχομένοις (dat. pl. masc. of pres. mid. ptc. of μάχομαι, "fight") is temp. and agrees with αὐτοῖς. "While they were fighting" is the best tr. (or "as they were fighting," NASB). Συνήλλασσεν (3rd sg. impf. act. indic. of συναλλάσσω) is tendential, "he tried to reconcile." Εἰς εἰρήνην is used adv., "peacefully." His attempt is brokered as a question under the cond. of their brotherhood. Ἱνατί (replacing the LXX διὰ τί) is a contraction of ἵνα τί γένηται, "to what end?" (BDF §12[3]). Ἀδικεῖτε (2nd pl. pres. act. indic. of ἀδικέω) ἀλλήλους is " . . . are you harming one another?" The pl. is a change from the sg. in the LXX and will revert in the next verse.

7:27 The speaker is described with the ptc. ἀδικῶν (nom. sg. masc. of pres. act. ptc. of ἀδικέω; subst.) that, with the acc. obj. πλησίον [πλησίος, -α, -ον, subst.], means "the one harming his neighbor." The vb. ἀπώσατο (3rd sg. aor. mid. indic. of ἀπωθέω) is often tr. lit., "pushed aside" (CSB, KJV, NASB, ESV, NET). However, in 7:39 the sense is metaphorical: "reject." It is likely the sense here (BHGNT 129). What follows is a dir. quote from Exod 2:14. The question is rhetorical—"Who appointed (κατέστησεν, 3rd sg. aor. act. indic. of καθίστημι) you . . . ?"—so it has the force of "no one appointed you."

7:28 Again, a verbatim citation of Exod 2:14 in the LXX. The neg. μή expects a "no" answer (BDAG 646b–c; ZG 372). The inf. ἀνελεῖν (aor. act. inf. of ἀναιρέω, "kill") is compl. to the following θέλεις (2nd sg. pres. act. indic. of θέλω). The relative clause ὃν τρόπον is "internally headed" (i.e., the antecedent is τρόπον); together it functions as an adv. acc. of manner (BHGNT 130). It is a common LXX idiomatic expression mng. "in the way that" (BDAG 1017a; ZG 372). The specificity of ἐχθὲς ἀνεῖλες (2nd sg. aor. act. indic. of ἀναιρέω), "you killed yesterday," was certainly not lost on Moses.

7:29 Stephen summarized the rest of the events of Exodus 2. Moses fled (ἔφυγεν, 3rd sg. aor. act. indic. of φεύγω) at the impetus of the man's words. The prep. phrase ἐν τῷ λόγῳ τούτῳ is causal (Bruce, *Acts of the Apostles*, 199; R 589). Πάροικος (nom. sg. masc. of πάροικος, -ον, "stranger," likely suggested by Exod 2:22) is the pred. nom. compl. of ἐγένετο (3rd sg. aor. mid. indic. of γίνομαι). On οὗ, see 1:13. That he sired (ἐγέννησεν, 3rd sg. aor. act. indic. of γεννάω) two sons is not mentioned in the LXX, but this seems to be the implication of Exod 4:20.

7:30 Καί continues the previous v. Πληρωθέντων (gen. pl. neut. of aor. pass. ptc. of πληρόω, gen. abs., temp.). See 7:23 on the use of πληρόω and age. "After forty years" follows the rabbinic tradition of dividing Moses's life into three periods of forty years and puts the events of Exod 3:2 in the second (Schnabel 374, 376). Ὤφθη (3rd sg. aor. pass. indic. of ὁράω; see 7:2, 26) takes the distant ἄγγελος as its subj. The gen. πυρός (πῦρ, -ός, τό) is an attrib. gen. mng. "burning" and modifies βάτου (gen. sg. fem. of βάτος, -ου, ἡ or ὁ, "bush"). The best tr. is "in the flame of a burning bush" (CSB, NIV, NLT, NET).

7:31 Two low-level developmental conjs. (δέ) with temp. ptcs. move the story forward in this verse. The first, ἰδών (nom. sg. masc. of aor. act. ptc. of ὁράω; temp.) assumes the events of the previous v. as background. The impf. ἐθαύμαζεν (3rd sg. impf. act. indic. of θαυμάζω) suggests ongoing activity. When it takes a dir. obj. (ὅραμα, acc. sg. neut. of ὅραμα, -ατος, τό), the mng. is "was marvelling at the sight." The second ptc., προσερχομένου (gen. sg. masc. of pres. mid. ptc. of προσέρχομαι), is a temp. gen. abs. complemented by the inf. κατανοῆσαι (aor. act. inf. of κατανοέω, "observe"). The use of ἐγένετο (3rd sg. aor. mid. indic. of γίνομαι) with φωνὴ κυρίου creates a dramatic event.

7:32 Stephen paraphrased Exod 3:6. The first sentence is verbless (assuming εἰμί). The ptc. γενόμενος (nom. sg. masc. of pres. mid. ptc. of γίνομαι) functions as a being vb. and takes the nom. pred. adj. ἔντρομος (nom. sg. masc. of ἔντρομος, -ον, "terrified") as the compl. Ἐτόλμα (3rd sg. impf. act. indic. of τολμάω, "dare") is compl. by κατανοῆσαι (aor. act. inf. of κατανοέω, "observe"). This suggests throughout the event Moses was averting his gaze.

7:33 This v. strongly resembles Exod 3:5. Λῦσον is the 2nd sg. aor. act. impv. of λύω. Ὑπόδημα (acc. pl. neut. of ὑπόδημα, -ατος, τό, "sandal") is modified by ποδῶν (descriptive gen. with σου [poss. gen.]). The ground (γάρ) is expressed with a pred. nom. cstr. The subj., τόπος, is modified by a prep. phrase with a rel. pron. phrase as the obj. of the prep. (ἐφ'ᾧ ἕστηκας, 2nd sg. pf. act. indic. of ἵστημι). The compl. is γῆ ἁγία, "holy ground."

7:34 The first clause is a dir. quote of Exod 3:7 (LXX). Thus, the unusual phrase ἰδὼν εἶδον is a tr. of the Heb. qal inf. cstr. Typically, in LXX-influenced Gk., it is tr. by an aor. ptc. (in this case, nom. sg. masc. of aor. act. ptc. of ὁράω) and an aor. of the same vb. (here, 1st sg. aor. act. indic. of ὁράω; see Turner, *Style,* 47). The sense is emphatic: "I have certainly seen" (CSB, NLT, NET). Στεναγμοῦ (gen. sg. masc. of στεναγμός, -οῦ, ὁ, "groaning") is gen. because ἤκουσα (1st sg. aor. act. indic. of ἀκούω) often takes a gen. obj. Κατέβην (1st sg. aor. act. indic. of καταβαίνω) takes the inf. ἐξελέσθαι (aor. mid. inf. of ἐξαιρέω, "deliver"; purp.) to complete the thought. The mid. means "rescue" (BDAG 344a, ZG 370), suggesting some self-interest in the action. At καί the text follows Exod 3:10 (LXX) closely. Καὶ νῦν δεῦρο tr. the Heb. "Come now" (wə 'attāh ləḵāh). Ἀποστείλω (1st sg. aor. act. subjunc. of ἀποστέλλω) is a rare use (Matt 7:4, Luke 6:42, and here) of a sg. hortatory subjunc. The sense may be more voluntative, as "Let me send . . ." doesn't tr. the Heb. or fit the pres. context (most EVV, "I will send"; BHGNT 134; R 931; Wallace 464).

7:35 This v. contains Stephen's comment on the story so far (Beale and Carson 563). Τοῦτον τὸν Μωϋσῆν is the acc. dir. obj. of ἠρνήσαντο (3rd pl. aor. mid. indic. of ἀρνέομαι), with the sense of "reject." The use of οὗτος with "Moses" in the next three vv. is reminiscent of the people's ref. to Moses in Exod 32:1 as they proposed flagrant idolatry. If intentional (likely, given the citation at 7:40) Stephen was making a subtle comp. to the failure at Sinai throughout his description of Moses. Their words to him are given in a rather long parenthetical rel. pron. phrase. Εἰπόντες (nom. pl. masc. of aor. act. ptc. of λέγω) introduces a restatement of Exod 2:14 (see v. 27). Τοῦτον reinstates Moses as the topic emphasized at the beginning, the dir. obj. of ἀπέσταλκεν (3rd sg. aor. act. indic. of ἀποστέλλω). Ὀφθέντος is the gen. sg. masc. of aor. pass. ptc. of ὁράω. On βάτῳ (dat. sg. fem.), see 7:30.

7:36 Οὗτος continues the ref. to Moses. Stephen summarized the exodus with the vb. ἐξήγαγεν (3rd sg. aor. act. indic. of ἐξάγω, "lead out" [also used in Exod 32:1]). The ptc. ποιήσας (nom. sg. masc. of aor. act. ptc. of ποιέω) is either attend. circum. or manner. It is likely the latter (Rogers and Rogers 244). Τέρατα (acc. pl. neut. of τέρας, -ατος, τό) καὶ σημεῖα, "wonders and signs," is the dir. obj. of the ptc. These are performed in three places expressed as compound objs. of the prep. ἐν (γῇ Αἰγύπτῳ ["Egypt"], ἐρυθρᾷ [dat. sg. fem. of ἐρυθρός, -ά, -όν] θαλάσσῃ ["red sea"], and ἐρήμῳ ["desert"]).

7:37 Οὗτος is again paired with "Moses," but the latter is now a pred. nom. Εἴπας (nom. sg. masc. of aor. act. ptc. of λέγω) is an attrib. ptc. mng. "the Moses who said" (CSB, RSV, NASB, ESV). The content is a citation of Deut 18:15. Both προφήτην (dir. obj.) and ὑμῖν (dat. of advantage) are fronted for emphasis. Ἀναστήσει is the 3rd sg. fut. act. indic. of ἀνίστημι. The phrase ὡς ἐμέ refers to Moses.

7:38 Οὗτος still ref. to Moses (the proper name, however, is no longer used). Γενόμενος (nom. sg. masc. of aor. mid. ptc. of γίνομαι; subst.) is a pred. nom. that emphasizes Moses's presence on Mount Sinai. Ἐκκλησίᾳ is best tr. "congregation" (RSV, NASB, ESV, NET). Λαλοῦντος (gen. sg. masc. of pres. act. ptc. of λαλέω, attrib.) modifies ἀγγέλου, perhaps an indirect ref. to the rabbinic teaching that the law was mediated through angels. That Moses received (ἐδέξατο, 3rd sg. aor. mid. indic. of δέχομαι) "living oracles" (λόγια [acc. pl. neut. of λόγιον, -ου, τό, "divine utterance"; dir. obj.] ζῶντα [acc. pl. neut. of pres. act. ptc. of ζάω; attrib.]) was Stephen's positive comment on the law's validity (i.e., not in the Exodus text; Beale and Carson 564). Δοῦναι is an aor. act. inf. denoting purp.

b. Israel's Idolatrous Response (7:39–44)

7:39 Ὧι continues the previous sentence and ref. to Moses. Ἠθέλησαν is the 3rd pl. aor. act. indic. of θέλω. Γενέσθαι (aor. act. inf. of γίνομαι; compl.) functions as a being vb. with the subst. adj. ὑπήκοοι (nom. pl. masc. of ὑπήκοος, -ον, "obedient ones"; takes the dat. ᾧ) as a pred. adj. Πατέρες is the subj. of ἠθέλησαν. The vb. ἀπώσαντο (3rd pl. aor. mid. indic. of ἀπωθέω) should be understood as "they rejected" (NLT; on the mng., see 7:27). The mng. of ἐστράφησαν (3rd pl. aor. pass. indic. of στρέφω, "turned") ἐν ταῖς καρδίαις αὐτῶν εἰς Αἴγυπτον is debated. It could mean:

1. they began to long for Egypt. This would be the more natural way to take the phrase (ZG 373, BHGNT 137).
2. they had made the decision to turn around and return to Egypt.

The ref. is often suggested to be the rebellion at Kadesh Barnea, Num 14:3–4 (see, e.g., BHGNT 137; Schnabel 381) but the golden calf incident is the immediate context, see below. The phrase might be a theological statement regarding idolatry.

7:40 Much of this v. is a citation of Exod 32:1 introduced with εἰπόντες (nom. pl. masc. of aor. act. ptc. of λέγω). Their demand is for Aaron to make (ποίησον, 2nd sg. aor. act. impv. of ποιέω) replacement gods to lead them. Προπορεύσονται (3rd pl. fut. mid. indic. of προπορεύομαι) is common in the LXX (thirty-four times) but appears in the NT twice (see Luke 1:76) and only in OT citations. For Μωϋσῆς οὗτος, see 7:35; here it is also a hanging nom. For ἐξήγαγεν, see 7:36. The phrase τί ἐγένετο (3rd sg. aor. mid. indic. of γίνομαι) αὐτῷ (dat. of disadvantage) has τί as its subj. and should be tr. "what happened to him."

7:41 Ἐμοσχοποίησαν (3rd pl. aor. act. indic. of μοσχοποιέω, "make a calf") is a word only found in Christian literature (BDAG 660a). Perhaps coined by Luke, it seems to be based on Exod 31:4 ἐποίησεν . . . μόσχον ("he made . . . a calf"). Ἀνήγαγον (3rd pl. aor. act. indic. of ἀνάγω, "offer up") takes the dat. indir. obj. εἰδώλῳ ("to the idol"). Stephen changed the sg. of the LXX to a pl., charging the people with complicity (Beale and Carson 565). This is the charge Stephen will repeat to present Israel at the end of the speech. The last clause echoes classic OT criticism/mockery of idolatry (see, e.g., Isa 44:15). Although pass. in form, εὐφραίνοντο (3rd pl. impf. pass. indic. of εὐφραίνω, "rejoice") is act. in sense (BDAG 415a–b).

7:42 Δέ indicates a major development in the golden calf incident, signified also by introducing θεός as the subj. of the next clauses. Stephen moved away from the Exodus narrative to its long-term results (Beale and Carson 565). In what follows there are several informal similarities to Rom 1:22–25 (e.g., παρέδωκεν; Robertson, *Pictures*, 92). Ἔστρεψεν (3rd sg. aor. act. indic. of στρέφω) is variously understood:

1. It may be intrans., understood as "God turned away" (CSB; see also RSV, NASB). The sense would be that he changed his attitude toward them (Barrett 1.368; Bruce, *Acts of the Apostles*, 203; ZG 373).
2. It may be trans., sharing αὐτούς as the dir. obj. with παρέδωκεν. Thus, "God turned away from them" (see NLT, NIV, NET; BHGNT 138; Bock 298–99). Since the vb. is strongly linked to παρέδωκεν (3rd sg. aor. act. indic. of παραδίδωμι, "hand over") it is likely the two vbs. do share the dir. obj. Furthermore, although the vb. is occasionally instrans., the trans. use is more common (Barrett 1.368).

Λατρεύειν (pres. act. inf. of λατρεύω, purp.) takes the dat. στρατιᾷ (dat. sg. fem. of στρατιά, -ᾶς, ἡ, "host"; a ref. to celestial bodies, Barrett 1.368; Bock 299). Καθὼς γέγραπται (3rd sg. pf. pass. indic. of γράφω) signals an OT citation (βίβλῳ τῶν προφητῶν is "the book of the prophets" [i.e., the Twelve Prophets], in this case, Amos 5:25–26). Μή expects a neg. answer, suggesting inappropriate sacrifices (i.e., to other deities, Bock 299). Προσηνέγκατε is the 2nd pl. aor. act. indic. of προσφέρω, "offer." The phrase οἶκος (nom. as voc.) Ἰσραήλ (descriptive gen.) is in an emphatic position.

7:43 Ἀνελάβετε (2nd pl. aor. act. indic. of ἀναλαμβάνω) takes a compound dir. obj.: τὴν σκηνὴν τοῦ Μόλοχ (gen. sg. masc. of Μόλοχ, ὁ; a Canaanite sky deity, "the tent of Moloch") and τὸ ἄστρον (ἄστρον, -ου, τό, "star") τοῦ θεοῦ [ὑμῶν] Ῥαιφάν (gen. sg. masc. of Ῥαιφάν, ὁ; Heb. is kīyūn = Saturn, BDAG 657c, 903a; "the star of your god, Rephan"). Τύπους is an acc. of appos., agreeing with σκηνήν and ἄστρον, defining them as "images" they made. A further indictment is said in a rel. pron. phrase (οὕς) with ἐποιήσατε (2nd pl. aor. act. indic. of ποιέω) followed by the inf. of purp. προσκυνεῖν (pres. act. inf. of προσκυνέω). The result was deportation. Μετοικιῶ is the 1st sg. fut. act. indic. of μετοικίζω, "deport." The prep. ἐπέκεινα, "beyond," takes the gen. Βαβυλῶνος (gen. sg. fem. of Βαβθλών, -ῶνος, ἡ) as its obj. "I will send you into exile beyond Babylon."

7:44 Ἡ σκηνὴ τοῦ μαρτυρίου ("tent of testimony") is in contrast to Moloch's tent in the previous v. Καθὼς διετάξατο (3rd sg. aor. mid. indic. of διατάσσω) means "just as he ordered." The subj. is λαλῶν (nom. sg. masc. of pres. act. ptc. of λαλέω; subst., i.e., God). Ποιῆσαι is the aor. act. inf. of ποιέω. The antecedent of the dir. obj. αὐτήν is σκηνή. Although τύπος in the previous v. is an idol, here it means "example." Ἑωράκει is the 3rd sg. plpf. act. indic. of ὁράω.

c. God's Provision of a Place to Worship (7:45–50)

7:45 Stephen transitioned to the generations after Moses (Barrett 1.369). The antecedent of ἥν (dir. obj.) is σκηνή. The subj. of εἰσήγαγον (3rd pl. aor. act. indic. of εἰσάγω, "bring into") is οἱ πατέρες ἡμῶν. Διαδεξάμενοι is the nom. pl. masc. of aor. mid. ptc. of διαδέχομαι, "receive in turn"; temp. (Bruce, *Acts of the Apostles*, 205). The best tr. is "and having received it in their turn, our fathers brought it in" (NASB). Ἰησοῦ refers to Joshua. Ἐν τῇ κατασχέσει (dat. sg. fem. of κατάσχεσις, -εως, ἡ, "possession") is a temp. expression mng. "when they took possession" (Bruce, *Acts of the Apostles*, 205). BDAG (528c) suggests there is an assumed "land," associated with ἐθνῶν, i.e., "land of the Gentiles." Ὧν (rel. pron.) is a gen. by attraction to ἐθνῶν (see 1:1). Ἐξῶσεν is the 3rd sg. aor. act. indic. of ἐξωθέω, "push out." Ἕως τῶν ἡμερῶν Δαυίδ summarizes the generations until the united monarchy.

7:46 Although technically a rel. pron., ὅς is often (and rightly) tr. as a pron. (NET). Εὗρεν (3rd sg. aor. act. indic. of εὑρίσκω) is used to express God granting favor (χάριν) to someone. The rel. pron. as the subj. of ᾐτήσατο (3rd sg. aor. mid. indic. of αἰτέω, mid. of pers. interest) makes David the implied ref. Σκήνωμα (acc. sg. neut. of σκήνωμα, -ατος, τό) refers to a dwelling place. Most EVV prefer the reading, "God of Jacob" (CSB, RSV, NASB, NLT, NIV) but a few choose the var. rdg. "house of Jacob" (e.g., NET; BHGNT 141).

7:47 Δέ suggests the building of the temple was a major movement. Οἰκοδόμησεν is the 3rd sg. aor. act. indic. of οἰκοδομέω, "build." The pron. αὐτῷ is a dat. of advantage. The antecedent is dependent on the rdg. in v. 46: if "God of Jacob," then the ref. is "a house for him" (i.e., God); if "house for Jacob," then he built a house for "it."

7:48 Stephen then made a theological point as a contrast (ἀλλ'). Ὁ ὕψιστος (nom. sg. masc. ὕψιστος, -η, -ον, "highest"; subst. superl. adj.) is a euphemism for God that highlights his transcendence. Χειροποιήτοις (dat. pl. masc. of χειροποίητος, -ον) is a subst.

adj. mng. "made by human hands" that is the obj. of the prep. ἐν. Most EVV make the implied noun explicit (see, e.g., CSB, "sanctuaries"). Κατοικεῖ is the 3rd sg. pres. act. indic. of κατοικέω. Ὁ προφήτης λέγει ("the prophet says") introduces the citation in the following v.

7:49–50 The passage cited is Isa 66:1 with minor deviations from the LXX. The first clause assumes εἰμί with οὐρανός as a pred. nom. (μοι is a poss. dat.). The second clause is linked by the developmental conj. δέ. The clause mirrors the syntax of the first (ὑποπόδιον, nom. sg. neut. of ὑποπόδιον, -ου, τό, "footstool," is a pred. nom.). Ποδῶν is a gen. of ref. "for my feet." Ποῖον ("what kind of") introduces a rhetorical question, with a fut. vb. οἰκοδομήσετε (encl. accent from poss. dat. μοι; 2nd pl. fut. act. indic. of οἰκοδομέω, mng. "Will you build?"). The gist of the rhetorical question is, "You cannot build a suitable house for me." The final clause uses τίς τόπος ("what place") as the subj. of an assumed vb. Most EVV assume εἰμί (CSB, RSV, NASB, NLT, NET). However, the gen. καταπαύσεώς (gen. sg. fem. of κατάπαυσις, -εως, ἡ) with μου ("my resting place") makes that difficult. It is better to assume another οἰκοδομήσετε (cf. NLT, "Could you build me such a resting place?"). The force of the second rhetorical question is also "you cannot build. . . ." Ἐποίησεν is the 3rd sg. aor. act. indic. of ποιέω.

d. Stephen's Counteraccusation (7:51–53)

7:51 Stephen abruptly shifted to address the hearers with inflammatory vocs. (BHGNT 143). The accused now becomes the accuser (Robertson, *Pictures*, 96). Bruce speculates that the ref. to the temple in the previous v. brought an angry outburst from the audience (Bruce, *Acts of the Apostles*, 208). It is an interruption, but more likely for the direction Stephen was headed. His address σκληροτράχηλοι (voc. pl. masc. of σκληροτράχηλος, -ον, "stiff-necked"; subst.) is often a condemnation of Israel (cf. Exod 33:3). Likewise, ἀπερίτμητοι (voc. pl. masc. of ἀπερίτμητος, -ον, "uncircumcised") with καρδίαις τοῖς ὠσίν (dats. of ref.) is a combination of denunciations found in the OT (cf. Jer 9:26, "hearts"; Jer 6:10, "ears"; see Beale and Carson 569). The combination of the emphatic ὑμεῖς, the pres. ἀντιπίπτετε (2nd pl. pres. act. indic. of ἀντιπίπτω, "resist"), and the adv. ἀεί is a pointed indictment of the hearers, mng. "YOU always resist." Stephen separated himself from the audience, implying Christians were not participating in the sins of the fathers (i.e., resisting what God was doing, Beale and Carson 569). The vb. takes the dat. τῷ πνεύματι τῷ ἁγίῳ as the dir. obj. The final clause assumes either εἰμί or ποιέω with little difference in meaning. Stephen intercepted and denied the excuse "we would not have acted like them" (cf. Matt 23:30).

7:52 The last vv. of Stephen's defense substantiate the previous statement in the form of another rhetorical question. Τίνα (acc. sg. masc.) is the dir. obj. of ἐδίωξαν (3rd pl. aor. act. indic. of διώκω). The next clause switches to a declarative format. Ἀπέκτειναν (3rd pl. aor. act. indic. of ἀποκτείνω, "kill") takes the ensuing subst. ptc. προκαταγγείλαντας (acc. pl. masc. of aor. act. ptc. of προκαταγγέλλω, "foretell") as the dir. obj. Ἐλεύσεως (gen. sg. fem. of ἔλευσις, -εως, ἡ, "arrival," gen. obj. of περί) may have already been a messianic term (Bruce, *Acts of the Apostles*, 208). Νῦν ("now") implies the fulfillment of the previous oracles. Ἐγένεσθε (2nd pl. aor. act. indic. of γίνομαι) functions as a being vb. with ὑμεῖς as the subj. and προδόται (nom. pl. masc. of προδότης, -ου, ὁ, "betrayers") and φονεῖς (nom. pl. masc. of φονεύς, -έως, ὁ, "murderers").

7:53 While by form οἵτινες is an indef. rel. pron., functionally it replaces the def. rel. pron. οἵ to avoid confusion with the art. (the Koinē period is well before the arrival of accents). "You who . . ." is the best tr. (see, e.g., NASB, NIV). Εἰς διαταγάς (acc. pl. fem. of διαταγή, -ῆς, ἡ, "commandment") ἀγγέλων is variously interpreted. A preliminary decision is what kind of gen. is ἀγγέλων? If it is a subj. gen. it suggests the angels are doing the commanding. Given διαταγάς means a commandment or direction, the subj. gen. would indicate that the reception of the law was commanded by angels. This seems unlikely. If obj., they are the recipients of the command (i.e., from God to deliver the law). The sense of εἰς has been variously interpreted. It might be:

1. a pred. modifier, i.e., "as decrees of angels" (RSV, NASB, ESV; BHGNT 144).
2. instr., i.e., "under the direction of angels" (CSB) or "by the command of the angels" (KJV, NET; ZG 374; Z §33). BDAG (237c) suggests "*you received the law by . . . directions of angels* (i.e., by angels under God's direction [to transmit it])" (emphasis in original).

At stake is the force of Stephen's accusation. If the first option is taken, Stephen's charge of breaking the law is in the realm of hypocrisy: "although you valued the law as . . . ." If the second, the tone is a charge of hubris as they break the law.

3. Stephen's Martyrdom (7:54–8:1a)

7:54 The response is predictable. Ἀκούοντες (nom. pl. masc. of pres. act. ptc. of ἀκούω) is temp. For the mng. of διεπρίοντο (3rd pl. impf. pass. indic. of διαπρίω, "infuriated") ταῖς καρδίαις, see 5:33. Ἔβρυχον (3rd pl. impf. act. indic. of βρύχω, "gnashing") τοὺς ὀδόντας (acc. pl. masc. of ὀδούς, ὀδόντος, ὁ, "teeth"; dir. obj.) is an idiom describing intense anger. Both impfs. are inceptive (Bock 310). The former idiom is internally focused. The latter is more external (Barrett 1.382; note: ἐπ' αὐτόν, "at him").

7:55 Ὑπάρχων (nom. sg. masc. of pres. act. ptc. of ὑπάρχω) is likely causal. Ἀτενίσας (nom. sg. masc. of aor. act. ptc. of ἀτενίζω, "look at") is either temp. or attend. circum. The main vb., εἶδεν (3rd sg. aor. act. indic. of ὁράω), shows Stephen seeing the unseeable as a compound dir. obj.: δόξαν θεοῦ and Ἰησοῦν ("the glory of God" and "Jesus"). Ἑστῶτα (acc. sg. masc. of pf. act. ptc. of ἵστημι; subst.) is likely a double-acc. with Ἰησοῦν. The position of Jesus is ἐκ δεξιῶν ("at the right [hand]," a locat. phrase common in biblical literature [twenty-two times NT; forty-six times LXX]; see also next v.).

7:56 The v. is a first-person restatement (εἶπεν, 3rd sg. aor. act. indic. of λέγω) of 7:55. Θεωρῶ (1st sg. pres. act. indic. of θεωρέω) takes a compound dir. obj.; the latter obj. is in a double-acc. obj./compl. cstr. The first obj. is οὐρανούς modified by the ptc. διηνοιγμένους (acc. pl. masc. of pf. pass. ptc. of διανοίγω, "open"; attrib.). The second obj. is the phrase τὸν υἱὸν τοῦ ἀνθρώπου. Although common in the Synoptics, this is the only use in Acts. Ἑστῶτα (acc. pl. masc. of ἵστημι) is the compl. of υἱόν. It places an emphasis on what the Son is doing while at the ultimate place of power and privilege (ἐκ δεξιῶν; BHGNT 145; see also previous v.). The exact significance of "standing" instead of the normal "sitting" (see Ps 110:1) is disputed. In the vacuum of a stated reason, the conjectures are legion (Barrett 1.384–85, lists eleven different views). The three most likely are below. Jesus stands . . .

1. to welcome Stephen as a vindicated martyr. This view suggests standing is the posture of a king pleased with his subject (see Johnson 139).
2. to intercede for Stephen. In this view, standing is the posture of prayer. Keener notes that some have connected it to the Samaritan doctrine that Moses interceded as world ruler during a period called "the standing" (Keener 2.1441). While possible, Keener rightly rejects it as too remote.
3. as a witness against the mob. Bruce (*Acts of the Apostles,* 210) develops this from the affirmation that Jesus acknowledges the one who acknowledged him (Luke 12:8). Jesus then stands as a witness in the heavenly court for Stephen. This would also be a witness against the judgment of the Sanhedrin. Keener notes that judges sat while hearing but stood to deliver a verdict. Furthermore, God is often depicted as rising to judge his people (Keener 2.1442–43). For example, in Isa 3:13–15 God rises to judge the elders of his people and asks, "What do you mean by crushing My people and grinding the face of the poor?" (NASB).

Without a sure statement the exegete should hold all these opinions lightly. Ultimately what we do know is that Jesus's claim in Luke 22:69 to be seated at the right hand of God was rightly interpreted by the Jewish leadership as a claim to deity. Thus, they executed him for blasphemy. Stephen makes the same claim and will be executed on the same charge.

7:57 The conj. δέ marks a significant movement in the narrative, with three actions. The ptc. κράξαντες (nom. pl. masc. of aor. act. ptc. κράζω, "cry out") is attend. circum. (BHGNT 146; Rogers and Rogers 245). The instr. dat. φωνῇ μεγάλῃ presents the crowd with a unified sound and should be tr. "with a loud voice" (see, e.g., NASB, ESV, NET). The second action is a reaction to what they considered blasphemy (συνέσχον, 3rd pl. aor. act. indic. of συνέχω, "cover" their ears). Finally, ὥρμησαν (3rd pl. aor. act. indic. of ὁρμάω, "rush") is also presented as a unified action (ὁμοθυμαδόν, "together," see comments at 1:14). It is unstated who is the "they" that does the violence. The scene is composed of the Synagogue of the Freedmen, the elders, the scribes, and the false witnesses (see 6:12–13). The last group named is at 6:15: the Sanhedrin. It is likely all participated, but stoning was done by the witnesses in typical proceedings. While Stephen's stoning is best described as "paralegal zeal" (Bock 314), the events likely followed the fuzzy outlines of normal procedure. The hostility of the Sanhedrin has been consistent throughout the narrative. Their tactics to stop the growing movement had been intensifying. At Stephen's declaration, they turned to murder.

7:58 Ἐκβαλλόντες (nom. pl. masc. of aor. act. ptc. of ἐκβάλλω; temp.) introduces the sequence that leads to the homicide. Ἔξω τῆς πόλεως fits normal judicial procedure, but vigilante flash mobs also could take targets outside (Keener 2.1454). Ἐλιθοβόλουν (3rd pl. impf. act. indic. of λιθοβολέω) is ingressive, "they began to stone. . . ." That the crowd stripped their cloaks is unusual. Normally, the condemned man was stripped, cast down a cliff, and stoned. That the crowd did so is formally unprecedented. It

might be that Luke was showing the shame and guilt of the crowd, whether they knew it or not (Keener 2.1454). That they laid (ἀπέθεντο, 3rd pl. aor. indic. act. of ἀποτίθημι) their cloaks at Saul's feet shows his complicity with some sort of delegated authority and likely indicates the actual absence of the Sanhedrin. The pass. ptc. of καλέω is typical in naming conventions (καλομένου, gen. sg. masc. of pres. pass. ptc. of καλέω).
7:59 Formally the ptc. ἐπικαλούμενον (acc. sg. masc. of pres. mid. ptc. of ἐπικαλέω) must be an attrib. ptc. modifying Στέφανον. If temp., it would have to be a gen. abs. since the subj. has changed from the main vb., ἐλιθοβόλουν (3rd pl. impf. act. indic. of λιθοβολέω, "stone"; BHGNT 147). However, since the aspect of the ptc. is in play, the sense of the combination of the impf. vb. and the ptc. is "and they were stoning Stephen as he was calling out." Λέγοντα is the acc. sg. masc. of pres. act. ptc. of λέγω; pleonastic. Stephen's prayer to receive δέξαι (2nd sg. aor. mid. impv. of δέχομαι) resembles Jesus's recorded in Luke 23:46, except that Jesus is addressed (κύριε Ἰησοῦ) rather than the Father. This demonstrates the deity of Christ in earliest literature (Bruce, *Acts of the Apostles*, 212).
7:60 Θεὶς (nom. sg. masc. of aor. act. ptc. of τίθημι) τὰ γόνατα (acc. pl. neut. of γονεύς, -έως, τὸ, "knee") is a common form in Luke (22:41; Acts 9:40; 20:36; 21:5), indicating intense prayer (Thompson 349). Ἔκραξεν (3rd sg. aor. act. indic. of κράζω, "cry out") φωνῇ μεγάλῃ (instr. dat.) is a nearly identical expression to the mob's cry in v. 58. The prayer also echoes Jesus's words on the cross (see Luke 23:34; although bracketed by UBS[5] it was probably original; Thompson 365). The contrast is stark: they cried for his blood; Stephen cried out for mercy for his assailants. The cstr. μὴ στήσῃς (2nd sg. aor. act. subjunc. of ἵστημι) functions as a negated aor. impv. With αὐτοῖς (dat. pl. masc., disadvantage, "against them"), it means "do not count against them" (Barrett 1.387). The neut. τοῦτο ref. to the whole saying. It is the dir. obj. of εἰπών (nom. sg. masc. of aor. act. ptc. of λέγω). In the aor., κοιμάομαι may be either mid. or pass. without a difference in mng., so ἐκοιμήθη (3rd sg. aor. pass. indic. of κοιμάω) is "he slept," a euphemism for death (BHGNT 147).
8:1a If there were any doubts about Saul's loyalties, 8:1a makes them clear. Ἦν συνευδοκῶν (nom. sg. masc. of pres. act. ptc. of συνευδοκέω) is a periph. impf. mng. "he was consenting." It suggests a prolonged attitude (Haenchen 293; cf. Acts 26:10). The vb. takes the dat. obj. ἀναιρέσει (dat. sg. fem. of ἀναίρεσις, -εως, ἡ, "murder").

HOMILETICAL SUGGESTIONS

Humanity's Amazing Propensity to Idolatry (7:2–50)

1. We can reject God's truth for ridiculous substitutes (vv. 2–43)
2. We can turn the truth of God into an idol apart from God (vv. 44–50)

A Spirit-Empowered Witness (7:2–8:1a)

1. Knows the Bible (7:2–46)
2. Addresses and corrects culture (vv. 47–54)
3. Pleases God (vv. 55–56)
4. Willing to glorify God in persecution (vv. 57–8:1a)

B. PALESTINE AND SYRIA: PHILIP, SAUL, AND PETER (8:1B–9:30)

The persecution by Saul serves two purposes. It is the bridge to Philip's ministry (one of the seven in 6:5, for the apostle Philip would have remained in Jerusalem, 8:1). It also anticipates Saul's role to be radically changed later.

The section has two major characters: Philip and Saul. The story, however, is more geographically arranged, so there are four major divisions: Samaria, Judea, Saul's conversion, and Antioch. Philip's ministry to Samaritans and Ethiopians is a bridge to the Gentiles. It is also in dir. fulfillment of the promise/command of Jesus at Acts 1:8. Typical in Acts, the movement of the gospel is done by the act of God and not the plan of men. God allows the persecution that sends thousands of evangelists throughout Judea. God leads Philip to the Samaritans and affirms it to the apostles, planting the idea that Christianity is not a Jewish sect. God arranges the encounter with the Ethiopian. Finally, Christ converts Saul independently. Clearly the Christian movement is a wave the believers are riding rather than a plan they concocted.

1. Saul the Persecutor (8:1b–3)

8:1b For the temp. expression with ἐγένετο, see 4:5. Διωγμός (nom. sg. masc. of διωγμός, -οῦ, ὁ) μέγας means a severe persecution (BDAG 253d). The phrase τὴν ἐν Ἱεροσολύμοις uses the art. to make an adj. of the prep. phrase modifying ἐκκλησίαν (BHGNT 148). Διεσπάρησαν is the 3rd pl. aor. act. indic. of διασπείρω, "scatter." Κατὰ τὰς χώρας has the sense of "over the countries" (BDAG 511b) with the epex. gen. Ἰουδαίας καὶ Σαμαρείας (gen. sg. fem. of Σαμάρεια, -ας, ἡ, "Samaria"). The phrase recalls 1:8, where the two nouns are also joined by καί, implying fulfillment. The prep. phrase πλὴν τῶν ἀποστόλων leaves the apostles in Jerusalem.

8:2 Συνεκόμισαν is the 3rd sg. aor. act. indic. of συγκομίζω, "bury." The subj. ἄνδρες εὐλαβεῖς (nom. pl. masc. of εὐλαβής, -ές) means "devout men" but the sense is debated:

1. It might mean Jews who were regarded as pious about the law (Barrett 1.392; Haenchen 294). In defense of this view, all believers but the apostles had left Jerusalem. If so, the loud lamentation (κοπετὸν [acc. sg. masc. of κοπετός, -οῦ, ὁ, "mourning," NT hapax] μέγαν) for Stephen is a protest against his murder, for lamentation was not allowed for one condemned (Str-B 2:686).

2. It might mean Jewish Christians (Bruce, *Acts of the Apostles*, 215). It would seem likely that if they were Jews, Luke would have been specific. If so, their actions were still a protest against the act and showed respect for Stephen.

8:3 The vb. ἐλυμαίνετο (3rd sg. impf. mid. indic. of λυμαίνω [the act. form appears late, BDAG 604b], "ravaging, destroying") is a particularly picturesque word. It often describes a wild animal (Rogers and Rogers 245). The entirety of the rest of the v. unpacks the details of the violence. Εἰσπορευόμενος (nom. sg. masc. of pres. mid. ptc. of εἰσπορεύομαι, "enter") and σύρων (nom. sg. masc. of pres. act. ptc. of σύρω, "drag off") are best understood as attend. circum. to παρεδίδου (3rd sg. impf. indic. act. of παραδίδωμι). It is best understood as customary, "he would hand over"). See CSB: "He would enter house after house, drag off men and women, and put them in prison." The prep. phrase κατὰ τοὺς οἴκους has a distributive sense and means "house to house"

(BDAG 512a). Τε . . . καί makes the point that both men and women were "equally offensive" (Barrett 1.393).

2. The Gospel Spreads to Samaria through Philip (8:4–25)

8:4 On μὲν οὖν, see 1:6. The subj. of this sentence is the art. ptc. διασπαρέντες (nom. pl. masc. of aor. pass. ptc. of διασπείρω, "scatter"; subst.) The ref. is to ἐκκλησίαν in the previous v. Without a stated obj., διῆλθον (3rd pl. aor. act. indic. of διέρχομαι) is best tr. "they went about" (RSV, NASB, ESV). The ptc. εὐαγγελιζόμενοι (nom. pl. masc. of pres. mid. ptc. of εὐαγγελίζομαι [on the voice, see 5:42]) is compl. to the vb. On τὸν λόγον, see 4:31.

8:5 Δέ, often left untranslated (CSB, ESV, NET, NASB—NLT's "for example" is pure interpretation), introduces Philip's role as a new development. Κατελθών is the nom. sg. masc. of aor. act. ptc. of κατέρχομαι, "descend"; temp. Although Philip went north, in Sem. idiom any direction from Jerusalem is "down" because of its exalted status (cf. 3:1). Ἐκήρυσσεν is the 3rd sg. impf. act. indic. of κηρύσσω, "preach."

8:6 Προσεῖχον (3rd pl. impf. act. indic. of προσέχω, "pay attention") sets the tone for Philip's ongoing ministry in Samaria. Λεγομένοις is the dat. pl. neut. of pres. pass. ptc. of λέγω; subst. (προσέχω takes a dat. obj.). The adj. ὁμοθυμαδόν, as earlier, may mean "in one accord" or "as one" here, although "together" in the sense of "all" is possible (see CSB). The phrase ἐν τῷ ἀκούειν αὐτοὺς καὶ βλέπειν τὰ σημεῖα (see 2:1) is a compound prep. phrase that is a temp. expression in Luke-Acts for contemporaneous time: "as they heard and saw" (Bruce, *Acts of the Apostles*, 217; Z §276). Ἐποίει is the 3rd sg. impf. act. indic. of ποιέω.

8:7–8 Γάρ explains the σημεῖα in the previous v. Grammatically, the v. is difficult, (given the UBS[5] text) if the subj. of the sentence is πολλοί, for the vb. ἐξήρχοντο (3rd pl. impf. mid. indic. of ἐξέρχομαι) seems to have the demons as the subj. There are three possible solutions without charging Luke with incompetence (often called "mental telescoping," Barrett 1.404; Bruce, *Acts of the Apostles*, 217):

1. Πολλοί is the subj. of ἐξήρχοντο, and the implication is that the many were driven out of the city (Barrett 1.403–404). This is unsatisfactory for it implies not deliverance but exile.
2. Πολλοί is a hanging nom. (nom. abs., pendent nom.) and is grammatically separate from the rest of the clause. It would have the sense of "in the case of many having unclean spirits" (NET [note], NASB; BHGNT 151—their suggestion of taking πνεύματα ἀκάθαρτα as the subj. is not necessary.
3. Accept the rdg. of Πολλῶν in byz. In this case πνεύματα ἀκάθαρτα is the nom. subj. of the vb. (See RSV, NIV, NET [although the note cites option 2], ESV, CSB). The word order, in this view, is unnatural and the ms. support is quite late (except for the boharic Coptic version).

On ἐγένετο δέ, see 4:5. Πολλὴ χαρά ("much joy") is the result of the ministry of healing.

8:9 Δέ marks a new development involving the introduction of a man named (on ὀνόματι, see 5:1) Σίμων. Προϋπῆρχεν (3rd sg. impf. act. indic. of προϋπάρχω, "existing before") with the compl. ptc. μαγεύων (nom. sg. masc. of pres. act. ptc. of μαγεύω) means "was formerly practicing magic" (BDAG 608b, RSV, NASB, NET). Joined by καί, ἐξιστάνων (nom. sg. masc. of pres. act. ptc. of ἐξίστημι) is also compl. with the sense of "was amazing the nation of Samaria." Λέγων (nom. sg. masc. of pres. act. ptc. of λέγω; attend. circum.) takes ἑαυτόν as its obj. The inf. εἶναί (pres. inf. of εἰμί) indicates indir. speech (taking τινα . . . μέγαν as an obj.). Together it has the sense of "claiming to be someone great" (CSB, NLT, NASB, ESV, NET, [NIV, "boasted"]).

8:10 The rel. pron. (ᾧ) ref. to Simon. as the obj. of προσεῖχον (3rd pl. impf. indic. act. of προσέχω, "pay attention"). Πάντες (subst. adj.) is the subj. of the vb. Ἀπὸ μικροῦ ἕως μεγάλου "from small to large" has an elative sense "from the least to the greatest" (KJV, RSV, NASB, ESV, NET). The ptc. λέγοντες (nom. pl. masc. of pres. act. ptc. of λέγω; attend. circum.) introduces dir. speech. On the pass. καλουμένη (nom. sg. fem. of pres. pass. ptc. of καλέω; attrib.) with titles, see 1:12. The best rendering of the phrase given that it is an attrib. ptc. is "the great power of God" (CSB, NASB, NIV).

8:11 Προσεῖχον (see previous v.) takes the dat. αὐτῷ as its obj. Διά is causal, taking ἐξεστακέναι (pf. act. inf. of ἐξίστημι) with the sense of "because he had amazed them." The dat. ἱκανῷ χρόνῳ ("for a considerable time") as a span of time is normally in the acc., but in Koinē there are occasions where there is no difference (Z §39). The adj. ἱκανός used with time indications (common in Acts) means "many, considerable" (BDAG 472d). The dat. μαγείαις (dat. pl. fem. of μαγεία, -ας, ἡ) is instrumental, "with his sorceries."

8:12 Δέ shows the next important step, in this case, contrasting: "but." The adv. ὅτε, "when," introduces a cause-and-effect sequence. The cause is upon the belief of the people. Ἐπίστευσαν (3rd pl. aor. act. indic. of πιστεύω) takes the dat. τῷ Φιλίππῳ εὐαγγελιζομένῳ (dat. sg. masc. of pres. act. ptc. of εὐαγγελίζομαι; attrib., on the voice, see 5:42) as the obj. The content of the gospel is the kingdom of God and the name of Jesus (likely the same use of ὄνομα as authority [see 3:6] for the rule is closely connected to Jesus's name [Bruce, *Acts of the Apostles*, 220]). The effect is obedience to the faith, expressed in baptism (ἐβαπτίζοντο, 3rd pl. impf. pass. indic. of βαπτίζω). The phrase ἄνδρες τε καὶ γυναῖκες, "both men and women," expresses a wide-ranging response.

8:13 Δέ is often tr. "even" here (see, e.g., CSB, NASB); a nontemporal "now" expresses the developmental aspect well. The nom. sg. masc. αὐτός is the intensive use of the pron. (i.e., in the pred. position), "Simon himself." His belief (ἐπίστευσεν, 3rd sg. aor. act. indic. of πιστεύω), given the encounter below, should be understood as superficial. Βαπτισθείς is the nom. sg. masc. of aor. pass. ptc. of βαπτίζω; temp. Προσκαρτερῶν (nom. sg. masc. of pres. act. ptc. of προσκαρτερέω, "to be devoted to"; periph. impf. with the preceding ἦν, emphasizing the prog. nature) takes a dat. dir. obj. (Φιλίππῳ), "he was following after Philip." Θεωρῶν is the nom. sg. masc. of pres. act. ptc. of θεωρέω; temp. It is best to take γινομένας (acc. pl. fem. of pres. pass. ptc. of γίνομαι) as a pass. attrib. ptc. with the mng. "the signs and great miracles being performed." Intentionally ironic, it is now Simon who is amazed (see 8:9, 11; ἐξίστατο, 3rd sg. impf. mid. indic. of ἐξίστημι, "to amaze").

8:14 Ἀκούσαντες is the nom. pl. masc. of aor. act. ptc. of ἀκούω; temp. Ὅτι introduces indir. speech. That Samaria had received (δέδεκται, 3rd sg. pf. mid. indic. of δέχομαι) τὸν λόγον τοῦ θεοῦ (gen. of source or poss.) suggests the ref. of the phrase is the gospel. The response is to send (ἀπέστειλαν, 3rd pl. aor. act. indic. of ἀποστέλλω) Peter and John to investigate. The reason this is necessary is in the next vv.

8:15–16 On οἵτινες, see 7:53. The ref. is to Peter and John. Καταβάντες (nom. pl. masc. of aor. act. ptc. of καταβαίνω) is temp. (on the use of the vb., see 8:5). They prayed (προσηύξαντο, 3rd pl. aor. mid. indic. of προσεύχομαι) for the purp. (indic. by ὅπως + subjunc.) that the Samaritan believers would receive (λάβωσιν, 3rd pl. aor. act. subjunc. of λαμβάνω) the Holy Spirit. The adv. οὐδέπω indicates that it was unthinkable that a believer should not have the Holy Spirit. Γάρ signals the reason such an action was necessary. The vb. of the clause is the plpf. periph. ἦν . . . ἐπιπεπτωκός (nom. sg. neut. of pf. act. ptc. of ἐπιπίπτω). "Had not yet fallen" is the best tr. (RSV, NASB). Their baptismal experience is described with an unusual pf. periph. pass. cstr. using the impf. ὑπῆρχον (3rd pl. impf. act. ind. of ὑπάρχω; rather than ἦσαν) and the pf. pass. ptc. βεβαπτισμένοι (nom. pl. masc. of pf. pass. ptc. of βαπτίζω, "they had only been baptized"; so CSB, RSV, ESV, NLT). The phrase εἰς τὸ ὄνομα τοῦ κυρίου Ἰησου is different than Luke's normal ἐν or ἐπί (εἰς is used elsewhere only at 19:5). In its base sense, it means "to become the property of" (Barrett 1.411–12). The use here is likely no more than a synonym for ἐν (Z §106). Thus, the belief of the Samaritans is affirmed; but since the lack of the Holy Spirit required a visit from the apostles, the experience was completely unexpected and unusual.

8:17 The laying on of hands had a series of symbolic meanings. Here the giving of a blessing seems to fit the context best (Barrett 1.412). Most EVV tr. the impf. vb. in both clauses (ἐπετίθεσαν, 3rd pl. impf. act. indic. of ἐπιτίθημι; and ἐλάμβανον, 3rd pl. impf. act. indic. of λαμβάνω, as aors. [RSV, ESV, NET]). However, the vbs. are either inceptive, "they began placing . . . and . . . were receiving" (NASB), or a progressive signifying ongoing activity (i.e., on individuals).

8:18 The narrative turns (δέ) to Simon's response. Ἰδών is the nom. sg. masc. of aor. act. ptc. of ὁράω; temp. Ὅτι identifies what Simon saw: through the laying on of hands (τῶν χειρῶν, obj. gen.) by the apostles (ἀποστόλων, poss. gen.) the Spirit was given (δίδοται, 3rd sg. pres. pass. indic. of δίδωμι, pres. from retained dir. speech). Προσήνεγκεν (3rd sg. aor. act. indic. of προσφέρω) means "he offered." Χρήματα (acc. pl. neut. of χρῆμα, -ατος, τό), a generic word for "money," is defined at 8:20 as "silver."

8:19 Luke switches to a dir. quotation (λέγων, nom. sg. masc. of pres. act. ptc. of λέγω). There has hardly been a more self-serving request. Δότε (2nd pl. aor. act. impv. of δίδωμι) takes ἐξουσίαν ταύτην as the dir. obj. followed by the crasis κἀμοὶ (καὶ + μοι, "also to me," indir. obj.). The conj. ἵνα reveals a rather entrepreneurial purp. The clause ᾧ ἐάν + subjunc. (here, ἐπιθῶ, 1st sg. aor. act. subjunc. of ἐπιτίθημι, "lay upon") has generally taken the place of the more formal indef. rel. pron. in Koinē (cf. 7:53). Λαμβάνῃ (3rd sg. pres. act. subjunc. of λαμβάνω) is governed by the previous ἵνα.

8:20 Peter's response is essentially a curse expressed in the opt. (BHGNT 157; Keener 2.1531). Ἀργύριον (nom. sg. neut. of ἀργύριον, -ου, τό, "silver"; likely used generically, "money" [BDAG 128d]) σου (poss. gen.) is followed immediately by σὺν σοί ("with you") creating a stunning barrage of sigmas, probably intentional. Εἴη is the 3rd sg. pres. opt. of εἰμί. The opt. is relegated to wishes in Koinē. In this case, from an apostle, it is a curse on the money and an indictment of Simon. Εἰς ἀπώλειαν (acc. sg. fem. of ἀπώλεια, -ας, ἡ, "perish" [ZG 376]). Ὅτι (causal) introduces the reason for the curse. Δωρεάν (acc. sg. fem. of δωρεά, -ᾶς, ἡ, "gift"; dir. obj.) is fronted for emphasis, in contrast to an obj. for sale. Ἐνόμισας (2nd sg. aor. act. indic. of νομίζω, "think") is compl. by the inf. κτᾶσθαι (pres. mid. inf. of κτάομαι, "to obtain") and creates the sense of "you thought you could obtain" (CSB, RSV, NASB, ESV). Διὰ χρημάτων (see 4:37; 8:18) indicates means, "through money."

8:21 Peter continued the indictment of Simon. Οὐκ ἔστιν σοι has the sense of "you have no . . ." (CSB, NASB, NET). Μερὶς (nom. sg. fem. of μερίς, -ίδος, ἡ) οὐδέ κλῆρος (nom. sg. masc. of κλῆρος, -ου, ὁ), mng. "portion nor share," is likely stacked for emphasis with the mng. "abs. no part" (Barrett 1.414; BHGNT 158). The mng. of the prep. phrase ἐν τῷ λόγῳ τούτῳ is debated:

1. it could mean, "in this matter" (BDAG 600b; BHGNT 158; CSB, KJV, RSV, NASB, ESV, NET) following a Sem. idiom.
2. it could mean "in this message," either participation in the gospel (Keener 2.1531; Rogers and Rogers 247; ZG 376) or the ministry (TNIV). Barrett (1:415) notes that the mng. "gospel" is more common in Acts. Since Simon is said to be doomed (8:20), it is likely Peter intended "the gospel" as participation in Christ. See Haenchen 305.

Γάρ indicates Peter's confirmation of the previous conclusion. Καρδία is a common metaphor for the inner part of a person (see 5:4). The pred. adj. εὐθεῖα (nom. sg. fem. of εὐθύς, -εῖα, -ύ), "immediately," appears in negated form (as it is here) to apply to the wicked (Keener 2.1532).

8:22 The course of action demanded in light of Simon's alienation is twofold. First, he should repent (μετανόησον, 2nd sg. aor. act. impv. of μετανοέω; see 2:38.). The sin to repent of is expressed in a prep. phrase ἀπὸ τῆς κακίας σου ταύτης ("from this wickedness of yours," RSV, NASB, NRSV, ESV); it is specifically the monetary offer. The second command is to pray (δεήθητι, 2nd sg. aor. pass. impv. of δέομαι). While the word is often tr. "pray," it is only appropriate when the ref. is a deity. The basic mng. of the word is "to ask" (cf. 8:34 below, used in ref. to Philip). The gen. τοῦ κυρίου is an obj. gen. typical of δέομαι. Εἰ ἄρα is used to introduce an indir. hypothetical statement (BDAG 127b; Bock 335). The sin to be forgiven (ἀφεθήσεται, 3rd sg. fut. pass. indic. of ἀφίημι) is the intent (ἐπίνοια, nom. sg. fem. of ἐπίνοια, -ας, ἡ) of his heart.

The specificity of the sin to be repented has led some scholars to suggest that Simon was a believer in sin rather than an unbeliever exposed by his sin. Some have even despaired of a solution (see Bock 334 for a fuller discussion). Peter's grounds for repentance in 8:23 would seem to put that at rest.

8:23 The vb. ὁρῶ (1st sg. pres. act. indic. of ὁράω) either takes a double acc. as its obj., σε (acc. sg. masc.) and ὄντα (acc. sg. masc. of pres. ptc. of εἰμί, BHGNT 159; MIT), or the ptc. is used as a marker for indir. discourse (Rogers and Rogers 247; KJV, RSV, NLT, NIV, NRSV, TNIV, NET). The sense is little changed in either case. The noun phrases χολὴν πικρίας and σύνδεσμον ἀδικίας serve as a compound obj. of the prep. εἰς (a functional equiv. to ἐν, Barrett 1.415). The exact mng. of the phrase is determined by the tr. of the words and their modifiers.

The identification of the second set is clearer than the first. Since they are parallel structures closely connected by καί, the mng. of the latter is closely connected to the mng. of the former. Modifying "chain" (σύνδεσμον, gen. sg. masc. of σύνδεσμος, -ου, ὁ), ἀδικίας ("unrighteousness") cannot be an attrib. gen., "in unrighteous chains." So, it is unlikely the first phrase (χολὴν [gen. sg. fem. of χολή, -ῆς, ἡ, "gall"] πικρίας [gen. sg. fem. of πικρία, -ας, ἡ, "bitter"]) is "bitter poison" even as an idiomatic "bitterly envious" (NET). It is possible that the gen. adjs. are gen. of means, i.e., "by bitterness" and "by iniquity" (NKJV). However, this necessitates the conversion of the head nouns to vbs. and eliminating εἰς. This seems unlikely. It is best to see them both as gens. of description: the poison is his bitterness and the chain is his unrighteousness (KJV, RSV, NASB, NRSV); both describe Simon's unredeemed state.

8:24 Simon's response (a pleonastic cstr., see 4:19) is either a request or dismissive sarcasm. Since sarcasm would have fit with Luke's theme that "Christianity has nothing to do with magic" (Bock 336), it is unlikely it would go unmentioned. Certainty is not forthcoming, but the ambiguity might be intentional to warn of the dangers of syncretism. Δεήθητε (2nd pl. aor. pass. impv. of δέομαι) ὑμεῖς is emphatic by the redundant pron. (Barrett 1.417). Ὅπως μηδὲν ἐπέλθῃ (3rd sg. aor. act. subjunc. of ἐπέρχομαι) is a neg. purp. cstr. "so that nothing . . . would come upon me." The rel. pron. phrase ὧν εἰρήκατε (2nd pl. pf. act. indic. of λέγω) functions as a gen. of ref. modifying the subj. μηδέν (BHGNT 159).

8:25 On μὲν οὖν, see 1:6. This v. is transitional, belonging to both sections by wrapping up and pointing forward (Levinsohn 272; Barrett 1.418). The two subst. ptcs. διαμαρτυράμενοι (nom. pl. masc. of aor. mid. ptc. of διαμαρτύρομαι, "testify") and λαλήσαντες (nom. pl. masc. of aor. act. ptc. of λαλέω) are likely a ref. to Peter and John (Barrett 1:418). Given the situation of persecution, ὑπέστρεφον (3rd pl. impf. act. indic. of ὑποστρέφω, "return") εἰς Ἱεροσόλυμα reinforces the identification. On τε, see 1:15. Πολλάς . . . κώμας (acc. pl. fem. of κώμη, -ης, ἡ; mng. "many villages") is the dir. obj. of εὐηγγελίζοντο (3rd pl. impf. mid. indic. of εὐαγγελίζομαι; on the voice, see 5:42), "evangelizing" (for a list of all the ways it may take an obj., see Bruce, *Acts of the Apostles*, 224).

HOMILETICAL SUGGESTIONS

The Church's Proper Response to Persecution (8:1–25)

1. Respond to persecution in proclamation (vv. 1–4)
2. Preach the gospel to all people (vv. 5–8)
3. Even in revival, evaluate supposed converts (vv. 8–25)

Preaching the Word in Power (8:4–25)

1. Preaching the Word subdues the supernatural (vv. 4–8)
2. Preaching the Word exposes the swindlers (vv. 9–13)
3. Preaching the Word warns the superficial (vv. 14–25)

3. Philip and the Ethiopian Eunuch (8:26–40)

8:26 The use of δέ, the introduction of a new character, and spatiotemporal shift mark a new movement in the story line. The combination of ἐλάλησεν (3rd sg. aor. act. indic. of λαλέω) and λέγων (nom. sg. masc. of pres. act. ptc. of λέγω) introduces dir. speech. Most modern EVV leave the ptc. untranslated. Ἄγγελος . . . κυρίου is anar. as typical of the introduction of a new participant (Levinsohn 150). He is to be distinguished from the OT "angel of the Lord" (on contextual and theological grounds rather than the use of the art). The command of the angel is twofold: ἀνάστηθι (2nd sg. aor. act. impv. of ἀνίστημι, "arise") and πορεύου (2nd sg. pres. mid. impv. of πορεύομαι; "go") is a Sem. idiom that suggests "go right now" (see Jonah 1:2; BHGNT 161). The mng. of κατὰ μεσημβρίαν (acc. sg. fem. of μεσημβρία, -ας, ἡ) is debated. Because the word may mean either "noon" or "south" two views are possible:

1. It could refer to a time of day. For some, this understanding is preferred precisely because no one traveled during the heat of the day (Barrett 1.423; Keener 2.1547–48). Thus, the angel is setting up a divine appointment by giving the departure time.
2. It may also be a direction, "toward the south" (BDAG 511b). The position of the midday sun was considered southerly. Elsewhere (Acts 22:6), when the ref. is temp., the prep. is περί (although the use there may be an approximate time). The sense of "Go right now" would suggest a direction (BHGNT 162; Schnabel 424). The implication of a "divine appointment" is still relevant to this interpretation.

The specific road to be taken is the one going down (καταβαίνουσαν, acc. sg. fem. of pres. act. ptc. of καταβαίνω; attrib.). The use of εἰς Γάζαν (acc. sg. fem. of Γάζα, -ης, ἡ; a city on the southwest coast of Palestine) indicates the destination point. That it is a specific road he is to take is more evidence of a "divine appointment" to be made on the road. The exact identification of the road cannot be determined abs. The last phrase (αὕτη ἐστὶν ἔρημος) likely modifies the fem. noun "Γάζα" and refers to "old Gaza" (known as ἡ ἔρημος Γάζα, i.e., the deserted Gaza) for the town was left desolate and the roads leading there were not considered desert (Barrett 1.423; Witherington 294).

8:27–28 Ἀναστὰς (nom. sg. masc. of aor. act. ptc. of ἀνίστημι) ἐπορεύθη (3rd sg. aor. pass. indic. of πορεύομαι) is technically an attend. circum. or temp. ptc. and finite vb. cstr., but the presentation is intended to mirror the command in v. 26. On καὶ ἰδού, see 1:10. The description of the famous Ethiopian eunuch is a complicated series of nouns, adj., and sub. clauses that all function as a subj. phrase of the vb. in v. 28. It begins with three noms. in agreement with ἀνήρ: Αἰθίοψ (nom. sg. masc. of Αἰθίοψ, -οπος, ὁ, a ref. to the region in Africa south of Egypt, "Ethiopia"), εὐνοῦχος (nom. sg. masc. of εὐνοῦχος, -ου, ὁ, "eunuch"), and finally δυνάστης (nom. sg. masc. of δυνάστης, -ου, ὁ, "court official"). The last noun is modified by the proper noun Κανδάκης (gen. sg. fem. of Κανδάκη, -ης, ἡ, "Candace"; gen. of descr.). She is βασιλίσσης (gen. sg. fem. of βασίλισσα, -ης, ἡ) Αἰθιόπων, "Queen of Ethiopia." This Ethiopia is likely the Nubian kingdom with Meröe as the capital (Keener 2.1551). Because Luke gives the indigenous term "Candace" that roughly means "queen," many have accused Luke of being confused (see Keener's discussion, 2:1574–75). However, it is no different than Mark 10:46, where Bartimaeus ("son of Timaeus") is described with "the son of Timaeus," assuming the language barrier. Two rel. pron. clauses (ὅς) complete the subj. complex. In the first, ἐπί has the sense of "over" (BDAG 365b). The obj. of the prep. πάσης τῆς γάζης (gen. sg. fem. of γάζα, -ης, ἡ, "treasure") employs πᾶς in the pred. pos., with the mng. "of the whole treasury" (likely a play on words with the name of the city). The second phrase tells his reason for having gone to Jerusalem. Ἐληλύθει is the 3rd sg. plpf. act. indic. of ἔρχομαι. Προσκυνήσων (nom. sg. masc. of fut. act. ptc. of προσκυνέω; purp.) is an example of the rare fut. ptc. Zerwick notes that it is used exclusively in Acts to indicate the purp. of movement (Z §95). It describes action after the main vb. so that it is best to tr. it like the inf., "to worship."

On τε, see 1:15. The vb. is finally expressed in v. 28 in a compound periph. impf. cstr. ἦν . . . ὑποστρέφων (nom. sg. masc. of pres. act. ptc. of ὑποστρέφω) . . . καθήμενος (nom. sg. masc. of pres. mid. ptc. of κάθημαι), mng. "he was returning and sitting. . . ." The ἅρματος (gen. sg. neut. of ἅρμα, -ατος, τό) was prob. not the familiar war chariot but a traveling chariot more like a covered wagon (BDAG 132a; Keener 2.1579–80). Reading (ἀνεγίνωσκεν, 3rd sg. impf. indic. act. of ἀναγινώσκω, "read") of the day was always done out loud, so it was easy to recognize that it was the prophet Isaiah (Keener 2.1583).

8:29 The theme of supernatural leading continues with the Spirit's direction to Philip. The instruction is in the form of a compound impv. Πρόσελθε (2nd sg. aor. act. impv. of προσέρχομαι) and κολλήθητι (2nd sg. aor. pass. impv. of κολλάω, "be joined"). The latter takes a dat. sg. masc. obj., τῷ ἅρματι (see 8:28) τούτῳ and has the sense of "stick to this chariot" (BDAG 556a).

8:30 Again, being obedient, Philip ran toward (προσδραμών, nom. sg. masc. of aor. act. ptc. of προστρέχω, "run up to"; attend. circum. or temp.) the chariot and heard (ἤκουσεν 3rd sg. aor. act. indic. of ἀκούω) the official reading a ms. The vb. often takes a gen. dir. obj.; thus, αὐτοῦ. It also takes the compl. ἀναγινώσκοντος (gen. sg. masc. of pres. act. ptc. of ἀναγινώσκω, "read"). Ἠσαΐαν τὸν προφήτην is the obj. of the ptc. and identifies the specific book. Philip's question is introduced by ἄρα (to be distinguished from ἆρα at 8:22 by the accent, generally untranslatable), which indicates a dir. question with a heightened tone intensified by γε (BDAG 127b; see Barrett 1.428 for a list of scholarly conjectures). "Do you really . . . ?" might be the best expression of it (Barrett 1.428). The question is a play on words with γινώσκω. Γινώσκεις (2nd sg. pres. act. indic. of γινώσκω) is followed by ἃ ἀναγινώσκεις (2nd sg. pres. act. indic. of ἀναγινώσκω), "What you are reading?"

8:31 In his response, the art. ὁ is used as a pron. Πῶς γάρ ("for how . . .") is tr. in most EVV as "Well, how. . . ." It is better to understand an implied neg. answer, "Of course not, for . . ." for which γάρ is the grounds (BHGNT 164; Barrett 1.428; Rogers and Rogers 247). Technically, ἂν δυναίμην (1st sg. pres. mid. opt. of δύναμαι) expresses the apod. of a fourth-class cond. (fut. less probable) with the mng. "How would I be able?" The prot., ἐὰν μή τις ὁδηγήσει (3rd sg. fut. act. indic. of ὁδηγέω, "guide") με, as a third-class cond. expects the subjunc. (as in the textual vars.). However, the sub-stitution of the fut. makes the fulfillment more likely (BHGNT 164). Overall, it is an elegant expression, presenting the official as a highly intelligent, literate man (Keener 2.1585). On τε, see 1:15. Παρεκάλεσεν is the 3rd sg. aor. act. indic. of παρακαλέω, "invite." The most natural way to understand the ptc. ἀναβάντα (acc. sg. masc. of aor. act. ptc. of ἀναβαίνω) as attend. circum. to καθίσαι (aor. act. inf. of καθίζω; purp.), "to come up and sit" (CSB, RSV, NASB, NIV, ESV).

8:32 In these two verses, a citation of Isa 53:7–8 is introduced by a pred. nom. cstr. The subj., περιοχή (nom. sg. fem. of περιοχή, -ῆς, ἡ), is a seige or a stronghold in the LXX (cf. Zech 12:2; Bock 343). The idea is a portion cut out, the content. In the NT period, it typically was used for a portion of Scripture. Γραφῆς is a part. gen. Ἀνεγίνωσκεν is the 3rd sg. impf. act. indic. of ἀναγινώσκω. The pred. nom. compl. is a cataphoric οὗτος pointing to the citation. Isaiah 53:7 is quoted verbatim from the LXX. Ἤχθη is the 3rd sg. aor. pass. indic. of ἄγω, "led." The prep. phrase ἐπὶ σφαγήν (acc. sg. fem. of σφαγή, -ῆς, ἡ) denotes the purp. of the leading: slaughter. The next phrase continues the analogy of a lamb (ἀμνός, nom. sg. masc. of ἀμνός, -ου, ὁ; subj.) in a pred. adj. cstr. with an implied vb. Κείραντος (gen. sg. masc. of aor. act. ptc. of κείρω, "shear"; subst.) is the gen. obj. of ἐναντίον, "before." The acc. αὐτόν is often tr. possessively in EVV. However, it is formally the obj. of the ptc.; "before the one shearing it" expresses it well. The pred. adj. compl. is ἄφωνος (nom. sg. masc. of ἄφωνος, -ον, "silent"). The adv. οὕτως completes the comp.: "likewise" (BDAG 742b). The pres. vb. ἀνοίγει (3rd sg. pres. act. indic. of ἀνοίγω) is in agreement in pers. and num. with an implied ἦν of the previous phrase but is likely a historical pres. highlighting the servant's silence.

8:33 Isaiah 53:8 is quoted verbatim except the last two clauses are left off. Ἐν τῇ ταπεινώσει (dat. sg. fem. of ταπείνωσις, -εως, ἡ, "humiliation") is likely manner, "in humiliation." The subj. ἡ κρίσις αὐτοῦ is best rendered "his justice." Ἤρθη (3rd sg. aor. pass. indic. of αἴρω) has the sense of "taken away" (BDAG 28a). Next, a rhetorical question expresses a sense of barrenness. The use of διηγήσεται (3rd sg. fut. mid. indic. of διηγέομαι, "relate fully") with τίς as the subj. is tr. as, "Who will relate his descendants?" implying "no one can relate . . . ." Ὅτι is causal. Αἴρεται (3rd sg. pres. pass. indic. of αἴρω) recalls the first vb. of the v. except in the pres. tense. It is likely, as before, a historical pres. for a vivid portrayal of the enduring loss (BHGNT 165).

8:34 The eunuch's question to Philip is introduced as dir. speech with a pleonastic ptc. cstr. (see 4:19), ἀποκριθεὶς (nom. sg. masc. of aor. pass. ptc. of ἀποκρίνομαι) . . . εἶπεν (3rd sg. aor. act. indic. of λέγω). Δέομαι (1st sg. pres. mid. indic. of δέομαι) is followed by the gen. of the person addressed (σου). Περὶ τίνος is fronted as the heart of the question. Τοῦτο refers to the words of the prophet in the Scripture. Περὶ ἑτέρου with the indef. pron. τινός is best tr. "about someone else?" (RSV, NRSV, ESV).

8:35 Ἀνοίξας (nom. sg. masc. of aor. act. ptc. of ἀνοίγω; attend. circum.) . . . στόμα (dir. obj.) is a common phrase in the LXX and continued in the NT. The Sem. expression points to a solemn pronouncement that follows (Z §363). It is followed by ἀρξάμενος (gen. sg. masc. of aor. mid. ptc. of ἄρχω; attend. circum.) ἀπὸ τῆς γραφῆς ταύτης that suggests Isaiah 53 was only the beginning point of Philip's teaching. Εὐηγγελίσατο (3rd sg. aor. mid. indic. of εὐαγγελίζομαι; on the voice, see 5:42) . . . Ἰησοῦν is an unusual phrase. It would suggest Jesus is the content of the gospel.

8:36 The phrase ὡς δὲ ἐπορεύοντο (3rd pl. impf. mid. indic. of πορεύομαι) is a temp. expression indicating contemporaneous activity. Κατὰ τὴν ὁδόν means "along the road." Ἦλθον is the 3rd pl. aor. act. indic. of ἔρχομαι. Φησιν (3rd sg. pres. act. indic. of φημί, "said"; historical pres.) introduces dir. speech. Ἰδοὺ ὕδωρ implies a ὧδέ ἐστιν, "here is." Κωλύει (3rd sg. pres. act. indic. of κωλύω, "hinder, prevent, forbid") is followed by βαπτισθῆναι (aor. pass. inf. of βαπτίζω; compl.): "What is there to prevent me from being baptized?" (BDAG 580a).

8:37 This v. is one of the more infamous textual vars. that is judged to be a Western addition to the book of Acts (see introduction) that was placed into the TR by Erasmus in its 2nd ed. (see Metzger 315–16). Note that it does not appear in the Robinson-Pierpont Byzantine text edition as well.

8:38 The phrase ἐκέλευσεν (3rd sg. aor. act. indic. of κελεύω, "command") στῆναι (aor. act. inf. of ἵστημι; compl.) τὸ ἅρμα (acc. sg. neut. of ἅρμα, -ατος, τό) has the sense of "to stop the chariot." Κατέβησαν (3rd pl. aor. act. indic. of καταβαίνω, "descend"). Ἀμφότεροι (nom. pl. masc.; subst.; "both," by def. no sg. form) is the subj. of the sentence. The prep. phrase εἰς τὸ ὕδωρ means "into the water." The appos. ὅ τε Φίλιππος καὶ ὁ εὐνοῦχος is a clarification of ἀμφότεροι (incl. a redundant τε . . . καί "both . . . and"). Ἐβάπτισεν is the 3rd sg. aor. act. indic. of βαπτίζω.

8:39–40a Δέ marks a new development in the story. Ἀνέβησαν (3rd pl. aor. act. indic. of ἀναβαίνω, "arise"). On ἐκ τοῦ ὕδατος, see the comments on εἰς at 8:38. The vb. ἥρπασεν (3rd sg. aor. act. indic. of ἁρπάζω, "snatch away"), with πνεῦμα κυρίου as the subj. phrase, describes a miraculous relocation of Philip. Ἄζωτον (acc. sg. fem. of Ἄζωτος, -ου, ἡ) is Ashdod of the OT. It was one of the five Philistine cities on the coast of southern Palestine (BDAG 23b). This relocation is made explicit by εἶδεν (3rd sg. aor. act. indic. of ὁράω) αὐτὸν οὐκέτι. The last clause relates the eunuch's travel in a much more standard way. Ἐπορεύετο (3rd sg. impf. mid. indic. of πορεύομαι). Χαίρων is the nom. sg. masc. of pres. act. ptc. of χαίρω; manner. Ultimately the use of γάρ in this context is a conundrum. Most commentators ignore the issue. Most EVV tr. it "and" or "but," following a line of thought that it may take on the mng. of δέ (BDAG 189b; Z §473; ZG 378). Culy and Parsons are probably more on target to consider the versification may have confused us. If we include the first clause of v. 40, we may understand it introducing a compound sentence: "The eunuch did not see him anymore, since he went on his way rejoicing but Philip ended up (εὑρέθη, 3rd sg. aor. pass. indic. of εὑρίσκω, "was found") in Azotus" (BHGNT 168).

8:40b The ptc. διερχόμενος (nom. sg. masc. of pres. mid. ptc. of διέρχομαι) is either temp. or attend. circum. If the latter, since the vb. is impf. (εὐηγγελίζετο, 3rd sg. impf. mid. indic. of εὐαγγελίζομαι; on the voice, see 5:42), there is little difference in mng. (see HCSB). The dir. obj. phrase τὰς πόλεις πάσας, "all the cities," expands the ministry to more than just Azotus. The use of ἕως "until" suggests at Caesarea (Καισαρείαν, acc. sg. fem. of Καισάρεια, -ας, ἡ) he settled down a bit. The entire phrase is a temp. ref. employing the subst. inf. τοῦ ἐλθεῖν (aor. act. inf. of ἔρχομαι) as the obj. of ἕως with αὐτόν as its subj.

HOMILETICAL SUGGESTIONS

The Believer and Divine Appointments (8:26–40)

1. Keep "divine appointments" (vv. 26–28)
2. Listen to the Spirit's instructions (vv. 29–30)
3. Be able to explain Scripture (vv. 31–35)
4. Follow through with the matters of obedience (vv. 36–40)

4. Saul's Conversion (9:1–19a)

9:1–2 The art. of previous ref. (ὁ) and ἔτι recall not only the person but the actions of Saul at 8:3. Ἐμπνέων (nom. sg. masc. of pres. act. ptc. of ἐμπνέω, "breathe") takes a compound gen. as its obj. (see BDF §174): ἀπειλῆς (gen. sg. fem. of ἀπειλή, -ῆς, ἡ, "threat") and φόνου (gen. sg. masc. of φόνος, -ου, ὁ, "murder"). They are rendered "murderous threats" by BDAG 100a (NIV, TNIV), treating them as hendiadys. Haenchen (319) defers but not on grammatical grounds. The prep. phrase εἰς τοὺς μαθητὰς τοῦ κυρίου is best rendered "against the disciples . . ." (RSV, NASB, ESV).

Προσελθών (nom. sg. masc. of aor. act. ptc. of προσέρχομαι; temp.) takes a dat. obj. τῷ ἀρχιερεῖ (dat. sg. masc.). The vb. ᾐτήσατο (3rd sg. aor. mid. indic. of αἰτέω) in the mid. means "he requested"). Ἐπιστολάς (acc. pl. fem. of ἐπιστολή, -ῆς, ἡ, "letters") are some sort of extradition authority (cf. 1 Macc 15:21; Bock 355). Πρὸς τὰς συναγωγάς indicates the recipient of the letter; εἰς Δαμασκόν (acc. sg. fem. of Δαμασκός, -οῦ, ἡ, "Damascus") is the city of destination. The best rendering would be "letters to the Damascus synagogues." The purp. of the letters (ὅπως) is expressed with a third-class cond. (uncertain but still likely, ἐάν + a subjunc. in the prot.). Εὕρῃ (3rd sg. aor. act. subjunc. of εὑρίσκω) takes τινας ("some") as dir. obj. Τῆς ὁδοῦ (part. gen.) is a primitive ref. to Christians. "The Way" is an appropriate title for a sect within Judaism; after Antioch and the unmediated inclusion of Gentiles, something else was needed (cf. Acts 11:26). The title has OT precedents (Schnabel 442; see, e.g., Isa 35:8; 40:3). Ὄντας (acc. pl. masc. of pres. ptc. of εἰμί) is attrib. to τινας. The distance between the ptc. and τινας possibly suggests uncertainty ("any who might be"; Barrett 1.448; Rogers and Rogers 248). Ἄνδρας τε καὶ γυναῖκας is best understood as an apos. statement agreeing with τινας. Δεδεμένους (acc. pl. masc. of pf. pass. ptc. of δέω, "bind") is attrib. to an understood αὐτούς (cf. RSV, NASB, "bring them bound. . ."). Ἀγάγῃ is the 3rd sg. aor. act. subjunc. of ἄγω.

9:3 On the temp. cstr. ἐν . . . τῷ πορεύεσθαι (pres. mid. inf. of πορεύομαι), see 2:1. "Now as he journeyed" is the best tr. (see KJV, RSV, NASB). Ἐγένετο is the 3rd sg. aor. mid. indic. of γίνομαι, "happen." Αὐτόν (acc. sg. masc.) is the subj. of ἐγγίζειν (pres. act. inf. of ἐγγίζω). Ἐξαίφνης is an adv. mng. "suddenly." On τε, see 1:15. Περιήστραψεν (3rd sg. aor. act. indic. of περιαστράπτω, "shine around"). Zerwick suggests *flashed round about* like lightning" (ZG 378). The source of the light (φῶς) is ἐκ τοῦ οὐρανοῦ ("from heaven"), which certainly suggests more than "from the sky."

9:4 Πεσών is the nom. sg. masc. of aor. act. ptc. of πίπτω, attend. circum. For the clause ἤκουσεν (3rd sg. aor. act. indic. of ἀκούω) φωνήν, using the acc. instead of the gen., see 9:7 below. Λέγουσαν (acc. sg. fem. of pres. act. ptc. of λέγω) introduces dir. speech. The double voc. Σαοὺλ Σαούλ is common of formal addresses in theophanies (Bruce, *Acts of the Apostles*, 235). In Luke (see, e.g., 10:41) it often has the tone of fond rebuke (Thompson 181). Given the context of persecution, urgency (like Luke 8:24; see Thompson 137) may make more sense. Τί ("why" = διὰ τί [ZG 378]) διώκεις (2nd sg. pres. act. indic. of διώκω) is prog. in force, "Why are you persecuting me?" (CSB, NASB, ESV). The identification of Jesus with his church is hard to miss.

9:5 The exchange between Saul and Christ is almost entirely one-sided once the speaker is identified. Τίς εἶ (2nd sg. pres. indic. of εἰμί), "Who are you," is a typical inquiry. The voc. sg. masc. κύριε is likely more than merely polite given the circumstances (Bruce, *Acts of the Apostles*, 235) but falls short of a divine ascription. The reply assumes a vb. of speaking. Ἐγώ εἰμι Ἰησοῦς is emphatic by the redundant pron. It is not likely that it has a ref. to the covenant name of God. In the rel. pron. phrase, σὺ διώκεις (2nd sg. pres. act. of διώκω) is likewise emphatic and in ominous contrast to the former cstr.

9:6 Ἀλλ' denotes contrast, likely assuming what follows is a change in direction and attitude (Barrett 1.451). Ἀνάστηθι (2nd sg. aor. act. impv. of ἀνίστημι, "arise") is reminiscent of Philip (see comments at 8:26). Εἴσελθε is the 2nd sg. aor. act. impv. of εἰσέρχομαι, "go into." Λαληθήσεταί is the 3rd sg. fut. pass. indic. of λαλέω. The statement of obligation using δεῖ (see 1:21) is rather straightforward (compl. inf. ποιεῖν [pres. act. inf.] with σε [acc. sg. masc., subj.]). Ὅ τί is written as an indef. rel. pron. (acc. sg. neut. of ὅστις). However, the rarity of the indef. rel. pron. cstr. in indir. questions in Koinē has led to some conjecture:

1. It may be as in the text, an indef. rel. pron. introducing an indir. question. This is common in CGk. for indir. questions, but not so in Koinē (BDF §300). Robertson saw this as evidence of Luke's "literary language" (R 731). If so, the whole phrase functions as the dir. obj. of the inf.

2. Culy and Parsons suggest that the accents are misinterpreted (none would be in a *scriptio continua* ms.). Instead they suggest the art., with an encl. accent from τι, which in turn has an encl. accent from σε. If so, the art. nominalizes the whole phrase that functions as the dir. obj. of λαληθήσεταί (BHGNT 172).

   The mng. is not changed either way.

9:7 Συνοδεύοντες (nom. pl. masc. of pres. act. ptc. of συνοδεύω, "travel with"; attrib.) takes a dat. obj. αὐτῷ and modifies ἄνδρες. Εἱστήκεισαν (3rd pl. plpf. indic. act. of ἵστημι) is used with the emphasis not on standing but just being there; as such it takes ἐνεοί (nom. pl. masc. of ἐνεός, -ά, -όν, "speechless") as a pred. adj. (see 26:6). Ἀκούοντες (nom. pl. masc. of pres. act. ptc. of ἀκούω) with the gen. τῆς φωνῆς as dir. obj. creates an apparent contradiction with 22:9. There those standing did not hear the voice. Three primary solutions occur:

1. At 9:4 and 22:10 the acc. of φωνή is used, while the gen. is used at 9:7. According to Robertson (R 506), the CGk. sense where the acc. has the sense of "understanding" but the gen. "merely hearing" is in force at 9:7 (see also Turner, *Insights,* 87–90). Several EVV seem to take this understanding (e.g.,

NLT, NASB, NIV, ESV, TNIV, NET). Wallace, however, notes that upon closer scrutiny this distinction seems imposed on the vb. He notes, if the distinction were true, "the exceptions, in fact, are seemingly more numerous than the rule!" (Wallace 133). The mistake is to assume that the distinction is always present. BDAG notes that in the gen. it can take on this mng. (BDAG 37d). Luke, however, is inconsistent with the cases (See BDF §172 [2]). So, while it may have this mng., it cannot rest on the cases alone.

2. As early as Chrysostom there is a view that what the men were hearing was Saul speaking to apparently no one (Bruce, *Acts of the Apostles*, 236). However, the art. used at 9:7 is the art. of previous ref. Thus, it refers to 9:4 as well.

3. Polhill (235) makes the distinction between the accounts at chs. 9 and 22 in that at 22:14 he adds a "voice from his mouth" (i.e., speaking). At 9:7, there is nothing to imply that there is anything heard more than a sound (see Witherington 312–13). Combined with the possible distinction of mng. in case use, this position is preferable.

9:8 After the theophany, Saul did exactly as Jesus ordered, employing the same vb. (ἠγέρθη, 3rd sg. aor. pass. indic. of ἐγείρω; the pass. is equiv. to the act. here: Paul did the standing [contra Haenchen 323]; see Z §231, most EVV "Saul arose"). However, there are two unexpected developments. First, he was blind. Ἀνεῳγμένων is the gen. pl. masc. of pf. pass. ptc. of ἀνοίγω; gen. abs., temp.). Οὐδὲν ἔβλεπεν (3rd sg. impf. act. indic. of βλέπω) means "he was seeing nothing." And second, his companions had to help him. Χειραγωγοῦντες is the nom. pl. masc. of pres. act. ptc. of χειραγωγέω, "lead by the hand"; manner. It is a helpless state (Bock 359) that was, at least, somewhat humiliating for Saul. Εἰσήγαγον is the 3rd pl. impf. act. indic. of εἰσάγω, "lead in."

9:9 Saul's condition and its duration are described using a periph. impf. ἦν (3rd sg. impf. indic. of εἰμί) . . . βλέπων (nom. sg. masc. of pres. act. ptc. of βλέπω). It is a continuing blindness. The acc. of time ἡμέρας τρεῖς ("for three days," CSB, RSV, NLT, ESV, NET) describes a duration. The fast is total. Μὴ ἔφαγεν (3rd sg. aor. act. indic. of ἐσθίω) is "he did not eat." Οὐδὲ ἔπιεν (3rd sg. aor. act. indic. of πίνω) augments the prev. clause, "nor did he drink." The fast is voluntary (not like the loss of sight), processing and preparing for what lies ahead (Bock 359).

9:10 On ὀνόματι, see 5:1. The Lord spoke (εἶπεν, 3rd sg. aor. act. indic. of λέγω) to Ananias (see 22:12) "in a vision" (ἐν ὁράματι, dat. sg. neut. of ὅραμα, -ατος, τό, "a vision"; means). Ἀνανία is voc. sg. masc. The response ἰδοὺ ἐγώ used abs. is frequent in the LXX (Bruce, *Acts of the Apostles*, 237; see, e.g., Gen 22:1; 1 Sam 3:4) and implies readiness to obey (Barrett 1.453).

9:11 On ἀναστὰς πορεύθητι, see 8:26. The ptc. is attend. circum. and takes on impv. force, "arise" (BHGNT 174). The basic command is twofold: "Go" and "seek" (ζήτησον, 2nd sg. aor. act. impv. of ζητέω). Each impv. is modified by a descriptive phrase. The first is a specific address, ἐπὶ τὴν ῥύμην (acc. sg. fem. of ῥύμη, -ης, ἡ, "street"), further modified by καλουμένην (acc. sg. fem. of pres. pass. ptc. of καλέω) Εὐθεῖαν (acc. sg. fem. of εὐθύς, -εῖα, -ύ, "straight"; acc. obj. of the ptc.). The second impv. vb. takes "a Tarsian (Ταρσέα acc. sg. masc. of Ταρσεύς, -έως, ὁ) named Saul" as its obj. The grounds for the command is emphatic with ἰδού (see 1:10). Γὰρ προσεύχεται (3rd sg. pres. mid. indic. of προσεύχομαι) suggests that Ananias was the answer to Saul's prayer.

9:12 Specifically, Saul has had a sim. experience (see also Cornelius in the next ch.). Εἶδεν (3rd sg. aor. act. indic. of ὁράω) takes a double-acc. cstr. with ἄνδρα . . . Ἀνανίαν and the ptcs. below. On ὁράματι, see 5:1. The vision functions as a command to Ananias although they are compound compl. ptcs. to "saw" (BHGNT 174). Εἰσελθόντα is the acc. sg. masc. of aor. act. ptc. of εἰσέρχομαι. Ἐπιθέντα is the acc. sg. masc. of aor. act. ptc. of ἐπιτίθημι. The purp. is expressed with ὅπως ἀναβλέψῃ (3rd sg. aor. act. subjunc. of ἀναβλέπω, "regain sight").

9:13 Ananias was understandably hesitant. Ἤκουσα is the 1st sg. aor. act. indic. of ἀκούω. The adj. rel. pron. ὅσα takes κακά as its antecedent and functions as the dir. obj. of the vb. Even without πᾶς it may take the mng. "all that." Thus, BDAG renders it "all the harm that he has done" (BDAG 729b; see MM 461b). Τοῖς ἁγίοις is a dat. of disadvantage with the poss. gen. σου, "to your saints." Ἐποίησεν is the 3rd sg. aor. act. indic. of ποιέω.

9:14 Ananias feared the enemy with the authority of the state behind him. The adv. ὧδε ("here, in this place") describes Saul's authority reaching to Damascus. The pl. ἀρχιερέων may describe the ruling class that was made up of the former high priests and their families (Bruce, *Acts of the Apostles*, 238). Δῆσαι is the aor. act. inf. of δέω, "bind"; epex. Ἐπικαλουμένους (acc. pl. masc. of pres. pass. ptc. of ἐπικαλέω; subst., obj. of the inf.) takes ὄνομα as its obj. It is a ref. to Joel 3:5, taken in Acts 2:21 to refer to Christians.

9:15 Jesus's response is an exhortation/grounds cstr. The command πορεύου (2nd sg. pres. mid. impv. of πορεύομαι) and the grounds to follow negates Ananias's fears. Ὅτι is causal. Ἐκλογῆς (gen. sg. fem. of ἐκλογή, -ῆς, ἡ) is an attrib. gen. modifying σκεῦος (nom. sg. neut. of σκεῦος, -ους, τό, "object, vessel") with μοι (poss. dat.). It is best rendered "my chosen vessel." The tr. "vessel" is superior to "instrument" (CSB, RSV, NLT, NASB, NRS, ESV, TNIV, NET) because the image is of a container filled for a purp., in this case filled with the gospel. The gen. inf. cstr. τοῦ βαστάσαι (aor. act. inf. of βαστάζω, "carry") τὸ ὄνομά μου is a summation of the Christian message (Barrett 1.456) and implies submission to Jesus's authority (i.e., salvation; see 2:21). The recipients of his mission are listed with a τε . . . καὶ . . . τε cstr., unique in the NT, a bit complicated by the postpositive nature of τε. Robertson notes that the basic cstr. is used when there is an essential "inner bond" (R 1179). In this case, the conceptual unity is that these need the gospel. Ἐθνῶν τε καὶ βασιλέων (gen. objs. of ἐνώπιον, "before") should be "both Gentiles and kings." Υἱῶν τε Ἰσραήλ is the final item ". . . and the sons of Israel."

9:16 There are numerous ways to interpret the use of γάρ here.

1. It is possible that γάρ is merely a synonym for δέ (BHGNT 177). However, it is generally best to look for a sense that is closer to the basic mng. of the word.

2. The γάρ possibly is a second basis for the impv. "Go" in the sense of an implied promise of safety. "Go, for he is my vessel . . . because I will show him . . ." (BHGNT 177, as possible).

3. Barrett suggests that it is the grounds for a safe approach to Paul. This construction interprets the conj. under an assumed cond. (Barrett 1.457).

The emphatic ἐγώ in conj. with ὑποδείξω (1st sg. fut. act. indic. of ὑποδείκνυμι, "show") makes the most sense with the second option, although safety was certainly on Ananias's mind. On ὅσα, see. v. 14; on δεῖ, see 1:21. Ὑπὲρ τοῦ ὀνόματός μου, "for my name," designates the reason for suffering (παθεῖν, aor. act. inf.; compl., constantive, ZG 379).

9:17 The first three vbs. describe Ananias's obedience. Ἀπῆλθεν is the 3rd sg. aor. act. indic. of ἀπέρχομαι, "depart." Εἰσῆλθεν is the 3rd sg. aor. act. indic. of εἰσέρχομαι. The cstr. of the ptc., ἐπιθείς (nom. sg. masc. of aor. act. ptc. of ἐπιτίθημι), and the vb., εἶπεν, expresses the two as a unit with the finite vb. the foregrounded mat. This is the fulfillment of the implied command of 9:12. The address Σαοὺλ ἀδελφέ (voc. sg. masc.), "brother Saul," implies recognition of Saul's chosen status and his otherwise unstated conversion (Bruce, *Acts of the Apostles*, 239). Ἀπέσταλκεν is the 3rd sg. pf. act. indic. of ἀποστέλλω, "sent." Ἰησοῦς begins an appos. phrase. Ὀφθείς (nom. sg. masc. of aor. pass. ptc. ὁράω; subst.) takes the sense of "appeared" (ZG 371, see 2:3). The rel. pron. ᾗ is fem. by form but has the masc. 1st decl. as its antecedent. Ἤρχου is the 2nd sg. impf. mid. indic. of ἔρχομαι. Ὅπως picks up the main vb. and denotes purp. The following subjuncs. compl. the phrase. Ἀναβλέψῃς is the 2nd sg. aor. act. subjunc. of ἀναβλέπω ("regain sight"), and πλησθῇς is the 2nd sg. aor. pass. subjunc. of πίμπλημι ("be filled").

9:18–19a The results are instantaneous (καὶ εὐθέως). Ἀπέπεσαν is the 3rd sg. aor. act. indic. of ἀποπίπτω, "fall off." Αὐτοῦ ἀπὸ τῶν ὀφθαλμῶν is in unusual word order for the poss. use of the gen. pron. (see BHGNT 178). However, it makes cleaner sense than most other options; thus, most EVV "from his eyes." Ὡς is a comp. particle ("like") suggesting λεπίδες (nom. pl. fem. of λεπίς, -ίδος, ἡ, "scales"; NT hapax, subj.) describes the appearance of whatever was covering Paul's eyes. The final clause has three vbs. joined by τε καί . . . καί, describing Paul's condition and actions in response. Ἀνέβλεψέν (3rd sg. aor. act. indic. of ἀναβλέπω) is the new condition. The second element expresses Paul's faith response with a ptc. ἀναστάς (nom. sg. masc. of aor. act. ptc. of ἀνίστημι; attend. circum.) and the vb. ἐβαπτίσθη (3rd sg. aor. pass. indic. of βαπτίζω, "baptized"). The third element describes a practical response. After eating (19a, λαβών [masc.nom. sg. aor. act. ptc. of λαμβάνω; temp.] with the obj. of the ptc. τροφήν [acc. sg. fem. of τροφή, -ης, ἡ, "food"]), Saul recovered strength (ἐνίσχυσεν, 3rd sg. aor. act. indic. of ἐνισχύω).

FOR FURTHER STUDY

17. The Conversion of Paul (9:1–19)

Awwad, J. B. "From Saul to Paul: The Conversion of Paul the Apostle." *Theological Review* 32, (2011): 3–14.

Bird, M. F. "A Funny Thing Happened on the Way to Damascus." In *Introducing Paul: The Man, His Mission and His Message*, 30–37. Downers Grove, IL: IVP Academic, 2008.

Dunn, J. D. G. "'A Light to the Gentiles': The Significance of the Damascus Road Christophany for Paul." In *Jesus, Paul and the Law: Studies in Mark and Galatians.* Louisville: Westminster /John Knox, 1990.

Everts, J. M. *DPL*, 156–63.

Hengel, M., and A. M. Schwemer. *Between Damascus and Antioch: The Unknown Years.* Louisville: Westminster/John Knox, 1997.

Hurtado, L. W. "Convert, Apostate or Apostle to the Nations: The 'Conversion' of Paul in Recent Scholarship." *SR* 22 (1993): 273–84.

Kern, Philip H. "Paul's Conversion and Luke's Portrayal of Character in Acts 8–10." *TynBul* 54 (2003): 63–80.

Lake, K. "The Conversion of Paul and the Events Immediately Following It." In *Additional Notes to the Commentary*, by Kirsopp Lake and Henry J. Cadbury, 188–95. Vol. 5 of *The Beginnings of Christianity*. London: Macmillan, 1933.

Longenecker, R., ed. *The Road from Damascus: The Impact of Paul's Conversion on His Life, Thought, and Ministry.* Grand Rapids: Eerdmans, 1997.

Quarles, C. "The Damascus Road." In *The Illustrated Life of Paul*, 17–41. Nashville: B&H Academic, 2014.

HOMILETICAL SUGGESTIONS

The Making of a Missionary (9:1–19a)

Not every testimony is exactly like Paul's, but they are similar
1. All of Christ's missionaries began on a misguided quest (vv. 1–2)
2. All of Christ's missionaries have a humbling encounter with Jesus (vv. 3–9)
3. Christ provides help for all his missionaries (vv. 10–12)
4. Christ sets his missionaries apart for ministry (vv. 13–19a)

"In His Name" (9:14–16)

1. It expresses the status of believers (v. 14)
2. It expresses the message of believers (vv. 15, 27)
3. It expresses the cause of suffering for believers (vv. 16 [21])

5. Saul's Post-Conversion Days (9:19b–30)

a. In Damascus (9:19b–25)

9:19b Ἐγένετο δέ is not the Sem. use of 4:5 but is the main vb. best tr. "now he was. . . ." The phrase ἡμέρας τινάς has the sense of "several days" (BDAG 1009a), summarizing his initial stay after conversion in Damascus. In comp. with Gal 1:17–21 and 2 Cor 11:32, Luke has left out some details (e.g., a trip to Arabia [Gal 1:7; 2 Cor 11:32]). Luke compresses the narrative that ostensibly covered a span of one to three years, but the general outline is in agreement, although there are apparent differences in some details (see Bock Johnson 173; Keener 2.1668–69; Witherington 303–15).

These are perhaps due to Luke's compression for a literary purp. (fairly common in ancient literature, Keener 2.1668).

9:20 Saul wasted no time before beginning to evangelize (καὶ εὐθέως). Ἐκήρυσσεν (3rd sg. impf. act. indic. of κηρύσσω) takes Ἰησοῦν as its obj. and is likely inceptive: "he began to preach" (Robertson, *Pictures,* 122; cf. NLT, NASB). The conj. ὅτι indicates indir. speech. The synagogues were a natural place for a rabbi to begin. It was also Paul's pattern throughout his ministry (cf. Rom 1:16). The content is a pred. nom. cstr. with οὗτος as the subj. and υἱός as the compl. The phrase occurs only here in Acts and is best understood messianically (Bock 365; Bruce 240; cf. Paul's sermon in ch. 13), although other included nuances are certainly possible (Keener 2.1671–72).

9:21 The subst. ptc. ἀκούοντες is the subj. of the vbs. ἐξίσταντο (3rd pl. impf. mid. indic. of ἐξίστημι, "they were continually astonished") and ἔλεγον (3rd pl. impf. indic. act. of λέγω, "saying"). The question that follows is presented as dir. speech and expects a yes answer. It begins with a pred. nom. cstr. οὗτός ἐστιν ὁ πορθήσας (nom. sg. masc. of aor. act. ptc. of πορθέω, "the one who devastated"; subst.). Πορθέω denotes "violent oppression and plundering" (Johnson 171). The ptc. takes another subst. ptc. phrase as its obj., ἐπικαλουμένους (acc. pl. masc. of pres. pass. ptc. of ἐπικαλέω) τὸ ὄνομα τοῦτο (on the mng., see 9:14). They continue, citing his purp. for coming to Damascus (suggesting word got there before Saul did). Εἰς τοῦτο means "for this reason" and points forward to the ἵνα clause. Ἐλήλύθει is the 3rd sg. plpf. act. indic. of ἔρχομαι. Δεδεμένους (acc. pl. masc. of pf. pass. ptc. of δέω) is likely the compl. in a double-acc. cstr. with αὐτούς. Thus, most EVV tr. the clause "so that he might bring (ἀγάγῃ, 3rd sg. aor. act. subjunc. of ἄγω) them bound." The prep. phrase ἐπὶ τοὺς ἀρχιερεῖς is common of legal proceedings and has the sense of "before the high priests" (RSV, NASB, NRSV, ESV; on the pl., see 9:14).

9:22 Μᾶλλον intensifies the vb. ἐνεδυναμοῦτο (3rd sg. impf. mid. indic. of ἐνδυναμόω, "strengthened"): "Saul grew stronger" (BDAG 613d). Thus, the impf. vb. συνέχυννεν (3rd sg. impf. act. indic. of συγχέω) likely has a prog. sense, "he was confounding." Κατοικοῦντας (acc. pl. masc. of pres. act. ptc. of κατοικέω) is an attrib. ptc. modifying Ἰουδαίους: "the Jews dwelling in Damascus." Συμβιβάζων (nom. sg. masc. of pres. act. ptc. of συμβιβάζω; means, best tr. "by proving") is only used in Acts in the NT (see 16:10; 19:33). The content of the proof is a pred. nom. cstr. intro. by ὅτι, "that this one (Jesus) is the Christ."

9:23 Ὡς with the impf. has the sense of "while" (BDAG 1106a). Ἐπληροῦντο is the 3rd pl. impf. pass. indic. of πληρόω. On ἱκανός and time, see 8:11. The impf. combined with ὡς indicates the plot was hatched during this time. Συνεβουλεύσαντο (3rd pl. aor. mid. indic. of συμβουλεύω, "plot") is used only here in Acts. It is compl. by the inf. ἀνελεῖν (aor. act. inf. of ἀναιρέω, "kill"). In some manner King Aretas is involved (mentioned by name in 2 Cor 11:32; Haenchen 331). Bruce (*Acts of the Apostles,* 242) notes that it is not unlikely that the Jews had enlisted government help in the matter. There is no doubt that in Saul, Aretas and the Jewish leadership had a common irritant and were working together.

9:24 Ἐγνώσθη (3rd sg. aor. pass. indic. of γινώσκω, "known") takes the dat. Σαύλῳ (dat. sg. masc.), the dat. is commonly associated with the pass. of γινώσκω (BDAG

200a). Ἐπιβουλή is the nom. sg. fem. of ἐπιβουλή, -ῆς, ἡ, "plot against"; subj. Luke does not tell how they knew, possibly a leak from Paul's former associates (Keener 2.1674). Παρετηροῦντο is the 3rd pl. impf. mid. indic. of παρατηρέω, "watched scrupulously." Πύλας is the acc. pl. fem. of πύλη, -ῆς, ἡ, "gates"; dir. obj. The phrase ἡμέρας τε καὶ νυκτός (gen. of time) suggests a kind of time. However, "both by day and night" is cumbersome in Eng., thus it is expressed by the Eng. adv. idiom "day and night" by most EVV.

9:25 Λαβόντες is the nom. pl. masc. of aor. act. ptc. of λαμβάνω; attend. circum. The gen. αὐτοῦ suggests Saul's disciples (the var. αὐτόν [acc. sg. masc.] suggests Paul himself; Haenchen prefers the var. [332] for no stated reason). That Paul had made disciples suggests a lengthy stay in Damascus, lending credence to a purposeful condensation of the tale. Νυκτός (gen. sg. fem.) is a gen. of time, "by night." The prep. phrase διὰ τοῦ τείχους (acc. pl. neut. of τεῖχος, -ους, τό), "through the wall," suggests an opening through which Saul was lowered (καθῆκαν, 3rd pl. aor. act. indic. of καθίημι, "lower"). Paul identifies it as a window in 2 Cor 11:33 (Barrett 1.467). Χαλάσαντες is the nom. pl. masc. of aor. act. ptc. of χαλάω; it means, best tr., "by letting down." Ἐν σπυρίδι (dat. sg. fem. of σπυρίς, -ίδος, ἡ, a sizable basket [see Matt 15:37]; Paul uses the generic word in 2 Cor 11:33) is tr. "in a large basket" (NASB).

b. In Jerusalem (9:26–30)

9:26 Δέ marks a development in the story line. Παραγενόμενος is the nom. sg. masc. of aor. mid. ptc. of παραγίνομαι; temp. Ἐπείραζεν (3rd sg. aor. act. indic. of πειράζω, "attempt") is compl. by the inf. κολλᾶσθαι (pres. pass. inf. of κολλάω, "join closely"; ZG 380). Ἐφοβοῦντο is the 3rd pl. impf. mid. indic. of φοβέομαι. The ptc. phrase μὴ πιστεύοντες (nom. pl. masc. of pres. act. ptc. of πιστεύω; causal) means "because (they) were not believing" (see RSV, "for"; NET, "because"; CSB, "since"). It introduces indir. speech that typically employs the pres. ἐστίν (BHGNT 182). Here it is in a pred. nom. cstr. "That he was a disciple" is the best rendering (KJV, RSV, NASB, NRSV, ESV, NET).

9:27 On Βαρναβᾶς, see 4:37. Ἐπιλαβόμενος (nom. sg. masc. of aor. mid. ptc. of ἐπιλαμβάνομαι, "take hold of"; attend. circum.) possibly takes αὐτόν as its obj. The pron. may, however, be the fronted obj. of ἤγαγεν (3rd sg. aor. act. indic. of ἄγω; see BDAG 16b; BHGNT 183; ZG 380). There is no major impact on the mng. That the pl. ἀποστόλους (acc. pl. masc., obj. of prep.) is used should not be seen as a contradiction to Gal 1:18–19. The pl. does not demand the total Twelve but may be generalizing (Bruce, *Acts of the Apostles*, 243). Paul includes Peter and James as apostles, so too could Luke, whose purp. was to show solidarity with Jerusalem (Paul's was to show his independence; Keener 2.1687).

Barnabas fully explained (διηγήσατο, 3rd sg. aor. mid. indic. of διηγέομαι) Paul's testimony (expressed in indir. speech). It is divided into two segments by the repetition of πῶς. The first is the event on the Damascus road. He saw the Lord (εἶδεν, 3rd sg. aor. act. indic. of ὁράω) who spoke to him (ἐλάλησεν, 3rd sg. aor. act. indic. of λαλέω). Second are the events in Damascus. Ἐπαρρησιάσατο is the 3rd sg. aor. mid. indic. of παρρησιάζομαι, "speak boldly." It is always used of a bold, open proclamation (Barrett

1.469). The prep. phrase ἐν τῷ ὀνόματι τοῦ Ἰησοῦ suggests speaking as an authorized agent (see 3:6).

9:28 The initial phrase is a marvel of compactness. It features a compound periph. impf. with three ptcs. compl. the cstr. The first two, εἰσπορευόμενος (nom. sg. masc. of pres. mid. ptc. of εἰσπορεύομαι, "enter") and ἐκπορευόμενος (nom. sg. masc. of pres. mid. ptc. of ἐκπορεύομαι, "depart"), are closely joined by καί, representing one thought (a LXX expression, ZG 381). "Moving about freely" is a good tr. (NASB, NIV, TNIV). The last ptc. of the three periphs. is παρρησιαζόμενος (nom. sg. masc. of pres. mid. ptc. of παρρησιάζομαι, "speak boldly"; on the vb., see above). On ἐν τῷ ὀνόματι, see 9:27.

9:29 Ἐλάλει (3rd sg. impf. act. indic. of λαλέω) τε καὶ συνεζήτει (3rd sg. impf. act. indic. of συζητέω) is, technically, "He was both speaking and disputing." Πρός used with people (Ἑλληνιστάς is the acc. masc. pl. of Ἑλληνιστής, Gk.-speaking Jews) is "with." These were likely associated with Stephen's assailants or the very people themselves (Bock 370). At the very least, Paul has taken on Stephen's role in disputing with the Hellenists (Barrett 1.470). The art. οἱ (nom. pl. masc., subj.) is used as a pers. pron. Ἐπεχείρουν (3rd pl. impf. indic. act. of ἐπιχειρέω, "they were attempting") describes the response. It is compl. by the inf. ἀνελεῖν (aor. act. inf. of ἀναιρέω, "kill"). They desired to treat Paul as they did Stephen.

9:30 Ἐπιγνόντες (nom. pl. masc. of aor. act. ptc. of ἐπιγινώσκω, "recognize"; temp.) has the sense of "when they recognized this." Κατήγαγον is the 3rd pl. aor. act. indic. of κατάγω, "take down." Εἰς Καισάρειαν (acc. sg. fem. of Καισάρεια, -ας, ἡ) is the immediate destination, "unto Caesarea." Ἐξαπέστειλαν (3rd pl. aor. act. indic. of ἐξαποστέλλω, "send out") has the sense of "they sent him off" (CSB, RSV, NRSV, ESV, NIV, TNIV). Εἰς Ταρσόν (acc. sg. fem. of Ταρσός, -οῦ, ἡ, "Tarsus," capital of Cilicia) is the ultimate destination, "unto Tarsus."

C. SUMMARY: JUDEA, GALILEE, AND SAMARIA (9:31)

9:31 Although short, this v. must be considered a summary (Barrett 1.472; Bruce, *Acts of the Apostles*, 245) that signals peace for the persecuted church (Haenchen 333). On μὲν οὖν, see 1:6. Καθ᾽ ὅλης, lit. "according to the whole," means "throughout" (CSB, KJV, RSV, NASB, NLT, NIV, NRSV, ESV, TNIV). Εἶχεν is the 3rd sg. impf. act. indic. of ἔχω. The compound temp. ptcs. οἰκοδομουμένη (nom. sg. fem. of pres. pass. ptc. of οἰκοδομέω, "edify") and πορευομένη (nom. sg. fem. of pres. mid. ptc. of πορεύομαι, in the sense of conducting one's life, "walking" [BDAG 853d]) make the most sense relative to the last finite vb. ἐπληθύνετο (3rd sg. impf. pass. indic. of πληθύνω, "it was multiplied"). Most EVV, however, understand the first ptc. to modify εἶχεν and the last phrases to modify ἐπληθύνετο. The use of the two prep. phrases are equivalent to dats. of sphere and describe a bidirectional relationship. Τῷ φόβῳ (dat. sg. masc.) τοῦ κυρίου indicates a respectful obedience toward God, while τῇ παρακλήσει (dat. sg. masc.) ἁγίου πνεύματος (gen. sg. neut.) describes an inner consoling activity from God.

HOMILETICAL SUGGESTIONS

Help along the Way (9:19b–31)

1. The bold evangelizing convert among his old friends (vv. 19b–25)
   a. First he amazed (vv. 19b–22)
   b. Then he enraged (vv. 23–25)
2. The bold evangelizing convert among his new friends (vv. 26–31)
   a. The intercession of a disciple eased the queasy (vv. 26–27)
   b. The intercession of the disciples rescued the preacher (vv. 28–31)

FOR FURTHER STUDY

18. Acts, Galatians, 2 Corinthians, and Pauline Chronology (9:23–25)

Alexander, L. C. A. *DPL*, 115–23.

Campbell, D. A. "An Anchor for Pauline Chronology: Paul's Flight from 'the Ethnarch of King Aretas' (2 Corinthians 11:32–33)." *JBL* 121 (2002): 279–302.

Hemer, C. J. "Observations on Pauline Chronology." In *Pauline Studies: Essays Presented to Professor F. F. Bruce on his 70th Birthday*, 3–8. Grand Rapids: Eerdmans, 1980.

Morgado, J., Jr. "Paul in Jerusalem: A Comparison of His Visits in Acts and Galatians." *JETS* 37 (1994): 55–68.

Townsend, J. T. "Acts 9:1–29 and Early Church Tradition." *SBL Seminar Papers* 27 (1988): 119–31.

Wainwright, A. W. "The Historical Value of Acts 9:19b–30." In *SE*, 589–94. Berlin: Akademie, 1973.

IV. Continued Expansion: The First Gentile Converts (9:32–12:24)

The movement to include Gentiles in the people of God apart from circumcision (i.e., as Gentiles) has been clear in the narrative. From Jews embracing Jesus as their Messiah, to Samaritans, to proselytes, the gospel has been moving outward from ethnic Israel (while still calling her) to the nations (1:8). The conversion and calling of Saul was also in preparation for the Gentile mission (put on hold until these events). With the conversion of the God-fearer Cornelius, the process to put the question of Gentile inclusion to rest begins to proceed.

A. THE PROOF OF GENTILE CONVERSION (9:32–11:18)

The incident in Caesarea is a watershed moment in Acts, with the salvation of a sympathetic but uncircumcised Gentile. Since the initiator of Cornelius's conversion was God, and since the reception of the Holy Spirit was undeniable, the issue of an unmediated inclusion of Gentiles is also undeniable. This incident continues Luke's theme that the progress of the gospel ethnically and geographically was a movement of God. It is also important that Peter (the apostle and pastor to the Jews) is the main protagonist. Given his status among the disciples, Peter's participation validates the event as few others could.

The story contains four movements. First, a man with a Gk. name (Aeneas) was healed (9:32–35). Second, a disciple named Tabitha (whose name is tr. into Gk. as Dorcas) was raised from the dead (9:36–42). These two events showed that Peter was following God's direction and ministering powerfully in the area. He is innocent of some underhanded agenda. The Cornelius event is narrated (9:43–10:48). The final scene is a firsthand report of what happened in Joppa that concludes with apostolic confirmation (11:1–18). There is no indication that a break with Judaism is the intent. The theological undercurrent was that the inclusion of the Gentiles was not a break with Judaism but the fulfillment of it (Barrett 1.478).

1. The Healing of Aeneas (9:32–35)

9:32 On ἐγένετο δέ, see 4:5. Πέτρον (acc. sg. masc.) διερχόμενον (acc. sg. masc. of pres. mid. ptc. of διέρχομαι; temp.) is the acc. subj. of the inf. κατελθεῖν (aor. act. inf. of κατέρχομαι, "go down"). The inf. phrase functions as the subj. of ἐγένετο (BHGNT 185). Διὰ πάντων (gen. sg. neut.) is a subst. adj., "all places." Κατοικοῦντας (acc. pl. masc. of pres. act. ptc. of κατοικέω; subst.) is followed by Λύδδα (acc. sg. fem. of Λύδδα, -ας, ἡ; in Acts [see 9:38], neut. or indecl. elsewhere; is "Lod" in the OT [see Neh 11:35], southeast of Joppa), an acc. of respect, "at Lydda."

9:33 Εὗρεν (3rd sg. aor. act. indic. of εὑρίσκω) suggests Peter stumbled upon the man (Barrett 1.480). Aeneas is a Gk. name, perhaps proleptic of the emphasis on Gentiles in this section. The prep. phrase ἐξ ἐτῶν ὀκτώ expresses duration (ZG 381). It is best rendered "for eight years" (see, e.g., RSV, NLT, NIV, etc.) modifying κατακείμενον (acc. sg. masc. of pres. mid. ptc. of κατάκειμαι, "recline"; attrib. to ἄνθρωπον). The phrase ἦν παραλελυμένος (nom. sg. masc. of pf. pass. ptc. of παραλύω) is a periph. plpf., "had been paralyzed."

9:34 Peter directly addressed the man. Αἰνέα is the voc. sg. masc. of Αἰνέας, -ου, ὁ. Ἰᾶταί (3rd sg. pres. mid. indic. of ἰάομαι, "heal") is an instantaneous pres. (KMP 259–60; see also Bruce, *Acts of the Apostles*, 247, "aoristic"). Ἀνάστηθι is the 2nd sg. aor. act. impv. of ἀνίστημι, "get up." The phrase στρῶσον (2nd sg. aor. act. impv. of στρωννύω, "spread") σεαυτῷ is an idiomatic phrase mng. "make your own bed" (BDAG 949a; CSB, RSV, NASB, ESV, NET). Ἀνέστη is the 3rd sg. aor. act. indic. of ἀνίστημι.

9:35 Εἶδαν is the 3rd pl. aor. act. indic. of ὁράω. Πάντες is likely hyperbole for a large number (Bock 377). Κατοικοῦντες is the nom. pl. masc. of pres. act. ptc. of κατοικέω; subst. The location Λύδδα (see 9:32) now includes Σαρῶνα (acc. sg. masc. of Σαρων (Σαρρων, -ωνος, ὁ [accent uncertain], "Sharon"; acc. of respect). Sharon includes the coastal plain stretching to Mt. Carmel (Barrett 1.482; Bruce, *Acts of the Apostles*, 247). On οἵτινες, see 7:53. Conversion is expressed with ἐπέστρεψαν (3rd pl. aor. act. indic. of ἐπιστρέφω, "turn toward").

2. The Raising of Tabitha (Dorcas) (9:36–42)

9:36 The location changes to ἐν Ἰόππῃ ("in Joppa"), on the coast. Μαθήτρια (nom. sg. fem. of μαθήτρια, -ας, ἡ) is a female disciple. Ταβιθά (nom. sg. fem., undeclined) is an Aram. name. Διερμηνευομένη (nom. sg. fem. of pres. pass. ptc. of διερμηνεύω, "translate") λέγεται (3rd sg. pres. pass. indic. of λέγω) is a stock phrase for translation. Δορκάς (nom. sg. fem. of Δορκάς, -άδος, ἡ) is "gazelle." She is described with a pred. adj. cstr. with πλήρης, "full," followed by gens. of content (typical with πλήρης) ἔργων ἀγαθῶν . . . ἐλεημοσυνῶν (gen. pl. fem. of ἐλεημοσύνη, -ης, ἡ), "good works" and "alms." Ἐποίει is the 3rd sg. impf. act. indic. of ποιέω.

9:37 On ἐγένετο δέ, see 4:5. Ἀσθενήσασαν is the acc. sg. fem. of aor. act. ptc. of ἀσθενέω; temp. Αὐτήν (acc. sg. fem.) is the subj. of the inf. ἀποθανεῖν (aor. act. inf. ἀποθνήσκω) mng. "she died." Λούσαντες is the nom. pl. masc. of aor. act. ptc. of λούω, "having washed"; attend. circum. or temp. Ἔθηκαν is the 3rd pl. aor. act. indic. of τίθημι, "place." Ἐν ὑπερῴῳ (dat. sg. neut. of ὑπερῷον, -ου, τό) refers to an upper-story room.

9:38 Οὔσης (gen. sg. fem. of pres. act. ptc. of εἰμί) is a causal gen. abs. mng. "because it was near." On Λύδδας (gen. sg. fem. of Λύδδα, -ας, ἡ; subj. of ptc.), see 9:32. Ἀκούσαντες is the nom. pl. masc. of aor. act. ptc. of ἀκούω; temp.) The clause Πέτρος ἐστὶν ἐν αὐτῇ, introduced by ὅτι, is indir. speech, explaining the pres. tense. Ἀπέστειλαν is the 3rd pl. aor. act. indic. of ἀποστέλλω, "send." Παρακαλοῦντες (nom. pl. masc. of pres. act. ptc. of παρακαλέω; purp.) introduces dir. speech. Μὴ ὀκνήσῃς (2nd sg. aor. act. subjunc. of ὀκνέω) is an aor. prohibition, "do not delay." The vb. is compl. by διελθεῖν (aor. act. inf. of διέρχομαι).

9:39 Ἀναστάς (nom. sg. masc. of aor. act. ptc. of ἀνίστημι; attend. circum.) and συνῆλθεν (3rd sg. aor. act. indic. of συνέρχομαι; attend. circum.) suggest Peter's response was immediate. The cstr. ὃν παραγενόμενον (acc. sg. masc. of aor. mid. ptc. of παραγίνομαι; attrib. [lit., "him who had arrived"]) functions like a gen. abs. However, as a rel. pron. it is the dir. obj. of ἀνήγαγον (3rd pl. aor. act. indic. of ἀνάγω, "lead up"; see BHGNT 189). Ὑπερῷον (acc. sg. neut. of ὑπερῷον, -ου, τό, "upper story," cf. 1:13). Παρέστησαν is the 3rd pl. aor. act. indic. of παρίστημι. Κλαίουσαι is the nom. pl. fem. of pres. act. ptc. of κλαίω; manner. It is difficult to know whether the widows (αἱ χῆραι) are an order of widows or those dependent on Dorcas (see Keener 2.1718). That they seem to be the recipients of Dorcas's ministry suggests the latter. That "they showed" (ἐπιδεικνύμεναι, nom. pl. fem. of pres. mid. ptc. of ἐπιδείκνυμι; manner) is in the mid. voice may suggest clothes on the women (BDF §316[1]; Bruce, *Acts of the Apostles*, 249; Z §234), or merely that had been given by her (Barrett 1.485; BHGNT 189). No doubt, however, they were made (ἐποίει, 3rd sg. impf. act. indic. of ποιέω) while (οὖσα, nom. sg. fem. of pres. ptc. of εἰμί; temp.) Dorcas was alive.

9:40 Ἐκβαλών is the nom. sg. masc. of aor. act. ptc. of ἐκβάλλω; temp. The masc. obj. πάντας (acc. pl. masc.) rather than fem. suggests more than the women were present (Barrett 1.485, see v. 41). "Everyone" is a good rendering (MIT, CEB). On θείς (nom. sg. masc. of aor. act. ptc. of τίθημι; temp.) τὰ γόνατα, see 7:60. Προσηύξατο is the 3rd sg. aor. act. indic. of προσεύχομαι. Ἐπιστρέψας is the nom. sg. masc. of aor. act. ptc. of ἐπιστρέφω; attend. circum. Peter's command, Ταβιθά (voc. sg. fem., undecl.) ἀνάστηθι (2nd sg. aor. act. impv. of ἀνίστημι), is sim. to Aeneas's earlier (9:34). The art. ἡ functions as a pron. subj. Ἤνοιξεν is the 3rd sg. aor. act. indic. of ἀνοίγω, "open." Ἰδοῦσα is the nom. sg. fem. of aor. act. ptc. of ὁράω; temp. Ἀνεκάθισεν is the 3rd sg. aor. act. indic. of ἀνακαθίζω, "sit up."

9:41 Δούς is the acc. sg. masc. of aor. act. ptc. of δίδωμι; temp. Ἀνέστησεν is the 3rd sg. aor. act. indic. of ἀνίστημι, "lift up." The ptc. φωνήσας (nom. sg. masc. of aor. act. ptc. of φωνέω) is necessary because he had dismissed them all earlier. It takes a compound dir. obj. (ἁγίους . . . χήρας, "the saints" and "widows"). The vb. παρέστησεν (3rd sg. aor. act. indic. of παρίστημι, "present") takes a double acc. with the dir. obj. αὐτήν and ζῶσαν (acc. sg. fem. of pres. act. ptc. of ζάω) as a compl. ptc.

9:42 Luke summarized the effects of the miracle. Ἐγένετο (3rd sg. aor. mid. indic. of γίνομαι) functions like a cop. here and takes a pred. adj. γνωστόν (nom. sg. neut. of γνωστός, -ή, -όν, "known"). On καθ᾽ ὅλης, see 9:31. Ἰόππης is the gen. sg. fem. of Ἰόππη, -ης, ἡ, "Joppa"; gen. of place. The added information, ἐπίστευσαν (3rd pl. aor.

act. indic. of πιστεύω) πολλοί ("many believed"), transforms the event from mere news to evangelism. On ἐπὶ τὸν κύριον, see 9:35.

HOMILETICAL SUGGESTIONS

Something to Talk About (9:32–43)

Changed lives is a platform for the gospel
1. Sickness can be a platform for the gospel (vv. 32–35)
2. Death of a saint can be a platform for the gospel (vv. 36–43)

3. The Conversion of Cornelius (9:43–10:48)

Keener (2:1730) suggests that several allusions to Jonah appear in the text: Joppa (1:3/9:43); reluctance (1:17/10:16); "arise and go" (3:2/10:20); Gentiles' faith (3:5/10:43); hostile response (4:1/10:14; 11:2); God's response (4:2–11/10:15; 11:17–18). While some parallels are more convincing than others, the thread seems legitimate to apply. At the very least, the allusions demonstrate that God's care for Gentiles is not a new-covenant innovation.

a. Cornelius's Vision (9:43–10:8)

9:43 The introduction of a new character with the formulaic "it came to pass" (on ἐγένετο δέ, see 4:5) begins a new section (although some disagree; see BHGNT 191). On ἡμέρας ἱκανάς, see 8:11. The use of μεῖναι (aor. act. inf. of μένω, compl.) without an acc. subj. is unusual, but clearly Peter is meant (Barrett 1.486). Παρά with a dat. obj. (τινι Σίμωνι, "a certain Simon") suggests someone's house (BDAG 757a). Βυρσεῖ is the dat. sg. masc. of βυρσεύς, -έως, ὁ, "a tanner"; appos. The inf. phrase is either a pred. nom. phrase and the vb. is impers. ("it came to pass" KJV, NKJV) or it is the subj. of the vb. ("He/Peter stayed . . . ," RSV, NLT, NASB, NIV, NRSV, ESV, TNIV, NET).

10:1 The main vb. is an implied copulative vb. that takes Ἀνὴρ . . . τις as the subj. If not, the vb. is in v. 3, although likely too distant. His location is expressed as "in Caesarea" (Καισαρείᾳ, dat. sg. fem. of Καισάρεια, -ας, ἡ). The other noms. "Cornelius" (Κορνήλιος, nom. sg. masc. of Κορνήλιος, -ου, ὁ) and "centurion" (ἑκατοντάρχης, nom. sg. masc. of ἑκατοντάρχης, -ου, ὁ) are appos. to the subj. On ὀνόματι, see 5:1. A σπείρης (gen. sg. fem. of σπεῖρα, -ης, ἡ, "cohort"; obj. of ἐκ) is one-tenth of a legion (c. 600 men, BDAG 936a–b). Ostensibly, Cornelius would have been one of six centurions (Barrett 1.499). Καλουμένης is the gen. sg. fem. of pres. pass. ptc. of καλέω; attrib. Ἰταλικῆς is the gen. sg. masc. of Ἰταλικός, -ή, -όν, "Italian"; subst. adj. Both σπεῖρα and Ἰταλικός are Latin loanwords: *cohors italica*, "Italian cohort." Cornelius would have been a Roman citizen, perhaps retired and settled in Caesarea (Barrett 1.499; although not certain, his status as a God-fearer would make this more likely).

10:2 The noms. in this v. continue the description of Cornelius and are most likely in appos. to ἀνήρ in 10:1. The structure is a subst. adj. (εὐσεβής, nom. sg. masc. of εὐσεβής, -ές, "a pious man") followed by three subst. attrib. ptcs. The first, φοβούμενος (nom. sg. masc. of pres. mid. ptc. of φοβέομαι), takes θεόν as a dir. obj. (and a prep.

phrase incl. his whole house). This is one of several terms to describe a "God-fearer": one who is a Gentile who embraced the God of Israel, but had not fully entered the covenant (i.e., not a full proselyte [Johnson 182]). The second, ποιῶν (nom. sg. masc. of pres. act. indic. of ποιέω), takes ἐλεημοσύνας (acc. pl. fem. of ἐλεημοσύνη, -ης, ἡ, "charities, alms"). Finally, δεόμενος (nom. sg. masc. of pre. mid. ptc. of δέομαι [takes a gen. θεοῦ]) is qualified by διὰ παντός, mng. "regularly" (NLT, NIV, TNIV, NET).

10:3 Εἶδεν is the 3rd sg. aor. act. indic. of ὁράω. The prep. phrase ἐν ὁράματι, "in a vision," is used ten times in Acts for a visionary experience (see 9:10). Φανερῶς is an adv. mng. "clearly" in this context. The combination of the near synonyms ὡσεὶ περί only occurs here in the Gk. Bible and creates an interpretive difficulty. Three solutions are possible:

1. The *byz.* omits περί. It is unlikely, nearly unthinkable, that someone should add the prep. creating such a difficulty. Other turbulence in the transmission (e.g., ℵ* substitutes ὡς) would suggest a number of readers saw a difficulty in ὡσεὶ περί. Therefore, most reject the rdg. although the simplicity of it is appealing.

2. Culy and Parsons suggest the rdg. as it stands is not describing the time of day the vision occurred. Instead, the combination of the adv. and prep. suggest the clarity of the vision. They tr. the phrase "as if it were mid-afternoon" (BHGNT 193). Few have followed them, although their interpretation takes seriously the grammar and should be seriously considered.

3. Finally, most EVV tr. the phrase as an approximation of the time of day. This is consistent with the use of both words. One assumes it is a redundancy. If so, the time of day the vision was received is important as it was a time of prayer at the temple (Bruce, *Acts of the Apostles*, 253; Keener 2.1750).

Although the acc. normally describes an extent of time, here it is a point—something not unheard of in CGk. (R 471). The final two ptcs. (εἰσελθόντα, acc. sg. masc. of aor. act. ptc. of εἰσέρχομαι and εἰπόντα, acc. sg. masc. of aor. act. ptc. of λέγω) are the compls. in a double-acc. cstr.

10:4 The best understanding of the art. ὁ is that it functions as the pron. subj. of εἶπεν. After ἀτενίσας (nom. sg. masc. of aor. act. ptc. of ἀτενίζω, "stare"; attend. circum.) the person viewed is expressed in the dat. (αὐτῷ). The ptc. γενόμενος (nom. sg. masc. of aor. mid. ptc. of γίνομαι) takes the pred. adj. ἔμφοβος (nom. sg. masc. of ἔμφοβος, -ον, "terrified"). Together the ptcs. function as background information to what Cornelius states. The tr. "and he stared at him in terror" (RSV, NLT, NRSV) conveys the mng. best. The address κύριε is simply a respectful address, i.e., without theological significance (Bruce, *Acts of the Apostles*, 254). The response of the angel demonstrates God's approval of Cornelius's actions. His prayers and charitable deeds have gone up (ἀνέβησαν, 3rd pl. aor. act. indic. of ἀναβαίνω) before God. The prep. phrase εἰς μνημόσυνον (acc. sg. neut. of μνημόσυνον, -ου, τό, "memorial") functions much like an acc. of ref. "as a memorial" (RSV, NASB, NIV, NRSV, TNIV, NET).

Barrett takes God's remembering Cornelius on the basis of his actions as indicating that Cornelius deserved salvation. He openly ponders whether this is in contradiction to Pauline theology that sees God's grace as incongruous (Barrett 1.503). Such a contradiction is unnecessary if we consider the place in salvation history. The beginning of Acts clearly takes place in a period where the old covenant and new covenant are "overlapping" (if only practically). In other words, those who were "of Israel" in the old covenant (see, e.g., Rom 9:6) need to be brought into the new. On this understanding, the large Jewish expansion early is understandable. One would expect those "of Israel" to be brought to faith in Christ. Likewise, Cornelius as a God-fearer was one already acceptable to Jews of the time (Keener 2.1755). He is as close to God as the Jews, as evidenced by his offerings (Schnabel 486–87). So then, the "memorial" language is God's acceptance of Cornelius's faith in him. No merit-based salvation is meant. Thus, there is no contradiction with Paul.

FOR FURTHER STUDY

19. God-Fearers (10:2)

*Hemer, C. J. "Appendix 2: The God-Fearers." In BASHH, 444–47.

Koch, D. "The God-Fearers between Facts and Fiction: Two *Theosebeis*-Inscriptions from Aphrodisias and Their Bearing for the New Testament." *ST* 60 (2006): 62–90.

Lake, K. "Proselytes and God Fearers." In *Beginnings* 5, 74–96.

*Levinskaya I. BAFCS, 5.51–126.

McKnight, S. *DNTB*, 835–47.

Wilcox, M. "The 'God-Fearers' in Acts, a Reconsideration." *JSNT* 13 (1981): 102–22.

10:5–6 The angel's instructions were to send (πέμψον, 2nd sg. aor. act. impv. of πέμπω) men to Joppa to summon (μετάπεμψαι, 2nd sg. aor. mid. impv of μεταπέμπω) Peter. He is described as Σίμωνα τινα ("a certain Simon") called (ἐπικαλεῖται, 3rd. sg. pres. pass. indic. of ἐπικαλέω) Peter. The angel described Peter's whereabouts. Ξενίζεται (3rd sg. pres. pass. indic. of ξενίζω, "being hosted") is a term of showing hospitality. Παρά and the dat. describe "at the house of. . ." (BDAG 757a), so most EVV tr. the phrase "lodging/staying with Simon, a tanner" (CSB, RSV, NLT, NASB, NIV, NRSV, ESV, TNIV). The location of the house is expressed by a poss. dat. rel. pron. (ᾧ) phrase: "whose house is by the sea."

10:7–8 Ὡς is temp.: "when" (see 1:10). The subj. of ἀπῆλθεν (3rd sg. aor. act. indic. of ἀπέρχομαι, "depart"), ὁ ἄγγελος ὁ λαλῶν (nom. sg. masc. of pres. act. ptc. of λαλέω; attrib.), is simultaneous to the main vb. The tense and the use of ὡς depicts Cornelius's summoning (φωνήσας, nom. sg. masc. of aor. act. ptc. of φωνέω; temp.) two servants as simultaneous to the angel's departure, i.e., an immediate obedience. Οἰκετῶν (gen. pl. masc. of οἰκέτης, -ου, ὁ; part. gen.) is a house servant. The στρατιώτην εὐσεβῆ ("a pious soldier") seems to be a protective escort for the servants. Προσκαρτερούντων (gen. pl. masc. of pres. act. ptc. of προσκαρτερέω; subst., part. gen., followed by the dat. of pers. [αὐτῷ]). BDAG identifies the group as military aides (BDAG 881a). Thus, the tr. "personal attendants" (NLT, NASB, NIV) is warranted. Ἐξηγησάμενος (nom. sg. masc. of aor. mid. ptc. of ἐξηγέομαι, "explain"; temp.). Ἀπέστειλεν is the 3rd sg. aor. act. indic. of ἀποστέλλω. The prep. phrase εἰς τὴν Ἰόππην employs the art. of previous ref.

b. Peter's Vision (10:9–16)

10:9 Τῇ δὲ ἐπαύριον is an idiomatic phrase mng. "on the next day." Τῇ (ref. an implied ἡμέρᾳ) is a dat. of time indicating a point in time. The gen. abs. phrase uses two ptcs., ὁδοιπορούντων (gen. pl. masc. of pres. act. ptc. of ὁδοιπορέω, "travel"; temp.) and ἐγγιζόντων (gen. pl. masc. of pres. act. ptc. of ἐγγίζω, "draw near"; temp.) that are simultaneous to Peter's actions. Ἀνέβη is the 3rd sg. aor. act. indic. of ἀναβαίνω, "ascend." The prep. phrase ἐπὶ τὸ δῶμα (acc. sg. neut. of δῶμα, -ατος, τό, "rooftop") expresses the destination. The purp. is denoted by the inf. προσεύξασθαι (aor. mid. inf. of προσεύχομαι, "pray"). "The eighth hour" (ὥραν ἕκτην [acc. sg. fem. of ἕκτος, -η, -ον]) is around noon. This is not an organized time to pray but perhaps a convention of those who prayed three times a day (Bruce, *Acts of the Apostles*, 254) or simply an indication that Peter regularly used the siesta time to pray (Keener 2.1762).

10:10 Ἐγένετο functions as a copulative vb. taking πρόσπεινος (nom. sg. masc. of πρόσπεινος, -ον, "hungry") as a pred. adj. Ἤθελεν (3rd sg. impf. act. indic. of θέλω, "want") is compl. by γεύσασθαι (aor. mid. inf. of γεύομαι). It is lit. "to taste," but here the mng. is "to dine" (BDAG 195b). The gen. abs. phrase with παρασκευαζόντων (gen. pl. masc. of pres. act. ptc. of παρασκευάζω; temp.) is best tr. "while they were preparing (lunch)." A trance (ἔκστασις, nom. sg. fem. of ἔκστασις, -εως, ἡ) in CGk. thought came from outside the person; thus, the language makes it the subj. of ἐγένετο rather than Peter. Most EVV tr. it "he fell into a trance."

10:11 Θεωρεῖ (3rd sg. pres. act. indic. of θεωρέω) is one of the rare historical pres. in Acts. Levinsohn notes that in Luke-Acts there are only five nonspeech historical pres. (only here and 10:27 in Acts) that serve to mark the associated information as significant and highlight what follows (Levinsohn 208). The obj. of the vb. is a compound dir. obj., each with a ptc. compl. The first, οὐρανόν (acc. sg. masc. of οὐρανός), takes ἀνεῳγμένον (acc. sg. masc. of pf. pass. ptc. of ἀνοίγω) as a compl. The compl. of the second dir. obj, καταβαῖνον (acc. sg. neut. of καταβαίνω, "coming down"; compl.), is fronted. The obj. σκεῦός (acc. sg. neut. of σκεῦος, -ους, τό) suggests any kind of container. Modified by τι, the best mng. is "something" (RSV, NLT, NIV, NRSV, ESV, TNIV, NET, NJB). It is described as "like a large linen cloth" (ὀθόνην, acc. sg. fem. of ὀθόνη, -ης, ἡ), that is, a sheet. The dat. phrase τέσσαρσιν ἀρχαῖς is a dat. of means modifying the ptc. καθιέμενον (acc. sg. neut. of pres. pass. ptc. of καθίημι; manner), together mng. "being lowered by four corners."

10:12 The contents are related by a prep. phrase with a rel. pron. as the obj. (ἐν ᾧ). Ὑπῆρχεν is the 3rd sg. impf. act. indic. of ὑπάρχω; impers., with a compound pred. nom. compl. The first, πάντα τὰ τετράποδα (nom. pl. neut. of τετράπους, -ους, τό), means "all kinds of four-footed things." The second, ἑρπετὰ (nom. pl. neut. of ἑρπετόν, -οῦ, τό) τῆς γῆς, is "creeping things of the earth" (i.e., reptiles, BHGNT 197). The third, πετεινὰ (nom. pl. neut. of πετεινόν, -οῦ, τό) τοῦ οὐρανοῦ, is "birds of the air." The gen. is likely balancing the previous γῆς.

10:13 The use of ἐγένετο and an anar. φωνή ("a voice came") gives the impression of detachment. Ἀναστάς (nom. sg. masc. of aor. act. ptc. of ἀνίστημι) as an attend. circum. ptc. in this context is impv., "arise," with the sense of urgency rather than simply "get up" (BHGNT 197). Peter (Πέτρε voc. sg. masc. of Πέτρος, -ου, ὁ) is given two commands. Θῦσον (2nd sg. aor. act. impv. of θύω, "slay") is closely connected to ceremonial slaying (BDAG 463b). So then, Barrett suggests it is a religious act Peter is commanded to do (Barrett 1.507). However, Bruce notes that in other contexts θύω (cf. Luke 15:23, 27, and 30) has no cultic mng., so too here (Bruce, *Acts of the Apostles*, 255). Φάγε is the 2nd sg. aor. act. impv. of ἐσθίω, "eat."

10:14 Peter's response was neg. (μηδαμῶς, adv., "by no means," BDAG 647a). The address κύριε (voc. sg. masc.) indicates Peter's recognition of the speaker. Ὅτι is causal. Οὐδέποτε ἔφαγον (1st sg. aor. act. indic. of ἐσθίω) πᾶν is a Sem. idiom mng. "I never ate anything" (Bruce, *Acts of the Apostles*, 255; Z §446). The vb. has a compound dir. obj. of subst. adjs., κοινόν (acc. sg. neut. of κοινός, -ή, -όν, "common") and ἀκάθαρτον (acc. sg. neut. of ἀκάθαρτος, -ον, "unclean"). Luke had made a point at 9:43 that Peter was staying at the home of a tanner, who regularly touched dead bodies (ceremonially unclean). Since Peter referred to food, he cannot be charged with hypocrisy but perhaps being selective. There is no indication that Peter's own opinions regarding Gentiles and the gospel are being addressed. What is clearly and dramatically being addressed is God's will on the matter.

10:15 Φωνή is unexpectedly anar. Ἐκ δευτέρου is a temp. expression mng. "for a second time" (BDAG 221a). The rel. pron. ἅ is "headless" (= "that which"). Θεός is likely a third person expression, identifying the speaker as Christ. Ἐκαθάρισεν is the 3rd sg. aor. act. indic. of καθαρίζω, "cleanse." Σύ is emphatic. Κοίνου (2nd sg. pres. act. impv. of κοινόω, "make common") implies ongoing activity, in this case, "stop what you are doing" (Bock 389; Bruce, *Acts of the Apostles*, 256).

10:16 Τοῦτο ("this") refers to the conversation, not the sheet coming down (Barrett 1.510). The prep. ἐπί is used often with numbers. Here with the adv. τρίς ("three times") the mng. is "This happened three times" (see, e.g., CSB, RSV, NASB, NIV). Ἀνελήμφθη (3rd sg. aor. pass. indic. of ἀναλαμβάνω, "it was taken up") is likely a divine pass. (Rogers and Rogers 252). The subj. σκεῦος (nom. sg. neut. of σκεῦος, -ους, τό, "vessel") is here best tr. "the object" (see 10:11, CSB, NET).

c. Transition to Caesarea (10:17–23a)

10:17 Ὡς is temp. (see 1:10); "while." Ἐν ἑαυτῷ is adv., mng. "inwardly" (RSV, ESV). Διηπόρει is the 3rd sg. impf. act. indic. of διαπορέω, "greatly perplexed." Τί ἂν εἴη (3rd sg. pres. opt. of εἰμί) with the presence of ἄν makes the opt. most likely a potential opt. (i.e., an incomplete 4th class cond., Wallace 485; Z §356; ZG 383). With the rel. pron. clause operating as the dir. obj., the mng. is "[if he could understand] what the vision (ὅραμα, nom. sg. neut. of ὅραμα, -ατος, τό) that he saw might be (i.e., mean)?" On ἰδού, see 1:10. It functions as a transition to the men sent (ἀπεσταλμένοι, nom. pl. masc. of pf. pass. ptc. of ἀποστέλλω; attrib.) by Cornelius. Their activities upon arrival at Joppa are expressed compactly with a temp. ptc. διερωτήσαντες (nom. pl. masc. of aor. act. ptc. of διερωτάω, "inquire"). This is followed by an acc. of ref. (οἰκίαν, acc. sg. fem. of οἰκία, -ας, ἡ). Ἐπέστησαν is the 3rd pl. aor. act. indic. of ἐφίστημι, "stand at." "At/before the gate" is the best tr. of ἐπὶ τὸν πυλῶνα (acc. sg. masc. of πυλών, -ῶνος, ὁ, "gate") (CSB, KJV, RSV, NIV, ESV, TNIV). The presence of a gate at the house suggests that Simon had an above-average level of wealth (BDAG 897b).

10:18 The exact mng. of the ptc. φωνήσαντες (nom. pl. masc. of aor. act. ptc. of φωνέω) is debated (see BHGNT 199). It is either:

1. a ptc. of means "by calling out,"
2. a ptc. of attend. circum. "they called out and . . . ," or
3. a temp. ptc. with the sense "after calling out they were asking." This would seem to make the most sense of an encounter at the gates. Typically, one calls out for attention, then asks for information once someone responds (Rogers and Rogers 252).

Ἐπυνθάνοντο is the 3rd pl. impf. mid. indic. of πυνθάνομαι, "inquiring." The inquiry is a dir. question (as indicated by ἐνθάδε, "here," rather than ἐκεῖ, "there," Barrett 1.510; Bruce, *Acts of the Apostles*, 257). On ξενίζεται, see 10:6.

10:19 Διενθυμουμένου (gen. sg. masc. of pres. mid. ptc. of διενθυμέομαι) with Πέτρου is a temp. gen. abs. phrase mng. "while Peter was pondering." On ἰδού, see 1:10. Ζητοῦντες (nom. pl. masc. of pres. act. ptc. of ζητέω). It is grammatically possible that the ptc. and the nouns are a nom. abs. phrase. However, the lack of a finite vb. (ostensibly with another subj.) makes the identification uncertain (although ἰδού doesn't require a complete sentence, BHGNT 200). Most EVV tr. it as if there were an implied εἰσίν (i.e., a pres. periph. cstr.). Either way the mng. is clear.

10:20 Several EVV tr. ἀλλ᾿ apart from a contrast (see, e.g., KJV, "therefore," or NIV, TNIV, "so,") or simply omit it (see, e.g., ESV, CSB). Zerwick proposes it indicates urgency (ZG 384). However, in that a specific contrast is difficult to see, and it is in an impv. context, it is very sim. to the use at 9:6. As there, it is best to supply an implied contrast from the context. Something like "three men are seeking you, you might be tempted not to trust them, but arise . . ." seems to be the intent (Barrett 1.511). Ἀναστάς (nom. sg. masc. of aor. act. ptc. of ἀνίστημι; attend. circum.) with the impv. κατάβηθι (2nd sg. aor. act. impv. of καταβαίνω) has the sense of "Arise and go down . . . ," i.e., "downstairs" (NLT, NASB, NIV, TNIV). Καὶ πορεύου (2nd sg. pres. mid. impv. of πορεύομαι) with σὺν αὐτοῖς indicates Peter was to be escorted by the three. Διακρινόμενος (nom. sg. masc. of pres. mid. ptc. of διακρίνω) in the mid. means "doubting" (BDAG 231b) with the subst. adj. as the dir. obj. means "doubting nothing" or "without hesitation" (RSV, NRSV, NET). Ὅτι is causal. The pron. ἐγώ (nom. sg.) is emphatic as a redundant nom. pron. Ἀπέσταλκα is the 1st sg. pf. act. indic. of ἀποστέλλω, "sent."

10:21 It is unlikely that Peter was the one who first answered the men (contra Barrett 1:511). The impf. of v. 18 suggests the asking was ongoing when Peter arrived. On ἰδού, see 1:10. Ἐγώ εἰμι means "I am the man" (as in most EVV). Ζητεῖτε is the 2nd pl. pres. act. indic. of ζητέω, "seek." Τίς (nom. sg. masc., interr. pron., "what") assumes a copulative vb. in the first clause of Peter's question. Αἰτία (nom. sg. fem., "reason" or "cause") is a pred. nom. Δι᾿ ἥν (with the acc. rel. pron. as the prep. obj.) is causal. Πάρεστε is the 2nd pl. pres. act. indic. of πάρειμι, "you are present." Altogether the mng. is "what is the reason for your coming?" (KJV, RSV, NASB, NRSV).

10:22 This v. rehearses much of what we have already learned about Cornelius through three nom. of appos. modifying Κορνήλιος. He is a centurion (ἑκατοντάρχης, nom. sg. masc. of ἑκατοντάρχης, -ου, ὁ). The second nom., ἀνήρ, is modified by the adj.

δίκαιος ("righteous") and the attrib. ptc. phrase φοβούμενος (nom. sg. masc. of pres. mid. ptc. of φοβέομαι) τὸν θεόν, "fearing God." Third, he is a man with a good report (μαρτυρούμενος, nom. sg. masc. of pres. pass. ptc. of μαρτυρέω; attrib.) from the Jews. Haenchen (351) notes that the phrase ἔθνους τῶν Ἰουδαίων rather than λαός is appropriate from a Gentile. Ἐχρηματίσθη (3rd sg. aor. pass. indic. of χρηματίζω, "instructed") is to receive a divine instruction, the contents of which are expressed in an inf. (BDAG 1089a). In this case it is twofold: μεταπέμψασθαί (aor. mid. inf. of μεταπέμπω, "summon") and ἀκοῦσαι (aor. act. inf. of ἀκούω) with ῥήματα ("words") as its obj.

10:23a Οὖν suggests obedience to the word of the Holy Spirit (BHGNT 202). Εἰσκαλεσάμενος (nom. sg. masc. of aor. mid. ptc. of εἰσκαλέομαι; temp.) is to invite verbally rather than a formal written summons (MM 188b). It is the normal word to use in such a setting. On ἐξένισεν (3rd sg. aor. act. indic. of ξενίζω), see 10:6.

d. Cornelius's Conversion (10:23b–48)

10:23b Ἀναστάς is the nom. sg. masc. of aor. act. ptc. of ἀνίστημι; attend. circum. Outside of the impv. a sense of urgency might not be in play. On τῇ δὲ ἐπαύριον, see 10:9. Ἐξῆλθεν is the 3rd sg. aor. act. indic. of ἐξέρχομαι, "depart"). Τινες τῶν ἀδελφῶν (part. gen.) is later specified as six (see 11:12; Bruce, *Acts of the Apostles*, 258; Schnabel 495). The second τῶν makes an adj. of the prep. phrase ἀπὸ Ἰόππης. Συνῆλθον is the 3rd pl. aor. act. indic. of συνέρχομαι, "accompany."

10:24 A second ἐπαύριον phrase (see 10:9) marks day four of the story (Barrett 1.513). When Peter entered (εἰσῆλθεν, 3rd sg. aor. act. indic. of εἰσέρχομαι) Caesarea, Cornelius had been preparing for an audience. The periph. impf. ἦν προσδοκῶν (nom. sg. masc. of pres. act. ptc. of προσδοκάω, "wait for") is qualified by the temp. ptc. συγκαλεσάμενος (nom. sg. masc. of aor. mid. ptc. of συγκαλέω, "call together"). Two classes make up the group: first, his relatives (συγγενεῖς, acc. pl. masc. of συγγενής, -ές, "kinsmen"; subst. adj.); second, his close friends. Both are dear to Cornelius. Ἀναγκαίους (acc. pl. masc. of ἀναγκαῖος, -α, -ον; attrib. adj.) has the basic mng. of "necessary," but it is "intimate" when modifying "family" or, as here, "friends" (φίλους, acc. pl. masc. of φίλος, -η, -ον) (see BDAG 60d).

10:25 Elsewhere an initial ἐγένετο often is a Sem. idiom (see 4:5) mng. "it came to pass." Here that is not the mng. because the inf. is art. in the gen. and the v. begins with ὡς. The art. gen. inf. has no sense of purp. as normal (Haenchen 330) but is another Sem. influence. It has "some futurity to it" (Rogers and Rogers 253). The best tr. is "it happened, as Peter was about to enter . . ." (i.e., the encounter takes place in front of the home). Cornelius's reception of Peter suggests he thought of Peter as no normal man. The reception is introduced by two ptcs. of attend. circum.: συναντήσας (nom. sg. masc. of aor. act. ptc. of συναντάω, "meet"; takes a dat. obj.) and πεσών (nom. sg. masc. of aor. act. ptc. of πίπτω). Both are background information to the main vb. προσεκύνησεν (3rd sg. aor. act. indic. of προσκυνέω, "worship"). "Met him, fell at his feet, and worshiped him" expresses it well (KJV, RSV, NASB, ESV).

10:26 The vb. ἤγειρεν (3rd sg. aor. act. indic. of ἐγείρω) implies a gentle rejection of Cornelius's action. While attend. circum., the ptc. λέγων (nom. sg. masc. of pres. act. ptc. of λέγω) in the pres. implies speaking simultaneously with lifting. Ἀνάστηθι is the

2nd sg. aor. act. impv. of ἀνίστημι, "arise." Peter affirmed he had no exalted status with two emphatic uses of a pron. and an adv. καί ("also"). First, the nom. ἐγώ is redundant and emphatic. Second, αὐτός is the intensive use, mng. "myself." All three highlight the anar. pred. nom. ἄνθρωπος, mng. "I too am just a man" (NASB).

10:27 Συνομιλῶν (nom. sg. masc. of pres. act. ptc. of συνομιλέω, "talk with") is temp., mng. "as he was conversing . . . ." The vb. tenses shifting from aor. εἰσῆλθεν (3rd sg. aor. act. indic. of εἰσέρχομαι) to the pres. εὑρίσκει (3rd sg. pres. act. indic. of εὑρίσκω; historical pres.) may suggest surprise on Peter's part (BHGNT 205; see 10:11 for an alt. view). Συνεληλυθότας (acc. pl. masc. of pf. act. ptc. of συνέρχομαι, "gather"; temp.) functions in a double-acc. cstr. with the subst. adj. πολλούς (acc. pl. masc. of πολύς, πολλή, πολύ).

10:28 This v. functions as an explanation of Peter's vision (Haenchen 350). Ἔφη is the 3rd sg. aor. (or impf.) act. indic. of φημί, "said." On τε, see 1:15. Ὑμεῖς (nom. pl. masc. pron., "you") is redundant and emphatic. Ἐπίστασθε (2nd pl. pres. mid. indic. of ἐπίσταμαι, "understand") is only used rarely outside of Acts (nine of fourteen are in Acts). The adv. ὡς introduces the content as indir. speech (R 1046; Bock 393): "how that" (also see R 969). The adj. ἀθέμιτον (nom. sg. neut. of ἀθέμιτος, -ον, "forbidden"; pred. adj.) is only used twice in the NT (here and 1 Pet 4:3). Ἀνδρὶ Ἰουδαίῳ (dat. sg. masc.) is a dat. of ref.: "Jewish man." Κολλᾶσθαι (pres. pass. inf. of κολλάω, "join closely"; epex., i.e., "associate") is paired with προσέρχεσθαι (pres. mid. inf. of προσέρχομαι, "visit,"; epex.; Rogers and Rogers 253). The person visited is in the dat. (BDAG 878a). Rather than "Gentile," Peter used the more benign term ἀλλοφύλῳ (dat. sg. masc. of ἀλλόφυλος, -ον, "foreigner"). The prohibition does not refer to a specific OT law but to Jewish convention regarding impurity (Barrett 1.515–16; Keener 2.1787–92). Barrett cites Jub. 22.16, "keep yourself separate from the nations, and do not eat with them; and do not imitate their rituals, nor associate with them," for the reasons of a permeating impurity from the worship and practice of idolatry (Barrett 1.515). In return, non-Jews thought the Jews very antisocial and suspicious for their separation (Witherington 353). At any rate, Peter rejected it with an advers. κἀμοί (crasis of καί and ἐγώ [dat. sg., indir. obj.], "but to me"). Ἔδειξεν (3rd sg. aor. act. indic. of δείκνυμι, "show") takes the inf. λέγειν (pres. act. inf. of λέγω) as a dir. obj. (R 1037). The inf. takes a double-acc. cstr. with compound compls. (κοινὸν . . . ἀκάθαρτον, "common or unclean") and ἄνθρωπον as the obj. Most EVV apply μηδένα (acc. sg. masc.) to ἄνθρωπον, mng. "no man" or "anyone." God has shown Peter that the gospel is for all people.

10:29 Peter's response to the vision was unqualified obedience. Ἀναντιρρήτως (adv., "without objection") is only used here in the NT. The cognate adj. is used at 19:36: "incontestable" (Bock 394). Μεταπεμφθείς is the nom. sg. masc. of aor. pass. ptc. of μεταπέμπω, "summon"; temp. Note the repetition of the vb. μεταπέμπω in Peter's request (πυνθάνομαι, 1st sg. pres. mid. indic. of πυνθάνομαι, "ask."). He knows why God summoned him; how did Cornelius know? Λόγῳ, a dat. of ref., in this context is "for what reason" or "cause" (NASB, see MM 379d; BDAG 601a). With τίνι (dat. sg. masc. of τίς, interr. pron., adj.) modifying it, "why" is a good tr. (see, e.g., CSB, RSV, NIV). Μετεπέμψασθέ is the 2nd pl. aor. mid. indic. of μεταπέμπω, "summon."

10:30 Ἔφη is the 3rd sg. aor./impf. act. indic. of φημί ("he said"). The phrase ἀπὸ τετάρτης ἡμέρας μέχρι ταύτης τῆς ὥρας is lit. "from the fourth day until this hour." In Eng. convention it is the third day (see NIV, TNIV, NJB), but the reckoning is inclusive; that is, it includes the day of the event (see Bock 394; Keener 2.1793). A second problem is that, with the phrase following, it suggests Cornelius was praying continually since the event he was about to describe. He clearly intends to place the event at the ninth hour four days previous. At issue is mainly the prep. μέχρι ("until"). The solution is that it is either a Sem. idiom (tr. Heb. *'aḏ*) or a Gk. idiom yet to be fully recognized. The lack of serious textual vars. suggests the early Gk. scribes saw no problem with the cstr. (Barrett 1.517). Ἤμην (1st sg. impf. act. indic. of εἰμί) and προσευχόμενος (nom. sg. masc. of pres. mid. ptc. of προσεύχομαι) form a periph. impf. The obj. τὴν ἐνάτην ("the ninth") refers to prescribed prayers at the ninth hour. On ἰδού, see 1:10. Ἔστη is the 3rd sg. aor. act. indic. of ἵστημι. Ἐσθῆτι λαμπρᾷ (dat. sg. fem. of λαμπρός, -ά, -όν; obj. of prep.) means either "bright/clean clothing" or "radiant clothing" (Keener 2.1793).

10:31–32 After φησίν (3rd sg. pres. act. indic. of φημί, "says"; historical pres.), much of these vv. are a repetition of 10:4–6 (see specifics there). Εἰσηκούσθη is the 3rd sg. aor. pass. indic. of εἰσακούω, "heard." Ἐμνήσθησαν is the 3rd pl. aor. pass. indic. of μιμνήσκομαι, "remembered." Πέμψον is the 2nd sg. aor. act. impv. of πέμπω. Μετακάλεσαι is the 2nd sg. aor. act. impv. of μετακαλέω, "summon." Ξενίζεται is the 3rd sg. pres. pass. indic. of ξενίζω, "lodged."

10:33 Cornelius's response is immediate (ἐξαυτῆς, adv., "at once"). Ἔπεμψα is the 1st sg. aor. act. indic. of πέμπω. The nom. pron. σύ is emphatic. The expression καλῶς (adv., "well") ἐποίησας (2nd sg. aor. act. indic. of ποιέω) is an expression of thanks (Bruce, *Acts of the Apostles*, 260). Most EVV tr. it with an expression of kindness, "It was good/kind of you . . . ." Several scholars (see, e.g., Barrett 1.518; Bruce, *Acts of the Apostles*, 260; and T 80) suggest the aor. ptc. παραγενόμενος (nom. sg. masc. of aor. mid. ptc. of παραγίνομαι, "arrive" denotes simultaneous action. However, that seems unnecessary. Only at the arrival has the act of kindness been completed. Thus, a logical sequence of 1) arriving, and 2) having done well, warrants the aor. ptc. (although the aor. ptc. is not necessarily subsequent rel. time, BDF §339). The nom. pron. ἡμεῖς is emphatic (like σύ above). With "before God" (ἐνώπιον τοῦ θεοῦ) between the subj. and the vb. (πάρεσμεν is the 1st pl. pres. act. indic. of πάρειμι, "present") the stakes are elevated. Ἀκοῦσαι is the aor. act. inf. of ἀκούω; purp. Τὰ προστεταγμένα (acc. pl. neut. of pf. pass. ptc. of προστάσσω, "command"; subst.) is the obj. of the inf., mng. "the things having been commanded."

10:34 Several matters mark Peter's response as solemn. First, Luke uses the stock phrase ἀνοίξας . . . τὸ στόμα (see 8:35). Second, since Peter had already been introduced to the scene, the anar. use (one would expect the art. of previous ref.) indicates the speech to follow is a significant development (Levinsohn 197; BHGNT 209). Finally, the prep. phrase ἐπ' ἀληθείας (adv. mng. "truly") represents a choice to elongate the expression. Καταλαμβάνομαι (1st sg. pres. mid. indic. of καταλαμβάνω) in the mid. means "to grasp, understand" (BDAG 520a). Ὅτι summarizes the perception (i.e., indir. discourse without an actual recast statement, Wallace 456). The statement is a pred. nom. cstr. with προσωπολήμπτης (nom. sg. masc., "one who shows partiality") as the pred. nom. This completes the mng. of the vision begun in v. 28.

10:35 Peter contrasted (ἀλλ᾿) what God does not do (v. 34) with what he does, with a pred. adj. cstr. The subjs. are two subst. ptcs., φοβούμενος (nom. sg. masc. of pres. mid. ptc. of φοβέομαι; subst.) and ἐργαζόμενος (nom. sg. masc. of pres. mid. ptc. of ἐργάζομαι; subst.). The latter has the obj. δικαιοσύνην, with the mng. "the one doing what is right" (BDAG 389b). The pred. adj. is δεκτός (nom. sg. masc. of δεκτός, -ή, -όν, "acceptable").

10:36–38 This passage is one of the main exhibits that leads scholars to conclude Acts is an unrevised document (BHGNT 210; see Barrett 1.521, "untranslatable"; Witherington 356; and, with typical reserve, Bruce, *Acts of the Apostles*, 261 calls it "awkward"). Bock's descriptive label "complex" (Bock 396) is preferred. The first difficulty is to establish the text. Most scholars accept the more difficult Alexandrian rdg. that includes ὅν (v. 36) and the ptc. ἀρξάμενος (see below, v. 37) rather than the less troublesome acc. or omission. Both those vars. seem to be attempts to "fix" the text (Bruce, *Acts of the Apostles*, 262; the latter might be unintentional, BHGNT 210) and should be rejected. It does, however, identify the interpretive problems for us.

When ὅν is included the question reverts to how should we then regard the acc. λόγον? The presence of the rel. pron. makes it impossible to be the obj. of ἀπέστειλεν (3rd sg. aor. act. indic. of ἀποστέλλω). That function belongs to the rel. pron. It is best, with most EVV, to take the acc. λόγον (acc. sg. masc.) as the obj. of οἴδατε (2nd pl. pf. act. indic. of οἶδα) in v. 37 (see, e.g., RSV, NIV, TNIV, NET; BHGNT 210). The mng. then is "you know the word that he sent to Israel . . . ." Εὐαγγελιζόμενος (nom. sg. masc. of pres. act. ptc. of εὐαγγελίζω; temp.) takes the obj. εἰρήνην. The clause οὗτός ἐστιν πάντων κύριος ("he is Lord of all") is a parenthetical comment on Ιησοῦ Χριστου. Since λόγον is the dir. obj., the phrase τὸ γενόμενον (acc. sg. neut. of aor. mid. ptc. of γίνομαι; attrib.) ῥῆμα in. v. 37 is a Sem. mng. "the thing that happened" and is appos. and resumptive to the dir. obj. (BHGNT 211; Bruce, *Acts of the Apostles*, 262). On καθ᾿ ὅλης, see 9:31.

The second difficulty is how to take the ptc. ἀρξάμενος (nom. sg. masc. of aor. mid. ptc. of ἀρχόμαι). Since it is nom. it cannot modify the previous ptc. as an attrib. (hence the acc. var.). Older commentators refer to the nom. as impossible to be "syntactically construed" (Metzger 333) and "a piece of careless and uncorrected writing" (Barrett 1.524). This assessment is no longer justified. In more recent commentaries the cstr. has been identified as part of Luke's particular idiolect. Like the expression in Luke 23:5, it modifies an implicit idea, epex. of τὸ γενόμενον ῥῆμα (see Thompson 359; BHGNT Luke 705; BDF §137[3] "used absolutely in a quasi-adverbial sense"). The public ministry of Christ began in Galilee after (μετά + acc.) John's preaching (ἐκήρυξεν, 3rd sg. aor. act. indic. of κηρύσσω) about baptism.

The acc. Ἰησοῦν is appos. to αὐτόν but fronted to demonstrate it is the focus of the sentence, although not the formal subj. (BHGNT 211; Bruce, *Acts of the Apostles*, 262; Bock 398). The acc. art. makes the phrase τὸν ἀπὸ Ναζαρέθ attrib. adj. to Ἰησοῦν. He was anointed (ἔχρισεν, 3rd sg. aor. act. indic. of χρίω) with the Holy Spirit (πνεύματι ἁγίῳ, both dat. sg. neut.) and power (δυνάμει, dat. sg. fem.; both are instr. dats.) is perhaps an allusion to Ps Sol. 17:37 (Bruce, *Acts of the Apostles*, 262) or more likely Isa 61:1 (Beale and Carson 580). Formally διῆλθεν (3rd sg. aor. act. indic. of διέρχομαι) is rendered "passed through," but without a specific object the best rendering is "went about" (CSB, KJV, RSV, NASB, NRSV, ESV). Both the following ptcs. are ptcs. of manner: εὐεργετῶν (nom. sg. masc. of pres. act. ptc. of εὐεργετέω, "do good works") and ἰώμενος (nom. sg. masc. of pres. mid. ptc. of ἰάομαι, "heal"). Καταδυναστευομένους (acc. pl. masc. of pres. pass. ptc. of καταδυναστεύω, "oppress"; subst.) is only used in the NT here and Jas 2:6, although thirty-two times in the LXX. The agent of the oppression is ὑπὸ τοῦ διαβόλου, and it likely has both physical and spiritual dimensions. Ὅτι is causal. That "God was with him" is also sim. to Ps Sol. 17:38 (a passage about the Messiah, Bock 398).

10:39 The testimony continues with Peter's affirmation of being an eyewitness to Jesus's ministry. The phrase ἡμεῖς μάρτυρες is a pred. nom. cstr. with an assumed ἐσμέν (unlike the sim. clause in 2:32). Ἐποίησεν is the 3rd sg. aor. act indic. of ποιέω. Most EVV omit the adv. καί ("also"). Ἀνεῖλαν is the 3rd pl. aor. act. indic. of ἀναιρέω ("take up," i.e., to kill). Κρεμάσαντες (nom. pl. masc. of aor. act ptc. of κρεμάννυμι) is a ptc. of manner, "by hanging." Ref. the cross as ξύλον occurs only five times in the NT (Acts 5:30; 10:40; 13:29; Gal 3:13; 1 Pet 2:24). Twice Paul uses the term; three times it is Peter, who all three times uses the prep. phrase ἐπὶ ξύλου. Given Paul's usage, it likely has a ref. to Deut 21:22–23 and the mng. of the death as under a curse.

10:40 His death is followed by the report of resurrection. Ἤγειρεν is the 3rd sg. aor. act. indic. of ἐγείρω. Τῇ τρίτῃ ἡμέρᾳ (dat. sg. fem.) is a dat. of time signifying a point in time, "on the third day." Ἔδωκεν is the 3rd sg. aor. act. indic. of δίδωμι. Γενέσθαι (aor. mid. inf. of γίνομαι) compl. the vb. Ἐμφανῆ (acc. sg. masc. of ἐμφανής, -ές, "visible"; pred. adj.) is lit. "he granted him to become visible" but has the sense of "allowed him to be seen" (See NLT, CEB).

10:41 Much of this v. is a compound indir. obj. phrase of an implicit "He was visible." Παντὶ τῷ λαῷ (dat. sg. masc. of λαός, -οῦ, ὁ), "to all the people," refers to the people of Israel. In contrast (ἀλλά), the disciples were eyewitnesses (μάρτυσιν, dat. sg. masc. of μάρτυς, μάρτυρος, ὁ; indir. obj. of the same implied clause). This status is emphasized throughout the rest of the v. The subst. ptc. προκεχειροτονημένοις (dat. pl. masc. of pf. pass. ptc. of προχειροτονέω, "choose beforehand"; NT hapax), mng. "the ones who had been chosen," is attrib. to μάρτυσιν. The eyewitness status is emphasized even more through an appos. pron. phrase ἡμῖν (dat. pl. of ἐγώ; appos.) On οἵτινες, see 7:53. The clause features a compound vb. cstr., συνεφάγομεν (1st pl. aor. act. indic. of συνεσθίω, "eat together") and συνεπίομεν (1st pl. aor. act. indic. of συμπίνω, "drink together"). Both take αὐτῷ as dir. obj. The inf. phrase τὸ ἀναστῆναι αὐτόν (aor. act. inf. of ἀνίστημι) functions as the obj. of the prep. μετά, mng. "after he was raised."

10:42 Παρήγγειλεν (3rd sg. aor. act. indic. of παραγγέλλω, "command") takes a dat. obj. (ἡμῖν) and a compl. inf. (BDAG 760b). In this case it is a compound cstr., κηρύξαι (aor. act. inf. of κηρύσσω) and διαμαρτύρασθαι (aor. mid. inf. of διαμαρτύρομαι, "solemnly testify"). The content of the command is introduced as indir. speech by ὅτι, expressed as a pred. nom. with the vb. ἐστίν. The pron. οὗτος (nom. sg. masc.; subj.) refers to Christ. The pred. nom. is a subst. ptc. that functions much like a double-acc.

cstr., but is in a pred. nom. cstr. with a compl., ὡρισμένος (nom. sg. masc. of pf. pass. ptc. of ὁρίζω), mng. "the one having been appointed." Κριτής (masc. nom. sg. of κριτής, -οῦ, ὁ) is the compl., mng. "as judge." Ζώντων (gen. pl. masc. of pres. act. ptc.) and νεκρῶν (gen. pl. masc.; subst. adj.) are both obj. gens., "the living and the dead."

10:43 The dat. of ref., τούτῳ, is fronted as the topic of the sentence even though προφῆται (nom. pl. masc. of προφήτης) is the subj. of the main vb. μαρτυροῦσιν (3rd pl. pres. act. indic. of μαρτυρέω). Ἄφεσιν (acc. sg. fem. of ἄφεσις -έσεως, ἡ, "forgiveness") is the obj. of λαβεῖν (aor. act. inf. of λαμβάνω; purp.). Διὰ τοῦ ὀνόματος ("through the name") expresses the means of gaining forgiveness, recalling the use at 2:21. The acc. subst. ptc. phrase πάντα πιστεύοντα (acc. sg. masc. of pres. act. ptc. of πιστεύω) is the subj. of the inf. That it is "all the ones believing" is particularly germane to this Gentile context (Schnabel 504).

10:44 God's confirmation is seen in the dispensing of the Spirit (Bock 400). Ἔτι λαλοῦντος (gen. sg. masc. of pres. act. ptc. of λαλέω; temp., gen. abs.) describes the Spirit's falling (ἐπέπεσεν, 3rd sg. aor. act. indic. of ἐπιπίπτω) while Peter was still speaking. Ἀκούοντας (acc. pl. masc. of pres. act. ptc. of ἀκούω; subst., obj. of prep.) describes the entirety of the audience.

10:45 Ἐξέστησαν is the 3rd pl. aor. act. indic. of ἐξίστημι, "amaze." Ἐκ περιτομῆς in the attrib. position (between οἱ and πιστοί) functions as an adj.: "the believers of the circumcision." Ὅσοι (nom. pl. masc. of ὅσος, -η, -ον, "as many as") limits "the circumcision" to those who came (συνῆλθαν, 3rd pl. aor. act. indic. of συνέρχομαι) with Peter. Ὅτι is causal. The adv. καί makes it clear that it was not the falling of the Spirit that was unexpected but falling upon the Gentiles (ἐπὶ τὰ ἔθνη). That prep. is fronted for emphasis. Ἁγίου πνεύματος is an epex. gen., "the gift which is the Holy Spirit" (BHGNT 215). Ἐκκέχυται is the 3rd sg. pf. pass. indic. of ἐκχέω; in the sequence of vb. tenses (i.e., rel. time), the pf. comes before the aor. ἐξέστησαν, so it functions like a plpf.: "it had been poured out" (Barrett 1.529; BDF §345). It is a common term for the coming of the Spirit in Acts (see 2:17, 18, 33; 22:20).

10:46a Γάρ gives the basis for identifying that it is the Spirit falling. Ἤκουον (3rd pl. impf. act. indic. of ἀκούω) takes a double-gen. obj.-compl. cstr. αὐτῶν (gen. pl. masc.) as the obj. and two ptcs. Λαλούντων (gen. pl. masc. of pres. act. ptc. of λαλέω) is the first compl. Γλώσσαις (dat. pl. fem. of γλῶσσα; instr.) ref. to the same experience as at Acts 2:4. It is most likely that they understood what was being said for the content is the second compl. μεγαλυνόντων (gen. pl. masc. of pres. act. ptc. of μεγαλύνω, "magnify"). God (Θεόν) is the object of their praise.

10:46b–47 Ἀπεκρίθη (3rd sg. aor. pass. indic. of ἀποκρίνομαι) is used even though technically he "answers" no one. Most EVV follow Bruce's advice and simply tr. it "said" (Bruce, *Acts of the Apostles*, 264). Μήτι (interr. particle) introduces a question that expects a "no" answer (Bock 401). Δύναται (3rd sg. pres. mid. indic. of δύναμαι) takes an inf. compl. (κωλῦσαι, aor. act. inf. of κωλύω, "forbid") that takes ὕδωρ (acc. sg. neut. of ὕδωρ, -ατος, τό, "water") as its obj. The inf. with a gen. art. (τοῦ μὴ βαπτισθῆναι, aor. pass. inf. of βαπτίζω) indicates purp. Τούτους (acc. pl. masc. of οὗτος, αὕτη, τοῦτο) is the subj. of the inf. Οἵτινες (see 7:53) modifies τούτους. Ἔλαβον is the 3rd pl. aor. act. indic. of λαμβάνω. The last phrase, ὡς καὶ ἡμεῖς, is lit. "as also we," best rendered "just as we have" (NIV, ESV, TNIV, NJB). Peter connected the purification of the Spirit to a transformed heart (Schnabel 505), thus qualification for baptism.

10:48 Peter's question in the previous v. was clearly rhetorical, for he next ordered (προσέταξεν, 3rd sg. aor. act. indic. of προστάσσω) baptism (βαπτισθῆναι, aor. pass. inf. of βαπτίζω). The prep. phrase ἐν τῷ ὀνόματι Ἰησοῦ Χριστοῦ differs from 2:38's ἐπί . . . , in that at Pentecost the appeal was to come to Christ. Here it is the result of coming to Christ (on this use of ὄνομα, see 2:21). Wanting to hear more, the new believers (the unexpressed subj., Barrett 1.531) requested (ἠρώτησαν, 3rd pl. aor. act. indic. of ἐρωτάω) to stay (ἐπιμεῖναι, aor. act. inf. of ἐπιμένω; compl.) ostensibly for more on Jesus. On ἡμέρας τινὰς, see 9:19.

HOMILETICAL SUGGESTIONS

The Candidate for Baptism (10:1–48)

1. They are drawn by God to Christ (vv. 1–23)
2. They hear the true gospel (vv. 24–43)
3. They make Christ their King (vv. 44–48)

4. Apostolic Confirmation (11:1–18)

11:1 Δέ marks a shift in the story to the report and defense of the event. Ἤκουσαν is the 3rd pl. aor. act. indic. of ἀκούω. Οἱ ὄντες (nom. pl. masc. of pres. ptc. of εἰμί; attrib.) modifies ἀδελφοί (nom. pl. masc. of ἀδελφός, -οῦ, ὁ, "brothers"). The prep. phrase κατὰ τὴν Ἰουδαίαν expresses extent, "throughout Judea" (CSB, NASB, NIV, ESV, TNIV, NET; see BDF §225). The limitation of the phrase is a tacit recognition that there were also brothers in Samaria and Damascus. It was, however, the Judean group that would be troubled with Gentile fellowship. The conj. ὅτι introduces indir. speech. Καί is adv. Ἐδέξαντο is the 3rd pl. aor. mid. indic. of δέχομαι, "receive." Τὸν λόγον τοῦ θεου is a ref. to the gospel (see 8:14).

11:2 On ἀνέβη (3rd sg. aor. act. indic. of ἀναβαίνω, "ascend") in ref. to Jerusalem, see 3:1. Διεκρίνοντο (3rd pl. impf. mid. indic. of διακρίνω) with the prep. phrase πρὸς αὐτόν (lit. "with him," but many EVV tr. simply as the dir. obj.), has the sense of "they were criticizing him" (BDAG 231b) or "took issue with him" (NASB, NET). Οἱ (nom. pl. masc. of ὁ) nominalizes the prep. phrase ἐκ περιτομῆς ("those of the circumcision"). Since there is no demand for circumcising the Gentile converts, they cannot be identified with the Judaizers of 15:5 (Schnabel 408).

11:3 Λέγοντες (nom. pl. masc. of pres. act. ptc. of λέγω) ὅτι has been interpreted as an indir. interr., "why?" (Bruce, *Acts of the Apostles*, 267; Barrett 1.537). However, it is a normal example of ὅτι *recatativum* (i.e., it introduces the essence of the complaint as dir. speech [Keener 2.1818]). The circumcision party does not question but accuses Peter of table fellowship with Gentiles (Bock 408). It is a purity issue that has failed to grasp the newness of the new covenant. See Luke 5:36, "The new is not just a patch that can be added to the old" (Thompson 95). The obj. of the vb. εἰσῆλθες (2nd sg. aor. act. indic. of εἰσέρχομαι, "enter") is not specified, but one may infer "house" (BDAG

294a; ZG 386). Πρὸς ἄνδρας with the vb. suggests a goal, "to men" (BDAG 874b). "Men" is modified by an attrib. ptc. phrase. Ἀκροβυστίαν (acc. sg. fem. of ἀκροβυστία, -ας, ἡ, "uncircumcision") is the obj. of ἔχοντας (acc. pl. masc. of pres. act. ptc. of ἔχω). The phrase is best rendered as "to uncircumcised men" (RSV, NASB, ESV, NET). Συνέφαγες (2nd sg. aor. act. indic. of συνεσθίω, "eat with") takes the dat. αὐτοῖς as its obj. and completes the complaint.

11:4–5 Peter's reply did not address table fellowship directly. He reported the Lord's activity in saving these Gentiles, making table fellowship a moot point: they are now brothers and sisters. Ἀρξάμενος (nom. sg. masc. of aor. mid. ptc. of ἄρχω) has been variously classified. It might be:

1. pleonastic (i.e., redundant, BDF §419; Barrett 1.538–39; Bruce, *Acts of the Apostles*, 268). That would explain why there is no compl. inf. as is often the case with ἄρχομαι.

2. Λέγων (nom. sg. masc. of pres. act. ptc. of λέγω), however, is clearly pleonastic and, if 1 were correct, creates the difficulty of having two pleonastic ptc. reduplicate the same word (ἐξετίθετο, 3rd sg. impf. mid. indic. of ἐκτίθημι, "explain"). So the second option is that it is an attend. circum. ptc. This suggests that Peter started from the beginning of the story, not beginning to speak (BHGNT 218; Rogers and Rogers 254).

Καθεξῆς is an adv. mng. "in order." Compare with 10:10–17 for many details of 11:5–12. Ἤμην (1st sg. impf. indic. of εἰμί) . . . προσευχόμενος (nom. sg. masc. of pres. mid. ptc. of προσεύχομαι; periph. impf. mng. "I was praying") has an emphatic ἐγώ as its subj. Εἶδον (1st sg. aor. act. indic. of ὁράω) is modified by ἐν ἐκστάσει (dat. sg. fem. of ἔκστασις, -εως, ἡ), an adv. temp. expression mng. "while in a trance." Ὅραμα (acc. sg. neut. of ὅραμα, -ατος, τό) is the dir. obj. of εἶδον. Καταβαῖνον (acc. sg. neut. of pres. act. ptc. of καταβαίνω) is compl. to σκεῦος (acc. sg. neut. of σκεῦος, -ους, τό) that is in appos. to ὅραμα. Τι ὡς is best tr. "something like" and is appos. and epex. to σκεῦος. Τέσσαρσιν ἀρχαῖς (both dat. pl. masc.) is an instr. of means, "by four corners." Καθιεμένην (acc. sg. fem. of pres. pass. ptc. καθίημι) is best tr. "being lowered." The prep. ἄχρι ("unto") in the last clause suggests the sheet was coming directly at Peter. Thus the tr. "right down to me" (NASB).

11:6 Verse 6 is complicated by three verbal forms mng. "see" in one sense or another. Most EVV drop one of them. The first is the attend. circum. ptc. ἀτενίσας (nom. sg. masc. of aor. act. ptc. of ἀτενίζω), which, with the prep. phrase, is "having stared into it." The main vb. of the clause κατενόουν (1st sg. impf. act. indic. of κατανοέω) is best understood as an iter. impf. (Wallace 549), "I was observing carefully." The final vb. εἶδον (1st sg. aor. act. indic. of ὁράω) relates what he saw with the same description that 10:11 expressed as dir. objs. The exception is θηρία (acc. pl. neut. of θηρίον, -ου, τό, "wild animal").

11:7 Peter continued. Ἤκουσα (1st sg. aor. act. indic. of ἀκούω) καί (adv.) is "I also heard . . ." Φωνῆς is the gen. dir. obj. of the vb. The ptc. λεγούσης (gen. sg. fem. of pres. act. ptc. of λέγω) with the pron. indir. obj. functions as a compl. ptc., "saying to me." On the phrase ἀναστάς, Πέτρε, θῦσον καὶ φάγε, see 10:13. Ἀναστάς is the nom. sg. masc. of aor. act. ptc. of ἀνίστημι; attend. circum.

11:8 Peter's reported response (εἶπον, 1st sg. aor. act. indic. of λέγω) is a close repetition of 10:14. Notably the clause εἰσῆλθεν (3rd sg. aor. act. indic. of εἰσέρχομαι) εἰς τὸ στόμα μου replaces ἔφαγον. Some word order is also different.

11:9 Again, the report is sim. to 10:15. The first part employs synonyms and word order changes. Ἀπεκρίθη is the 3rd sg. of aor. pass. ptc. of ἀποκρίνομαι. On ἐκ δευτέρου and the clause ἃ ὁ θεὸς ἐκαθάρισεν, σὺ μὴ κοίνου, see the comments at 10:15.

11:10 For details, see 10:16. The report is very sim. except that ἀνεσπάσθη (3rd sg. aor. pass. indic. of ἀνασπάω) and πάλιν, "it was taken up again," replaces εὐθὺς ἀνελήμφθη. Also, ἅπαντα (acc. pl. neut. of ἅπας, ἅπασα, ἅπαν, "all things"; dir. obj.) replaces τὸ σκεῦος.

11:11 On καὶ ἰδού, see 1:10. Ἐξαυτῆς is an adv. mng. "immediately." Ἐπέστησαν is the 3rd sg. aor. act. indic. of ἐφίστημι, "stand." The prep. phrase ἐπὶ τὴν οἰκίαν describes the men at the gate (see 10:17). Ἀπεσταλμένοι (nom. pl. masc. of pf. pass. ptc. of ἀποστέλλω) is attrib. modifying ἄνδρες (BHGNT 221; Rogers and Rogers 255).

11:12 Εἶπεν (3rd sg. aor. act. indic. of λέγω) is still part of Peter's speech. Peter expressed the Spirit's instruction in indir. speech with an inf. (συνελθεῖν, aor. act. inf. of συνέρχομαι). The expression μηδὲν διακρίναντα (acc. sg. masc. of aor. act. ptc. of διακρίνω, "doubt, waver"; manner), "without hesitation," is reminiscent of 10:20 (see also 10:29). Peter gave new information in that with him came (ἦλθον, 3rd pl. aor. act. indic. of ἔρχομαι) οἱ ἓξ ἀδελφοί (nom. pl. masc. of ἀδελφός, -οῦ, ὁ) οὗτοι, "these six brothers." Since they were from the circumcision (see 10:45), Peter indicated he was not the only one who entered the house (εἰσήλθομεν, 1st pl. aor. act. indic. of εἰσέρχομαι; see Johnson 198).

11:13 Ἀπήγγειλεν (3rd sg. aor. act. indic. of ἀπαγγέλλω) has the sense of "he explained," referring to the previous ref. of ἀνδρός. Πῶς introduces indir. speech (like 9:27). Εἶδεν is the 3rd sg. aor. act. indic. of ὁράω. Two compl. ptcs. expand the event. The first, σταθέντα (acc. sg. masc. of aor. pass. ptc. of ἵστημι), reinforces the actual presence of the angel. The second, εἰπόντα (acc. sg. masc. of aor. act. ptc. of λέγω), introduces the commands of the angel. The command is twofold: "send" (ἀπόστειλον, 2nd sg. aor. act. impv. of ἀποστέλλω) assumes a dir. obj., "men." The second is to "summon" (μετάπεμψαι, 2nd sg. aor. mid. impv. of μεταπέμπω) Simon, called (ἐπικαλούμενον, acc. sg. masc. of pres. pass. ptc. of ἐπικαλέω) "Peter."

11:14 The fut. vb. λαλήσει (3rd sg. fut. act. indic. of λαλέω) suggests the purp. of the meeting. The content/purp. of the words (ῥήματα, acc. pl. neut. of ῥῆμα, -ατος, τό) is expressed in a prep. phrase, ἐν οἷς. It identifies the purp. as salvation (σωθήσῃ, 2nd sg. fut. pass. indic. of σῴζω). Καὶ πᾶς ὁ οἶκός σου, "and your whole house," is not a promise for "household salvation" but indicates that the words are for everyone in his house, not just Cornelius.

11:15 On the temp. phrase with ἐν and the inf., see 2:1. In this case, the inf. ἄρξασθαι (aor. mid. inf. of ἄρχομαι) is compl. by another inf., λαλεῖν (pres. act. inf. of λαλέω). Ἐπέπεσεν is the 3rd sg. aor. act. indic. of ἐπιπίπτω, "fell upon." The last clause assumes a repetition of ἐπέπεσεν. Ὥσπερ . . . ἐν ἀρχῇ ("just as . . . in the beginning") recalls the events at Pentecost (Bruce, *Acts of the Apostles*, 269).

11:16 Ἐμνήσθην (1st sg. aor. pass. indic. of μιμνήσκομαι) takes the gen. ῥήματος (gen. sg. neut. of ῥῆμα, -ατος, τό) as its dir. obj. Ὡς, sim. to ὅτι in this context, introduces dir. speech (BDAG 1105c). The impf. ἔλεγεν (3rd sg. impf. act. indic. of λέγω) is possibly the "pluperfective impf." (see Wallace 550, although he cites it otherwise), "he had said" (cf. NIV, NRSV; see the tr. in BHGNT 217). In Luke, John states these words. Rather than a misattribution (see Barrett 1.542) the impf. may suggest repeated teaching by Jesus as ref. at 1:5 (thus, Wallace [549] suggests it is customary or iter.). The saying itself is identical to 1:5 except for a minor word-order variation. See comments there. That Peter assigned the baptism to the conversion of Cornelius and his house suggests strongly βαπτισθήσεσθε (2nd pl. fut. pass. indic. of βαπτίζω) ἐν πνεύματι ἁγίῳ ("in the Holy Spirit") refers to the initial indwelling of the Spirit.

11:17 Peter's ultimate defense is presented in a cond. sentence. Τὴν ἴσην (acc. sg. fem. of ἴσος, -η, -ον, "equal") δωρεάν (acc. sg. fem. of δωρεά, -ᾶς, ἡ; dir. obj.) is fronted for emphasis, "the same gift." The antecedent and classification of the ptc. πιστεύσασιν (dat. pl. masc. of aor. act. ptc. of πιστεύω) is debated.

1. If it modifies αὐτοῖς, the ref. is to the house of Cornelius. "He gave to those who believed" (attrib.) or "those after believing" (temp.) is the sense. Barrett prefers it if "Luke is thinking logically" (Barrett 1.542). Grammatically, the distance between the constituents makes this an unlikely choice.

2. It might modify both αὐτοῖς and ἡμῖν. Several twentieth-century scholars prefer this solution (Barrett 1.542; Bruce, *Acts of the Apostles*, 269; Haenchen 355). Theologically, this is Peter's point. However, grammatically the nearer ἡμῖν is more likely (BHGNT 223). If so, he highlights that the Jews had to first believe as well. The next question then is, what is the classification?

3. If it is attrib. to ἡμῖν, it should be tr. " . . . to us who believed" (KJV, NIV, TNIV, CEB; BHGNT 217, 224). One would expect it more in the attrib. position if this were the case.

4. If it is a temp. ptc. modifying ἡμῖν, the tr. should be "after we believed . . ." (NASB, NET). EVV that tr. it "when we believed" (KJV, RSV, NLT, NRSV, ESV) run the risk of suggesting the moment of belief was Pentecost (clearly not the case). Instead, Peter is merely stating the logical sequence of belief and baptism. He does not here give credence to the Pentecostal doctrine of Spirit baptism after salvation (see comments at 11:21).

In the apod., the presence of δυνατός (nom. sg. masc. of δυνατός, -ή, -όν, "able") as a pred. adj. forces us to consider ἐγὼ τίς as a pred. nom. cstr. with an assumed being vb: "Who was I?" (because you cannot have a pred. adj. and a pred. nom. in the same sentence, BHGNT 224; see also BDF §298; Bruce, *Acts of the Apostles*, 270; T 89). The final clause with ἤμην (1st sg. impf. indic. of εἰμί) takes the pred. adj. δυνατός with κωλῦσαι (aor. act. inf. of κωλύω, "forbid") as a compl. inf. The best rendering is "Who was I? Was I able to forbid God?" Thus, Peter called for a judgment.

11:18 Ἀκούσαντες (nom. pl. masc. of aor. act. ptc. of ἀκούω) is best classified as a temp. ptc. "after hearing these things" (ταῦτα, acc. pl. neut. of οὗτος, αὕτη, τοῦτο). Ἡσύχασαν (3rd pl. aor. act. indic. of ἡσυχάζω) is an ingressive aor., "they grew silent." This is best understood as "stopped disputing" (see KJV, NLT, NIV, TNIV, NET).

'Εδόξασαν is the 3rd pl. aor. act. indic. of δοξάζω. Λέγοντες (nom. pl. masc. of pres. act. ptc. of λέγω) introduces the content of their praise. Ἔθνεσιν (dat. pl. neut. of ἔθνος, -ους, τό) is fronted for emphasis. The dir. obj., τὴν μετάνοιαν εἰς ζωήν ("repentance unto life"), is also fronted and recalls Peter's invitation in Acts 2. Repentance is understood to be an integral part of salvation, even though it was not mentioned in the story above. Ἔδωκεν is the 3rd sg. aor. act. indic. of δίδωμι.

HOMILETICAL SUGGESTIONS

When Racism Meets the Gospel (11:1–18)

1. A biased accusation: unbiblical attitudes about Gentiles (vv. 1–3)
2. An unbiased report: God made Gentiles brothers without circumcision (vv. 4–17)
3. A humble realization and retraction (v. 18)

B. GENTILE CONVERSION IN ANTIOCH AND
THE RETURN OF PAUL (11:19–26)

This section introduces the founding of the church at Antioch. It describes an influx of Gentiles into the church and Barnabas's stabilizing influence. It brings Paul back on the scene, staging the larger Gentile mission. The import here is momentous. The unmediated inclusion of the Gentiles was confessed almost theoretically in the previous section. Here, enthusiastic evangelists are seeking them out with great success. With the inclusion of Gentiles, Christianity cannot be merely a sect within Judaism (as the term, "the Way," might suggest, cf. 9:2). Another name seemed appropriate. Here it is a dimin. of "Christ," signifying a follower of Christ (BDF §5[2]). Grammatically, it is sim. to words like Ἡρῳδιανοί ("Herodians") that are also dimin. Given that Χριστός is a title rather than a proper name at this time, something like "Messianists" is appropriate (Johnson 205). There is little warrant for the popular notion that the term itself indicates the character of the disciples.

11:19 On μὲν οὖν, see 1:16. Διασπαρέντες (nom. pl. masc. of aor. pass. ptc. of διασπείρω) is subst.: "those having been scattered." While the prep. ἀπό often has a sense of separation, in the phrase ἀπὸ τῆς θλίψεως it indicates source and takes a causal force, "because of the persecution" (ZG 388; see also Bruce, *Acts of the Apostles*, 271; Rogers and Rogers 255). Γενομένης is the gen. sg. fem. of aor. mid. ptc. of γίνομαι; attrib. Ἐπὶ Στεφάνῳ should not be taken in the sense of "against Stephen" (contra BDAG 366a) but in a causal sense "over Stephen" (ZG 389; Z §126). Διῆλθον is the 3rd pl. aor. act. indic. of διέρχομαι, "pass through." The prep. ἕως sets the limit to the travel, mng. "as far as." Μηδενί ("to no one") is the indir. obj. of λαλοῦντες (nom. sg. masc. of pres. act. ptc. of λαλέω; manner [BHGNT 225]). Τὸν λόγον (acc. sg. obj. of the ptc.), as usual for Acts, refers to the gospel. Εἰ μή (mng. "except") qualifies the statement with another indir. obj. phrase μόνον Ἰουδαίοις ("to Jews alone").

11:20 Ἦσαν (3rd pl. impf. indic. of εἰμί) takes τινες (nom. pl. masc. of τὶς, τὶ) as a pred. nom. with the prep. phrase functioning as a part. gen. ἐξ αὐτῶν. The best tr. is "there were some of them" (see, e.g., RSV, NASB, NET). Ἄνδρες is likely a nom. of appos. to τινες as Κύπριοι (nom. pl. masc. of Κύπριος, -ου, ὁ, "Cyprians") and Κυρηναῖοι (nom. pl. masc. of Κυρηναῖος, -ου, ὁ, "Cyrenians") are to ἄνδρες. Ἐλθόντες is the nom. pl. masc. of aor. act. ptc. of ἔρχομαι; temp. Ἐλάλουν (3rd pl. impf. indic. act. of λαλέω) is likely an ingressive impf., "they began speaking" (see NASB, NET, TNIV, NLT, NIV, CEB). Καί is adv., "also." Ἑλληνιστάς earlier was likely Gk.-speaking Jews. Here in Antioch, that does not seem to be the case, for it is cast as unusual (Barrett 1.550–51; Keener 2.1842). Εὐαγγελιζόμενοι is the nom. pl. masc. of pres. mid. ptc. of εὐαγγελίζομαι; manner.

11:21 Ἦν is the 3rd sg. impf. indic. of εἰμί. The subj. phrase χεὶρ (nom. sg. fem. of χείρ, χειρός, ἡ, "hand") κυρίου is euphemistic, mng. something like "the power of the Lord." Or it may denote the Holy Spirit (see Bruce, *Acts of the Apostles*, 272; Johnson 203). Either way, it endorses the work as an act of God (Haenchen 366). Ἀριθμός (nom. sg. masc. of ἀριθμός, -οῦ, ὁ, "number") is a collective sg. properly followed by a sg. subst. ptc. (πιστεύσας, nom. sg. masc. of aor. act. ptc. of πιστεύω): "a great number who believed . . ." (Barrett 1.551). Ἐπέστρεψεν (3rd sg. aor. act. indic. of ἐπιστρέφω, "turn") is in agreement with ἀριθμός. One should comp. the use of the aor. ptc. and the vb. here with the sim. cstr. at 11:17, regarding receiving the Spirit. It is inconceivable that there is any stretch of time between believing and turning to the Lord. Instead a logical sequence is in mind at both places.

11:22 Ἠκούσθη (3rd sg. aor. pass. indic. of ἀκούω) ὁ λόγος εἰς τὰ ὦτα (acc. pl. neut. of οὖς, -ωτός, τό, "ears"; obj. of prep.) is another euphemism with the mng. "when the news reached . . ." (see CSB, NIV). Οὔσης (gen. sg. fem. of pres. ptc. of εἰμί; attrib.). Περὶ αὐτῶν refers to newly converted Gentiles in Antioch. Barnabas was then dispatched (ἐξαπέστειλαν, 3rd pl. aor. act. indic. of ἐξαποστέλλω, "send forth"). Διελθεῖν (aor. act. inf. of διέρχομαι, "pass through"; purp.) is in brackets in the UBS⁵, but likely original, given that it is more probable a scribe took out a redundant phrase than added one. Furthermore, it parallels the journey of the Cyprians and Cyrenians in v. 20.

11:23 It is possible that both ptcs., παραγενόμενος (nom. sg. masc. of aor. mid. ptc. of παραγίνομαι) and ἰδών (nom. sg. masc. of aor. act. ptc. of ὁράω), are causal. However, without denying their cause-and-effect nature, they are more likely temp. "After he arrived and saw . . ." would be the sense of it. Bock (415) suggests there is likely a wordplay between the obj. of the ptc. χάριν and the vb. For Ἐχάρη (3rd sg. aor. pass. indic. of χαίρω), "He was made glad" would be a lit. tr. Παρεκάλει is the 3rd sg. impf. act. indic. of παρακαλέω. The dat. of manner τῇ προθέσει τῆς καρδίας (lit., "with purp. of heart") might refer to Barnabas (see the ambivalent position in NASB). However, it is better to see it looking forward to προσμένειν (pres. act. inf. of προσμένω; in this context, it is to remain true, followed by dat. of pers. τῷ κυρίῳ, BHGNT 227). The force, then, is "to steadfastly remain true . . ." (see Bock 415).

11:24 The reason for the exhortation (ὅτι, causal) is a compound pred. nom. cstr. First, he is ἀνὴρ ἀγαθός (pred. nom) "a good man." The second pred. nom. is compound. He was full (πλήρης, nom. sg. masc. of πλήρης, -ες) of two things: πνεύματος ἁγίου (gen. objs. are typical of πλήρης) and πίστεως (gen. sg. fem.). Because this is the grounds for Barnabas's actions, it implies that those who would have opposed are neither good, filled, or faithful. Προσετέθη is the 3rd sg. aor. pass. indic. of προστίθημι. The phrase ὄχλος ἱκανός is best tr. "a large company" (see RSV). On ἱκανός and numeric expressions, see 8:11.

11:25–26 With the influx of new converts, Barnabas sought out Paul. The reason for Paul is not given, and speculation normally centers around his education. However, Keener suggests that Barnabas had heard Paul's testimony and remembered his calling to the Gentiles (Keener 2.1846). Ἐξῆλθεν is the 3rd sg. aor. act. indic. of ἐξέρχομαι. Ἀναζητῆσαι is the aor. act. inf. of ἀναζητέω, "seek out"; purp. Εὑρών is the nom. sg. masc. of aor. act. ptc. of εὑρίσκω; temp. Ἤγαγεν is the 3rd sg. aor. act. indic. of ἄγω. On ἐγένετο δέ with the compl. inf., see 4:5. Here it is a compound with three infs. The first is συναχθῆναι (aor. pass. inf. of συνάγω, "come together"). Αὐτοῖς is dat. pl. masc.; dat. of association "with them." Ἐνιαυτὸν ὅλον is an adv. expression (acc. of time) mng. "after a whole year." The subj. is implied. Ἐν τῇ ἐκκλησίᾳ is a locat. expression suggesting the place of worship (BHGNT 228). The best rendering is "they met with them in the church for a whole year." The second inf. phrase in the compound phrase is διδάξαι (aor. act. inf. of διδάσκω) ὄχλον ἱκανόν ("great crowds"; obj. of the prep.). The final inf. phrase (χρηματίσαι, aor. act. inf. of χρηματίζω) means "to take the name" (BDAG 1089b) and takes μαθητάς as the subj. and Χριστιανούς (acc. pl. masc. of Χριστιανός, -οῦ, ὁ, "Christians") as the obj.

FOR FURTHER STUDY

20. Clean and Unclean: Purity Issues in Acts

Bassler, J. "Luke and Paul on Impartiality." *Bib* 66 (1985): 546–52.

Chilton, B. *DLNT*, 989–96.

Hauck, F. *TDNT*, 3.423–31.

House, C. "Defilement by Association: Some Insights from the Usage of Κοινός/Κοινόω in Acts 20 and 11." AUSS 21 (1983): 143–53.

Kilgallen, J. J. "Clean, Acceptable, Saved: Acts 10." *ExpTim* 109 (1998): 301–2.

Klawans, J. "Notions of Gentile Impurity in Ancient Judaism." *AJS Review* 20 (1995): 285–312.

NIDNTTE, 2.568–78.

Parsons, M. C. "'Nothing Defiled AND Unclean': The Conjunction's Function in Acts 10:14." *PRSt* 27 (2000): 263–74.

Wall, R. W. "'Purity and Power' according to the Acts of the Apostles." *Wesleyan Theological Journal* 34 (1999): 64–82.

HOMILETICAL SUGGESTIONS

Planting a Great Church (11:19–30)

1. You need enthusiastic evangelists (vv. 19–21)
2. You need pastoral oversight (vv. 22–24)
3. You need a gifted and called teacher (vv. 25–27)
4. You need a missionary spirit (vv. 28–30)

C. EVENTS IN JERUSALEM (11:27–12:24)

This section is composed of three parts. First, there is a short report of a famine relief visit (11:27–30) sparked by a prophecy by Agabus (11:28). This placed the Antioch delegation (Saul and Barnabas) in Jerusalem when persecution again breaks out (12:1–17). The section subverts the notion of a Gentile church and a Jewish church. There is one church as the most Gentile church "remains in continuity with the mother church in Jerusalem" (Keener 2.1850; see also Schnabel 528). This solidarity included persecution. The final section (12:18–24) is the death of Herod Agrippa I under the judgment of God. It is also recorded in Josephus *Ant.* 19.343–50. While Luke's account is more compressed, there is no reason to suggest substantial contradictions (Keener 2.1967).

1. The Famine Relief Visit (11:27–30)

11:27 Ἐν ταύταις δὲ ταῖς ἡμέραις functions like a dat. of time, suggesting a point rather than an extent (i.e., "at this time," NASB, NRSV, NET). Κατῆλθον is the 3rd pl. aor. act. indic. of κατέρχομαι, "come down." Προφῆται (nom. pl. masc. of προφήτης, -ου, ὁ) is the first instance of the term referring specifically to Christian prophets in the NT.

11:28 Ἀναστάς is the nom. sg. masc. of aor. act. ptc. of ἀνίστημι. Ἐξ αὐτῶν functions like a part. gen. Ἐσήμανεν (3rd sg. aor. act. indic. of σημαίνω, "signify") in this context has a prophetic, forward-looking aspect. The inf. μέλλειν (pres. act. inf. of μέλλω) indicates indir. speech and takes a compl. inf. (ἔσεσθαι, fut. mid. inf. of εἰμί). The fut. inf. is rare in the NT. Given the forward-looking nature of μέλλω, the use here underlines the predictive nature of the speech. Ἐφ᾽ ὅλην τὴν οἰκουμένην (acc. sg. fem. of οἰκουμένη, -ης, ἡ, "upon the whole world") refers to the known inhabited world (BDAG 699b). Luke has an interest in fulfilled prophecy, so he makes a note that this happened ἐπὶ Κλαυδίου (temp.: "at the time of Claudius").

11:29 What specifically to do with the gen. μαθητῶν is difficult, although clearly it is a part. gen. The best option is to understand that it modifies τις. See NASB ". . . any of the disciples." Εὐπορεῖτο (3rd sg. impf. indic. mid. εὐπορέω) here has the act. sense (BDAG 410b) "as they prospered." The vb. ὥρισαν (3rd pl. aor. act. indic. of ὁρίζω, "determine") takes a compl. inf. πέμψαι (aor. act. inf. of πέμπω). Εἰς διακονίαν has the sense of "for support" (BDAG 230b) and assumes an obj. of some kind (i.e., "something"). Most EVV tr. it as a noun, "relief" (KJV, RSV, NLT, NRSV, NET, NJB). The phrase κατοικοῦσιν ἐν τῇ Ἰουδαίᾳ (dat. pl. masc. of pres. act. ptc. of κατοικέω) is placed in the attrib. position between the art. and its noun, "the brothers dwelling in Judea."

11:30 Although a rel. pron. phrase with an adv. καί, it is best to tr. ὃ καὶ ἐποίησαν (3rd pl. aor. act. indic. of ποιέω) as "this they did" (NLT; see also CSB, NASB, NIV, NRSV, TNIV, NJB). Ἀποστείλαντες is the nom. pl. masc. of aor. act. ptc. of ἀποστέλλω; means: "by sending."

FOR FURTHER STUDY

21. NT Prophets in Acts (11:27–30)

Aune, D. E. *Prophecy in Early Christianity*. Grand Rapids: Eerdmans, 1983.

Cousland, J. R. C. *DNTB*, 830–35.

Ellis, E. E. *Prophecy and Hermeneutic in Early Christianity*. Grand Rapids: Eerdmans 1978.

———. "The Role of the Christian Prophet in Acts." In *Apostolic History and the Gospel*. Edited by W. W. Ward and R. P. Martin, 129–44. Exeter: Paternoster 1970.

Friedrich. *TDNT*, 6.828–61.

Giles, K. N. *DLNT*, 971–77.

NIDNTTE, 4.161–74.

Turner, M. "The Spirit of Prophecy and the Power of Authoritative Preaching in Luke-Acts: A Question of Origins." *NTS* 38 (1992) 66–88.

2. Persecution in Jerusalem (12:1–17)

12:1–2 The phrase κατ᾽ ἐκεῖνον δὲ τὸν καιρόν expresses approximate time (BDAG 512a; BHGNT 231). Bruce (*Acts of the Apostles*, 279) locates it "perhaps after the prophecy of Agabus, but certainly before the famine." Ἡρῴδης ὁ βασιλεὺς is Herod Agrippa I, son of Aristobulus, the grandson of Herod the Great, king over Palestine from 41–44 (Bruce, *Acts of the Apostles*, 279–80; Robertson, *Pictures,* 163). Ἐπέβαλεν (3rd sg. aor. act. indic. of ἐπιβάλλω) with the dir. obj. τὰς χεῖρας (the art. functions as a poss. pron.) means "he laid his hands upon." Κακῶσαι is the aor. act. inf. of κακόω, "mistreat"; purp.; see the RSV's "laid violent hands." The art. τῶν (gen. pl. masc.) is a part. gen. and functions as a demonstrative pron. With τινας (acc. pl. masc. of τὶς, τὶ; obj. of the inf.), it is tr. "some of those from the church." Specifically, James (Ἰάκωβον), the brother of John (i.e., the other son of Zebedee). Luke's description is hauntingly swift, like the execution. Ἀνεῖλεν is the 3rd sg. aor. act. indic. of ἀναιρέω, "execute." Μαχαίρῃ is the dat. sg. fem. of μάχαιρα, -ας, ἡ, "with a sword"; instr. As an act of capital punishment, it indicates decapitation (Haenchen 382).

12:3 Ἰδών (nom. sg. masc. of aor. act. ptc. of ὁράω) is most likely temp., but a case can be made that it is causal (BHGNT 231). Ὅτι introduces the content of Herod's perception, and the following clause functions like indir. discourse, retaining the tense of the summarized speech (Z §346; ZG 389). Thus, ἀρεστόν (nom. sg. neut. of ἀρεστός, -η, -ον, "pleasing"; pred. adj.) ἐστιν is best tr. as a past tense.

In the Mishna *Sanh.* 9.1, the murderer and the citizens of an apostate idolatrous city (reminiscent of Jericho) are to be decapitated. James does not comfortably fit in either of these categories, nor would we really expect Herod to be adhering to it. The precise charge will remain unknown. However, that it pleased the Jews may be connected conceptually to the beguiled city. Moreover, the delight may be that decapitation was considered the most shameful of deaths (*Sanh.* 7:3; Str-B 2:706; Johnson 211).

Προσέθετο (3rd sg. aor. mid. indic. of προστίθημι) is typically "to add." However, it is common in the LXX paired with a compl. inf. to suggest something like "again" or "further" (BDAG 889a; BDF §435; Bruce, *Acts of the Apostles*, 281; R 552; ZG

389). "He proceeded to . . ." is the best tr. (see, e.g., CSB, KJV, NASB, NIV). The Heb. expression is in the mid., with compl. inf. συλλαβεῖν (aor. act. inf. of συλλαμβάνω, "arrest") following. The vb. ἦσαν (3rd pl. impf. indic. of εἰμί) is impers., "there were." But one may assume "these were." The notation ἡμέραι (nom. pl. fem. of ἡμέρα, -ας, ἡ; pred. nom.) τῶν ἀζύμων (subst. of the adj. ἄζυμος, -ον; gen. of descr., the pl. subst. refers to "the feast of unleavened bread") brings the death of Christ to mind for the reader (Johnson 211; Keener 2.1879).

12:4 Πιάσας is the nom. sg. masc. of aor. act. ptc. of πιάζω; temp. or attend. circum. Ἔθετο (3rd sg. aor. mid. indic. of τίθημι) in the mid. of special interest suggests Herod keeping Peter for his own purposes (i.e., death; Z §234). Παραδούς is the nom. sg. masc. of aor. act. ptc. of παραδίδωμι; attend. circum. The guard posted is excessive. Τέσσαρσιν τετραδίοις (dat. pl. neut. of τετράδιον, -ου, τό, "squad") is technically sixteen soldiers (four squads of four). Φυλάσσειν is the pres. act. inf. of φυλάσσω. The cause for jail rather than immediate execution is expressed in the causal ptc., βουλόμενος (nom. sg. masc. of pres. mid. ptc. of βούλομαι). Strictly, Passover immediately precedes the Feast of Unleavened Bread. However, the whole sequence may be referred to as "Passover" (Keener 2.1878; Johnson 2:11). "After the Passover" (μετὰ τὸ πάσχα) would be more politically sensitive for the king's plan. The phrase ἀναγαγεῖν (aor. act. inf. of ἀνάγω, "bring up"; purp.) . . . τῷ λαῷ likely refers to a public execution (Barrett 1.577; BHGNT 232).

12:5 On μὲν οὖν, see 1:6. Ἐτηρεῖτο (3rd sg. impf. pass. indic. of τηρέω, "keep"). The phrase ἦν . . . γινομένη (nom. sg. fem. of pres. pass. ptc. of γίνομαι) is a periph. impf. that, given the prep. of agency (ὑπὸ τῆς ἐκκλησίας, "by the church"), should be considered a pass.; "being made . . . by the church" expresses it well (RSV, NASB, ESV).

12:6 Ἤμελλεν (3rd sg. impf. indic. act. of μέλλω.) takes the compl. inf. προαγαγεῖν (aor. act. inf. of προάγω) and is likely inceptive (see Ὅτε): "was going to bring him forward/out" (RSV, NASB, ESV). Τῇ νυκτὶ ἐκείνῃ is dat. sg. fem.; dat. of time, "on that night." The phrase ἦν . . . κοιμώμενος (nom. sg. masc. of pres. mid. ptc. of κοιμάομαι) is another periph. impf., mng. "he was sleeping." Peter was μεταξὺ δύο στρατιωτῶν (gen. pl. masc. of στρατιώτης, -ου, ὁ, "between two soldiers") δεδεμένος (nom. sg. masc. of pf. pass. ptc. of δέω) with ἁλύσεσιν δυσίν (dat. pl. fem.; dat. of means, "with two chains"; see next v.). Two more guards (φύλακες, nom. pl. masc. of φύλαξ, -ακος, ὁ) ἐτήρουν (3rd pl. impf. act. indic. of τηρέω) keeping watch shows that Herod was "going the extra mile" to secure Peter. It may be due to the lack of success of previous jailings (cf. 5:19).

12:7 On καὶ ἰδού, see 1:10, appropriate for the appearance of an angel. Ἐπέστη is the 3rd sg. aor. act. indic. of ἐφίστημι, "stand over." Light or bright clothes is often assoc. with angels (see, e.g., Matt 28:3; 2 Cor 11:14). The phrase ἔλαμψεν (3rd sg. aor. act. indic. of λάμπω, "shine") ἐν τῷ οἰκήματι (dat. sg. neut. of οἴκημα, -ατος, τό, "room") suggests filling the room. Peter was, apparently, sleeping deeply. The angel had to strike him (πατάξας, nom. sg. masc. of aor. act. ptc. of πατάσσω, "strike"; temp.) on his side (πλευράν, acc. sg. fem. of πλευρά, -ᾶς, ἡ). Ἤγειρεν is the 3rd sg. aor. act. indic. of ἐγείρω. Λέγων (nom. sg. masc. of pres. act. ptc. of λέγω; attend. circum.) introduces dir. speech. Ἀνάστα (2nd sg. aor. act. impv. of ἀνίστημι, "arise") ἐν τάχει (dat. sg. neut.

of τάχος, -ους, τό) is lit. "in speed" but is used adv. (BDAG 992a), so "Quick, get up!" Ἐξέπεσαν is the 3rd pl. aor. act. indic. of ἐκπίπτω, "fell off." Αὐτοῦ is a poss. gen. modifying ἁλύσεις (nom. pl. fem. of ἅλυσις, -εως, ἡ, "chains"). The art. with ἐκ τῶν χειρῶν functions like a poss. pron., "from his hands."

12:8 The angel's direction is given in dir. speech with two impvs.: ζῶσαι (2nd sg. aor. mid. impv. sg. of ζωννύω, "gird up") and ὑπόδησαι (2nd sg. aor. mid. impv. of ὑποδέω, "tie up") his sandals. Peter complied (ἐποίησεν, 3rd sg. aor. act. indic. of ποιέω). The second speech is dir. citation. The angel commanded him to put on (περιβαλοῦ, 2nd sg. aor. mid. impv. of περιβάλλω) his cloak and to follow (ἀκολούθει, 2nd sg. pres. act. impv. of ἀκολουθέω) him.

12:9 Ἐξελθὼν (nom. sg. masc. of aor. act. ptc. of ἐξέρχομαι; attend. circum.). Ἠκολούθει is the 3rd sg. impf. indic. act. of ἀκολουθέω. Ringing remarkably true, Peter was in a daze, expressed as οὐκ ᾔδει (3rd sg. plpf. act. indic. of οἶδα, a functional aor., "knew"). On the tense of indir. speech, see 12:3. Ἀληθές (pred. adj., "true") ἐστιν τὸ γινόμενον (nom. sg. neut. of pres. mid. ptc. of γίνομαι; subst., subj. of the vb.) is lit. "what had happened was true." The content of his thoughts (ἐδόκει, 3rd sg. impf. act. indic. of δοκέω, "think") is again in indir. speech with an inf. (βλέπειν, pres. act. inf. of βλέπω) that takes ὅραμα (acc. sg. neut. of ὅραμα, -ατος, τό, "vision") as its dir. obj.

12:10 Διελθόντες is the nom. pl. masc. of aor. act. ptc. of διέρχομαι; temp. Φυλακήν is the acc. sg. fem. of φυλακή, -ῆς, ἡ, "prison"; obj. of ptc. Both the πρώτην and δευτέραν ("first" and "second") ref. to the guards posted at two inner gates (Bruce, *Acts of the Apostles*, 285). Ἦλθαν is the 3rd pl. aor. act. indic. of ἔρχομαι. Τὴν πύλην (acc. sg. fem. of πύλη, -ης, ἡ, "gate") τὴν σιδηρᾶν (acc. sg. fem. of σιδηροῦς, -ᾶ, -οῦν, "iron"), "the iron gate," ref. to the last, most fortified gate leading to the city (Bruce, *Acts of the Apostles*, 285). Φέρουσαν is the acc. sg. fem. of pres. act. ptc. of φέρω; attrib. Αὐτομάτη (nom. sg. fem. of αὐτόματος, -η, -ον, "by itself") technically agrees with the subj. (ἥτις) although used adv. Ἠνοίγη is the 3rd sg. aor. pass. indic. of ἀνοίγω, "open." Ἐξελθόντες is the nom. pl. masc. of aor. act. ptc. of ἐξέρχομαι; attend. circum. Προῆλθον (3rd pl. aor. act. indic. of προέρχομαι) is lit. "they went before." The dir. obj. ῥύμην (acc. sg. fem. of ῥύμη, -ης, ἡ) μίαν (lit., "one street" or "alley") likely refers to "one block" (BDAG 868b; Barrett 1.582; Schnabel 539). Εὐθέως ἀπέστη (3rd sg. aor. act. indic. of ἀφίστημι, "depart") describes a sudden departure.

12:11 The phrase ἐν ἑαυτῷ with a form of γίνομαι (γενόμενος, nom. sg. masc. of aor. mid. ptc. of γίνομαι; temp.) is common in Gk. for coming to a right mind (Barrett 1.582; the phrase is in contrast to 11:5 ἐν ἐκστάσει, Bruce, *Acts of the Apostles*, 284). Peter's confession: The Lord sent (ἐξαπέστειλεν, 3rd sg. aor. act. indic. of ἐξαποστέλλω, "send forth") the angel and delivered him (ἐξείλατο, 3rd sg. aor. mid. indic. of ἐξαιρέω). The deliverance is from the hand of Herod (i.e., the power of Herod) and πάσης τῆς προσδοκίας (gen. sg. fem. of προσδοκία, -ας, ἡ, "expectation") τοῦ λαοῦ τῶν Ἰουδαίων (i.e., that Peter would be put to death). Barrett suggests the last phrase signifies Peter's understanding that he now separated from unbelieving Judaism (Barrett 1.583; Schnabel 538).

12:12 Συνιδών is the nom. sg. masc. of aor. act. ptc. of συνοράω, "realize"; temp. That he went (ἦλθεν, 3rd sg. aor. act. indic. of ἔρχομαι) to Mary's house suggests it was a well-known meeting place. The series of gens. following Ἰωάννου are appos. John Mark will appear four more times in Acts (12:25; 13:13; 15:37, 39). The expression τοῦ ἐπικαλουμένου (gen. sg. masc. of pres. pass. ptc. of ἐπικαλέω; attrib.) Μάρκου is typical in Acts. It suggests Μᾶρκος is a Roman name (see 13:13, where he is simply "John"). That Paul refers to him as Barnabas's cousin (Col 4:10) suggests Mary was Barnabas's aunt in some way. Since the house belonged the Mary, she was likely widowed. On οὗ, see 1:13. Ἦσαν (3rd pl. impf. indic. of εἰμί) takes the subst. adj. ἱκανοί (nom. pl. masc. of ἱκανός, -ά, -όν, "many") as its subj. Συνηθροισμένοι (nom. pl. masc. of pf. pass. ptc. of συναθροίζω, "gather"; subst., pred. nom.) and προσευχόμενοι (nom. pl. masc. of pres. mid. ptc. of προσεύχομαι; subst., pred. nom.) are compound pred. nom. compls.

12:13 Κρούσαντος is the gen. sg. masc. of aor. act. ptc. of κρούω, "knock"; temp. That there is a gate (πυλῶνος, gen. sg. masc. of πυλών, -ῶνος, ὁ) and a servant girl (παιδίσκη, nom. sg. fem. of παιδίσκη, -ης, ἡ, dimin. of παῖς) suggests Mary's wealth. Ὑπακοῦσαι (aor. act. inf. of ὑπακούω, "answer") is common of responding to a knock (BDAG 1029a). Mentioning the name Ῥόδη (nom. sg. fem. of Ῥόδη, -ης, ἡ, "Rhoda") might suggest a young member of the family rather than a slave (Barrett 1.584).

12:14 Ἐπιγνοῦσα is the nom. sg. fem. of aor. act. ptc. of ἐπιγινώσκω; temp. The prep. phrase ἀπὸ τῆς χαρᾶς is best rendered "for joy" (BDAG 106b) as it gives the reason the gate (πυλῶνα, acc. sg. masc. of πυλών, -ῶνος, ὁ) is not opened (ἤνοιξεν, 3rd sg. aor. act. indic. of ἀνοίγω). Εἰσδραμοῦσα (nom. sg. fem. of aor. act. ptc. of εἰστρέχω, "run into"; temp.) presumes a room where they were praying. Ἀπήγγειλεν (3rd sg. aor. act. indic. of ἀπαγγέλλω, "announce") introduces indir. speech using an inf. (ἑστάναι, pf. act. inf. of ἵστημι). "That Peter was standing" is a good tr. (RSV, NRSV, ESV, NET, NJB).

12:15 The art. οἱ functions as a pron. subj. of εἶπαν (3rd pl. aor. act. indic. of λέγω). In dir. speech, Luke reported a blunt accusation: μαίνῃ (2nd sg. pres. mid. indic. of μαίνομαι), "You are mad!" The art. ἡ also functions as a pron. subj. (τὸ διϊσχυρίζετο, 3rd sg. impf. mid. indic. of διϊσχυρίζομαι, "insist"). On the sense of οὕτως ἔχειν, see 7:1; it is an inf. due to indir. speech. Οἱ is another art. used as the pron. subj. to ἔλεγον (3rd pl. impf. act. indic. of λέγω). The vb. ἐστίν is impers. "It is . . ." The pred. nom. ὁ ἄγγελος is likely a ref. to the belief that each person had a guardian angel who resembled and looked after them (see Schnabel 540; Bock 429). Note that Luke merely reports; he does not endorse the idea.

12:16 Perhaps the most entertaining scene in the NT is that Peter continued (ἐπέμενεν, 3rd sg. impf. indic. act. of ἐπιμένω) knocking (κρούων, nom. sg. masc. of pres. act. ptc. of κρούω; compl.) at the gate while the discussion was ensuing. Ἀνοίξαντες is the nom. pl. masc. of aor. act. ptc. of ἀνοίγω; temp. Εἶδαν is the 3rd pl. aor. act. indic. of ὁράω. Ἐξέστησαν is the 3rd pl. aor. act. indic. of ἐξίστημι, "amazed."

12:17 Κατασείσας (masc. sg. nom. of aor. act. ptc. of κατασείω, "motion, gesture"; temp. or attend. circum.) is the first of four instances in Acts where a speaker gestures before making an address (see 13:16, 19:33, and 21:40). It was often an orator's gesture in antiquity (Barrett 1.586). The inf. σιγᾶν (pres. act. inf. of σιγάω, "say nothing") indic. the purp. is to hush the excited house (see Bruce, *Acts of the Apostles*, 286). Peter's recitation (διηγήσατο, 3rd sg. aor. mid. indic. of διηγέομαι, "describe in detail") of his escape (ἐξήγαγεν, 3rd sg. aor. act. indic. of ἐξάγω, "bring out") from prison (φυλακῆς, gen. sg. fem. of φυλακή, -ης, ἡ; obj. of prep.) is given in summary form. It turns to dir. speech with εἶπέν (on τε, see 1:15). Ἀπαγγείλατε (2nd pl. aor. act. impv. of ἀπαγγέλλω, "tell") takes dats. "James and the brothers" (Ἰακώβῳ καὶ τοῖς ἀδελφοῖς) as indir. objs. and "these things" (ταῦτα) as the obj. This is the first mention of James in the book of Acts. The instruction and the lack of introduction (cf. 12:2, where James the son of Zebedee is identified) demonstrates both his leadership in the Jerusalem church and his fame (Barrett 1:586; Johnson 213–14). "The brothers" are likely James's fellow elders (Bruce, *Acts of the Apostles*, 286). Peter's departure (ἐξελθών, nom. sg. masc. of aor. act. ptc. of ἐξέρχομαι; attend. circum.) and travel (ἐπορεύθη, 3rd sg. aor. pass. indic. of πορεύομαι) "to another place" (εἰς ἕτερον τόπον) has received much conjecture. All that can be known is that he left in safety (Johnson 214).

3. The Death of Herod Agrippa I (12:18–24)

It is not totally clear why the fate of Agrippa is mentioned. It is likely, however, that it rounds off the demonstration of the justice of God. The righteous apostle was set free, but the unrighteous king was struck by the hand of God.

12:18 Γενομένης is the gen. sg. fem. of aor. mid. ptc. of γίνομαι; gen. abs., temp. The vb. ἦν (3rd sg. impf. indic. of εἰμί) is impers., "there was." The pred. nom. τάραχος modified by οὐκ ὀλίγος is "no small disturbance" (NASB). Ἐν τοῖς στρατιώταις (dat. pl. masc. of στρατιώτης, -ου, ὁ), "among the soldiers," is understandable given their responsibilities and the repercussions (see next v.). Ἄρα "enlivens the question" (BDAG 127b). Τί ὁ Πέτρος ἐγένετο (3rd sg. aor. mid. indic. of γίνομαι) means "what had become of Peter" (BDAG 1007a; CSB, KJV, RSV, NIV, NRSV, ESV, TNIV, NET, NJB).

12:19 Herod ordered a search (ἐπιζητήσας, nom. sg. masc. of aor. act. ptc. of ἐπιζητέω, "seek after"; temp.) that was unsuccessful (εὑρών, nom. sg. masc. of aor. act. ptc. of εὑρίσκω, with μὴ, "not finding"). Ἀνακρίνας is the nom. sg. masc. of aor. act. ptc. of ἀνακρίνω, "examine"; attend. circum. Φύλακας (acc. pl. masc. of φύλαξ, -ακος, ὁ) is the dir. obj. of ἐκέλευσεν (3rd sg. aor. act. indic. of κελεύω, "order"). The compl. inf. ἀπαχθῆναι (aor. pass. inf. of ἀπάγω) technically means "to be led away." It certainly means incarceration. It more likely also signifies an execution (see Luke 23:26 of Jesus), as most agree (most EVV, Barrett 1.588; Bruce, *Acts of the Apostles*, 287; Johnson 214; MM 51b). Herod then retires (κατελθών, nom. sg. masc. of aor. act. ptc. of κατέρχομαι) to Caesarea for an extended stay (διέτριβεν, 3rd sg. impf. indic. act. of διατρίβω, "remain").

12:20 Ἦν . . . θυμομαχῶν (nom. sg. masc. of pres. act. ptc. of θυμομαχέω; periph. impf., NT hapax) is normally tr. "very angry" in EVV. "Irate" or "furious" seems to be a better rendering (see Vulg. *iratus*). Τυρίοις (dat. pl. masc. of Τύριος, -ου, ὁ) . . . Σιδωνίοις (dat. pl. masc. of Σιδώνιος, -ία, -ιον,) are dats. of disadvantage and best tr., "with the Tyrians and Sidonians." Since ὁμοθυμαδόν is always "together" in Acts, the vb. παρῆσαν (3rd pl. impf. act. indic. of πάρειμι, "appear") presents a joint audience with Herod. Likely it was gained through bribing (the euphemistic sense of πείσαντες, nom. pl. masc. of aor. act. ptc. of πείθω) Blastus. Τόν functions as a rel. pron. Ἐπὶ τοῦ κοιτῶνος (gen. sg. masc. of κοιτών, -ῶνος, ὁ) τοῦ βασιλέως is lit. "over the bedroom of the king." He was the official who administered the living quarters of the king and controlled access to him (Keener 2.1060). The delegation was requesting (ἠτοῦντο, 3rd pl. impf. mid. indic. of αἰτέω) peace because they were dependent on the king for food (διά + the acc. art. + τρέφεσθαι, pres. pass. inf. of τρέφω, "feed").

12:21 In context, τακτῇ (dat. sg. fem. of τακτός, -ή, -όν) . . . ἡμέρᾳ is a dat. of time, "on the appointed day." It must be an arrangement with the Tyrian and Sidonian delegation. Thus, πρὸς αὐτούς ("to them") at the end of the v. must at least include them as well. The event seems to be designed to pander to Herod's well-endowed ego. He dresses (ἐνδυσάμενος, nom. sg. masc. of aor. mid. ptc. of ἐνδύω; temp.) in ἐσθῆτα (acc. sg. fem. of ἐσθής, -ῆτος, ἡ) βασιλικήν (acc. sg. fem. of βασιλικός, -ή, -όν): "royal clothing." He sits (καθίσας, nom. sg. masc. of aor. act. ptc. of καθίζω, temp.) on a βήματος (gen. sg. neut. of βῆμα, -ατος, τό). For a king, it would imply a throne (Johnson 214). Ἐδημηγόρει (3rd sg. impf. act. indic. of δημηγορέω) is "he was delivering a public address."

12:22 Δῆμος (nom. sg. masc. of δῆμος, -ου, ὁ) ref. to the people of the city, Caesarea. The content of their cries (ἐπεφώνει, 3rd sg. impf. indic. act. of ἐπιφωνέω, "shout out") assumes a copulative vb. (ἐστίν, "it is"). Θεοῦ must suggest Herod was called a god rather than the conduit for God.

12:23 Παραχρῆμα is an adv. mng. "immediately." Luke identifies Herod's assailant (ἐπάταξεν, 3rd sg. aor. act. indic. of πατάσσω, "strike") as an angel. The prep. phrase ἀνθ' ὧν is a causal idiomatic expression mng. "in return for which = because" (BDAG 88a; BHGNT 241; MM 47a). The cause is that he did not give (ἔδωκεν, 3rd sg. aor. act. indic. of δίδωμι) glory to God; that is, he was stealing God's glory. The nature of the angel's blow is expressed with γενόμενος (nom. sg. masc. of aor. mid. ptc. of γίνομαι; temp.) σκωληκόβρωτος (nom. sg. masc. of σκωληκόβρωτος, -ον; pred. adj.: "eaten by worms"). Such a grisly death is reminiscent of his grandfather's gruesome end as reported by Josephus (*Ant.* 19:169; *J.W.* 1.656). Herod's death (ἐξέψυξεν, 3rd sg. aor. act. indic. of ἐκψύχω, "expire") according to Josephus (*Ant.* 19:343–50) was five days later. Luke has often declined a detailed chronology in favor of getting to the point (cf. Luke 24/Acts 1). One need not posit a great variance between the accounts. Keener notes some have suggested a ruptured appendix with an accompanying infestation of worms, a note common in the deaths of tyrants (Keener 2.1967–69).

12:24 As his custom, Luke summarizes. In Acts, λόγος τοῦ θεοῦ ("word of God") is normally a ref. to the gospel. The impfs. ηὔξανεν (3rd sg. impf. act. indic. of αὐξάνω) and ἐπληθύνετο (3rd sg. impf. pass. indic. of πληθύνω) are likely a doublet to express a wide expansion (BHGNT 242). The pass. of the latter is likely a divine pass. ("was growing and being multiplied").

HOMILETICAL SUGGESTIONS

Human Attempts to Stifle the Gospel (12:1–25)

1. Some individuals will suffer (vv. 1–4).
   a. There may be individuals who suffer death (vv. 1–3)

    b.   There may be individuals who suffer imprisonment (v. 4)

2. Some individuals may be granted divine deliverance (vv. 5–10)
3. The church is to pray and obey (vv. 5, 11–17)
4. God will ultimately bring justice to the persecutors (vv. 18–23)
5. The Word of God is unbound (vv. 24–25)

Self-Idolatry: Cause and Effect (12:18–25)

1. The cause of Herod's death (vv. 18–22)
   a. Herod prepared to entertain the crowd
   b. Herod enjoyed the flattery of the crowd
   c. Herod accepted their deification of him
   d. Most of all, Herod only had a superficial relationship to God

2. The results of Herod's sin (v. 23)
   a. God sent an angel to strike him down
   b. His death was grisly
   c. What happened after his death is even more grisly

3. The man who would stop the gospel could not contain it (vv. 24–25)

V. The Gentile Mission:
Part 1, Asia Minor (12:25–16:5)

This section of Acts is about the gospel penetrating Asia Minor (Luke arranges his story geographically) to complete Jesus's instructions to go to the ends of the earth (1:8), and Gentile inclusion in the church. One would think the Cornelius episode would have finally put to rest the matter of Gentiles included as Gentiles. Unfortunately, the issue of Gentile inclusion was not settled until the Jerusalem Council of Acts 15. The section is composed of three parts: the first missionary journey (12:25–14:28); the Jerusalem Council (15:1–33); and the beginning of the second missionary journey (15:36–16:5).

A. FIRST MISSIONARY JOURNEY (12:25–14:28)

While technically a misnomer, Paul's so-called first missionary journey (Acts 12:25–14:28; one could term "Damascus, Arabia, Jerusalem, Syria/Cilicia and Antioch" [Schnabel 548] earlier evangelistic journeys), is the first prolonged attempt at bringing the gospel to the nations. It is also the first step by Paul to fulfill his calling at his conversion (Keener 2.1982). As with other encounters, the impetus is from the Holy Spirit (a theme in Acts); it was not a plan of human beings (Barrett 1.599).

1. Syrian Antioch: Sent Out (12:25–13:3)

12:25 Barnabas and Saul now return (ὑπέστρεψαν, 3rd pl. aor. act. indic. of ὑποστρέφω) to Antioch. Since 11:30 has the apostles in Jerusalem, the use of εἰς Ἰερουσαλήμ has spawned textual var. of ἐξ and ἀπό. Recent scholars on the witness of esp. $\mathfrak{P}^{74}$ take ἐξ as the rdg. (i.e., "from Jerusalem," Keener 2.1981; see BHGNT 242). This is unlikely. Instead one need only understand that the prep. modifies the following ptc. phrase (however unusual), πληρώσαντες (nom. pl. masc. of aor. act. ptc. of πληρόω; temp.) τὴν διακονίαν. Συμπαραλαβόντες is the nom. pl. masc. of aor. act. ptc. of συμπαραλαμβάνω, "bring." On John Mark, see 12:12.

13:1 Ἦσαν (3rd pl. impf. act. indic. of εἰμί; impers. "there were") introduces a pred. nom. cstr with a compound compl., προφῆται ("prophets") and διδάσκαλοι ("teachers"), at the end of the clause. Κατὰ τὴν οὖσαν (acc. sg. fem. of pres. ptc. of εἰμί;

attrib.) ἐκκλησίαν is a spatial marker mng. "in the congregation there" (BDAG 511b; BDF §474). The following list of five names is presented as two sets in series marked by τε (τε . . . καὶ . . . καὶ . . . τε . . . καί). It may be that the division is for stylistic reasons (Barrett 1.603; BHGNT 244) or it may be a division of prophets and teachers (presumably in order). It is more notable that the list is cosmopolitan in its makeup. Συμεών ("Simon," indecl.), who has the nickname Νίγερ (transliterated Lat. mng. "Black"; possibly an African, Bruce, *Acts of the Apostles*, 292), is a Jewish Christian with a Lat. and Heb. name. Λούκιος ὁ Κυρηναῖος (nom. sg. masc. of Κυρηναῖος, -ου, ὁ), "Lucius the Cyrenian," is undoubtedly Gentile. Μαναήν is clearly well connected politically. He is σύντροφος (nom. sg. masc. of σύντροφος, -ον, "brought up together with") of Herod the tetrarch (i.e., Antipas; Bruce, *Acts of the Apostles*, 293). We know Barnabas was a Levite, and Paul a (former?) rabbi.

13:2 The temp. gen. abs. in the pres. tense (λειτουργούντων, gen. pl. masc. of pres. act. ptc. of λειτουργέω, "worshiping," and νηστευόντων, gen. pl. masc. of pres. act. ptc. of νηστεύω, "fast") particularly emphasize that the message of the Holy Spirit came as they were in the process. There is no indication of a special occasion for the fast. Ἀφορίσατε is the 2nd pl. aor. act. impv. of ἀφορίζω, "separate." The particle δή is used 317 times in the LXX but only five in the NT (three in Luke-Acts, see 15:36). Although relatively weak (BHGNT 244), when used with commands it suggests a greater urgency (BDAG 222a; BDF §451). The dat. sg. masc. μοι is a dat. of advantage. The purp. of the separation (εἰς) is apparently known to Barnabas and Saul, suggested by the rel. pron. phrase with a pf. vb., ὃ προσκέκλημαι (1st sg. pf. mid. indic. of προσκαλέομαι) αὐτούς. The implication would be they were waiting for the Spirit to affirm their desire.

13:3 The response is given in three attend. circum. ptcs. and a finite vb. First, they held a specific fast (suggested by the aor., νηστεύσαντες, nom. pl. masc. of aor. act. ptc. of νηστεύω, "fast"). Then came a time of prayer (προσευξάμενοι, nom. pl. masc. of aor. mid. ptc. of προσεύχομαι). Finally was a commissioning expressed as "laying (ἐπιθέντες, nom. sg. masc. aor. act. ptc. of ἐπιτίθημι) hands on them." The departure is stated succinctly, probably for effect. Ἀπέλυσαν is the 3rd pl. aor. act. indic. of ἀπολύω, mng. "they released (them)."

HOMILETICAL SUGGESTIONS

The Church and Those Called by God (12:25–13:3)

1. The leadership should be praying about the Spirit's call (12:25–13:2)
2. The church should commission the called to their ministry (v. 3)

2. Cyprus: Proconsul Sergius Paulus Believes (13:4–12)

Cyprian Jews had previously been presented with the gospel when the church was persecuted (see 11:19). The island is the first step here not only because of Barnabas's familiarity but because the gospel had previously been "to no one except Jews." The encounter recalls Peter's confrontation with Simon Magus in Acts 8:9–24. The story, perhaps, has some validation of the Gentile mission and Paul. The major point, however, is the success on Cyprus.

13:4 On μὲν οὖν, see 1:6. Ἐκπεμφθέντες (nom. pl. masc. of aor. pass. ptc. of ἐκπέμπω, "send out"; temp.). The prep. phrase ὑπὸ τοῦ ἁγίου πνεύματος is a typical expression of the Holy Spirit's agency. Κατῆλθον (3rd pl. aor. act. indic. of κατέρχομαι, "descend") represents an initial step, for Σελεύκειαν (acc. sg. fem. of Σελεύκεια, -ας, ἡ, "Seleucia"; obj. of prep.) was the port of Antioch (Bruce, *Acts of the Apostles*, 295). Ἐκεῖθεν is an adv. mng. "from there." Ἀπέπλευσαν is the 3rd pl. aor. act. indic. of ἀποπλέω, "sail away." Κύπρον is acc. sg. masc. of Κύπρος, -ου, ἡ, "Cyprus."

13:5 Καὶ γενόμενοι (nom. pl. masc. of aor. mid. ptc. of γίνομαι; temp.) ἐν Σαλαμῖνι (dat. sg. fem. of Σαλαμίς, -ῖνος, ἡ, "Salamis") describes their landing in the important port city of Cyprus (Bruce, *Acts of the Apostles*, 295). Immediately, they got to their business. Κατήγγελλον is the 3rd pl. impf. act. indic. of καταγγέλλω, "preach." The dir. obj. τὸν λόγον τοῦ θεοῦ is typically "the gospel message" in Acts. The prep. phrase ἐν ταῖς συναγωγαῖς begins the pattern that will be repeated throughout the Gentile mission, "to the Jew first . . ." (see Rom 1:16). The vb. εἶχον (3rd pl. impf. act. indic. of ἔχω) takes a double-acc. cstr.: Ἰωάννην (dir. obj.) ὑπηρέτην (acc. sg. masc. of ὑπηρέτης, -ου, ὁ; compl.), together mng. "John as an assistant."

13:6 Διελθόντες is the nom. pl. masc. of aor. act. ptc. of διέρχομαι; temp. The obj. of the ptc. is ὅλην τὴν νῆσον (acc. sg. fem. of νῆσος, -ου, ἡ), "the whole island." Extent is expressed by ἄχρι Πάφου (gen. sg. masc. of Πάφος, -ου, ἡ), "until Paphos." This suggests a more strenuous evangelistic effort than merely going to Paphos (about eighty-three miles west, essentially from one coast to the other). Εὖρον is the 3rd pl. aor. act. indic. of εὑρίσκω. The dir. obj. ἄνδρα is followed by a series of masc. acc. sgs.: τινὰ μάγον (of μάγος, -οῦ, ὁ), "a certain magician"; ψευδοπροφήτην (of ψευδοπροφήτης, -ου, ὁ), "false prophet"; and Ἰουδαῖον, "Jewish." The first two are appos. to ἄνδρα. The last one (Ἰουδαῖον) is likely appos. to ψευδοπροφήτην, so it is a "Jewish false-prophet." One need not infer that since "Jew" shows up in this smorgasbord of heresy that Luke is anti-Sem. (contra Barrett 1.613). As a magician the person described was clearly beyond the religious sensibilities of the Jews as well. The UBS⁵ rdg. is the more difficult, lit. "to whom (was) the name of Bar-Jesus." The name Βαριησοῦ (gen. sg. masc. of Βαριησοῦς, -οῦ, ὁ) means "son of Joshua" and has no relation to Christ.

13:7 The magician was in the company of (σύν) a high-level official of Rome, τῷ ἀνθυπάτῳ (dat. sg. masc. of ἀνθύπατος, -ου, ὁ). The Vulg. tr. it correctly as *proconsule* ("proconsul"). Presumably the man held the imperium for the whole island. Σεργίῳ (dat. sg. masc. of Σέργιος, -ου, ὁ; a Roman surname [gens]) Παύλῳ is "Sergius Paulus." While we do not have a record of his proconsulship (the records are incomplete), we do have inscriptional evidence of a Claudian senator named "Lucius Sergius Paulus" (Keener 2.2014, citing CIL 6.31545.3; see also Barrett 1.613–14 and Bruce, *Acts of the Apostles*, 297). It would not be unusual for him to be traveling with an eastern magician because they were thought to have "the best magic" (Keener 2.2013). Sergius Paulus is described as ἀνδρὶ συνετῷ (dat. sg. masc. of συνετός, -ή, -όν), "an intelligent man." He requested (προσκαλεσάμενος, nom. sg. masc. of aor. mid. ptc. of προσκαλέομαι; temp.) an audience of Barnabas and Saul. Ἐπεζήτησεν (3rd sg. aor. act. indic. of ἐπιζητέω, "seek after") is compl. by the inf. ἀκοῦσαι (aor. act. inf. of ἀκούω). On τὸν λόγον τοῦ θεοῦ (i.e., the gospel), see 4:31.

13:8 We are introduced to the name Ἐλύμας (nom. sg. masc. of Ἐλύμας, -α, ὁ), who opposed (ἀνθίστατο, 3rd sg. impf. mid. indic. of ἀνθίστημι) the missionaries. He is identified as the same magician Βαριησοῦ (13:6) by the use of the art. of previous ref. in ὁ μάγος. Οὕτως γάρ introduces the substantiation for identifying (presumably) "Elymas" with "magician." In doing so, a number of questions arise for interpreters trying to understand how this is so, for "Elymus" does not translate Βαριησοῦ.

1. The Western text reads ἕτοιμας (the major exemplar, Beza, was corrected to the current rdg.), "ready." A number of Sem. conjectures regarding "Elymus" as some sort of sim. term have been proposed. None have won the day (Barrett 1.615). Some want to connect it to a Cyprian Jewish magician in Josephus named "Atomos" ("indivisible," *Ant.* 20:142; see Johnson 223). It remains unclear how that fulfills Luke's usage. Besides, the textual unlikelihood for the basis for these interpretations leads to rejecting them.

2. The Arabic *Alim* ("wiseman" or "magician") has been proposed. However, the chance that this would be meaningful for Luke or his readers is remote.

3. Ἐλύμας might be a pun related to the Heb. word for "dreamer," *ḥolem*. False prophets and dreamers are connected at Deut 13:31.

4. The term μεθερμηνεύεται (3rd sg. pres. pass. indic. of μεθερμηνεύω, "being translated") is used at Acts 4:36 of Barnabas with less than a word-for-word basis but on cognitive grounds. Here Luke may be doing something sim. Something like this may be regarding *ḥolem* or another term yet unrecognized.

The ptc. ζητῶν (nom. sg. masc. of pres. act. ptc. of ζητέω) is compl. by διαστρέψαι (aor. act. inf. of διαστρέφω, "mislead") Since in Eng. we do not say "mislead from the faith," the tr. in most EVV is "to turn away from."

13:9 The art. ὁ functions as a rel. pron. that introduces the Roman name for Saul (Σαῦλος). Using adv. καί, he is "also Paul" (see the Vulg. "*qui et Paulus*"). Ὁ καί is the normal way in Gk. to introduce an alternate name (Bruce, *Acts of the Apostles*, 298). From this point forward Saul will be referred to as Παῦλος (the term Σαῦλος will not appear again in Acts). Bruce notes that he is in mostly Gentile contexts from now on (Bruce, *Acts of the Apostles*, 298). Two preliminaries give the background for Paul's verbal response (in v. 10). He is filled (πλησθείς, nom. sg. masc. of aor. pass. ptc. of πίμπλημι, "fill"; temp.) with the Holy Spirit and he stares (ἀτενίσας, nom. sg. masc. of aor. act. ptc. of ἀτενίζω, "stare"; attend. circum.) at Elymas.

13:10 The exclamatory particle ὦ carries a deep emotional tone (Wallace 68–69). Runge refers to it as an overly specific "thematic address" that sets the stage for Paul's statement (Runge 359). The adj. πλήρης (voc. sg. masc. of πλήρης, -ες, "full") is a subst. adj. in appos. to υἱέ (voc. sg. masc. of υἱός, -οῦ, ὁ, "son"). The series of gens. that follow are gens. of content, παντὸς δόλου (gen. sg. masc. of δόλος, -ου, ὁ, mng. "of all guile") and πάσης ῥᾳδιουργίας (gen. sg. fem. of ῥᾳδιουργία, -ας, ἡ, mng. "of all deceit"). "Son" (υἱέ) is almost certainly a play on the name Βαριησοῦ. Διαβόλου (gen. sg. masc. of διάβολος, -ον; subst. "devil") is a gen. of relationship. Nearly dir. adjacent to υἱέ is the second voc. (ἐχθρέ, voc. sg. masc. of ἐχθρός, -ά, -όν; subst. adj., "enemy"). Πάσης δικαιοσύνης (gen. sg. fem. of δικαιοσύνη, -ης, ἡ) is a gen. of ref. mng. "regarding all righteousness." Παύσῃ (2nd sg. fut. mid. indic. of παύω) is in the form of a question but is more of an accusation (BHGNT 248). It is compl. by διαστρέφων (nom. sg. masc. of pres. act. ptc. of διαστρέφω, "distort"). Εὐθείας is the acc. sg. fem. of εὐθύς, "straight" (see also at 9:11).

13:11 Καὶ νῦν ἰδού (cf. 20:22, 25), common in the LXX (see BDF §442), combines καὶ νῦν (see 4:29) and ἰδού (see 1:10). The expression is very solemn. On χεὶρ κυρίου, see 11:21. Paul announces a curse on the man with ἔσῃ (2nd sg. fut. mid. indic. of εἰμί) and τυφλός (nom. sg. masc. of τυφλός, -ή, -όν) as the pred. adj. This is followed by a negated (μή) ptc. βλέπων (nom. sg. masc. of pres. act. ptc. of βλέπω) that is attrib. to τυφλός (BHGNT 249; Rogers and Rogers 260). The noun ἥλιον (acc. sg. masc. of ἥλιος, -ου, ὁ, "sun") is the obj. of ptc. The prep. phrase ἄχρι καιροῦ (lit., "up to a season") has a sense of "for a time." The results are instantaneous (παραχρῆμα adv. "immediately"). Luke described the event from the perception of the magician. Ἔπεσεν is the 3rd sg. aor. act. indic. of πίπτω, "fall." Although there is a compound subj., the sg. vb. suggests it is a matter of hendiadys; that is, ἀχλύς (nom. sg. fem. of ἀχλύς, -ύος, ἡ, "mist") and σκότος (nom. sg. neut. of σκότος, -ους, τό, "darkness") should be "mist and darkness fell" (BHGNT 249). Bruce (via Hobart) suggests ἀχλύς is used in medical writing to describe an inflammation that produces a cloudy appearance (Bruce, *Acts of the Apostles*, 297; see also Barrett 1.618; Rogers and Rogers 260). Περιάγων is the nom. sg. masc. of pres. act. ptc. of περιάγω, "go about"; attend. circum. Ἐζήτει is the 3rd sg. impf. act. indic. of ζητέω, "seek." The dir. obj. is χειραγωγούς (acc. pl. masc. of χειραγωγός, -οῦ, ὁ, "one who leads by the hand")

13:12 Ἰδών (nom. sg. masc. of aor. act. ptc. of ὁράω) is temp. On ἀνθύπατος (nom. sg. masc.), see 13:7. Γεγονός (acc. sg. neut. of pf. act. ptc. of γίνομαι) is the subst. obj. of ἰδών. Ἐπίστευσεν is the 3rd sg. aor. act. indic. of πιστεύω. Ἐκπλησσόμενος (nom. sg. masc. of pres. mid. ptc. of ἐκπλήσσομαι; causal) is best rendered "because he was astonished/amazed" (see, e.g., CSB, RSV, NIV, ESV). What he believed is expressed as "teaching" (διδαχῇ) that should include the symbolic import of the miracle as well as the gospel. Κυρίου is an obj. gen., "about the Lord" (NLT, NIV, NRSV, TNIV, NET, NJB).

FOR FURTHER STUDY

22. *Magic in Acts and Early Christianity (13:6–8)*

Arnold, C. E. *DLNT*, 701–5.
Aune, D. E. "'Magic' in Early Christianity and Its Ancient Mediterranean Context: A Survey of Some Recent Scholarship." *Annali Di Storia Dell'Esegesi* 24 (2007): 229–94.
Klauck J. *Magic and Paganism in Early Christianity: The World of the Acts of the Apostles*. Translated by Brian McNeil. Minneapolis: Fortress 2003.
Porter, S. E. "Magic in the Book of Acts." In *Kind of Magic: Understanding Magic in the New Testament and Its Religious Environment*, 107–21. London: T&T Clark, 2007.
Twelftree, G. "Jesus and Magic in Luke-Acts." In *Jesus and Paul: Global Perspectives in Honor of James D. G. Dunn for His 70th birthday*, 46–58. London: T&T Clark, 2009.

HOMILETICAL SUGGESTIONS

Wolves in Sheep's Clothing (13:4–12)

1. The wolf will hinder the gospel (vv. 4–8)
2. The wolf will be exposed by the shepherd (vv. 9–11)
3. The discerning person will embrace the truth (v. 12)

3. Pisidian Antioch: Gentiles Believe despite Jewish Opposition (13:13–52)

Paul's visit to Pisidian Antioch accomplishes several matters. First, it presents Paul's typical synagogue sermon in his longest speech in Acts (twenty-five vv.). It demonstrates Paul's gospel is utterly orthodox (some similarities to Peter's sermons are likely included for this purp.—see, e.g., the quote of Psalm 16). It also demonstrates the pattern of "to the Jew first, then the Gentiles." Finally, the reaction to the speech gives the historical foundations for preaching to the Gentiles (Keener 2.2026; Schnabel 565). The preaching focuses on the fulfillment of God's promises in Christ: he is Israel's promised Messiah (Schnabel 566).

a. In the Synagogue (13:13–16)

13:13 Ἀναχθέντες is the nom. pl. masc. of aor. pass. ptc. of ἀνάγω, "having put to sea"; temp. Employing a pers. pron. use of the art., the phrase οἱ περὶ Παῦλον (lit. "the ones with Paul," BHGNT 250) is a CGk. idiom that includes Paul but identifies him as the leader (Bruce, *Acts of the Apostles*, 300; T 270). Ἦλθον is the 3rd pl. aor. act. indic. of ἔρχομαι. Εἰς Πέργην (acc. sg. fem. of Πέργη, -ης, ἡ) τῆς Παμφυλίας (gen. sg. fem. of Παμφυλία, -ας, ἡ) identifies the ultimate destination as "Perga of Pamphylia"; Perga is twelve miles from the seaport of Attalia (southern Asia Minor, Bruce, *Acts of the Apostles*, 300; Johnson 229). The defection of John Mark (merely Ἰωάννης [nom. sg. masc. of Ἰωάννης, -ου, ὁ] here) is briefly expressed (anticipating 15:38–39). The ptc. ἀποχωρήσας (nom. sg. masc. of aor. act. ptc. of ἀποχωρέω; attend. circum.) is often tr. merely "left." The word with ἀπ' αὐτῶν means "to desert" (BDAG 125a; BHGNT 251). Ὑπέστρεψεν is the 3rd sg. aor. act. indic. of ὑποστρέφω, "return."

13:14 Διελθόντες is the nom. pl. masc. of aor. act. ptc. of διέρχομαι, "go on from"; temp. (BDAG 244b; ZG 393). Παρεγένοντο is the 3rd pl. aor. mid. indic. of παραγίνομαι, "arrive." Ἀντιόχειαν τὴν Πισιδίαν (acc. sg. fem. of Πισίδιος, -ου, ὁ; acc. of ref.) is identified to distinguish it from Syrian Antioch. Continuing the pattern, the group enters (εἰσελθόντες, nom. pl. masc. of aor. act. ptc. of εἰσέρχομαι) the synagogue. Ἡμέρᾳ is a dat. of time ("on the day"). The neut. gen. (descr.) pl. σαββάτων, as in a number of LXX texts (e.g., Exod 35:3; Lev 24:8), ref. to one Sabbath day, not many (BDAG 909d; BDF §141[3]). Ἐκάθισαν is the 3rd pl. aor. act. indic. of καθίζω, "sit down."

13:15 The description of the synagogue service begins with a reading (ἀνάγνωσιν, acc. sg. fem. of ἀνάγνωσις, obj. of μετά "after") of the Law and the Prophets. The leaders of the synagogue (ἀρχισυνάγωγοι, nom. pl. masc. subj.) send (ἀπέστειλαν, 3rd pl. aor. act. indic. of ἀποστέλλω, "send") πρὸς αὐτούς, presumably Paul's entourage. On the address ἄνδρες ἀδελφοί, see 1:16. The synagogue ruler invites them to speak by a cond.

sentence (εἴ marks the prot.). Ἐστίν is impers. with λόγος παρακλήσεως as the pred. nom. Τίς, then, is adj. Together it is, "if there is a certain word of exhortation among you." Πρὸς τὸν λαόν modifies "word of exhortation" and means "for the people." The apod. is a simple command λέγετε (2nd pl. pres. act. impv. of λέγω, "speak").

13:16 Paul jumped at the chance. Ἀναστάς is the nom. sg. masc. of aor. act. ptc. of ἀνίστημι; attend. circum. Κατασείσας (nom. sg. masc. of aor. act. ptc. of κατασείω, "gesture"; temp.) takes an instr. dat. τῇ (functions as a poss.) χειρί, "with his hands." On the address Ἄνδρες Ἰσραηλῖται, see 2:22. On οἱ φοβούμενοι τὸν θεόν, see 10:2, 35. Ἀκούσατε (2nd pl. aor. act. impv. of ἀκούω) is best tr. "listen" (CSB, RSV, NRSV, ESV, NET, NJB).

b. Paul's Sermon (13:17-41)

1) Israel until David's Greater Son (13:17-25)

13:17 He begins by placing the subj., θεός, at a prominent position. Israel's relationship to God is built with a cstr. around a gen. of relationship, τοῦ λαοῦ τούτου (functions adjectively) Ἰσραήλ (gen. of appos.) "of this people Israel." Paul then noted three actions (see Schnabel 574-75). First, he chose (ἐξελέξατο, 3rd sg. aor. mid. indic. of ἐκλέγομαι, "choose") "our fathers." Second, he exalted (ὕψωσεν, 3rd sg. aor. act. indic. of ὑψόω) "the people." The prep. phrase ἐν τῇ παροικίᾳ (dat. sg. fem. of παροικία, -ας, ἡ, "time in a foreign land") limits the ref. to "the sojourning" in Egypt. The art. is likely a monadic use, that is, the well-known sojourn. Third, a display of God's power is expressed as μετὰ βραχίονος (gen. sg. masc. of βραχίων, -ονος, ὁ) ὑψηλοῦ (gen. sg. masc. of ὑψηλός, -ή, -όν; attrib. gen.), "with a high arm." It is a phrase that often describes the exodus (ten of twelve times in the LXX, cf. Exod 6:1; 6:6; Deut 4:34; 5:15). Ἐξήγαγεν is the 3rd sg. aor. act. indic. of ἐξάγω, "lead out." The antecedent of αὐτῆς is Αἰγύπτου (gen. sg. fem. of Αἴγυπτος, -ου, ἡ), thus "out of it" in Eng.

13:18 Ὡς expresses an approximation (BDAG 1105b). The noun phrase τεσσερακονταετῆ (acc. sg. masc. of τεσσερακονταετής, -ές) χρόνον are accs. of time expressing a stretch of time, "and for . . . about forty years" (CSB, RSV, NASB, NIV, NRSV, ESV, TNIV, NJB). Ἐτροποφόρησεν (3rd sg. aor. act. indic. of τροποφορέω, "to put up with someone else's manners/moods") refers to God's dealings with the wilderness generation (αὐτούς).

13:19-20 Paul jumps from Moses to Joshua with καθελών (masc. nom. sg. of aor. act. ptc. of καθαιρέω, "conquer"; temp.), which takes ἔθνη ἑπτά (neut. acc. sgs.), "seven nations," as the dir. obj. The list is given in Deut 7:1. God is still the subj. of κατεκληρονόμησεν (3rd sg. aor. act. indic. of κατακληρονομέω, "divide as an inheritance"). The adv. ὡς is, again, approximate (see 3:18). The neut. dat. pls., ἔτεσιν τετρακοσίοις καὶ πεντήκοντα ("about 450 years"), are uses of the dat. to express an extent of time. It is unusual but known in HGk. (Z §54). Καὶ μετὰ ταῦτα ("after these things") in the pres. position applies the period to the sojourning (400 years), wilderness wanderings (forty years), and inheritance division (c. ten years) (see Bruce, *Acts of the Apostles*, 264). A textual var. that places it at the front of the v. applies the period to the judges, creating a chronological problem with 1 Kgs 6:1 (i.e., 480 years from the exodus to Solomon's fourth year). Ἔδωκεν is the 3rd sg. aor. act. indic. of δίδωμι. Κριτάς is the acc. pl. masc. of κριτής, -οῦ, ὁ, "judges"; dir. obj. The last phrase employing the adv. ἕως ("until") identifies Σαμουήλ (gen. sg. masc. of indecl. Σαμουήλ, ὁ) [τοῦ] προφήτου, "Samuel the prophet" as the last judge of Israel.

13:21 Κἀκεῖθεν is a crasis (καί + ἐκεῖθεν), here meaning "from that time" or "afterwards" (Barrett 1.635). Most EVV have simply "then." Ἠτήσαντο (3rd pl. aor. mid. indic. of αἰτέω) is, most likely, a mid. of pers. interest: "they asked for themselves" (BHGNT 254; Bruce, *Acts of the Apostles*, 305; Rogers and Rogers 261). God gave them Saul, son of Kish, ἐκ φυλῆς Βενιαμίν ("from the tribe of Benjamin"). The length of Saul's reign is clouded in obscurity. The MT of 1 Sam 13:1 is corrupt (it states "two years"). Paul's statement here, ἔτη τεσσεράκοντα (see 13:18; acc. of time, "forty years") agrees with the Gk. of Josephus *Ant.* 6:378 (eighteen with Samuel, twenty-two apart from him = forty). However, at 10:143 Josephus says twenty (although the latter, comparing it with the earlier, may be an approximation of Saul's independent reign). The Latin version of the *Ant.* has twenty at 6:378 (Johnson 232). There is no reason to accuse Luke (or Paul) of error at this point.

13:22 Μεταστήσας is the nom. sg. masc. of aor. act. ptc. of μεθίστημι, "remove"; temp. Ἤγειρεν is the 3rd sg. aor. act. indic. of ἐγείρω, "raise." Αὐτοῖς is a dat. of advantage (for them) or poss. (their). Εἰς βασιλέα functions much like a double-acc. cstr. as a pred. acc. modifying τὸν Δαυίδ: "to be king" (BDAG 213a; ZG 393). The statement is a blended quote of Ps 88:19 (89:10 LXX directed to "his elect one" [MT], hence the sg. ᾧ) and 1 Sam 13:14. Since Ps 88:1 refers to the Davidic covenant, it is no stretch to place it in a Christological context. Καί is adv.: "also." Μαρτυρήσας is the nom. sg. masc. of aor. act. ptc. of μαρτυρέω. Εὗρον is the 1st sg. aor. act. indic. of εὑρίσκω, "find." Δαυίδ (dir. obj.) is further identified with τὸν τοῦ Ἰεσσαί (gen. sg. masc. of indecl. Ἰεσσαί, ὁ; gen. of relationship). The art. τοῦ makes the case of the noninflected loanword, Ἰεσσαί, explicit. The art. τόν functions much like a pron. (it is hard to say it "nominalizes" a noun phrase, BHGNT 255). Ἄνδρα is an acc. of appos. further identifying Δαυίδ. Κατὰ τὴν καρδίαν μου, normally tr. "after my heart," expresses conformity to a standard. The expressed standard, καρδίαν μου, is a ref. to the will of God (BDAG 509b). This is further explained by the rel. pron. phrase that he will do (ποιήσει, 3rd sg. fut. act. indic. of ποιέω) πάντα τὰ θελήματά (dir. obj.) μου (lit. "all my wills").

13:23 Τούτου is a subst. gen. of source, "from this one." Ἤγαγεν (3rd sg. aor. act. indic. of ἄγω, "lead") is best tr. "God brought" (BDAG 16c; CSB, RSV, NASB, NIV, NRSV, ESV, NET). The vb. is modified by ἀπὸ τοῦ σπέρματος (lit. "from his seed," i.e., descendants) and κατ' ἐπαγγελίαν ("according to the promise"). The dir. obj. σωτῆρα (acc. sg. masc. of σωτήρ, -ῆρος, ὁ, "savior") is identified with an acc. of appos., Ἰησοῦν.

13:24 Προκηρύξαντος (gen. sg. masc. of aor. act. ptc. of προκηρύσσω, "proclaim publicly"; gen. abs., temp., NT hapax) takes Ἰωάννου (gen. sg. masc. of Ἰωάννης, -ου, ὁ, "John") as its subj. The gen. abs. modifies the previous v. As such, it highlights a topic construction (BHGNT 256). Πρὸ προσώπου, lit. "before his face," here is "presence." Τῆς εἰσόδου (gen. sg. fem. of εἴσοδος, -ου, ἡ, "entrance") αὐτοῦ modifies the prep. phrase, anticipating the presentation of Jesus. Βάπτισμα (acc. sg. neut. of βάπτισμα, -ατος, τό) takes μετανοίας (gen. sg. fem. of μετάνοια, -ας, ἡ) as a descr. gen., "a baptism of repentance." The gen. abs. phrase is compl. by the indir. obj. τῷ λαῷ Ἰσραήλ, "to all the people of Israel."

13:25 The adv. ὡς is temp., "as." Ἐπλήρου is the 3rd sg. impf. indic. act. of πληρόω, "fulfill," i.e., nearing the end of his ministry (BHGNT 256). The acc. dir. obj. describes John's ministry as a δρόμον (acc. sg. neut. of δρόμον, -ου, τό), "race." Ἔλεγεν (3rd sg. impf. act. indic. of λέγω) introduces a dir. question (τί). The vb. ὑπονοεῖτε (2nd pl. pres. act. indic. of ὑπονοέω, "suppose") takes a compl. inf. εἶναι (pres. act. inf. of εἰμί) with the sense of "What do you suppose I am?" The negated phrase εἰμί (1st sg. pres. indic.) is impers. with ἐγώ as the pred. nom., best tr. "It is not I." In contrast (ἀλλ᾽) the one is coming. On ἰδού, see 1:10. Ἔρχεται is the 3rd sg. pres. mid. indic. of ἔρχομαι. Μετ᾽ ἐμέ is sequential ("after me"). Εἰμί (see above) has ἄξιος ("worthy") as the pred. nom. Λῦσαι (aor. act. inf. of λύω) is compl. to ἄξιος.

2) The Gospel (13:26–37)

13:26 A long list of vocs. turns the address from history to evangelism. On the voc. Ἄνδρες ἀδελφοί, see 1:16. The second is υἱοί (voc. pl. masc.; appos.) γένους (gen. sg. neut. of γένος, -ους, τό; gen. of source mng. "from the family") Ἀβραάμ (gen. sg. masc. of indecl. Ἀβραάμ, ὁ, mng. "of Abraham," it needs no art. to specify case for it could be no other case). Next is not appos. but another addressee, as indicated by καί and ἐν ὑμῖν (BHGNT 258; Rogers and Rogers 261). "God-fearers" is expressed with a subst. ptc. φοβούμενοι (nom. pl. masc. of pres. mid. ptc. of φοβέομαι; subst.). It is unlikely that these are proselytes (as Barrett 1.639 supposes) but used in the same sense as Cornelius. Two items are fronted for emphasis: ἡμῖν (dat. pl. of ἐγώ, indir. obj.) and the subj. phrase ὁ λόγος τῆς σωτηρίας ταύτης ("the word of this salvation"). Finally, ἐξαπεστάλη (3rd sg. aor. pass. indic. of ἐξαποστέλλω, "send forth") has an official sense (BDAG 346a), that is, from God.

13:27 Paul explicitly separates his hearers from the following accusation by identifying the culprits as the inhabitants (κατοικοῦντες, nom. pl. masc. of pres. act. ptc. of κατοικέω; subst.) of Jerusalem and their rulers (ἄρχοντες, nom. pl. masc. of ἄρχων, -οντος, ὁ). A causal ptc. (ἀγνοήσαντες, nom. pl. masc. of aor. act. ptc. of ἀγνοέω, "not know") gives the reason they condemned Jesus. Ἀναγινωσκομένας (acc. pl. fem. of pres. pass. ptc. of ἀναγινώσκω; attrib.) is best tr. "which are being read." Κατὰ πᾶν σάββατον, in the attrib. position to the ptc., has a distributive prep. and a form of πᾶς. Therefore, it is redundant and emphatic (BHGNT 259). "Read every single Sabbath" would be a good rendering. Κρίναντες (nom. pl. masc. of aor. act. ptc. of κρίνω; means) followed immediately by ἐπλήρωσαν (3rd pl. aor. act. indic. of πληρόω) has the sense "by condemning they fulfilled the utterances of the prophets." The entire verse rather spirals to the point. They condemned because they were ignorant; by condemning they fulfilled the very words they heard every Sunday. Such a spiral has a very Pauline flavor.

13:28 The acc. μηδεμίαν (acc. sg. fem. of μηδείς, "not one") negates αἰτίαν (acc. sg. fem. of αἰτία, -ας, ἡ, "cause or reason") with the obj. gen. θανάτου is best tr. "not a single cause for death." Εὑρόντες (nom. pl. masc. of aor. act. ptc. of εὑρίσκω) is concessive, "although finding." The vb. ᾐτήσαντο (3rd pl. aor. mid. indic. of αἰτέω) in the mid. has the sense of a demand (BDAG 30b). The demand is given in indir. speech with an inf. ἀναιρεθῆναι (aor. pass. inf. of ἀναιρέω); with the acc. obj. it means "for him to be killed."

13:29–30 Ὡς is temp., "when." Ἐτέλεσαν (3rd pl. aor. act. indic. of τελέω) is lit. "they completed"; here, "they fulfilled." Γεγραμμένα (acc. pl. neut. of pf. pass. ptc. of γράφω) is a subst. dir. obj.: "the things having been written." Καθελόντες (nom. pl. masc. of aor. act. ptc. of καθαιρέω, "take down"; attend. circum.) assumes "him" as the obj. of the ptc. Ἔθηκαν (3rd pl. aor. act. indic. of τίθημι) also assumes an obj. Emphatic in its brevity and import, Paul bluntly affirms the resurrection. Ἤγειρεν is the 3rd sg. aor. act. indic. of ἐγείρω, "raise."

13:31 The validity of the resurrection is offered through the eyewitness accounts. Ὤφθη (3rd sg. aor. pass. indic. of ὁράω) in the pass. is "he appeared" (see 2:3). Ἐπὶ ἡμέρας expresses an extent of time (R 602; BDAG 367b; MM 235a).The comp. adj. πλείους takes an elative force (Wallace 260). The sense is "over a period of very many days." Συναναβᾶσιν (dat. pl. masc. of aor. act. ptc. of συναναβαίνω, "go up with"; subst.) is the dir. obj. of ὤφθη (BDAG 719d). The ptc. takes a dat. of the pers. accompanied (αὐτῷ, BDAG 965a; BHGNT 260). Ἀπὸ τῆς Γαλιλαίας εἰς Ἰερουσαλήμ represents the ones who had accompanied Jesus in his ministry (Barrett 1.644; Haenchen 395). On οἵτινες, see 5:16. It is the subj. in a pred. nom. cstr., with εἰσίν (3rd pl. pres. indic. of εἰμί) and μάρτυρες (nom. pl. masc. of μάρτυς, μάρτυρος, ὁ, "witness") as the compls. Altogether Paul's statements resemble in substance his recitation of the gospel in 1 Cor 15:3–7.

13:32 Ἡμεῖς is emphatic (by position and redundancy, Haenchen 411) in the sense of a contrast with the orig. disciples. Likewise, ὑμᾶς is emphasized by position. It is part of a double-acc. cstr. as the dir. obj. of the vb. (Barrett 1.645; BDF §152[2]; Bruce, *Acts of the Apostles*, 309; R 474). Εὐαγγελιζόμεθα (1st pl. pres. mid. indic. of εὐαγγελίζω) is used in its base sense of "bring good news." The prep. phrase πρὸς τοὺς πατέρας ἐπαγγελίαν (in the attrib. poss.) modifies the compl. of the double-acc. cstr. ἐπαγγελίαν (acc. sg. fem. of ἐπαγγελία, -ας, ἡ). Γενομένην (acc. sg. fem. of aor. mid. ptc. of γίνομαι; attrib.) is the only time an attrib. ptc. appears in this position in Acts (i.e., anar. following an art. noun; BHGNT 261): "the promise made to our fathers."

13:33 Ὅτι defines the content of the promise to the fathers (Barrett 1.646; Bruce [*Acts of the Apostles*, 309] calls it the third obj. of the previous v.). The dir. obj. ταύτην is fronted and puts it in focus (BHGNT 261). Most EVV render ἐκπεπλήρωκεν (3rd sg. pf. act. indic. of ἐκπληρόω) as "fulfilled." However, the vb. has a causative sense, with the mng. "he has made good" (MM 197d). The indir. obj. clause features a textual var. that is difficult to adjudicate with certainty.

1. A number of early mss. read merely ἡμῶν (𝔓⁷⁴ ℵ A B C* D). If so, the rdg. is "to our children." This makes the promise applicable to the children of the hearers. Scholars often reject it as a "nonsense" rdg. (Metzger 410). It is the most difficult, the shortest, and the earliest rdg. (see NASB).

2. Later mss read αὐτῶν ἡμῖν (C³ E L P et al.) instead. If so, the rdg. is "to us their children." The earliest extant appearance is Chrysostom (c. 407). After that, it is the sixth- and ninth-century correctors of C. The sense is a bit clearer and the promise is available to the hearers.

The means of the fulfillment is the raising up of Jesus. Ἀναστήσας (nom. sg. masc. of aor. act. ptc. of ἀνίστημι) is a ptc. of means, mng. "by having raised." What the vb. refers to may be variously interpreted:

1. Some assert that it does not refer to resurrection but "bringing him on the stage of history" (Barrett 1.645; see also Bruce, *Acts of the Apostles*, 309; Schnabel 581). Three basic reasons are: a) the resurrection is directly cited below (v. 34); b) The ref. to Psalm 2 below is to his baptism (Barrett 1.645); and c) in v. 22 David is said to be raised up in this manner and this v. parallels that mng. (Bruce, *Acts of the Apostles*, 309).

2. Others affirm it does refer to the resurrection. The resurrection is mentioned in v. 30, making this a continuation of the flow of thought (Haenchen 411). Furthermore, the connection to Jesus's baptism is tenuous (sonship is affirmed at his baptism, not necessarily Psalm 2). The ref. to the resurrection in v. 34 seems to build on this ref. Finally, if γεννάω refers to enthronement (see below), resurrection is more likely to be the specific event.

Ὡς καί introduces Scripture as the grounds. Γέγραπται is the 3rd. sg. pf. pass. indic. of γράφω. The quote from the LXX is a pred. nom. cstr. υἱός μου εἶ (2nd sg. pres. indic. of εἰμί) σύ. The vb. γεγέννηκά (1st sg. pf. act. indic. of γεννάω) has no sense of "coming into existence" in this context. Instead, as an enthronement song, the vb. refers to the installment as king (see Keener 2.2068). It is not becoming or being adopted as Son, but a public declaration by resurrection (Bock 468).

13:34 Ὅτι δέ introduces a disputed phrase followed by substantiation (BHGNT 262). It offers the interpretation of the second Scripture citation before it is cited, thus the tr. "and as for the fact that . . ." (RSV, NASB, ESV, NET ["regarding the fact"], CSB ["as to his raising"]). Ἀνέστησεν (3rd sg. aor. act. indic. of ἀνίστημι) clearly refers to the resurrection here (ἐκ νεκρῶν). The mng. of resurrection is defined as a permanent state of life, using the special fut. pointing verbal form μέλλοντα (acc. sg. masc. of pres. act. ptc. of μέλλω; result) that takes a compl. inf., ὑποστρέφειν (pres. act. inf. of ὑποστρέφω, "return") to corruption. Μηκέτι (no longer) presumes decay is the present state. Οὕτως εἴρηκεν (3rd sg. pf. act. indic. of λέγω) introduces two Scriptures that together validate the resurrection. Δώσω is the 1st sg. fut. act. indic. of δίδωμι.

Τὰ ὅσια (acc. pl. neut. of ὅσιος, -ία, -ον, "holy, righteous") refers to the holy things of God thus, the divine promises (BDAG 728b; ZG 395 "gracious promises") given to David. Δαυίδ is indecl. Culy and Parsons suggest it may be a gen. (BHGNT 262). While morphologically other cases are possible, there is little doubt that David is the recipient of the promises whatever the case. The holy things are also described as πιστά (acc. pl. neut. πιστός, -ή, -όν), "faithful." Louw and Nida tr. it, "I will give to you the divine promises made to David, promises that can be trusted" (LN 33.290). Isaiah 55:3 invites the hearers to come and partake of a permanent covenant that is made based on God's promises to David (at least 2 Sam 7:15 but more likely considering all the fut. promises to David as available to the people of God).

13:35 Most EVV, following BDAG (251c), take διότι in the sense of "therefore." The best rendering is inferential, given the covenantal promise to David. "For also" seems to connect the resurrection of Jesus to the promises to David by specifically citing it. Ἐν ἑτέρῳ is likely another "psalm," but "elsewhere" (NIV) or another "passage" (CSB), or "text" (NJB), more precisely tr. the idiom. There is obvious connection thematically in the contexts, but Paul also employs the rabbinic hermeneutic principle of *gezerah shevah*, utilizing analogous words to connect distant texts (Keener 2.2073). Here the connection is δίδωμι (δώσεις, 2nd sg. fut. act. indic., "you will not allow" in this context) and ὅσιος, -ία, -ον (ὅσιόν, acc. sg. masc., subst, mng. "holy One") as well as another ref. to διαφθορά (διαφθοράν, acc. sg. fem., "decay"). The final term Paul had already used to define the nature of resurrection. In doing so, he had given his hearers reason to interpret for themselves the cited psalm, although in the next v. he makes it explicit.

13:36 On μέν, see 13:37. The two dat. noun phrases following ὑπηρετήσας (nom. sg. masc. of aor. act. ptc. of ὑπηρετέω, "serve"; temp.) has been interpreted at least three ways (see Barrett 1.649).

1. Since the vb. takes a dat. of the pers. served as dir. obj., ἰδίᾳ γενεᾷ, "his own generation," is the explicit pers. although fronted. If so, τῇ . . . βουλῇ (with τοῦ θεοῦ in the attrib. poss.) is a dat. of means, "by the will of God" (KJV, NKJV). Barrett (1:649) rightly suggests cautiously that this is the most natural rdg.
2. Yet, the position of ἰδίᾳ γενεᾷ may suggest it is a dat. of time ("in his own generation"). However, one would expect an acc. cstr., but see 13:19. If so, τῇ . . . βουλῇ is the dir. obj. Bruce suggests v. 22 is analogous to this rdg. (Bruce, *Acts of the Apostles*, 311). Most modern EVV follow this rdg. (see also Johnson 235; Keener 2.2073).
3. Finally, τῇ . . . βουλῇ might modify ἐκοιμήθη (3rd sg. aor. pass. indic. of κοιμάομαι, "sleep"), suggesting his death was normal and natural. This is the least natural rdg.

The phrase "gathered (προσετέθη, 3rd sg. aor. pass. indic. of προστίθημι, "add") to his fathers" is a stock phrase regarding death in the OT (Judg 2:10; 2 Kgs 22:20). In contrast to the "holy one," David experienced (εἶδεν, 3rd sg. aor. act. inidic. of ὁράω) decay (διαφθοράν, acc. sg. fem. of διαφθορά, -ᾶς, ἡ).

13:37 Δέ concludes a lengthy μέν . . . δέ cstr. highlighting the contrast between David and Christ (BHGNT 263; Bruce, *Acts of the Apostles*, 311). The one whom God raised (ἤγειρεν, 3rd sg. aor. act. indic. of ἐγείρω, ref. to Jesus) did not decay (εἶδεν διαφθοράν, see 13:34, 35, and 36).

3) Paul's Appeal (13:38–41)

Particularly in the appeal to respond, a Pauline stamp can be discerned. Paul appeals to belief to be justified from our sins. Attempts to tr. δικαιόω as "freed" (RSV) is unlikely, esp. in a Jewish context. The forensic mng. is certainly warranted (see NLT, "declared right with God"). Although the grammar is difficult, the inability of the law to save anyone is in line with the Paul we meet in the letters.

13:38–39 Paul's address (on γνωστὸν . . . ἔστω, see 2:14) is solemn. On the voc. ἄνδρες ἀδελφοί, see 1:16. The two together slow down the reader and mark the following statement as highly important. Ὅτι introduces the content of what is to be known.

Τούτου ref. to Christ as the source of the forgiveness proclaimed (καταγγέλλεται, 3rd sg. pres. pass. indic. of καταγγέλλω). Ἀπὸ πάντων (gen. pl. neut. of πᾶς, πᾶσα, πᾶν) belongs to the clause in v. 39 but is fronted for focus (BHGNT 264). The rel. pron. ὧν is likely a gen. by attraction to πάντων (Z §21 seems to identify it thus). On attraction, see 1:2; this instance has both low agentivity and prominence. If so, it would normally function as the dir. obj. of the vb., here, ἠδυνήθητε (2nd pl. aor. pass. indic. of δύναμαι compl. by δικαιωθῆναι aor. pass. inf. of δικαιόω, "justify"). The best rendering would be "from everything, which you cannot be justified. . . ." Ἐν νόμῳ Μωϋσέως is best considered instr. of means, "by the law of Moses" (see Bruce, *Acts of the Apostles*, 312). The upshot is that the law cannot produce justification at all (not that it can produce some, contra Witherington 413). The thought is complete by v. 39. Ἐν τούτῳ is instr., "by him." Πᾶς ὁ πιστεύων (nom. sg. masc. of pres. act. ptc. of πιστεύω; subst.) is the subj. of δικαιοῦται (3rd sg. pres. pass. indic. of δικαιόω). Together it has the sense "and by him everyone who believes is justified from all things, which is not possible under the law of Moses."

13:40 Βλέπετε (2nd pl. pres. act. impv. of βλέπω) has the sense of "pay attention." The neg. subjunc. as a prohibition, μὴ ἐπέλθῃ (3rd sg. aor. act. subjunc. of ἐπέρχομαι), takes εἰρημένον (nom. sg. neut. of pf. act. ptc. of λέγω; subst.) as the subjunc. The prep. phrase ἐν τοῖς προφήταις, as a locat., points to v. 41 as another scriptural citation.

13:41 What is obliquely referred to as something that would "come upon you" in the previous v. is explicitly "to perish" in the citation of Hab 1:5. Paul is citing an analogy in Scripture rather than a promise-and-fulfillment motif. In Habakkuk the Chaldeans are coming upon the scoffers who don't believe; Paul now applies it eschatologically to his hearers (Bruce, *Acts of the Apostles*, 312), that is, "Your situation is very similar!" Three impvs. are addressed to "despisers" of God's message (καταφρονηταί, voc. pl. masc. of καταφρονητής, -οῦ, ὁ). The LXX rdg. of "despisers" rather than "among the Gentiles" in the MT is found at Qumran (1QpHab 2.1, 3, 5; see Barrett 1.653; Bruce, *Acts of the Apostles*, 312). The first impv., ἴδετε (2nd pl. aor. act. impv. of ὁράω), is normally a poetic call for attention ("Behold"). Here it is mitigated a bit by being in a series. The second, θαυμάσατε (2nd pl. aor. act. impv. of θαυμάζω), indicates something out of the ordinary is seen. The third, ἀφανίσθητε (2nd pl. aor. pass. impv. of ἀφανίζω, "perish"), is shocking. Ὅτι is causal, giving the reason they perish. Ἔργον ἐργάζομαι ἐγώ is highly emphatic by repetition of lexemes and the redundant pron. The work (ἔργον), however, is rejected emphatically, expressed by the double neg. (οὐ μή) in the apod. of a third-class cond. (truly hypothetical). With πιστεύσητε (2nd pl. aor. act. subj. of πιστεύω, prohibitory subjunc.) the neg. has the sense of complete rejection. The prot. (introduced by ἐάν) takes the concessive sense "even if." In Paul's appropriation of the text, he takes the place of the man who "explains in detail" (ἐκδιηγῆται, 3rd sg. pres. mid. subjunc. of ἐκδιηγέομαι).

HOMILETICAL SUGGESTIONS

The Gospel as God's Promise to Israel (13:17–41)

1. Understand God's promise (vv. 17–25)
2. Understand that Jesus fulfills God's promise (vv. 26–37)
3. Believe on Jesus to receive God's promise for the forgiveness of sin (vv. 38–41)

c. The Response (13:42–52)

In v. 42, the KJV and NKJV specify Jews leaving the synagogue and Gentiles urging based on the *byz.* text. It seems to be an attempt to clarify, given the later context. However, it makes the move to the Gentiles more abrupt. As it stands, the move is more organic and fits with Luke's theme that God is leading the movement. It also fits with Paul's pattern of "to the Jew first and also the Gentiles," seen in Cyprus as well. This mandate is expressed as a compelling necessity in v. 46. Barrett states, "The Christian message was the fulfilment of Israelite history and especially of Israelite prophecy. No other people had so clear a right to hear what God now had to say . . ." (Barrett 1.656).

13:42 Ἐξιόντων is the gen. pl. masc. of pres. act. ptc. of ἔξειμι, "depart"; gen. abs., temp. The subj. of the gen. abs., αὐτῶν, must ref. to Paul and Barnabas for, by definition, the subj. of a gen. abs. must be different than the subj. of the main vb. (παρεκάλουν, 3rd pl. impf. indic. act. of παρακαλέω, "urge"). That subj. is not explicit but easily understood to be the hearers of the sermon, often tr. "the people" for clarity (see, e.g., CSB, RSV, NASB, NIV, ESV). Μεταξύ is used adj. in the attrib. position modifying σάββατον, mng. "next" (Barrett 1.654; Bruce, *Acts of the Apostles*, 313; ZG 395). As the obj. of the prep. εἰς, the mng. is "on the next Sabbath" (one would expect ἐν, but see BDF §206). The content of the urging is in indir. speech employing the inf. λαληθῆναι (aor. pass. inf. of λαλέω) and the subj. τὰ ῥήματα ταῦτα ("these words").

13:43 Λυθείσης (gen. sg. fem. of aor. pass. ptc. of λύω; gen. abs., temp.) refers to the discharge of the synagogue, mng. "after the synagogue was dismissed." Paul and Barnabas were followed (ἠκολούθησαν, 3rd pl. impf. act. indic. of ἀκολουθέω, takes the dats. Παύλῳ and Βαρναβᾷ as dir. objs.). The ref. of the phrase σεβομένων (gen. pl. masc. of pres. mid. ptc. of σέβω, "worship"; attrib.) προσηλύτων is to those Gentiles who had offered a sacrifice and been baptized, circumcised, and faithful rather than to "God-fearers" (see ch. 10). It is best tr. "worshiping proselytes" (Barrett 1.654; Bruce, *Acts of the Apostles*, 313; Haenchen 413; Keener 2.2093). On οἵτινες, see 7:53; the antecedent is Paul and Barnabas. Προσλαλοῦντες is the nom. pl. masc. of pres. act. ptc. of προσλαλέω; attend. circum. The impf. ἔπειθον (3rd pl. impf. indic. of πείθω) is likely tendential (Rogers and Rogers 262), "attempting to persuade." This fits with the impf. use of πείθω (Z §252). The mng. of the phrase "to continue (προσμένειν, pres. act. inf. of προσμένω; indir. speech) in the grace of God" is disputed:

1. Some take it to mean successful evangelism. The new converts would then endure in the faith (Barrett 1.654; Bock 462; Haenchen 413; Johnson 252). The vb. προσμένω frequently occurs as a call to endurance for young believers (Keener 2.2093). It does not necessarily imply apostasy is something a real Christian does.
2. The phrase may be a ref. to faithful Jews and proselytes to continue to live pious lives (BHGNT 267). It is highly unlikely that Paul and Barnabas would be satisfied with any piety apart from Christ.

13:44 The arrival of the next Sabbath is expressed with a dat. of time (τῷ ἐρχομένῳ [dat. sg. masc. of pres. mid. ptc. of ἔρχομαι; attrib.] σαββάτῳ) best rendered "on the next Sabbath" (NIV, TNIV, NET). Σχεδόν (adv., mng. "almost"; three times in NT, twice in Acts [19:26]). Πᾶσα ἡ πόλις is fronted for emphasis, noting the surprising size (BHGNT 267). Συνήχθη is the 3rd sg. aor. pass. indic. of συνάγω. Ἀκοῦσαι is the aor. act. inf. of ἀκούω; purp. The dir. obj. phrase τὸν λόγον τοῦ κυρίου is equivalent to "the word of God" that, in Acts, means the gospel.

13:45 Luke presents the opposition on the shallowest of terms. When they saw (ἰδόντες, nom. pl. masc. of aor. act. ptc. of ὁράω; temp.) the crowd the Jews became jealous (ἐπλήσθησαν, 3rd pl. aor. pass. indic. of πίμπλημι, with a gen. dir. obj. ζήλου [gen. sg. masc. of ζῆλος, -ου, ὁ]). Ἀντέλεγον (3rd pl. impf. act. indic. of ἀντιλέγω, "dispute") takes a dat. dir. obj. phrase τοῖς . . . λαλουμένοις (dat. pl. neut. of pres. act. ptc. of λαλέω), with Paul as the agent (ὑπὸ Παύλου). Βλασφημοῦντες (nom. pl. masc. of pres. act. ptc. of βλασφημέω) is either manner, describing how the Jews spoke out against Paul (see NJB, "used blasphemies to contradict"), or (as most EVV) it is a ptc. of means, "by blaspheming [him]" (i.e., "reviling him," ESV, NET; "insulting him," CSB; BHGNT 268).* Many take it as attend. circum. (Rogers and Rogers 262). See NRSV, "and blaspheming, they contradicted" and KJV, NKJV, "contradicting and blaspheming." Adjudication is not certain, but a contentious, ugly meeting is.

13:46 The report shifts from only Paul speaking to include Barnabas as well. The term παρρησιασάμενοί (nom. pl. masc. of aor. mid. ptc. of παρρησιάζομαι; manner) means "having spoken boldly"; as a vb. of speaking it acts as an adv. to εἶπαν (3rd pl. aor. act. indic. of λέγω; see RSV, NASB, ESV, "spoke out boldly," CSB, "boldly replied" [BHGNT 268]). Παρρησιάζομαι (seven times in Acts, twice outside) is intended to produce a "prophetic coloration of his characters" (Johnson 241; ἰδού below has the same affect, see 1:10). Ὑμῖν (dat. of indir. obj.) is fronted for emphasis (BHGNT 268). Ἀναγκαῖον (nom. sg. neut. of ἀναγκαῖος, -α, -ον; pred. adj. with impers. ἦν, "it was necessary") is cstr. much like δεῖ with an acc. subj. (τὸν λόγον) of a compl. inf. (λαληθῆναι, aor. pass. inf. of λαλέω). Paul's mandate of Jew first is indicated by the ordinal πρῶτον ("first"). They now present a cause-and-effect situation introduced by ἐπειδή ("since"). The consequences of rejecting the gospel (ἀπωθεῖσθε, 2nd pl. pres. mid. indic. of ἀπωθέω; lit. "you pushed aside," a graphic term for rejection [Bock 463]) is expressed ironically and sarcastically. In the debate arena, they assume the hearers affirm the word of God, so the only understanding of their rejection (because the missionaries are correct) is that they judged (κρίνετε, 2nd pl. pres. act. indic. of κρίνω) themselves unworthy of eternal life. Thus, the effect: Paul and Barnabas turn to the Gentiles (στρεφόμεθα, 1st pl. pres. pass. indic. of στρέφω, "turn"; the pass. has an act. force [BDAG 948d]).

13:47 Γάρ defends the turn to the Gentiles by introducing Isa 49:6 as a command (ἐντέταλται, 3rd sg. pf. mid. indic. of ἐντέλλομαι). The command to the servant of Isaiah is likewise the command to Paul and Barnabas (Bock 464). Τέθεικά (1st sg. pf. act. indic. of τίθημι) has the sense of "ordained/appointed" (NET). Εἰς φῶς is best understood to function as a pred. modifier (R 482–83; BHGNT 269, "as a light"). Ἐθνῶν is an obj. gen. The phrase τοῦ εἶναί σε (subj. of the inf.) is likely the result of being appointed light; "so that you would be. . ." is a lit. tr. Because εἰς σωτηρίαν appears with a parallel cstr. (εἰς φῶς), it is likely the same syntax (see Luke 2:32, where φῶς is in parallel cstr. with σωτηρία). If so, the second εἰς σωτηρίαν also functions as a pred. modifier. However, it is unlikely the missionaries intend to represent themselves "as salvation." Since the quote is closer to the MT than the LXX (Bock 464) one should consider that the Heb. "my salvation" ‍(yəšûʿātī) lies behind the intent of the citation. Thus, the NJB tr. it "so that my salvation may reach." The parallel to ἐσχάτου τῆς γῆς found in Acts 1:8 is apparent. Implicitly the fulfillment of Jesus's words is associated with the turn to the Gentiles.

13:48 The pres. ptc ἀκούοντα (nom. pl. neut. of pres. act. ptc. of ἀκούω; temp) presents simultaneous action to the response of the Gentiles (ἔχαιρον, 3rd pl. impf. act. indic. of χαίρω and ἐδόξαζον, 3rd pl. impf. act. indic. of δοξάζω). Ἐπίστευσαν is the 3rd pl. aor. act. indic. of πιστεύω. The subord. rel. pron. ὅσοι ("as many as") identifies those who believed. The cstr. ἦσαν τεταγμένοι (nom. pl. masc. of pf. pass. ptc. of τάσσω, "put in place"; periph. plpf.) is best "as many as had been appointed" (NASB) or "all who had been appointed" (CSB). Ζωὴν αἰώνιον represents the second and last appearance of this phrase "eternal life" in Acts (see 13:46). Altogether the statement "is as unqualified a statement of absolute predestination . . . as found anywhere in the NT" (Barrett 1.658). No word of a double-predestination is stated. Luke clearly saw no contradiction between human responsibility and divine sovereignty (Keener 2.2102).

13:49 Διεφέρετο is the 3rd sg. impf. pass. indic. of διαφέρω, "carry through." The subj. phrase ὁ λόγος τοῦ κυρίου (like ὁ λόγος τοῦ θεοῦ) consistently refers to the gospel in Acts. Χώρας (gen. sg. fem. of χώρα, -ας, ἡ, "region") refers to the area around Pisidian Antioch. The evangelism was likely done by assistants to Paul and Barnabas (Barrett 1.659; Haenchen 414).

13:50 The successful missionary activity likely added to the Jewish angst. Παρώτρυναν (3rd pl. aor. act. indic. of παροτρύνω, "incite") is only used here in biblical literature with the idea of rousing the emotions (BDAG 780c). Two groups are stirred up. First, γυναῖκας is surrounded by two adj. items. Σεβομένας (acc. pl. fem. of pres. mid. ptc. of σέβω; attrib.) in the mid. is "worshiping," i.e., Gentile proselytes (BHGNT 333). Εὐσχήμονας (acc. pl. fem. of εὐσχήμων, -ον) is "honorable" in the sense of "nobil-ity" (BDAG 414a; *TDNT* 2.770–72). These highborn wives surely had influence (Haenchen 414) on the second group (perhaps, in part, their husbands [Schnabel 590]). The subst. adj. πρώτους designates the "leading men" of the city. They purposed to stir up (ἐπήγειραν, 3rd pl. aor. act. indic. of ἐπεγείρω) persecution (διωγμὸν acc. sg. masc. of διωγμός, -οῦ, ὁ) against Paul and Barnabas. The persecution takes the form of exile (ἐξέβαλον, 3rd pl. aor. act. indic. of ἐκβάλλω). Ὁρίων (gen. pl. neut. of ὅριον, -ου, τό; obj. of prep.) refers to the region or district.

13:51 The subst. ptc. ἐκτιναξάμενοι (nom. pl. masc. of aor. mid. ptc. of ἐκτινάσσω) with the obj. κονιορτόν (acc. sg. masc. of κονιορτός, -οῦ, ὁ, "dust") is lit. "ones shaking the dust off their feet." However, the idiomatic phrase is best tr. as an attend. circum. or temp. ptc. phrase in Eng. (BHGNT 271). Jesus's sim. injunction in Luke 9:5; 10:11 and Matt 10:15 is reflective of the Jewish custom of declaring the place to be pagan with no community within it (Str-B 1:571; Barrett 1.660; see also Thompson 148). The action is ἐπ' αὐτούς ("against them"), signifying a denouncement of the Jews within Antioch. From there they went to Iconium.

13:52 As was his custom, Luke summarizes regarding the spiritual health of the disciples (presumably in Antioch). They are filled (ἐπληροῦντο, 3rd pl. impf. act. indic. of πληρόω) with joy and the Holy Spirit.

FOR FURTHER STUDY

23. Divine Sovereignty in Acts (13:48)

Cosgrove, C. H. "The Divine Dei in Luke-Acts: Investigations into the Lukan
    Understanding of God's Providence." *NovT* 26 (1984): 168–90.
Lescelius, R. H. "Foreknowledge: Prescience or Predestination?" *Reformation & Revival*
    12 (2003): 25–39.
Ng, E. Y. L. "Ἦσαν Τεταγμένοι in Acts 13:48: Mid. Voice or Passive Voice? Implications
    for the Doctrine of Divine Election." *CGST Journal* 50 (2011): 185–99.
Str-B, 2.726

HOMILETICAL SUGGESTIONS

When Truth Challenges Power and Privilege (13:42–52)

1. Many intellectually honest will be interested (vv. 42–44)
2. Many personally threatened will respond in jealousy and slander (vv. 45–48)
3. When slander doesn't work, they stir up persecution (vv. 49–50)
4. That the Word of God cannot be stopped produces joy (vv. 51–52)

4. South Galatia: Iconium, Derbe, Lystra (14:1–23)

Persecution and persistence permeate this section on the evangelization of the cities of southern Galatia. At Iconium (14:1–6), a lengthy successful ministry resulted in persecution by the rulers. Lystra and Derbe are treated together (14:7–20). At Lystra (14:7–19) there was not the great success. To their dismay, Paul and Barnabas were the object of idolatry, then persecution, stirred up by Jews from Antioch. At Derbe (14:21) they have great success. On a return trip through these towns they emphasized the necessity to endure persecution (which they have exemplified), and they appointed elders in every church. The return trip to Antioch, where they stay for a long period of time, is the topic of 14:24–28.

a. Iconium (14:1–7)

14:1 On ἐγένετο δέ, see 4:5. The phrase κατὰ τὸ αὐτό may be taken in two ways:

1. Barrett makes the convincing case that it is not "together" (so BDAG 513a) but "in the same manner," referring to their practice of "to the Jew first" (Barrett 1.667; Bruce, *Acts of the Apostles*, 317; NIV, CSB "as usual").
2. Many EVV take the phrase to modify ἐγένετο with the inf. εἰσελθεῖν (aor. act. inf. of εἰσέρχομαι) as epex., with the mng. "the same thing happened: Paul and Barnabas went . . ." (NLT, CEB, see also NRSV; Schnabel 602).

With the adv., οὕτως ὥστε is "they spoke in such a way" (NASB ["manner"], NET, ESV, CSB, ZG 396). Πιστεῦσαι (aor. act. inf. of πιστεύω) indicates result and takes the phrase πολὺ πλῆθος as its subj. ("a great many"). The gen. pls. Ἰουδαίων τε καὶ Ἑλλήνων ("of both Jews and Greeks") are part. gens.

14:2 Ἀπειθήσαντες (nom. pl. masc. of aor. act. ptc. of ἀπειθέω; attrib.) modifies Ἰουδαῖοι, mng. "unbelieving Jews." Ἐπήγειραν is the 3rd pl. aor. act. indic. of ἐπεγείρω, "stir up." BDAG (502a) suggests ἐκάκωσαν (3rd pl. aor. act. indic. of κακόω, "embitter") τὰς ψυχὰς τῶν ἐθνῶν κατὰ τῶν ἀδελφῶν should be tr. "poisoned the minds of the Gentiles against the brothers."

14:3 On ἱκανόν, see 7:20, 8:11 (with χρόνον, "for a long time"). On μὲν οὖν, see 1:6. Διέτριψαν is the 3rd pl. aor. act. indic. of διατρίβω, "continue." Παρρησιαζόμενοι is the nom. pl. masc. of pres. mid. ptc. of παρρησιάζομαι, "speak boldly"; manner. Ἐπὶ τῷ κυρίῳ (with dat. obj.) is best a causal cstr. (NASB, Barrett 1.670; Bruce, *Acts of the Apostles*, 278; Z §126). Μαρτυροῦντι is the dat. sg. masc. of pres. act. ptc. of μαρτυρέω; attrib. Χάριτος may be attrib., "to his gracious word," or obj., "the word about his grace." Διδόντι (dat. sg. masc. of pres. act. ptc. of δίδωμι) is a ptc. of means, mng. "by granting" (Haenchen 420; Rogers and Rogers 263). Γίνεσθαι (pres. mid. inf. of γίνομαι) works with δίδωμι to make a causal cstr. (BHGNT 273). "By causing signs and wonders to come through their hands" is a good rendering. Luke's point seems to be that the word of God is not hindered (somewhat forecasting the end of the book).

14:4 The attitude of Iconium regarding the missionaries was divided (ἐσχίσθη, 3rd sg. aor. pass. indic. of σχίζω). In contrast to the leading men, the subj. of the vb. (πλῆθος, many EVV "people") modified by a part. gen. πόλεως presents a less unified front. The division is expressed in a typical μὲν . . . δέ cstr., almost strictly parallel. Each clause employs the art. as an indef. pron. (οἱ, mng. "some") and σὺν with the dat. of party (Ἰουδαίοις /ἀποστόλοις). Only the first clause has an expressed vb., ἦσαν (3rd pl. impf. indic. of εἰμί). The pl. of ἀπόστολος must include Barnabas as well as Paul. The sense of it, then, should be with the mng. "missionary" (see 1:26).

14:5 Ὡς is temp., "when." Ἐγένετο (3rd sg. aor. mid. indic. of γίνομαι) has ὁρμή (nom. sg. fem. of ὁρμή, -ῆς, ἡ, "an attempt") as either the subj. (BDAG 724a; RSV, NASB) or the pred. nom. of an impers. vb. (BDF §393[6]; BHGNT 274; KJV, NIV). There is no difference in mng. Ὁρμή in CGk. meant "a violent motion toward" (i.e., "rush"). The present usage keeps its violent overtones but falls short of "rush" (Barrett 1.672). Ἐθνῶν and Ἰουδαίων are both gen. of means connected by τε καί, "by both Gentiles and Jews." Σύν adds their rulers (ἄρχουσιν) to the plot. Two infs. give the content of the plot: ὑβρίσαι (aor. act. inf. of ὑβρίζω, "harm") and λιθοβολῆσαι (aor. act. inf. of λιθοβολέω, "stone").

14:6–7 Συνιδόντες is the nom. pl. masc. of aor. act. ptc. of συνοράω, "aware"; attend. circum. Κατέφυγον (3rd pl. impf. aor. act. of καταφεύγω), the preferred prep., intensifies φεύγω to "they escaped" (ZG 397). The general destination is the cities of Lyconia (the specific destinations are indicated by accs. of ref.; i.e., "namely . . ." Barrett 1.673), Λύστραν (acc. sg. fem. of Λύστρα, -ας, ἡ, "Lystra"; the word does appear as a neut. as well [cf. 14:8], see BDAG 605c; BDF §57), Δέρβην (acc. sg. fem. of Δέρβη, -ης, ἡ, "Derbe"), and περίχωρον (acc. sg. fem. of περίχωρος, -ον, "the surrounding region"; subst.). Κἀκεῖ is a crasis of καὶ ἐκεῖ, "and there." It is followed by a periph. impf. εὐαγγελιζόμενοι (nom. pl. masc. of pres. mid. ptc. of εὐαγγελίζομαι; on its voice, see 5:42) ἦσαν (3rd pl. impf. indic. of εἰμί).

b. Lystra and Derbe (14:8–23)

14:8 Τις ἀνήρ ("a certain man") commonly introduces a new character and scene. Ἐν Λύστροις (dat. neut. pl. of Λύστρα, -ων, τά) sets the scene in Lystra. The adj. phrase ἀδύνατος . . . τοῖς ποσίν locat. of place) is lit. "powerless in his feet," describing one who cannot walk. Ἐκάθητο is the 3rd sg. impf. mid. indic. of κάθημαι, "sit." It is followed by a second adj. phrase describing the extent of his handicap: χωλός (nom. pl. masc. of χωλός, -ή, -όν, "lame") ἐκ κοιλίας μητρὸς αὐτοῦ is lit. "lame from his mother's womb," often tr. "from birth" (CSB, RSV, NLT, NIV). The difficulty is heightened with a rel. pron. (ὅς) clause. Οὐδέποτε περιεπάτησεν (3rd sg. aor. act. indic. of περιπατέω) is lit. "who never walked." The lengthy description is to demonstrate the magnitude of the healing to come. The unnamed man had insufficient physical structures to enable locomotion. Walking could only be possible if these structures are provided/created for him.

14:9 Ἤκουσεν (3rd sg. aor. act. indic. of ἀκούω) takes a double obj./compl. cstr. in the gen. Παύλου (gen. sg. masc.) and λαλοῦντος (gen. sg. masc. of pres. act. ptc. of λαλέω). The topic switches to Paul in the subj. clause. Ἀτενίσας is the acc. sg. masc. of aor. act. ptc. of ἀτενίζω, "look intently at"; temp. It takes a dat. of pers. (αὐτῷ). Ἰδών (nom. sg. masc. of aor. act. ptc. of ὁράω; temp.) has a cognitive dimension here ("recognizing"), so ὅτι introduces the content of the knowledge. Since πίστιν has no obj., it is likely not a ref. to saving faith but the expectation or hope for healing (Bock 475). Thus, τοῦ σωθῆναι (aor. pass. inf. of σῴζω) is a purp. cstr. (contra BDF §400[2]; Z §384) most likely mng. "that he might be healed," although some double-entendre is not unlikely (Johnson 247; Schnabel 606).

14:10 The miracle is stated in the briefest of terms. With a loud voice (μεγάλῃ φωνῇ), Paul commands him to rise (ἀνάστηθι, 2nd sg. aor. act. impv. of ἀνίστημι). Ὀρθός (nom. sg. masc. of ὀρθός, -ή, -όν) is used adv. (Johnson 247), mng. "stand up straight" (MIT). The dir. mention of the feet (ἐπὶ τοὺς πόδας) recalls that they were the man's problem. The contrast between the aor. ἥλατο (3rd sg. aor. mid. indic. of ἅλλομαι, "leap") and the impf. περιεπάτει (3rd sg. impf. act. indic. of περιπατέω; inceptive) suggests "he jumped up and began to walk around."

14:11 The crowd's (ὄχλοι) response is disturbing. Ἰδόντες is the nom. pl. masc. of aor. act. ptc. of ὁράω; temp. or causal. Ὅ is a headless rel. pron., "that which." Ἐποίησεν is the 3rd sg. aor. act. indic. of ποιέω. Ἐπῆραν is the 3rd pl. aor. act. indic. of ἐπαίρω, "lift up." Λυκαονιστί is an adv. mng. "in the Lycaonian language." Λέγοντες is the nom. pl. masc. of pres. act. ptc. of λέγω; pleonastic. Ὁμοιωθέντες (nom. pl. masc. of aor. pass. ptc. of ὁμοιόω, "make like"; attend. circum.) takes a dat. obj. (ἀνθρώποις), mng. "having become like men." Κατέβησαν is the 3rd pl. aor. act. indic. of καταβαίνω.

14:12 Ἐκάλουν (3rd pl. impf. act. indic. of καλέω) takes a comp. double-acc. structure; Βαρναβᾶν Δία (Barnabas, Zeus) and Παῦλον Ἑρμῆν (Paul, Hermes): the head of the Gk. pantheon and his messenger. Ὁ ἡγούμενος (nom. sg. masc. of pres. mid. ptc. of ἡγέομαι; subst., pred. nom.) τοῦ λόγου is lit. "the leader of the word," that is, "chief speaker" (CSB, KJV, NASB, NIV, NRSV, ESV, TNIV, NET).

14:13 On τε, see 1:15. The ptc. phrase τοῦ ὄντος (gen. sg. masc. of pres. ptc. of εἰμί; attrib.) πρὸ τῆς πόλεως modifying Διός (gen. sg. masc. of Ζεύς, Διός, ὁ) refers to a temple at the gates of the city (Haenchen 427). Ταύρους (acc. pl. masc. of ταῦρος, -ου, ὁ, "bull") καὶ στέμματα (acc. pl. neut. of στέμμα, -ατος, τό, "garlands of wool and flowers," BDAG 942c) are the objs. of the ptc. ἐνέγκας (acc. sg. masc. of aor. act. ptc. of φέρω; temp.). They are fronted for emphasis. Ἐπὶ τοὺς πυλῶνας ("unto the gates") refers to both objs. Ἤθελεν is the 3rd sg. impf. act. indic. of θέλω. Θύειν is the pres. act. inf. of θύω, "sacrifice"; compl. Altogether it was an incredibly expensive, albeit misguided, gesture.

14:14 To their horror, Paul and Barnabas found themselves the objs. of idolatry. Ἀκούσαντες is the nom. pl. masc. of aor. act. ptc. of ἀκούω; temp. The subj. ἀπόστολοι is accompanied by the attrib. masc. nom. sgs. Βαρναβᾶς and Παῦλος (see 14:4). Ripping (διαρρήξαντες, nom. pl. masc. of aor. act. ptc. of διαρρήγνυμι, "tear"; attend. circum.) their cloaks is a common expression of great distress (Johnson 248). Running (ἐξεπήδησαν, 3rd pl. aor. act. indic. of ἐκπηδάω, "rush out") throughout the crowd shouting (κράζοντες, nom. pl. masc. of pres. act. ptc. of κράζω; manner) to stop the misidentification and idolatry demonstrates an authentic revulsion to idolatry.

14:15 Λέγοντες (nom. pl. masc. of pres. act. ptc. of λέγω) is joined by καί to the previous ptc., so while it introduces dir. speech, it is still a ptc. of manner (BHGNT 278). The question posed is rhetorical, with the mng. "Stop doing these things!" (Haenchen 428). Ποιεῖτε is the 2nd pl. pres. act. indic. of ποιέω. The basis for the implied command follows. The redundant ἡμεῖς is emphatic, the subj. of a pred. nom. clause with ἐσμεν (1st pl. pres. indic. of εἰμί). Ὁμοιοπαθεῖς (nom. pl. masc. of ὁμοιοπαθής, -ές, "of like nature") modifies the pl. pred. nom. ἄνθρωποι. Εὐαγγελιζόμενοι (nom. pl. masc. of pres. mid. ptc. of εὐαγγελίζομαι; indir. discourse; on its voice, see 5:42). The prep. phrase ἀπὸ τούτων τῶν ματαίων (gen. pl. neut. of μάταιος, -αία, -αιον; subst., obj. of prep.) means "from these useless things." The inf. ἐπιστρέφειν (pres. act. inf. of ἐπιστρέφω) might be an expression of indir. speech (BHGNT 279; R 1036). It is more likely compl. and here virtually identical to the inf. of purp. (BDF §392[3]; the Western text makes purp. explicit with ὅπως). The obj. of the ptc. is the living (ζῶντα, acc. sg. masc. of pres. act. ptc. of ζάω; attrib.) God.

The actions of God explained from here to v. 17 form the foundation for evangelizing the nations, for the passage describes his relationship to them, the reason for their distance to him, and his continual witness to them. Although closely resembling Exod 20:11 and Ps 146:6 (LXX 145), it is a common refrain in the OT (Barrett 1.680; see also Acts 17:24). The vb. ἐποίησεν (3rd sg. aor. act. indic. of ποιέω) is followed by four objs. in the acc: heaven (οὐρανόν), the earth (γῆν), the sea (θάλασσαν), and everything (πάντα) in them (all).

14:16 The dat. παρῳχημέναις (dat. pl. fem. of pf. mid. ptc. of παροίχομαι; attrib.) is lit. "having been past" but best tr. "in the previous generations" (γενεαῖς, dat. pl. fem. of γενεά, -ᾶς, ἡ; obj. of prep.) in Eng. Εἴασεν (3rd sg. aor. act. indic. of ἐάω, "permit") is completed by πορεύεσθαι (pres. mid. inf. of πορεύομαι; compl.). Ὁδοῖς (dat. pl. fem. of ὁδός) is a dat. of manner, "in their own ways."

14:17 Καίτοι (crasis of καί and τοί) is concessive, "and yet" (NASB), "although" (CSB). Ἀφῆκεν (3rd sg. aor. act. indic. of ἀφίημι) is negated (οὐκ) and takes a double-acc. cstr. with the fronted ἀμάρτυρον (acc. sg. masc. of ἀμάρτυρος, -οῦ, ὁ, "without a witness") as a compl. and a refl. αὐτόν as the dir. obj. The ptc. ἀγαθουργῶν (nom. sg. masc. of pres. act. ptc. of ἀγαθοεργέω) is likely causal "because he was doing good," (RSV) although many EVV take it to be means, "by doing good" (NASB, NRSV, ESV, NET, NJB). The rest of the v. explains the content of "doing good." These all are objs. of the causal/means (and thus epex., BHGNT 280) ptc. διδούς (nom. sg. masc. of pres. act. ptc. of δίδωμι). The first was fronted οὐρανόθεν (adv. "from heaven," the position favors modifying the subsequent noun and not the ptc.) ὑετούς (acc. pl. masc. of ὑετός, -οῦ, ὁ, "rain"). Second is καιρούς καρποφόρους (acc. pl. masc. of καρποφόρος, -ον, "fruit-bearing"; NT hapax), mng. "fruitful seasons." The statement regarding God's benefits is capped off with an adv. result ptc. ἐμπιπλῶν (nom. sg. masc. of pres. act. ptc. of ἐμπίπλημι, "satisfy"), followed by fem. gen. sgs., gens. of content, τροφῆς (of τροφή, -ῆς, ἡ, "food") and εὐφροσύνης (of εὐφροσύνη, -ης, ἡ, "gladness").

14:18 Λέγοντες (nom. pl. masc. of pres. act. ptc. of λέγω) is either means ("by saying these things," most EVV; "with," e.g., RSV, NJB) or concessive ("even though . . . ," e.g., NASB, CSB), most likely the former. The adv. μόλις ("with difficulty," or "barely" [CSB], used twice outside of Acts in NT) modifies κατέπαυσαν (3rd pl. aor. act. indic. of καταπαύω, "stop, dissuade") and suggests a narrow mg. of error. The gen. art. inf. τοῦ μὴ θύειν (while technically a negated result cstr., BHGNT 280) after vbs. of hindering means "from" (ZG 398), that is, "from sacrifice."

14:19 Jews from Antioch and Iconium arrived; ἐπῆλθαν (3rd pl. aor. act. indic. of ἐπέρχομαι, "arrive") suggests almost an Old West posse. The crowd is quickly turned (perhaps disillusioned by the team's denials of deity). Πείσαντες is the nom. pl. masc. of aor. act. ptc. of πείθω; temp. Λιθάσαντες is the nom. pl. masc. of aor. act. ptc. of λιθάζω, "stone"; temp. The use of the impf. ἔσυρον (3rd pl. impf. indic. act. of σύρω, "drag") suggests the disciples (in the next v.) intervened in the process (Barrett 1.684). Νομίζοντες (nom. pl. masc. of pres. act. ptc. of νομίζω) is causal, mng. "because they supposed." Τεθνηκέναι is the pf. act. inf. of θνήσκω, "die"; compl.

14:20 Κυκλωσάντων (gen. pl. masc. of aor. act. ptc. of κυκλόω, "encircle"; gen. abs., temp.) is an interesting choice of words. BDAG 574b places it under "with hostile intent," suggesting an intervention (Johnson 253). Ἀναστάς is the acc. sg. masc. of aor. act. ptc. of ἀνίστημι; attend. circum. There is no indication Paul rose from the dead (see νομίζω above). Both preservation from or healing of injuries are miraculous, though (Barrett 1.684; Bock 479). Paul enters εἰσῆλθεν (3rd sg. aor. act. indic. of εἰσέρχομαι) the city. On the next day (τῇ ἐπαύριον, see 10:9) he left, ἐξῆλθεν (3rd sg. aor. act. indic. of ἐξέρχομαι) εἰς Δέρβην, "for Derbe."

14:21 The ptcs. εὐαγγελισάμενοί (nom. pl. masc. of aor. mid. ptc. of εὐαγγελίζω, temp., [on its voice, see 5:42]) and μαθητεύσαντες (nom. pl. masc. of aor. act. ptc. of μαθητεύω, "make a disciple"; temp. [the only time used in Acts] modified by ἱκανούς) briefly describe the visit to Derbe, although the last ptc. implies a longer time (Schnabel 613). Ὑπέστρεψαν is the 3rd pl. aor. act. indic. of ὑποστρέφω. The order suggests a return trip in the order they came; an act of great bravery (Bruce, *Acts of the Apostles*, 326; Bock 482).

14:22 The reason to return through the cities is pastoral (Johnson 254). Ἐπιστηρίζοντες (nom. pl. masc. of pres. act. ptc. of ἐπιστηρίζω, "strengthen"; purp.) τὰς ψυχάς refers to the spiritual health of the disciples (μαθητῶν). Thus, the following ptc., παρακαλοῦντες (nom. pl. masc. of pres. act. ptc. of παρακαλέω), while indir. speech., is also epex. They strengthened by encouraging. The ptc. is compl. by ἐμμένειν (pres. act. inf. of ἐμμένω), mng. "to remain" in the faith. It is almost identical to 13:43 (cf. also 11:23), likely with the same mng.: a call to endurance (Barrett 1.686, understandable in the face of persecution seen). Καὶ ὅτι switches to dir. speech (Johnson 254). It introduces another dimension of the exhortation, that suffering (πολλῶν θλίψεων, "many troubles") is an unavoidable (δεῖ) part of the journey to enter (εἰσελθεῖν, aor. act. inf. of εἰσέρχομαι) the kingdom.

14:23 The ptc. χειροτονήσαντες (nom. pl. masc. of aor. act. ptc. of χειροτονέω, "appoint"; temp.) has Paul and Barnabas as the subj. Κατ᾽ ἐκκλησίαν is distributive; "in every church" with the pl. πρεσβυτέρους without a doubt refers to a plurality of elders in every church (for single-elder a sg. is necessary). Προσευξάμενοι (masc. nom. pl. of aor. mid. ptc. of προσεύχομαι; attend. circum.) μετὰ νηστειῶν ("with fasting") implies an accompanying fast (not the means of worship). To entrust (παρέθεντο, 3rd pl. aor. mid. indic. of παρατίθημι) to the Lord is not a statement of abandonment, but of confidence in the Lord's providence, suggesting worthiness. The object is somewhat vague, but surely means the entirety of the church, not just the elders (BHGNT 283). Πεπιστεύκεισαν is the 3rd pl. plpf. indic. act. of πιστεύω.

HOMILETICAL SUGGESTIONS

God's Continuing Witness to the Nations (14:15–17)

1. God made and therefore owns everything (v. 15)
2. He allowed the nations to go their own ways (v. 16)
3. Even there he was declaring himself (v. 17)

The Missionary Response to Persecution (14:1–23)

1. Preach boldly and know when to move on (vv. 1–7)
2. Understand commitment to the truth may lead to persecution (vv. 8–20)
3. Prepare the church continually to remain steadfast (vv. 21–23)

5. Return to Syrian Antioch (14:24–28)

14:24–25 Their trip through Galatia is related rather briefly, referencing, at first, regions not cities. They go through (διελθόντες, nom. pl. masc. of aor. act. ptc. of διέρχομαι; temp.) Pisidia (east toward Antioch). The vb. ἦλθον (3rd pl. aor. act. indic. of ἔρχομαι) and the prep. εἰς relay the destination (due south to Pamphylia). After evangelizing (λαλήσαντες, nom. pl. masc. of aor. act. ptc. λαλέω; temp., with the obj. τὸν λόγον) the city of Perga, they went southwest (κατέβησαν, 3rd pl aor. act. indic. of καταβαίνω) to the city of Attalia.

14:26 Κἀκεῖθεν, see 13:21. Ἀπέπλευσαν is the 3rd pl. aor. act. indic. of ἀποπλέω, "set sail." That it was appropriate to return to Syrian Antioch is expressed by ὅθεν ("from where") with a periph. plpf. ἦσαν παραδεδομένοι (nom. pl. masc. of pf. pass. ptc. of παραδίδωμι), mng. "they had been entrusted." Τῇ χάριτι with the vb. has the sense "to place under the good favor of God." Ἐπλήρωσαν (3rd pl. aor. act. indic. of πληρόω) refers to the implicit mandate of παραδίδωμι and the explicit commission at 13:2. The phrase suggests the reason for the return to Syrian Antioch was, at least in part, because they had fulfilled the original mandate.

14:27 Two temp. ptcs. set up the report to the church at Antioch. The first is the landing (παραγενόμενοι is the nom. pl. masc. of aor. mid. of παραγίνομαι; temp.) at Antioch. The second is gathering (συναγαγόντες, nom. pl. masc. of aor. act. ptc. of συνάγω; temp.) the church. The impf. ἀνήγγελλον (3rd pl. impf. indic. act. of ἀναγγέλλω, "report") suggests a long meeting. The rel. pron. ὅσα is lit. "as many as," but may be understood as "everything that" (BDF §304; sim. KJV, RSV, NLT, NASB, NIV, CSB). Zerwick notes that it also may be exclamatory, "What great things!" (ZG 399). The latter fits the lexical stock of the pron. best. Ἐποίησεν (3rd sg. aor. act. indic. of ποιέω) with God as the subj. and modified by μετ' αὐτῶν (ref. to the apostles, indic. association, BHGNT 284 [see 7:9]) indicates the success was the work of God through available servants. Ἤνοιξεν (3rd sg. aor. act. indic. of ἀνοίγω) introduces a metaphor regarding the Gentiles' openness to the gospel at the hand of God. Θύραν πίστεως (lit. a gen. of content) completes the metaphor, "a door of faith."

14:28 Διέτριβον is the 3rd pl. impf. indic. act. of διατρίβω, "continue." The acc. of time (χρόνον) is modified by litotes (οὐκ ὀλίγον): "not short" means "a long time" (e.g., KJV, NASB, NIV). The tr. however loses the rhetorical effect of litotes that is a form of understatement for effect.

B. JERUSALEM COUNCIL (15:1–35)

The Jerusalem Council dealt with the first great theological crisis of the church. The crisis had been brewing since Cornelius (Acts 10) but its roots went further back. Luke has shown the gospel taking root (at the Lord's direction) farther and farther from Judaism. From Jews to Samaritans, to proselytes, to God-fearers, and with the church at Antioch to Gentiles completely separate from Judaism. To the circumcision party of the church this surely was an irritant that kept growing. The last group was the proverbial straw on the camel's back. The apostles had given no quarter regarding Gentile inclusion, having witnessed God's validation. At the Jerusalem Council, the official stance of the church was hammered out.

1. Setting (15:1–5)

15:1 Just as the church at Syrian Antioch was riding high, trouble showed up in the form of unnamed Jewish "Christians" (τινες, "some men") who came (κατελθόντες, nom. pl. masc. of aor. act. ptc. of κατέρχομαι, "come down"; temp.) from Jerusalem teaching heresy. The impf. ἐδίδασκον (3rd pl. impf. act. indic. of διδάσκω) is either progressive (RSV, ESV, NIV, TNIV), indicating numerous encounters, or inceptive (Barrett 2.699), "began teaching" (NASB, NET). It is more ominous that the obj. of the teaching is ἀδελφούς and not τὸν λαόν (i.e., they are not evangelizing). The content of their teaching (indicated by ὅτι) goes against the direction of God's movement since ch. 8. It is presented in a neg. third-class cond. (indicated by ἐὰν μή). With περιτμηθῆτε (2nd pl. aor. pass. subjunc. of περιτέμνω) the phrase is "unless you are circumcised." The dat. ἔθει (dat. sg. neut. of ἔθος, -ους, τό, dat. of rule [BHGNT 285] sometimes called "cause" [ZG 399 "by reason of"]) with the gen. Μωϋσέως is "according to the custom of Moses." The apod. is chilling: οὐ δύνασθε (2nd pl. pres. mid. indic. of δύναμαι) with the compl. inf. σωθῆναι (aor. pass. inf. of σῴζω), "you are not able to be saved."

15:2 Γενομένης (gen. sg. fem. of aor. mid. ptc. of γίνομαι; gen. abs., temp.) takes στάσεως (gen. sg. fem. of στάσις, -εως, ἡ, "strife, disunion") and ζητήσεως (gen. sg. fem. of ζήτησις, -εως, ἡ, "debate") as the compound subj. of the ptc. On οὐκ ὀλίγης (litotes), see 14:28. The dat. sg. masc. nouns Παύλῳ and Βαρναβᾷ are dats. of respect. Ἔταξαν (3rd pl. aor. act. indic. of τάσσω), "they appointed," presumably ref. to the church. It takes the compl. inf. ἀναβαίνειν and a threefold dir. obj. (Παῦλον καὶ Βαρναβᾶν καί τινας ἄλλους). Three prep. phrases set up the parameters of the meeting: πρός, the invitees (ἀποστόλους and πρεσβυτέρους); εἰς, the place (Ἰερουσαλήμ); and περί, the topic (ζητήματος [gen. sg. neut. of ζήτημα, -ατος, τό] τούτου, "this dispute").

15:3 On μὲν οὖν, see 1:6; the presence here suggests the trans. nature of the passage (Barrett 2.702). Προπεμφθέντες (nom. pl. masc. of aor. pass. indic. of προπέμπω, "assist") is the subj. of the vb. (BHGNT 285). It assumes a variety of provisions/arrangements for a journey (BDAG 873c), made explicitly by the church (ὑπό). Διήρχοντο is the 3rd pl. impf. mid. indic. of διέρχομαι, "go through." That it mentions both (τε . . . καί) Phoenicia (Φοινίκην, acc. sg. fem. of Φοινίκη, -ης, ἡ) and Samaria (Σαμάρειαν, acc. sg. fem. of Σαμάρεια, -ας, ἡ) suggests they took a dir. route. The ptc. ἐκδιηγούμενοι (nom. pl. masc. of pres. mid. ptc. of ἐκδιηγέομαι, "tell [in detail]"; attend. circum.) expresses their activity relating the conversion (ἐπιστροφήν) of the Gentiles. Ἐποίουν

(3rd pl. impf. act. indic. of ποιέω) is the same subj. (the embassy from Antioch) and is causative (Z §227; see also Rogers and Rogers 265). The response is great joy (χαρὰν μεγάλην). Πᾶσιν τοῖς ἀδελφοῖς is a dat. of agency phrase mng. "by all the brothers." This response demonstrates that Gentile inclusion is not only welcome but celebrated in the churches.

15:4 Upon arrival (παραγενόμενοι, nom. pl. masc. of aor. mid. of παραγίνομαι; temp.) they were well received (παρεδέχθησαν, 3rd pl. aor. pass. indic. of παραδέχομαι). The prep. ἀπό takes on the domain of ὑπό with the pass. (Z §90). It takes three gen. objs., ἐκκλησίας . . . ἀποστόλων . . . πρεσβυτέρων ("the church, the apostles, and the elders"). The list sets up a contr. with the objectors in v. 5. Ἀνήγγειλάν is the 3rd pl. aor. act. indic. of ἀναγγέλλω, "report." On ὅσα see 14:27. The vb. ἐποίησεν (3rd sg. aor. act. indic. of ποιέω) is modified by μετ᾽ αὐτῶν that is instr.: "by means of" (MM 401a).

15:5 Ἐξανέστησαν is the 3rd pl. aor. act. indic. of ἐξανίστημι, "rise up." The art. τῶν functions as a pron. nominalizing the prep. phrase ἀπὸ τῆς αἱρέσεως (gen. sg. fem. of αἵρεσις, -εως, ἡ, "sect, party") τῶν Φαρισαίων (gen. pl. masc. of Φαρισαῖος, -ου, ὁ; part. gen.). The statement should not be read in the typical neg. overtones. In the Gospel, Luke's position regarding the Pharisees is not wholly neg. (contra Johnson 260). Since the nature of a theological conservative is to resist change, what happened here had to be huge for them. Luke's description of them is πεπιστευκότες (nom. pl. masc. of pf. act. ptc. of πιστεύω; attrib.) without qualification. Surely among them there was a continuum of the necessity from "for salvation" to "for fellowship" (see Bruce, *Acts of the Apostles*, 334). Although clearly some continued in this vein, the conclusion of the council would suggest major concession by them. Λέγοντες (nom. pl. masc. of pres. act. ptc. of λέγω; attend. circum.) introduces their contention. It is expressed (indic. by ὅτι) with "robust rigor" by δεῖ, "must" (Schnabel 632). The content of the necessity is a pair of compl. infs.: περιτέμνειν (pres. act. inf. of περιτέμνω, "circumcise") and παραγγέλλειν (pres. act. inf. of παραγγέλλω, "command"). The latter has its own compl. inf. τηρεῖν (pres. act. inf. of τηρέω) with the obj. τὸν νόμον Μωϋσέως, "the law of Moses."

2. The Formal Council: Dispute and Testimony (15:6–12)

15:6 Συνήχθησάν (3rd pl. aor. pass. indic. of συνάγω, "gather") is the start of more formal proceedings (although "council" in modern terms might be somewhat anachronistic). While others were in attendance (see v. 22), that the decision would not be a vote by the church (Barrett 2.713) is implied by the subj. of the vb., ἀπόστολοι and πρεσβύτεροι joined by τε . . . καί (both apostles and elders). Ἰδεῖν is the aor. act. inf. of ὁράω; purp. Λόγου (gen. sg. masc.; obj. of prep.) has the sense "matter."

15:7 Peter, not Paul and Barnabas, led off the testimony. Gentile inclusion unmediated by Judaism is presented not as an aberration from Antioch. Instead, it was defended by one of Jerusalem's own. Πολλῆς . . . ζητήσεως (gen. sg. fem. of ζήτησις, "much debate") is fronted for emphasis before the ptc. γενομένης (gen. sg. fem. of aor. mid. ptc. of γίνομαι; gen. abs., temp.), likely indicating a rigorous discussion. Ἀναστάς is the nom. sg. masc. of aor. act. ptc. of ἀνίστημι; attend. circum. On ἄνδρες ἀδελφοί, see 1:16. The phrase ὑμεῖς ἐπίστασθε (2nd pl. pres. mid. indic. of ἐπίσταμαι), mng. "you know," is emphatic by the redundant pron. The prep. phrase ἀφ᾽ ἡμερῶν ἀρχαίων (an idiomatic

phrase mng. "in the early days," RSV, NASB, ESV) is limited by ἐν ὑμῖν and refers
to the events in Acts 10 (Johnson 261). Ἐξελέξατο (3rd sg. aor. mid. indic. of ἐκλέγω,
"choose") takes a complicated dir. obj. cstr. of two inf. phrases. Ἔθνη (acc. pl. neut.
of ἔθνος, -ους, τό) is the subj. of the first ἀκοῦσαι (aor. act. inf. of ἀκούω) that has its
own obj., λόγον τοῦ εὐαγγελίου ("the gospel message"). Πιστεῦσαι (aor. act. inf.) is the
second obj. in the comp.

15:8 The attrib. adj. καρδιογνώστης modifies θεός and is best rendered "the God who
knows the heart." Ἐμαρτύρησεν is the 3rd sg. aor. act. indic. of μαρτυρέω. Αὐτοῖς refers
to the Gentiles. Δούς (acc. pl. masc. of aor. act. ptc. of δίδωμι) is a ptc. of means, "by
giving." Καθὼς καὶ ἡμῖν ("just as to us") places the Gentile and Jewish believers on
equal terms, prefiguring his entire argument.

15:9 Οὐθέν (acc. sg. neut. adj. of οὐθείς; subst., dir. obj.) is fronted for emphasis, mng.
"nothing." Διέκρινεν is the 3rd sg. aor. act. indic. of διακρίνω, "discriminate." The prep.
μεταξύ ("between") identifies the constituents that God considered the same. The τε
καί cstr. with the gens. ἡμῶν and αὐτῶν highlights the equal consideration but is hard
to tr. smoothly into Eng. Most EVV simply have "and." The dat. τῇ πίστει can be
interpreted two ways (although both views affirm the necessity of faith in salvation):

1. As a dat. of ref. pointing backward. The mng. then is "He made no distinction
   between us and them *regarding (our) faith* (BHGNT 288; Keener 2.2234).
2. As a dat. of means pointing forward, modifying the ptc. καθαρίσας (nom. sg.
   masc. of aor. act. ptc. of καθαρίζω). The mng. in this case is "having cleansed
   their hearts by faith" (Barrett 2.717; Bock 449; Haenchen 445; Schnabel
   634).

15:10 Νῦν οὖν is inferential given God's obvious opinion on the matter. The question
introduced by τί ("why?") is rhetorical. Πειράζετε (2nd pl. pres. act. indic. of πειράζω,
"test") τὸν θεόν is a common OT theme (see, e.g., Exod 17:2; Num 14:22; Ps 78:41,
56) based on Deut 6:16. The force of the rhetorical question (tinted with accusation)
definitely includes a warning: "Stop testing God." The rest of Peter's case refutes an
absurd expectation by merely stating it (see Barrett 2.717). Ἐπιθεῖναι (aor. act. inf. of
ἐπιτίθημι, epex. inf. [Bruce, *Acts of the Apostles*, 336; BHGNT 290]) ζυγόν has a Sem.
flavor and should be tr. "by putting a yoke" (Z §392; RSV, NASB, NIV, ESV, NET,
NJB). By the use of the term μαθητῶν (poss. gen.), Peter gives no ground to question
the status of the believing Gentiles. However, since the term is generic of believers,
there is also an inference to Jewish Christians as well regarding the law made explicit
below. The rel. pron. ὅν takes ζυγόν (acc. sg. masc. of ζυγός, -οῦ, ὁ, "yoke") as its
antecedent. The neg. οὔτε . . . οὔτε ("neither . . . nor") comp. like items ("our Fathers"
and "us"). Ἰσχύσαμεν (1st pl. aor. act. indic. of ἰσχύω, "be able") takes the compl. inf.
βαστάσαι (aor. act. inf. of βαστάζω, "bear").

15:11 Ἀλλά presents the contrast to the absurd thought in v. 10, so "on the contrary . . ."
is a good rendering (NRSV, NET, MIT). Διὰ τῆς χάριτος might modify πιστεύομεν (1st
pl. pres. act. indic. of πιστεύω), mng. "we believe through the grace . . ." (KJV, MIT).
However, it is more likely it is fronted for emphasis and modifies σωθῆναι (aor. pass.
inf. of σῴζω) with the mng. "saved through the grace . . ." (most EVV take it this way,
Barrett 2.719; BHGNT 290; Bruce, *Acts of the Apostles*, 337; Haenchen 446). Most

EVV rightly take the inf. to be indir. speech, "we believe that we are saved. . . ." Καθ'
ὃν τρόπον κἀκεῖνοι is an idiomatic phrase mng. "in the same way they are" (it is best to
keep the assumed εἰμί in the same tense as the main vb. and not migrate it to the fut.
". . . they will" as RSV, ESV).

15:12 Surprisingly, the contribution of Paul and Barnabas is a rather short summary. It
was supporting evidence to Peter's stance. Ἐσίγησεν (3rd sg. aor. act. indic. of σιγάω)
as an ingressive aor. is "they became silent." Πᾶν τὸ πλῆθος ("the whole multitude")
likely includes the gallery as well (Barrett 2.721). Ἤκουον (3rd sg. impf. act. indic.
of ἀκούω; the switch from sg. to pl. is normal for collective sgs. like πλῆθος [ZG
400]) takes the gens. Βαρναβᾶ (gen. sg. masc. of Βαρναβᾶς, -ᾶ, ὁ, "Barnabas") and
Παύλου as dir. objs. and the compl. ptc. ἐξηγουμένων (gen. pl. masc. of pres. mid. ptc.
of ἐξηγέομαι, "declare [in detail]," Luke tends to use the term in eyewitness accounts
[Keener 3.2240]). The rel. pron. ὅσα takes the internal σημεῖα and τέρατα (acc. pl.
fem. of τέρας, -ατος, τό; strikingly, the last time for either word in Acts) and is likely
exclamatory, "What great signs and wonders!" (see ZG 400 [ref. to 14:27], 399).

3. James's Response on Behalf of the Jerusalem Church (15:13–21)

15:13 Σιγῆσαι (aor. act. inf. of σιγάω) takes αὐτούς (ref. to Paul and Barnabas) as its
subj. and is the obj. of the prep. Μετά, lit. "after they became silent,"; it is best tr. "after
they finished" (RSV, NIV, NRSV). Ἀπεκρίθη (3rd sg. aor. pass. indic. of ἀποκρίνομαι) is
in a pleonastic cstr. with λέγων (nom. sg. masc. of pres. act. ptc. of λέγω). Essentially,
"James (Ἰάκωβος) replied" (RSV, NSRV, ESV). The cstr., however, is solemn (MM
64d; Z §229). On ἄνδρες ἀδελφοί, see 1:16. Ἀκούσατέ (2nd pl. aor. act. impv. of ἀκούω)
takes μου as dir. obj. mng. "listen to me."

15:14 Συμεών (nom. sg. masc.; subj.) is an archaic form (see Luke 2:25, 34; Rev
7:7; and, significantly, 2 Pet 1:1) only used elsewhere in Acts at 13:1 of a prophet.
Ἐξηγήσατο is the 3rd sg. aor. mid. indic. of ἐξηγέομαι (see v. 12). Καθώς after words
of speaking introduces indir. speech (BDAG 494a); "how" in most EVV. Ἐπεσκέψατο
(3rd sg. aor. mid. indic. of ἐπισκέπτομαι, "visit") is modified by an adv. πρῶτον, "first."
Λαβεῖν (aor. act. inf. of λαμβάνω; purp.) indicates the intent of the visitation. Λαὸν τῷ
ὀνόματι (dat. of advantage) αὐτοῦ is "a people for his name."

15:15 Τούτῳ (dat. dir. obj.) is fronted for emphasis. Συμφωνοῦσιν is the 3rd pl. pres.
act. indic. of συμφωνέω, "agree." Λόγοι with προφητῶν (poss. gen.) might be a ref. to
the Book of the Twelve, or a clue that there will be other allusions as well (Beale and
Carson 589; Witherington 459). It surely is a ref. to Scripture introduced by καθὼς
γέγραπται (3rd sg. pf. act. indic. of γράφω).

15:16 The citation is a rather free ref. of Amos 9:11, with μετὰ ταῦτα ("after these
things") as James's setting the context (Bock 503, although sim. to Jer 12:15). There
may be a common text between the LXX and Qumran at places (see, e.g., CD 7.15,
16), but this does not suggest the quotation is extremely close (for more, see Barrett
2.725–27). God's actions are described as compound: ἀναστρέψω (1st sg. fut. act. indic.
of ἀναστρέφω ("I will return") and ἀνοικοδομήσω (1st sg. fut. act. indic. of ἀνοικοδομέω,
"I will rebuild"). The dir. obj. phrase, σκηνὴν Δαυὶδ ("tent of David") τὴν πεπτωκυῖαν
(acc. sg. fem. of pf. act. ptc. of πίπτω; attrib.), is lit. "David's fallen tent" (CSB, NIV,

TNIV). The ref. in the LXX refers to the eschatological people of God that understand σκηνή as "tabernacle" (Barrett [2:725] notes the possibility that the MT does as well, for the restoration of the king includes the kingdom). All the 3rd pers. prons. that follow, though fem. (in agreement with σκηνή) should be tr. "it." The subst. ptc. phrase κατεσκαμμένα (acc. pl. neut. of pf. pass. ptc. of κατασκάπτω, "tear down") αὐτῆς is the dir. obj. of ἀνοικοδομήσω (1st sg. fut. act. indic. of ἀνοικοδομέω, "rebuild"). Ἀνορθώσω is the 1st sg. fut. act. indic. of ἀνορθόω, "restore" (see Heb 12:12).

15:17–18 Ὅπως with ἐκζητήσωσιν (3rd pl. aor. act. subjunc. of ἐκζητέω, "seek") produces a statement of purp. (BDAG 718b; BDF §369; R 986). In this case, the purp. of the restoration is that the κατάλοιποι (nom. pl. masc. of κατάλοιπος, -ον; subst. adj., mng. "remaining people") would seek the Lord (κύριον). Most take the καί as epex., clarifying the previous subj. (see, e.g., Bruce, *Acts of the Apostles*, 341). Ἔθνη (nom. pl. neut. of ἔθνος, -ους, τό) is in appos. to κατάλοιποι. Ἐπικέκληται (3rd sg. pf. pass. indic. of ἐπικαλέω) takes ὄνομά as the subj. and is lit. "upon whom my name is called." However, it is idiomatic of ownership. "Someone's name is called over someone to designate the latter as the property of the former" (BDAG 373b; see also Keener 3.2252). Thus, "I have called to be my own" (NET) is correct. The redundant prep. phrase ἐπ᾽ αὐτούς is a lit. tr. of the MT that requires it to add gender to its rel. pron. (Barrett 2.727). Most EVV skip it. The conclusion is typical of the prophets. Λέγει (3rd sg. pres. act. indic. of λέγω) κύριος, "the Lord says." The latter is modified by the attrib. ptc. ποιῶν (nom. sg. masc. of pres. act. ptc. of ποιέω). Ταῦτα is the obj. of the ptc., mng. "who is doing these things." Amos 9:11 stops at ταῦτα. In v. 18, γνωστά (acc. pl. neut. of γνωστός, -ή, -όν, "be known") ἀπ᾽ αἰῶνος ("things forever known") is therefore either James's own comment or an oblique ref. to Isa 45:21 (Beale and Carson 591), likely a little of both.

Marshall noted the following regarding this text: James's "after these things" means after something else had happened—that is, after God's judgment is turned away. The phrase "rebuild its ruins" refers to the temple, not resurrection or the dynasty of David. The temple, however, is not a physical building but the eschatological people of God. Allusions to Zech 8:22; Jer 12:15; and Isa 45:21 also point to the inclusion of the Gentiles. The phrase "all the nations" declares God's ownership of all people. These, among other matters, make it clear the restored temple is the church. The inclusion of the Gentiles (widely attested in the prophets) as already belonging to God would imply no need to become Jews first (Beale and Carson 992; see also Schnabel 641; Witherington 459).

FOR FURTHER STUDY

24. Jerusalem Council: James, Amos 9, and the Inclusion of the Gentiles (15:13–21)

Bauckham, R. "James and the Gentiles (Acts 15.13–21). In *History, Literature and Society in the Book of Acts*. Edited by B. Witherington III, 154–84. Cambridge: Cambridge University Press, 1996.

———. "James and the Jerusalem Church." In BAFCS 1, 415–80.

Beale and Carson, 592–93.

Bennema, C. "The Ethnic Conflict in Early Christianity: An Appraisal of Bauckham's
Proposal on the Antioch Crisis and the Jerusalem Council." *JETS* 56 (2013): 753–63.
Lake, K. "The Apostolic Council." In *Beginnings* 5, 195–212.

15:19 Διό (inferential conj.) builds on both the testimony and the Scripture. Ἐγὼ
κρίνω (1st sg. pres. act. indic.of κρίνω, "judge") is emphatic. It is difficult to know
the exact sense of the statement. Is it a binding pronouncement (Witherington 467),
James's personal but weighty opinion (Haenchen 449), or is he making a motion in a
meeting (Bruce, *Acts of the Apostles*, 341)? The use of παρενοχλεῖν (pres. act. inf. of
παρενοχλέω, mng. "to cause another annoyance" [Johnson 266]) without an acc. subj.
expresses the whole as James's decision (Barrett 2.729; most EVV incorrectly add
"we"). Since Acts 16:4 and 21:25 imply a decision by the apostles and elders, some
mid. ground may be in order. James, as the leader of the Jerusalem church, has decided
that he (and by extension, that church) will not pester the Gentiles. Then he offers a
suggestion for peace. The prep. phrase ἀπὸ τῶν ἐθνῶν (functioning like a part. gen.)
modifies the ptc. ἐπιστρέφουσιν (dat. pl. masc. of pres. act. ptc. of ἐπιστρέφω; subst.),
mng. "the ones from the Gentiles turning" to God.

15:20 Ἀλλ' offers a contrast to "harassing." Ἐπιστεῖλαι is the aor. act. inf. of ἐπιστέλλω,
"write a letter." The gen. art. with the inf., τοῦ ἀπέχεσθαι (pres. mid. inf. of ἀπέχω), is a
purp. statement. The mid. voice suggests a voluntary action (i.e., he is not imposing a
new law, even though intrans.). "Refrain" is a good tr. In this mng., it takes a gen. obj.
(BDAG 103a, technically a gen. of separation; Z §386). The four items that are pro-
hibited are each a part of common pagan temple worship (the following is condensed
from Witherington 460–64; see also BHGNT 295). These terms should be considered
as four separate pagan activities in the venue of their temples. First, ἀλισγημάτων (gen.
pl. neut. of ἀλίσγημα, -ατος, τό) τῶν εἰδώλων (gen. pl. neut. of εἴδωλον, -ου, τό), "pollution of idols," is a generic term that includes eating in the presence of idols. Second,
πορνείας (gen. sg. fem. of πορνεία, -ας, ἡ), if in a temple context, means "prostitution,"
in a social context any sexual immorality. Third, πνικτοῦ (gen. sg. neut. of πνικτός, -ή,
-όν; subst.) means "something strangled," referring to ritual sacrifice. Fourth, αἵματος
likely refers to ritual drinking of blood. The point is not only those things that are
particularly offensive to Jews but renouncing idolatry both ritually and culturally (see
1 Thess 1:9; 1 Pet 4:3). The suggestion is that they needed to make it clear that while
they agree Gentiles can enter the kingdom as Gentiles, there must be a clean break
with idolatry. There is no space for syncretism of any sort.

15:21 The support (γάρ) is scriptural (Μωϋσῆς is a euphemism; see "being read"
below). Ἐκ γενεῶν ἀρχαίων is lit. "from generations of antiquity," best rendered "since
ancient times." Both instances of κατά are distributive ("in each city" and "on every
Sabbath"). Κηρύσσοντας (acc. pl. masc. of pres. act. ptc. of κηρύσσω; subst.) is the
obj. of the vb. ἔχει (3rd sg. pres. act. indic. of ἔχω). Αὐτόν is the obj. of the ptc. ref. to
Moses. Together it means "Moses has had someone preaching him." Ἀναγινωσκόμενος
(nom. sg. masc. of pres. pass. ptc. of ἀναγινώσκω; temp.) is either a temp., "being
read," or means "by being read" because it modifies "Moses" (BHGNT 296).

   The larger question regards just how does this support the conclusion James has
drawn?

It would seem that the best understanding is not so much regarding table fellow-ship (though surely included) but concern for previous foundational teaching. For generations, Moses has been taught in these cities, specifically rejecting idolatry and its accompanying filth. For Gentile Christians to ignore this for a cultural assimilation would: (a) violate the Scripture; (b) impede Jewish evangelism; and (c) create a disrup-tion in fellowship. Keener, although rejecting the view taken here, is certainly correct when he states, "Whatever else may be said, these rules at the least allowed Gentiles to be seen as God-fearers rather than as idolaters" (3.2269).

4. The Letter Sent to the Gentile Churches (15:22–29)

15:22 James's suggestion is received by consensus. Ἔδοξεν (3rd sg. aor. act. indic. of δοκέω) is impers. ("it seemed best"), with the dat. of pers. perceiving: ἀποστόλοις, πρεσβυτέροις, and ὅλῃ τῇ ἐκκλησίᾳ ("apostles, elders, and the whole church"). Ἐκλεξαμένους (acc. pl. masc. of aor. mid. ptc. of ἐκλέγω) is temp., mng. "after elect-ing." One would expect a dat. pl. (as in some mss.). However, the acc. is acceptable because it modifies the unexpressed obj. of the inf. (it would be acc.; the series of dats. are the same ref. as this understood obj., Z §394). The compl. inf. πέμψαι (aor. act. inf. of πέμπω) compl. the idea of the finite verb. The rest of the v. identifies a delegation to Antioch. Καλούμενον is the acc. sg. masc. of pres. pass. ptc. of καλέω; subst. The dele-gation is identified as ἄνδρας ἡγουμένους (acc. pl. masc. of pres. mid. ptc. of ἡγέομαι; attrib.), mng. "leading men."

15:23 Γράψαντες (nom. pl. masc. of aor. act. ptc. of γράφω) is likely temp., "after writing," modifying the inf. πέμψαι in v. 22. The ptc. also assumes a demonstrative pron. obj. "this" (see NASB, NET, NJB, ["this letter"], RSV, NIV, NRSV, ESV, TNIV, ["the following letter"]). Διὰ χειρὸς αὐτῶν ("through their hands"). The letter's address is typical of first-century letters. The sender is expressed in the nom. (ἀπόστολοι, πρεσβύτεροι, ἀδελφοί) without a vb. (assuming some form of γράφω). The recipients are in the dat. (ἀδελφοῖς) located by κατά as Antioch, Syria, and Cilicia. Τοῖς ἐξ ἐθνῶν employs the art. as a nominalizer of the prep. phrase functioning as an appos. noun "the ones of the Gentiles." Χαίρειν (pres. act. inf. of χαίρω) is common in greetings, lit. mng. "rejoice"; here it is best rendered "greetings" (see Acts 23:26 and, intriguingly, Jas 1:1 as the only other examples in the NT).

15:24 The next three verses are one long sentence. Ἠκούσαμεν is the 1st pl. aor. act. indic. of ἀκούω. The conj. ὅτι introduces indir. speech, giving the content of the report. If the ptc. ἐξελθόντες (nom. pl. masc. of aor. act. indic. of ἐξέρχομαι, "go out") is orig. (see Metzger 385), ἐξ ἡμῶν modifies it, implying distance from the Jerusalem church. Ἐτάραξαν is the 3rd pl. aor. act. indic. of ταράσσω, "trouble." Λόγοις is a dat. of means, "by words." Ἀνασκευάζοντες (nom. pl. masc. of pres. act. ptc. of ἀνασκευάζω, "upset") indicates result. With ψυχάς as the obj., the mng. is "upsetting your souls." Οἷς reaches back to τινές (referring to the Judaizers) and is dat. for διεστειλάμεθα (1st pl. aor. mid. indic. of διαστέλλω, "give orders"), taking a dat. obj. This, of course, is negated (οὐ).

15:25 On ἔδοξεν and the dat., see 15:22. Γενομένοις (dat. pl. masc. of aor. mid. ptc. of γίνομαι) is best understood as a temp. ptc. (although see BHGNT 299). Ὁμοθυμαδόν is typically "together" in Acts (see 1:14); if so, the mng. is "after gathering together" (Johnson 274), implying the council. Ἐκλεξαμένοις (dat. pl. masc. of aor. mid. ptc. of ἐκλέγω; temp.) is best, "after choosing." Πέμψαι is the aor. act. inf. of πέμπω. The previously mentioned delegation (ἄνδρας) is joined by Barnabas and Paul (described as ἀγαπητοῖς).

15:26 Ἀνθρώποις is in appos. to Barnabas and Paul. Παραδεδωκόσιν (dat. pl. masc. of pf. act. ptc. of παραδίδωμι; attrib.) τὰς ψυχὰς αὐτῶν is lit. "handing over their souls." Most EVV tr. it "risked their lives." Johnson, however, calls it "overly dramatic" (Johnson 276). Several, like Johnson, are now suggesting "devoted their lives for our Lord Jesus Christ" is a better tr. (Barrett 2.742; Bruce, *Acts of the Apostles*, 345).

15:27 The conj. οὖν is inferential. Ἀπεστάλκαμεν (1st pl. pf. act. indic. of ἀποστέλλω) identifies the rest of the party (Judas and Silas). The mng. of καὶ αὐτούς is difficult. The antecedent is clearly Judas and Silas. Most are considering it some form of refl. use of the pron. (see, e.g., R 687). Καί, then, is adv., "also" (see NASB). Barrett may be correct that the oddity of the expression is due to a Sem. influence (Barrett 1.743). Διὰ λόγου, lit. "through word," is often tr. "by word of mouth" (CSB, KJV, RSV, NASB), mng. "in person" (as opposed to a letter, BDF §223; T 267). Ἀπαγγέλλοντας (acc. pl. masc. of pres. act. ptc. of ἀπαγγέλλω) is obviously for purp. In CGk. one would expect a fut. ptc, (see 8:27), but these were growing rare in the Koinē period; a present can take its place (BDF §339; Barrett 2.743; R 1129). Τὰ αὐτά (the obj. of the ptc.) is the identifying use of the pron., mng. "the same things."

15:28 On ἔδοξεν, see 15:22. Μηδὲν πλέον . . . βάρος (acc. sg. neut. of βάρος, -ους, τό, "no more burden") is the obj. of ἐπιτίθεσθαι (pres. pass. inf. ἐπιτίθημι; compl.). Used as a prep., πλήν introduces the exception. Its gen. obj. is the adv. (never an adj. in the NT, BDAG 358c) ἐπάναγκες that is nominalized by the art. τῶν: "these necessary things."

15:29 The prohibition is very sim. to v. 20 (e.g., on ἀπέχεσθαι, see there). The letter's prohibition essentially says the same as James's suggestion except it substitutes a few synonyms and has some minor deviation in word order. The "pollution of idols" is now εἰδωλοθύτων (gen. neut. pl. of εἰδωλόθυτος, -ον, "something sacrificed to idols"). Αἵματος ("blood") and πνικτῶν (gen. pl. neut. of πνικτός, -ή, -όν, "strangled") are reversed, but with the same mng. Πορνείας (gen. sg. fem. of πορνεία, -ας, ἡ, "fornication") rounds off the list. Διατηροῦντες (nom. pl. masc. of pres. act. ptc. of διατηρέω, "keep, maintain") takes the refl. pron. ἑαυτούς, "keeping yourselves," and functions as the prot. of a cond. cstr. (Wallace [633] notes it might be means). The apod., εὖ πράξετε (2nd pl. fut. act. indic. of πράσσω),"you will do well," is without explanation (as v. 21). Ἔρρωσθε (2nd pl. pf. pass. impv. of ῥώννυμι) is lit. "be strong" but is a stereotypical way to end a letter (BDAG 909a); thus, "farewell" in many EVV.

HOMILETICAL SUGGESTIONS

The First Great Theological Debate in the Church (15:1–29)

1. The problem: how are Gentiles to be admitted to the people of God? (vv. 1–5)
2. The evidence: the opinion and experience of the apostles (vv. 6–12)

a. Peter: salvation is by grace through faith (vv. 6–11)
b. Paul and Barnabas: corroborated by the missionary journey (v. 12)

3. The solution: filter the experience through the Scriptures (vv. 13–20)

a. James: the experience agrees with Scripture (vv. 13–18)
b. Proposal: they must altogether abandon idolatry (vv. 19–21)
c. Communicate to the Gentiles (vv. 22–29)

5. Return to Syrian Antioch (15:30–35)

15:30–31 On μὲν οὖν, see 1:6. Ἀπολυθέντες (nom. pl. masc. of aor. pass. ptc. of ἀπολύω, "depart"; subst.) is the subj. of κατῆλθον (3rd pl. aor. act. indic. of κατέρχομαι, "go down"). Ἀντιόχειαν (acc. sg. fem. of Ἀντιόχεια, -ας, ἡ) is Syrian Antioch. Συναγαγόντες is the nom. pl. masc. of aor. act. ptc. of συνάγω, "gather"; temp. Ἐπέδωκαν is the 3rd pl. aor. act. indic. of ἐπιδίδωμι, "deliver" (with ἐπιστολήν [acc. sg. fem. of ἐπιστολή, -ῆς, ἡ, "letter"] as the dir. obj.). Ἀναγνόντες is the nom. pl. masc. of aor. act. ptc. of ἀναγινώσκω; temp. Ἐχάρησαν is the 3rd pl. aor. pass. indic. of χαίρω. Ἐπὶ τῇ παρακλήσει is causal (BHGNT 301), mng. "for this encouragement."

15:32 On καὶ αὐτοί, see 15:29. With προφῆται ὄντες (nom. pl. masc. of pres. ptc. of εἰμί; attrib.) it means "also being prophets themselves," that is, as well as Paul and Barnabas (Bruce, *Acts of the Apostles*, 348). Διὰ λόγου πολλοῦ is lit. "through a large word," mng. "with a long speech" (BDAG 599c; NET). The effect of the speech was παρεκάλεσαν (3rd pl. aor. act. indic. of παρακαλέω, "encourage") and ἐπεστήριξαν (3rd pl. aor. act. indic. of ἐπιστηρίζω, "strengthen").

15:33 Ποιήσαντες (nom. pl. masc. of aor. act. ptc. of ποιέω), as a temp. ptc. with χρόνον as the obj., is a usage of ποιέω that is found in CGk., mng. "having spent some time" (Barrett 2.749; Bruce, *Acts of the Apostles*, 348). The unexpressed subj. of ἀπελύθησαν (3rd pl. aor. pass. indic. of ἀπολύω) is the Jerusalem delegation. Μετ᾽ εἰρήνης, lit. "with peace," implies a blessing. The ref. of πρὸς τοὺς ἀποστείλαντας (acc. pl. masc. of aor. act. ptc. of ἀποστέλλω; subst.) αὐτούς. (lit., "to the ones having sent them") is the Jerusalem church.

15:34 This v. is omitted in the better texts. It is a Western expansion that is found in the TR, not represented in the *byz.* text-type. Metzger believed the insertion was to explain the presence of Silas at v. 40 (Metzger 302).

15:35 In contrast, Paul and Barnabas continued (διέτριβον, 3rd pl impf. act. indic. of διατρίβω) in Antioch. The two ptcs. describing their activities (both nom. pl. masc. forms; attend. circum.) are "teaching" (διδάσκοντες, pres. act. ptc. of διδάσκω) and "evangelizing" (εὐαγγελιζόμενοι, pres. mid. ptc. of εὐαγγελίζω; on the voice, see 5:42). Καί is adv. Τὸν λόγον τοῦ κυρίου (an acc. dir. obj. phrase) is normally the gospel in Acts. Here it may be more comprehensive, but see εὐαγγελίζω above.

C. SECOND MISSIONARY JOURNEY BEGINS (15:36–16:5)

1. Paul and Barnabas Separate (15:36–41)

15:36 Μετὰ δέ τινας ἡμέρας ("after some days") is another of Luke's unspecified but lengthy stretches of time. Paul makes a proposal to Barnabas. Ἐπιστρέψαντες is the nom. pl. masc. of aor. act. ptc. of ἐπιστρέφω; attend. circum. On δή, see 13:2. Ἐπισκεψώμεθα (1st pl. aor. act. subjunc. of ἐπισκέπτομαι) is a hortatory subjunc. mng. "let us visit." Although κατὰ πόλιν πᾶσαν (distributive, "in every city") is sg., the sense is pl., so the rel. pron. αἷς is also pl. (BDF §296 "*constructio ad sensum*"). Barrett proposes the prep. is emphatic, suggesting a comprehensive program (2:753). Κατηγγείλαμεν is the 1st pl. aor. act. indic. of καταγγέλλω, "proclaim." Zerwick (ZG 402) suggests that with πῶς, the vb. ἔχουσιν (3rd pl. pres. act. indic. of ἔχω) takes on the force of a being vb. so, "how they are doing."

15:37 Barnabas, agreeably, offers an additional proposal. It is expressed with a compl. cstr.: ἐβούλετο (3rd sg. impf. mid. indic. of βούλομαι) and συμπαραλαβεῖν (aor. act. inf. of συμπαραλαμβάνω, "take along"; compl.). The obj. is John Mark (lit. "John, the one called . . . :" καλούμενον [acc. sg. masc. of pres. pass. ptc. of καλέω; attrib.]).

15:38 The cstr. of Paul's objection places an acc. obj. phrase describing John Mark between the vb. (ἠξίου, 3rd sg. impf. indic. act. of ἀξιόω, "consider worthy"; in the impf. always with the sense of "thought it good," BHGNT 304) and its negated inf. compl. (συμπαραλαμβάνειν, pres. act. inf. of συμπαραλαμβάνω, "take along"). Culy and Parsons suggest this cstr. presents John Mark and his previous abandonment as the topic (BHGNT 304). This is also suggested by the repetitive use of τοῦτον at the end of the v. (see Haenchen 474). He is described with a twofold subst. ptc.: "the one who deserted" (ἀποστάντα, acc. sg. masc. of aor. act. ptc. of ἀφίστημι) and "the one who had not gone with them" (συνελθόντα, acc. sg. masc. of aor. act. ptc. of συνέρχομαι; neg. by μή).

15:39 The vb. ἐγένετο (3rd sg. aor. mid. indic. of γίνομαι) is impers., best tr. "there arose" (RSV, ESV). Παροξυσμός (nom. sg. masc. of παροξυσμός, -οῦ, ὁ, "a sharp disagreement"; only used elsewhere in the NT in Heb 10:24) is a pred. nom. The cstr. ὥστε ἀποχωρισθῆναι (aor. pass. inf. of ἀποχωρίζω) is a result clause that takes αὐτούς as its subj., mng. "so that they separated." Ὥστε also governs ἐκπλεῦσαι (aor. act. inf. of ἐκπλέω, "sail away") at the end of the v. (Rogers and Rogers 268). The latter inf. takes παραλαβόντα (acc. sg. masc. of aor. act. ptc. of παραλαμβάνω) as an attend. circum., mng. "he took along John Mark and sailed away." The choice of Cyprus is likely because it was Barnabas's homeland. It should also be noted that Mark was his cousin (Col 4:10).

15:40–41 Ἐπιλεξάμενος (nom. sg. masc. of aor. mid. ptc. of ἐπιλέγω; attend. circum.) means "to call" or "name" in the act. and is "select" in the mid. (BDAG 374d–375a). Paul is the focus so ἐξῆλθεν (3rd sg. aor. act. indic. of ἐξέρχομαι, "depart.") is sg. On παραδοθείς (nom. sg. masc. of aor. pass. ptc. of παραδίδωμι, "entrust"; temp.) τῇ χάριτι τοῦ κυρίου, see 14:23. Διήρχετο (3rd sg. impf. mid. indic. of διέρχομαι, "go through") in the sg. continues the focus on Paul. The ptc. ἐπιστηρίζων (nom. sg. masc. of pres.

act. ptc. of ἐπιστηρίζω, "strengthen") might be manner, but is likely attend. circum. (BHGNT 305; Rogers and Rogers 268).

HOMILETICAL SUGGESTIONS

Even Missionaries Have Arguments (15:35–41)

1. Disputes may begin with good intentions (vv. 35–36)
2. Disputes will occur with unmovable opinions (vv. 37–38)
3. Disputes may be unsettled and still further the gospel (vv. 39–41)

2. Paul and Silas Deliver Decisions of Jerusalem Council, Take Timothy (16:1–5)

16:1 The sg. κατήντησεν (3rd sg. aor. act. indic. of καταντάω,"arrived") still ref. to Paul alone. On καὶ ἰδού, see 1:10. Τις modifies μαθητής (nom. sg. masc.) adjectively, "a certain disciple." It introduces Timothy (Τιμόθεος, nom. sg. masc.) in a pred. nom. cstr. with ἦν. Timothy is further described with appos. nom. υἱός with a compound gen. series: γυναικὸς Ἰουδαίας πιστῆς ("a Jewish believing woman") and πατρὸς . . . Ἕλληνος ("a Greek father").

16:2 Timothy was highly recommended. Ἐμαρτυρεῖτο is the 3rd sg. impf. pass. indic. of μαρτυρέω ("he was being well spoken of"). Ἐν Λύστροις καὶ Ἰκονίῳ is in the attrib. position between ἀδελφῶν (gen. pl. masc. of ἀδελφός, -ου, ὁ) and its art. (τῶν). All of which functions as the obj. of the prep. ὑπό, indicating agency.

16:3 Τοῦτον (acc. sg. masc. of οὗτος, dir. obj.) is fronted to keep Timothy in focus (BHGNT 307). Ἠθέλησεν (3rd sg. aor. act. indic. of θέλω) takes the compl. inf. ἐξελθεῖν (aor. act. inf. of ἐξέρχομαι, "depart"). Λαβών is the nom. sg. masc. of aor. act. ptc. of λαμβάνω; attend. circum. Περιέτεμεν is the 3rd sg. aor. act. indic. of περιτέμνω, "circumcise." There is no need to assume Paul did so personally (see Wallace 413). Διά is causal with the acc. phrase τοὺς Ἰουδαίους τοὺς ὄντας (acc. pl. masc. of pres. ptc. of εἰμί; attrib.). The pl. ἐν τοῖς τόποις ἐκείνοις (dat. pl. masc.) refers to Lystra and Iconium (see v. 2). Γάρ is also causal. Ἤδεισαν (3rd pl. plpf. act. indic. of οἶδα) functions as an aor., "they knew." Ὅτι presents the content of οἶδα (indir. speech). It is in a pred. nom. cstr. with ὑπῆρχεν (3rd sg. impf. act. indic. of ὑπάρχω). Because indir. speech uses the same tense as the dir. speech would, the impf. rather than a pres. means Timothy's father was dead at the time (Barrett 2.762; Bruce, *Acts of the Apostles*, 352; Z §346). The purp. of the circumcision is not stated but is likely to stabilize Timothy's status among Jews (Keener 3.2316). To other Jews, Timothy would be considered of Jewish descent because his mother was, but nonconforming from his lack of circumcision. To Gentiles he would be considered "practically a Jew because he was brought up in his mother's religion" (Bruce, *Acts of the Apostles*, 353). Paul's practice of beginning in the synagogue made Timothy's circumcision a matter of wisdom with no salvific significance.

16:4 Ὡς is temporal. Διεπορεύοντο is the 3rd pl. impf. act. indic. of διαπορεύομαι, "were passing through." Παρεδίδοσαν is the 3rd pl. impf. act. indic. of παραδίδωμι, "delivered." Φυλάσσειν (pres. act. inf. of φυλάσσω, "guard"; purp.) takes τὰ δόγματα τὰ κεκριμένα (acc. pl. neut. of pf. pass. ptc. of κρίνω; attrib.) as its obj., mng. "the decrees having been decided." The prep. ὑπό expresses agency. Τῶν (gen. pl. masc.) acts as a pron. nominalizing the prep. phrase ("those in Jerusalem").

16:5 On μὲν οὖν, see 1:6. Luke's characteristic summary is presented in a parallel str. with a vb. followed by a bare dat. The first is ἐστερεοῦντο (3rd pl. impf. pass. indic. of στερεόω "strengthen"). Πίστει is a locat. of sphere. The second leg of the parallel is ἐπερίσσευον (3rd pl. impf. act. indic. of περισσεύω, "grow"). Ἀριθμῷ (dat. sg. masc. of ἀριθμός, -οῦ, ὁ, "number") is a dat. of ref. defining the area of growth. Καθ᾽ ἡμέραν is distributive, mng. "daily."

HOMILETICAL SUGGESTIONS

Discipleship as a Continuing Process (16:1–5)

1. Always be looking for someone to mentor (v. 1)
2. Seek the opinion of those in the know (v. 2)
3. Prepare for future ministry (v. 4)
4. Engage in present ministry (v. 5)

VI. The Gentile Mission: Part Two, Greece (16:6–19:20)

Luke's focus is on the evangelization of the Gk. peninsula even though it begins in Asia Minor. The missionaries' steps are directed by God throughout. There are some similarities to Peter's experiences (e.g., Paul's imprisonment). However, the difference is that instead of escape, God used it this time for evangelism. The point seems to be God is still moving, but for his own purposes. The section is in two parts. The first narrates the conclusion of the second missionary journey (16:6–18:20). The second describes the third missionary journey to 19:20. At 19:21, while still ministering in the Gk. world, the focus turns to Rome.

A. CONTINUING THE SECOND MISSIONARY JOURNEY (16:6–18:23)

1. Ministry in Philippi (16:6–40)

A major part of Luke's presentation is that the gospel goes from Jerusalem to the ends of the earth at the leading of Christ. Here that leading is shown through blocking attempts. The team's efforts were almost comical as they probed northern Asia Minor for the next step. Attempts were made at Phrygia, Galatia, Bithynia, Mysia, and Troas, but the Spirit prevented them. It was not until a vision of a Macedonian man that the team had direction.

a. Paul's Vision of the Macedonian (16:6–10)

16:6 Διῆλθον (3rd pl. aor. act. indic. of διέρχομαι, "go through") switches to the plural, indicating Paul's intent to take Timothy is completed. The acc. sg. fem. dir. obj. phrase Φρυγίαν (of Φρυγία, -ας, ἡ, "Phrygia") καὶ Γαλατικὴν (of Φαλατική, -ης, ἡ) χώραν has a great deal of dispute, mostly over the so-called north or south Galatian theory. The most natural way is to read Phrygia and Galatia as adjs. modifying "region" sharing the art. (Keener 3.2324–25; although see R 787–88). If so, it is one region, not two. Κωλυθέντες (nom. pl. masc. of aor. pass. ptc. of κωλύω, "forbid") and λαλῆσαι (aor. act. inf. of λαλέω; compl.) in Ἀσίᾳ (dat. sg. fem. of Ἀσία, -ας, ἡ) pushes them northwest to "Mysia" (see v. 7).

16:7 Ἐλθόντες is the nom. pl. masc. of aor. act. ptc. of ἔρχομαι; temp. Κατὰ τὴν Μυσίαν (acc. sg. fem. of Μυσία, -ας, ἡ) is used spatially, "up to Mysia" (BDAG 511d). Ἐπείραζον (3rd pl. impf. act. indic. of πειράζω, "try") takes a compl. inf. πορευθῆναι (aor. pass. inf. of πορεύομαι). Εἰς τὴν Βιθυνίαν (acc. sg. fem. of Βιθυνία, -ας, ἡ, "Bithynia") refers to a region northeast of Mysia. However, Luke continues his theme of divine direction of the mission with a prohibition. Εἴασεν (3rd sg. aor. act. indic. of ἐάω, "allowed"; a typically Lukan word, nine times in Luke-Acts) refers to the "Spirit of Jesus."

16:8 Παρελθόντες (nom. pl. masc. of aor. act. ptc. of παρέρχομαι; temp.) takes Mysia as dir. obj. They obviously now go southeast (κατέβησαν, 3rd pl. aor. act. indic.), winding up in Troas (Τρῳάδα, acc. sg. fem. of Τρῳάς, -άδος, ἡ).

16:9 On the vb. ὤφθη (3rd sg. aor. pass. indic. of ὁράω), see 2:3. Luke is careful to avoid language that would imply Paul was asleep (Haenchen 488). The phrase διὰ [τῆς] νυκτός ("during the night") is the space/extent that the event happened (Z §115). Furthermore, ὅραμα (nom. sg. neut. of ὅραμα, -ατος, τό) is better "a vision" (see 10:17), describing a divine message. Ἀνὴρ Μακεδών (nom. sg. masc. of Μακεδών, -όνος, ὁ, "Macedonian") τις suggests an unknown man. The cstr. ἦν ἑστώς (nom. sg. masc. of pf. act. ptc. of ἵστημι) is a technically a periph. plpf., but ἵστημι in an intrans. pf. or plpf. means to be in a standing position (BDAG 482d), mng. no more than the following pres. (BHGNT 309). Ἦν governs both the following ptcs. (both nom. sg. masc. pres. act. ptcs.) as well, making them periph. impfs.: παρακαλῶν (of παρακαλέω, "was urging") and λέγων (of λέγω, "was saying," introducing dir. speech). Διαβάς (nom. sg. masc. of aor. act. ptc. of διαβαίνω) is attend. circum., here an impv. "cross over." Βοήθησον (2nd sg. aor. act. impv. of βοηθέω, "help") takes a dat. of advantage as the object aided (ἡμῖν).

16:10 The response was instantaneous. Ὡς is temp. "when." Εἶδεν is the 3rd sg. aor. act. indic. of ὁράω. The switch to the 1st pl. ἐζητήσαμεν (1st pl. aor. act. indic. of ζητέω, "sought") is loaded with implications regarding the origins of Acts (for a longer discussion, see the introduction). The opinion here is that it represents the beginning of eyewitness accounts. Ἐξελθεῖν (aor. act. inf. of ἐξέρχομαι) is compl. συμβιβάζοντες (nom. pl. masc. of pres. act. ptc. of συμβιβάζω, "concluding") is causal. Ὅτι introduces the content of the conclusion. Προσκέκληται (3rd sg. pf. mid. indic. of προσκαλέω) takes a dir. obj. (ἡμᾶς, acc. pl.) and a compl. inf. εὐαγγελίσασθαι (aor. mid. inf. of εὐαγγελίζω; on the voice, see 5:42). Αὐτούς (acc. pl. masc.) ref. to the Macedonians.

FOR FURTHER STUDY

25. The So-Called We Passages (16:10–17; 20:5–15; 21:1–18; 27:1–28:16)

Cadbury, H. J. "'We' and 'I' Passages." NTS 3 (1957): 128–32.

Haenchen, E. "'We' in Acts and the Itinerary." JTC (1965): 65–99.

Hemer, C. J. "The Authorship and Sources of Acts." In BASHH, 308–410.

———. "First Person Narrative." TynBul 36 (1985): 79–109.

Porter, S. E. "Excurses: The 'We' Passages." In BAFCS 2, 545–74. Witherington, 480–86.

b. The First Converts in Europe (16:11–15)

16:11 Ἀναχθέντες (nom. pl. masc. of aor. pass. ptc. of ἀνάγω; temp.) is lit. "having set sail" (i.e., from Troas). Εὐθυδρομήσαμεν (1st pl. aor. act. indic. of εὐθυδρομέω) is a nautical term mng. "run a straight course" (BDAG 406a). Σαμοθράκην (acc. sg. fem. of Σαμοθράκη, -ης, ἡ, "Samothrace") is a mountainous island in the northern Aegean. Τῇ δὲ ἐπιούσῃ (dat. sg. fem. of pres. act. ptc. of ἔπειμι, "come upon, come near"; attrib. to an assumed ἡμέρα) is a dat. of time mng. "on the next day." Whether Νέαν πόλιν (UBS⁵) or Νεάπολιν (*byz.*) is irrelevant in mng. (but two words would be CGk.; Bruce, *Acts of the Apostles*, 356). Neapolis was the port-city of Philippi (Bruce, *Acts of the Apostles*, 356).

16:12 On κἀκεῖθεν, see 13:21. The rel. pron. phrase (on ἥτις, see 3:23; 7:53) gives the rationale of going to Philippi. The phrase πρώτη[ς] μερίδος (gen. sg. fem. of μερίς, -ίδος, ἡ, "part") τῆς Μακεδονίας πόλις is notoriously difficult both textually and grammatically. The problem is best solved through establishing the text, then sorting out the grammar.

This takes two steps:

1) Πρώτη[ς], as in the UBS⁵, is a conjectural emendation by the committee not supported in any Gk. ms. tradition (some Vulg. mss. read *primae partis* or *primae parte;* Bruce, *Acts of the Apostles*, 357). The idea is to render Philippi as part of the first district of Macedonia (as a part. gen., MIT ["Macedonia was in four districts"]). As appealing as it is, the lack of textual support is insurmountable. Πρώτη, then, must modify πόλις. The objection has normally been that Philippi was not the capital city, nor πρώτη a formal title (BASHH 114; Bruce, *Acts of the Apostles*, 357; ZG 404). However, for that clearly to be the mng., it must be ἡ πρώτη (Barrett 2.779). It might be first in the sense of proximity or importance (the latter would be a matter of opinion [BASHH 114]). The opinion here is that "leading" is the best understanding.

2) An art. τῆς modifies μερίδος in a wide variety of mss. (the art. after μερίδος is best supported by Vaticanus, which alone has swayed some). If art., μερίδος is likely demonstrative, "that portion," and "Μακεδονίας" is likely in appos. to μερίδος (Barrett 2.778), mng. "leading city of that Macedonian district" (RSV, NLT, NASB, NIV, TNIV, NET, NJB).

The second descr., mercifully uncomplicated, correctly identifies Philippi as κολωνία (nom. sg. fem. of κολωνία, -ας, ἡ, "colony"; in appos. to πόλις). Ἦμεν (1st pl. impf. act. indic. of εἰμί) and διατρίβοντες (nom. pl. masc. of pres. act. ptc. of διατρίβω, "continue") are a periph. impf. that with ἡμέρας τινάς indicates an indefinite period of time.

16:13 On τε, see 1:15. On ἡμέρα . . . σαββάτων, see 13:14. The trip outside (ἐξήλθομεν, 1st pl. aor. act. indic. of ἐξέρχομαι) the city gates was to gather beside a river (παρὰ ποταμόν [acc. sg. masc. of ποταμός, -οῦ, ὁ, "river"]). Ἐνομίζομεν (1st pl. impf. act. indic. of νομίζω, "suppose") is often as opposed to reality (BDAG 675c). If so, the meeting with the women says nothing about their status as Jews or Gentiles but explains why the missionaries went to the river (a custom for Jews without a synagogue, Johnson 292). The content of their assumption is given in indir. speech with εἶναι (pres. inf. of εἰμί). It is impers., "there was. . . ." Προσευχὴν (acc. sg. fem., obj. of the inf.) in this context is "a place of prayer" (BDAG 879a; not necessarily a building, Barrett 2.781). Καθίσαντες is the nom. pl. masc. of aor. act. ptc. of καθίζω; temp. The vb. ἐλαλοῦμεν (1st pl. impf. act. indic. of λαλέω) takes γυναιξίν (dat. pl. fem. of γυνή, -αικός, ἡ) as an indir. obj. The latter is modified by συνελθούσαις (dat. pl. fem. of aor. act. ptc. of συνέρχομαι; attrib.); mng. "who had gathered."

16:14 Τις γυνή (nom. sg. fem. of γυνή, -αικός, ἡ), mng. "a certain woman," is highlighted among the women. On ὀνόματι, see 5:1. Λυδία (nom. sg. fem. of Λυδία, -ας, ἡ, "Lydia"; appos.) is introduced as a seller of purple (πορφυρόπωλις, nom. sg. fem. of πορφυρόπωλις, -ιδος, ἡ; appos.), indicating Lydia's wealth (Keener 3.2400). It was a trade deeply connected to Thyatira (Θυατείρων, neut. gen. pl. of Θυάτειρα; gen. of source, Bock 534; Keener 3.2395). Σεβομένη (nom. sg. fem. of pres. mid. ptc. of σέβω, "worship") is likely referring to a God-fearer (Haenchen 494; Keener 3.2393), given the obj. θεόν. Ἤκουεν is the 3rd sg. impf. act. indic. of ἀκούω. The rel. pron. ἧς is a gen. of poss. (modifying καρδίαν). Διήνοιξεν (3rd sg. aor. act. indic. of διανοίγω, "open") with "heart" is to "enable someone to perceive" (BDAG 234c). Προσέχειν (pres. act. inf. of προσέχω, "give heed to" with dat. obj.; result), suggests something more like "to receive," given Lydia's baptism at 16:15. Λαλουμένοις is the dat. pl. neut. of pres. pass. ptc. of λαλέω; subst.

16:15 Ὡς is temporal. Ἐβαπτίσθη (3rd sg. aor. pass. indic. of βαπτίζω) and ὁ οἶκος αὐτῆς need not imply anything thing other than a great movement of God in the extended family (incl. servants and other dependents; Bruce, *Acts of the Apostles*, 359). Παρεκάλεσεν (3rd sg. aor. act. indic. of παρακαλέω) λέγουσα (nom. sg. fem. of pres. act. ptc. of λέγω; pleonastic) has a solemn tone. The request is expressed as a first-class cond. statement. The prot. (with εἰ) is indir. speech. Κεκρίκατέ (2nd pl. pf. act. indic. of κρίνω) εἶναι (pres. inf. of εἰμί) takes πιστήν (acc. sg. fem. of πιστός, -ήν, -όν) as the obj. The apod. opens with εἰσελθόντες (nom. pl. masc. of aor. act. ptc. of εἰσέρχομαι; attend. circum.). Finally, μένετε (2nd pl. pres. act. impv. of μένω, "stay") expresses the essence of the request. Παρεβιάσατο (3rd sg. aor. mid. indic. of παραβιάζομαι, "strongly urge"; see Luke 24:29 as the only other instance in the NT). The dir. obj., ἡμᾶς, reintroduces the author in the narrative.

HOMILETICAL SUGGESTIONS

The Basics of Evangelism (16:11–15)

1. Find an interested crowd (vv. 11–13)
2. Present the gospel (v. 14)
3. Follow through with discipleship (v. 15)

c. Disturbance in Philippi (16:16–24)

16:16 On ἐγένετο δέ, see 4:5. Πορευομένων is the gen. sg. masc. of pres. mid. ptc. of πορεύομαι; gen. abs. The art. in the prep. phrase εἰς τὴν προσευχήν is likely the art. of previous ref. indicating "the place of prayer" (see v. 13). Παιδίσκην (acc. sg. fem. of παιδίσκη, -ης, ἡ, "female slave"; subj. of the inf.) is "slave" because she has "masters"

(Barrett 2.784; always "slave" in NT but "young girl" in CGk.). Ἔχουσαν (acc. sg. fem. of pres. act. ptc. of ἔχω; attrib.) takes πνεῦμα πύθωνα (acc. sg. masc. of πύθων, -ωνος, ὁ) as its obj. Lit. "a spirit of Python," it echoes the priestesses of Delphi. They were thought to be hosting the god speaking through them (a term for "pregnant" later came to be "ventriloquism," probably implying speech in a strange voice [Keener 3.2424]). On the use of the inf. (ὑπαντῆσαι aor. act. inf. of ὑπαντάω, "meet"), see 4:5, Z §389. She brought (παρεῖχεν, 3rd sg. impf. indic. act. of παρέχω) great profit (ἐργασίαν, acc. sg. fem. of ἐργασία, -ας, ἡ, "profit, gain"; dir. obj.). Μαντευομένη (nom. sg. fem. of pres. mid. ptc. of μαντεύομαι) is a ptc. of means, mng. "by doing divination."

16:17 Κατακολουθοῦσα (nom. sg. fem. of pres. act. ptc. of κατακολουθέω, "follow after"; attend. circum.) takes a compound dat. obj. (Παύλῳ and ἡμῖν). Ἔκραζεν is the 3rd sg. impf. act. indic. of κράζω. Λέγουσα (nom. sg. fem. of pres. act. ptc. of λέγω; pleonastic) introduces dir. speech. It is a pred. nom. cstr. with εἰσίν (3rd pl. pres. indic. of εἰμί). The referent of the poss. gen. phrase τοῦ θεοῦ τοῦ ὑψίστου (gen. sg. masc. of ὕψιστος, -η, -ον, "most high"; attrib.) is ambiguous in the setting. It was common among the Greeks for Zeus (Bruce, *Acts of the Apostles*, 360; Schnabel 683). It is esp. noteworthy that it was used by a Pythian prophetess (Barrett 2.786). Καταγγέλλουσιν (3rd pl. pres. act. indic. of καταγγέλλω, "announce") takes a dat. obj., ὑμῖν. The anar. phrase ὁδόν (acc. sg. fem. of ὁδός, -οῦ, ἡ; dir. obj.) σωτηρίας (gen. sg. fem. of σωτηρία, -ᾶς, ἡ; descr.) is likely indef., "a way of salvation" (Bruce, *Acts of the Apostles*, 361; Schnabel 683). Thus, the "endorsement" implicitly allows for other ways of salvation; something Christianity would never accept (cf. 4:12; see Robertson, *Pictures*, 255).

16:18 The antecedent of the acc. sg. neut. τοῦτο (dir. obj.) is generic, ref. to the girl's actions as a whole. Ἐποίει is the 3rd sg. impf. act. indic. of ποιέω. Ἐπὶ πολλὰς ἡμέρας expresses an extent of time (BDAG 367b), i.e., "for many days." Διαπονηθείς (nom. sg. masc. of aor. pass. ptc. of διαπονέομαι, "grow greatly annoyed"; attend. cirucm.) and ἐπιστρέψας (nom. sg. masc. of aor. act. ptc. of ἐπιστρέφω; attend. circum.) are virtually simultaneous. Πνεύματι is the indir. obj. to εἶπεν (3rd sg. aor. act. indic. of λέγω), ref. to the possessing spirit in the girl. Paul commands (παραγγέλλω, 1st sg. pres. act. indic. of παραγγέλλω) by the authority of Jesus (ἐν ὀνόματι Ἰησοῦ Χριστοῦ, see 3:6). Ἐξελθεῖν is the aor. act. inf. of ἐξέρχομαι, "to come out"; compl. Luke's description uses the same vb. that Paul commanded (ἐξῆλθεν, 3rd sg. aor. act. indic. of ἐξέρχομαι). The identifying (adj.) use of αὐτός, -ή, -ό (αὐτῇ, dat. sg. fem.) as a dat. of time modifying ὥρᾳ (dat. sg. fem. of ὥρα, -ας, ἡ) is lit. "at the same hour" but mng. "immediately" (Barrett 2.788; Haenchen 496; cf. CSB "right away").

16:19 The response from her masters was not positive. Ἰδόντες is the nom. pl. masc. of aor. act. ptc. of ὁράω; temp. (poss. causal). Ὅτι points to the content of the sight. Again, the use of the same vb. as the exorcism (ἐξῆλθεν, 3rd sg. aor. act. indic. of ἐξέρχομαι) is likely intentional (Bruce, *Acts of the Apostles*, 361). Not only was the demon expelled, so was the hope for profit (ἐργασίας, gen. sg. fem. of ἐργασία, -ας, ἡ). Ἐπιλαβόμενοι is the nom. pl. masc. of aor. mid. ptc. of ἐπιλαμβάνομαι; attend. circum. Εἵλκυσαν is the 3rd pl. aor. act. indic. of ἕλκω, "drag." The destination (ἀγοράν, acc. sg. fem. of ἀγορά, -ᾶς, ἡ) is unfortunately tr. "marketplace" in nearly every EVV. In Philippi, it would be the central public square (the forum). It would be the place where the rulers (ἄρχοντας, acc. pl. masc. of ἄρχων, -οντος, ὁ) were (see Keener 3.2467; Schnabel 685).

16:20–21 Προσαγαγόντες is the nom. pl. masc. of aor. act. ptc. of προσάγω, "bring forward"; temp., takes a dat. obj. In Philippi, στρατηγοῖς (dat. pl. masc. of στρατηγός, -οῦ, ὁ) is the common name for the *duoviri*, a pair of praetors who were the city's highest officials (BDAG 947d–48a; BAFCS 3:123; MM 593a). The charges presented are fictitious. Εἶπαν is the 3rd pl. aor. act. indic. of λέγω. Ἐκταράσσουσιν is the 3rd pl. pres. act. indic. of ἐκταράσσω, "agitate." An appeal to xenophobia is apparent with the fronted ἡμῶν, i.e., not their city. This is made explicit with Ἰουδαῖοι ὑπάρχοντες, (nom. pl. masc. of pres. act. ptc. of ὑπάρχω; attrib.) "being Jews."

Καταγγέλλουσιν is the 3rd pl. pres. act. indic. of καταγγέλλω, "broadly proclaim," with ἔθη (acc. pl. neut. of ἔθος, -ους, τό, "customs") as the dir. obj. In a legal setting, the impers. vb. ἔξεστιν (3rd sg. pres. act. indic. of ἔξεστι) is best "not legal" (CSB) or "lawful" (RSV, NASB NRSV, ESV). It takes a pair of compl. infs., παραδέχεσθαι (aor. mid. inf. of παραδέχομαι, "receive") and ποιεῖν (pres. act. inf. of ποιέω). Ῥωμαίοις οὖσιν (dat. pl. masc. of pres. ptc. of εἰμί) is causal, mng. "because we are Romans." The charge was fallacious. While new cults were illegal, Judaism (Paul and Silas are identified as Jews) was a tolerated religion where even proselyting was permitted (Bruce, *Acts of the Apostles*, 362; SW 81). The charge is an emotional xenophobia designed to play on the suspicions of the Romans regarding Jews (Johnson 295).

16:22 Συνεπέστη is the 3rd sg. aor. act. indic. of συνεφίστημι, "join in an uprising." Κατ᾽ αὐτῶν is "against them." Customary before a beating (Keener 3.2477), the στρατηγοί (nom. pl. masc. of στρατηγός, -οῦ, ὁ, see 16:20) tear off (περιρήξαντες, nom. pl. masc. of aor. act. ptc. of περιρήγνυμι; temp., NT hapax) the victims' robes (ἱμάτια acc. pl. neut. of ἱμάτιον, -ου, τό). Ἐκέλευον (3rd pl. impf. act. indic. of κελεύω, "order") is compl. by ῥαβδίζειν (pres. act. inf. of ῥαβδίζω, "beat with a rod"). The order is surely part of Paul's list in 2 Cor 11:25.

16:23 On τε, see 1:15. Ἐπιθέντες is the nom. pl. masc. of aor. act. ptc. of ἐπιτίθημι; temp. The adj. πολλάς ("many") is fronted and distant from its head noun for emphasis (πληγάς, acc. pl. fem. of πληγή, -ῆς, ἡ, "wounds"). The beating was severe (not limited to the Jewish thirty-nine lashes, Keener 3.2479) and instant. The order would have been "go, lictors, strip off their garments; let them be scourged" (Rogers and Rogers 271). Lictors were men (with rods; see 16:35, ῥαβδούχους) who preceded those holding imperium in public processions. If the officials were of praetor rank, they would have six lictors each (Keener 3.2477–48; see also *TDNT* 6.971). Ἔβαλον is the 3rd pl. aor. act. indic. of βάλλω. Παραγγείλαντες (nom. pl. masc. of aor. act. ptc. of παραγγέλλω) takes a dat. obj. (δεσμοφύλακι, dat. sg. masc. of δεσμοφύλαξ, -ακος, ὁ, "jailor"; all three NT uses in ch. 16). Τηρεῖν is the pres. act. inf. of τηρέω, indir. speech. With the adv. ἀσφαλῶς, it means "to guard securely."

16:24 Παραγγελίαν (acc. sg. fem. of παραγγελία, -ας, ἡ, "order") as the dir. obj. of λαβὼν (nom. sg. masc. of aor. act. ptc. of λαμβάνω) expresses "having received the order." The order is taken seriously. Paul and Silas are placed in a highly secure situation. First, the jailor placed them (ἔβαλεν, 3rd sg. aor. act. indic. of βάλλω) in the inner prison cell. The comp. adj. ἐσωτέραν (acc. sg. fem. of ἐσώτερος, -α, -ον) is superl. in force, "the innermost prison" (BHGNT 317; Bruce, *Acts of the Apostles*, 363). Second, he locked them in stocks. Ἠσφαλίσατο (3rd sg. aor. mid. indic. of ἀσφαλίζω, "fasten, secure") εἰς τὸ ξύλον (acc. sg. neut. of ξύλον, -ου, τό) is lit. "he fastened them to the wood," i.e., a wooden device.

d. Deliverance in Custody (16:25–34)

16:25 Κατὰ . . . τὸ μεσονύκτιον (acc. sg. neut. of μεσονύκτιον, -ου, τό) represents an approximation, "about midnight" (BDAG 512b; CSB, RSV, NASB, NIV, ESV, NET). Προσευχόμενοι is the nom. pl. masc. of pres. mid. ptc. of προσεύχομαι; attend. circum. The trans. ὕμνουν (3rd pl. impf. indic. act. of ὑμνέω) means "they were singing in praise to" the obj. (i.e., θεόν, BDAG 1027c). Ἐπηκροῶντο (3rd pl. impf. mid. indic. of ἐπακροάομαι) has the sense of "they were overhearing" (specifically the other prisoners, δέσμιοι, nom. pl. masc. of δέσμιος, -ου, ὁ; subj.).

16:26 Throughout this v. the surprise factor is subtly highlighted. The adv. ἄφνω is rare (three times in NT, only in Acts). With the fronted σεισμός (nom. sg. masc. of σεισμός, -οῦ, ὁ, "earthquake") it highlights the surprise of the event. Ἐγένετο is the 3rd sg. aor. mid. indic. of γίνομαι. The inf. (σαλευθῆναι aor. pass. inf. of σαλεύω, "shake," with θεμέλια [acc. pl. neut. of θεμέλιον, "foundations"] as the subj.) with ὥστε is normally result; however, given the pass. and the presentation, a divine purp. cannot be ruled out (see BDAG 1107c; BDF §391[3]; R 900; Z §352). The description of the doors of the prison is in a sim. cstr. Ἠνεῴχθησαν (3rd pl. aor. pass. indic. of ἀνοίγω, "were opened") has an adv. παραχρῆμα ("immediately," only used two times outside of Luke-Acts) with subj. θύραι (nom. pl. fem. of θύρα, "doors"). Ἀνέθη (3rd sg. aor. pass. indic. of ἀνίημι, "was released"), although a neut. pl. (δεσμά, nom. pl. neut. of δεσμός, -οῦ, ὁ, "chains"), is presented distributively through πάντων (see Barrett 2.794) which is subst. ("of every man") and fronted for the surprise factor (BHGNT 319).

16:27 Shame and dishonor may have played a part in the jailor's despair. However, for failing in his duties, the jailor could expect severe penalties as a public example. Given the large number of escapees, he was clearly overwhelmed at the prospect (see Bruce, *Acts of the Apostles*, 364; Johnson 301; Witherington 497). The next two vv. are a complex contrast cstr. In the first v., three adv. ptcs. precede the main vb., giving the background to the jailor's suicide attempt. The ptc. following the main vb. gives the reason. Regarding the preceding ptcs., the first two are temp. Γενόμενος (nom. sg. masc. of aor. mid. ptc. of γίνομαι) presents a pred. adj. cstr. The jailor becomes awake (ἔξυπνος, nom. sg. masc. of ἔξυπνος, -ον; pred. adj.). Ἰδών (nom. sg. masc. of aor. act. ptc. of ὁράω) takes as an obj. "the opened doors" (ἀνεῳγμένας, acc. pl. fem. of pf. pass. ptc. of ἀνοίγω [adj. modifying θύρας, acc. pl. fem. of θύρα, -ας, ἡ]). The third ptc. is attend. circum. Σπασάμενος (nom. sg. masc. of aor. mid. ptc. of σπάω, "draw out") with the obj. μάχαιραν (acc. sg. fem. of μάχαιρα, -ας, ἡ) is "having drawn a sword." The finite vb. of the sentence finally appears. Ἤμελλεν (3rd sg. impf. indic. act. of μέλλω) takes a compl. inf. ἀναιρεῖν (pres. act. inf. of ἀναιρέω) with the refl. pron. It is, "he was going to kill himself." The ptc. following the finite vb. is causal. Νομίζων is the nom. sg. masc. of pres. act. ptc. of νομίζω, "suppose." Ἐκπεφευγέναι (pf. act. inf. of ἐκφεύγω, "escape") expresses indir. speech.

16:28 Ἐφώνησεν (3rd sg. aor. act. indic. of φωνέω, "cry out") is modified by the instr. dat. μεγάλῃ φωνῇ ("with a loud voice"). Λέγων is the nom. sg. masc. of pres. act. ptc. of λέγω; pleonastic. The negated πράξῃς (2nd sg. aor. act. subjunc. of πράσσω) is a prohibitive subjunc. (Z §242). The grounds (γάρ) for the exhortation is a pred. adj. cstr. with ἐσμεν (1st pl. pres. indic. of εἰμί) and the pred. adv. ἐνθάδε (indecl.), "here."

16:29 The switch in subj. from Paul to the jailor is not explicit but clear. Some add "jailor" for clarity (see, e.g., NLT, NIV, NRSV, ESV, NET). His response to Paul and Silas is one of immense respect. Αἰτήσας (nom. sg. masc. of aor. act. ptc. of αἰτέω; attend. circum.) with the dir. obj. φῶτα (acc. pl. neut. of φῶς, -ῶτος, τό) is best tr. "and he called for lights" (RSV, NLT, NASB, NIV, NRSV, ESV). Εἰσεπήδησεν (3rd sg. aor. act. indic. of εἰσπηδάω, "rush in") is a rare word in biblical literature (Amos 5:19 [fleeing a lion] and here), typically signifying a vigorous action in secular literature (Bruce, *Acts of the Apostles*, 364). Γενόμενος (nom. sg. masc. of aor. mid. ptc. of γίνομαι; attend. circum.) takes ἔντρομος (nom. sg. masc. of ἔντρομος, -ον) as a pred. adj. It is lit. "having become trembling" but means something like "and tremors came upon him." Most EVV simply tr. it as an adv. to the main vb. "he fell trembling." Προσέπεσεν (3rd sg. aor. act. indic. of προσπίπτω, "fall before") takes dat. objs. (Παύλῳ and Σιλᾷ, "Paul and Silas"; BDAG 884b). Given Paul's reaction (cf. 14:13–14) there is no indication of worship.

16:30 The jailor then leads (προαγαγών, nom. sg. masc. of aor. act. ptc. of προάγω; temp.,) the missionaries outside (ἔξω). Ἔφη is the 3rd sg. aor. act. indic. of φημί, "say." The voc. κύριοι (voc. pl. masc. of κύριος, -ου, ὁ) means "sirs" (see Barrett 2.796; Schnabel 691; a term not used for prisoners, to be sure). On δεῖ, see 1:21. Ποιεῖν is the pres. act. inf. of ποιέω; compl. Ἵνα introduces a purp. expression with σωθῶ (1st sg. aor. pass. subjunc. of σῴζω). The question is clearly about eternal salvation. It presupposes the jailor had overheard part of an interrogation of Paul and Silas, or otherwise had basic information that these events corroborated.

16:31 The pls. οἱ (used as a pron.) and εἶπαν (3rd. pl. aor. act. indic. of λέγω) suggest what follows (although in dir. speech) summarizes the conversation (Bock 542). Πίστευσον (2nd sg. aor. act. impv. of πιστεύω, "believe") in the aor. signifies the entrance into the state with a note of urgency (Rogers and Rogers 272). The obj. of belief is found in the prep. phrase ἐπὶ τὸν κύριον Ἰησοῦν. The result is σωθήσῃ (2nd sg. fut. pass. indic. of σῴζω, "you will be saved"). The final phrase, "you and your house" (σὺ καὶ ὁ οἶκός σου), may be understood as the subj. with the concord on the one in focus (i.e., the jailor, BHGNT 321; KJV, RSV, NJB). However, it is more likely that it is an appos. statement giving additional information, " . . . you and your household" (so CSB, RSV, NIV, NRSV, ESV, TNIV, NET). If so, salvation will come to the household in the same way; by their own belief, not the jailor's.

16:32 It is not stated exactly where this conversation takes place. It is most likely in the jailor's quarters, for his household is present. The mention of the household in v. 31 leads to their evangelism. Ἐλάλησαν is the 3rd pl. aor. act. indic. of λαλέω. The dir. obj. phrase is τὸν λόγον τοῦ κυρίου (typically the gospel in Luke). Τοῖς functions as a pron. mng. "all those" (NET, MIT).

16:33 Παραλαβών (nom. sg. masc. of aor. act. ptc. of παραλαμβάνω) may suggest "took them in as guests" (Barrett 2.798). On the use of ἐν ἐκείνῃ τῇ ὥρᾳ, see 16:18 (cf.

ZG 406, "even at that hour of night" [NLT]). Although a little strange, ἔλουσεν (3rd sg. aor. act. indic. of λούω, "wash") ἀπὸ τῶν πληγῶν is an idiom for "he washed their wounds" (BDAG 603c). Ἐβαπτίσθη (3rd sg. aor. pass. indic. of βαπτίζω). The nom. αὐτός is emphatic. Αὐτοῦ is a gen. of relationship referring to the jailor's household. On παραχρῆμα, see 16:26.

16:34 Ἀναγαγών is the nom. sg. masc. of aor. act. ptc. of ἀνάγω; temp. Παρέθηκεν (3rd sg. aor. act. indic. of παρατίθημι) and τράπεζαν (acc. sg. fem. of τράπεζα, -ης, ἡ, "table") is lit. "he set a table before them," mng. "a meal" (CSB, NLT, NIV, TNIV, NJB). Ἠγαλλιάσατο is the 3rd sg. aor. mid. indic. of ἀγαλλιάω, "rejoice." Πανοικεί (indecl., "the whole house") functions like a subst. adj. It appears only here in biblical literature but commonly in the papyri (MM 476d–77a). Πεπιστευκώς (nom. sg. masc. of pf. act. ptc. of πιστεύω; causal) takes a dat. dir. obj. (θεῷ).

HOMILETICAL SUGGESTIONS

The Devil's Attempt to Silence the Gospel (16:16–34)

1. The plan behind a deceitful commendation (vv. 16–18)
   a. An attempt to lull the believers
   b. An attempt to place falsehood on the same plane as truth
   c. The apostolic response (exorcism)
2. The plan behind an illegal arrest and beating (vv. 19–25)
   a. An attempt to discourage the evangelists
   b. An attempt to silence the evangelists
   c. The apostolic response (praise)
3. The divine plan triumphs (vv. 25–34)
   a. A divine intervention
   b. An apostolic intervention
   c. A household saved

e. Final Adjudication (16:35–40)

16:35 Ἡμέρας δὲ γενομένης (gen. sg. fem. of aor. mid. ptc. of γίνομαι) is a temp. gen. abs. phrase mng. "when it was day" (RSV, ESV) or "when it was daylight" (i.e., at dawn, NIV, TNIV). The praetors (οἱ στρατηγοί) sent (ἀπέστειλαν, 3rd pl. aor. act. indic. of ἀποστέλλω) men to carry a message. The dir. obj. of the vb. is ῥαβδούχους (acc. pl. masc. of ῥαβδοῦχος, -ου, ὁ; Latin "*Lictor*," Keener 3.2525). They are possibly the very men who beat the missionaries earlier (Bock 543). Λέγοντες (nom. pl. masc. of pres. act. ptc. of λέγω) introduces the message to the jailor. Ἀπόλυσον is the 2nd sg. aor. act. impv. of ἀπολύω, "release."

16:36 The message is relayed (ἀπήγγειλεν, 3rd sg. aor. act. indic. of ἀπαγγέλλω) to Paul by the jailor (δεσμοφύλαξ, nom. sg. masc. of δεσμοφύλαξ, -ακος, ὁ). Ὅτι introduces dir. speech. ἀπέσταλκαν is the 3rd pl. pf. act. indic. of ἀποστέλλω. Ἵνα introduces a purp. clause with ἀπολυθῆτε (2nd pl. aor. pass. subjunc. of ἀπολύω), "to release you"

(CSB, NASB, NET ["to be released"]). The jailor then, expecting them to jump at it, sends his blessing. Ἐξελθόντες (nom. pl. masc. of aor. act. ptc. of ἐξέρχομαι; attend. circum., impv. force, Rogers and Rogers 272). Πορεύεσθε (2nd pl. pres. act. impv. of πορεύομαι) with ἐν εἰρήνῃ means "come out now and go in peace" (CSB, RSV, NASB, NSRV). The release was likely an assumption that the punishment received was enough (Bruce, *Acts of the Apostles*, 366) and perhaps an indication of the baseless nature of the charges.

16:37 Paul's response (ἔφη, 3rd sg. aor. act. indic. of φημί, "say") is to the lictors (αὐτούς). Δείραντες is the nom. pl. masc. of aor. act. ptc. of δέρω, "beat"; attend. circum. Δημοσίᾳ (dat. sg. fem. of δημόσιος, -ία, -ιον) is a dat. of manner (KMP 132), mng. "publicly." Ἀκατακρίτους (acc. pl. masc. of ἀκατάκριτος, -ον) , mng. "without due process" (CSB "without a trial"), is a subst. adj. modifying ἡμᾶς. The phrase ἀνθρώπους Ῥωμαίους (acc. pl. masc. of Ῥωμαῖος, -α, -ον) modifying ὑπάρχοντας (acc. pl. masc. of pres. act. ptc. of ὑπάρχω) is concessive, mng. "although being Roman" (see NIV, TNIV, NET, MIT, NJB, i.e., citizens). Paul elaborated on the shameful treatment. Note the continuity of ἔβαλαν (3rd pl. aor. act. indic. of βάλλω) with εἰς φυλακήν (acc. sg. fem. of φυλακή, -ης, ἡ), "thrown into prison," and ἐκβάλλουσιν (3rd pl. pres. act. indic. of ἐκβάλλω), "secretly (λάθρᾳ) thrown out." Bruce notes the terms are discourteous (Bruce *Acts of the Apostles*, 367). Οὐ γάρ is an emphatic way of rejecting a proposal (BHGNT 323). Ἐλθόντες (nom. pl. masc. of aor. act. ptc. of ἔρχομαι) as attend. circum. is taking on the sense of the 3rd. pl. aor. act. impv. ἐξαγαγέτωσαν (of ἐξάγω) mng. "let them come out and escort us out" (a more courteous term).

16:38 The lictors (ῥαβδοῦχοι, nom. pl. masc. of ῥαβδοῦχος, -ου, ὁ) relayed the message (on ἀπήγγειλαν, see v. 36). Ἐφοβήθησαν (3rd pl. aor. pass. indic. of φοβέομαι) is ingressive: "they became fearful." The following causal ptc. explains their fear: they heard (ἀκούσαντες, nom. pl. masc. of aor. act. ptc. of ἀκούω) Paul and Silas were Romans. As Keener notes "to beat and imprison Roman citizens without trial (Acts 16:37) was itself a criminal offense" (Keener 3.2517).

16:39 Ἐλθόντες is the nom. pl. masc. of aor. act. ptc. of ἔρχομαι, attend. circum. Παρεκάλεσαν (3rd pl. aor. act. indic. of παρακαλέω) means "were conciliatory" toward them (BDAG 765d; although "reassure" doesn't fit the context, nor does "apologized" [RSV, NLT, NRSV, ESV, NET]; "appease" is better [CSB, NIV, TNIV]). Paul had used ἐξάγω in v. 36. Surely intentional, Luke uses the same word (ἐξαγαγόντες, nom. pl. masc. of aor. act. ptc. of ἐξάγω; attend. circum.), best tr. "escorted," in contr. to βάλλω (NIV, TNIV). The missionaries were asked (ἠρώτων, 3rd pl. impf. act. indic. of ἐρωτάω) to leave the city (ἀπελθεῖν, aor. act. inf. of ἀπέρχομαι; indir. speech; KMP 371).

16:40 Luke quickly wraps up the visit to Philippi. On ἐξελθόντες, see v. 39. They returned to Lydia's home (εἰσῆλθον, 3rd pl. aor. act. indic. of εἰσέρχομαι). Ἰδόντες is the nom. pl. masc. of aor. act. ptc. of ὁράω; attend. circum. Here the sense of παρεκάλεσαν (3rd pl. aor. act. indic. of παρακαλέω) is "encouraged." With ἐξῆλθαν (3rd pl. aor. act. indic. of ἐξέρχομαι), the "we passages" are suspended until 20:5. Bruce notes that Luke was left at Philippi (cf. Phil 4:14; Bruce, *Acts of the Apostles*, 367).

HOMILETICAL SUGGESTIONS

When God Directs the Ministry (16:6–40)

Introduction: God speaks (vv. 6–10)
What follows is true only if God has spoken.
    1. Expect God to move (vv. 11–15)
    2. Expect opposition (vv. 16–24)
    3. Expect a counter operation (vv. 25–34)
Conclusion: vindication (vv. 35–40)
It comes in many forms, some only in heaven.

2. Ministry in Thessalonica (17:1–9)

17:1 Διοδεύσαντες is the nom. pl. masc. of aor. act. ptc. of διοδεύω, "pass through"; temp. (unique to Luke, cf. Luke 8:1). They went southwest on the *Via Egnatia* (Bruce, *Acts of the Apostles*, 368) to Amphipolis (Ἀμφίπολιν, acc. sg. fem. of Ἀμφίπολις, -εως, ἡ) and Apollonia (Ἀπολλωνίαν, acc. sg. fem. of Ἀπολλονία, -ας, ἡ; both objs. of the ptc.), each an overnight stop (BASHH 108). Ultimately, they came (ἦλθον, 3rd pl. aor. act. indic. of ἔρχομαι) to Thessalonica (Θεσσαλονίκην, acc. sg. fem. of Θεσσαλονίκη, -ης, ἡ; dir. obj.). The comment regarding a Jewish synagogue (an impers. ἦν with a pred. nom. συναγωγή) would suggest none were in the previous cities (Haenchen 506); that is, they had a small Jewish population (however, see Z §217).

17:2 Κατὰ . . . τὸ εἰωθός (acc. sg. neut. of pf. act. ptc. of εἴωθα, "be accustomed"; an obsolete pres., subst.) with the poss. dat. Παύλῳ means "according to Paul's custom" (NASB). Εἰσῆλθεν is the 3rd sg. aor. act. indic. of εἰσέρχομαι. Ἐπὶ σάββατα (acc. pl. neut. of σάββατον, -ου, τό) τρία is disputed:

    1. It could mean "for three weeks" (RSV). In this view, ἐπί refers to a period of time. If so, problems with the Thessalonian correspondence arise. There, it looks like the ministry was longer than three weeks (see Keener 3.2539).
    2. It could mean he argued (διελέξατο, 3rd sg. aor. mid. indic. of διαλέγομαι) "for three Sabbaths." That Paul's custom is mentioned earlier, this is a more likely mng. (Barrett 2.809). If so, it is possible that it is "three consecutive Sabbaths" (NLT ["in a row"], NJB; Haenchen 507). It is better, however, to simply note "three Sabbaths," leaving room for a longer ministry (KJV, NASB, NIV, NRSV, ESV, TNIV, NET).

17:3 Διανοίγων (nom. sg. masc. of pres. act. ptc. of διανοίγω, "explain"; manner) and παρατιθέμενος (nom. sg. masc. of pres. mid. ptc. of παρατίθημι; manner) in the mid. means "demonstrating" [BDAG 772a]). The first ὅτι indicates the content of the explanation. Ἔδει (3rd sg. impf. act. indic. of δεῖ) has χριστόν as the subj. and compound compl. infs. (παθεῖν, aor. act. inf. of πάσχω, "suffer," and ἀναστῆναι, aor. act. indic. of ἀνίστημι, "to rise"). The second ὅτι clearly introduces dir. speech (as the first might as well, Barrett 2.811). Οὗτος is best understood as the subj. of ἐστιν. Thus, ὁ χριστός is the pred. nom. with the art. of previous ref. The presence of Ἰησοῦς complicates the matter. It is likely in appos. to οὗτος. Given the word order it is best tr. "This man is the

Christ: namely, Jesus . . ." (see Barrett 2.811, NRSV). Most EVV follow the grammar as, "This Jesus, whom . . . is the Christ." The pron. ἐγώ is emphatic. Καταγγέλλω is the 1st sg. pres. act. indic. of καταγγέλλω, "proclaim."

17:4 Ἐξ αὐτῶν functions as a part. gen. (ZG 407; Z §81). Ἐπείσθησαν is the 3rd pl. aor. pass. indic. of πείθω, "persuade." Προσεκληρώθησαν (3rd pl. aor. pass. indic. of προσκληρόω, "to be attached to, join"; NT hapax) with masc. sg. dats. as the obj. (Παύλῳ and Σιλᾷ) means "were joined to Paul and Silas." On τε, see 1:15. The gen. σεβομένων (gen. pl. masc. of pres. mid. ptc. of σέβω, "worship") Ἑλλήνων (gen. pl. masc. of Ἑλλήν, -ηνος, ὁ; together mng. "devout Greeks," i.e., devout to God [Barrett 2.812; Schnabel 705]; i.e., "God-fearers") is a part. gen. to πλῆθος (masc. nom. sg of πλῆθος, -ους, τό, "crowd." The part. gen. phrase, γυναικῶν . . . πρώτων (gen. pl. fem. of πρῶτος, -η, -ον) means "leading women" (Bruce, *Acts of the Apostles*, 369) and modifies the following subst. adj. phrase οὐκ ὀλίγαι (nom. pl. fem. of ὀλίγος, -η, -ον) mng. "not a few" (on the litotes, see 14:28).

17:5 This v. is two complicated sentences joined by καί. In the first, three ptcs. set up a riot provoked by Thessalonian Jews. The first, ζηλώσαντες (nom. pl. masc. of aor. act. ptc. of ζηλόω), is causal, giving the reason for the riot. The next two are attend. circum. Προσλαβόμενοι (nom. pl. masc. of aor. mid. ptc. of προσλαμβάνω) in the mid. means "having taken along." Ἀγοραίων (gen. pl. masc. of ἀγοραῖος; gen. of source) is lit. "from the market" but represents a group of questionable character (BDAG 15a; cf. ESV "rabble"). This is made explicit by the ptc.'s obj. phrase ἄνδρας τινὰς πονηρούς (masc. acc. pls.; obj. of the ptc.), "some wicked men." The final background ptc., ὀχλοποιήσαντες (nom. pl. masc. of aor. act. ptc. of ὀχλοποιέω, "form a mob"), is only known in Plutarch *Aemilius Paullus 38* outside of Acts (Bruce, *Acts of the Apostles*, 370), a NT hapax. Ἐθορύβουν is the 3rd pl. impf. act. indic. of θορυβέω, "set in an uproar." With the obj. πόλιν (acc. sg. fem. of πόλις, -εως, ἡ) it surely means "started a riot in the city" (CSB, NIV, TNIV, MIT).

The second sentence begins with the temp. ptc. ἐπιστάντες (nom. pl. masc. of aor. act. ptc. of ἐφίστημι, "approach"), by context, with the intent to harm (see comments in BHGNT 327). It takes a dat. obj. (BDAG 418d, technically a dat. of disadvantage) οἰκίᾳ (dat. sg. fem. of οἰκία, -ας, ἡ). Ἰάσονος (gen. sg. masc. of Ἰάσων, -ονος, ὁ, "Jason"; poss. gen.). Ἐζήτουν is the 3rd pl. impf. act. indic. of ζητέω, "seek." Προαγαγεῖν is the aor. act. inf. of προάγω, "drag"; purp. Δῆμον (acc. sg. masc. of δῆμος, -ου, ὁ) is the popular assembly in a democracy (BDAG 223b; Johnson 307; Schnabel 706).

17:6 Most EVV tr. the neg. ptc. εὑρόντες (nom. pl. masc. of aor. act. ptc. of εὑρίσκω; causal or temp.) as "when they did not find. . . ." The combination of the impf. ἔσυρον (3rd pl. act. indic. of σύρω, "drag"), the prep. phrase ἐπὶ τοὺς πολιτάρχας (acc. pl. masc. of πολιτάρχης, -ου, ὁ; rulers of Thessalonica), and the pres. ptc. βοῶντες (nom. pl. masc. of pres. act. ptc. of βοάω, "shout") creates a vivid account of the mob's mistreatment. Ὅτι introduces dir. speech and is not tr. in most EVV. The accusation is in the form of a pred. nom. Οἰκουμένην (acc. sg. fem. of οἰκουμένη, -ης, ἡ, "world") is the obj. of ἀναστατώσαντες (nom. pl. masc. of aor. act. ptc. of ἀναστατόω, "disturb"; subst., pred. nom.). Οὗτοι (subst., mng. "these men") is the subj. of an assumed being vb. The adv. ἐνθάδε ("here") modifies πάρεισιν (3rd pl. pres. act. indic. of πάρειμι, "arrive").

17:7 Ὑποδέδεκται (3rd sg. pf. mid. indic. of ὑποδέχομαι, "receive") has Ἰάσων (nom. sg. masc. of Ἰάσων, -ονος, ὁ, "Jason") as its subj. Ἀπέναντι (prep., "against") takes the gen. δογμάτων (gen. pl. neut. of δόγμα, -ατος, τό, "decree"). Πράσσουσιν is the 3rd pl. pres. act. indic. of πράσσω, "do." Λέγοντες (nom. pl. masc. of pres. act. ptc. of λέγω; means) is how they violate the decrees. Βασιλέα (acc. sg. masc. of βασιλεύς, -έως, ὁ; fronted for emphasis) is the obj. of εἶναι (pres. inf. of εἰμί; indir. speech; impers., mng. "there is"). In the Western Empire, Romans historically detested the idea of a king. In the East, however, it was the basic term for Caesar, and the charge is the most serious possible (Bruce, *Acts of the Apostles*, 371).

17:8 Ἐτάραξαν (3rd pl. aor. act. indic. of ταράσσω, "trouble") takes a compound dir. obj., ὄχλον (acc. sg. masc. of ὄχλος, -ου, ὁ) and πολιτάρχας (acc. pl. masc. of πολιτάρχης, -ου, ὁ, see 17:6). Ἀκούοντας (acc. pl. masc. of pres. act. ptc. of ἀκούω) is temp.,"when they heard" (most EVV).

17:9 Λαβόντες (nom. pl. masc. of aor. act. ptc. of λαμβάνω) with the subst. adj. obj. ἱκανὸν (acc. sg. neut. of ἱκανός, -η, -ον) here is "to take bail" (BDAG 472c), a Latinism from the legal system (Bruce, *Acts of the Apostles*, 372). It is likely Jason and the others were forced to guarantee Paul and Silas's "good behavior" and quiet departure. Paul may allude to this in places like 1 Thess 2:17 (Bruce, *Acts of the Apostles*, 372; Schnabel 709). Ἀπέλυσαν is the 3rd pl. aor. act. indic. of ἀπολύω, "release." There is no doubt the young church continued to suffer persecution (see Keener's treatment, 3:2557–58).

3. Ministry in Berea (17:10–15)

17:10 Because of the situation's severity (and perhaps the bond enacted), the brothers act immediately (adv. εὐθέως) and by night (διὰ νυκτός, the space of time, see Z §115). Ἐξέπεμψαν is the 3rd pl. aor. act. indic. of ἐκπέμπω, "send out." Βέροιαν (acc. sg. fem. of Βέροια, -ας, ἡ, "Berea") is well off the *Via Egnatia*. It was likely chosen for that very reason (twenty-five miles inland, Keener 3.2561). On οἵτινες, see 7:53. The ref. is Paul and Silas. Παραγενόμενοι is the nom. pl. masc. of aor. mid. ptc. of παραγίνομαι; temp. The vb. ἀπῄεσαν (3rd pl. impf. act. indic. of ἄπειμι, "go away") is a NT hapax whose exact mng. here is unclear. Bruce suggests the ἀπ' pref. is "practically otiose" (Bruce, *Acts of the Apostles*, 373). Zerwick more plausibly suggests it is "the notion of going where they were accustomed to go" (Z §133), the synagogue.

17:11 The Bereans' character is expressed in a pred. adj. cstr. with οὗτοι ("these men") as the subj. and a comp. adj. εὐγενέστεροι (nom. pl. masc. of εὐγενής, -ές). The latter is lit. "more highborn" but came to mean merely "noble" and is likely in contrast to ἀγοραίων in v. 5 (Keener 3.2563). The art. τῶν nominalizes the prep. phrase and is a gen. of comp. "than those in Thessalonica." On οἵτινες, see 7:53. Ἐδέξαντο (3rd pl. aor. mid. indic. of δέχομαι, "receive"). The dir. obj. λόγον, as elsewhere, is a ref. to the gospel. Μετὰ πάσης προθυμίας (gen. pl. fem. of προθυμία,-ας, ἡ; subst. adj.) means "with all goodwill" (see BDAG 870a; *TDNT* 7.699). Καθ' ἡμέραν (acc. sg. fem. of ἡμέρα) is distributive: "daily." Ἀνακρίνοντες is the nom. pl. masc. of pres. act. ptc. of ἀνακρίνω, "examine"; manner. The final clause is an expression in CGk. style. In an indir. question, in a historical context, the opt. ἔχοι (3rd sg. pres. act. opt. of ἔχω) took the place of an indic. (Bruce, *Acts of the Apostles*, 373; Wallace 484). On οὕτως with ἔχω, see 7:1. It is best rendered "to see if these things were so" (RSV, ESV, NET).

17:12 On μὲν οὖν, see 1:6. Ἐξ αὐτῶν functions a part. gen. Ἐπίστευσαν is the 3rd pl. aor. act. indic. of πιστεύω, "believe." Καί (ascensive) is best rendered "including." Believing Gk. (Ἑλληνίδων [gen. pl. fem. of Ἑλληνίς, -ίδος, ἡ) women (γυναικῶν; in appos. to αὐτῶν) are described as εὐσχημόνων (gen. pl. fem. of εὐσχήμων, -ον); together mng. "prominent Greek women." Luke also uses litotes (see 14:28) to note many men as well (presumably likewise prominent, BAFCS 2.114–17).

17:13 Ὡς is temp., "when." Ἔγνωσαν is the 3rd pl. aor. act. indic. of γινώσκω. The subj. οἱ . . . Ἰουδαῖοι ("the Jews") is specified as ἀπὸ τῆς Θεσσαλονίκης ("from Thessalonica"). Ὅτι relates the content of the knowledge in indir. speech. Καί is adv., "also." Κατηγγέλη is the 3rd sg. aor. indic. pass. of καταγγέλλω, "preach." The phrase ὁ λόγος τοῦ θεου ref. to the gospel. The opponents came (ἦλθον, 3rd pl. aor. act. indic. of ἔρχομαι) there also (κἀκεῖ crasis of καὶ ἐκει). Culy and Parsons note that the two ptcs. σαλεύοντες (nom. pl. masc. of pres. act. ptc. of σαλεύω, "stir up"; purp.) and ταράσσοντες (nom. pl. masc. of pres. act. ptc. of ταράσσω, "trouble, disturb"; purp.) are likely a doublet mng. "to thoroughly stir up" (BHGNT 330).

17:14 The response of the new community is hasty (εὐθέως . . . τότε; ESV, CSB, "then . . . immediately"). Ἐξαπέστειλαν is the 3rd pl. aor. act. indic. of ἐξαποστέλλω, "send away." Πορεύεσθαι (pres. mid. inf. of πορεύομαι) likely expresses purp. The stacking of preps. with ἕως (ἕως ἐπὶ) is not uncommon (see BDAG 423d–24a). It is likely one concept (Haenchen 509) best tr. "as far as" (Barrett 2.819–20; BHGNT 331). Ὑπέμειναν (3rd pl. aor. act. indic. of ὑπομένω) implies staying in a place while others depart: "they stayed behind" (BDAG 1039b, *TDNT* 4.581). On τε, see 1:15. The second τε is part of a τε . . . και cstr.: "Both Silas and Timothy" (the compound subj. of the vb.). The animosity was directly aimed at Paul (Schnabel 711).

17:15 It is unclear whether Paul goes by land or sea (it was a favorable season for sailing, BASHH 116). However, καθιστάνοντες (nom. pl. masc. of pres. act. ptc. of καθίστημι, "bring, take"; subst.) as the subj. of ἤγαγον (3rd pl. aor. act. indic. of ἄγω) makes it clear he was not alone in the travel. The prep. phrase ἕως Ἀθηνῶν (gen. pl. fem. of Ἀθῆναι, -ῶν, αἱ, "Athens") sets the destination. For the return trip, the escorts received (λαβόντες, nom. pl. masc. of aor. act. ptc. of λαμβάνω; temp.) instructions (ἐντολήν, acc. sg. fem. of ἐντολή, -ῆς, ἡ, "an order") for those left behind. Ἵνα introduces a purp. clause. Ὡς τάχιστα (superl. of ταχέως [BDF §60 (2), lit., "language"]; NT hapax) has the sense of "as quickly as possible" (BDAG 992d). Ἔλθωσιν is the 3rd pl. aor. act. subjunc. of ἔρχομαι. The main vb. of the clause, ἐξῄεσαν (3rd pl. impf. act. indic. of ἔξειμι, "depart," i.e., with the instructions) ref. to the escorts.

HOMILETICAL SUGGESTIONS

Jealous Opposition to the Gospel (17:1–15)

1. Jealousy seeks to harm the messengers (vv. 1–9)
2. Jealousy pursues the messengers at great distances (vv. 10–15)

4. Ministry in Athens (17:16–34)

a. Paul's Arrival (17:16–21)

17:16 In Athens (Ἀθῆναις, dat. pl. fem. of Ἀθῆναι, -ῶν, αἱ), Paul waited (ἐκδεχομένου, gen. sg. masc. of pres. mid. ptc. of ἐκδέχομαι; gen. abs., temp.) for Silas and Timothy to return. The phrase is in the gen. abs. because πνεῦμα ("spirit"; i.e., Paul's spirit) is the subj. of the main vb. Παρωξύνετο (3rd sg. impf. pass. indic. of παροξύνω, "provoke") has the sense of emotional distress. The word is likely intentionally vague to cover a range of emotions (grief, anger, concern, etc.). Θεωροῦντος (gen. sg. masc. of pres. act. ptc. of θεωρέω; gen. abs [switch in subj.], causal) takes πόλιν (dat. sg. fem. of πόλις, πόλεως, ἡ) as the dir. obj. Οὖσαν is the acc. sg. fem. of pres. ptc. of εἰμί; compl. in a double-acc. cstr. (BHGNT 333). Κατείδωλον (NT hapax, a distinctly Christian word after the NT, likely coined here) is based on a common custom using κατ-, mng. "full of. . . ." Most of these refer to vegetation, so Barrett suggests "a forest of idols" (Barrett 2.827). Paul had been in Gentile cities for quite some time, yet found Athens disturbing. It was known even among the pagans as overrun by idols. Keener noted that it was estimated that Rhodes had 73,000 idols and Athens had no fewer (Keener 3:2574).

17:17 On μὲν οὖν, see 1:6. Paul continued his practice of evangelism in the synagogues (διελέγετο, 3rd sg. impf. mid. of διαλέγομαι, "dispute"). Ἰουδαίοις . . . σεβομένοις are dats. of assoc., "with Jews and God-fearers." Paul also disputed in the Agora (ἐν τῇ ἀγορᾷ, dat. sg. fem. of ἀγορά, -ᾶς, ἡ, "marketplace"). Κατὰ πᾶσαν ἡμέραν is likely an emphatic distributive "every single day" (BHGNT 334; possibly in contr. with synagogues on the Sabbath). Παρατυγχάνοντας (acc. pl. masc. of pres. act. ptc. of παρατυγχάνω, "happen to be near"; subst., NT hapax) as the obj. of πρός means "with those who happen to be near."

17:18 Καί is adv., "also." Τινές (nom. pl. masc. of τίς, τί; subj.) is followed by a part. gen. (modified by two gen. pl. masc. subst. adjs: Ἐπικουρείων [of Ἐπικούρειος, -ή, -όν, "Epicurean"] and Στοϊκῶν [of Στοϊκός, -ή, -όν, "Stoic"]) φιλοσόφων (gen. pl. masc. of φιλόσοφος, -ου, ὁ, "philosophers"). These two philosophical schools (both founded around 300 BC) were in stark contrast to each other (see Johnson 313). The Epicureans devalued religion, thought the gods disinterested in humanity, and sought pleasure as the highest goal of humanity (Bruce, *Acts of the Apostles*, 376). The Stoics, on the other hand, considered the gods more immanent. They sought consistency on a rational basis and self-sufficiency (Bruce, *Acts of the Apostles*, 377). Both found a common opponent in the gospel but resorted to name-calling. Συνέβαλλον (3rd pl. impf. act. indic. of συμβάλλω, "converse") takes a dat. obj. (αὐτῷ). The response is in two directions. First, ἔλεγον (3rd pl. impf. act. indic. of λέγω) introduces indir. speech. The sentence is the apod. of an incomplete fourth-class cond. (fut. less probable). The implicit prot. is "If he could say anything that made sense!" (Wallace 484). Τί (interr. pron. acc. sg. neut. of τίς, τί; dir. obj.) with the indef. particle ἄν means "what would. . . ." Θέλοι is the 3rd sg. pres. act. opt. of θέλω; potential opt. Σπερμολόγος (nom. sg. masc. of σπερμολόγος, -ον; often tr. "babbler") refers to one picking up scraps of information (Bruce, *Acts of the Apostles*, 377, "a seed-picker") and communicating it in an unsophisticated way (BDAG 937d). Louw and Nida add that it is given in pretense of intelligence. Thus, he is "an ignorant showoff" (LN 27.19). Λέγειν is the pres. act. inf. of λέγω; indir. speech. Οὗτος is also generally disparaging when the person is present (Barrett 2.830).

The second opinion is fairer. Οἱ functions as a pron., best rendered "others." Δοκεῖ is the 3rd sg. pres. act. indic. of δοκέω, "seem"; takes a compl. inf. εἶναι (pres. inf. of εἰμί). The latter takes a pred. in the nom. case (by the irregular constraint δοκέω has on the inf. BHGNT 335, i.e., instead of the expected acc.). Ξένων (gen. pl. neut. of ξένος, -η, -ον,) δαιμονίων (normally "demon" in the NT, but here of "semi-divine being," BDAG 210a) is an obj. gen. phrase, fronted for emphasis modifying καταγγελεύς (nom. sg. masc. of καταγγελεύς, -έως, ὁ, "a preacher"; NT hapax). Luke's explanation of their conclusion (causal ὅτι) fronts the acc. sg. dir. objs. (Ἰησοῦν and ἀνάστασιν) "Jesus and the resurrection" to the vb. εὐηγγελίζετο (3rd pl. impf. mid. indic. of εὐαγγελίζω [on the voice, see 5:42]). It is often suggested from the pl. δαιμονίων that the philosophers, with little contact with the concept of resurrection, were assuming two gods; perhaps Jesus and Anastasia (Witherington 515).

17:19 Ἐπιλαβόμενοί (nom. pl. masc. of aor. mid. ptc. of ἐπιλαμβάνομαι, "take hold"; attend. circum., twelve times in Luke-Acts, two times elsewhere). On τε, see 1:15. This ptc. takes a gen. obj. (αὐτοῦ, ref. to Paul). Ἄρειον πάγον (acc. masc. sg. of Ἄρειος πάγος, ὁ; prep. obj.), lit. "Mars Hill," is a ref. to the council of Mars Hill. At this time, a body of local authorities adjudicating public-order issues, incl. religious matters (Barrett 2.832; Bruce, *Acts of the Apostles*, 378). Luke typically referred to local courts with local names. Ἤγαγον is the 3rd pl. aor. act. indic. of ἄγω, "lead." Λέγοντες is the nom. pl. masc. of pres. act. ptc. of λέγω; attend. circum. Δυνάμεθα (1st pl. pres. mid. indic. of δύναμαι; presents a polite request) is compl. by the inf. γνῶναι (aor. act. inf. of γινώσκω), mng. "may we know. . . ." Thus, it is not so much an arrest but an inquiry. The requested content is in a pred. nom. cstr. with an assumed vb. Τίς (nom. sg. fem. of τίς, τί; interr. pron.) is the subj. The compl. is the noun phrase ἡ καινὴ αὕτη . . . διδαχή, "this new teaching." Ὑπὸ σοῦ λαλουμένη (nom. sg. fem. of pres. pass. ptc. of λαλέω; attrib.) is lit. "being spoken by you."

17:20 Γάρ introduces the grounds for the request. Ξενίζοντα (acc. pl. neut. of pres. act. ptc. of ξενίζω; subst.) with τινα (acc. pl. neut., indef. pron.) functions as the dir. obj., "some strange things." Εἰσφέρεις is the 2nd sg. pres. act. indic. of εἰσφέρω, "introduce." Βουλόμεθα (1st pl. pres. mid. indic. of βούλομαι) takes a compl. inf. (γνῶναι aor. act. inf. of γινώσκω), mng. "we want to know." The information sought is expressed in an idiom introduced by the interr. pron. τίνα (acc. pl. neut.). Lit. the statement is "what these things [ταῦτα] want [θέλει, 3rd sg. pres. act. indic. of θέλω] to be [εἶναι, pres. inf. of εἰμί; compl.]." It is best rendered "what these things mean" (KJV, RSV, NASB, ESV, MIT).

17:21 This v. is Luke's comment on the Athenians. The sentence has a compound subj. First, Ἀθηναῖοι (nom. pl. masc. of Ἀθηναῖος, -α, -ον) . . . πάντες is "all the Athenians." Second, ἐπιδημοῦντες (nom. pl. masc. of pres. act. ptc. of ἐπιδημέω; attrib.) modifies ξένοι (nom. pl. masc. of ξένος, -η, -ον; subst. adj.), mng. "the visiting strangers." Εἰς οὐδὲν ἕτερον (acc. sg. neut. of ἕτερος, -α, -ον) and the vb. ηὐκαίρουν (3rd pl. impf. act. indic. of εὐκαιρέω, habitual impf.) means "used to spend time in nothing else" (BDAG

407a). Ἤ . . . ἤ is "than . . . or" (with a comp.). Λέγειν τι and ἀκούειν τι (pres. act. infs. + acc. sg. neut. indef. pron.) take καινότερον (acc. sg. neut. comp. adj. of καινός, -ή, -όν superl. in mng. [ZG 410]; Z §150) in a double-acc. cstr., best rendered "than to say or to hear the newest thing."

b. Paul's Speech on the Areopagus (17:22–34)

Quite a number of scholars see parallels with Socrates's death in the narrative (Plato, *Apology* 17a; Barrett 2.834; NICNT, 333; Keener 3.2604). Like Socrates, Paul began in the Agora, debated with philosophers, was "charged" with introducing new gods, and was brought before the Areopagus council. If so, on some level it comp. Paul to Socrates (Keener 3.2604). There are no formal charges, and it is likely a combination of curiosity and investigation. Paul's argument is that the God he preaches is the unknown God of an altar he had seen (17:22–23). Archaeology has yet to find such an altar, but the literature freq. refers to them (Keener 3.2632). The sermon has three movements. Each repeat a key word in the previous section as the first word of the section: 17:24, Θεός, who God is; 17:26, ποιέω, what he desires from humans; 17:29, γένος, how we should respond. Hemer sums it up well: "The nature of God is thus explained against the backdrop of the Athenians' own terminology, as Paul gently exposes the inconsistency between the transcendent reality to which their thinkers aspired and the man-made images of Athens" (BASHH 423).

17:22 Σταθείς is the nom. pl. masc. of aor. pass. ptc. of ἵστημι; attend. circum. Ἐν μέσῳ τοῦ Ἀρείου πάγου (gen. sg. masc. of ὁ Ἄρειος πάγος, "Areopagus") places Paul in the place of inquiry in front of the council (Barrett 2.834). Ἔφη (3rd sg. aor. act. indic. of φημί) introduces dir. speech. On ἄνδρες Ἀθηναῖοι (voc. pl. masc. of Ἀθηναῖος, -α, -ον), compare 1:11, 16; 2:22. Κατὰ πάντα is distributive, "in every way." Ὡς modifies the comp. adj. δεισιδαιμονεστέρους (acc. pl. masc. of δεισιδαίμων, -ον, "religious") that in turn is the compl. in a double-acc. cstr. (BHGNT 336; ὑμᾶς, dir. obj.) mng. "how very religious you are." Θεωρῶ is the 1st sg. pres. act. indic. of θεωρέω, "see."

17:23 Γάρ indicates substantiation. Two temp. ptcs. set up Paul's defense. Διερχόμενος (nom. sg. masc. of pres. mid. ptc. of διέρχομαι; temp.) and ἀναθεωρῶν (nom. pl. masc. of pres. act. ptc. of ἀναθεωρέω, "carefully observe," perhaps "one after another" [ZG 410]). The dir. obj. σεβάσματα (acc. pl. neut. of σέβασμα, -ατος, τό, "objects of worship") is a conscious choice to avoid inflammatory language (Haenchen 521). Εὗρον is the 1st sg. aor. act. indic. of εὑρίσκω. Καί is adv., "also." Βωόν is the acc. sg. masc. of βωμός, -οῦ, ὁ, "an altar"; dir. obj. Ἐπεγέγραπτο (3rd sg. plpf. pass. indic. of ἐπιγράφω, "inscribe") quotes Ἀγνώστῳ (dat. sg. masc. of ἄγνωστος, -ον) θεῷ "to an Unknown God." Ἀγνοοῦντες (nom. pl. masc. of pres. act. ptc. of ἀγνοέω, "not know"; attrib.) modifies εὐσεβεῖτε (2nd pl. pres. act. indic. of εὐσεβέω), mng. "you ignorantly worship." Τοῦτο ("this") refers to the previous clause and is the dir. obj. of καταγγέλλω (1st sg. pres. act. indic. of καταγγέλλω, "announce").

17:24 God is introduced in a long nom. phrase that recalls Isa 42:5 (Haenchen 522). Θεός (subj.) is modified by an attrib. ptc. ποιήσας (nom. sg. masc. of aor. act. ptc. of ποιέω). It takes a compound obj.: κόσμον (acc. sg. masc. of κόσμος, -ου, ὁ) and πάντα τά (acc. pl. neut. art. functioning as a pron.; lit., "all the things" in it (ἐν αὐτῷ). Οὗτος (resumptive after such a long phrase, BHGNT 337) is the subj. of an assumed ἐστίν. Οὐρανοῦ (gen. sg. masc. of οὐρανός, -οῦ, ὁ) and γῆς (gen. sg. fem. of γῆ, -ῆς, ἡ) modifies κύριος (pred. nom.). Ὑπάρχων (nom. sg. masc. of pres. act. ptc. of ὑπάρχω) is causal, laying the grounds for the statement that follows. The adj. χειροποιήτοις (dat. pl. neut. of χειροποίητος, -η, -ον, "made by hand" [attrib. to ναοῖς dat. pl. masc. of ναός, -οῦ, τό, "temple"]) is not the inflammatory statement of 7:48. The word essentially means "man-made" (BDAG 1083c; MM 687c; ZG 410). As such it would not be offensive to a Gentile about a pagan shrine. To be sure, those regarding the OT hearing or reading it would recognize echoes of prophetic criticism (see, e.g., Isa 16:12 LXX). Κατοικεῖ is the 3rd sg. pres. act. indic. of κατοικέω, "dwell" (neg. by οὐκ). Thus, the true God is transcendent.

17:25 Οὐδέ, "neither," negates the initial statement. Ὑπὸ χειρῶν ἀνθρωπίνων (gen. pl. fem. of ἀνθρώπινος, -η, -ον, "human"; agent of pass. vb. mng. "by human hands") plays off χειροποιήτοις in v. 24). Θεραπεύεται (3rd pl. pres. pass. indic. of θεραπεύω) is normally "to heal" in the NT. Here it is "to serve" (BDAG 453a). Προσδεόμενός (nom. sg. masc. of pres. mid. ptc. of προσδέομαι, NT hapax) is causal, "as if he needed" in most EVV. The positive statement is all-inclusive. Αὐτός is emphatic. This runs counter to the Gk. belief that the gods needed offerings to be happy (Robertson, *Pictures*, 287). Διδούς (acc. sg. masc. of pres. act. ptc. of δίδωμι) is causal, "because he is giving. . . ." The dir. obj. is compound: ζωόν (acc. sg. fem. of ζωή, -ῆς, ἡ), πνοήν (acc. sg. fem. of πνοή, -ῆς, ἡ, "breath"), and τὰ πάντα (acc. pl. neut. of πᾶς, πᾶσα, πᾶν, subst. adj., "all things").

17:26 Vv. 26–27 is an example of periodism: a long sentence with nuance, allusion, and subtlety (something the educated enjoyed). The basic str. is a finite vb. clause, "he made" (building off v. 25) with two inf. of purp. clauses; "to dwell all over the earth" (v. 26) and "to seek him" (v. 27) (Witherington 526). Ἐποίησέν is the 3rd sg. aor. act. indic. of ποιέω. On τε, see 1:15. Ἐξ ἑνός indicates source, "from one man." Πᾶν ἔθνος is the acc. sg. neut. of ἔθνος, -ους, τό; dir. obj. mng. "every nation." The first inf. clause explains the distribution of humanity as a work of God. Κατοικεῖν is the pres. act. indic. of κατοικέω; purp., "to dwell." Ἐπὶ παντὸς προσώπου τῆς γῆς is lit. "upon all the face of the earth" but is best tr. "over the whole earth" (cf. Gen 1:28). The rest of the v. is a comment on the Dispersion, likely based on Deut 32:8 (see Beale and Carson 595). The aor. ptc. ὁρίσας (nom. sg. masc. of aor. act. ptc. ὁρίζω, "determine") suggests the determination took place before creation (Bruce, *Acts of the Apostles*, 383). Two phrases joined by καί outline two determinations. First, "allotted seasons" is προστεταγμένους (acc. pl. masc. of pf. pass. ptc. of προστάσσω; attrib.) modifying καιρούς (acc. pl. masc. of καιρός, -οῦ, ὁ). It most naturally refers to periods of time (contra BHGNT 339). Second, "boundaries of where they live" is ὁροθεσίας (acc. pl. fem. of ὁροθεσία, -ας, ἡ, "borders;" biblical hapax) modified by κατοικίας (gen. sg. fem. of κατοικία, -ας, ἡ, "habitation"; attrib. gen.) and a poss. pron. (αὐτῶν). Witherington (526) notes the idea presented runs counter to the Athenian beliefs of ethnic exclusivity.

17:27 Ζητεῖν (pres. act. inf. of ζητέω) is the second purp. of creation. It should not be seen as a purp. of the Dispersion (the implication of NIV, NRSV, TNIV, NET, NJB). Thus, it is a statement on the nature of humanity; created to seek God (Schnabel 735).

However, presently their success in seeking is only remotely possible. Εἰ introduces the prot. of an incomplete fourth-class cond. (the most hypothetical of all cond. forms, Wallace 702; see also Keener 3.2652; Z §403). Ἄρα γε intensifies the remote possibility (see R 1190, who tr. the cond. and ἄρα as "if haply"). The prot. features two potential opt. vbs. The first, ψηλαφήσειαν (3rd pl. aor. opt. indic. of ψηλαφάω), is used four times in the NT, mng. always neg., "to grope about" like a blind man (BDAG 1098a; Bock 567; Keener 3.2652; Witherington 528). The second, εὕροιεν (3rd pl. aor. opt. indic. of εὑρίσκω), completes the search. The mng. is "if, by a stroke of blind luck, they grope around and find him. . . ." It assumes an apod. of something like "he would fellowship with them." The polite implication is that humans innately neither know God nor know how to find him (Schnabel 735). Καί γε is concessive, "although" (Bruce, *Acts of the Apostles*, 383). Οὐ μακράν (a fixed fem. acc. form., indecl., "far"; on litotes, see 14:28) means "close to." The expression ἀπὸ . . . ἡμῶν (part. gen.) makes his proximity personal. Ὑπάρχοντα is the acc. sg. masc. of pres. act. ptc. of ὑπάρχω; attrib. to θεόν.

17:28 Γάρ substantiates the previous clause. Ἐν . . . ἐσμέν is certainly a quotation, likely of Epimenides (BASHH 118; Bruce, *Acts of the Apostles*, 385; Keener 3.2659). Three vbs. declare humanity's proximity to him (ἐν αὐτῷ = "in the power of," Barrett 2.847; or "by him," Witherington 529). The first is ζῶμεν, 1st pl. pres. act. indic. of ζάω. Second, κινούμεθα (1st pl. pres. pass. indic. of κινέω) in the pass. has an intrans. mng. (BDAG 545b; ZG 411), "move about." Finally, ἐσμέν (1st pl. pres. indic. of εἰμί), often tr. "we have our being" (KJV, RSV), is better "we exist/are" (NLT, NASB, NET), avoiding pantheistic overtones (see Johnson 316).

Τινες ("some") recognizes the statement was common (Barrett 2.848). Καθ᾽ ὑμᾶς takes the place of the simple poss. (Z §130). Ποιητῶν (gen. pl. masc. of ποιητής, -οῦ, ὁ, "poet") is a part. gen. Εἰρήκασιν is the 3rd pl. pf. act. indic. of λέγω. Together the phrase means "some of your poets have said." The quote is closest to Aratus Soli, although it was Cleanthes who was profusely quoted (Keener 3.2659). It begins with τοῦ (which is rarely tr.). It is best to take the gen. sg. masc. art. as a pron. and a gen. of source, "from him" (BHGNT 340). Καί is adv., "also." Γένος (nom. sg. neut. of γένος, -ους, τό) is the pred. nom. of ἐσμέν (1st pl. pres. indic. of εἰμί), mng. "offspring." The citations are speaking to/of Zeus. Paul, however, applies it to "the unknown God." In doing so, he subtly proposes the abandonment of idolatry.

17:29 Γένος (see 17:28) is the pred. nom. of ὑπάρχοντες (nom. pl. masc. of pres. act. ptc. of ὑπάρχω; causal). Neg. ὀφείλομεν (1st pl. pres. act. indic. of ὀφείλω) compl. by νομίζειν (pres. act. inf. of νομίζω) is "we ought not to think. . . ." Χρυσῷ (dat. sg. masc. of χρυσός, -οῦ, ὁ, "gold"), ἀργύρῳ (dat. sg. masc. of ἄργυρος, -ου, ὁ, "silver"; [see intro. for the significance of the nondiminutive form]), and λίθῳ (dat. sg. masc. of λίθος, -ου, ὁ), are in the dat., because ὅμοιον takes a dat. Χαράγματι (dat. sg. neut. of χάραγμα, -ατος, τό; appos. to previous list) means "an image" but implying artisanship (BDAG 1077d). It is modified by two gens. of means: τέχνης (gen. sg. fem. of τέχνη, -ης, ἡ, "skill, trade") and ἐνθυμήσεως (gen. sg. fem. of ἐνθύμησις, -εως, ἡ, "thought, reflection, idea") with the poss. gen. ἀνθρώπου; together, the phrase is "the skill and imagination of man" (see NET). Τὸ θεῖον (acc. sg. neut. of θεῖος, θεία, θεῖον, "divine") is the obj. of εἶναι (pres. inf. of εἰμί; indir. speech). The art. clearly makes it a neut. subst. adj., "the divine essence."

17:30 On μὲν οὖν, see 1:6. Paul transitions to his closing. Χρόνους (acc. pl. masc. of χρόνος, -ου, ὁ) τῆς ἀγνοίας (gen. sg. fem. of ἄγνοια, -ας, ἡ; descr. gen.) is "times of ignorance" (cf. ESV, CSB). The phrase is the obj. of ὑπεριδών (nom. pl. masc. of aor. act. ptc. of ὑπεροράω, "overlook"; concessive). Paul does not suggest universalism. Humans everywhere are accountable for their sins. Even when they don't have the law, violating natural law is enough to condemn (see Rom 2:14–16). They were not judged for their ignorance. The overlooking here is the specific season of ignorance regarding who God is. It recalls the inscription "to the unknown God" at the beginning of the speech (Bock 569; Schnabel 739). This makes the adversative transition τὰ νῦν all the more striking. As of right now, things are different. Instead of passing over, he commands (παραγγέλλει, 3rd sg. pres. act. indic. of παραγγέλλω) repentance (μετανοεῖν, pres. act. inf. of μετανοέω [see 2:38], compl.): a "radical change of attitude and life" (Robertson, *Pictures,* 290).

17:31 Καθότι in HGk. is "because" (ZG 411). God has fixed (ἔστησεν, 3rd sg. aor. act. indic. of ἵστημι, "appoint") a day. The rel. pron. phrase is an allusion to Ps 9:9 LXX. Μέλλει (3rd sg. pres. act. indic. of μέλλω) takes a compl. inf. (κρίνειν, pres. act. inf. of κρίνω), mng. "he will judge." The dir. obj. οἰκουμένην (acc. sg. fem. of οἰκουμένη, -ης, ἡ) ref. to all the inhabitants of the world. Ἐν δικαιοσύνῃ is either the standard of judgment (BHGNT 341) or the manner that the judge operates (Barrett 2.852; R 550 [adv.]; ZG 411; Z §117). Certainty is impossible, but the two mngs. are not far apart. What follows with ἐν ἀνδρί is clearly instr. "by the man" (BDF §219[1]). We expect the acc. but ᾧ is dat. by attraction to ἀνδρί. Ὥρισεν is the 3rd sg. aor. act. indic. of ὁρίζω, "appoint." Πίστιν (acc. sg. fem. of πίστις, -εως, ἡ) and παρασχών (nom. sg. masc. of aor. act. ptc. of παρέχω, "grant, show"; attend. cirucm.) together means "providing proof" (BDAG 818d; BHGNT 342; Bruce, *Acts of the Apostles*, 386). That proof is the resurrection (Ἀναστήσας, nom. sg. masc. of aor. act. ptc. of ἀνίστημι; means).

17:32 The response turns on hearing the resurrection. Ἀκούσαντες is the nom. sg. masc. of aor. act. ptc. of ἀκούω; temp., (perhaps causal). The v. is in a μὲν. . . δέ cstr. Οἱ is used as a pron. subj. of both clauses and is tr. "some." In the first, the vb. ἐχλεύαζον (3rd pl. impf. act. indic. of χλευάζω) is likely an inceptive impf., "began to mock" (Rogers and Rogers 276). In the second, εἶπαν (3rd pl. aor. act. indic. of λέγω) introduces the fact that some take the first step toward faith: listening (ἀκουσόμεθά, 1st pl. fut. mid. indic. of ἀκούω). The adv. καί ("also") and πάλιν ("again") has the sense of "some more."

17:33 Οὕτως signals the end of the formal meeting. Ἐξῆλθεν is the 3rd sg. aor. act. indic. of ἐξέρχομαι. Opinions on the success of the meeting differ. In terms of what the meeting was ostensibly about, Paul was successful in not being banned from Athens. In fact, he accomplished what Socrates did not. He left without formal charges.

17:34 There were also some converts among the hearers. Κολληθέντες is the nom. pl. masc. of aor. pass. ptc. of κολλάω, "join oneself to"; it takes a dat. of pers. (αὐτῷ). Ἐπίστευσαν is the 3rd pl. aor. act. indic. of πιστεύω. The list includes women and unnamed others, but the most interesting is Διονύσιος ὁ Ἀρεοπαγίτης (nom. sg. masc. of

Ἀρεοπαγίτης, -ου, ὁ), "Dionysius the Areopagite." Luke surely means one of the council members (Johnson 318), one of the most prestigious converts so far (with Sergius
Paulus, Keener 3.2678).

HOMILETICAL SUGGESTIONS

Who Is God? (17:24–31)

1. He is the creator of all things (vv. 24–25)
2. God's purposes in creating human beings (vv. 26–28)
   a. To fill the earth (v. 26)
   b. To seek him (v. 27)
3. How human beings should respond? (vv. 29–31)
   a. Renounce idolatry (v. 29)
   b. Repent of sin (v. 30)

FOR FURTHER STUDY

26. The Areopagus Address (17:22–31)

Barrett, C. K. "Paul's Speech on the Areopagus." In *New Testament Christianity for Africa
and the World: Essays in Honour of Harry Sawyerr*, 69–77. London: SPCK, 1974.
Gärtner, B. *The Areopagus Speech and Natural Revelation.* Lund: Gleerup, 1955.
Gempf, C. *DPL*, 51–54.
Hemer, C. J. "The Speeches of Acts: II. The Areopagus Address." *TynBul* 40 (1989):
239–59.
McRay, J. R. *DNTB*, 140–41.
Ramsey, W.M. *St. Paul the Traveler and Roman Citizen*, 237–52. New York: Putnam,
1896.
Sandnes, K. O. "Paul and Socrates: The Aim of Paul's Areopagus Speech." *JSNT* 50 (June
1993): 13–26.

5. Ministry in Corinth (18:1–17)

a. Initial Ministry in Corinth (18:1–11)

18:1 Μετὰ ταῦτα as a transition is common in John but unusual in Acts (only three
times). Χωρισθείς is nom. pl. masc. of aor. pass. ptc. of χωρίζω; attend. circum. Ἦλθεν
is the 3rd sg. aor. act. indic. of ἔρχομαι. Εἰς Κόρινθον (acc. sg. fem. of Κόρινθος, -ου, ἡ,
"Corinth") is about forty miles west of Athens (Bock 577). Under the Roman republic
it had been destroyed and lay barren for 100 years until Julius Caesar rebuilt it as a
Roman colony. It was a major center of commerce, culture, and entertainment in Paul's
time (Bruce, *Acts of the Apostles*, 389–90; Haenchen 533; Witherington 537–38).
18:2 Paul is the subj. of εὑρών (nom. sg. masc. of aor. act. ptc. of εὑρίσκω; attend. circum.) that takes a compound obj. The first, τινα Ἰουδαῖον ("a certain Jew") is identified
as Aquila (Ἀκύλαν, acc. sg. masc. of Ἀκύλας, -αν, ὁ; in appos. to Ἰουδαῖον). On ὀνόματι,

see 5:1. Ἐληλυθότα is the acc. sg. masc. of pf. act. ptc. of ἔρχομαι, attrib. (poss. causal). Ποντικόν (acc. sg. masc. of Ποντικός, -ή, -όν, "from Pontus"; appos. to Aquila) with γένει (dat. sg. neut. of γένος, -ους, τό; dat. of ref. [Z §53]) means "a native of Pontus" (ZG 412). The second obj. is Πρίσκιλλαν (acc. sg. fem. Πρίσκιλλα, -ης, ἡ, dimin. of Πρίσκα). Διά and the art. inf. τό διατεταχέναι (pf. act. inf. of διατάσσω, "command") with Κλαύδιον (acc. sg. masc. of Κλαύδιος, -ου, ὁ, "Claudius"; subj. of inf.) is tr. by most EVV "because Claudius had ordered/commanded." The content of the order is a compl. inf. χωρίζεσθαι (pres. pass. inf. of χωρίζω, "expel"). The ref. is to the famous "edict of Claudius" that expelled Jews from Rome on account of a "Chrestus" (c. AD 49–50; Bruce, *Acts of the Apostles*, 390–91). Finally, the main vb. (with Paul as the subj.) is προσῆλθεν (3rd sg. aor. act. indic. of προσέρχομαι), "he came to them."

18:3 Another causal cstr., διά takes the art. inf. τό . . . εἶναι (pres. inf. of εἰμί) as the prep. obj. The inf. takes ὁμότεχνον (acc. sg. neut. of ὁμότεχνος, -ον, "practicing the same trade") as the obj. of the inf. (in this case a pred. adj. because of the being vb., BHGNT 344). Ἔμενεν is the 3rd sg. impf. act. indic. of μένω. Ἠργάζετο is the 3rd sg. impf. mid. indic. of ἐργάζομαι. Ἦσαν (3rd pl. impf. act. indic. of εἰμί) takes σκηνοποιοί (nom. pl. masc. of σκηνοποιός, -οῦ, ὁ, "tent makers"; pred. nom., widely used for "leather workers," Bruce, *Acts of the Apostles*, 392). Τέχνῃ (dat. sg. fem. of τέχνη, -ης, ἡ) is a dat. of ref. mng. "by trade" (see R 487, "instr.").

18:4 Διελέγετο is the 3rd sg. impf. mid. indic. of διαλέγομαι, "converse, discuss, argue." Κατὰ πᾶν σάββατον is distributive, "on every Sabbath." Ἔπειθέν (3rd sg. impf. act. indic. of πείθω) with the acc. pls. Ἰουδαίους and Ἕλληνας (masc. of Ἕλλην, -ηνος, ὁ) in a τε . . . καί cstr. means "he was persuading both Jews and Greeks." Often the impf. is identified as tendential "attempted to persuade" (Barrett 2.864; Haenchen 534; Robertson, *Pictures*, 296; Z 273). However, Luke's frequent use of the impf. would suggest otherwise. There is no contextual reason to suggest anything other than successful preaching (see Schnabel 758). The summary style of these vv. suggests a lengthy Corinthian ministry.

18:5 Ὡς is temp., "when." Upon Silas and Timothy's arrival (κατῆλθον, 3rd pl. aor. act. indic. of κατέρχομαι, "come down"; see 1 Thess 3:6), Paul began to concentrate solely on preaching. Συνείχετο (3rd sg. impf. mid. indic. of συνέχω, "occupied with") is likely mid. instead of pass. (BHGNT 345) and an inceptive impf. "he began to occupy himself" (see NASB, NET), since previously he was doing secular work (Barrett 2.866; Bruce, *Acts of the Apostles*, 392; Haenchen 534). The vb. takes masc. sg. dat. obj. λόγῳ, "in the gospel," that is, "with preaching" to the Jews (Johnson 323). Διαμαρτυρόμενος is the nom. sg. masc. of pres. mid. ptc. of διαμαρτύρομαι, "solemnly testify"; attend. circum. Εἶναι (pres. inf. of εἰμί) expresses indir. speech, giving the content of the preaching: "Jesus is the Christ" (a pred. acc., BHGNT 345; Wallace 194).

18:6 In a compound gen. abs. phrase, the Jews (αὐτῶν) oppose (ἀντιτασσομένων, gen. pl. masc. of pres. mid. ptc. of ἀντιτάσσω) and blaspheme (βλασφημούντων, gen. pl. masc. of pres. act. ptc. of βλασφημέω). On the latter, it is not stated whether Paul or Christ is the object; if Paul, "slandering" is best. That Paul shook his garments (ἐκτιναξάμενος, nom. sg. masc. of aor. mid. ptc. of ἐκτινάσσω, "shake off"; temp. [see

Neh 5:13—possibly sim. to shaking dust off one's feet, Beale and Carson 595]) suggests Christ is the obj. His parting shot is in two clauses, both assuming a being vb. The first, τὸ αἷμα ὑμῶν ἐπὶ τὴν κεφαλὴν ὑμῶν ("your blood is on your head"), is an OT formula (cf. Lev 20:9; Deut 21:5; esp. Ezek 33:1–6; Beale and Carson 595, "a firm basis in LXX diction") signifying Paul was free from responsibility for their souls. Καθαρὸς ἐγώ is a pred. adj. cstr., lit. mng. "I am clean." In the phrase ἀπὸ τοῦ νῦν, the τοῦ nominalizes the adv. "now" as the obj. of the prep., mng. "from now on" (ZG 412). Πορεύσομαι is the 1st sg. fut. mid. indic. of πορεύομαι, with the prep. phrase εἰς τὰ ἔθνη ("to the Gentiles") as the destination.

18:7 Μεταβάς is the nom. sg. masc. of aor. act. ptc. of μεταβαίνω, "go/pass over"; temp. Ἐκεῖθεν (adv. "there") refers to the synagogue. He went into (εἰσῆλθεν, 3rd sg. aor. mid. indic of εἰσέρχομαι) the house of Titus Justus (Τιτίου Ἰούστου [masc. gen. sgs. of Τίτιος], -ου, ὁ and Ἰοῦστος, -ου, ὁ; on ὀνόματι, see 5:1). Σεβομένου (gen. sg. masc. of pres. mid. ptc. of σέβω, "worship"; attrib.) with the obj. θεόν identifies him as a God-fearer. Spatially, the house is adjacent (συνομοροῦσα fem. nom. sg. pres. act. ptc. of συνομορέω, periph., lit. "sharing a boundary" [ZG 412], i.e., "next door," most EVV tr. as a pred. adj.). It takes a dat. obj. συναγωγῇ ("to the Synagogue"). Thus, Paul's move was neither spatially or theologically distant. It is likely that the move was because he had become a believer, although it is also possible he was merely a decent and hospitable man.

18:8 The mission to the synagogue was successful. The conversion of Crispus (Κρίσπος, nom. sg. masc. of Κρίσπος, -ου, ὁ) is reported (likely the same as the one in 1 Cor 1:14, Barrett 2.868). He is identified with an appos. nom. as the ἀρχισυνάγωγος (nom. sg. masc. of ἀρχισυνάγωγος, -ου, ὁ, "leader of the synagogue"). The aor. ἐπίστευσεν (3rd sg. aor. act. indic. of πιστεύω) is perhaps inceptive (ZG 412), "he became a believer" (NRSV, NJB), as did his whole house (ὅλῳ τῷ οἴκῳ). Further success is noted in that many Corinthians (πολλοὶ τῶν Κορινθίων [gen. pl. masc. of Κορίνθιος, -ου, ὁ, "Corinthian"; part. gen.]) believed. The term is broad enough to cover both Jews and Gentiles in Corinth. Ἀκούοντες (nom. pl. masc. of pres. act. ptc. of ἀκούω) has no formal obj. and either ref. to the conversion of Crispus (see NASB, HCSB) and his family or Paul (cf. RSV, ESV). Ἐπίστευον (3rd pl. impf. act. indic. of πιστεύω; perhaps inceptive impf., note previous instance, NRSV) and ἐβαπτίζοντο (3rd pl. impf. pass. indic. of βαπτίζω, "baptize") note the formal follow-through of conversion.

18:9 Continuing Luke's theme that the mission is led by Christ, Paul received a vision (ὁράματος, gen. sg. neut., of ὅραμα, ὁράματος, τό; obj. of prep.). Even though it happens at night (ἐν νυκτί, dat. sg. fem. of νύξ, νυκτός, ἡ), it is not a dream (ὕπνος). The neg. impv. μὴ φοβοῦ (2nd sg. pres. pass. impv. of φοβέομαι) is a formula to allay apprehension (Wallace 725; suggesting Paul was awake). In contrast, Paul is to speak (λάλει 2nd sg. pres. act. impv. of λαλέω) and not become silent (μὴ σιωπήσῃς, 2nd sg. aor. subjunc. indic. of σιωπάω, inceptive. aor.). Noting the use of tenses, Robertson suggests "stop fearing, go on speaking, and do not become afraid" (Robertson, *Pictures,* 271). On litotes, see 14:28.

18:10 Διότι (causal conj., CGk. expression, mostly by Luke and Paul, BDF §456) gives the grounds for the commands. Ἐγώ as a redundant nom. is emphatic, possibly an allusion to Exod 3:12 (Barrett 2.870). The implicit promise is explicit with οὐδεὶς ἐπιθήσεταί (3rd sg. fut. mid. indic. of ἐπιτίθημι). The mid. with the dat. obj. (σοι) means "will attack you." The gen. art. inf. τοῦ κακῶσαί (aor. act. inf. of κακόω, "exasperate") is a result clause (T 141). Thus, Paul might be attacked, but none will successfully harm him. The grounds (διότι) for the conclusion is a pred. nom. cstr. with λαός ("people") as the compl. of an impers. ἐστίν. Μοι (dat. sg. masc. of ἐγώ) is a poss. dat. Πολύς modifies λαός. Lit. it is "there are many people to me"; most EVV tr. "I have many people." The promise is that Christ has plans for these to come to him (Schnabel 761), so Paul will not be hindered by successful persecution.

18:11 Indirectly, the statement of the duration of Paul's stay is the fulfillment of the promise made in the vision. While lit. "sat, settled," ἐκάθισεν (3rd sg. aor. act. indic. of καθίζω), is unusual in Gk. (Barrett 2.870; see Luke 24:49), it is the best rendering for this context (Z 253; ZG 413; NASB). The length of stay is expressed in accs. of time, conveying duration, ἐνιαυτόν (acc. sg. masc. of ἐνιαυτός, -οῦ, ὁ, "a year") and μῆνας (acc. pl. masc. of μήν, μηνός, ὁ) ἕξ, "six months." It is the entirety of Paul's stay in Corinth (Haenchen 536). The ptc. διδάσκων (nom. sg. masc. of pres. act. ptc. of διδάσκω) is attend. circum. (διδάσκω is always pres. as a ptc. suggesting why the expected aor. is not used here, BHGNT 348). The dir. obj. phrase, λόγον τοῦ θεοῦ ("the word of God"), is "the gospel and all it entails" (Bock 580).

HOMILETICAL SUGGESTIONS

Taking Advantage of the Possibilities (18:1–11)

1. Transition: Paul is bivocational (vv. 1–4)
2. Penetration: Paul has support to focus on his work (vv. 5–8)
3. Saturation: Christ validates the vision (vv. 9–11)

b. Jewish Charges before Gallio (18:12–17)

Gallio was the older brother of the well-known orator Seneca. After a respectable career, he was forced to commit suicide at the same time his brother was (Barrett 2.870; Haenchen 536). His arrival in Corinth is one of the chronological anchors in the time line (confirmed by inscriptions at Delphi; Bruce, *Acts of the Apostles*, 395).

18:12 Γαλλίωνος (gen. sg. masc. of Γαλλίων, -ωνος, ὁ) is the gen. subj. of the gen. abs. phrase. The appos. gen. ἀνθυπάτου (gen. sg. masc. of ἀνθύπατος, -ου, ὁ; four times in NT, all in Acts) is best "proconsul." Ὄντος is the gen. sg. masc. of pres. ptc. of εἰμί. Ἀχαΐας (gen. sg. fem. of Ἀχαΐα, -ας, ἡ; descr.) is the Roman provincial name of the Greek peninsula (BDAG 159d). As a temp. gen. abs. phrase it should be rendered, "while Gallio was proconsul of Achaia" (CSB, NASB, NIV, TNIV, NET, MIT, NJB), likely early in his proconsulship (Bruce [*Acts of the Apostles*, 395] notes that this is likely between July and October of AD 51). Κατεπέστησαν (3rd pl. aor. act. indic. of κατεφίστημι) with the adv. ὁμοθυμαδόν means "a united attack" (CSB, RSV, NIV, ESV). The vb. takes a dat. obj. (Παύλῳ) mng. "against Paul." Ἤγαγον is the 3rd pl.

aor. act. indic. of ἄγω. Ἐπὶ τὸ βῆμα (mng. a destination) ref. to a raised platform where judicial decisions were made (Johnson 328), so "into the court" (ZG 413).

18:13 Λέγοντες is the nom. pl. masc. of pres. act. ptc. of λέγω. Ὅτι introduces dir. speech. Ἀναπείθει (3rd sg. pres. act. indic. of ἀναπείθω, "incites;" NT hapax) perhaps has the implication of an evil persuasion (MM 37a). The prep. phrase παρὰ τὸν νόμον is "contrary to the law" (BDAG 758b) in an emphatic position (Barrett 2.872). The question is whether it is Jewish or Roman law. Since Gallio interprets it as Jewish law later, it is best to take it so here (Bruce, *Acts of the Apostles*, 396, and he noted no Roman law was broken). It might possibly be a fumbling attempt to remove Christianity from the protective umbrella of Judaism (Witherington 552). Οὗτος (nom. sg. masc.; subj.) is a bit dismissive. The dir. obj. τοὺς ἀνθρώπους (acc. pl. masc.) is likely "our men." Σέβεσθαι (pres. mid. inf. of σέβω, "worship") is compl. to ἀναπείθει.

18:14 Μέλλοντος (gen. sg. masc. of pres. act. ptc. of μέλλω; gen. abs., temp.) is compl. by ἀνοίγειν (pres. act. inf. of ἀνοίγω), mng. "as Paul was about to open." In τὸ στόμα (acc. sg. neut., obj. of inf.) the art. is poss., mng. "his mouth." Εἶπεν is the 3rd sg. aor. act. indic. of λέγω. Gallio speaks in a second-class cond. cstr. (contrary to fact, εἰ + indic. vb. in the prot. and ἄν in the apod., the only one in Acts, BHGNT 350). In this clause, ἦν (3rd sg. impf. indic. of εἰμί) is impers. (on μέν, see 1:1) with a compound pred. adj. cstr. with two nom. sg. neut. adjs. The first, ἀδίκημά (of ἀδίκημα, -ατος, τό) τι, is "some wrongdoing." The second, ῥᾳδιούργημα (of ῥᾳδιούργημα, -ατος, τό) πονηρόν, is "wicked crime." Ὦ Ἰουδαῖοι (voc. pl. masc.) may belong to the apod. (NET). It is more likely, however, that the phrase concludes the prot., ". . . , O Jews" (cf. NASB, ESV). The position of the voc. deep in the sentence may indicate address to an inferior (BHGNT 197–98). It is more likely that Luke was conforming to CGk. style, where the particle is neither emphatic nor placed initially (see Wallace 69). Such language would be expected of an educated man like Gallio. Κατὰ λόγον may be taken a variety of ways (mostly depending on the mng. of λόγος):

1. In the sense of what is natural. Lit. it would be "according to reason," but best rendered "rightly." Several EVV tr. it "it would be reasonable" (Haenchen 536; CSB, NASB, NIV, TNIV).

2. It might be "according to the matter." Barrett renders it "of course" (Barrett 2.873; BHGNT 350)

3. It may be connected to ἀνεσχόμην (1st sg. aor. mid. indic. of ἀνέχομαι, "endure") as a legal idiom that means "to accept a case" (Bruce, *Acts of the Apostles*, 396; NLT, NET). While it has been often proposed, actual usage of the phrase as an idiom is not readily apparent (Barrett 2.874).

18:15–16 Gallio switches to a first-class cond. (assumed true) with εἰ and an indic. vb. Ζητήματά (nom. pl. neut. of ζήτημα, -ατος, τό, "question") is the pred. nom. with ἐστιν. Περί takes three gen. objs.: λόγου (inexplicably tr. as a pl. in most EVV, better "message" or "teaching," BDAG 599c); ὀνομάτων (gen. pl. neut. of ὄνομα, -ατος, τό, could be "persons" [as 1:15], although without good reason, lit. makes sense, BHGNT 350; Bruce, *Acts of the Apostles*, 396; ["titles"] ZG 413); and νόμου ("law"). Τοῦ nominalizes the prep. phrase καθ᾽ ὑμᾶς as an adj. phrase, distancing it from Roman law. Most EVV tr. it "your law" (see Z §130). The apod. is terse. Ὄψεσθε (2nd pl. fut. mid. indic.

of ὁράω, impv.) with an intensive use of the pron. αὐτοί, is lit. "you yourselves must see" [to it] and may be a Latinism (Barrett 2.874; Schnabel 764). Κριτής (nom. sg. fem. of κριτής, -οῦ, ὁ, "judge") is the pred. nom. to the inf. εἶναι at the end of the verse. One would expect an acc., but sometimes with εἰμί the nom. is used (BHGNT 351). Ἐγώ is emphatic. Τούτων is best "of these things." The neg. βούλομαι (1st sg. pres. mid. indic. of βούλομαι) is "I do not want." It takes a compl. inf. εἶναι. Sherwin-White notes that this is the precise wording of a magistrate "refusing to exercise his *arbitrium iudicantis* within a matter *extra-ordinem*"(SW 102; see Witherington 554). Ἀπήλασεν (3rd sg. aor. act. indic. of ἀπελαύνω, "drive away"; NT hapax) is a rather forceful dismissal of the charges (Barrett 2.875; Schnabel 765), perhaps even by the lictors (Haenchen 536).

18:17 Ἐπιλαβόμενοι (nom. pl. masc. of aor. mid. ptc. of ἐπιλαμβάνομαι, "take hold of"; attend. circum., a rather hostile word [Haenchen 537]) takes the vague subst. adj. πάντες as the subj. The Western text (then the *byz.*) clarifies with "Greeks," which is a good assumption (although not the original rdg.) given the dismissal (Bruce, *Acts of the Apostles*, 397). The obj. of the ptc., Sosthenes (Σωσθένην, acc. sg. masc. of Σωσθένης, -ους, ὁ), is identified with the appos. acc. ἀρχισυνάγωγον (acc. sg. masc. of ἀρχισυνάγωγος, -ου, ὁ). He was either Crispus's successor or colleague. No dir. evidence connects him to the same name in 1 Cor 1:1, although he was quite possibly the same person. Ἔτυπτον is the 3rd pl. impf. act. indic. of τύπτω, "beat." Ἔμπροσθεν τοῦ βήματος (gen. sg. neut. of βῆμα, -ατος, τό; mng."before the Bema") suggests an immediate attack. Οὐδέν τούτων (part. gen.) is evident in CGk. (BDF §176[3]). Ἔμελεν (3rd sg. impf. act. indic. of μέλω, "a care/concern"; only occurs in the 3rd sg. in the NT). "None of these things were a concern to Gallio" is the best rendering (see NET).

HOMILETICAL SUGGESTIONS

Paul in the Courts of Men (18:12–17)

1. False charges (vv. 12–13)
2. Dismissal (vv. 14–15)
3. Humiliation (vv. 16–17)

6. Return Trip (18:18–23)

18:18 Προσμείνας is the nom. sg. masc. of aor. act. ptc. of προσμένω, "remain longer, further"; temp. The obj. of the ptc., ἡμέρας ἱκανάς (see 8:11), means "considerable days," often tr. "for some time" (CSB, NLT, NIV, TNIV, NJB). Ἀδελφοῖς (dat. pl. masc. of ἀδελφός, -οῦ, ὁ) is the obj. of ἀποταξάμενος (nom. sg. masc. of aor. mid. ptc. of ἀποτάσσω, "say farewell"). Ἐξέπλει (3rd sg. impf. act. indic. of ἐκπλέω, "sail away") is likely inceptive, "he was beginning to set sail" (Barrett 2.877; ZG 414). Συρίαν (acc. pl. fem. of Συρία, -ας, ἡ) will specifically be Antioch via Jerusalem. Priscilla (nom. sg. fem. of Πρίσκιλλα, -ης, ἡ) and Aquila (nom. sg. masc. of Ἀκύλας, acc. -αν, ὁ) join him (compound subjs. of an elided being vb.). Κειράμενος is the nom. sg. masc. of aor. mid. ptc. of κείρω, "shear"; temp. The mid. is used when shaving a part of yourself (ZG 414). The shaving is before he set sail, for ἐν Κεγχρεαῖς (dat. pl. fem. of Κεγχρεαί, -ῶν, αἱ, "Cenchrea") is the port city of Corinth. Εἶχεν is the 3rd sg. impf. act. indic. of ἔχω, lit. "he was having"; in this context, with εὐχήν (acc. sg. fem. of εὐχή, -ῆς, ἡ, "vow") as the dir. obj., it is best "he was under a vow" (NRSV, ESV). Specifically, it was likely the end of the Nazirite vow (Bruce, *Acts of the Apostles*, 398, although, he notes, it was a private vow, not formal, for circumstances did not permit the latter).

18:19 Κατήντησαν is the 3rd pl. aor. act. indic. of καταντάω, temp., "having arrived." Εἰς Ἔφεσον (acc. sg. fem. of Ἔφεσος, -ου, ἡ, Ephesus) is the destination. Κἀκείνους (crasis of καὶ + ἐκεῖνος "and them") likely ref. to Πρίσκιλλα and Ἀκύλας of the previous v. Κατέλιπεν is the 3rd sg. aor. act. indic. of καταλείπω, "left." Αὐτοῦ functions as a deictic adv., "there" (BDAG 154a; ZG 414). Barrett (2:878) suggests that αὐτὸς δὲ εἰσελθών (nom. pl. masc. of aor. act. ptc. of εἰσέρχομαι) introduces v. 20 with the result that Paul left Priscilla and Aquila in Ephesus, while he continued on his journey. Supporting this is that the two are still in Ephesus at 18:26, after Paul had left (18:23). The position here, however, well before Paul leaves Ephesus, on the very heels of his arriving, suggests that Paul entered the synagogue by himself (thus, αὐτός is refl. here). Διελέξατο is the 3rd sg. aor. mid. indic. of διαλέγομαι, "discuss, argue." Ἰουδαίοις is dat. pl. masc.; dat. of assoc., "with the Jews."

18:20 Ἐρωτώντων (gen. pl. masc. of pres. act. ptc. of ἐρωτάω; gen. abs.) is concessive, with the subj. αὐτῶν, mng. "although they were asking." Ἐπὶ πλείονα χρόνον means "for more time" (see 13:31 for a sim. cstr., Z §125). It modifies the inf. μεῖναι (aor. act. inf. of μένω), with the mng. "to stay longer" (NRSV, ESV, NJB; CSB: "longer time"). Paul declined (neg. [οὐκ] ἐπένευσεν, 3rd sg. aor. act. indic. of ἐπινεύω, "to give consent [by a nod]").

18:21 In contrast to consenting (ἀλλ'), Paul bid farewell (ἀποταξάμενος, nom. sg. masc. of aor. mid. ptc. of ἀποτάσσω; temp.). Εἰπών (nom. sg. masc. of aor. act. ptc. of λέγω) introduces dir. speech. Ἀνακάμψω is the 1st sg. fut. act. indic. of ἀνακάμπτω, "return." The caveat is expressed in a gen. abs. phrase θεοῦ θέλοντος (gen. sg. masc. of pres. act. ptc. of θέλω) that is best taken as cond. (Wallace 633), "if God is willing." Ἀνήχθη is the 3rd sg. aor. pass. indic. of ἀνάγω, "put out to sea."

18:22 Luke relates the trip in three steps. First, κατελθών (nom. sg. masc. of aor. act. ptc. of κατέρχομαι, "go down"; temp.) to Caesarea (εἰς Καισάρειαν [acc. sg. fem. of Καισάρεια, -ας, ἡ]). Second, ἀναβάς (nom. sg. masc. of aor. act. ptc. of ἀναβαίνω, "go up"; temp.) with ἀσπασάμενος (nom. sg. masc. of aor. mid. ptc. of ἀσπάζομαι; temp.). "Having greeted the church" should be understood as the Jerusalem church. Ἀναβαίνω is so ubiquitously a ref. to Jerusalem (see 3:1), it is very likely here as well, esp. given the use of κατέβη (3rd sg. aor. act. indic. of καταβαίνω) to refer to Antioch. The vb. would not be used to describe a trip from Caesarea to Antioch (Bruce, *Acts of the Apostles*, 400).

18:23 Ποιήσας (nom. sg. masc. of aor. act. ptc. of ποιέω) with the acc. obj. χρόνον τινά (acc. sg. masc.) means "having spent some time." Ἐξῆλθεν is the 3rd sg. aor. act. indic. of ἐξέρχομαι, "departed." Διερχόμενος is the nom. sg. masc. of pres. mid. ptc. of διέρχομαι. Καθεξῆς, "successively," suggests a systematic return to the churches planted (Barrett 2.881; ZG 414 "one after the other"). On τὴν Γαλατικὴν χώραν καὶ Φρυγίαν, see 16:6). Ἐπιστηρίζων (nom. sg. masc. of pres. act. ptc. of ἐπιστηρίζω, "strengthen") takes the obj. πάντας τοὺς μαθητάς, "all the disciples."

HOMILETICAL SUGGESTIONS

Always Evangelizing (18:1–23)

1. Sowing in transition (vv. 1–11)
2. Sowing in opposition (vv. 12–17; cf. 1 Cor 1:1)
3. Sowing in preparation for more (vv. 18–23)

B. THIRD MISSIONARY JOURNEY (18:24–19:20)

Although a third missionary journey is started, Luke is still describing the evangelization of Asia Minor. The first two sections describing Apollos and the disciples
of John the Baptist are linked by their association with John. Luke exalts John but
puts him in the proper perspective to Christ. This continues an approach begun in the
Gospel of Luke. In Luke 1 and 2, John is shown to be great, but inferior to Jesus in
terms of his parents, his birth, and his mission (see Thompson 14). Luke continues
the theme in Acts. In the next two scenes Luke describes those who were followers of
John (in Ephesus of all places!). The first, Apollos, seems to need only more accurate
information about Jesus. This he receives from Aquila and Priscilla. The second is a
group of John's disciples who needed more than instruction; they needed salvation.
The group's initiation into Christianity is treated along the lines of Jews, Samaritans,
and Gentiles with the manifestation of tongues. In this way, Luke pictures them as a
strategic group, likely because a John-the-Baptist movement lasted well into the fourth
century (Witherington 569; see also Barrett 2.885).

1. Remnants of the Baptist Instructed and Converted (18:23–19:8)

a. Apollos Instructed by Priscilla and Aquila (18:24–28)

18:24 Ἰουδαῖος δέ τις transitions to a new section and introduces a new character, "a certain Jew." He is described by three appos. noms.: Ἀπολλῶς (nom. sg. masc. of Ἀπολλῶς,
-ῶ, ὁ, "Apollos"; on ὀνόματι, see 5:1), Ἀλεξανδρεύς (nom. sg. masc. of Ἀλεξανδρεύς,
-έως, ὁ; subst. adj. "an Alexandrian"; on γένει, see 18:2), and Ἀνήρ, modified by λόγιος
(nom. sg. masc., λόγιος, -ία, -ιον; attrib. adj., best tr. "an eloquent man" [MM 378c]).
Κατήντησεν is the 3rd sg. aor. act. indic. of καταντάω, "arrive." Δυνατός is a pred. nom.
with the attrib. ptc. ὤν (nom. sg. masc. of pres. ptc. of εἰμί), mng."who was mighty."
With ἐν ταῖς γραφαῖς ("in the Scriptures") the sense is "well-versed" (RSV, NRSV,
NET). "Competent" (ESV, CSB) seems to downgrade the mng.
18:25 Ἦν κατηχημένος (nom. sg. masc. of pf. pass. ptc. of κατηχέω, "teach, instruct")
is a periph. plpf. mng. "he had been instructed." Ὁδόν is an acc. of ref. With τοῦ κυρίου,
it is "regarding the way of the Lord." Ζέων (nom. sg. masc. of pres. act. ptc. of ζέω;
attrib.) lit. means "boiling"; religiously it means "with burning zeal" (BDAG 426d).
Most EVV somewhat tepidly tr. it "fervent in spirit." Luke characterizes his ministry
with two impfs.: ἐλάλει (3rd sg. impf. act. indic. of λαλέω) and ἐδίδασκεν (3rd sg. impf.
act. indic. of διδάσκω). Ἀκριβῶς (adv., "accurately") modifies both vbs. Ἐπιστάμενος
(nom. sg. masc. of pres. mid. ptc. of ἐπίσταμαι, "understand") is best understood as a
concessive ptc. with the dir. obj. βάπτισμα (acc. sg. neut. of βάπτισμα, -ατος, τό, "baptism"), mng. "although he only understood the baptism of John."
18:26 On τε, see 1:15. Ἤρξατο (3rd sg. aor. mid. indic. of ἄρχομαι) and παρρησιάζεσθαι
(pres. mid. inf. of παρρησιάζομαι; compl.) means "he began to speak boldly."
Ἀκούσαντες (nom. pl. masc. of aor. act. ptc. of ἀκούω; temp.), with the gen. sg. masc.
dir. obj. αὐτοῦ, suggests Priscilla and Aquila also were attending the synagogue.
Προσελάβοντο (3rd pl. aor. mid. indic. of προσλαμβάνω) in the mid. means "they took

him aside." Ἀκριβέστερον (acc. sg. masc. of ἀκριβῶς; comp. adj., "more accurately") modifies ἐξέθεντο (3rd pl. aor. mid. indic. of ἐκτίθημι, "explain"). Τὴν ὁδόν (acc. sg. fem. of ὁδός, -οῦ, ἡ; dir. obj.) ref. to Christianity. Apollos's knowledge of Jesus was not so much wrong as incomplete (Schnabel 786).

18:27 Βουλομένου (gen. sg. masc. of pres. mid. ptc. of βούλομαι; gen. abs., temp.) is compl. by διελθεῖν (aor. act. inf. of διέρχομαι), mng. "when he wanted to go through." The ultimate destination is Ἀχαΐαν (acc. sg. fem. of Ἀχαΐα, -ας, ἡ, "Achaia"; obj. of prep.), essentially the Greek peninsula. Apollos was apparently well known to churches in Achaia after this (cf. 1 Cor 1:12). Προτρεψάμενοι (nom. pl. masc. of aor. mid. ptc. of προτρέπω, "encourage"; temp., NT hapax) in the nom. pl. identifies the brothers (ἀδελφοί) as the subj. Ἔγραψαν is the 3rd pl. aor. act. indic. of γράφω. Ἀποδέξασθαι is the aor. mid. inf. of ἀποδέχομαι, "receive gladly"; purp. Παραγενόμενος is the nom. sg. masc. of aor. mid. ptc. of παραγίνομαι; temp. Συνεβάλετο (3rd sg. aor. mid. indic. of συμβάλλω) πολύ is "greatly helped" with the obj. in the dat. (πεπιστευκόσιν dat. pl. masc. of pf. act. ptc. of πιστεύω; subst.).

18:28 The help is defined by the substantiation given (γάρ). Two parallel clauses with fronted advs. set the tone of Apollos's ministry. First, εὐτόνως (adv., "mightily") is emphatic. Ἰουδαίοις (dat. pl. masc. of Ἰουδαῖος, -αία, -αῖον) suggests Apollos was teaching in the synagogues. Διακατηλέγχετο (3rd sg. impf. mid. indic. of διακατελέγχομαι) has the sense of arguing overwhelmingly. The second of the parallel clauses is also introduced by an adv., δημοσίᾳ ("publicly"). The ptc. ἐπιδεικνύς (nom. sg. masc. of pres. act. ptc. of ἐπιδείκνυμι) most likely means "by proving." The source is through his exposition of Scripture (διὰ τῶν γραφῶν). The obj. of his proof is given in indir. speech with an inf. εἶναι (pres. inf. of εἰμί) as the vb. in a pred. nom. cstr. (but with accs. due to the inf.). The art. marks τὸν χριστόν as the subj. and, thus, Ἰησοῦν is the pred.: "the Christ is Jesus."

b. Disciples of John Converted (19:1–7)

19:1 On ἐγένετο δέ, see 4:5. On the temp. cstr. ἐν τῷ . . . inf. (εἶναι, pres. inf. of εἰμί), see 2:1. Παῦλον is the subj. of the later infs. (both in the temp. cstr.). Διελθόντα is the acc. sg. masc. of aor. act. ptc. of διέρχομαι, "go through"; temp. Τὰ ἀνωτερικά (acc. pl. neut. of ἀνωτερικός, -ή, -όν, "upper") μέρη is lit. "the upper part," i.e., the interior [BDAG 77d; ZG 415]). [Κατ]ελθεῖν (aor. act. inf. of κατέρχομαι, "came) continues the temp. cstr., as does εὑρεῖν (aor. act. inf. of εὑρίσκω) with τινας μαθητάς ("certain disciples) as the dir. obj.

19:2 Εἶπέν is the 3rd sg. aor. act. indic. of λέγω. On τε, see 1:15. Εἰ introduces a dir. question (BHGNT 359; Z §401 [perhaps Sem., ZG 415]; see also Turner, *Style,* 54). Πνεῦμα ἅγιον is the dir. obj. Ἐλάβετε is the 2nd pl. aor. act. of λαμβάνω. Πιστεύσαντες (nom. pl. masc. of aor. act. ptc. of πιστεύω; temp.). The aor. ptc. has been interpreted to mean the possibility/necessity of receiving the Holy Spirit after conversion (Keener discusses it at length, 3:2818). Grammatically, "rel. time" of the ptc. is not a hard-and-fast rule (see BDF §339). This is esp. true when there is a sequence that describes instantaneous actions (cf. 11:17 and 21). Such are often said to be simultaneous (see R 861–62, 1113). Paul's question is fundamentally about their belief that would be evidenced by receiving the Spirit. Given that these "disciples" know nothing of the Spirit (see below) and are rebaptized (something neither the Samaritans [ch. 8] nor Apollos were required to do), it suggests an incomplete knowledge about Jesus to a degree that they are not converted (Schnabel 788). The art. οἱ functions as a pron. The conj. ἀλλ᾽ is emphatic. (BHGNT 359). Zerwick suggests an implied "not only did we not receive . . . but . . ." (ZG 415). Ἔστιν is impers. Ἠκούσαμεν is the 1st pl. aor. act. indic. of ἀκούω. Keener rightly asserts that this does not necessarily mean ignorance, but something like "is given" or "poured out" (Keener 3.2819; cf. John 7:39).

19:3 Εἶπέν is the 3rd sg. aor. act. indic. of λέγω. On τε, see 1:15. Εἰς τί is best understood as equiv. to an instr. ἐν (T 255; Z §101). Ἐβαπτίσθητε is the 2nd pl. aor. pass. indic. of βαπτίζω. Οἱ functions as a pers. pron. Εἶπαν is the 3rd pl. aor. act. indic. of λέγω. Εἰς τὸ Ἰωάννου is sim. to Paul's question; "with John's baptism" is the best rendering (NJB).

19:4 Paul's repsonse was both respectful and accurate. Εἶπεν is the 3rd sg. aor. act. indic. of λέγω. Ἐβάπτισεν (3rd sg. aor. act. indic. of βαπτίζω) βάπτισμα (acc. sg. neut. of βάπτισμα, -ατος, τό, "baptism") is a cstr. with a cognate acc., lit. "John baptized a baptism . . .," followed by a descriptive gen. μετανοίας (gen. sg. fem. of μετάνοια, -ας, ἡ, "repentance"). Λαῷ (dat. sg. masc. of λαός, -οῦ, ὁ), the indir. obj. of λέγων (nom. sg. masc. of pres. act. ptc. of λέγω; attend. circum.), begins indir. speech. Εἰς τὸν ἐρχόμενον (acc. sg. masc. of pres. mid. ptc. of ἔρχομαι; subst. obj. of prep.) and μετ᾽ αὐτόν places the emphasis on the obj. of faith. The conj. ἵνα indicates indir. speech, so the subjunc. that follows (πιστεύσωσιν, 3rd pl. aor. act. subjunc. of πιστεύω) takes an "ought to" sense, "they should believe." Paul directly identifies him distinctly with τοῦτ᾽ (nom. sg. neut. of οὗτος, αὕτη, τοῦτο) ἔστιν that indicates an explanation (cf.1:19). Εἰς τὸν Ἰησοῦν ("in Jesus"), then, specifically identifies the coming one. Paul is implying that if they are followers of John, they must become followers of Jesus (Schnabel 789).

19:5 The disciples of John apparently agreed. Ἀκούσαντες is the nom. pl. masc. of aor. act. ptc. of ἀκούω; temp. Ἐβαπτίσθησαν is the 3rd pl. aor. pass. indic. of βαπτίζω, "baptize." On εἰς τὸ ὄνομα, see 8:16. The descriptive phrase τοῦ κυρίου Ἰησοῦ specifies their improved understanding of Jesus: he is Lord.

19:6 Sim. to the Samaritans in ch. 8, upon the laying on of hands (ἐπιθέντος, gen. sg. masc. of aor. act. ptc. of ἐπιτίθημι; gen. abs., temp. with Παύλου as the subj.), the Spirit came upon them (ἦλθεν, 3rd sg. aor. act. indic. of ἔρχομαι). The evidence of the Spirit is expressed in two 3rd pl. impf. indic. act. vbs., (in a τε . . . καί cstr.) ἐλάλουν (λαλέω [on γλώσσαις, see 2:4]) and ἐπροφήτευον (προφητεύω, "prophesy"). Christian prophets have already been introduced into Acts (see 11:27; 13:1; 15:32). Luke clearly links the verb form to a Spirit-empowered utterance, not limited to praise (see Keener 3.2824).

19:7 Ἦσαν (3rd pl. impf. indic. of εἰμί) πάντες in the attrib. position means the group (οἱ . . . ἄνδρες; subj.) is referred to as a whole (Z §188). The adv. ὡσεί indicates the exact number, not an approximation (Bruce, *Acts of the Apostles*, 407): twelve (δώδεκα).

FOR FURTHER STUDY

27. John the Baptist beyond the Gospels (18:25; 19:3)

Barrett, C K. "Apollos and the Twelve Disciples of Ephesus." In *New Testament Age: Essays in Honor of Bo Reicke*, 29–39. Macon, GA: Mercer University Press, 1984.
Cummins, S. A. *DJG²*, 436–44.
Erickson, R. J. "The Jailing of John and the Baptism of Jesus: Luke 3:19–21." *JETS* 36 (1993): 455–66.
Hollenbach, P. W. *ABD*, 3.887–99.
Michaels, J. R. "Paul and John the Baptist: an Odd Couple?" *TynBul* 42 (1991): 245–60.
Taylor, J. E. *The Immerser: John the Baptist within Second Temple Judaism*. Grand Rapids: Eerdmans, 1997.

HOMILETICAL SUGGESTIONS

How Do You Approach Partially True Doctrine? (18:23–19:7)

1. Some only need better instruction: Apollos (vv. 23–28)
2. Some desperately need the gospel: John's disciples (vv. 1–7)

2. Paul's Ministry to the Ephesian Jews (19:8–10)

19:8 Paul follows his custom of entering (εἰσελθών, nom. sg. masc. of aor. act. ptc. of εἰσέρχομαι) the synagogues. Ἐπί (often in Luke for an extent of time, Z §125) μῆνας (acc. pl. masc. of μήν, μηνός, ὁ) τρεῖς means "for three months." Ἐπαρρησιάζετο is the 3rd sg. impf. mid. indic. of παρρησιάζομαι, "speak boldly." Two adv. ptcs. of manner unpack the mng. of the ptc: Διαλεγόμενος (nom. sg. masc. of pres. mid. ptc. of διαλέγομαι, "discuss, argue") and πείθων (nom. pl. masc. of pres. act. ptc. of πείθω). The content of Paul's urgings is in the prep. phrase περὶ τῆς βασιλείας τοῦ θεοῦ, "concerning the kingdom of God."

19:9 Ὡς is temporal, "when." Τινες (nom. pl. masc. of τὶς, τί; indef. pron.) is the subj. of the compound verbs ἐσκληρύνοντο (3rd pl. impf. pass. indic. of σκληρύνω, "harden"; likely inceptive) and ἠπείθουν (3rd pl. impf. act. indic. of ἀπειθέω, "disobey, be disobedient"). The latter has the sense of coming to faith, so "would not believe" is appropriate (see also RSV "disbelieved" and ESV "continued in unbelief"). The expression of their hardened disbelief is "speaking evil" (κακολογοῦντες, nom. pl. masc. of pres. act. ptc. of κακολογέω); corresponding to βλασφημούντων in 18:6 (Bruce, *Acts of the Apostles*, 408). Τὴν ὁδόν (acc. sg. fem. of ὁδός, -οῦ, ἡ; obj. of ptc.) is still a term for Christianity (cf. 9:2). The prep. phrase ἐνώπιον τοῦ πλήθους, "before the multitudes" (likely the unbelieving citizens, Barrett 2.904), signifies a public ridiculing of Paul and his message. Ἀποστάς is the nom. sg. masc. of aor. act. ptc. of ἀφίστημι, "go away, withdraw"; attend. circum. Ἀφώρισεν (3rd sg. aor. act. indic. of ἀφορίζω, "separate") with the dir. obj. Μαθητάς (acc. pl. masc. of μαθητής, -οῦ, ὁ) is best "he withdrew . . . and took the disciples." Καθ' ἡμέραν is distributive, "daily." Διαλεγόμενος (see v. 8) is technically attend. circum. but unpacks the purp. of gathering the disciples elsewhere.

A σχολῇ (dat. sg. fem. of σχολή, -ῆς, ἡ) is usually a public lecture hall or auditorium (Witherington 575; see also Bruce, *Acts of the Apostles*, 408). That it is "of Tyrannus" (Τυράννου, gen. sg. masc. of Τύραννος, -ου, ὁ; poss. gen.) likely means he was either the hall's most famous client, or that he owned it (Keener 3.2828). The Western text adds plausible historical detail, "from the fifth hour until the tenth" (i.e., from 11:00 a.m. to 4:00 p.m.; see Metzger 417 and the introduction for comments).

19:10 The aor. (ἐγένετο, 3rd sg. aor. mid. indic. of γίνομαι) rather than the impf. views the time period as a whole. With the prep. phrase ἐπὶ ἔτη δύο, it means "this lasted for two years" (Barrett 2.905). The conj. ὥστε marks a result, anticipating the later inf. The subst. ptc. κατοικοῦντας (acc. pl. masc. of pres. act. ptc. of κατοικέω) with the acc. dir. obj. Ἀσίαν (acc. sg. fem. of Ἀσία, -ας, ἡ) means "all the inhabitants of Asia" (ZG 416) and refers to the Roman province. Ἀκοῦσαι (aor. act. inf. of ἀκούω) completes the result clause. As usual in Acts, λόγον τοῦ κυρίου refers to the gospel. Jews and Greeks are joined in a τε . . . καί cstr., "both . . . and." Schnabel (794) points out that the claim is not that every individual or that Paul personally gave the gospel to every city but that the gospel had been proclaimed and took root throughout the province.

3. Miracles at Ephesus (19:11–20)

19:11 Δυνάμεις (acc. pl. fem. of δύναμις, -εως, ἡ) as a fronted dir. obj. makes the miracles the focus of the sentence. On τε, see 1:15. The phrase οὐ τὰς τυχούσας (acc. pl. fem. of aor. act. ptc. of τυγχάνω, "happen"; subst.) is lit. "not the one that happens to be" (i.e., the first thing you meet, BDAG 1019c; on litotes, see 14:28; on the use of οὐ with a ptc., see 7:5), hence "no ordinary miracles—that is, "extraordinary" (NASB, NIV, ESV, TNIV, NET, MIT). God (Θεός) performs (ἐποίει, 3rd sg. impf. act. indic. of ποιέω) the signs, even though Paul was the agent (διὰ τῶν χειρῶν Παύλου, "through Paul's hands").

19:12 The sentence is complicated. The conj. ὥστε indicates result. It takes three infs. in this v., each with modifying prep. phrases and acc. subjs. Καί is adv., "also." Ἐπὶ τοὺς ἀσθενοῦντας (acc. pl. masc. of pres. act. ptc. of ἀσθενέω; subst.) is destination, "to the sick." The first of the infs., ἀποφέρεσθαι (pres. pass. inf. of ἀποφέρω), "carry off," with "from his skin" [χρωτός gen. sg. masc. of χρώς, χρωτός, ὁ]) takes the alternating accs. as subjs., σουδάρια (acc. pl. neut. of σουδάριον, -ου, τό, "face cloths"; cf. Luke 19:20) and σιμικίνθια (acc. pl. neut. of σιμικίνθιον, -ου, τό, "aprons"). Both are Latinisms from the commercial world (BDF §5). Ἀπαλλάσσεσθαι (pres. pass. inf. of ἀπαλλάσσω, "depart") with the acc. subj. of the inf. νόσους (acc. pl. fem. of νόσος, -ου, ἡ) is best rendered "and their diseases were lifted from them." The final element of this result cstr. regards the evil spirits (πνεύματα τὰ πονηρα, neut. acc. pls.; subj. of the inf.). The final inf. in the series is ἐκπορεύεσθαι (pres. mid. inf. of ἐκπορεύομαι, "expel").

19:13 Ἐπεχείρησαν (3rd pl. aor. act. indic. of ἐπιχειρέω), lit. "they took in hand," has the sense of "they attempted" (BDAG 386d). The subj. τινες (nom. pl. masc. of τὶς, τί) is followed by a part. gen. phrase τῶν περιερχομένων (gen. pl. masc. of pres. mid. ptc. of περιέρχομαι; attrib.) Ἰουδαίων ἐξορκιστῶν (gen. pl. masc. of ἐξορκιστής, -οῦ, ὁ), best tr. "itinerant Jewish exorcists" (RSV, NRSV, ESV, NET, NJB). The initial vb. takes a compl. inf. ὀνομάζειν (pres. act. inf., "call"). The use of ἐπί is in the sense of "over"

(BDAG 363c). The obj. of the prep. is the ptc. phrase τοὺς ἔχοντας (acc. pl. masc. of pres. act. ptc. of ἔχω; subst.) τὰ πνεύματα τὰ πονηρά ("wicked spirits"). The obj. of the inf. is τὸ ὄνομα (acc. sg. neut. of ὄνομα, -ατος, τό). Λέγοντες (nom. pl. masc. of pres. act. ptc. of λέγω; attend. circum.) introduces dir. speech. Ὁρκίζω (1st sg. pres. act. indic.) is typical of exorcism. "I adjure" is followed by an acc. of ref. Ἰησοῦν (Wallace 206; BHGNT 365). Jesus is identified as the one Paul preaches (κηρύσσει, 3rd sg. pres. act. indic. of κηρύσσω).

19:14 Ἦσαν (3rd pl. impf. indic. of εἰμί) is the initial vb. of a periph. cstr. Τινος (gen. sg. masc. of τις) Σκευᾶ (gen. sg. masc. of Σκευᾶς, -ᾶ, ὁ; gen. of source) is "of a certain Sceva." He is identified with an appos. gen. as a Ιουδαίου ἀρχιερέως (gen. sg. masc. of ἀρχιερεύς, -έως, ὁ), "Jewish high priest." Ἑπτὰ υἱοί ("seven sons") is the subj. Luke's short description suggests that Sceva (a Latin cognomen) was likely a member of the priestly aristocracy in the Dispersion (Schnabel 797). Ποιοῦντες (nom. pl. masc. of pres. act. ptc. of ποιέω) completes the periph. impf. (begun with the initial word).

19:15 Ἀποκριθέν is the nom. sg. neut. of aor. pass. ptc. of ἀποκρίνομαι; pleonastic (see 4:19). Τὸ πνεῦμα τὸ πονηρόν ("the wicked spirit") is the subj. of εἶπεν (3rd sg. aor. act. indic. of λέγω; dir. speech). The statement is a μὲν . . . δέ cstr. with Ἰησοῦν (dir. obj.) fronted for emphasis. Γινώσκω is the 1st sg. pres. act. indic. of γινώσκω. Παῦλον is the dir. obj. of ἐπίσταμαι (1st sg. pres. mid. indic. of ἐπίσταμαι, "know"). The distinction between the vbs. is "recognize" and "am aquainted with" (Robertson, *Pictures,* 318). The contr. phrase (δέ) is a question in a pred. nom. cstr. Ὑμεῖς (nom. pl. of σύ; pred. nom.) is fronted before τίνες (nom. pl. masc. of τίς, τί; interr. pron., subj.) for emphasis (Barrett 2.910). Ἐστέ is the 2nd pl. pres. indic. of εἰμί. The question is likely rhetorical with the sense of "I do not recognize you." In other words, Jesus's name is "not simply a theurgic technique to be used by anyone" (Johnson 341) but only by believers (Haenchen 564).

19:16 The results were both shameful and comical. The exorcists were attacked (ἐφαλόμενος, nom. sg. masc. of aor. mid. ptc. of ἐφάλλομαι, "leap upon"; temp.). Κατακυριεύσας (nom. sg. masc. of aor. act. ptc. of κατακυριεύω, "subdue"; attend. circum.) takes a gen. obj. ἀμφοτέρων (gen. pl. masc. of ἀμφότεροι, -αι, -α; normally "both" but in latter and *byz.* Gk. it means "all," Bruce, *Acts of the Apostles,* 411). Ἴσχυσεν (3rd sg. aor. act. indic. of ἰσχύω) with κατ' αὐτῶν is lit. "he prevailed against them" (KJV). Ὥστε takes an inf. with two acc. objs. fronted for emphasis (γυμνούς [acc. pl. masc. of γυμνός, -ή, -όν, "naked"; describing a state] and τετραυματισμένους [acc. pl. masc. of pf. pass. ptc. of τραυματίζω; manner, "having been wounded"], BHGNT 367). Ἐκφυγεῖν (aor. act. inf. of ἐκφεύγω, "run away") completes the result phrase (with both pride and bodies wounded). Thus, they came to expel the demon but were themselves expelled in the most embarrassing fashion.

19:17 Ἐγένετο is the 3rd sg. aor. mid. indic. of γίνομαι and the dir. obj. γνωστόν (acc. sg. neut. of γνωστός, -ή, -όν) mng. "this became known" (CSB, RSV, NASB, NIV, NRSV, ESV). The indir. obj. is in the form of a τε . . . καί cstr. with masc. dat. pls. Ἰουδαίοις and Ἕλλησιν (dat. pl. masc. of Ἕλλην, -ηνος, ὁ), "both Jews and Greeks." On κατοικοῦσιν (dat. sg. masc. of pres. act. ptc. of κατοικέω), subst., and the acc. of place (in this case Ἔφεσον [nom. sg. fem. of Ἔφεσος, -ου, ἡ, "Ephesus"]), see 19:10.

Ἐπέπεσεν is the 3rd sg. aor. act. indic. of ἐπιπίπτω, "fall." Ἐμεγαλύνετο (3rd sg. impf. pass. indic. of μεγαλύνω, "magnify") takes ὄνομα as the subj.

19:18 Πολλοί is the nom. pl. masc. of πολύς, πολλή, πολύ, "many"; subj. On τε, see 1:15. Πεπιστευκότων (gen. pl. masc. of pf. act. ptc. of πιστεύω) is a subst. part. gen. "of the ones having believed." Ἤρχοντο is the 3rd pl. impf. indic. act. of ἔρχομαι. The vb. is followed by two ptcs. of manner (or attend. circum.): ἐξομολογούμενοι (nom. pl. masc. of pres. mid. ptc. of ἐξομολογέω) and ἀναγγέλλοντες (nom. pl. masc. of pres. act. ptc. of ἀναγγέλλω), mng. "confessing and announcing." Since the deed (πράξεις, acc. pl. fem. of πρᾶξις, -εως, ἡ; obj. of ptc.) is likely in the sense of "their spells" (BDAG 860a; Bruce, *Acts of the Apostles*, 412; MM 533d), the essence is an open confession of general sinfulness and, in particular, dabbling in the occult.

19:19 Ἱκανοί (nom. pl. masc. of ἱκανός, -ή, -όν'; subj.) is "many" (NASB) or "a number" (RSV, ESV). Περίεργα (acc. pl. neut. of περίεργος, -ον) in the neut. pl. is "things belonging to magic." It is the obj. of the subst. ptc. πραξάντων (gen. pl. masc. of aor. act. ptc. of πράσσω; part. gen.); together it has the sense, "of the ones who practiced magic" (BDAG 860d). Συνενέγκαντες (nom. pl. masc. of aor. act. ptc. of συμφέρω, "bring together into a heap"; attend. circum.) The art. τάς modifies the dir. obj. βίβλους and functions as a poss. pron.: "their books." Ephesus was particularly noted for the popularity of such books (so much so some are called ἐφέσια γράμματα, "Ephesian writings," Witherington 582–83). Κατέκαιον is the 3rd pl. impf. act. indic. of κατακαίω, "burn." Ἐνώπιον πάντων ("before all") is a public demonstration of repentance. Since the power of such "spells" was believed to lie in their secrecy, publicly denouncing them would render them useless in their minds (Bruce, *Acts of the Apostles*, 412). The magnitude of the event is given with a monetary value. Συνεψήφισαν is the 3rd pl. aor. act. indic. of συμψηφίζω, "count up." Τιμάς is the acc. pl. fem. of τιμή, -ῆς, ἡ, "the price"; dir. obj. Εὗρον is the 3rd pl. aor. act. indic. of εὑρίσκω. Ἀργυρίου is the gen. sg. neut. of ἀργύριον, -ου, τό; gen. of price modifying μυριάδας (acc. pl. fem. of μυριάς, -άδος, ἡ, "ten thousand") πέντε, mng. "worth fifty thousand pieces of silver." The Roman denarius and the Greek drachma are about the same weight (Johnson 342). Given a single denarius is about a day's wage, the value of the books was impressive.

19:20 While typical of Luke's summaries and no doubt about the general mng., the specifics could be variously interpreted. If κράτος (acc. sg. neut. of κράτος, -ους, τό) is modified by τοῦ κυρίου (gen. sg. masc.), it means "by the might of the Lord" (Barrett 2.914; BHGNT 369). Most commentators (see, e.g., Bruce, *Acts of the Apostles*, 413), however, agree that it modifies λόγος, ref. to the gospel (though in a unique word order). Ηὔξανεν is the 3rd sg. impf. act. indic. of αὐξάνω, "grow." Ἴσχυεν (3rd sg. impf. indic. act. of ἰσχύω) is lit. "it was strong;" most EVV have "prevailing."

FOR FURTHER STUDY

28. The Miracles in Ephesus (19:11–20)

Bates, Matthew W. "Why Do the Seven Sons of Sceva Fail?: Exorcism, Magic, and Oath Enforcement in Acts 19,13–17." *RB* 118 (2011): 408–21.

Davids, P. H. *DLNT*, 747–52.

Kenner, C. S. *Miracles: The Credibility of the New Testament Accounts.* 2 vols. Grand
    Rapids: Baker Academic, 2011.
Porter, S. E. "Magic in the Book of Acts." In *Kind of Magic: Understanding Magic in the
    New Testament and its Religious Environment*, 107–21. London: T&T Clark, 2007.
Twelftree, G. "Jesus and Magic in Luke-Acts." In *Jesus and Paul: Global Perspectives in
    Honor of James D. G. Dunn for His 70th birthday*, 46–58. London: T&T Clark, 2009.
————. *Paul and the Miraculous: A Historical Reconstruction.* Grand Rapids: Baker
    Academic, 2013.

HOMILETICAL SUGGESTIONS

Not Your Ordinary Ministry (19:11–20)

What Happens When God Does Something Unusual?
1. It provokes the copycat without authority (vv. 13–16)
2. It provokes true repentance (vv. 17–20)

VII. To the Ends of the Earth: On to Rome (19:21–28:31)

At 19:10 Luke commented that all the Asians had heard the gospel. It was not only a statement of the success of the missionaries but a clue that Paul's mission to Asia was coming to an end. At 19:21 the new move is expressly stated as Rome. From this point forward, Rome is the focus of the narrative, even though Paul will not get there until ch. 28. The purp. of these chs. is to demonstrate God's faithfulness in the fulfillment of his purposes. Paul's intent was to revisit and to strengthen the churches along the way, then organize and implement a visit to Rome (Schnabel 801).

A. FROM EPHESUS TO JERUSALEM (19:21–21:16)

This unit demonstrates Luke's "dramatic flair" (Witherington 583). Paul's last days in Ephesus show how deeply Christianity had penetrated Ephesus, prepares the reader for future hostility, and displays the providence of God to fulfill his purposes.

1. Ephesus: Opposition by Demetrius (19:21–41)

19:21 Ὡς is temp., "when." Ἐπληρώθη (3rd sg. aor. pass. indic. of πληρόω) takes a neut. pl. subj. (ταῦτα, nom. pl. neut. of οὗτος). Ἔθετο (3rd sg. aor. mid. indic. of τίθημι) modified by ἐν τῷ πνεύματι is best understood as an idiom (like Luke 21:14 with καρδία, a Heb., T 139) mng. "resolved" (Barrett 2.919; ZG 417; NIV, TNIV, NJB). Διελθών (nom. sg. masc. of aor. act. ptc. of διέρχομαι; temp.) is best understood as background information to the inf. It is not unusual to see the nom. instead of the normal acc. with infs. (cf. Luke 19:37, BHGNT 371). Most EVV tr. it as attend. circum., "to pass through." Taking the fem. sg. acc. objs. Μακεδονίαν (of Μακεδονία, -ας, ἡ, "Macedonia") and Ἀχαΐαν (of Ἀχαΐα, -ας, ἡ, "Achaia"), a major purp. seems to be the collection for the Jerusalem saints (cf. 20:4; 1 Cor 16:1–4; Bruce, *Acts of the Apostles*, 413; Johnson 346). Πορεύεσθαι (pres. mid. inf. of πορεύομαι) is a compl. inf. Εἰς Ἱεροσόλυμα is the destination. The use of dir. speech (indicated by εἰπών, nom. sg. masc. of aor. act. ptc. of λέγω; attend. circum.) is saved for the final clause, highlighting Paul's ultimate goal (Schnabel 801). Τὸ γενέσθαι (aor. mid. inf.; obj. of prep.) με (subj. of inf.) with the adv. ἐκεῖ is best "after I have been there." Δεῖ is the so-called divine must (Bock 605; Keener 3.2861). He must see (ἰδεῖν, aor. act. inf.; compl.) Rome because it is God's will (likely an allusion to 1:8, Barrett 2.920).

19:22 Ἀποστείλας is the nom. sg. masc. of aor. act. ptc. of ἀποστέλλω; attend. circum. Εἰς τὴν Μακεδονίαν (see 19:21, "to Macedonia") indicates destination (see below, where it is location). Δύο (acc. sg. masc. indecl.) is modified by the part. gen. subst. ptc. διακονούντων (gen. pl. masc. of pres. act. ptc. of διακονέω, "serve") mng. "two of his helpers." Τιμόθεον and Ἔραστον (masc. acc. sgs. of Τιμόθεος, -ου, ὁ, "Timothy," and Ἔραστος, ου, ὁ, "Erastus") are appos. to δύο. Αὐτός is emphatic in contrast to the two sent. Ἐπέσχεν (3rd sg. aor. act. indic. of ἐπέχω, "stay"; cf. MM 232b) with the acc. χρόνον means "for a while." Εἰς τὴν Ἀσίαν is used in a locat. sense "at Asia" (R 593; BDF §205).

19:23 Ἐγένετο δέ is a significant development but not the Sem. use (Barrett 2.922). It is impers. in a pred. nom. cstr., "there was." Κατὰ τὸν καιρόν describes contemporaneous time (BDAG 512a, note the art. of previous ref.); that is, during Paul's time in Ephesus. Modified by ἐκεῖνον, it means "during that time." Τάραχος (nom. sg. masc. of τάραχος, -ου, ὁ; pred. nom.) with the adv. litotes (see 14:28) οὐκ ὀλίγος means "no small trouble." The cause of the trouble is περὶ τῆς ὁδοῦ (cf. 9:2), Christianity.

19:24 Δημήτριος (nom. sg. masc. of Δημήτριος, -ου, ὁ) τις is "a certain Demetrius" (on ὀνόματι, see 5:1). He is identified with a long appos. nom. phrase describing his trade. Ἀργυροκόπος is the nom. sg. masc. of ἀργυροκόπος, -ου, ὁ, "silversmith." Ποιῶν (nom. sg. masc. of pres. act. ptc. of ποιέω) with the obj. phrase ναοὺς ἀργυροῦς (acc. pl. masc. of ἀργυροῦς, -ᾶ, -οῦν, "made of silver") Ἀρτέμιδος (gen. sg. fem. of Ἄρτεμις, -ιδος, ἡ, "Artemis") means "silver shrines of Artemis." Bruce notes the Ephesian Artemis was not the Gk. goddess but an ancient local deity, "a Mother-goddess of Asia Minor" (Bruce, *Acts of the Apostles*, 415). The entire noun phrase is the subj. to παρείχετο (3rd sg. impf. mid. indic. of παρέχω, "grant"). Τεχνίταις is the dat. pl. masc. of τεχνίτης, -ου, ὁ; indir. obj. "to the Artisans." Another litotes (see 14:28), οὐκ ὀλίγην ἐργασίαν (acc. sg. fem. of ἐργασία, -ας, ἡ, "profit, gain"; dir. obj.), is "no small profit."

19:25 The rel. pron. οὕς refers to the craftsmen and is the obj. of the ptc. συναθροίσας (nom. sg. masc. of aor. act. ptc. of συναθροίζω, "gather together"; temp.). Καί identifies a second group (thus, a compound dir. obj.). Ἐργάτας (acc. pl. masc. of ἐργάτης, -ου, ὁ) is lit. "the workers," who Barrett identifies as "relatively unskilled workmen" (Barrett 2.924). The noun phrase has a prep. phrase in the attrib. position, περὶ τὰ τοιαῦτα, mng. "on sim. lines" (ZG 417). Ἐπίστασθε is the 2nd pl. pres. mid. indic. of ἐπίσταμαι, "know." Ὅτι gives the content of the knowledge. Ἐκ ταύτης τῆς ἐργασίας (gen. sg. fem. of ἐργασία, -ας, ἡ, "trade, business"; see 19:24 for a sim. domain), "from this business," functions like a pred. nom. Εὐπορία (nom. sg. fem. of εὐπορία, -ας, ἡ, "prosperity") is the subj. of ἐστιν and is modified by a poss. dat. (ἡμῖν).

19:26 The stacking of vbs. of perception, θεωρεῖτε (2nd pl. pres. act. indic. of θεωρέω) and ἀκούετε (2nd pl. pres. act. indic. of ἀκούω), heightens the magnitude of his complaint. The οὐ μόνον . . . ἀλλά cstr. is another way of magnifying the effect of the missionaries by stacking escalating similarities, in this case, regions. Ἐφέσου (gen. sg. fem. of Ἔφεσος, -ου, ἡ, "Ephesus"; gen. of place [KMP 100; R 494]). Σχεδόν (adv., three times in the NT, two times in Acts; see 13:44) modifies πάσης τῆς Ἀσίας (fem. gen. sg., gen. of place), mng. "nearly all of Asia." The use of the demonstrative Παῦλος οὗτος is hostile and dismissive. Πείσας (nom. sg. masc. of aor. act. ptc. of πείθω; attend. circum.) is backgrounded to the main vb. μετέστησεν (3rd sg. aor. act. indic. of μεθίστημι, "turn"). Ἱκανὸν ὄχλον is the dir. obj., "a considerable crowd." Λέγων (nom. sg. masc. of pres. act. ptc. of λέγω) ὅτι introduces indir. speech. It is in the form of a pred. nom. cstr. with οἱ διὰ χειρῶν γινόμενοι as a subj. phrase "those made by hand" (i.e., "handmade gods," NLT). The neg. (οὐκ) copulative vb. εἰσίν (3rd pl. pres. indic. of εἰμί) takes θεοί as the pred. nom.

19:27 Another οὐ μόνον . . . ἀλλά cstr. (see 19:26) sets up a "from bad to worse" point of view. The sentence is complicated, but understanding the main vb. and its str. will be very helpful before a phrase-by-phrase analysis. Κινδυνεύει (3rd sg. pres. act. indic. of κινδυνεύω) is "to run a risk." It often takes an inf. to express that risk (Barrett 2.926; MM 344b). Demetrius will outline three risks posed by Christianity: business disrepute; goddess disregard; goddess diminishment.

Τοῦτο is most likely an acc. sg. neut. modifying τὸ μέρος that means (with the poss. dat. ἡμῖν) "this business of ours." If so, κινδυνεύει is impers., "there is a risk that." It is possible that it is a nom. cstr. and the subj. of the vb. However, it is smoother to tr. it as the acc. subj. of the first inf. controlled by the vb., ἐλθεῖν (aor. act. inf. of ἔρχομαι). Εἰς ἀπελεγμόν (acc. sg. masc. of ἀπελεγμός, -οῦ, ὁ, "refutation, exposure, discredit"; NT hapax) completes the risk, mng. "unto disrepute."

The second and third parts are a religious statement. Καί is adv., "also." Τὸ . . . ἱερόν has in the attrib. position the poss. gen. sg. fem. phrase τῆς μεγάλης θεᾶς (of θεά, -ᾶς, ἡ; NT hapax) Ἀρτέμιδος (of Ἄρτεμις, -ιδος, ἡ; appos.), mng. "the temple of the great goddess Artemis." The acc. phrase is the subj. of the inf. λογισθῆναι (aor. pass. inf. of λογίζομαι) that is second inf. under the control of κινδυνεύει. Like the previous clause, a prep. phrase completes the risk: εἰς οὐθέυ, "as nothing." Μέλλειν (pres. act. inf. of μέλλω) is the third inf. and is the third risk taking the compl. inf. καθαιρεῖσθαι (pres. pass. inf. of καθαιρέω, "pull down") that in turn takes a poss. gen. sg. fem. phrase τῆς μεγαλειότητος (of μεγαλειότης, -ητος, ἡ;) αὐτῆς. It is best, "run the risk of . . . pulling down her majesty." While hyperbolic the last rel. pron. phrase "which all Asia (nom. sg. fem. of Ἀσία, -ας, ἡ) and the world" (οἰκουμένη, nom. sg. fem. of οἰκουμένη, -ης, ἡ) builds off the fact that the temples were widely distributed (at least thirty-three temples are known; Bruce, *Acts of the Apostles*, 417). Σέβεται is the 3rd sg. pres. mid. indic. of σέβω, "worship."

19:28 Ἀκούσαντες (nom. pl. masc. of aor. act. ptc. of ἀκούω; temp.) Γενόμενοι (nom. pl. masc. of aor. mid. ptc. of γίνομαι; temp.) takes the pred. adj. πλήρεις (nom. pl. masc. of πλήρης, -ες) that is followed by a gen. of content θυμοῦ, "full of anger"—that is, "enraged" (RSV, NRSV, ESV, NET). Ἔκραζον (3rd pl impf. act. indic. of κράζω) is likely progressive, "they were continually crying out." Λέγοντες (nom. pl. masc. of pres. act. ptc. of λέγω) is pleonastic, introducing dir. speech. The implication of the impf. is a chant. It is in the form of a pred. adj. cstr. with an assumed being vb. Μεγάλη (nom. sg. fem.), although fronted, is the pred. adj. The subj. is ἡ Ἄρτεμις (nom. sg. fem. of Ἄρτεμις, -ιδος, ἡ) modified by Ἐφεσίων (gen. pl. masc. of Ἐφέσιος,

-ία, -ιον; poss. gen., "of the Ephesians") to distinguish from the Gk. goddess of the same name.

19:29 Ἐπλήσθη (3rd sg. aor. pass. indic. of πίμπλημι, "fill," i.e., the city) takes the gen. of content συγχύσεως (gen. sg. fem. of σύγχυσις, -εως, ἡ, "confusion, tumult"; NT hapax). CSB, KJV, RSV, NASB, NSRV, and ESV tr. it "confusion," but contextually to tr. the phrase "in an uproar" is a better fit (see NIV, TNIV, NET, NJB). Ὥρμησάν (3rd pl aor. act indic. of ὁρμάω, "rush"; see 7:57) with ὁμοθυμαδόν (adv., "together") indicates a mobbish action. Εἰς τὸ θέατρον (acc. sg. neut. of θέατρον, -ου, τό, "theater") is the destination. Coming after the main vb., συναρπάσαντες (nom. pl. masc. of aor. act. ptc. of συναρπάζω, "drag away"; attend. circum.) defines the rush to the theater as a seizure. The objs. of the ptc. are the Macedonians Gaius and Aristarchus, identified as Paul's traveling companions (συνεκδήμους, acc. pl. masc. of συνέκδημος, -ου, ὁ).

19:30 The question of Paul's whereabouts is answered in a gen. abs. cstr. βουλομένου (gen. sg. masc. of pres. mid. ptc. of βούλομαι; temp.) takes a compl. inf. of εἰσελθεῖν (aor. act. inf. of εἰσέρχομαι, "enter"). Εἰς τὸν δῆμον (acc. sg. masc. of δῆμος, -ου, ὁ) might refer to a crowd, but it is best understood as destination, for the term δῆμος is the normal name for the popular assembly of a Gk. city-state (Bruce, *Acts of the Apostles*, 418; although not an official meeting, Schnabel 806). The neg. impf. εἴων (3rd pl. impf. act. indic. of ἐάω), "the disciples were not allowing," suggests a lively discussion.

19:31 Καί is adv., "also." Τινές (indef. pron.) is modified by the part. gen. Ἀσιαρχῶν (gen. pl. masc. of Ἀσιάρχης, -ου, ὁ, "Asiarchs"; NT hapax). Ὄντες (nom. pl. masc. of pres. ptc. of εἰμί; attrib.) takes φίλοι (nom. pl. masc. of φίλος, -ου, ὁ) as a pred. nom. Πέμψαντες (nom. pl. masc. of aor. act. ptc. of πέμπω; attend. circum.). Παρεκάλουν (3rd pl. impf. act. indic. of παρακαλέω, "urge"). The neg. inf. expresses indir. speech, giving the content of the message. Μὴ δοῦναι (aor. act. inf. of δίδωμι) with the refl. pron. ἑαυτόν is lit. "not to give himself," tr. by most EVV as "not to venture" (ZG 418), that is, to the theater.

19:32 Μὲν οὖν (see 1:6) is resumptive back to the assembly (Barrett 2.376). Robertson notes "the use of ἄλλος-ἄλλο = 'one one thing, one another'" and is "almost reciprocal" (R 747, see 2:12 and 21:34). With Ἔκραζον (3rd pl. impf. act. indic. of κράζω) in the impf., the picture is of an uproarious mess. Γάρ introduces the cause of the uproar, the assembly (ἐκκλησία, nom. sg. fem. of ἐκκλησία, -ας, ἡ). The plpf. periph. cstr. (συγκεχυμένη, nom. sg. fem. of pf. pass. ptc. of συγχέω) with the initial ἦν is "had been confused." Οἱ πλείους (nom. pl. masc. of πολύς, subst. adj., subj.) is "the majority." Οὐκ ᾔδεισαν (3rd pl. plpf. act. indic. of οἶδα; functionally an aor.) is "they did not know." Τίνος ἕνεκα is in reversed order normal for prep. (R 425). It is lit. "for the sake of what," but merely means "why?" Συνεληλύθεισαν is the 3rd pl. plpf. act. indic. of συνέρχομαι, "gather."

19:33 The tr. of this verse is layered in conjecture and little certainty. Johnson notes, "the entire sequence involving Alexander is obscure" (349). Here are the three major interpretations:

1. Most commentators understand ἐκ . . . τοῦ ὄχλου assumes a subj. (τινες) and functions as a part. gen. (Barrett 2.932; BDF §162[2.6]; BHGNT 377; see Z §80). In this way, it is said to be the subj. of συνεβίβασαν (3rd pl. aor. act.

indic. of συμβιβάζω). If so, what is the mng. of the vb.? Of the four possible semantic domains, the trans. use of the vb. favors "advise, instructed" (see BDAG 957a; BHGNT 377; Bock [vaguely] 611; Haenchen 574; Schnabel 808). Most EVV that take this option use "prompted" (RSV, NASB, NRSV, ESV, NET): "Some of the crowd prompted . . ."

2. Bruce agrees with the use of the initial prep. phrase but complains that understanding of συμβιβάζω as "instruct" is unlikely but "just possible" (Bruce, *Acts of the Apostles*, 419). He prefers "conjectured." It is impossible, in this rdg., to take Ἀλέξανδρον (acc. sg. masc. of Ἀλέξανδρος, -ου, ὁ) as the dir. obj. The tr. of the NET assumes it to be an acc. of ref., i.e., "it was about Alexander." They then take the following gen. abs. phrase προβαλόντων (gen. pl. masc. of aor. act. ptc. of προβάλλω) . . . τῶν Ἰουδαίων to be causal, "because the Jews pushed him toward the front." The difficulty is the interpretation of Ἀλέξανδρον. Its strength is that it fits the context of an attempted apology nicely.

3. The KJV, NKJV tr. as "they drew Alexander out of the multitude." This view takes ἐκ . . . τοῦ ὄχλου adv. (its natural mng., Barrett 2.932). However, it depends on the Western rdg. (also attested in *byz.* text) προεβίβασαν (3rd pl. aor. act. indic. of προβιβάζω, "bring forward") for συμβιβάζω. Συμβιβάζω is the earliest rdg., the more difficult rdg., and is the best explanation for the origin of the others (it is highly unlikely a scribe would change προβιβάζω to συμβιβάζω).

Whatever view is taken, Alexander attempts a defense. Κατασείσας is the acc. sg. masc. of aor. act. ptc. of κατασείω, "make a sign"; attend. circum. Witherington notes this was the typical orator's gesture asking for silence (Witherington 596–97). Ἤθελεν (3rd sg. impf. act. indic. of θέλω) takes a compl. inf. ἀπολογεῖσθαι (pres. mid. inf. of ἀπολογέομαι, "give a defense") with δήμῳ (dat. sg. masc. of δῆμος, -ου, ὁ; indir. obj.); the best tr. is "he wanted to make a defense to the assembly." Alexander is a Jew likely wanting to distance his group from Paul.

19:34 Ἐπιγνόντες is the nom. pl. masc. of aor. act. ptc. of ἐπιγινώσκω; temp. Ὅτι introduces indir. speech, thus the pres. tense of ἐστιν (3rd sg. pres. indic. of εἰμί) is retaining the orig. tense. Ἰουδαῖός ("Jew") is a pred. nom. Altogether one expects a gen. abs. since the subj. of the main vb. is different. Most refer to it as a "sense construction" (Barrett 2.933; Bruce, *Acts of the Apostles*, 419; Haenchen 575) as sometimes these are found in the nom. rather than oblique cases by attraction to the unspoken subj. throughout (i.e., the crowd, see T 316; BHGNT 378). Φωνή is likely the subj. of ἐγένετο (3rd sg. aor. mid. indic. of γίνομαι) and modified by the adj. μία, "one voice arose" (cf. NASB). It may also be pred. nom. of an impers. vb., "there arose one voice." The prep. phrase ἐκ πάντων ("from all") is an oblique ref. to the unspoken subj.: the crowd. Ὡς ἐπὶ ὥρας δύο is an approximation mng. "for about two hours."

Κραζόντων (gen. pl. masc. of pres. act. ptc. of κράζω; attend. circum.) introduces dir. speech, in agreement with πάντων, "shouting." Μεγάλη ἡ Ἄρτεμις (nom. sg. fem. of Ἄρτεμις, -ιδος, ἡ) Ἐφεσίων (gen. pl. masc. of Ἐφέσιος, -ία, -ιον, "Ephesian") is a pred. adj. cstr. assuming a being vb., in the order pred. adj., subj., and descriptive gen., "great is Artemis of the Ephesians."

19:35 Καταστείλας (nom. sg. masc. of aor. act. ptc. of καταστέλλω, "restrain"). Γραμματεύς (nom. sg. masc. of γραμματεύς, -έως, ὁ) is normally "scribe." In this context, it refers to the chief executive magistrate in a city who implemented the decrees of the assembly (BASHH 122; Haenchen 575). Φησίν is the 3rd sg. pres. act. indic. of φημί, "say." On the voc. Άνδρες (with the appos. Ἐφέσιοι [voc. pl. masc. of Ἐφέσιος, -ία, -ιον, "Ephesian"]), see 1:11. The phrase τίς . . . ἐστιν ἀνθρώπων employs an interr. pron. as a pred. nom., an impers. being vb. and a part. gen. mng. "who is there among men." Γάρ is often used in questions where Eng. leaves it unstructured (BDF §452[1]). Barrett notes that "it either emphasizes the question . . . or it assumes an unexpressed accusation or admonition, 'you must really restrain yourselves, for . . .'" (Barrett 2.935; see Bruce, *Acts of the Apostles*, 420 "[Be quiet], for"). Γινώσκει is the 3rd sg. pres. act. indic. of γινώσκω. Immediate apprehension of a fact in Gk. takes an acc. (here the phrase τὴν Ἐφεσίων πόλιν, acc. sg. fem. of πόλις) and a participle (οὖσαν, acc. sg. fem. of pres. ptc. of εἰμί) and functions much like indir. speech (Z §168). Νεωκόρον (acc. sg. masc. of νεωκόρος, -ου, ὁ; pred. acc. by attraction to πόλιν) is a "temple guardian," modified by a compound gen. phrase: Ἀρτέμιδος (gen. sg. fem. of Άρτεμις, -ιδος, ἡ) and διοπετοῦς (gen. sg. neut. of διοπετής, -ες; subst. adj.), "the thing having fallen from the sky."

19:36 Ἀναντιρρήτων (gen. pl. neut. of ἀναντίρρητος, -ον, "undeniable"; NT hapax) is a pred. adj. Οὖν expresses the implication of the principle in the previous v. Ὄντων (gen. pl. masc. of pres. ptc. of εἰμί) modified by τούτων is a causal gen. abs. phrase. Δέον, the ptc. form of δεῖ (cf. 1 Pet 1:16 and 1 Tim 5:13 for the only other NT occurrences; nom. sg. neut. of pres. act. ptc.), is a periph. pres. cstr. with ἐστίν. The ptc. takes two compl. infs. The use of κατεσταλμένους (acc. pl. masc. of pf. pass. ptc. of καταστέλλω, "restrain, quiet") and ὑπάρχειν (pres. act. inf. of ὑπάρχω) expresses a continuing action after the state is achieved, "you must calm down" (cf. NASB). Μηδὲν προπετές (acc. sg. neut. of προπετής, -ές) is "nothing rash." It modifies the second inf., πράσσειν (pres. act. inf. of πράσσω).

19:37 Ἠγάγετε is the 2nd pl. aor. act. indic. of ἄγω, "bring." Γάρ introduces the grounds for the command of the previous v. The men (ἄνδρας, acc. pl. masc. of ἀνήρ, ἀνδρός, ὁ; dir. obj.) are described as neither ἱεροσύλους (acc. pl. masc. of ἱερόσυλος, -ον, "temple-robbers"; NT hapax, cf. cognate at Rom 2:22; perhaps mng. "sacrilegious," BDAG 471c) nor βλασφημοῦντας (acc. pl. masc. of pres. act. ptc. of βλασφημέω; subst.), with the obj. phrase τὴν θεόν (acc. sg. masc., but note the acc. sg. fem. art., not uncommon, BHGNT 380) ἡμῶν best rendered "blasphemers of our goddess." The official's defense should be understood in the sense of broken laws. First, these men have not been seen trying to rob the treasuries of the temple (something the Ephesians feared from previous such attempts; see Johnson 350; Witherington 598). Second, they have not been heard slandering the goddess in particular. Demetrius's charge was rather general concerning idols made by hands. The claim of Ephesus was that the idol fell from the sky (see 19:35; Bruce, *Acts of the Apostles*, 420).

19:38 Εἰ introduces a first-class cond., an argument assumed true. It begins with a compound subj.: Δημήτριος (nom. sg. masc. of Δημήτριος, -ου, ὁ) and τεχνῖται (nom. pl. masc. of τεχνίτης, -ου, ὁ, "craftsman"; see 19:21). Ἔχουσιν (3rd pl. pres. act. indic. of ἔχω) with λόγον (acc. sg. masc., of λόγος,-ου, ὁ; dir. obj.) likely is the language of the court, "have a case" (Barrett 2.937; BHGNT 380). It is also likely that ἀγοραῖοι (nom. pl. masc. of ἀγοραῖος, -ον, lit. "pertaining to a market"; BDAG 14b) ἄγονται (3rd pl. pres. pass. indic. of ἄγω) is a Latinism mng. "the courts are open" (assuming "days;" BDF §5; see also MM 6b; BASHH 123). Ἀνθύπατοί (nom. pl. masc. of ἀνθύπατος, -ου, ὁ, "proconsul") is the pred. nom. of an impers. εἰσιν (3rd pl. pres. indic. of εἰμί), "there are proconsuls." Ἐγκαλείτωσαν (3rd pl. pres. act. impv. of ἐγκαλέω), followed by a dat. of disadvantage, ἀλλήλοις, is "let them bring charges against one another" (CSB, RSV, NASB, NRSV, ESV).

19:39 On εἰ, see v. 38. The phrase τι περαιτέρω (comp. adv.), "anything further" (the dir. obj. of the following vb., NT hapax), is challenged by a significant var. περὶ ἑτέρων ("concerning other things"). Metzger and most EVV prefer the former for contextual fit, arising by a mistake in hearing (Metzger 419). Ἐπιζητεῖτε is the 2nd pl. pres. act. indic. of ἐπιζητέω, "seek." The prep. phrase ἐν τῇ ἐννόμῳ (dat. sg. fem. of ἔννομος, -ον) ἐκκλησίᾳ means "in the lawful assembly." Ἐπιλυθήσεται is the 3rd sg. fut. pass. indic. of ἐπιλύω, "resolve, decide, settle."

19:40–41 Zerwick suggests καὶ γάρ is a Latinism for *etenim*, "for in fact" (ZG 419). Even so, it likely is a second grounds for dispersing (see v. 35). On κινδυνεύομεν (1st pl. pres. act. indic. of κινδυνεύω, "run a risk"), see 19:27. Ἐγκαλεῖσθαι is the pres. pass. inf. of ἐγκαλέω (compl.), with the gen. of content giving the charge, στάσεως (gen. sg. fem. of στάσις, -εως, ἡ), mng. "to be charged with rebellion." In the prep. phrase περὶ τῆς σήμερον, the art. nominalizes the adj. "today." That it is fem. suggests, most likely, ἐκκλησίας ("assembly") is in mind (Bruce, *Acts of the Apostles*, 421). Neg. by μηδενός, αἰτίου (gen. sg. neut. of αἴτιος, -ια, -ον, "cause, source") is the subj. of the ptc. ὑπάρχοντος (gen. sg. masc. of pres. act. ptc. of ὑπάρχω; gen. abs., causal). It is best tr. "because there is no cause." The rel. pron.'s antecedent in περὶ οὗ is most likely αἰτίου, "concerning which." Neg. by [οὐ'] (on incl. the var., see Metzger 420 "the least unsatisfactory rdg."), δυνησόμεθα (1st pl. fut. mid. indic. of mid. δύναμαι) takes a compl. inf. ἀποδοῦναι (aor. act. inf. of ἀποδίδωμι) and λόγον (acc. sg. masc. of λόγος, -ου, ὁ) is the obj. of the inf. It is best tr. "concerning which we will not be able to give a reason." The double neg. (μηδενός/οὐ) is likely a colloq. that generated the textual var. (BHGNT 381). The bigger issue in the text is the relatively unnecessary prep. phrase περὶ οὗ. These form fertile grounds for suggesting textual emendations (see Barrett 2.939–40). Ultimately, the text is understandable as it stands (although somewhat turbulent). It is clear that the official is declaring an indefensible gathering. Thus, he dismisses it (ἀπέλυσεν, 3rd sg. aor. act.indic. of ἀπολύω).

HOMILETICAL SUGGESTIONS

When the Gospel Takes Root in Your Town (19:21–41)

1. Expect pagan business to suffer (vv. 28–34)
2. Expect some proprietors to attack God's messengers (vv. 28–34)
3. Expect God to move to enact his purposes (vv. 35–41)

2. Paul's Journey to Macedonia and Greece, Seven Days in Troas (20:1–12)

20:1 On the temp. cstr. μετά with an aor. inf. (here, παύσασθαι, aor. mid. inf. of παύω; intrans. mid.), see 1:3. Θόρυβον (acc. sg. masc. of θόρυβος, -ου, ὁ, "clamor"; subj. of the inf.) is closely associated with sound (Barrett 2.945). The cstr. means "after the uproar stopped." Three nom. sg. masc. of aor. temp. ptcs. set the backdrop for Paul's departure: Μεταπεμψάμενος (mid. ptc. of μεταπέμπω, "summon"), παρακαλέσας (act. ptc. of παρακαλέω, "encourage, exhort"), and ἀσπασάμενος (mid. ptc. of ἀσπάζομαι, "say farewell"; BDAG 144a). Ἐξῆλθεν is the 3rd sg. aor. act. indic. of ἐξέρχομαι.

20:2 Paul's Macedonia visit is appropriately treated in the briefest of terms for the visit seems to be limited. Διελθών is the nom. sg. masc. of aor. act. ptc. of διέρχομαι; temp. Τὰ μέρη ἐκεῖνα is the obj. of the ptc., "those parts." Παρακαλέσας is the nom. sg. masc. of aor. act. ptc. of παρακαλέω; temp. Λόγῳ πολλῷ is a dat. of means, "with a long message" (cf. 15:32; BDAG 599c; NET). Ἦλθεν is the 3rd sg. aor. act. indic. of ἔρχομαι. Since εἰς and a place name is generally destination in Acts, the best tr. of the phrase is "he came to Greece" (RSV, NASB, NSRV, ESV, NET).

20:3 On τε, see 1:15. The phrase ποιήσας (nom. sg. masc. of aor. act. ptc. of ποιέω) μῆνας (acc. pl. masc. of μήν, μηνός, ὁ) τρεῖς is idiomatic, mng. "having stayed three months" (cf. 15:33; Barrett 2.946; BHGNT 383; ZG 420). Γενομένης (gen. sg. fem. of aor. mid. ptc. of γίνομαι; gen. abs.; temp.) takes ἐπιβουλῆς (gen. sg. fem. of ἐπιβουλή-ης, ἡ, "a plot") and a dat. of disadvantage, αὐτῷ ("against him"). Μέλλοντι (dat. sg. masc. of pres. act. ptc. of μέλλω; temp.), the compl. inf. ἀνάγεσθαι (pres. mid. inf. of ἀνάγω), and the prep. phrase of destination εἰς τὴν Συρίαν (acc. sg. fem. of Συρία, -ας, ἡ) is "as he was about to set sail for Syria" (cf. NASB, ESV, CSB). The phrase ἐγένετο (3rd sg. aor. mid. indic. of γίνομαι) γνώμης (gen. sg. fem. of γνώμη, -ης, ἡ, "mind"; technically a gen. of source, BDF §162[7]; R 514) is likely idiomatic, mng. "he made the decision." Τοῦ ὑποστρέφειν (pres. act. inf. of ὑποστρέφω) is a purp. cstr. with the gen. art., mng. "to return." The change of route is διὰ Μακεδονίας (gen. sg. fem. of Μακεδονία, -ας, ἡ), "through Macedonia," rather than by sea (Bock 618).

20:4–5 It is best to take vv. 4 and 5 together as a delegation to carry the offering to Jerusalem for the saints (see 1 Cor 16:1–2; 2 Cor 8–9), representing the Gentile churches. The list includes representatives from most regions of Paul's evangelism except, notably, Corinth and Philippi (see Schnabel 833). The list, however, is of Paul's traveling companions and may not be the whole group that will converge at Jerusalem. Συνείπετο (3rd sg. impf. mid. indic. of συνέπομαι, "accompany") takes Σώπατρος (nom. sg. masc. of Σώπατρος, -ου, ὁ) Πύρρου (gen. sg. masc. of Πύρρος, -ου, ὁ; gen. of rel.) Βεροιαῖος (nom. sg. masc. of Βεροιαῖος, -α, -ον, "of Berea"; attrib.), mng. "Sopater, son of Pyhrrus, of Berea." A new sentence begins (indicated by δέ) that will take a series of nom. names as the compound subj. It begins with Θεσσαλονικέων (gen. pl. masc. of Θεσσαλονικεύς, -έως, ὁ; part. gen.,) "of the Thessalonians." These are identified as "Aristarchus and Secundus" (nom. sg. masc.; Ἀρίσταρχος of Ἀρίσταρχος, -ου, ὁ and Σεκοῦνδος of Σεκοῦνδος, -ου, ὁ). From Galatia, Gaius (both nom. sg. masc.; Γάϊος [of Γάϊος, -ου, ὁ] Δερβαῖος [of Δερβαῖος, -α, -ον, "Derbian"]) and Timothy (Τιμόθεος, nom. sg. masc. of Τιμόθεος, -ου, ὁ), who appears without a city (likely Lystra; Bruce, *Acts of the Apostles*, 371). Lastly, the Asians (Ἀσιανοί nom. pl. masc. of Ἀσιανός, -οῦ, ὁ) are "Tychicus and Trophimus" (nom. sg. masc. of Τύχικος, -ου, ὁ, and Τρόφιμος, -ου, ὁ). These may be the subj. of an implied vb. or, as Culy and Parsons suggest, the οὗτοι in v. 5 is resumptive and these are the subj. of v. 5 (see BHGNT 384). Προελθόντες is the nom. pl. masc. of aor. act. ptc. of προέρχομαι, "go ahead"; temp. Because ἔμενον (3rd pl. impf. act. indic. of μένω) takes the acc. pl. masc. ἡμᾶς ("us"), the "we passages" resume (Barrett 2.949). Τρῳάδι (dat. sg. fem. of Τρῳάς, -άδος, ἡ) is Troas.

20:6 The emphatic ἡμεῖς is in contrast to the advancement of the delegation. Ἐξεπλεύσαμεν is the 1st pl. aor. act. indic. of ἐκπλέω, "sail away". The temp. expression μετὰ τὰς ἡμέρας τῶν ἀζύμων (gen. pl. masc. of ἄζυμος, -ον) is lit. "after the days of Azuma" (i.e., Feast of Unleavened Bread). It suggests that Luke is still using the Jewish religious calendar (Barrett 2.949; Keener 3.2960) and that Paul celebrated Easter with the Macedonians (Rogers and Rogers 284). Ἤλθομεν (1st pl aor. act. indic. of ἔρχομαι) πρὸς αὐτούς ("to them") is the delegation; εἰς Τρῳάδα (acc. sg. fem. of Τρῳάς, -άδος, ἡ) is the destination. Ἄχρι ἡμερῶν πέντε (lit. "until five days") is an unusual expression for an extent of time. BDAG tr. it "within five days" (BDAG 160d). The clause διετρίψαμεν (1st pl. aor. act. indic. of διατρίβω) ἡμέρας ἑπτά (acc. of time, extent) is "we stayed for seven days."

20:7 Ἐν δὲ τῇ μιᾷ τῶν σαββάτων is a temp. phrase (a point in time) mng. "on the first day of the week." What follows is likely on a Sunday evening–early Monday morning. The believers are meeting on a Sunday, but this may or may not indicate formal time of worship. Luke may include the ref. to connect Eutychus's resurrection to Jesus's (see Keener 3.2967–68). Συνηγμένων (gen. pl. masc. of pf. pass. ptc. of συνάγω; gen. abs., temp.) takes ἡμῶν as the subj., mng. "when we had gathered." Κλάσαι (aor. act. inf. of κλάω; purp.) ἄρτον means "eat a community meal" (Bock 619; the Lord's Supper is an imposition on the phrase here; Bruce, *Acts of the Apostles*, 425 suggests the communal meal would include ordinance). Paul's speech employing διελέγετο (3rd sg. impf. mid. indic. of διαλέγομαι) does not imply an argument, as elsewhere in Acts. We should assume "was preaching to them." Μέλλων (nom. sg. masc. of pres. act. ptc. of μέλλω; causal) with the compl. inf. ἐξιέναι (pres. act. inf. of ἔξειμι) is best "because he was going to depart the next day." Παρέτεινέν is the 3rd sg. impf. act. indic. of παρατείνω, "extend"; NT hapax. The art. τὸν λόγον is best tr. "his message." Μέχρι μεσονυκτίου (gen. sg. neut. of μεσονύκτιον, -ου, τό) is "until midnight."

20:8 The dir. obj. phrase λαμπάδες ἱκαναί (cf. Acts 8:11), most often tr. "many lamps," is likely torches. Ἐν τῷ ὑπερῴῳ, "in the upper room," is the upper story of the building. The rel. pron. phrase is comprised of a periph. plpf. ἦμεν συνηγμένοι (nom. pl. masc. of pf. pass. ptc. of συνάγω), "where we had been gathered."

20:9 Καθεζόμενος (nom. sg. masc. of pres. mid. ptc. of καθέζομαι, "sit"; attrib.) modifies the noun phrase τις νεανίας (nom. sg. masc. of νεανίας, -ου, ὁ, "a youth") On ὀνόματι, see 5:1. Εὔτυχος (nom. sg. masc. of Εὔτυχος, -ου, ὁ) means "fortunate" (BASHH 233; a common name, Barrett 2.953). Θυρίδος is the gen. sg. fem. of θυρίς, -ίδος, ἡ, "window." Καταφερόμενος (nom. sg. masc. of pres. pass. ptc. of καταφέρω, "bring down"; attrib.) with the dat. of means (masc. dat. sgs. ὕπνῳ [of ὕπνος, -ου, ὁ] βαθεῖ [of βαθύς, -εῖα, -ύ]) means "being overcome by deep sleep." Bruce suggests "dropping off to sleep" (in contr. to the aor. ptc. later where he succumbs, perhaps "nodding off" [*Acts of the Apostles*, 426]). Διαλεγομένου (gen. sg. masc. of pres. mid. ptc. of διαλέγομαι; gen. abs., temp.) modified by ἐπὶ πλεῖον in this friendly context means "reasoning still longer" (cf. RSV, NSRV, ESV; NIV's "on and on" is unnecessarily pejorative). Κατενεχθείς (nom. sg. masc. of aor. pass. ptc. of καταφέρω; attend. circum.) with ἀπὸ τοῦ ὕπνου (gen. sg. masc. of ὕπνος, -ου, ὁ) denoting agency (BDF §210; cf. 2:22) is describing the completed state, "having been overcome by sleep" (note the art. of previous ref.; Eutychus lost his fight with sleep). Ἔπεσεν (3rd sg. aor. act. indic. of πίπτω, "fall." Τριστέγου (gen. sg. neut. of τρίστεγον, -ου, τό, "third story") relays the seriousness of the fall. Ἤρθη is the 3rd sg. aor. pass. indic. of αἴρω, "take up, lift." Luke avoids ὡς νεκρός (see, e.g., Rev 1:17) in favor of the bare νεκρός (nom. sg. masc. of νεκρός, -ά, -όν) to express the fact that Eutychus was truly dead (Barrett 2.954).

20:10 Καταβάς (nom. sg. masc. of aor. act. ptc. of καταβαίνω; attend. circum.) is appropriate for having to race down the stairways to get outside to the fallen youth. Ἐπέπεσεν is the 3rd sg. aor. act. indic. of ἐπιπίπτω with the dat. αὐτῷ, mng. "he threw himself upon him" (BDAG 377b). Συμπεριλαβών (nom. sg. masc. of aor. act. ptc. of συμπεριλαμβάνω; attend. circum.) is "having embraced." Εἶπεν (3rd sg. aor. act. indic. of λέγω) introduces dir. speech. Μὴ θορυβεῖσθε (2nd pl. pres. pass. impv. of θορυβέω) is likely more proactive than stopping an action in progress (see BHGNT 285), mng. "don't be disturbed." The grounds (γάρ) is "his life" (ἡ . . . ψυχὴ αὐτοῦ) was in him, that is, "he's alive!" There is no grammatical reason to assume Paul means he didn't die. Furthermore, if it were so, the story would be pointless.

20:11 Four aor. temp. ptcs. complete Paul's visit in Troas before he leaves. Ἀναβάς is the nom. sg. masc. of aor. act. ptc. of ἀναβαίνω. Κλάσας is the nom. sg. masc. of aor. act. ptc. of κλάω, "break" (only of bread in NT). Γευσάμενος (nom. sg. masc. of aor. mid. ptc. of γεύομαι), lit. "having tasted," is the eating of another meal, not the Lord's Supper (contra NLT). The presence of τε associates the prep. phrase ἐφ' ἱκανόν with ὁμιλήσας (nom. sg. masc. of aor. act. ptc. of ὁμιλέω, "speak, converse, address"; two times in both Luke and Acts, denoting conversation). Here it is in a temp. expression mng. "having talked for a long time." It is expressly ἄχρι αὐγῆς (gen. sg. fem. of αὐγή, -ῆς, ἡ, "daybreak"), "until dawn." Οὕτως, lit. "thus," is best in Eng., "then." Ἐξῆλθεν is the 3rd sg. aor. act. indic. of ἐξέρχομαι, "depart."

20:12 On the heels of Paul's departure, ἤγαγον (3rd pl. aor. act. indic. of ἄγω, "bring") refers to Paul's hearers. The phrase τὸν παῖδα ζῶντα (acc. sg. masc. of pres. act. ptc. of ζάω) is an obj.-compl. double acc. (BHGNT 388). The clause is best tr. "they took the boy away alive." Παρεκλήθησαν is the 3rd pl. aor. pass. indic. of παρακαλέω, "they were comforted." Οὐ μετρίως is a NT hapax ("not moderately"); on litotes, see 14:28.

HOMILETICAL SUGGESTIONS

Opposition and Grace on the Journey (20:1–12)

1. Opposition from Jews, foiled by wisdom (vv. 1–6)
2. Opposition from tragedy, foiled by divine intervention (vv. 7–12)

3. Paul's Farewell to the Ephesian Elders (20:13–38)

Paul's emotional farewell speech has a narrative setting (vv. 13–17) followed by a speech of five movements: his faithful ministry in Ephesus (vv. 18–21); his future plans (vv. 22–24); his expectation regarding Ephesus (vv. 25–27); his admonition to the elders (vv. 28–32); and, finally, a benediction, farewell, and departure (vv. 32–38). These themes are sim. to Jesus's address in Luke 21 (Barrett 2.964).

Literarily, the speech is a genre common in antiquity: the farewell address in which the protagonist says farewell (often before his death) and instructs his disciples for future conduct. In the context of the book as whole, it sums up Paul's unrestricted ministry before a lengthy captivity period (an undertone of apologetic can also be heard). It has much to teach modern followers of Jesus about ministry and life perspectives (surely also Luke's purpose).

The speech is Paul's only speech to believers in Acts (Bruce, *Acts of the Apostles*, 429). Not surprisingly, it contains a series of parallels to expressions in Paul's letters. These are not merely pasted phrases of one familiar with the letters. It is "unmistakably Paul" (Johnson 367). Noting that it comes in a "we section," Bruce (*Acts of the Apostles*, 429) suggests that Luke heard it himself (cf. 21:1). For parallels, see Bruce, *Acts of the Apostles*, 430–37; Keener 3.3001; Witherington 610–11.

a. Setting (20:13–17)

20:13 Continuing the 1st pl. narration, ἡμεῖς is emphatic in contrast to Paul's mode of travel later. Προελθόντες is the nom. pl. masc. of aor. act. ptc. of προέρχομαι, "go ahead"; attend. circum. Ἀνήχθημεν is the 1st pl. aor. act. indic. of ἀνάγω, "set sail." The destination was Ἄσσον (acc. sg. fem. of Ἄσσος, -ου, ἡ, "Assos"), a town south-south-east of Troy (Troas). The purp. expressed by μέλλοντες (nom. pl. masc. of pres. act. ptc. of μέλλω) is compl. by ἀναλαμβάνειν (pres. act. inf. of ἀναλαμβάνω, "pick up"). The reason is introduced by γάρ. The syntax of the ptc. διατεταγμένος (nom. sg. masc. of pf. mid. ptc. of διατάσσω, "having commanded") is not clear. The vb. ἦν (3rd sg. impf. indic. of εἰμί) signals a periph. cstr. although whether it goes with this ptc. or the following (μέλλων) is debated. Normally the vb. precedes the ptc. in such cstrs.; if so, διατεταγμένος is likely result.* The mng. is little changed either way (BHGNT 389): Paul commanded them to go on without him for he had other plans. Μέλλων (nom. sg. masc. of pres. act. ptc. of μέλλω; periph. impf.) compl. by πεζεύειν (pres. act. inf. of πεζεύω) is "he was going to go by foot." On the emphatic αὐτός, see μεῖς above. Bruce notes that the overland trip was shorter than by ship (a direct route), esp. if the winds were contrary. Thus, Paul stayed behind to make sure everything was fine, then intended to meet them in Assos (Bruce, *Acts of the Apostles*, 427).

20:14 Ὡς is temp., "when." Συνέβαλλεν (3rd sg. impf. act. indic. of συμβάλλω, "meet") takes a dat. obj. ἡμῖν, mng. "when he met us." Ἀναλαβόντες is the nom. pl. masc. of aor. act. ptc. of ἀναλαμβάνω, "pick up"; temp. Ἤλθομεν is the 1st pl. aor. act. indic. of ἔρχομαι, "go." Εἰς Μιτυλήνην (acc. sg. fem. of Μιτυλήνη, -ης, ἡ, "Mitylene") is Luke's typical expression of destination.

20:15 Κἀκεῖθεν is a crasis for καὶ ἐκεῖθεν, "from there." Ἀποπλεύσαντες is the nom. pl. masc. of aor. act. ptc. of ἀποπλέω, "sail away"; temp.). Ἐπιούσῃ (dat. sg. fem. of pres. act. ptc. of ἔπειμι) is a subst., dat. of time (assuming ἡμέρᾳ), mng. "on the next day." Κατηντήσαμεν is the 1st pl. aor. act. indic. of καταντάω, "arrive." The prep. ἄντικρυς is a NT hapax mng. "opposite of . . ." with a gen. obj. (Χίου gen. sg. fem. of Χίος, -ου, ἡ, "Chios;" an island southwest of Mitylene). Ἑτέρᾳ (a dat. of time, "another"), like the previous temp. ref., assumes ἡμέρᾳ, "on the next day." Παρεβάλομεν is the 1st pl. aor. act. indic. of παραβάλλω, "cross over," with the destination of Samos (εἰς Σάμον [acc. sg. fem. of Σάμος, -ου, ἡ]), an island west of Ephesus. Τῇ . . . ἐχομένῃ (dat. sg. fem. of pres. mid. ptc. of ἔχω; subst., dat. of time) refers to the third day (also assuming ἡμέρᾳ), "on the next day." Μίλητον (acc. sg. fem. of Μίλητος, -ου, ἡ, "Miletus") is a seaport city south of Ephesus.

20:16 The reason (γάρ) for the stop at Miletus was Paul's decision (κεκρίκει, 3rd sg. plpf. act. indic. of κρίνω, "decide") to save time. The plpf. suggests the decision had been made at the outset (i.e., he chose that ship because of the decision) rather than a spur-of-the-moment decision (Johnson 356). The vb. takes an inf. of indir. speech, παραπλεῦσαι (aor. act. inf. of παραπλέω, "sail past"), ref. to Ephesus. The negated purp. clause (ὅπως and the subjunc. γένηται [3rd sg. aor. mid. subjunc. of γίνομαι]) explains why. Χρονοτριβῆσαι (aor. act. inf. of χρονοτριβέω, "spend time") functions like a pred. nom. of γένηται. It is best tr. "in order to avoid spending time" (ZG 422; cf. NIV, TNIV, NJB). Γάρ is again explanatory. Ἔσπευδεν is the 3rd sg. impf. act. indic. of σπεύδω, "hurry." The haste is explained by a potential opt. phrase (i.e., fourth-class cond.; see KMP 208; Wallace 702). The mng. is clear but sorting out the grammar is difficult. BDF (§384[2(2)]) notes that hypothetical cstrs. appear without ἄν in the prot. Thus, εἰ δυνατὸν εἴη (3rd sg. pres. opt. of εἰμί) αὐτῷ (dat. of ref.) is "if it would be possible for him." The subj. of the vb. (see BHGNT 390) is in the form of indir. speech employing an inf. γενέσθαι (aor. mid. inf. of γίνομαι). It presents a remote possibility to be in Jerusalem (εἰς = ἐν here) on the day of Pentecost. Robertson says Pentecost was a month away, and the acc. (an extent of time) suggests he wants to be there for the whole day (Robertson, *Pictures,* 346).

20:17 At Miletus, Paul sent (πέμψας, nom. sg. masc. of aor. act. ptc. of πέμπω; attend. circum.) to Ephesus. Μετεκαλέσατο (3rd sg. aor. mid. indic. of μετακαλέω, "summon") takes πρεσβυτέρους (acc. pl. masc. of πρεσβύτερος, -α, -ον; comp. adj., subst.), "the elders," as the dir. obj. Streamlining his time is likely still on his mind, so he summoned the leaders of the church rather than holding an open meeting.

b. Introduction: Paul's Faithful Ministry in Ephesus (20:18–21)

20:18 Ὡς is temp., "when." Παρεγένοντο is the 3rd pl. aor. mid. indic. of παραγίνομαι, "arrive." Εἶπεν is the 3rd sg. aor. act. indic. of λέγω. With the emphatic pers. pron.

ὑμεῖς, ἐπίστασθε (2nd pl. pres. mid. indic. of ἐπίσταμαι, "know") sets up the Ephesian elders as witnesses of a sort. The statement ἀπὸ πρώτης ἡμέρας ἀφ᾽ ἧς ἐπέβην (1st sg. aor. indic. act. of ἐπιβαίνω, "set foot") εἰς τὴν Ἀσίαν (acc. sg. fem. of Ἀσία, -ας, ἡ) emphasizes the extent of time ("from the first day I set foot in Asia"). Πῶς introduces the content of the knowledge. By using it rather than ὅτι, Luke emphasized the manner of his conduct (BHGNT 392). Τὸν πάντα χρόνον is an acc. of time phrase, ref. the extent. Ἐγενόμην is the 1st sg. aor. mid. indic. of γίνομαι. Because the emphasis is on manner rather than the mere fact of his stay, "how I lived among you the whole time" is the best tr. (cf. RSV, NIV, NSRV, ESV, TNIV, NET).

20:19 Δουλεύων (nom. sg. masc. of pres. act. ptc. of δουλεύω) may either be epex. of πῶς (v. 18, BHGNT 393) or manner (Rogers and Rogers 285). In either classification, Paul is describing his manner of life as authentically Christian. Μετά controls three gens.: ταπεινοφροσύνης (gen. sg. fem. of ταπεινοφροσύνη, -ης, ἡ, with πάσης mng. "complete humility"); δακρύων (gen. pl. neut. of δάκρυον, -ου, τό, "tear"); and πειρασμῶν (gen. pl. masc. of πειρασμός, -οῦ, ὁ) with συμβάντων (gen. pl. masc. of aor. act. ptc. of συμβαίνω, "happen"; attrib.), mng. "the trials that happened." Ἐν ταῖς ἐπιβουλαῖς (dat. pl. fem. of ἐπιβουλή, -ῆς, ἡ) is instr. of means, "by the plots." Those who plotted are identified with a poss. gen. Ἰουδαίων ("of the Jews").

20:20 The adv. ὡς continues what the Ephesian elders know. Ὑπεστειλάμην is the 1st sg. aor. mid. indic. of ὑποστέλλω, "hold back." Συμφερόντων (gen. pl. neut. of pres. act. ptc. of συμφέρω), "be profitable"; subst., part. gen.) is best tr. "of the profitable things." Τοῦ μή controls the next two infs.: ἀναγγεῖλαι (aor. act. inf. of ἀναγγέλλω, "announce") and διδάξαι (aor. act. inf. of διδάσκω). The syntax is disputed:

1. Bruce suggests the inf. is epex. of "the profitable things" (cf. Rogers and Rogers 285). This is possible, but the cstr. of the gen. art. and the inf. is technically a result/purp. expression (see BDF §400); it is best to understand it in that way.

2. Barrett suggests it is a consec. cstr. (i.e., result). The sense then is "I held back nothing with the result that I announced to you. . . ." But the statement is intentional, which is the dividing line between result and purpose.

3. It is likely purp. (BHGNT 393). But the double neg. must be considered. For Robertson, the neg. is redundant and emphatic (R 1094). If so, the second should not be tr. In this sense, it would be a positive statement. It is likely, however, that the distance across clauses is too great to treat it so. Given a purp. statement, it is best rendered "lest I failed to. . . ." The content of the teaching is in v. 21.

Paul's declaration is consistent: publicly (δημοσίᾳ) and in each house (κατ᾽ οἴκους, the distributive use, ZG 422). This is likely in contrast to the hypocrisy of the false teachers (Johnson 360–61).

20:21 Διαμαρτυρόμενος (nom. sg. masc. of pres. mid. ptc. of διαμαρτύρομαι, "solemnly testify") is epex. to ὡς in v. 21, thus the content of the proclamation. Ἰουδαίοις τε καὶ Ἕλλησιν (indir. objs., "to both Jews and Greeks") is a typical Pauline phrase. The cstr. found in τὴν . . . μετάνοιαν (acc. sg. fem. of μετάνοια, -ας, ἡ, "repentance") καὶ πίστιν (one art. covering two nouns joined by καί, the so-called Sharp's rule) means they considered some form of unity (Barrett 2.969; BHGNT 393; Wallace 289; Z §184). Given the content, it is expressing two elements of conversion (Barrett 2.969). Furthermore, because repentance is εἰς θεόν, and faith is εἰς τὸν κύριον ἡμῶν Ἰησοῦν, the statement has trinitarian implications.

c. Paul's Intent to Go to Jerusalem (20:22–24)

20:22 On καὶ νῦν ἰδού, see 13:11. Δεδεμένος (nom. sg. masc. of pf. pass. ptc. of δέω, "bind"; causal) takes the dat. τῷ πνεύματι. The noun is an instr. dat. of agency if referring to the Holy Spirit; dat. of ref. if Paul's spirit. Given Luke's emphasis on the Spirit's leading in Acts, and the context, the former is more likely. Ἐγὼ . . . πορεύομαι is emphatic and likely progressive, "I am going. . . ." Εἰς Ἰερουσαλήμ indicates destination. Συναντήσοντά (acc. pl. neut. of fut. act. ptc. of συναντάω, "happen") is subst., mng. "the things going to happen." It takes a dat. of (dis)advantage, μοι, and is the obj. of the concessive ptc. εἰδώς (nom. sg. masc. of pf. act. ptc. of οἶδα).

20:23 Πλήν ("except") sets up what Paul does know through the Holy Spirit. The Spirit's testimony has been κατὰ πόλιν (distributive, "in each city"). Διαμαρτύρεταί is the 3rd sg. pres. mid. indic. of διαμαρτύρομαι, "solemnly testify." Λέγον (nom. sg. neut. of pres. act. ptc. of λέγω) ὅτι introduces indir. speech. Δεσμά (nom. pl. neut. of δεσμός, -οῦ, ὁ, "bond" [only neut. in the pl. in the NT]) and θλίψεις ("bonds and afflictions") are fronted for emphasis. Μένουσιν is the 3rd pl. pres. act. indic. of μένω, "wait."

20:24 The v. is difficult, with textual variations and emendations corroborating this assessment (see Barrett 2.971). As the text stands, οὐδενὸς λόγου is a gen. of price, lit. "not worth a word." Ποιοῦμαι (1st sg. pres. mid. indic. of ποιέω) in the mid. has the sense of "I consider." It takes a double-acc. cstr. (obj.-compl.). The dir. obj. is ψυχήν (the art. is used like a poss. pron., "my life"). The compl. in the cstr. is τιμίαν ἐμαυτῷ (lit. "precious to myself") that picks up the initial λόγου to complete its mng. All EVV tr. the clause idiomatically; BDAG (599b) does about as well as anyone: "I do not consider my life worth a single word." The distance between constituents makes the last part of the interpretation difficult, so Culy and Parsons consider οὐδενὸς λόγου a gen. of respect with the resulting tr. "On no account do I consider my life precious to me" (BHGNT 395). The sense is clear either way.

Ὡς with an inf. (τελειῶσαι aor. act. inf. of τελειόω) creates a purp. clause (BDAG 1106b; the only one in the NT, R 987), "in order to complete." The inf. takes a double obj., "my race" (δρόμον acc. sg. masc. of δρόμος, -ου, ὁ, "race") and διακονίαν ("ministry"). The rel. clause defines the ministry. In terms of sanctioning authority, it is the highest. Ἔλαβον (1st sg. aor. act. indic. of λαμβάνω, "receive") is modified by παρὰ τοῦ κυρίου Ἰησου ("from the Lord Jesus"). Διαμαρτύρασθαι (aor. mid. inf. of διαμαρτύρομαι, "solemnly testify") is a purp. statement. It is the essence of the commission. The inf. takes εὐαγγέλιον (acc. sg. neut. of εὐαγγέλλιον, -ου, τό) as its obj. Χάριτος is the gen. sg. fem. of χάρις, -ιτος, ἡ; obj. gen. Paul is likely ref. Jesus's words at 9:15 that he would take the gospel to "Gentiles, kings, and Israelites." Thus, Paul's attitude devalued his own life in favor of obedience to his calling.

d. Paul's Expectation regarding Ephesus (20:25–27)

20:25 On καὶ νῦν ἰδού, see 13:11. Ἐγώ is emphatic. Οἶδα ("I know") expresses Paul's confident assertion, given what has been revealed to him. Ὄψεσθε is the 2nd pl. fut. mid. indic. of ὁράω. Τὸ πρόσωπόν μου (dir. obj., lit. "my face") is a Heb. expression mng. "me" (ZG 422). Ὑμεῖς πάντες ("you all") is the nom. subj. phrase. It is modified by a prep. phrase with a rel. pron. clause as the obj. (ἐν οἷς). Διῆλθον is the 1st sg. aor. act. indic. of διέρχομαι, "pass through" (NASB "went about"). Κηρύσσων (nom. sg. masc. of pres. act. ptc. of κηρύσσω) is manner, mng. "by preaching."

20:26 Διότι (= δι᾿ ὅ, ZG 423), "therefore," is on the grounds of his faithful ministry. Μαρτύρομαι (1st sg. pres. mid. indic. of μαρτύρομαι, "affirm, insist") with ἐν τῇ σήμερον ἡμέρᾳ (lit. "in the today day," mng. "this very day") suggests a very solemn pronouncement (Schnabel 844). It is given in a pred. adj. cstr. fronting the adj. καθαρός (nom. sg. masc. of καθαρός, -α, -ον, "clean"). Ἀπὸ τοῦ αἵματος πάντων ("from the blood of all") is a ref. to Ezek 33:6 (Witherington 622; see also 18:6). Paul was not the watchman who didn't sound the trumpet, so he had no guilt regarding their rejection of Christ.

20:27 Γάρ introduces the grounds for the claim that is very sim. to 20:20, neatly wrapping up this part of the speech. Ὑπεστειλάμην (1st sg. aor. mid. indic. of ὑποστέλλω, "hold back"), with τοῦ μὴ ἀναγγεῖλαι (see 20:20; purp. although here the double neg. is redundant and emphatic), means "I did not refrain in order to announce." Here there is an obj., πᾶσαν τὴν βουλήν (acc. sg. fem. of βουλή, -ῆς, ἡ, "counsel") τοῦ θεοῦ, "the whole counsel of God." Thus, the grounds for his innocence was his declaration of God's word. Although it was physically impossible for him to witness to every Asian, he did consistently proclaim the gospel in the region and gave the Ephesians everything they needed to continue to evangelize their home.

e. Guard the Flock (20:28–31)

20:28 Προσέχετε (2nd pl. pres. act. impv. of προσέχω, "be on guard") takes a compound dat. dir. obj.: the refl. pron. ἑαυτοῖς ("for yourselves") and ποιμνίῳ (dat. sg. neut. of ποίμνιον, -ου, τό, "flock"). The prep. phrase ἐν ᾧ modifies "flock" and is best "among whom." The rel. clause employs a double-acc., obj.-compl. cstr. with the obj. ὑμᾶς ("you") fronted for emphasis. Πνεῦμα, "Spirit," is the subj. of ἔθετο (3rd sg. aor. mid. indic. of τίθημι; the mid. is used with a double-acc. cstr. with the mng. "he made x to be y" [BDAG 1004b]). The compl. is ἐπισκόπους (acc. pl. masc. of ἐπίσκοπος, -ου, ὁ, "overseers"). Ποιμαίνειν (pres. act. inf. of ποιμαίνω, "shepherd"; purp.) takes ἐκκλησίαν ("church") as the obj. of the inf. The precious nature of the church is revealed through the price paid for her. Περιεποιήσατο (3rd sg. aor. mid. indic. of περιποιέω, "purchase"). The subj. of περιεποιήσατο is unexpressed, leaving the ref. of ἰδίου ("of his own") somewhat vague. The implied subj. of the vb. is a 3rd sg. pron., likely ref. to θεοῦ. Thus, the adj. is likely referring to "his own *Son*" rather than "his own blood" (MM 298d; Bruce, *Acts of the Apostles*, 434; Bock 630; Schnabel 837; RSV, NET, MIT, NJB).

20:29 Ἐγὼ οἶδα ("I know") is emphatic. Εἰσελεύσονται (3rd pl. fut. mid. indic. of εἰσέρχομαι, "enter") is modified by μετὰ τὴν ἄφιξίν (acc. sg. fem. of ἄφιξις, -εως, ἡ; NT hapax) μου, "after my departure." Λύκοι (nom. pl. masc. of λύκος, -ου, ὁ, "wolf") βαρεῖς (nom. pl. masc. of βαρύς, -εῖα, -ύ, "fierce, cruel") is best "savage wolves" (NASB, NIV, NRSV, TNIV). It describes both the danger and attitude of false teachers. The neg. ptc. φειδόμενοι (nom. pl. masc. of pres. mid. ptc. of φείδομαι, "spare"; manner) is "by not sparing" taking a gen. obj., ποιμνίου (gen. sg. neut. of ποίμνιον, -ου, τό), "the flock."

20:30 Paul turned his attention to internal threats to the flock. Ἐξ ὑμῶν αὐτῶν highlights the surprise factor through fronting and employing of the intensive use of αὐτός, "from you yourselves!" Ἀναστήσονται (3rd pl. fut. mid. indic. of ἀνίστημι) is an intrans. mid. mng. "they will arise." Λαλοῦντες is the nom. pl. masc. of pres. act. ptc. of λαλέω; attend. circum. The obj. of the ptc. is a subst. ptc., διεστραμμένα (acc. pl. neut. of pf. pass. ptc. of διαστρέφω), mng. "perverse things" (representing heresy, Barrett 2.979). The art. inf. τοῦ ἀποσπᾶν (pres. act. inf. of ἀποσπάω, "draw away") indicates purp. It takes μαθητάς (acc. pl. masc. of μαθητής, -οῦ, ὁ) as its obj. Ὀπίσω with a gen. obj. (αὐτῶν) is "after them."

20:31 Διό, "therefore," is inferential. Γρηγορεῖτε (2nd pl. pres. act. impv. of γρηγορέω, "watch" or "be alert") in the pres. suggests ongoing vigilance (Bock 631) and is more robust than Προσέχετε at v. 28 (Johnson 364). Μνημονεύοντες (nom. pl. masc. of pres. act. ptc. of μνημονεύω, attend. circum., in this case, with impv. force) is "remembering." The content of the memory is introduced by ὅτι. Fronted for emphasis, the acc. of time τριετίαν (acc. sg. fem. of τριετής, -ες, "of/for three years") indicates an extent (Bruce [*Acts of the Apostles*, 435]: "a round number"). The acc. sg. nouns νύκτα and ἡμέραν are in appos. to τριετίαν. The neg. vb. ἐπαυσάμην (1st sg. aor. mid. indic. of παύω) is an intrans. mid. that is compl. by the ptc. νουθετῶν (nom. sg. masc. of pres. act. ptc. of νουθετέω, "warn"; only used elsewhere in Paul, Schnabel 849). The ptc. takes the phrase ἕνα ἕκαστον ("each one") as its obj.

f. Benediction and Farewell (20:32–38)

20:32 On καὶ τὰ νῦν, see 4:29. Παρατίθεμαι (1st sg. pres. mid. indic. of παρατίθημι) in the mid. is "entrust." It takes an acc. obj. (ὑμᾶς) and a dat. indir. obj., in this case, compound: θεῷ and the phrase τῷ λόγῳ τῆς χάριτος αὐτου ("the word of his grace"). Barrett's suggestion is that this is an example of hendiadys where "God" and "word" are one concept, i.e., God, active in his word (Barrett 2.981). Χάριτος, then, is an attrib. gen. and αὐτου modifies λόγῳ (BHGNT 398), mng. "his gracious message." In that rdg., the possibility of a mediated message is minimized; that is, it is dir. from God. In this understanding, although the following ptc. is grammatically in appos. to λόγῳ, God is the enabler. The subst. ptc. δυναμένῳ (dat. sg. masc. of pres. mid. ptc. of δύναμαι) is "which is able." It takes compound compl. aor. act. infs., οἰκοδομῆσαι (of οἰκοδομέω, "to edify") and δοῦναι (of δίδωμι, "to give"). Ἡγιασμένοις (dat. pl. masc of pf. pass. ptc. of ἁγιάζω) is the subst. obj. of prep., mng. "among all the ones who have been sanctified."

20:33–34 Fronted for emphasis, a series of alternating gen. sg. masc. dir. objs. (ἀργυρίου [of ἀργύριον, -ου, τό] . . . χρυσίου [of χρυσίον, -ου, τό] . . . ἱματισμοῦ [of ἱματισμός, -οῦ, ὁ], "silver . . . gold . . . cloak") are modified by a poss. gen. οὐδενός (gen. sg. masc., subst. "of no man"). The vb. ἐπεθύμησα (1st sg. aor. act. indic. of ἐπιθυμέω, "desire, covet") takes the gen. of a thing coveted (BDAG 370d). Paul possibly alludes to 1 Sam 12:3 as a prototypical disclaimer in a farewell address (Johnson 365). The phrase αὐτοὶ γινώσκετε (2nd pl. pres. act. indic. of γινώσκω) has the intensive use of the pron., mng. "you yourselves know." Ὅτι introduces the content. Fronted for emphasis, the phrase ταῖς χρείαις μου and the subst. ptc. οὖσιν (dat. pl. masc. of pres. ptc. of εἰμί) are compound dat. objs. of the following vb., mng. "my needs and the ones with me." Ὑπηρέτησαν is the 3rd pl. aor. act. indic. of ὑπηρετέω, "ministered." The sentence is completed with the introduction of the subj. χεῖρες (nom. pl. fem. of χείρ, -ιτος, ἡ, "hand"), with the pron. αὗται (nom. pl. fem. of οὗτος; demonstrative pron. used adj.) mng. "these hands." It was likely accompanied with a gesture. It is def. emphatic at the end of the sentence (Bruce, *Acts of the Apostles*, 436).

20:35 BDAG identifies πάντα as an acc. of ref., "at every opportunity" (BDAG 1037b; Barrett 2.982; see RSV, NASB, NIV, NRSV, ESV, TNIV, NET, NJB). This is likely correct because ὑπέδειξα (1st sg. aor. act. indic. of ὑποδείκνυμι, "show") normally takes a dat. of pers. (here "ὑμῖν"). The content (ὅτι) of what Paul showed is οὕτως κοπιῶντας (nom. sg. masc. of aor. act. ptc. of κοπιάω; means), best tr. "by laboring like this." On δεῖ, see 3:21. It takes two infs., ἀντιλαμβάνεσθαι (pres. mid. inf. of ἀντιλαμβάνω, "help") with ἀσθενούντων (gen. pl. masc. of pres. act. ptc. of ἀσθενέω; subst.) as the obj. (not in the acc. because ἀντιλαμβάνω takes a gen.). Μνημονεύειν (pres. act. inf. of μνημονεύω, "remember") is the second compl. inf. to δεῖ. On τε, see 1:15. The gen. obj. of the inf. is λόγων ("words"). Τοῦ κυρίου Ἰησοῦ is a poss. gen. that also serves to introduce an otherwise unknown saying of Jesus. Ὅτι may introduce dir. speech, but is more likely to be causal (BHGNT 399; Schnabel 851, NRSV). The latter is slightly more likely for the presence of εἶπεν. Bruce refers to the emphatic αὐτός as "reverential" and tr. it "the Master" (Bruce, *Acts of the Apostles*, 436). The pred. adj. μακάριόν . . . μᾶλλον is used instead of a comp. adj. With the impers. ἐστιν, it means "it is more blessed." The items comp. are compl. pres. act. infs.: διδόναι (of δίδωμι, "give") and λαμβάνειν (of λαμβάνω, "receive"). Although the statement is not in one of the four Gospels (technically called an "agrapha"), it is sim. to Luke 6:38 and 11:9. That it is not in a Gospel should not diminish the authenticity of the saying. Luke could just as easily have placed the saying in the Gospel. He likely reserved the saying for this spot (Bruce, *Acts of the Apostles*, 437; possibly because it is the place where he first heard it).

20:36 The meeting ends in prayer. Ταῦτα ("these things") is the obj. of the temp. ptc. εἰπών (nom. sg. masc. of aor. act. ptc. of λέγω). On θεὶς τὰ γόνατα, see 7:60. Προσηύξατο (3rd sg. of aor. mid. indic. of προσεύχομαι, "pray") is a fitting end of the speech.

20:37 Ἱκανὸς . . . κλαυθμός is a pred. nom. with an impers. ἐγένετο (3rd sg. aor. mid. indic. of γίνομαι), mng. "there was considerable weeping," perhaps loudly (ZG 424). Πάντων is gen. pl. masc.; gen. of source; "from all." Ἐπιπεσόντες (nom. sg. masc. of aor. act. ptc. of ἐπιπίπτω; attend. circum.) ἐπὶ τὸν τράχηλον (lit., "having fallen upon the neck") is an idiom mng. "they embraced" (BDAG 1014d; ZG 424; Barrett 2.98; it is common in LXX, an "emotional embrace"). Κατεφίλουν (3rd pl. impf. act. indic. of καταφιλέω) is either an ingressive impf. "they began kissing him" or iter. "repeatedly kissed" (NASB; most EVV, simply "kissed").

20:38 Ὀδυνώμενοι (nom. pl. masc. of pres. pass. ptc. of ὀδυνάω, "be pained/distressed") with the adv. μάλιστα mng. "being esp. in agony" (see Luke 16:24; Thompson 261). The rel. pron. ᾧ is dat. by attraction to λόγῳ. Εἰρήκει (3rd sg. plpf. indic. act. of λέγω) ref. 20:25. Ὅτι introduces indir. speech. The neg. (οὐκέτι) vb. μέλλουσιν (3rd pl. pres. act. indic. of μέλλω) with the compl. inf. θεωρεῖν (pres. act. inf. of θεωρέω) is best tr. "no longer going to see him." The last thing they did was to escort (προέπεμπον, 3rd pl. impf. indic. act. of προπέμπω) him to the ship.

FOR FURTHER STUDY

29. Paul's Farewell and Farewell Discourses (20:18–35)

Barrett, C. K. "Paul's Address to the Ephesian Elders." In *God's Christ and His People*, 107–21. Oslo: Universitetsforlaget, 1977.

Hemer, C. J. "The Speeches of Acts: Pt 1: The Ephesian Elders at Miletus." *TynBul* 40 (1989): 77–85.

Kellum, L. S. *DJG²*, 266–69.

Kurz, W. S. "Biblical Farewell Addresses." *TBT* 38 (2000): 69–73.

Lövestam, E. "Paul's Address at Miletus." *ST* 41 (1987): 1–10.

30. Sayings of Jesus Outside of the Gospels ("Agrapha") (20:35)

Charlesworth, J., and C. Evans. "Jesus in the Agrapha and Apocryphal Gospels." In *Studying the Historical Jesus: Evaluations of the State of Current Research*. Edited by B. Chilton and C. Evans, 483–91. NTTS 19: Leiden: Brill, 1994.

Theissen, G., and A. Merz. "Further Sources: Floating Traditions about Jesus." In *The Historical Jesus: A Comprehensive Guide*, 54–62. Minneapolis: Fortress, 1998.

Van Voorst, R. E. "The Agrapha: Scattered Sayings of Jesus." In *Jesus Outside the New Testament: An Introduction*, 179–84. Grand Rapids: Eerdmans, 2000.

HOMILETICAL SUGGESTIONS

Paul's Word for Elders (20:18–35)

1. Remember faithful ministry (vv. 18–20)
2. Be faithful to God's plan in hardship (vv. 22–24)
3. Be on the lookout for false teachers (vv. 25–27)
4. Guard the flock (vv. 28–31)
5. Trust God's grace and faithfully work (vv. 32–35)

4. Paul's Journey to Jerusalem (21:1–16)

21:1 Ὡς is temp., "when." On δὲ ἐγένετο, see 4:5. Ἀναχθῆναι (aor. pass. inf. of ἀνάγω) takes ἡμᾶς as the subj., "after we set sail." Ἀποσπασθέντας is the acc. pl. masc. of aor.

pass. ptc. of ἀποσπάω, "draw away"; temp. Εὐθυδρομήσαντες is the nom. pl. masc. of aor. act. ptc. of εὐθυδρομέω "set a straight course." Ἤλθομεν is the 1st pl. aor. act. indic. of ἔρχομαι. Εἰς (destination) Κῶ is an island in the Aegean Sea, south of Miletus. Τῇ assumes ἡμέρᾳ, in effect nominalizing the adv. ἑξῆς (only in Luke-Acts). As a dat. of time it is a temp. expression mng. "on the next (day)." Two more destinations are indicated by εἰς: Ῥόδον (acc. sg. fem. of Ῥόδος, -ου, ἡ,"Rhodes"; an island southeast of Kos) and Πάταρα (acc. sg. neut. of Πάταρα, -ων, τά, "Patara;" a city on the southwest coast of Asia Minor).

21:2 Εὑρόντες is the nom. pl. masc. of aor. act. ptc. of εὑρίσκω; temp. Πλοῖον is modified by the attrib. ptc. διαπερῶν (nom. sg. neut. of pres. act. ptc. of διαπεράω, "cross over") that takes εἰς Φοινίκην (fem. acc. sg. of Φοινίκη, -ης, ἡ), "to Phoenicia," as the destination (the Syrian coast). Ἐπιβάντες is the nom. pl. masc. of aor. act. ptc. of ἐπιβαίνω, "go aboard"; temp. Ἀνήχθημεν is the 1st pl. aor. pass. indic. of ἀνάγω, "put to sea."

21:3 This v. features a number of nautical terms that are difficult to tr. Ἀναφάναντες (nom. sg. masc. of aor. act. ptc. of ἀναφαίνω) takes Κύπρον (acc. sg. fem. of Κύπρος, -ου, ἡ, "Cyprus") as the obj. Lit. mng. "having made Cyprus visible" (i.e., by drawing near, BDF §309[1]), most EVV have "come in sight of Cyprus." Καταλιπόντες (nom. pl. masc. of aor. act. ptc. of καταλείπω, "leave"; temp.) takes εὐώνυμον (acc. sg. fem. of εὐώνυμος, -ον, "on the left") as the obj. The entire phrase means they sailed south of the island. The impf. ἐπλέομεν (1st pl. impf. act. indic. of πλέω) with the prep. phrase conveys "we were continuing to sail to Syria" (Rogers and Rogers 287). Κατήλθομεν (1st pl. aor. act. indic. of κατέρχομαι, "come down") is a nautical term for "reach the coast," that is, "landed" (ZG 424). Εἰς Τύρον (acc. sg. fem. of Τύρος, -ου, ἡ), "to Tyre," refers to a major seaport in Phoenicia (i.e., Syria). Ἐκεῖσε, adv. mng. "there," is used only two times in the NT, both in Acts. Τὸ πλοῖον is the subj. of the periph. impf. ptc. ἦν ἀποφορτιζόμενον (nom. sg. neut. of pres. mid. ptc. of ἀποφορτίζομαι), with the dir. obj. γόμον (acc. sg. masc. of γόμος, -ου, ὁ, "cargo"), mng. "the ship was unloading the cargo."

21:4 Ἀνευρόντες (nom. pl. masc. of aor. act. ptc. of ἀνευρίσκω, "seek out") assumes finding the obj. (μαθητάς, acc. pl. masc. of μαθητής, -ου, ὁ, "disciples"). Ἐπεμείναμεν is the 1st pl. aor. act. indic. of ἐπιμένω, "continue." Ἡμέρας ἑπτα is an acc. of time (extent). On αὐτοῦ, see 18:19. On οἵτινες, see 7:53. Ἔλεγον (3rd pl. impf. act. indic. of λέγω) is likely progressive: "kept telling Paul" (NASB, NET ["repeatedly"], NJB). The phrase διὰ τοῦ πνεύματος ("through the Spirit") is rather vague. It is expressed in indir. speech by a neg. inf. ἐπιβαίνειν (pres. act. inf. of ἐπιβαίνω), "not to embark" to Jerusalem. The major question is whether or not the Spirit commanded Paul not to go through prophetic utterance. Luke has already hinted at trouble in Jerusalem at 20:22–23. He clearly did not interpret them as a prohibition. Keener lists several interpretations (3:3082–83):

1. Paul disobeyed an inspired utterance of the Spirit. This seems extremely unlikely, given that the narrative is driven by their obedience to the Spirit's leading. Paul is certain he is acting in God's will.

2. Tyrian Christians were warning based on their hostility of Jews. Keener
   points out that Paul was Jewish and such was not the pattern of the Gentile
   church. Furthermore, nothing in the text points to this understanding.
3. Paul evaluated and rejected "prophetic speech." Again, this is not stated in the
   text. It would be unlikely to be expressed so vaguely.
4. Paul doesn't reject the warning but the application not to go. Later we see
   just such a thing in Agabus's prophecy (21:11). Grammatically the indir.
   command is the message of the disciples. "Through the Spirit" can certainly
   indicate the occasion for the interpretation.

21:5 On δὲ ἐγένετο and an inf., see 4:5. Ἐξαρτίσαι (aor. act. inf. of ἐξαρτίζω, "finish"), not used of time anywhere else, is probably a nautical term (Bruce, *Acts of
the Apostles*, 439). Ἐξελθόντες (nom. pl. masc. of aor. act. ptc. of ἐξέρχομαι; attend.
circum.). Ἐπορευόμεθα is the 1st pl. impf. mid. indic. of πορεύομαι. It will be modified
by two attend. circum. ptcs. at the final clause. But first there is a gen. abs. phrase:
προπεμπόντων (gen. pl. masc. of pres. act. ptc. of προπέμπω, "accompany"). Πάντων
is the subj. of the ptc. (Luke also notes wives and children). Ἕως ἔξω has the sense of
"until we were outside" (cf. RSV, NASB, ESV; ZG 425). On θέντες (nom. pl. masc.
of aor. act. ptc. of τίθημι; attend. circum.) τὰ γόνατα (acc. pl. neut. of γόνυ, -ατος, τό,
"knee"), see 7:60. Αἰγιαλόν (acc. sg. masc. of αἰγιαλός, -οῦ, ὁ) is a beach with sand
suitable to beach ships (BDAG 25c), "as opposed to ἀκτή used of a rocky shore"
(BASHH 125). Προσευξάμενοι is the nom. pl. masc. of aor. mid. ptc. of προσεύχομαι;
attend. circum.

21:6 Ἀπησπασάμεθα (1st pl. aor. mid. indic. of ἀπασπάζομαι) takes the obj. ἀλλήλους,
mng. "We said farewell to one another." They boarded (ἀνέβημεν, 1st pl. aor. act. indic.
of ἀναβαίνω). The Tyrian Christians returned (ὑπέστρεψαν, 3rd pl. aor. act. indic. of
ὑποστρέφω). Τὰ ἴδια refers to "their own homes."

21:7 The trip (πλοῦν, acc. sg. masc. of πλόος, -οῦς, ὁ, "voyage"; obj. of ptc., only
elsewhere at 27:10) from Tyre continued (διανύσαντες, nom. pl. masc. of aor. act. ptc.
of διανύω; temp., NT hapax). The ptc., often tr. "finished" (see KJV, RSV, NASB,
MIT), is also "continued" (BDAG 234d; Barrett 2.991; Bruce, *Acts of the Apostles*,
440; Rogers and Rogers 287); the latter seems to fit this context. Κατηντήσαμεν is the
1st pl. aor. act. indic. of καταντάω, "arrive." Πτολεμαΐδα (fem. sg. acc. of Πτολεμαΐς,
-ΐδος, ἡ, "Ptolemais") is a day's sailing journey. The pattern remains the same, greeting
(ἀσπασάμενοι, nom. pl. masc. of aor. mid. ptc. of ἀσπάζομαι) and lodging with brothers. They stayed (ἐμείναμεν, 1st pl. aor. act. indic. of μένω) for one day.

21:8 On τῇ δὲ ἐπαύριον, see 10:9. Ἐξελθόντες is the nom. pl. masc. of pres. act. ptc. of
ἐξέρχομαι; attend. circum. Ἤλθομεν is the 1st pl. aor. act. indic. of ἔρχομαι. Caesarea
(Καισάρειαν, fem. sg. acc. of Καισάρεια, -ας, ἡ; obj. of prep., destination) is Caesarea
Maritima (by the sea). Εἰσελθόντες is the nom. pl. masc. of aor. act. ptc. of εἰσέρχομαι;
attend. circum. Φιλίππου (gen. sg. masc. of Φίλιππος, -ου, ὁ; poss. gen.) is identified in
two ways. First, with a gen. of appos. εὐαγγελιστοῦ (gen. sg. masc. of εὐαγγελιστής, -ου,
ὁ, "evangelist"; only here, Eph 4:11, and 2 Tim 4:5). When we last saw Philip at 8:40 at
Caesarea, the vb. εὐαγγελίζομαι was used three times in that episode (Bruce, *Acts of the
Apostles*, 440). More than merely distinguishing him from the apostle Philip, sharing

the gospel seems to be his passion. The second identification is the attrib. ptc. phrase ὄντος (gen. sg. masc. of pres. ptc. of εἰμί) ἐκ τῶν ἑπτα, "being one of the seven," that is, the "deacons" of 6:5.

21:9 Philip's daughters are introduced with the poss. dat. τούτῳ in a pred. nom. cstr. ῏Ησαν (3rd pl. impf. indic. of εἰμί) is impers. ("there were") with the pred. nom. phrase of noun (θυγατέρες, "daughters") modified by two adjs. (τέσσαρες, "four," and παρθένοι [nom. pl. fem. of παρθένος, -ου, ἡ, "virgins"]) and an attrib. ptc. προφητεύουσαι (nom. pl. fem. of pres. act. ptc. of προφητεύω), lit. "four virgin prophesying daughters," but best tr. "four unmarried daughters, who prophesied" (ESV, NET).

21:10 Ἐπιμενόντων (gen. pl. masc. of pres. act. ptc. of ἐπιμένω, "continue"; gen. abs., temp.). The phrase ἡμέρας πλείους in the acc. is an extent of time, "for many days." Κατῆλθέν (3rd sg. aor. act. indic. of κατέρχομαι, "come down") takes τις as the subj., "a certain man." On ὀνόματι, see 5:1. Ἅγαβος (nom. masc. sg. of Ἅγαβος, -ου, ὁ), a Christian prophet, was last seen at 11:28.

21:11 Agabus follows the OT tradition, where prophets were often called to carry out symbolic acts (Haenchen 611). Three ptcs. of attend. circum. set up Agabus's message to Paul. First, logically, he arrives (ἐλθών, nom. sg. masc. of aor. act. ptc. of ἔρχομαι); second, he takes up (ἄρας, nom. sg. masc. of aor. act. ptc. of αἴρω) Paul's belt (ζώνην, acc. sg. fem. of ζώνη, -ης, ἡ). And third, he binds (δήσας, nom. sg. masc. of aor. act. ptc. of δέω) his hands and feet with it. Εἶπεν (3rd sg. aor. act. indic. of λέγω) introduces dir. speech. The only other place in the NT where τάδε λέγει (3rd sg. pres. act. indic. of λέγω) is employed is each of the letters in Revelation 2–3. It is, however, used 362 times in the LXX, mostly for the familiar "thus says the Lord." Agabus is clearly following in that tradition, except his referent is τὸ πνεῦμα τὸ ἅγιον ("the Holy Spirit"). Ἅνδρα (acc. sg. masc. of ἀνήρ, ἀνδρός, ὁ; dir. obj.) is fronted for emphasis. The rel. pron. οὗ is a gen. of poss. modifying the subj. (ζώνη nom. sg. fem. of ζώνη, -ης, ἡ, "belt") of a pred. nom. cstr. The content of the prophecy is a compound clause. Δήσουσιν (3rd pl. fut. act. indic. of δέω) takes Ἰουδαῖοι (nom. pl. masc., "Jews") as the subj. Παραδώσουσιν (3rd pl. fut. act. indic. of παραδίδωμι, "hand over") with the destination εἰς χεῖρας ἐθνῶν ("the hands of the Gentiles"). Both vbs. are predictive futs.

Many have noted Agabus's prophecy is not strictly accurate. The Jews do not bind Paul, nor do they turn him over to the Gentiles. The Romans rescue, then arrest, Paul (see Barrett 2.995–96; Witherington 631). The objection is overstated. If Luke had believed it not to be accurate it is unlikely he would have included it. Instead, he includes it to continue the point he's been making all along—the Spirit is continually warning Paul that trouble awaits him. Witherington suggests that NT prophecy is "general content" to be weighed and sifted (631). It is doubtful Agabus saw it that way; he was far too specific. Wallace identifies the vbs. as causative acts. (413). This is not uncommon for the act. voice (see 3:15, where Peter accuses the Jews of killing the author of life, clearly causative). So, later, Paul will be arrested at the instigation of the Jews and held in custody. It is unlikely there was no formal charge made by the Jews (Barrett 2.996).

21:12 Ὡς is temp., "when." Ἠκούσαμεν is the 1st pl. aor. act. indic. of ἀκούω. The subj. of παρεκαλοῦμεν (1st pl. pres. act. indic. of παρακαλέω, "urge") is presented in a τε καί cstr. "both we (ἡμεῖς) and the locals (ἐντόπιοι, nom. pl. masc. of ἐντόπιος, -ου, ὁ; NT hapax)." Τοῦ μὴ ἀναβαίνειν is a neg. purp. cstr. "not to go."

21:13 Paul's answer (ἀπεκρίθη, 3rd sg. aor. pass. indic. of ἀποκρίνομαι) is deeply emotional. Τί ποιεῖτε (2nd pl. pres. act. indic. of ποιέω), "what are you doing," takes two ptcs. of means. The first, κλαίοντες (nom. pl. masc. of pres. act. ptc. of κλαίω), is "by weeping." The second is muddled by Eng. idiom. Συνθρύπτοντές (nom. pl. masc. of pres. act. ptc. of συνθρύπτω, "break in pieces"; NT hapax) is something like "crushed to powder" (Barrett 2.997; MM 607d); with μου τὴν καρδίαν ("my heart") as its obj., it is unlikely to mean causing emotional distress but rather Paul's will, that is, "crushing my resolve." The gist of the statement is something along the lines of "what are you trying to accomplish by. . . ." Rhetorically, it is a prohibition, with the grounds (γάρ) Paul's readiness to suffer. On οὐ μόνον . . . ἀλλά, see 19:26. Δεθῆναι (aor. pass. inf. of δέω, "bind") and ἀποθανεῖν (aor. act. inf. of ἀποθνήσκω, "die") are compl. to ἑτοίμως ἔχω (1st sg. pres. act. indic. of ἔχω; with the adv. presents a state, ZG 435, "I am ready"), presenting an escalation of suffering Paul is willing to endure for Jesus's sake.

21:14 A neg. temp. (KJV, RSV, NLT, NIV, TNIV) or causative (NASB, NRSV, ESV, NET) ptc. πειθομένου (gen. sg. masc. of pres. pass. ptc. of πείθω; gen. abs.) means "when (or because) he would not be persuaded." Ἡσυχάσαμεν (1st pl. aor. act. indic of ἡσυχάζω) is an ingressive aor., "we grew silent." Εἰπόντες (nom. sg. masc. of aor. act. ptc. of λέγω) introduces dir. speech. Somewhat of a Christian stock phrase, the group joins Paul in commitment to the Lord's (κυρίου; poss. gen.) will (θέλημα; dir. obj.) by declaring γινέσθω (3rd sg. pres. mid. impv. of γίνομαι), "let it be done."

21:15 A temp. phrase (with δέ) signals the turn to Jerusalem, μετὰ . . . τὰς ἡμέρας ταύτας ("after these days"). Ἐπισκευασάμενοι (nom. pl. masc. of aor. mid. ptc. of ἐπισκευάζομαι, "equip"; temp.) is, perhaps, "saddled horses" (Bruce, *Acts of the Apostles*, 443; Robertson, *Pictures,* 366). Ἀνεβαίνομεν (1st pl. impf. act. indic. of ἀναβαίνω) is likely an ingressive impf. "started on our way" (NASB, NRSV, TNIV, NET).

21:16 Συνῆλθον is the 3rd pl. aor. act. indic. of συνέρχομαι, "they came." Καί is adv., "also." Τῶν μαθητῶν (gen. pl. masc. of μαθητής) is a part. gen. of an unexpressed subj. best tr. "some of the disciples from Caesarea" (BDF §164[2]; R 1003). Ἄγοντες (nom. pl. masc. of pres. act. ptc. of ἄγω), according to Barrett, takes the place of a fut. ptc., thus expressing purp. (Barrett 2.1002; see also BDF §339[2c]; although see R 892). Παρ' ᾧ (dat. sg. masc., "to whom") refers to the house of Mnason. Since Jerusalem was more than sixty miles away, even on horseback it takes more than a day. A place on the way is then necessary. Ξενισθῶμεν (1st pl. aor. pass. subjunc. of ξενίζω) is the vb. for the rel. clause, together mng. "to the one with whom we should be lodged." If so, Μνάσωνί and the dats. that follow are in appos. to the rel. pron. (BHGNT 408). However, most EVV, and grammarians, take it as a case of inverse attraction where the dat. is attracted to the case of the rel. pron.; i.e., it normally would be in the acc. (obj. of ἄγοντες). The mng. is not impacted either way. The following dats. are clearly in appos. to Mnason. Ἀρχαίῳ μαθητῇ may mean "an early disciple" (Bruce, *Acts of the Apostles*, 443), or "orig." (MM 80d)*, or "since Pentecost" (BASHH 170). Another possibility is that it means "of long standing" (Bruce, *Acts of the Apostles*, 443, citing *New Docs.* 1 §85).

HOMILETICAL SUGGESTIONS

Interpreting the Inner Voice of the Spirit (21:1–16)

1. The disciples interpreted the prompting to avoid Jerusalem (vv. 1–6)
2. The disciples interpreted Agabus's prophecy to avoid Jerusalem (vv. 7–12)
3. The apostle interpreted both as a warning to be prepared to suffer (vv. 13–16)

B. PAUL'S FINAL VISIT TO JERUSALEM AND HIS
REMOVAL TO CAESAREA (21:17–23:35)

Romans 15:31 carries a prayer request from Paul to the Roman Christians: "Pray that I may be rescued from the unbelievers in Judea, that my ministry to Jerusalem may be acceptable to the saints. . . ." In the following narrative both fears are addressed and, at least partly, answered in the affirmative. From 21:17–24:23, Luke narrates twelve days, highlighting the importance of Paul's arrest and interrogations in Luke's mind. Bruce likens it to Holy Week in the Gospels (Bruce, *Acts of the Apostles*, 444). Interestingly, Luke fails to mention the delivery of the collection (surely one of the main reasons for the trip). This is likely due to the arrest completely overshadowing the generosity of the Gentile churches (Schnabel 871). There is likely some tension among the Jewish brothers (see Bock 646). That it is alleviated through a show of solidarity demonstrates it was not at the point of complete division.

1. Paul's Visit with James and the Elders (21:17–26)

21:17 Γενομένων (gen. pl. masc. of aor. mid. ptc. of γίνομαι; gen. abs., temp.) introduces the arrival at (εἰς) Jerusalem. The response of the brothers is warm: ἀσμένως (adv., "gladly;" NT hapax) ἀπεδέξαντο (3rd pl. aor. mid. indic. of ἀποδέχομαι, "receive").

21:18 On τῇ δὲ ἐπιούσῃ, see 16:11. Εἰσῄει is the 3rd sg. impf. act. indic. of εἴσειμι, "enter"; it occurs three of four times in Acts, once in Heb 9:6. Σὺν ἡμῖν ("with us") indicates Luke's presence. The use of πρὸς Ἰάκωβον suggests James's importance (Barrett 2.1005). On τε, see 1:15. That they also included the presence (παρεγένοντο, 3rd pl. aor. mid. indic. of παραγίνομαι, "be present") of the elders (πρεσβύτεροι, subj. of vb.) suggests a formal meeting of a synagogue leadership (Barrett 2.1005). The lack of the Twelve suggests they are not in Jerusalem (Bruce, *Acts of the Apostles*, 444; Haenchen 608).

21:19 Ἀσπασάμενος is the nom. sg. masc. of aor. mid. ptc. of ἀσπάζομαι; temp. Ἐξηγεῖτο (3rd sg. impf. mid. indic. of ἐξηγέομαι, "tell, report, describe") is best tr. "he was relating in detail." Καθ' ἓν ἕκαστον is distributive, "one by one" (ZG 426). One would normally expect the rel. pron. ἅ instead of the gen. ὧν. One of two explanations is likely:

1. It is a headless rel. pron. that is a gen. of ref. (BHGNT 410), "regarding the things."
2. It is an attraction to an assumed τούτων in the previous clause, "each and every one 'of these things'" (BDAG 726c; Robertson, *Pictures,* 368; although see R 746). BDAG's list of parallels is suggestive of this opinion. Ἐποίησεν (3rd sg. aor. act. indic. of ποιέω) has θεός as the subj. Two prep. phrases finish the summary: ἐν τοῖς ἔθνεσιν ("among the Gentiles") and διὰ τῆς διακονίας αὐτοῦ ("through his ministry").

21:20 The response of the Jerusalem church does not suggest a hostile crowd. Ἀκούσαντες is the nom. pl. masc. of aor. act. ptc. of ἀκούω; subst. The vb. ἐδόξαζον (3rd pl. impf. act. indic. of δοξάζω) is perhaps ingressive, "they began praising" (Rogers and Rogers 288; NASB). BDF suggests a past action in progress with further qualification, "they praised God for some time and in various ways until they finally said . . ."

(BDF §327). Εἶπόν (3rd pl. aor. act. indic. of λέγω) introduces dir. speech. Θεωρεῖς is the 2nd sg. pres. act. indic. of θεωρέω. The cstr. πόσαι μυριάδες (nom. pl. masc. of μυριάς, -άδος, ἡ, "10,000"; but often simply an undefined large number; pred. nom. of an impers. εἰσίν, BHGNT 410) τῶν πεπιστευκότων (gen. pl. masc. of pf. act. ptc. of πιστεύω; subst., part. gen.) is best tr. "how many thousands . . . who have believed." Ἐν τοῖς Ἰουδαίοις modifies the ptc., "among the Jews." The last clause is a pred. adj. cstr. with πάντες as the subj., followed by the pred. adj. phrase ζηλωταὶ τοῦ νόμου (nom. pl. masc. of ζηλωτής, -ου, ὁ, "zealot"); with a gen. of ref., it is lit. "zealots for the law." Ὑπάρχουσιν (3rd pl. pres. act. indic. of ὑπάρχω) serves as the copulative vb.

21:21 Κατηχήθησαν is the 3rd pl. aor. pass. indic. of κατηχέω, "report, inform." Ὅτι introduces the content of the information. The cstr. of the clause is a double acc. (R 483; ZG 422). The first, ἀποστασίαν (acc. sg. fem. of ἀποστασία, -ας, ἡ, lit. "apostasy," better "abandonment" here), is fronted for emphasis. Διδάσκεις (2nd sg. pres. act. indic. of διδάσκω) is likely progressive, "you are teaching." The second acc. obj., τοὺς . . . Ἰουδαίους, is modified by a distributive prep. phrase, κατὰ τὰ ἔθνη πάντας, mng. "throughout all the nations," (see BDAG 511c; BHGNT 411). Λέγων introduces two specific charges that comprise the abandonment in indir. speech employing two negated infs. First, περιτέμνειν (pres. act. inf. of περιτέμνω, "circumcise") takes αὐτούς as the subj. and τέκνα as the obj.; in the second clause, τοῖς ἔθεσιν (dat. pl. neut. of ἔθος, -ου, τό, "in the customs") is locat. of sphere (R 522).

21:22 The phrase τί οὖν ἐστιν ("what, then, is it?") is often tr. "What shall we do?" (NIV, TNIV). However, given the proposal in v. 23, they don't seem to be asking for an opinion, so a rhetorical question is more likely, "What then is to be done?" (RSV, NASB, NRSV; cf. 1 Cor 14:15). Πάντως ἀκούσονται (3rd pl. fut. mid. indic. of ἀκούω) is "they will certainly hear." Ὅτι expresses the content of the hearing. Ἐλήλυθας is the 2nd sg. pf. act. indic. of ἔρχομαι.

21:23 The elders offer a proposal regarding four of their men. First, the men are introduced. Ποίησον is the 2nd sg. aor. act. impv. of ποιέω. A rel. pron. phrase (ὅ) functions as the dir. obj. Λέγομεν is the 1st pl. pres. act. indic. of λέγω. The proposal begins with an impers. εἰσίν (3rd pl. pres. indic. of εἰμί) in a pred. nom. cstr. followed by a dat. of association (ἡμῖν, "with us") then the pred. nom. Ἄνδρες τέσσαρες ("four men"). Εὐχήν (acc. sg. fem. of εὐχή, -ης, ἡ, "a vow") is the obj. of the ptc. ἔχοντες (nom. pl. masc. of pres. act. ptc. of ἔχω). The prep. phrase ἐφ᾽ ἑαυτῶν with the refl. pron. is best tr. "under a vow" (RSV, NASB, NRSV, NJB).

21:24 The statement of the actual proposal is complicated. It consists of the proposal with two impvs., a purp. clause with two vbs., the last modified by a rel. pron. phrase with two clauses itself. Τούτους (acc. pl. masc.) ref. to the men of the previous v. Παραλαβών (nom. sg. masc. of aor. act. ptc. of παραλαμβάνω; attend. circum.) has the impv. force of the first impv., ἁγνίσθητι (2nd sg. aor. pass. impv. of ἁγνίζω "be purified"; refl., most EVV "purify yourself"). The second impv. is δαπάνησον (2nd sg. aor. act. impv. of δαπανάω, "pay"). The purp. clause (ἵνα) uses two fut. indics. rather than the subjunc. to express something somewhere between purp. and result (Z §340; ZG 427; see also BDF §369[2]; R 984). Ξυρήσονται (3rd pl. fut. mid. indic. of ξυράω) is an intrans. mid., "they would shave" (i.e., complete a Nazirite vow; Bruce, *Acts of* *the Apostles*, 447). The art. in τὴν κεφαλήν is poss., and the sg. is distributive; most EVV, "their heads." Γνώσονται is the 3rd pl. fut. mid. indic. of γινώσκω. Ὅτι indicates the content of the knowledge. The rel. pron. ὧν (gen. pl. neut.) is a gen of ref. modifying κατήχηνται (3rd pl. pf. pass. indic. of κατηχέω), mng. "that of which they have been informed." Οὐδέν ἐστιν means "is nothing." In contrast (ἀλλά), Paul would demonstrate that he "walks orderly" (στοιχεῖς, 2nd sg. pres. act. indic. of στοιχέω): a Sem. idiom mng. "live uprightly" (ZG 427). The epex. ptc. φυλάσσων (nom. sg. masc. of pres. act. ptc. of φυλάσσω) explains it "guarding the law."

21:25 περὶ δέ means "now concerning . . ." (cf. 1 Cor 7:1, 25) with τῶν πεπιστευκότων ἐθνῶν (gen. pl. masc. of pf. act. ptc. of πιστεύω; attrib.) as the obj. of the prep. Ἡμεῖς is emphatic. Ἐπεστείλαμεν (1st pl. aor. act. indic. of ἐπιστέλλω, "write a letter") refers to the letter of Acts 15. "Saying" would have merely introduced the contents of the letter, but κρίναντες (nom. pl. masc. of aor. act. ptc. of κρίνω, temp., "judge") introduces the nature of the letter (a judgment) as well. Φυλάσσεσθαι (pres. mid. inf. of φυλάσσω) with a refl. αὐτούς and the dir. obj. τό . . . εἰδωλόθυτον means "to keep themselves from idolatry" (referring to idol feasts in pagan temples [Witherington 650]). For the rest of the list, see 15:29.

21:26 Paul does as requested (even the verbiage used is very sim.). Two temp. ptcs. set up Paul's entrance into the temple. Παραλαβών is the nom. sg. masc. of aor. act. ptc. of παραλαμβάνω, "take" (i.e., the men). Τῇ ἐχομένῃ (dat. sg. fem. of pres. mid. ptc. of ἔχω; attrib.) ἡμέρα (dat. of time) is a temp. expression mng. "on the next day." The second temp. ptc. (ἁγνισθείς, nom. sg. masc. of aor. pass. ptc. of ἁγνίζω, "purify") demonstrates Paul's participation in the ritual. Εἰσήει is the 3rd sg. impf. act. indic. of εἴσειμι, "enter." Διαγγέλλων (nom. masc. sg. of pres. act. ptc. of διαγγέλλω, "give notice of") is likely purp., i.e., intending to notify the priest in charge (Barrett 2.1015). Ἐκπλήρωσιν (acc. sg. fem. of ἐκπλήρωσις, -εως, ἡ, "completion") τῶν ἡμερῶν τοῦ ἁγνισμοῦ (gen. sg. masc. of ἁγνισμός, -οῦ, ὁ, "purification") is the content of the notification. Ἕως οὗ means "at which time" (BHGNT 414; BDAG 423b). Προσηνέχθη is the 3rd sg. aor. pass. indic. of προσφέρω, "offer." Ὑπὲρ ἑνὸς ἑκάστου ("for each one of them") indicates that each man had an individual offering (προσφορά, nom. sg. fem. of προσφορά, -ᾶς, ἡ; subj.).

2. Paul Arrested at the Temple (21:27–40)

21:27 Ὡς is temp., "when." Ἔμελλον (3rd pl. impf. act. indic. of μέλλω) takes ἑπτὰ ἡμέραι as the subj., and the compl. inf. συντελεῖσθαι (pres. pass. inf. of συντελέω), mng. "when the seven days were about to be completed." "Asian Jews" (οἱ ἀπὸ τῆς Ἀσίας [gen. sg. fem. of Ἀσια, -ας, ἡ, "Asia"] Ἰουδαῖοι) is fronted for some kind of emphasis, likely to distinguish from local Jews (esp. given the group's history). Θεασάμενοι (nom. pl. masc. of aor. mid. ptc. of θεάομαι) is temp., "having seen." Συνέχεον is the 3rd pl. impf. act. indic. of συγχέω, "stir up." Πάντα τὸν ὄχλον (masc. acc. sgs.) is the dir. obj., "the whole crowd." Ἐπέβαλον (3rd pl. aor. act. indic. of ἐπιβάλλω) . . . τὰς χεῖρας), lit. "they cast their hands," is best tr. "they seized" (NIV, TNIV, NET, NJB) or, more colloq., "they grabbed" (NLT). The "arrest" is a vigilante mob action.

21:28 Κράζοντες is the nom. pl. masc. of pres. act. ptc. of κράζω, "cry out"; attend. circum. On ἄνδρες Ἰσραηλῖται, see 1:15. βοηθεῖτε (2nd pl. pres. act. impv. of βοηθέω, "help") is as if some violence has happened (Robertson, *Pictures*, 376). Their charge is in the form of a pred. nom. cstr. with οὗτός ("this man") as the subj. and an art. pred. nom. (ὁ ἄνθρωπος), suggesting identification of a known entity. His identification is a complex attrib. ptc. phrase ὁ . . . διδάσκων (nom. sg. masc. of pres. act. ptc. of διδάσκω) is modified by a prep. phrase (κατά, "against") in an attrib. position with three gen. sg. masc. objs. (λαοῦ, νόμου, τόπου ["people," "law," and "this place"]) and an acc. obj. of the ptc. (πάντας πανταχῇ [adv.]) immediately following, mng. "everyone, everywhere" (ESV, NET). Ἔτι τε καί is an expression that builds on known facts and escalates it (BDAG 400b–c; BHGNT 415; ZG 427); "and has even . . ." (cf. NLT, NASB, ESV, NJB) or "more than that" (NRSV) is a good rendering. Ἕλληνας (acc. pl. masc. of Ἕλλην, -ηνος, ὁ, "Greek" [mng. Gentiles]), the dir. obj., is fronted for emphasis. Εἰσήγαγεν is the 3rd sg. aor. act. indic. of εἰσάγω, "bring." Κεκοίνωκεν (3rd sg. pf. act. indic. of κοινόω, "make common, impure, defile") in the pf. accents an enduring state. The defilement of the temple by bringing in Gentiles would have been an electrifying charge in the climate of the festival (Johnson 381). The charges, of course, are baseless.

21:29 The grounds (γάρ) for the accusation was an encounter previously in the city. Ἦσαν . . . προεωρακότες (nom. pl. masc. of pf. act. ptc. of προοράω, "see before"; periph. plpf., mng. "they had previously seen") refers to Trophimus, also from Asia. They had assumed (ἐνόμιζον, 3rd pl. impf. act. indic. of νομίζω, "suppose") Paul had brought (εἰσήγαγεν, 3rd sg. aor. act. indic. of εἰσάγω) him and others (given the pl. Ἕλληνας in v. 28) into the temple.

21:30 This event must have been a terrifying experience. Ἐκινήθη (3rd sg. aor. pass. indic. of κινέω) takes ἡ πόλις ὅλη, together mng. "the whole city was aroused." Ἐγένετο (3rd sg. aor. mid. indic. of γίνομαι) is impers. with συνδρομή (nom. sg. fem. of συνδρομή, -ῆς, ἡ, "running together"; see MM 604c, "a tumultuous concourse"; NT hapax) followed by a descriptive gen. λαοῦ. It expresses a mob of the inhabitants of Jerusalem forming and seizing (ἐπιλαβόμενοι, nom. pl. masc. of aor. mid. ptc. of ἐπιλαμβάνομαι, "take hold of") Paul. Εἷλκον is the 3rd pl. impf. act. indic. of ἕλκω, "drag." The doors were shut (ἐκλείσθησαν, 3rd pl. aor. pass. indic. of κλείω). A host of speculative reasons has been suggested: to prevent further contamination (Barrett 2.1021; Bruce, *Acts of the Apostles*, 450); to specifically protect from the stain of a murder (Robertson, *Pictures,* 379); to be a symbolic of rejection of Paul and his message (Bock 652; Johnson 382). What can be said is that it was probably done by the temple police as a common-sense act, given mob violence. The bigger point is that the Jews considered the place desecrated until the offender is dead (Witherington 656).

21:31 On τε, see 1:15. Ζητούντων (gen. masc. pl. of pres. act. ptc. of ζητέω; gen. abs., temp.) is compl. by ἀποκτεῖναι (aor. act. inf. of ἀποκτείνω, "kill"). Josephus (*J.W.* 5.244) notes the cohort was stationed during the festivals to guard against sedition. Ἀνέβη (3rd sg. aor. act. indic. of ἀναβαίνω) has φάσις (nom. sg. fem. of φάσις, -εως, ἡ, "a report, news") as the subj. The dat. indir. obj. χιλιάρχῳ (dat. sg. masc. of χιλίαρχος, -ου, ὁ) τῆς σπείρης (gen. sg. fem. of σπεῖρα, -ας, ἡ) is a specific Roman officer, "to the tribune of the cohort." Ὅτι introduces the content of the report. Συγχύννεται (3rd sg.

pres. pass. indic. of συγχέω) is often "in an uproar" (KJV, NLT, NIV, NRSV, TNIV) but "chaos" best keeps the relationship to the basic mng. of "confusion."

21:32 Ὅς refers to the tribune who is the unnamed subj. throughout the first clause. Παραλαβών (nom. sg. masc. of aor. act. ptc. of παραλαμβάνω, "take along"; attend. circum.) has compound acc. pl. masc. objs.: στρατιώτας (of στρατιώτης, -ου, ὁ) and ἑκατοντάρχας (of ἑκατοντάρχης, -ου, ὁ), "soldiers and centurions," suggesting at least 200 men [Bruce, *Acts of the Apostles*, 451]). Κατέδραμεν is the 3rd sg. aor. act. indic. of κατατρέχω, "run down" (i.e., from the fortress). Οἵ . . . ἰδόντες (nom. pl. masc. of aor. act. ptc. of ὁράω) is subst. The ptc. takes a compound obj., χιλίαρχον (acc. sg. masc. of χιλίαρχος, -ου, ὁ, "tribune") and στρατιώτας (acc. pl. masc. of στρατιώτης, -ου, ὁ, "soldier"). Ἐπαύσαντο (3rd pl. aor. mid. indic. of παύω, "stop"; intrans. mid.) is compl. by τύπτοντες (nom. pl. masc. of pres. act. ptc. of τύπτω, "beat"). Taken strictly, the subst. ptc. implies only those who saw the military approaching stopped beating Paul. However, the phrase is often tr. as temp. (cf., KJV, NIV, ESV). Culy and Parsons tr. as such and note that this option "may be preferable in English" (BHGNT 417).

21:33 Once the tribune arrived, he first placed Paul in custody. Ἐγγίσας is the nom. sg. masc. of aor. act. ptc. of ἐγγίζω; attend. circum. Ἐπελάβετο (3rd sg. aor. mid. indic. of ἐπιλαμβάνομαι) takes a gen. obj. αὐτοῦ, "he arrested him" (i.e., Paul). Ἐκέλευσεν (3rd sg. aor. act. indic. of κελεύω, "order"). The inf. (δεθῆναι, aor. pass. inf. of δέω, "bind") indicates indir. speech and is followed by a dat. of means, ἁλύσεσιν (dat. pl. fem. of ἅλυσις, -εως, ἡ) δυσίν, "by two chains." Ἐπυνθάνετο (3rd sg. impf. mid. indic. of πυνθάνομαι) is an ingressive impf., "he began asking" (NASB). The questions were τίς εἴη (3rd sg. pres. opt. of εἰμί), "Who might he be?" (an "oblique opt." in indir. speech, BDF §386[1]), and τί ἐστιν πεποιηκώς (nom. sg. masc. of pf. act. ptc. of ποιέω; periph. pf., emphasizing the stative aspect [KMP 342; BDF §352]), "What has he done?" The assumption is that Paul was some sort of wrongdoer.

21:34 On ἄλλοι δὲ ἄλλο τι, see 19:32. Ἐπεφώνουν (3rd pl. impf. act. indic. of ἐπιφωνέω) is a Lukan favorite, four times all in Luke-Acts, mng. "they were crying out." Ἐν τῷ ὄχλῳ is "among the crowd" and notes a disparate voice in the throng. The neg. gen. abs. phrase (δυναμένου [gen. sg. masc. of pres. mid. ptc. of δύναμαι] compl. by γνῶναι [aor. act. inf. of γινώσκω]) is highly unusual in that it is one of only five in the NT that does not change the subj. in the main clause. Three of five are said to be in Acts (here; 22:17; 28:6, BHGNT 418; though on 22:17 see below). Zerwick notes that the phenomenon occurs outside of the NT so merely to dismiss it as "clumsy" (BDF §423[4]) or an "abuse of the construction" (Barrett 2.1022) is unwarranted. Instead Zerwick proposes some sort of discord between clauses warrants the gen. abs. (§49). Levinson (178) suggests the discord between "experiencer" and "agent" is the reason for it. Τὸ ἀσφαλές (acc. sg. neut. of ἀσφαλής, -ες; obj. of the inf.) is best "for sure." The cause of the uncertainty is expressed with διὰ τὸν θόρυβον (acc. sg. masc. of θόρυβος, -ου, ὁ), mng. "because of the uproar." His order (ἐκέλευσεν, 3rd sg. aor. act. indic. of κελεύω) is expressed with the inf. ἄγεσθαι (aor. pass. inf. of ἄγω) with the destination of παρεμβολήν (acc. sg. fem. of παρεμβολή, -ῆς, ἡ, "barracks, fortress").

21:35 Ὅτε . . . ἐγένετο (3rd sg. aor. mid. indic. of γίνομαι) with the prep. phrase ἐπὶ τοὺς ἀναβαθμούς (acc. pl. masc. of ἀναβαθμός, -οῦ, ὁ) means "when he came to the flight of stairs" (i.e., the steps leading from the temple to the fortress). Συνέβη (3rd sg. aor. act. indic. of συμβαίνω, "come to pass"; NT hapax.) avoids a redundant ἐγένετο (Bruce, *Acts of the Apostles*, 452; Haenchen 617). The inf. phrase (βαστάζεσθαι, pres. pass. inf. of βαστάζω, "carry") is either the subj. of the vb. (BHGNT 418; R 392; 1043) or the obj. (BDF §393[5]), with no change of mng.

21:36 The conj. γάρ introduces the reason for the soldier's assist. Ἠκολούθει is the 3rd sg. impf. act. indic. of ἀκολουθέω. Κράζοντες (nom. sg. masc. of pres. act. ptc. of κράζω) introduces dir. speech. Schnabel (896) rightly notes that the crowd who could not speak with a unified voice finds it when they see Paul about to disappear. Αἶρε (2nd sg. pres. act. impv. of αἴρω) αὐτόν, lit. "take him away," is by force, in this case remove him by killing (BDAG 28d; BHGNT 419; Haenchen 617; ZG 428).

21:37 On τε, see 1:15. Μέλλων (nom. sg. masc. of pres. act. ptc. of μέλλω; temp.) is compl. by the inf. εἰσάγεσθαι (pres. pass. inf. of εἰσάγω), best tr. "as Paul was about to be dragged in." Λέγει and εἰ introduce a dir. question. Ἔξεστίν (3rd sg. pres. act. indic. of ἔξεστι) takes a dat. of ref. (μοι) and an inf. (εἰπεῖν), mng. "Is it permitted for me to speak . . . ?" Τι is the dir. obj., "something." The tribune's response (ἔφη, 3rd sg. aor. act. indic. of φημί) was surprise. Ἑλληνιστὶ γινώσκεις (2nd sg. pres. act. indic. of γινώσκω) is lit. "You know Greek?" (cf. NASB). It is not a request for a change of language.

21:38 The mng. of the opening phrase οὐκ ἄρα σὺ εἶ (2nd sg. pres. indic. of εἰμί) is debated. Is it a question or a conclusion drawn from the previous statement? Normally οὐκ expects an affirmative response and ἄρα is inferential (R 1177). If so, he is negating a previous supposition: "Then you are not . . ." (NASB, NRSV, NET, MIT). Αἰγύπτιος is the nom. masc. sg. of Αἰγύπτιος, -ία, -ιον, "Egyptian"; pred. nom. The Egyptian ref. is known to us from Josephus (*J.W.* 2.261–63). He was a false prophet suppressed by Felix (c. AD 54). The temp. phrase πρὸ τούτων τῶν ἡμερῶν ("before these days") is in the attrib. position to the attrib. ptcs. ἀναστατώσας (nom. sg. masc. of aor. act. ptc. of ἀναστατόω, "disturb, trouble, upset") and ἐξαγαγών (nom. sg. masc. of aor. act. ptc. of ἐξάγω): "who stirred up and led out." Τετρακισχιλίους (acc. pl. masc. of τετρακισχίλιοι, -ων, οἱ, "4,000"). Josephus has 30,000 men; most preferred Luke's account (see BASHH 127). Σικαρίων (gen. pl. masc. of σικάριος, -ου, ὁ; part. gen.) is lit. "dagger men." The word refers to assassins in wider usage. Here it is a group of vicious Jewish terrorists who had no problems using assassination to attain their goals (Witherington 662).

21:39 Paul's response is in a pred. nom. cstr. with ἄνθρωπος as the pred. nom. Μέν is solitarium (see 1:1). The phrase Ἰουδαῖος Ταρσεύς (nom. sg. masc. of Ταρσεύς, -έως, ὁ) . . . πολίτης (nom. sg. masc. of πολίτης, -ου, ὁ; nom. of appos.) is lit. "A Tarsean Jewish citizen." Τῆς Κιλικίας (gen. sg. fem. of Κιλικία, -ας, ἡ) identifies the region of the town. Οὐκ ἀσήμου (gen. sg. fem. of ἄσημος, -ον, "unimportant, insignificant") πόλεως (on litotes, see 14:28) is "not an insignificant city." Δέομαι (1st sg. pres. mid. indic. of δέομαι) with a gen. obj. (σου) is "I beg you" (RSV, NASB, NRSV, ESV) or simply "please" (NIV, TNIV, NET, NJB). Ἐπίτρεψόν (2nd sg. aor. act. impv. of ἐπιτρέπω) is compl. by λαλῆσαι (aor. act. inf. of λαλέω), mng. "allow me to speak."

21:40 Ἐπιτρέψαντος (gen. sg. masc. of aor. act. ptc. of ἐπιτρέπω) is a gen. abs. cstr. Ἑστώς (nom. sg. masc. of pf. act. ptc. of ἵστημι; attend. circum.) modified by the prep.

phrase ἐπὶ τῶν ἀναβαθμῶν (lit., "the ascending thing"; the previously mentioned staircase) is "he stood on the staircase." Κατέσεισεν (3rd sg. aor. act. indic. of κατασείω), followed by an instr. dat. τῇ χειρί, "he motioned with his hand." Πολλῆς . . . σιγῆς (gen. sg. fem. of σιγή, -ῆς, ἡ), "much silence," is either the subj. or the pred. in a gen. abs. cstr. with γενομένης (gen. sg. fem. of aor. mid. ptc. of γίνομαι; temp.), mng. "when a great hush came about" (cf. CSB). Προσεφώνησεν (3rd sg. aor. act. indic. of προσφωνέω) is modified with an instr. dat. phrase τῇ Ἑβραΐδι διαλέκτῳ (fem. dat. sgs. of Ἑβραΐς, -ΐδος, ἡ, "Hebrew," and διάλεκτος, -ου, ἡ, "language"). Most assume the specific language was Aramaic (cf. Johnson 384). However, the phrase may refer to Heb., although the former is more likely (Witherington 664). It is best tr. "he called out in the Hebrew language" ("Aramaic," NIV, NLT, CSB). Λέγων (nom. sg. masc. of pres. act. ptc. of λέγω) introduces the speech to follow.

HOMILETICAL SUGGESTIONS

When Things Go Wrong (21:17–40)

1. Good intentions: a show of solidarity (vv. 17–26)
2. Bad intentions: a show of violence (vv. 27–36)
3. God's intentions: a stage for the gospel (vv. 37–40)

3. Paul's Defense (22:1–29)

22:1 On Ἄνδρες ἀδελφοί, see 1:16; here Paul adds πατέρες. Ἀκούσατέ is the 2nd pl. aor. act. impv. of ἀκούω. Μου modifies the gen. obj. of the vb. ἀπολογίας (gen. sg. fem. of ἀπολογία, -ης, ἡ), "my defense." Πρὸς ὑμᾶς νυνί is in the attrib. position.

22:2 Ἀκούσαντες is the nom. pl. masc. of aor. act. ptc. of ἀκούω, temp. Ὅτι introduces indir. speech. Ἑβραΐδι διαλέκτῳ (see 21:40) is "the Hebrew/Aramaic language." Προσεφώνει is the 3rd sg. impf. indic. act. of προσφωνέω, "address." This v. virtually transposes the previous v., taking the dat. of people addressed (αὐτοῖς). The comp. adj. μᾶλλον with παρέσχον (3rd pl. aor. act. indic. of παρέχω) with the acc. obj. ἡσυχίαν (acc. sg. fem. of ἡσυχία, -ας, ἡ) means "they quieted down all the more" (cf. BDAG 440d). Φησίν (3rd pl. pres. act. indic. of φημί) resumes Paul's speech.

22:3 Paul first introduces himself with a pred. nom. cstr.: ἐγώ as the subj. with ἀνὴρ Ἰουδαῖος (Jewish man) as the pred. nom. It is followed by a series of attrib. ptcs. modifying ἀνήρ. Γεγεννημένος (nom. sg. masc. of pf. pass. ptc. of γεννάω) identifies his birthplace as ἐν Ταρσῷ (dat. sg. fem. of Ταρσός, -οῦ, ἡ; obj. of prep., mng. "in Tarsus"). Ἀνατεθραμμένος is the nom. sg. masc. of pf. pass. ptc. of ἀνατρέφω, "nurture." The use of δέ makes "in this city" (ἐν τῇ πόλει ταύτῃ) likely Jerusalem (BHGNT 423). The prep. phrase παρὰ τοὺς πόδας Γαμαλιήλ ("at the feet of Gamaliel") is fronted for emphasis. Πεπαιδευμένος (nom. sg. masc. of pf. pass. ptc. of παιδεύω) with the prep. phrase κατὰ ἀκρίβειαν (acc. sg. fem. of ἀκρίβεια, -ας, ἡ, "exactness, precision") τοῦ πατρῴου νόμου is "according to the strictness of the law of our forefathers" (ZG 429). Ὑπάρχων (nom. sg. masc. of pres. act. indic. of ὑπάρχω) is the last of the ptcs., taking a pred. nom. ζηλωτὴς with a gen. of ref. θεοῦ, "being zealous for God." He affirms the crowd's zeal as a parenthetical comment.

22:4 The rel. pron. ὅς has ἀνήρ in the previous v. as the antecedent. Ταύτην τὴν ὁδόν ("this way") ref. to Christianity (see 9:2). Ἐδίωξα (1st sg. aor. act. indic. of διώκω) is modified by ἄχρι θανάτου (lit. "until death"). Some consider it hyperbole (Haenchen [625] has it generalizing a single case [i.e., Stephen]). Barrett (2:1036) notes a synagogue beating could kill, but it seems more is in mind (see 26:10; cf. 9:1, 1 Tim 1:15; Bruce, *Acts of the Apostles*, 455; Keener 3.3225). It is followed by two ptcs. of manner, δεσμεύων (nom. sg. masc. of pres. act. ptc. of δεσμεύω) and παραδιδούς (nom. sg. masc. of pres. act. ptc. παραδίδωμι) "by binding and handing over." The τε . . . καί cstr., "both men and women," demonstrates the extent of his zeal.

22:5 Paul points to those who appointed him for corroboration. Μαρτυρεῖ (3rd sg. fut. act. indic. of μαρτυρέω) takes ἀρχιερεύς ("high priest") as the subj. Μοι is a dat. of advantage. Typical of Paul's epistolary style, the next clause has an elided vb. instead of repeating the previous, taking πᾶν τὸ πρεσβυτέριον (mng. "the whole body of elders") as the subj. The prep. phrase (παρ' ὧν) changes the Sanhedrin from witness to agent. Δεξάμενος is the nom. sg. masc. of aor. mid. ptc. of δέχομαι; attend. circum. Ἐπορευόμην is the 1st sg. impf. mid. indic. of πορεύομαι. Ἄξων (nom. sg. masc. of fut. act. ptc. of ἄγω; purp.); most EVV tr. it "to bring." Given the context, however, the lit. "drag" is warranted. Ὄντας (acc. pl. masc. of pres. ptc. of εἰμί, subst., obj. of ptc.) with ἐκεῖσε (in Koinē a virtual synonym for ἐκεῖ, BDF §103; Barrett 2.1037) in the attrib. position means "those living there." Δεδεμένους is the acc. pl. masc. of pf. pass. ptc. of δέω. The purp. is expressed in a ἵνα clause with τιμωρηθῶσιν (3rd pl. aor. pass. subjunc. of τιμωρέω), "so they may be punished."

22:6 On ἐγένετο δέ, see 4:5. It will ultimately take the inf. περιαστράψαι (see below) to complete the cstr. With μοι (dat. of advantage), the phrase begins, "Now it happened to me." The pron. is modified by two dat. sg. masc. pres. ptcs. that are tr. temp. by most EVV, "as I was going (πορευομένῳ, mid. of πορεύομαι) and drawing near (ἐγγίζοντι, act. of ἐγγίζω) to Damascus." Περὶ μεσημβρίαν (acc. sg. fem. of μεσημβρία, -ας, ἡ) expresses the time as an approximation, best tr. "about noon" (cf. CSB, ESV, NLT). Ἐξαίφνης is an adv. mng. "suddenly" (five times in NT, four in Luke-Acts). Περιαστράψαι is the aor. act. inf. of περιαστράπτω, "shine around." Φῶς ἱκανόν is the subj. of the inf., lit. "a great light." Since the adj. ἱκανός, -ή, -όν refers to large in extent, "intense" or "very bright" (NLT, NET) seems better than a mere "great" (RSV) describing the light.

22:7 On τε, see 1:15. Ἔπεσά is the 1st sg. aor. act. indic. of πίπτω. Ἔδαφος is the acc. sg. neut. of ἔδαφος, -ους, τό, "surface, ground" (obj. of prep., NT hapax; see cognate at Luke 19:44). Ἤκουσα (1st sg. aor. act. indic. of ἀκούω) takes the gen. sg. fem. obj. φωνῆς. Λεγούσης (gen. sg. fem. of pres. act. ptc. of λέγω) introduces dir. speech. On the contents, see 9:4.

22:8 Paul's recount is virtually identical to 9:5, except certain transpositions to the 1st sg. For example, Ἀπεκρίθην (1st sg. aor. pass. indic. of ἀποκρίνομαι) replaces εἶπεν in 9:5. Paul adds εἶπέν πρός με in setting up Jesus's response (assumed at 9:5). Jesus is also identified as Ναζωραῖος (nom. sg. masc. of Ναζωραῖος, -ου, ὁ), "the Nazorean" (see 2:22). For more specifics, see 9:5.

22:9 Paul described the phenomenon with a μὲν . . . δέ cstr. Ὄντες (nom. pl. masc. of pres. ptc. of εἰμί; subst.) is the subj. of the vb. ἐθεάσαντο (3rd pl. aor. mid. indic. of θεάομαι). In contrast (δέ), they did not hear (ἤκουσαν, 3rd pl. aor. act. indic. of ἀκούω) the speaker (λαλοῦντός, gen. sg. masc. of pres. act. ptc. of λαλέω; subst.). On the apparent discrepancy, see 9:4.

22:10 Paul's request for directions is not recorded in ch. 9. The clause τί ποιήσω (1st sg. aor. act. subjunc. of ποιέω) is a delib. subjunc., mng. "What should I do?" Ἀναστάς (nom. sg. masc. of aor. act. ptc. of ἀνίστημι; attend. circum.) takes on an impv. force, "arise." Πορεύου is the 2nd sg. pres. mid. impv. of πορεύομαι, "go." Κἀκεῖ is a crasis of καὶ ἐκεῖ, "and there." Σοι is the indir. obj. of the following vb., fronted for emphasis. Λαληθήσεται (3rd sg. fut. pass. indic. of λαλέω) is impers., "it will be told." The rel. pron. ὧν is gen. by attraction to the previous πάντων (one would expect ἅ as the obj. of the following vb. [R 717]). Τέτακταί (3rd sg. pf. pass. indic. of τάσσω) takes a dat. obj. (σοι), "it is appointed for you." Ποιῆσαι is the aor. act. inf. of ποιέω; indir. speech.

22:11 The parallels here to 2 Cor 4:6 are significant (Johnson 389). Ὡς is normally a temp. adv. in this position in Acts (BHGNT 427), although, in context, causal is possible ("since," Schnabel 904; NASB, NRSV, NET, MIT, NJB). The neg. vb. ἐνέβλεπον (1st sg. impf. act. indic. of ἐμβλέπω, "look at, gaze") is modified by a causal ἀπό that takes a long noun phrase as the obj. (τῆς δόξης τοῦ φωτὸς ἐκείνου, "from the glory of that light"). Χειραγωγούμενος (nom. sg. masc. of pres. pass. ptc. of χειραγωγέω) is instr. of means, "being led by the hands." The prep. of agency (ὑπό) takes the ptc. phrase τῶν συνόντων (gen. pl. masc. of pres. act. ptc. of σύνειμι; subst.) μοι (poss. dat.), mng. "by my companions."

22:12–13 In 9:10 Ananias is simply called μαθητής. Paul portrays him in terms that would appeal to pious Jews, giving us more information about the man (Bruce, *Acts of the Apostles*, 457; Johnson 389). V. 12 is a lengthy subj. phrase to the finite vb. in v. 13. Ἀνανίας . . . τις ("a certain Ananias") is followed by a series of phrases modifying the lead noun. He is first described by an appos. nom. phrase ἀνὴρ εὐλαβής (nom. sg. masc. of εὐλαβής, -ές) mng. "a devout man." Κατὰ τὸν νόμον ("according to the law") provides the standards for the assessment. Paul then cites his reputation (μαρτυρούμενος, nom. sg. masc. of pres. pass. ptc. of μαρτυρέω; attrib., here with the sense "being well respected") and those making the assessments through a prep. phrase, ὑπὸ πάντων τῶν κατοικούντων (gen. pl. masc. of pres. act. ptc. of κατοικέω; attrib.) Ἰουδαίων ("by all the Jews living there").

Still waiting on the main vb., two attend. circum. ptcs. narrate the approach to Paul. Ἐλθών (nom. sg. masc. of aor. act. ptc. of ἔρχομαι; modified by πρός με) and ἐπιστάς (nom. sg. masc. of aor. act. ptc. of ἐφίστημι) is lit. "having come to me and standing at [me]." The finite vb. of the sentence, εἶπέν (3rd sg. aor. act. indic. of λέγω), introduces dir. speech. Ἀνάβλεψον is the 2nd sg. aor. act. impv. of ἀναβλέπω, "receive sight." Κἀγώ is a crasis of καὶ ἐγώ. The phrase αὐτῇ τῇ ὥρᾳ (fem. dat. sgs., dat. of time) employs the identifying use of αὐτός, with the sense, "at that very hour." Ἀνέβλεψα (1st sg. aor. act. indic. of ἀναβλέπω) is a play on semantic domains of ἀναβλέπω ("regain sight/look up"). It must mean "I looked up," for it is modified by the prep. phrase εἰς αὐτόν (BHGNT 428; Robertson, *Pictures,* 391; ZG 430).

22:14 Εἶπεν (3rd sg. aor. act. indic. of λέγω) introduces dir. speech. The subj. of the vb. is the phrase θεὸς πατέρων ἡμῶν (i.e., not some innovation). Προεχειρίσατό (3rd sg. aor. mid. indic. of προχειρίζομαι, "appoint") takes σε as dir. obj. and three purp. infs. First, γνῶναι (aor. act. inf. of γινώσκω) with θέλημα as an obj., "his will"; second, ἰδεῖν (aor. act. inf. of ὁράω) with δίκαιον (subst., "the righteous one"); and, finally, ἀκοῦσαι (aor. act. inf. of ἀκούω) with φωνήν as an obj. The prep. phrase ἐκ τοῦ στόματος αὐτου describes an unmediated relationship with God.

22:15 Ὅτι is causal. Ἔσῃ (2nd sg. fut. mid. indic. of εἰμί) introduces a pred. nom. cstr. with μάρτυς as the pred. nom. Αὐτῷ is a dat. of advantage. Paul (prudently) does not specifically mention Gentiles (cf. v. 22; Barrett 2.1042). He does note his witness was to be πρὸς πάντας ἀνθρώπους ("to all men"). Ὧν (gen. pl. neut. rel. pron.) most likely is a gen. of ref., "about the things which." Ἑώρακας (2nd sg. pf. act. indic. of ὁράω) in the pf. in contrast to the aor. ἤκουσας (2nd sg. aor. act. indic. of ἀκούω) suggests a continuing effect on Paul from what he saw (BDF §342[2]).

22:16 Τί μέλλεις means, "Why are you delaying?" (a rare instance of the abs. use of μέλλω, BDAG 628c). Ἀναστάς (nom. sg. masc. of aor. act. ptc. of ἀνίστημι; attend. circum.) has an impv. sense, "arise." Βάπτισαι (2nd sg. aor. mid. impv. of βαπτίζω) and ἀπόλουσαι (2nd sg. aor. mid. impv. of ἀπολούω) are both permissive mids. (KMP 195; Wallace 427; Z §232; cf. 1 Cor 6:11). A refl. causative idea is "consent to baptism" and "let God wash away your sins." Thus, the consent (i.e., receiving the gospel), not the act of baptism, washes away sin. What is more, the aor. ptc. of means, ἐπικαλεσάμενος (nom. sg. masc. of aor. mid. ptc. of ἐπικαλέω; "by calling . . ." [NLT, MIT]), points to an action prior to the baptism/washing. The ptc. with the dir. obj. phrase, τὸ ὄνομα αὐτοῦ, echoes Peter's evangelistic appeal at Pentecost (cf. 2:21, 38).

22:17–18 On ἐγένετο δέ μοι, see 4:5; 22:6. It will take two infs. after temp. expressions regarding Paul. The first temp. expression employs the ptc. ὑποστρέψαντι (dat. sg. masc. of aor. act. ptc. of ὑποστρέφω; temp.), mng. "after I returned to Jerusalem." The second temp. expression is a gen. abs. (because the subj. is no longer Paul but a trance). Προσευχομένου is the gen. sg. masc. of pres. mid. ptc. of προσεύχομαι; temp. mng. (with the prep. phrase) "while I was praying in the temple." The first inf. is γενέσθαι (aor. mid. inf. of γίνομαι) with με as the subj. with ἐκστάσει (dat. sg. fem. of ἔκστασις, -εως, ἡ; obj. of prep.), mng. "I fell into a trance."

The second inf. is in v. 18. Ἰδεῖν (aor. act. inf. of ὁράω) takes αὐτόν as the subj. (presumably Christ; see ἐμοῦ at the end of the v.). Λέγοντά (acc. sg. masc. of pres. act. ptc. of λέγω) introduces dir. speech. It is a compound impv. clause. The first impv. is σπεῦσον (2nd sg. aor. act. impv. of σπεύδω, "hurry"). The second, ἔξελθε (2nd sg. aor. act. impv. of ἐξέρχομαι), is modified by two prep. phrases, ἐν τάχει and ἐξ Ἰερουσαλήμ, mng. "get quickly out of Jerusalem." The grounds for the command is their rejection of Paul's message about Christ. Παραδέξονταί is the 3rd pl. fut. mid. indic. of παραδέχομαι, "accept."

22:19 On κἀγώ, see 22:13. Εἶπον (1st sg. aor. act. indic. of λέγω) introduces Paul's response with dir. speech. He likely objects because he considered himself the very man to win his people (Bruce, *Acts of the Apostles*, 459; Keeener 3:3238; Schnabel 907; cf. Rom 9:1–3; 10:1). Rhetorically, it is included to appeal to his present hearers (Haenchen 627). Αὐτοί is emphatic. Ἐπίστανται is the 3rd pl. pres. mid. indic. of ἐπίσταμαι, "know." Ὅτι introduces the content. Ἐγὼ ἤμην (1st sg. impf. indic. of εἰμί) is emphatic, the first part of a compound periph. impf. cstr. Φυλακίζων is the nom. sg. masc. of pres. act. ptc. of φυλακίζω, "imprison." Δέρων is the nom. sg. masc. of pres. act. ptc. of δέρω, "beat." Κατά τὰς συναγωγάς is pl. distributive, mng. "in every synagogue" (KJV, RSV, NLT, NRSV), "synagogue after synagogue" (CSB), or, best, "one synagogue after another" (NASB, ESV). Πιστεύοντας is the acc. pl. masc. of pres. act. ptc. of πιστεύω; subst. obj. of previous ptcs.; "those who believe."

22:20 Paul continues. Ἐξεχύννετο (3rd sg. impf. pass. indic. of ἐκχέω) τὸ αἷμα is lit. "the blood was shed," referring to Stephen's death. Μάρτυρός (gen. of appos. to Στεφάνου), is best "witness" (CSB, RSV, NASB, NRSV, ESV, NET, NJB). "Martyr" (KJV, NIV, TNIV) is anachronistic. Αὐτός is the intensive use of the pron. ("I myself," NRSV, ESV, NET). It is the subj. of a compound periph. impf. Ἐφεστώς (nom. sg. masc. of pf. act. ptc. of ἐφίστημι, "stand") never occurs in the pres. ptc. form, suggesting, in function, it serves as a periph. impf. like the following pres. ptc. (BHGNT 432). Συνευδοκῶν is the nom. sg. masc. of pres. act. ptc. of συνευδοκέω, "approve (heartily)." Φυλάσσων is the nom. sg. masc. of pres. act. ptc. of φυλάσσω (with ἱμάτια as the obj.). Ἀναιρούντων is the gen. pl. masc. of pres. act. ptc. of ἀναιρέω; subst. gen. of poss., mng. "of the ones killing him."

22:21 Christ responded simply. Πορεύου is the 2nd sg. pres. mid. impv. of πορεύομαι, "go." Ὅτι is causal. Ἐγώ is emphatic. Ἐθνη μακράν, "distant nations," is the destination of ἐξαποστελῶ (1st. sg. fut. act. indic. of ἐξαποστέλλω, "send").

22:22 At the first mention of a friendly disposition toward Gentiles, the crowd cut Paul off. Ἤκουον (3rd pl. impf. indic. act. of ἀκούω) ἄχρι τούτου τοῦ λόγου is best "up to this word" (ESV). Ἐπῆραν (3rd pl. aor. act. indic. of ἐπαίρω) with φωνήν is "they raised their voice." Λέγοντες (nom. pl. masc. of pres. act. ptc. of λέγω) introduces dir. speech. Αἶρε (2nd sg. pres. act. impv. of αἴρω) ἀπὸ τῆς γῆς, "away . . . from the earth," is a demand for execution (cf. CSB "Wipe . . . off the face of the earth," see Luke 23:18). The grounds (γάρ) is the neg. καθῆκεν (3rd sg. impf. act. indic. of καθήκω [only at Rom 1:28 elsewhere]), compl. by ζῆν (pres. act. inf. of ζάω), mng. "he is not fit to live." The impf. suggesting what "ought to be" is consistent with CGk. (ZG 432; Z §319). It is possible that the crowd leapt to the conclusion that his mission to the Gentiles confirmed the likelihood that Trophimus had been brought into the temple. However, the response is similar to the crowd that was offended when Jesus mentioned that God's work included Gentiles in Luke 4:24–29 (Johnson 391). Thus, we cannot say for certain why the statement provoked such a response.

22:23–24 The response of the tribune is prefaced by a compound gen. abs. temp. phrase. The crowd was crying out (κραυγαζόντων, gen. pl. masc. of pres. act. ptc. of κραυγάζω); ripping (ῥιπτούντων, gen. pl. masc. of pres. act. ptc. of ῥίπτω) their cloaks; and casting (βαλλόντων, gen. pl. masc. of pres. act. ptc. of βάλλω) dust into the air. The

actions are clearly a rejection of Paul and his message. But the precise mng. of the
actions beyond shouting is unclear.

1. Witherington, citing Chrysostom, suggests "shaking off their cloaks" (tr.
   ῥίπτω). This would be similar to shaking the dust off one's feet. Flinging dust
   in the air would be symbolic of casting stones (Witherington 675; see also
   Schnabel 923, who tr. the vb. as "taking off," also suggesting preparation for
   some action; perhaps something like the stoning of Stephen).
2. Johnson suggests the cloaks were torn as a traditional display of indignation.
   Throwing dust is reminiscent of Acts 13:51 (Johnson 391).
3. Barrett suggests that ῥίπτω is casting off their cloaks and that casting the dust
   is a straightforward description. The upshot is that Luke describes a frenzied
   crowd gesturing in less-than-premeditated actions (Barrett 2.1046). The picture is meant to be chaotic furor over Paul.

In the face of such a frenzy, the tribune responded quickly. Ἐκέλευσεν is the 3rd sg.
aor. act. indic. of κελεύω, "order." The content is given by indir. speech with εἰσάγεσθαι
(pres. pass. inf. of εἰσάγω, "bring into" the fortress.) Εἴπας is the nom. sg. masc. of aor.
act. ptc. of λέγω; attend. circum. Μάστιξιν is the dat. sg. fem. of μάστιξ; dat. of means;
"by a whip" (likely fronted for emphasis). Ἀνετάζεσθαι (pres. pass. inf. of ἀνετάζω) is
indir. speech mng. "to judicially examine" (often by torture, ZG 432). Ἵνα expresses
the purp. of the examination, to get the facts. Ἐπιγνῷ is the 3rd sg. aor. act. subjunc. of
ἐπιγινώσκω. Δι᾽ ἣν αἰτίαν is lit. "because of which reason"; best tr. "to find out why"
(ESV). Ἐπεφώνουν (3rd pl. impf. act. indic. of ἐπιφωνέω) with the dat. of ref. αὐτῷ is
"they were shouting at him."

22:25 Ὡς is temp., "when." Προέτειναν (3rd pl. aor. act. indic. of προτείνω; NT hapax)
with αὐτόν is "they stretched him out," preparing Paul to be whipped. Ἱμᾶσιν (dat. pl.
masc. of ἱμάς, -άντος, ὁ) is either:

1. Purp., mng. "for the whips" or "lash" (cf. NLT, NIV, ESV, TNIV, NET, CSB;
   Barrett 2.1048)
2. Or it is instr. of means, "with thongs/straps" (cf. KJV, RSV, NASB, NRSV,
   NJB; BHGNT 434; Bock 664).

The tribune left, and the attending centurion (τὸν ἑστῶτα [acc. sg. masc. of pf. pass.
ptc. of ἵστημι; attrib.] ἑκατόνταρχον) was the ranking officer. Εἰ introduces a dir. question (see Z §401). The fronted dir. obj., ἄνθρωπον, is modified by two adjs., Ῥωμαῖον
(acc. sg. masc. of Ῥωμαῖος, -α, -ον, "Roman," i.e., a citizen) and ἀκατάκριτον (acc. sg.
masc. of ἀκατάκριτος, -ον, "uncondemned," i.e., without due process). Ἔξεστιν (3rd
sg. pres. act. indic. of ἔξεστι) as a question is "Is it lawful?" It takes a dat. of ref. (ὑμῖν)
and a compl. inf. (μαστίζειν, pres. act. inf. of μαστίζω, "flog"). The force of Paul's
query is to question the legality of the beating. He, however, poses it as a question to
demonstrate respect for the authority of the military (at least their power over him at
the moment). It is strategically wise, producing a "polite" shiver.

22:26 Hearing (ἀκούσας, nom. sg. masc. of aor. act. ptc. of ἀκούω; temp.) Paul, the
centurion rushes to (προσελθών, nom. sg. masc. of aor. act. ptc. of προσέρχομαι; attend.
circum.) the tribune (χιλιάρχῳ, dat. sg. masc. of χιλίαρχος, -ου, ὁ). Ἀπήγγειλεν is the 3rd

sg. aor. act. indic. of ἀπαγγέλλω. Λέγων (nom. sg. masc. of pres. act. ptc. of λέγω) introduces dir. speech. Τί μέλλεις (2nd sg. pres. act. indic. of μέλλω) with the compl. inf. ποιεῖν (pres. act. inf. of ποιέω) is lit. "What are you about to do?" It should be tr. avoiding a Western accusatory idiom (BHGNT 435). Given the γάρ in the next clause disclosing his Roman citizenship, "What are you going to do?" seems best (NIV, TNIV).

22:27 The tribune (χιλίαρχος, nom. sg. masc. of χιλίαρχος, -ου, ὁ) approached (προσελθών; see v. 26) Paul for his own interrogation of the prisoner. Λέγε is the 2nd sg. pres. act. impv. of λέγω. The question is a pred. nom. cstr. with εἶ (2nd sg. pres. indic. of εἰμί): "Are you a Roman?" Paul's answer (ἔφη, 3rd sg. aor. act. indic. of φημί) is the affirmative particle, ναί ("yes").

22:28 The tribune's (see above) reply (ἀπεκρίθη, 3rd sg. aor. pass. indic. of ἀποκρίνομαι) is in light of the offense he has already committed by nearly flogging a citizen. Purchasing a citizenship (as the tribune had) is a lesser status. So, the tribune probes with his own status (at the time, auxiliary soldiers were rarely citizens until discharge, Keener 3.3254). Ἐγώ is somewhat emphatic and implies a contrast with Paul. Πολλοῦ κεφαλαίου (gen. sg. neut. of κεφάλαιον, -ου, τό; gen. of price) with the vb. ἐκτησάμην (1st sg. aor. act. indic. of κτάομαι) is best "I acquired . . . with a large sum of money." At the time, or shortly before, Claudius was in the practice of selling citizenship (Keener 3.3253). Paul's status, however, was not so mercantile. Ἐγώ is also emphatic and in contrast. Δὲ καί likely emphasizes the vb. (Barrett 2.1050; cf. 1 Cor 15:15) γεγέννημαι (1st sg. pf. pass. indic. of γεννάω) mng. "I was actually born a Roman citizen" (Haenchen 634; NASB).

22:29 The effect is dramatic; without an order from the tribune, the interrogators back off (ἀπέστησαν, 3rd pl. aor. act. indic. of ἀφίστημι, "withdrew"). The subj. uses a subst. ptc. phrase οἱ μέλλοντες (nom. masc. pl. of pres. act. ptc. of μέλλω) with the compl. inf. ἀνετάζειν (pres. act. inf. of ἀνετάζω), lit. "those who were going to examine him," but the mng. is "to flog him." They apparently wanted to distance themselves in every way from what they were about to do. The tribune was fearful as well (ἐφοβήθη, 3rd sg. aor. pass. indic. of φοβέω). Ἐπιγνούς (nom. sg. masc. of aor. act. ptc. of ἐπιγινώσκω) is causal, "because he recognized." The content that drove the fear is expressed in two ὅτι clauses. The first is in a pred. nom. cstr. with ἐστίν, "He is a Roman" (Ῥωμαῖός, nom. sg. masc. of Ῥωμαῖος, -α, -ον; subst. adj.). The second is a periph. plpf. and identifies the tribune's infraction, ἦν δεδεκώς (nom. sg. masc. of pf. act. ptc. of δέω), with the obj. αὐτόν, mng. "he had bound him."

HOMILETICAL SUGGESTIONS

Sharing Your Testimony with Your Countrymen (22:1–29)

1. Tell God's actions (vv. 1–21)
   a. Like them, Paul was zealous for God (vv. 1–5)
   b. Jesus interrupted his journey (vv. 6–16)
   c. Jesus sent him on a new journey (vv. 17–21)
2. Trust the results to God (protection here, but not always promised) (vv. 22–29)

FOR FURTHER STUDY

31. Paul's Forensic Speeches (22–26)

Cadbury, H. J. "The Speeches in Acts." In *Beginnings* 5, 402–27.

Neyrey, J. "The Forensic Defense Speech and Paul's Trial Speeches in Acts 22–26: Form and Function." In *Luke-Acts: New Perspectives from the Society of Biblical Literature Seminar.* Edited by C. H. Talbert, 210–24. New York: Crossroad, 1984.

Winter, B. W. "The Importance of the *Captatio Benevolentiae* in the Speeches of Tertullus and Paul in Acts 24:1–21." *JTS* 42 (October 1991): 505–31.

———. "Official Proceedings and the Forensic Speeches in Acts 24–26." In BAFCS 1, 305–36.

Witherup, R. D. "Functional Redundancy in the Acts of the Apostles: A Case Study." *JSNT* 48 (1992): 67–86.

4. Paul before the Sanhedrin (22:30–23:11)

22:30 On τῇ δὲ ἐπαύριον, see 10:9. Βουλόμενος (nom. sg. masc. of pres. mid. ptc. of βούλομαι) takes the compl. inf. γνῶναι (aor. act. inf. of γινώσκω); with the obj. ἀσφαλές (acc. sg. neut. of ἀσφαλής, -ές), it is a causal phrase, "because he wanted to know the certainty." The art. τό (acc. sg. neut.) is an acc. of ref., nominalizing the following phrase as an appos. to ἀσφαλές mng. "regarding why (τί) he was accused (κατηγορεῖται, 3rd sg. pres. pass. indic. of κατηγορέω) by the Jews." The tribune then took three actions to set up an official inquiry. He released (ἔλυσεν, 3rd sg. aor. act. indic. of λύω) Paul. He ordered (ἐκέλευσεν, 3rd sg. aor. act. indic. of κελεύω) the chief priests and Sanhedrin to convene (συνελθεῖν, aor. act. inf. of συνέρχομαι, "gather"; compl.). Finally, he brought Paul forward (καταγαγών, nom. sg. masc. of aor. act. ptc. of κατάγω, "bring down"; attend. circum.) and stood him (ἔστησεν, 3rd sg. aor. act. indic. of ἵστημι) before them.

23:1 Ἀτενίσας (nom. sg. masc. of aor. act. ptc. of ἀτενίζω, "gaze intently"; attend. circum.) suggests Paul "sized up" his audience (Witherington 687). Συνεδρίῳ (dat. sg. neut. of συνέδριον, - ου, τό, "Sanhedrin") indicates destination. On ἄνδρες ἀδελφοί, see 1:11, 16. Ἐγώ is emphatic. The dat. phrase πάσῃ συνειδήσει ἀγαθῇ is a dat. of manner. Πεπολίτευμαι (1st sg. pf. mid. indic. of πολιτεύομαι) is used in a religious sense (τῷ θεῷ) regarding the proper course of life (Haenchen 637). "Citizenship" is likely a remote echo to the word (Barrett 2.1058; although see Witherington 687). The prep. phrase ἄχρι ταύτης τῆς ἡμέρας ("until this day") included his present Christianity (Barrett 2.1058).

23:2 The response to this opening statement was abrupt and violent—this time not from an unruly mob, but the highest source, the high priest Ananias. Ἐπέταξεν (3rd sg. aor. act. indic. of ἐπιτάσσω, "order") takes a dat. obj. παρεστῶσιν (dat. pl. masc. of pf. act. ptc. of παρίστημι; subst., with the dat. αὐτῷ, mng. "those standing by him") and an inf. of indir. speech (τύπτειν, pres. act. inf. of τύπτω, "strike"). That the obj. of the inf. is Paul's mouth is an insult (Keener 3.3271).

23:3 Paul's response was not as measured as his opening statement. He fired back verbally, in kind, employing τύπτειν (pres. act. inf. of τύπτω) as a compl. inf. to μέλλει (3rd sg. pres. act. indic. of μέλλω) and θεός as the subj., mng. "God is going to strike you." Bruce notes nine years later Ananias was struck down (perhaps by zealots; Bruce, *Acts of the Apostles*, 464). The address at the end of the sentence is particularly heated. Τοῖχε κεκονιαμένε (voc. sg. masc. of pf. pass. ptc. of κονιάω, "whitewash"; attrib. [the only voc. ptc. in the Gk. Bible) is together a "whitewashed wall": an allusion to hypocrisy (cf. Ezek 13:10; BDAG 1010a). Καὶ σύ ("and you") in a question denotes indignation (Barrett 2.1060). Κάθη is the 2nd sg. pres. mid. indic. of κάθημαι, "sit." Κρίνων is the nom. sg. masc. of pres. act. ptc. of κρίνω; attend. circum. Κατὰ τὸν νόμον followed by a second καί indicates a contrast to παρανομῶν (nom. sg. masc. of pres. act. ptc. of παρανομέω; concessive, NT hapax). The cstr. emphasizes the hypocrisy, mng. "according to the law . . . yet ("and at the same time," ZG 433) flouting the law." Κελεύεις is the 2nd sg. pres. act. indic. of κελεύω, "order." Τύπτεσθαι is the pres. pass. inf. of τύπτω; indir. speech, "strike." To strike Paul before a guilty verdict was contrary to the presumption of innocence in Jewish law (Bruce, *Acts of the Apostles*, 464; see, e.g., Lev 19:15) and the procedure of the court (*m. Sanh.* 3:6–8; see Witherington 689).

23:4 Παρεστῶτες (nom. pl. masc. of pf. act. ptc. of παρίστημι; subst., subj.) are perhaps the very ones who struck Paul (cf. John 18:22 and Jesus's experience; Bruce, *Acts of the Apostles*, 464). Ἀρχιερέα (acc. sg. masc. of ἀρχιερεύς, "high priest") τοῦ θεοῦ is an unusual expression to highlight the affront (Haenchen 6:38) and fronted for emphasis (BHGNT 440). Λοιδορεῖς is the 2nd sg. pres. act. indic. of λοιδορέω, "revile," (three times in NT). It may either be a rhetorical question or a statement without change in mng. (Barrett 2.1061).

23:5 Paul responds (ἔφη, 3rd sg. aor. act. indic. of φημί) in defense. The vb. ᾔδειν (1st sg. plpf. act. indic. of οἶδα, functions as an aor.) neg. is "I did not know." Ὅτι introduces what Paul did not know (a content conjunction, Wallace 678). The statement is a pred. nom. cstr. with ἀρχιερεύς as the pred. nom. There may be a number of reasons for Paul's ignorance. Bruce (*Acts of the Apostles*, 464) notes three explanations for his lack of recognition (see also Witherington 689):

1. Paul may have had vision problems. While popular, and attested in tradition, it is the most difficult to demonstrate here.
2. The high priest had changed since his last visit. So, while Paul may have known the change, he may not have seen him before. It would not be likely that the priest would be wearing his official robes outside of those duties (Keener 3.3279).
3. Paul may be speaking ironically, presuming the high priest could not act so unlawfully. If so, it is a prophetic criticism of the high priest (Johnson 397).

The substantiation (γάρ) is to the implication of his failure to identify the high priest, that he would not have spoken in this way. His basis is his allegience to the Torah. Γέγραπται (3rd sg. pf. pass. indic. of γράφω), "it is written," refers to Exod 22:27 (LXX). Ἐρεῖς (2nd sg. fut. act. indic. of λέγω) is an impv. fut. Κακῶς is an adv., "poorly."

23:6 Γνούς (nom. sg. masc. of aor. act. ptc. of γινώσκω; temp.) has the sense of "after he perceived." Given the lack of a just hearing, Paul likely framed the charge around the central evidence for Jesus as Messiah (the resurrection) to create both witness and chaos. The content of his perception (ὅτι) is expressed in contrasting pred. nom. clauses noting the political/religious composition of the audience. Τὸ ἓν μέρος is the subj. with the pred. gen. Σαδδουκαίων (gen. pl. masc. of Σαδδουκαῖος, -ου, ὁ, "Sadducees") in appos. to an implied αὐτῶν (BHGNT 441 [although one would expect the vb. form to be a ptc. in the gen. case, Wallace 102]). A parallel phrase (introduced by ἕτερον, "other") has Φαρισαίων ("Pharisees"). Ἔκραζεν is the 3rd sg. impf. act. indic. of κράζω. On ἄνδρες ἀδελφοί, see 1:11, 16. He identified himself as a Pharisee (Φαρισαῖός; pred. nom.). The phrase, "a son of a Pharisee" (υἱὸς Φαρισαίων) denotes a generational commitment, intensifying his pedigree. Ἐλπίδος καὶ ἀναστάσεως is likely hendiadys ("the hope of the resurrection," BDF 442[16]; ZG 433; Z §460), although καί is possibly epex. (BHGNT 442; Rogers and Rogers 294). Κρίνομαι is the 1st sg. pres. pass. indic. of κρίνω.

23:7 Εἰπόντος is the gen. sg. masc. of aor. act. ptc. of λέγω; gen. abs., temp. Ἐγένετο (3rd sg. aor. mid. indic. of γίνομαι) is impers., "there arose." Στάσις (nom. sg. fem. of στάσις, -εως, ἡ, "a dissension") is a pred. nom. (with the previous ἐγένετο). The nature of the noun requires the gens. Φαρισαίων καὶ Σαδδουκαίων (gen. pl. masc. of Σαδδουκαῖος, -ου, ὁ; together mng. "between the Pharisees and Sadducees," Wallace 137). Ἐσχίσθη is the 3rd sg. aor. pass. indic. of σχίζω, "divide."

23:8 The rationale (γάρ) for the appeal is the characterization of the sects in question, employing a μέν. . .δέ cstr. The Sadducee position is expressed as what they say (λέγουσιν, 3rd pl. pres. act. indic. of λέγω) with a neg. inf. of indir. speech (μὴ εἶναι, pres. inf. of εἰμί), best tr. "there is no . . . ," taking "resurrection" (ἀνάστασιν) as the dir. obj.

Luke's inclusion of μήτε ἄγγελον μήτε πνεῦμα ("neither angel nor spirit") regarding the Sadducees and the note that the Pharisees affirm (contrasting "say there is no" with "confess" [ὁμολογοῦσιν, 3rd pl. pres. act. indic. of ὁμολογέω]) ἀμφότερα (acc. pl. neut. of ἀμφότεροι, -αι, -α; subst., dir. obj., lit. "both things") is problematic. We do not have any other source regarding Sadducean denial of angels. Given their acceptance of the Pentateuch (that features angels) this seems unlikely. In truth, we have precious little information on the sect and no Sadducean document. We have Josephus *Ant.* 13.171; 18:16; *J.W.* 2:165, the Gospels, Acts, possibly 1 Enoch, and later rabbinic statements (Barrett 2.1066). The picture is remarkably sparse (Josephus never mentions resurrection either).

The suggestion that it was unlikely they denied angelic beings is likely true. However, as Witherington notes, "it may also be doubted that Luke, who is otherwise quite well informed about early Judaism, would have made such a major mistake about Sadducean beliefs" (Witherington 692). A variety of explanations have been offered; the two most likely are below:

    1. Luke as elsewhere used ἀμφότεροι (lit. "both") to describe more than two items (see 19:16). If so, Luke may have meant all in the series, to be rendered

"all" (BDAG 55d; Bruce, *Acts of the Apostles*, 466; most EVV). It may be that the surface reading is correct given the sparse evidence (Johnson 398).

2. It is possible, and grammatically likely, that the μήτε . . . μήτε cstr. are subsets of "resurrection." The sg. ἄγγελον seems misplaced if referring to the messengers of heaven. It could refer to a resurrection either in a body, like an angel, or as a spirit. Witherington (citing Daube) suggests the phrase ἄγγελον . . . πνεῦμα is "the realm of angel or spirit" that the good Jew spent awaiting resurrection (692).

23:9 Ἐγένετο (3rd sg. aor. mid. indic. of γίνομαι) is impers. ("there was"), taking κραυγὴ μεγάλη (fem. nom. sgs., "a great outcry") as a pred. nom. Ἀναστάντες is the nom. pl. masc. of aor. act. ptc. of ἀνίστημι; attend. cirucm.). Τινές ("some") is the fronted subj. of the vb., modified by three gens.: 1) γραμματέων (gen. pl. masc. of γραμματεύς, -έως, ὁ), a part. gen.; 2) μέρους (gen. sg. neut. of μέρος, -ους, τό, "party"), a poss. gen.; and 3) Φαρισαίων, a descriptive gen. ("scribes from the Pharisee party"). Διεμάχοντο is the 3rd pl. impf. mid. indic. of διαμάχομαι, "sharply contend." Λέγοντες (nom. pl. masc. of pres. act. ptc. of λέγω) introduces dir. speech. Οὐδὲν κακόν ("nothing evil"; dir. obj.) is fronted for emphasis. Εὑρίσκομεν is the 1st pl. pres. act. indic. of εὑρίσκω, "find." Culy and Parsons note three options for the cond. particle εἰ (BHGNT 443):

1. It may assume an apod. (as supplied in the *byz.* text, μὴ θεομαχῶμεν [1st pl. pres. act. subjunc. of θεομαχέω; hortatory, mng. "let us not fight against God"]; Bruce, *Acts of the Apostles*, 467; see BDF §482; R 1203, a speech cut short due to emotion).
2. It could introduce a dir. question, "What if . . ." (BDAG 278b; most EVV).
3. Finally, the UBS⁵ punctuates it as a question introducing dir. speech. (Did it really . . . [perhaps it did]). No real change of mng. occurs with each. Ἐλάλησεν is the 3rd sg. aor. act. indic. of λαλέω.

23:10 The strife quickly got out of hand. The crowd's response is expressed as a gen. abs. Γινομένης is the gen. sg. fem. of pres. mid. ptc. of γίνομαι; temp., mng. "when . . . arose." Πολλῆς (fronted for emphasis [BHGNT 444]) . . . στάσεως (gen. sg. fem. of στάσις, -εως, ἡ), "a great dissension," is the subj. of the ptc. The fear (φοβηθείς, nom. sg. masc. of aor. pass. ptc. of φοβέομαι) of the tribune leads to protective custody for Paul. The fear was μὴ διασπασθῇ (3rd sg. aor. pass. indic. of διασπάω), "lest Paul be torn apart." The order (ἐκέλευσεν, 3rd sg. aor. act. indic. of κελεύω) has three components expressed as indir. speech. The first is an attend. circum. ptc., καταβάν (acc. sg. neut. of aor. act. ptc. of καταβαίνω). In this case the force is impv. "go down." Two infs. of indir. speech complete the order: ἁρπάσαι (aor. act. inf. of ἁρπάζω) αὐτόν, "to seize him (Paul)"; and ἄγειν (pres act. inf. of ἄγω) "to bring" him into the fortress. That the same protective custody needed to happen with the Sanhedrin suggests they were no more in control of their hostility than the crowd (Johnson 399).

23:11 Τῇ δὲ ἐπιούσῃ νυκτί (dat. of time) is "on the next night" (cf. 7:26). Paul receives a visit reinforcing that Rome is the ultimate destination in sight (cf. 19:21). Ἐπιστάς (nom. sg. masc. of aor. act. ptc. of ἐφίστημι; attend. circum.) takes κύριος as the subj., mng. "The Lord stood over and . . . ." Θάρσει (2nd sg. pres. act. impv. of θαρσέω) is "take courage!" Most commentators take this as a vision (see Bruce, *Acts of the*

Apostles, 467; Johnson 399), although Luke elsewhere notes these specifically (see 9:10, 12; 16:9; 18:9; 22:17). The language of standing and speaking is closer to the-ophany and more like the visit of the angel at 27:23. The Lord substantiates (γάρ) the command with a comp. using ὡς "just as. . . ." Διεμαρτύρω is the 2nd sg. aor. mid. indic. of διαμαρτύρομαι, "you gave solemn testimony." The comp. completed with οὕτως ("in the same way"). On δεῖ, see 1:21. It takes the compl. inf. μαρτυρῆσαι (aor. act. inf. of μαρτυρέω), "you must bear witness" in Rome. As Barrett points out, Paul's appeal to the resurrection was not a clever trick to escape, but instead a testimony about Jesus (Barrett 2.1067). The visit by the Lord was certainly needed after such a day. But it was also needed to prepare Paul for what was next. There are no more miraculous escapes for Paul in Acts (Witherington 693).

HOMILETICAL SUGGESTIONS

Testifying before a Hostile Crowd (22:30–23:11)

1. Respect (even unrighteous) authority (22:30–23:5)
2. Stick to the main issue (here it is resurrection) (23:6–10)
3. Be encouraged that God is working long-term (23:11)

FOR FURTHER STUDY

32. Sadducees (23:8)

Daube, D. "On Acts 23: Sadducees and Angels." *JBL* 109 (1990): 493–97.
Keener, 3.3291–95.
Meyer, R. *TDNT*, 7:35–56.
NIDNTTE 4:228–31.
Porton, G. G. *ABD* 5:892–95.
———. *DNTB*, 1050–52.
Strauss, M. L. *DJG*², 823–25.

5. Paul's Removal to Caesarea (23:12–35)

The trip from Jerusalem to Caesarea is a tale of political intrigue and suspense. Although wildly entertaining in its movements, the story highlights God's providence as he directs Paul to fulfill his desire to go to Rome. Getting there was not a particu-larly straight path.

23:12 Γενομένης δὲ ἡμέρας is a temp. gen. abs. phrase mng. "when it was day." Ποιήσαντες (nom. pl. masc. of aor. act. ptc. of ποιέω; temp.) takes συστροφήν (acc. sg. fem. of συστροφή, -ῆς, ἡ, "a plot") as its obj. Ἀνεθεμάτισαν (3rd pl. aor. act. indic. of ἀναθεματίζω), often tr. "bound themselves with an oath" (cf. RSV, NASB, ESV), is lit. "they cursed themselves" (cf. KJV, CSB, "they bound themselves under a curse"). Λέγοντες (nom. pl. masc. of pres. act. ptc. of λέγω) introduces indir. speech with a pair of aor. act. infs. (φαγεῖν of ἐσθίω and πιεῖν of πίνω) in a μήτε . . . μήτε cstr. ("neither eat nor drink"). On ἕως οὗ, see 21:26, here mng. "before" (BDAG 423c). The subjunc. ἀποκτείνωσιν (3rd pl. aor. act. subjunc. of ἀποκτείνω) is used in an indef. temp. clause (see Wallace 480) expressing an action as a fut. contingency (see also R 974–76). It is best tr. "before they had killed Paul."

23:13 The vb. ἦσαν (3rd pl. impf. indic. of εἰμί) is often tr. as an impers. vb, but the subj. is at the end of the sentence (BHGNT 446). Πλείους (comp. adj. of πολύς, πολλή, πολύ, "more") is the pred. adj. of the vb., modified by the comp. gen. τεσσεράκοντα, mng. "more than forty men." The subj. of the vb. is the subst. ptc. ποιησάμενοι (nom. pl. masc. of aor. act. ptc. of ποιέω) with the obj. συνωμοσίαν (acc. sg. fem. of συνωμοσία, -ας, ἡ; "conspiracy, plot"; NT hapax) in the attrib. position.

23:14 On οἵτινες, see 7:53. The oath takers involve the Jewish leaders by approaching (προσελθόντες, nom. pl. masc. of aor. act. ptc. of προσέρχομαι) them and formalizing their oath. Εἶπαν (3rd pl. aor. act. indic. of λέγω) introduces dir. speech. The phrase ἀναθέματι (dat. sg. neut. of ἀνάθεμα, -ατος, τό; instr. dat., also "cognate dat." Johnson 403) ἀνεθεματίσαμεν (1st pl. aor. act. indic. of ἀναθεματίζω, "curse") with the refl. pron. ἑαυτοὺς (lit. "with a curse, we cursed ourselves") represents the Heb. inf. abs. (BDF §198[6]). The words used are related to the Heb. *herem*, the complete destruction vow (Keener 3.3304). Tr. like "we have strictly bound ourselves" (RSV) or "solemn oath" (NIV) seems domesticated. Perhaps "May we be completely destroyed" is best. There were offerings available for those unable to keep such an oath, so how serious it was is questionable (Keener 3.3304). The content of the oath is given with a neg. inf. of purp., γεύσασθαι (aor. mid. inf. of γεύομαι), "to taste nothing." On ἕως οὗ, see 23:12. On ἀποκτείνωμεν (1st pl.), see 23:12.

23:15 The conspirators suggest an illegal and sinister deception to the religious leaders of Jerusalem. Ὑμεῖς is emphatic in contrast to the ἡμεῖς of the conspirators later. Ἐμφανίσατε (2nd pl. aor. act. impv. of ἐμφανίζω, "inform") σὺν τῷ συνεδρίῳ ("with the council") signifies a group notification. Ὅπως καταγάγῃ (3rd sg. aor. act. subjunc. of κατάγω) is a purp. cstr. mng. "to bring him down." The conj. ὡς, in this case, indicates a pretense, "like" or "as if" (BDAG 1105d; Bruce, *Acts of the Apostles*, 524). Μέλλοντας (acc. pl. masc. of pres. act. ptc. of μέλλω) takes the compl. inf. διαγινώσκειν (pres. act. inf. of διαγινώσκω) to express "going to determine." Ἀκριβέστερον is a comp. adj. as an adv. "more accurately." On ἡμεῖς, see above. The prep. phrase πρὸ τοῦ ἐγγίσαι αὐτόν (aor. act. inf. of ἐγγίζω; subst., obj. of prep.) is "before he draws near"; that is, on the way to the court (cf. NLT). Ἕτοιμοί (nom. pl. masc. of ἕτοιμος, -η, -ον) is a pred. adj. Τοῦ ἀνελεῖν (aor. act. inf. of ἀναιρέω) is a purp. cstr. mng. "we are prepared to kill him." In essence, the conspirators were offering the leaders plausible deniability.

23:16 Somehow word gets out (ἀκούσας, nom. sg. masc. of aor. act. ptc. of ἀκούω; temp.) to ὁ υἱὸς τῆς ἀδελφῆς (lit., "the son of the sister," i.e., "Paul's nephew"). Ἐνέδραν (acc. sg. fem. of ἐνέδρα, -ας, ἡ, "ambush") is used here and 25:3 in the NT. The nephew's response is introduced by two ptcs. of attend. circum., Παραγενόμενος (nom. sg. masc. of aor. mid. ptc. of παραγίνομαι) and εἰσελθών (nom. sg. masc. of aor. act. ptc. of εἰσέρχομαι). Παρεμβολήν (acc. sg. fem. of παρεμβολή, -ῆς, ἡ; "barracks"; obj. of prep.) is a ref. to the fortress Antonia (BAFCS 3.137). Ἀπήγγειλεν is the 3rd sg. aor. act. indic. of ἀπαγγέλλω, "announce." The boy's access was likely due to the perception that he was not a threat and does not indicate Paul had free access to friends and visitors here (BAFCS 3.148–49).

23:17 Paul summoned (προσκαλεσάμενος, nom. sg. masc. of aor. mid. ptc. of προσκαλέω) a centurion. The phrase "one of the centurions" (ἕνα τῶν ἑκατονταρχῶν [gen. pl. masc. of ἑκατοντάρχης, -ου, ὁ; part. gen.]) suggests a large military presence. His word (ἔφη, 3rd sg. aor. act. indic. of φημί) is formally a command-grounds str., rhetorically a request. Ἀπάγαγε is the 2nd sg. aor. act. indic. of ἀπάγω, "take" with νεανίαν (acc. sg. masc. of νεανίας, -ου, ὁ, "young man") as the obj. The basis was the boy's news. Ἔχει (3rd sg. pres. act. indic. of ἔχω) takes τι as the dir. obj. with an epex. inf., ἀπαγγεῖλαί (aor. act. inf. of ἀπαγγέλλω), "he has something to tell him."

23:18 On μὲν οὖν, see 1:6. The centurion does exactly (with the same words) what Paul asked. Παραλαβών is the nom. sg. masc. of aor. act. ptc. of παραλαμβάνω; subst. Φησίν (3rd sg. pres. act. indic. of φημί) introduces dir. speech as a historic pres. ὁ . . . Παῦλος is the subj. of the centurion's statement (with δέσμιος [nom. sg. masc. of δέσμιος, -ου, ὁ] in the pred. pos., most EVV tr. "Paul the prisoner"). Προσκαλεσάμενός is the nom. sg. masc. of aor. mid. ptc. of προσκαλέω; attend. circum. With ἠρώτησεν (3rd sg. aor. act. indic. of ἐρωτάω) the aor. suggests a completed request (Barrett 2.1076). The rest of the v. is Paul's request nearly verbatim, converted to indir. speech. Ἀγαγεῖν is the aor. act. inf. of ἄγω, indir. speech, "bring." Ἔχοντά (acc. pl. masc. of pres. act. ptc. of ἔχω; causal), mng. "because he has," takes τι as the dir. obj. Λαλῆσαί is the aor. act. inf. of λαλέω, "say"; epex.

23:19 Ἐπιλαβόμενος is the nom. sg. masc. of aor. mid. ptc. of ἐπιλαμβάνομαι, "take hold of"; attend. circum. The tribune's actions suggest that reliable information regarding Paul or the incident is more than welcome. Given the volatility of the crowd and the empire's desire for peaceful provinces, the interest is understandable. He first withdraws (ἀναχωρήσας, nom. sg. masc. of aor. act. ptc. of ἀναχωρέω). Κατ᾽ ἰδίαν (lit., "according to his own") means no more than "aside," that is, privately (BDAG 467c). Then he begins investigating. Ἐπυνθάνετο (3rd sg. impf. mid. indic. of πυνθάνομαι, "ask") introduces dir. speech. The interr. τί is "what." Ἔχεις is the 2nd sg. pres. act. indic. of ἔχω. Ἀπαγγεῖλαί is the aor. act. inf. of ἀπαγγέλλω, epex., "report."

23:20 Paul's nephew related nearly verbatim the words of the assassins in v. 15, "as if the young man overheard" (Robertson, *Pictures,* 406). Εἶπεν . . . ὅτι introduces indir. speech. Συνέθεντο (3rd pl. aor. mid. indic. of συντίθημι) in the mid. is "they agreed" (i.e., the Ἰουδαῖοι). Τοῦ ἐρωτῆσαί (aor. act. inf. of ἐρωτάω) is technically a purp. cstr. (although little different than a mere inf.), "to ask you" (for an alt. view, see BHGNT 450). The cstr. ὅπως . . . καταγάγῃς (2nd sg. aor. act. subjunc. of κατάγω) is a purp. clause, "that you would bring down." For ὡς μέλλον τι ἀκριβέστερον, see 23:15. Πυνθάνεσθαι is the pres. mid. inf. of πυνθάνομαι, "to inquire"; compl.

23:21 The conj. οὖν is inferential. The subjunc. cstr. μὴ πεισθῇς (2nd sg. aor. pass. subjunc. of πείθω) is the normal aor. prohibitive, with αὐτοῖς (dat. of agency), lit. "do not be persuaded by them." The grounds (γάρ) for the prohibition is the planned ambush (ἐνεδρεύουσιν, 3rd pl. pres. act. indic. of ἐνεδρεύω, "lie in wait"). The prep. phrase ἐξ αὐτῶν ("from them") refers to the Jewish leadership. Ἄνδρες πλείους τεσσεράκοντα is very sim. to 23:13, mng. "more than forty men." Ἀνεθεμάτισαν (3rd pl. aor. act.

indic. of ἀναθεματίζω) with the refl. pron. ἑαυτοὺς is "they cursed themselves." On μήτε φαγεῖν μήτε πιεῖν ἕως οὗ, see 23:12. Καὶ νῦν εἰσιν (3rd pl. pres. indic. of εἰμί) sets up an impers. pred. adj. cstr. with ἕτοιμοι (see 21:15) as the adj. Προσδεχόμενοι is the nom. pl. masc. of pres. mid. ptc. of προσδέχομαι, "wait"; attend. circum. It is a rather suspenseful "and now they are waiting." The obj. of the ptc., "consent" (ἐπαγγελίαν acc. sg. fem. of ἐπαγγελία, -ας, ἡ), has ἀπὸ σοῦ ("from you") in the attrib. position.

23:22 On μὲν οὖν, see 1:6. It sets up the tribune's (χιλίαρχος, nom. sg. masc. of χιλίαρχος, -ου, ὁ) response. Ἀπέλυσεν is the 3rd sg. aor. act. indic. of ἀπολύω, "release." Παραγγείλας (nom. sg. masc. of aor. act. part. of παραγγέλλω; temp.) with the neg. ἐκλαλῆσαι (aor. act. indic. of ἐκλαλέω, indir. speech) has the sense "after charging him to tell no one." Ὅτι shifts from indir. to dir. speech. Ἐνεφάνισας is the 2nd sg. aor. act. indic. of ἐμφανίζω, "disclose."

23:23 The tribune's response was to prepare to move Paul under the cover of darkness with a sizeable force (justified given Sanhedrin complicity [Keener 3.2320]). Προσκαλεσάμενος is the nom. sg. masc. of aor. mid. ptc. of προσκαλέω, "summon"; temp. That he called two centurions (δύο . . . τῶν ἑκατονταρχῶν [gen. pl. masc. of ἑκατοντάρχης, -ου, ὁ; part. gen.]) likely means a company of over 200 men (even though centurions often had around eighty men [Keener 3.2320]). Bruce refers to it as "heavy infantry, cavalry, and light armed troops" (*Acts of the Apostles*, 470). The order was to assemble (ἑτοιμάσατε, 2nd pl. aor. act. impv. of ἑτοιμάζω, "prepare") 200 (διακοσίους [acc. pl. masc. of διακόσιοι, -αι, -α]) soldiers (στρατιώτας [acc. pl. masc. of στρατιώτης, -ου, ὁ]). Ὅπως πορευθῶσιν (3rd pl. pres. subjunc. of πορεύομαι) is a purp. clause explaining the destination (ἕως Καισαρείας [gen. sg. fem. of Καισάρεια, -ας, ἡ, "Caesarea"]). Καί is adv., "also." He added (both objs. of ἑτοιμάσατε) seventy (ἑβδομήκοντα, indecl.) cavalrymen (ἱππεῖς, nom. pl. masc. of ἱππεύς, -έως, ὁ) and 200 "spearmen" (δεξιολάβους, acc. pl. masc. of δεξιολάβος, -ου, ὁ). The last noun is not found in any contemporaneous literature (it does show up in the sixth century as a technical military term, Keener 3.3320). It is assumed that it was a military term at this time as well. It lit. means "taking in the right hand"; thus, Jerome's tr. *lancearios* ("spearmen") is likely correct (Barrett 2.1078). The temp. phrase ἀπὸ τρίτης ὥρας τῆς νυκτός likely is the starting point, so "no earlier than 9:00 p.m." (Haenchen 647).

23:24 On τε, see 1:15. Κτήνη (acc. pl. neut. of κτῆνος, -ους, τό, fronted obj. of the inf.) is lit. "beasts of burden" and can be a number of animals (Bruce, *Acts of the Apostles*, 470; "mounts" is a good tr., CSB, RSV, NASB, NRSV, ESV, NET). Παραστῆσαι (aor. act. inf. of παρίστημι, "provide") is indir. speech (see BDF §460). Ἵνα indicates a purp. clause. Ἐπιβιβάσαντες (nom. pl. masc. of aor. act. ptc. of ἐπιβιβάζω, "set on"; attend. circum.). The ultimate purpose is expressed as to "carry safely" (Διασώσωσιν, 3rd pl. aor. act. subjunc. of διασώζω) to Felix (Φήλικα, acc. sg. masc. of φῆλιξ, -ικος, ὁ), the Roman governor (ἡγεμόνα, acc. sg. masc. of ἡγεμών, -όνος, ὁ). The tribune was likely glad to hand him over.

23:25 The tribune sent a letter of which Luke at least includes the gist. Γράψας is the nom. sg. masc. of aor. act. ptc. of γράφω. Ἔχουσαν (acc. sg. fem. of pres. act. ptc. of ἔχω; attrib.) takes the obj. phrase τύπον (acc. sg. masc. of τύπος, -ου, ὁ) τοῦτον; together, lit. "having this form." Τύπος is used as rhetorical device to introduce an inserted letter, that is, the contents (BDAG 1020a; *New Docs* 1:77ff; but see BASHH 347–48). With Paul as the major witness of the events, we have reliable testimony if not the actual letter.

23:26 The letter followed conventional forms. The prescript includes sender in the nom. (Κλαύδιος Λυσίας, "Claudius Lysias"), the recipient in the dat. sg. masc. (κρατίστῳ [of κράτιστος, -η, -ον, cf. Luke 1:3] ἡγεμόνι Φήλικι [see 23:24]) "to the most-excellent governor Felix," and a greeting (χαίρειν, pres. act. inf. of χαίρω).

23:27 The dir. obj. of the main vb. is fronted, ἄνδρα τοῦτον ("this man"). Three ptc. phrases give the background information to Paul's deliverance. The first two ref. to Paul, the third to C. Lysias. Συλλημφθέντα is the acc. sg. masc. of aor. pass. ptc. of συλλαμβάνω, "seize" (i.e., "by the Jews"). Μέλλοντα (acc. sg. masc. of pres. act. ptc. of μέλλω) takes the compl. inf. ἀναιρεῖσθαι (pres. pass. inf. of ἀναιρέω) with the mng. "going to be killed" by them. A shift to the nom. makes C. Lysias the subj. of the next ptc., ἐπιστάς (nom. sg. masc. of aor. act. ptc. of ἐφίστημι, "stand at/near"). Finally, the main vb. is expressed: ἐξειλάμην (1st sg. aor. mid. indic. of ἐξαιρέω), "I rescued." It is not really possible for μαθών (nom. sg. masc. of aor. act. ptc. of μανθάνω, "learn") to mean "after that I learned . . ." (Barrett 2.1083). Nor is it likely accurate to repunctuate the sentence to associate with the next verse (as Johnson 403, 407). The conj. τε in the next v. would need to be with μαθών. The ptc. is best rendered "When I learned" (cf. NLT, NRSV). All might be resolved if we understand ἐξειλάμην to refer to the protective custody, conveniently skipping over the fact that the tribune had nearly flogged a Roman citizen (on this part Johnson [407] is correct). It is also quite possible that Lysias was representing himself inaccurately for his own benefit (Witherington 700). There is no doubt he was covering his own liability.

23:28 βουλόμενός (nom. sg. masc. of pres. mid. ptc. of βούλομαι) takes the compl. inf. ἐπιγνῶναι (aor. act. inf. of ἐπιγινώσκω). Δι᾽ ἣν is best tr. "for which." It modifies ἐνεκάλουν (3rd pl. impf. act. indic. of ἐγκαλέω, "charge"), that is, a legal accusation (see Barrett 2.1084). Κατήγαγον is the 1st sg. aor. act. indic. of κατάγω, "send down"; the destination (εἰς) was "their council."

23:29 C. Lysias continues with a rel. pron. clause (ὅν) modifying αὐτῷ in v. 28 (i.e., Paul). Εὗρον (1st sg. aor. act. indic. of εὑρίσκω) indicates the results of his investigation. It takes a double-acc. cstr. with the rel. pron. and two compl. The first is the nature of the offense. He was "being accused" (ἐγκαλούμενον, acc. sg. masc. of pres. pass. ptc. of ἐγκαλέω) regarding questions (ζητημάτων, gen. pl. neut. of ζήτημα, -ατος, τό; obj. of prep.) of Jewish law. The second is C. Lysias's opinon. Μηδέν neg. the ptc. delayed to nearly the end. The adj. ἄξιον ("worthy of") is modified by two descriptive gens., θανάτου (gen. sg. masc. of θάνατος, -ου, ὁ) and δεσμῶν (gen. pl. masc. of δεσμός, -ου, ὁ, "bonds"). The adj. is best understood as attrib. to "charge" below. Ἔχοντα is the acc. sg. masc. of pres. act. ptc. of ἔχω. Ἔγκλημα (acc. sg. neut. of ἔγκλημα, -τος, τό, "charge") is the obj. of ἔχοντα. Together, the phrase is "not having an accusation worthy of death or imprisonment." Most commentators note it important that the tribune exonerated Paul of criminal activity (see, e.g., Haenchen 648; Schnabel 938).

23:30 Μηνυθείσης (gen. sg. fem. of aor. pass. ptc. of μηνύω, "make known"; gen. abs., temp.) takes the inf. phrase ἐπιβουλῆς (gen. sg. fem. of ἐπιβουλή, -ῆς, ἡ; subj. of inf., gen. because of the gen. abs. BHGNT 455; ZG 436) . . . ἔσεσθαι (fut. mid. inf. of εἰμί; indir. speech). "That there would be a plot . . . was made known to me" is the sense of it. Bruce (*Acts of the Apostles*, 472) notes it is a mixed cstr., "the gen. abs. passing to an indirect statement." Ἔπεμψα is the 1st sg. aor. act. indic. of πέμπω; epistolary aor., "send." Παραγγείλας (nom. sg. masc. of aor. act. ptc. of παραγγέλλω; temp.) takes a dat. obj. κατηγόροις (dat. pl. masc. of κατήγορος, -ου, ὁ), mng. "I also ordered the accusers"). Λέγειν (pres. act. inf. of λέγω; compl.) in the legal arena with [τὰ] πρὸς αὐτὸν ἐπὶ σοῦ means "to state the things against him before you" (see Barrett 2.1085).

23:31 On μὲν οὖν, see 1:6; it signals the end of the letter by beginning a new section. Between the subj. (στρατιῶται, nom. pl. masc. of στρατιώτης, -ου, ὁ, "soldiers") and its vb. are two background events. First, they are obeying the orders of the tribune expressed as a prep. phrase, κατὰ τὸ διατεταγμένον (acc. sg. neut. of pf. pass. ptc. of διατάσσω; subst.), lit., "in accordance to their orders" (NASB, NET; ZG 436). The second is the ptc. ἀναλαβόντες (nom. pl. masc. of aor. act. ptc. of ἀναλαμβάνω, "take up"; attend. circum.). Ἤγαγον (3rd pl. aor. act. indic. of ἄγω) modified by διὰ νυκτός is best rendered "they brought him by night." The destination is Antipatris (Ἀντιπατρίδα, acc. sg. fem. of Ἀντιπατρίς, -ιδος, ἡ), some thirty-five to thirty-seven miles to the northwest (Barrett 2.1086).

23:32 On τῇ δὲ ἐπαύριον, see 10:9. The implied subj. of the ptc. ἐάσαντες (nom. pl. masc. of aor. act. ptc. of ἐάω, "let, permit"; attend. circum.) is the infantry of the previous v. or possibly the centurions. Ἱππεῖς (acc. pl. masc. of ἱππεύς, -έως, ὁ, "horsemen") is the obj. The inf. ἀπέρχεσθαι (pres. mid. inf. of ἀπέρχομαι, "depart") is compl. to the earlier ptc. Ὑπέστρεψαν (3rd pl. aor. act. indic. of ὑποστρέφω), to the fortress in Jerusalem. It is easy to get the impression the infantry made it the thirty-seven miles in one night. This is not possible on foot. It is more likely that once they got into the coastal plains the next morning, they turned back, while the cavalry went on to Antipatris (see Keener 3.3344; Schnabel 939).

23:33 On οἵτινες, see 7:53. The completion of the mission is expressed with two aor. attend. circum. ptcs. First, they arrived (εἰσελθόντες, nom. pl. masc. of aor. act. ptc. of εἰσέρχομαι) at Caesarea (Καισάρειαν, acc. sg. fem. of Καισάρεια, -ας, ἡ; prep. obj. [c. twenty-five miles from Antipatris, Barrett 2.1087]). Second, they delivered (ἀναδόντες, nom. pl. masc. of aor. act. ptc. of ἀναδίδωμι; NT hapax) the letter to the governor. The main vb. παρέστησαν (3rd pl. aor. act. indic. of παρίστημι, "present") is reserved for giving Paul to the governor.

23:34–35 Three temp. aor. ptc. phrases provide background to the main vb. in v. 35. Ἀναγνούς (nom. sg. masc. of aor. act. ptc. of ἀναγινώσκω, "read") assumes the letter previously delivered. The second ptc., ἐπερωτήσας (nom. sg. masc. of aor. act. ptc. of ἐπερωτάω, "ask") is modified by the prep. phrase ἐκ ποίας ἐπαρχείας (gen. sg. fem. of ἐπαρχεία, -ας, ἡ, "province"). It is lit. "from what kind of province?" but in HGk. ποίος = τίνος (Barrett 2.1087; Bruce, *Acts of the Apostles*, 473). If the more archaic sense is correct, it would suggest the governor is ascertaining whether or not Paul was from an imperial or senatorial province (an option Bruce denies). Even if it was so, once Felix learned (πυθόμενος, nom. sg. masc. of aor. mid. ptc. of πυνθάνομαι) that Paul was from

Cilicia (Κιλικίας, gen. sg. fem. of Κιλικία, -ας, ἡ; prep. obj.), there was no hope of kicking Paul to another province. He had jurisdiction (Keener 3.3346).

With the introduction of the main vb., the narrative shifts to dir. speech. Διακούσομαί (1st sg. fut. mid. indic. of διακούω, NT hapax, a legal term; Bruce, *Acts of the Apostles*, 474) with the poss. gen. σου is, "I will hear your case" (ZG 436). The vb. ἔφη (3rd sg. aor. act. indic. of φημί) is a rare occurrence, the word of speaking inserted after the speech has started (Barrett 2.1088 calls it "parenthetical"). Παραγένωνται is the 3rd pl. aor. mid. subjunc. (as required by ὅταν in an indef. temp. phrase) of παραγίνομαι, "whenever they arrive." Κελεύσας (nom. sg. masc. of aor. act. ptc. of κελεύω, "order") takes the compl. inf. φυλάσσεσθαι (pres. pass. inf. of φυλάσσω, "keep") and is attend. circum. to ἔφη. Robertson (R 864) identifies the ptc. as coincident, that is, simultaneous, (see also BHGNT 465).

HOMILETICAL SUGGESTIONS

The Irresistible Progress of God's Purposes (23:12–35)

1. Those resisting God's purposes are humiliated (vv. 12–22)
2. God's purposes may be supported through unlikely means (vv. 23–35)

C. PAUL'S CASE BEFORE FELIX, FESTUS, AND AGRIPPA (24:1–26:32)

In this section, Paul will give his defense before two Roman governors, a king, and many Jews in (at least partial) fulfillment of Acts 9:15 (". . . Gentiles, kings, and the children of Israel"). The procedure follows Roman jurisprudence of *extra ordinem* (SW 48, "an exemplary account;" BASHH 129–30; cf. BAFCS 3.158–67). The complicating factor (beyond political and religious intrigue) was that while the charges were political, the evidence was theological (SW 51). Thus, Felix procrastinated (for personal and, likely, professional gain) and put his successor in a bind.

1. The Jews' Charges against Paul (24:1–9)

Most of the recorded charge is a well-crafted *capitio benevolentiae*. The craftmanship then "tails away in a lame and impotent peroration" (Bruce, *Acts of the Apostles*, 475). Instead of a poor attempt by Luke at rhetoric, we should understand it as an intentional portrait of the speaker and the procedure (see the introduction). According to Keener the charge has an *exordium* (14:2–4); *narratio* (24:5–6); and *peroratio* (24:8), following rhetorical convention (Keener 4.3357). The actual charges are twofold: 1) sedition, and 2) an attempt to defile the temple (Witherington 707). Both were false, but if found guilty, they could incur the death penalty. The charges beyond the initial refrain are in summary form (24:9).

24:1 The new section is introduced by δέ and a temp. phrase ("after five days," presumably to prepare the case, Keener 4.3354). Κατέβη is the 3rd sg. aor. act. indic. of καταβαίνω, "go down." The company is the high priest, certain elders, and ῥήτορος (gen. sg. masc. ῥήτωρ, -ου, ὁ, "rhetor"; obj. of prep.) Τερτύλλου (gen. sg. masc. of Τέρτυλλος, -ου, ὁ) τινός ("an orator, a certain Tertullus"). He would have been the prosecuting attorney, given the Roman name, likely a Jewish Roman citizen to counterbalance Paul (Keener 4.3355–56). Without a doubt, he is a "hired gun." On οἵτινες, see 7:53. Ἐνεφάνισαν (3rd pl. aor. act. indic. of ἐμφανίζω, "inform") takes the dat. dir. obj. ἡγεμόνι (dat. sg. masc. of ἡγεμών, -όνος, ὁ, "governor"). Κατὰ τοῦ Παύλου is "against Paul."

24:2–3 Κληθέντος (gen. sg. masc. of aor. pass. ptc. of καλέω; gen. abs., temp.) likely refers to presenting Paul before the governor (since Tertullus is the subj. of the main vb., see Barrett 2.1094; BHGNT 459). Ἤρξατο (3rd sg. aor. mid. indic. of ἄρχομαι) takes the compl. inf. κατηγορεῖν (pres. act. inf. of κατηγορέω) mng. "he began to accuse," that is, "presented the charges" (cf. NLT, NIV, TNIV). Λέγων (nom. sg. masc. of pres. act. ptc. of λέγω) introduces dir. speech. The rhetor began with the customary political (and inaccurate) flattery (Keener 4.3364–65). Two causal pres. ptcs. note the great deeds of the governor. First, the general peace is attained (τυγχάνοντες, nom. pl. masc. of pres. act. ptc. of τυγχάνω) through him. Second, as a gen. abs. phrase (the subj. changes), improvements (διορθωμάτων, gen. pl. neut. of διόρθωμα, -ατος, τό, "improvement, reform"; subj. of ptc.) have come to be (γινομένων, gen. pl. neut. of pres. mid. ptc. of γίνομαι) through his providence (προνοίας, gen. sg. fem. of πρόνοια, -ας, ἡ; obj. of prep., only used here and Rom 14:13). The main clause begins (or the last clause ends) with an alliterative τε . . . καί cstr. (Bruce, *Acts of the Apostles*, 476) with πάντη (adv., "in every way") and πανταχοῦ (adv., "everywhere"). Ἀποδεχόμεθα

(1st pl. pres. mid. indic. of ἀποδέχομαι, "receive") is modified by the prep. phrase μετὰ πάσης εὐχαριστίας ("with all gratitude").

24:4 A neg. purp. clause, ἵνα . . . μή, expresses something he did not want to happen. Ἐπὶ πλεῖόν is "any longer" (cf. 20:9; BDAG 367c). The exact mng. of ἐγκόπτω (1st sg. pres. act. subjunc. of ἐγκόπτω) is debated (see BDAG 274b). It may mean "hinder, detain" (cf. RSV, NRSV, ESV, NET) or perhaps, "weary" (a LXX use, Haenchen 653; cf. KJV, TNIV). Given that the neg. vb. is modified by ἐπὶ πλεῖόν ("further") the former is best, for the trial has just started. Παρακαλῶ is the 1st sg. pres. act. indic. of παρακαλέω, "urge." Ἀκοῦσαί (aor. act. inf. of ἀκούω; indir. speech) takes an acc. subj. (σε) and a gen. obj. (ἡμῶν because the vb. takes a gen. obj.) The whole phrase functions as the obj. of παρακαλῶ, ". . . you to hear us." Συντόμως is an adv. mng. "briefly" (NT hapax [but see the longer ending of Mark 16:8]). The final phrase ἐπιεικείᾳ (dat. sg. fem. of ἐπιείκεια, -ας, ἡ, "clemency, graciousness") is a dat. of means, "by your kindness." It is possibly a legal term to suggest fair but favorable treatment (Barrett 2.1096).

24:5 Γάρ begins the actual charges against Paul (possibly assuming "we have accused him . . ."). Εὑρόντες (nom. pl. masc. of aor. act. ptc. of εὑρίσκω) takes a double-acc. cstr. First, Paul is called a λοιμόν (acc. sg. masc. of λοιμός, -οῦ, ὁ, "a pestilence"). Second, he is a fomenter (κινοῦντα, acc. sg. masc. of pres. act. ptc. of κινέω; subst., lit. "a mover") of a rebellion (στάσεις, acc. pl. fem. of στάσις, -εως, ἡ) among the Jews. Τοῖς nominalizes the following prep. phrase as an appos. to Ἰουδαίοις. It is clearly hyperbolic (BHGNT 460) and designed to trigger the governor. Πρωτοστάτην (acc. sg. masc. of πρωτοστάτης, -ου, ὁ) is a "leader" of the sect of the Nazarenes. The ref. is derogatory, in two areas. First, in this context, Ναζωραίων (gen. pl. masc. of Ναζωραῖος, -ου, ὁ, "Nazorean"), is likely a Jewish term, possibly building off the insignificance of Nazareth (Schnabel 955). Second, "sect" (αἱρέσεως, gen. sg. fem. of αἵρεσις, -έσεως, ἡ) implies theological aberration (see v. 14).

24:6 The antecedent of the rel. pron. in v. 5 ὅς is ἄνδρα, that is, Paul. Καί is adv., "also," adding another charge (Barrett 2.1099). Ἐπείρασεν (3rd sg. aor. act. indic. of πειράζω, "attempt") takes a compl. inf. (βεβηλῶσαι, aor. act. inf. of βεβηλόω, appropriate for a Gentile setting [cf. 21:28; Bruce, *Acts of the Apostles*, 477]), mng. "he attempted to defile." Ἐκρατήσαμεν (1st pl. aor. act. indic. of κρατέω, "arrest") adds an air of legality to what Luke presents as mob violence (Johnson 411).

24:7 An addition by the Western text inserts what is known as v. 7 and a clause in v. 8 that is found in the KJV, NASB, NKJV. The addition was included in the TR, but the Robinson-Pierpont *byz.* text does not include the addition. While some make a case for its originality (see Metzger 434), most scholars and modern EVV decline to include it.

24:8 Παρ' οὗ refers to Paul. Δυνήσῃ is the 2nd sg. fut. mid. indic. of δύναμαι. The expected compl. inf. comes after a ptc. phrase. Αὐτός is refl., "yourself," and is connected to ἀνακρίνας (nom. sg. masc. of aor. act. ptc. of ἀνακρίνω; means); together it is "by examining yourself." The inf. ἐπιγνῶναι (aor. act. inf. of ἐπιγινώσκω, "come to know") is compl. to δυνήσῃ. Tertullus finished up with an emphatic ἡμεῖς, subj. of κατηγοροῦμεν (1st pl. pres. act. indic. of κατηγορέω, "accuse"). The pron. is likely in contrast to Felix.

24:9 Luke finishes the report with the reaction of the fellow accusers mentioned at the beginning. The Jews joined in the attack (συνεπέθεντο, 3rd pl. aor. mid. indic. of συνεπιτίθημι, NT hapax [see Deut 32:27; MM 605c]). Καί is adv., "also." Φάσκοντες (nom. pl. masc. of pres. act. ptc. of φάσκω) is means, "by asserting" [see NRSV]). Ἔχειν is the pres. act. inf. of ἔχω, indir. speech.

2. Paul's Defense before Felix (24:10–27)

Paul's defense is a short acknowledgment of Felix (24:10); then Paul will 1) deny the charges altogether (24:11–13); 2) affirm his Christianity (24:14–16); and 3) affirm the issue is theological, not political (24:17–21). He will also insinuate guilt on those charging him, esp. noting the lacking presence of the supposed eyewitnesses (the Asian Jews; see Bock 694; Keener 4.3416). Their absence at the procedure (the legal term was *destitutio*) had strong legal consequences for them and was a valid objection to the charge of defiling the temple (SW 52). Paul's purp. is not purely self-centered, but he addressed three goals: to deny the charges, to affirm Christianity, and to give a powerful testimony to Christ (Keener 4.3387).

24:10 Paul responded (Ἀπεκρίθη, 3rd sg. aor. pass. indic. of ἀποκρίνομαι) after Felix motioned to him (νεύσαντος, gen. sg. masc. of aor. act. ptc. of νεύω, "nod"; gen. abs., temp.). The intent of the nod is indicated by the inf. λέγειν (pres. act. inf. of λέγω). Paul began his exordium with the customary compliments, but more truthful than Tertullius's pandering (Witherington 585). Paul merely notes that Felix had been κριτήν (acc. sg. masc. of κριτής, -ου, ὁ) ἐκ πολλῶν ἐτῶν, "a judge . . . for many years." The prep. phrase expresses the distance from the starting point (Robertson's "point of departure" [R 597]). The use of the ptc. ὄντα (acc. sg. masc. of pres. ptc. of εἰμί) is CGk. style to express indir. speech (HGk. uses the inf. or ὅτι more, Barrett 2.1101). The pres. tense conveys "past action still in progress" (R 892; T 59). Ἐπιστάμενος (nom. sg. masc. of pres. mid. ptc. of ἐπίσταμαι) is causal, "because I know . . ." (cf. CSB, KJV, NET, MIT). Εὐθύμως is an adv. ("gladly") modifying ἀπολογοῦμαι (1st sg. pres. mid. indic. of ἀπολογέομαι, "make a defense").

24:11 Δυναμένου (gen. sg. masc. of pres. mid. ptc. of δύναμαι; causal, gen. abs.) takes ἐπιγνῶναι (aor. act. inf. of ἐπιγινώσκω), together mng. "because you can come to know," that is, "ascertain" (RSV), "verify" (NIV, ESV, TNIV, NET, NJB). Ὅτι introduces the content of the knowledge. Οὐ πλείους (comp. adj., "no more than . . .") is fronted for emphasis. Εἰσίν (3rd pl. pres. indic. of εἰμί) is impers., "there are," with the pred. nom. phrase ἡμέραι δώδεκα ("twelve days"). Ἀνέβην (1st sg. aor. act. indic. of ἀναβαίνω, "go up"; see 3:1) is modified by a fut. ptc. προσκυνήσων (nom. sg. masc. of fut. act. ptc. of προσκυνέω) denoting purp., "to worship."

24:12 Paul makes two denials using οὔτε . . . ἤ ("neither . . . nor," cf. NASB) in a double-acc. cstr. with εὗρον (3rd pl. aor. act. indic. of εὑρίσκω) taking με and three ptc. phrases joined by οὔτε. The first is διαλεγόμενον (acc. sg. masc. of pres. mid. ptc. of διαλέγομαι, "dispute." The second denial is the ptc. phrase ἐπίστασιν (acc. sg. fem. of ἐπίστασις, -εως, ἡ, "a stop"; obj. of ptc.) ποιοῦντα (acc. sg. masc. of pres. act. ptc. of ποιέω; causal) ὄχλου. It is an idiom that lit. means "causing the stop of a crowd"; the sense here is "stirring up a crowd" (Robertson, *Pictures,* 416; cf. BDAG 839d; RSV,

NIV, NRSV, NET). The final denial is in two parts (οὔτε . . . οὔτε), "neither in the synagogue or in the city."

24:13 Οὐδέ introduces another denial of a different kind than the previous v.; the accusers cannot prove their charges. Παραστῆσαι (aor. act. inf. of παρίστημι, "prove") is compl. to δύνανταί (3rd pl. pres. act. indic. of δύναμαι), mng. "able to prove." Κατηγοροῦσίν (3rd pl. pres. act. indic. of κατηγορέω), "they accuse," takes a gen. obj. (μου).

24:14 Paul switched from denial to confession with ὁμολογῶ (1st sg. pres. act. indic. of ὁμολογέω). Ὅτι introduces the content of the confession. The prep. phrase is fronted before the vb. Τὴν ὁδόν is Paul's rejection of the prosecutor's terminology (Ναζωραίων), made clear by the rel. pron. clause (ἥν, modifying ὁδόν). Λέγουσιν is the 3rd pl. pres. act. indic. of λέγω, "they call." Οὕτως (adv., "thus") is resumptive. Λατρεύω (1st sg. pres. act. indic., "worship") takes a dat. obj., πατρῴῳ (dat. sg. masc. of πατρῷος, -α, -ον, "paternal" [see 22:3]) modifying θεῷ, mng. "our ancestral God." The vb. takes two ptcs. of attend. circum. The first is πιστεύων (nom. sg. masc. of pres. act. ptc. of πιστεύω). The obj. of the ptc. (in the dat.) is a compound obj. with πᾶσιν ("everything") covering both. Both are nominalized prep. phrases (each by τοῖς). The first is κατὰ τὸν νόμον ("according to the law") signifying his faith was not contrary to the law. The second is ἐν τοῖς προφήταις γεγραμμένοις (dat. pl. masc. of pf. pass. ptc. of γράφω), best tr. "the things written in the Prophets." The statement is not only another object of his faith but declaring the prophetic forecasting of the Messiah.

24:15 The second ptc. modifying λατρεύω is ἔχων (nom. sg. masc. of pres. act. ptc. of ἔχω), with ἐλπίδα (acc. sg. fem. of ἐλπίς, -ίδος, ἡ) as its obj. Αὐτοί in the intensive use, with οὗτοι, is "these themselves." The phrase is the subj. of προσδέχονται (3rd pl pres. mid. indic. of προσδέχομαι), lit. "they receive," here "accept." Ἀνάστασιν is the fronted obj. of the inf. μέλλειν (pres. act. inf. of μέλλω; indir. speech). It takes the inf. ἔσεσθαι (fut. mid. inf. of εἰμί), together mng. "that there will be a resurrection." It is completed by a τε καί cstr. with two gen. pl. masc. subst. adjs., obj. gens., δικαίων ("the righteous") and ἀδίκων ("the unrighteous").

24:16 Ἐν τούτῳ is causal but the exact source is debated:

1. It may refer to the fact of the resurrection in the previous clause. The rendering would be "because of this . . ." (see NLT, NASB, NET). It is possible that it has a Sem. origin (common in the LXX, Z §119).
2. It may be causal but without a dir. antecedent (Barrett 2.466; BHGNT 466; Bruce, *Acts of the Apostles*, 425). The cause then is a larger context (Robertson [*Pictures,* 418] suggests the confession of belief in vv. 14 and 15). However, since judgment is connected to resurrection (Haenchen 655), it is not necessary to look much further than v. 15.

Αὐτός is the intensive use of the pron., perhaps implying his accusers do not do as Paul. Ἀσκῶ is the 1st sg. pres. act. indic. of ἀσκέω, "practice, engage in"; NT hapax. Ἀπρόσκοπον (acc. sg. fem. of ἀπρόσκοπος, -ον) συνείδησιν is the obj. of the compl. inf. ἔχειν (pres. act. inf. of ἔχω), mng. "to have a clear conscience." On διὰ παντός, see 2:25.

24:17 Δέ marks a shift in Paul's argument. Δι' ἐτῶν . . . πλειόνων is a temp. expression mng. "after many years" (BDAG 224b; a CGk. expression, ZG 438). The cstr.

that follows is a vb. that takes a fut. ptc. with two objs. The word order, however, presents the first obj., ἐλεημοσύνας (acc. pl. fem. of ἐλεημοσύνη, -ης, ἡ, "alms") as somewhat emphatic. Ποιήσων (nom. sg. masc. of fut. act. ptc. of ποιέω) expresses purp. Παρεγενόμην (1st sg. aor. mid. indic. of παραγίνομαι, "arrived") is the main vb. The last obj. of the ptc. is προσφοράς (acc. pl. fem. of προσφορά, -ᾶς, ἡ, "offerings").

24:18 Ἐν αἷς is a temp. expression mng. "while/as I was doing this" (RSV, NRSV, ESV, CSB, likely ref. to the sacrifices [Barrett 2.1109]). Εὗρόν (3rd pl. aor. act. indic. of εὑρίσκω) takes a double-acc. cstr. with με and ἡγνισμένον (acc. sg. masc. of pf. pass. ptc. of ἁγνίζω, "purify"). Paul thus contradicts the charge of defilement in v. 6 (Haenchen 655). That he had neither a crowd (ὄχλου) nor a riot (θορύβου, gen. sg. masc. of θόρυβος, -ου, ὁ) at the time also denies the charge of sedition (see v. 5).

24:19 The initial noun phrase τινὲς δὲ ἀπὸ τῆς Ἀσίας Ἰουδαῖοι ("now some Jews from Asia") seems to be incomplete since there is no stated vb. The phrase may be taken in at least three different ways:

1. Culy and Parsons suggest τινὲς . . . Ἰουδαῖοι is the nom. pl. subj. of εὗρόν in v. 18 (BHGNT 467). In the textual tradition, the *byz.* text omits δέ and places the phrase in v. 18, making the same conclusion. It is not likely the orig. reading.
2. The use of δέ as an intersentence conj. suggests another understanding. Barrett proposes it creates a contrast to the preceding clause (Barrett 2.1108–9). Paul did not create a riot, but these Jews from Asia accused him of it. This would assume an elided vb., common in Paul (see Robertson, *Pictures,* 419).
3. The last option assumes a contrastive δέ, but the elided vb. accuses the Jews from Asia as the ones actually creating the riot (Haenchen 656).

Roman law demanded accusers to be present, so Paul notes that his accusers are absent. In the impf., ἔδει (3rd sg. impf. act. indic. of δεῖ) expresses something that should have been so (BDAG 214b–c), taking two pres. act. compl. infs., παρεῖναι (of πάρειμι) and κατηγορεῖν (of κατηγορέω), mng. "they should have been present before you to accuse." It is the apod. of a fourth-class cond. The vb. of the protasis ἔχοιεν (3rd pl. pres. act. opt. of ἐγώ) is the best potential opt. (KMP 208). The best explanation for the loss of ἄν is that it is a mixed cond. (Robertson, *Pictures,* 421). It is best tr. "if they had anything against me."

24:20 The particle ἤ, "or," presents Paul's demands (in lieu of the Asian Jewish presence) that legal charges be brought. Αὐτοί is intensive, modifying the pron. οὗτοι mng. "these men themselves." Εἰπάτωσαν (3rd pl. aor. act. impv. of λέγω) is "let them say." Εὗρον (3rd pl. aor. act. indic. of εὑρίσκω) has ἀδίκημα (nom. sg. neut. of ἀδίκημα, -ατος, τό, "crime") as the dir. obj. Because the subj. switches to Paul, the phrase is a gen. abs. στάντος (gen. sg. masc. of aor. act. ptc. of ἵστημι; temp.) with μου as the subj., mng. "when I stood (before the council)."

24:21 A second ἤ offers the resurrection as Paul's preferred object of investigation. Grammarians struggle over the lack of the art. with οὗτος in the prep. phrase. That cstr. normally signals it is in the pred. (cf. Luke 1:36; BDF §292; BDAG 741d). In the attrib., one would expect the art., but as Robertson points out, attrib. makes perfect sense here (R 702) and it is not unknown outside the NT (Robertson, *Pictures,* 421).

Μιᾶς ταύτης φωνῆς is lit. "this one sound," best tr. "this one statement" (CSB) or "thing" (NASB, ESV, NET). Ἧς is gen. by attraction to φωνῆς. The reduplicated form of the aor. vb. ἐκέκραξα (1st sg. aor. act. indic. of κράζω) is a form common in the LXX (Bruce, *Acts of the Apostles*, 481). It may be a reduplicated aor. of κράζω (R 348) or a compound vb. (κεκράζω, a form unattested elsewhere, BHGNT 468); both would mean "cry out." Ὅτι introduces the content of Paul's shout as dir. speech, περὶ ἀναστάσεως νεκρῶν, "about the resurrection of the dead." Ἑστώς is the nom. sg. masc. of pf. act. indic. of ἵστημι. Κρίνομαι is the 1st sg. pres. pass. indic. of κρίνω. Ἐφ᾽ ὑμῶν has the sense of "before you." Thus, Paul inserts the suggestion that his "crime" is not criminal but theological. Over such a case, Felix has no jurisdiction.

24:22 Ἀνεβάλετο (3rd sg. aor. mid. indic. of ἀναβάλλω, "adjourned") is a NT hapax, likely a legal term (BDAG 58d–59a). The aor. ptc. forms that follow take place before the dismissal. A comp. adj. ἀκριβέστερον (acc. sg. masc. of ἀκριβής, -ές, "more accurately") may either be comp. or elative in force.

1. If the former, Felix, likely through the proceedings, had gained more accurate information (i.e., than the accusers) about Christianity (Witherington 713; see BHGNT 469). If so, the proceedings were given by Luke in summary form.

2. If the latter, he came into the meeting with rather accurate knowlege (Barrett 2.1112; Bruce, *Acts of the Apostles*, 482; Z §148). Hemer suggests that his Jewish wife, Drusilla, could be the source (BASHH 131). Schnabel proposes there is no reason that a Roman governor would not know whether or not the Christians were a political threat by this time (Schnabel 963).

3. A third option is that it is comp. but without an obj. (see R 654). In this mng. it would mean, "more accurately than expected," that is, more than the Sanhedrin expected (Robertson, *Pictures,* 421). That the ptc. εἰδώς (nom. sg. masc. of pf. act. ptc. of οἶδα) is causal suggests that Felix did not need to hear the rest of Paul's case because of his knowledge of "the Way," pointing to either 1 or 3.

Εἴπας (nom. sg. masc. of aor. act. ptc. of λεγω) introduces dir. speech in an indef. temp. clause using ὅταν ("whenever") and καταβῇ (3rd sg. aor. act. subjunc. of καταβαίνω) referring to the tribune. Διαγνώσομαι is the 1st sg. fut. mid. indic. of διαγινώσκω, "decide." Τά nominalizes καθ᾽ ὑμᾶς. It is best tr. "your case" (cf. RSV, NASB, NET, ESV).

24:23 Διαταξάμενος (nom. sg. masc. of aor. mid. ptc. of διατάσσω, "order") takes a dat. (ἑκατοντάρχῃ, dat. sg. fem. of ἑκατοντάρχης, -ου, ὁ, "centurion") and three infs. of indir. speech defining the order. The first, τηρεῖσθαι (pres. pass. inf. of τηρέω, "keep"), is best understood as "in custody" (RSV). The second, ἔχειν (pres. act. inf. of ἔχω), with the obj. ἄνεσιν (acc. sg. fem. of ἄνεσις, -εως, ἡ), is best "to have some liberty" (RSV, ESV). The third inf., κωλύειν (pres. act. inf. of κωλύω), is neg., mng. "to forbid no one." It takes an inf. of purp. ὑπηρετεῖν (pres. act. inf. of ὑπηρετέω, "minister"; compl.). The charge is very sim. to the one delivered to Agrippa in Josephus *Ant.* 18:235 (see Johnson 412). Josephus described that detention (see 18:203–4) as including daily baths, meals, and visits from friends and servants, bringing food and other things to ease him (see also Haenchen 656). Paul's may not have been so lenient but it was *custodia liberior.*

24:24 Felix later (lit. "after some days") interviewed Paul, arriving (παραγενόμενος, nom. sg. masc. of pres. mid. ptc. of παραγίνομαι; attend. circum.) with his wife Drusilla (Δρουσίλλῃ, dat. sg. fem. of Δρούσιλλα, -ης, ἡ; sister of Herod Agrippa II, Barrett 2.1113). She is described with ἰδίᾳ (dat. sg. fem. of ἴδιος, -α, -ον, lit. "her own," but here merely a poss. [Bruce, *Acts of the Apostles*, 483]) and an attrib. ptc. phrase οὔσῃ (dat. sg. fem. of pres. ptc. of εἰμί) Ἰουδαίᾳ (dat. sg. fem. of Ἰουδαῖος, -α, -ον), "who was a Jewish woman." Μετεπέμψατο is the 3rd sg. aor. act. indic. of μεταπέμπω, "summon." Whether or not the summons was for religious curiosity or not, Felix *et ux* heard (ἤκουσεν, 3rd sg. aor. act. indic. of ἀκούω) about the faith. The prep. phrase εἰς Χριστὸν Ἰησοῦν is in the attrib. poss. to πίστεως (gen. sg. fem. of πίστις, -εως, ἡ; obj. of prep.) and suggests "faith in Messiah Jesus" (Johnson 419), that is, evangelism.

24:25 Διαλεγομένου (gen. sg. masc. of pres. mid. ptc. of διαλέγομαι, "discuss"; gen. abs., temp.) refers to Paul. The content of his teaching is summarized by three objs. of the prep. περί. Δικαιοσύνης has been interpreted as the Gk. moralists did, mng. "justice" (Keener 4.3434). For the epistolary Paul, "righteousness" is both ethical and forensic; demands for right action and a declaration from God (Schnabel 966; see Bock 695). There is no reason to abandon the Paul we know here. Ἐγκρατείας (gen. sg. fem. of ἐγκράτεια, -ας, ἡ, "self-control") was the mastery over the desires, a virtue in Gk. and Roman teaching (Barrett 2.1114–15), but for Paul only available through the Holy Spirit (cf. Gal 5:23). Τοῦ κρίματος τοῦ μέλλοντος (gen. sg. masc. of pres. act. ptc. of μέλλω) is "the coming judgment." What makes a discussion of righteousness and self-control fearful is standing before a holy God. As Bruce stated, these were "three subjects Felix and Drusilla certainly needed to hear about" (Bruce, *Acts of the Apostles*, 483). Felix's emotional response is ἔμφοβος γενόμενος (nom. sg. masc. of aor. mid. ptc. of γίνομαι; attend. circum.), "became terrified," for as Robertson noted, they did not possess righteousness, did not practice self-control, and were certain to be overtaken by the judgment (Robertson, *Pictures,* 422). Τὸ νῦν ἔχον (acc. sg. neut. of pres. act. ptc. of ἔχω) is a temp. idiomatic expression mng. "for the present" (BDAG 422c); with πορεύου (2nd sg. pres. mid. impv. of πορεύομαι) it means, "Go, for now" (cf. CSB). Καιρὸν . . . μεταλαβών (nom. sg. masc. of aor. act. ptc. pf μεταλαμβάνω; temp.) is lit. "having come into time," best rendered "when I find time" (NASB). Μετακαλέσομαί is the 1st sg. fut. mid. indic. of μετακαλέω, "summon."

24:26 Another reason for the delay is expressed in a coincident cstr. (BHGNT 471; R 1139–40), ἅμα (adv. mng. "at the same time") ἐλπίζων (nom. sg. masc. of pres. act. ptc. of ἐλπίζω). Χρήματα is nom. sg. neut., "money"; here "a bribe" is best (common in antiquity). Δοθήσεται is the 3rd sg. fut. pass. indic. of δίδωμι. Διό ("wherefore") suggests that fut. meetings were in hopes of the bribe. Πυκνότερον (comp. adv. as elative [T 30] mng. "quite often," cf. NLT, NASB, CSB) modifies the ptc. μεταπεμπόμενος (nom. sg. masc. of pres. mid. ptc. of μεταπέμπω, "summon"). Ὡμίλει is the 3rd sg. impf. act. indic. of ὁμιλέω, "converse."

24:27 Διετίας (gen. sg. fem. of διετία, -ης, ἡ, "two years"; subj. of ptc.) πληρωθείσης (gen. sg. fem. of aor. pass. ptc. of πληρόω; gen. abs., temp.) is a temp. expression with the sense "after two years had passed" (cf. NET, CSB). The phrase ἔλαβεν (3rd sg. aor. act. indic. of λαμβάνω) διάδοχον (acc. sg. masc. of διάδοχος, -ου, ὁ, "successor"; dir. obj., NT hapax) is an expression mng. "received as successor." Πόρκιον Φῆστον (masc. acc. sgs. of Πόρκιος, -ου, ὁ and Φῆστος, -ου, ὁ, "Porcius Festus") is an appos. to διάδοχον naming him as successor (as a case can be made for a double-acc. cstr.). Felix's (indicated by θέλων [nom. sg. masc. of pres. act. indic. of θέλω; attend. circum.]) desire to appease the Jews (καταθέσθαι, aor. mid. inf. of κατατίθημι, "grant [a favor]"; MM 333d suggests some expected reciprocity, only here and 25:9 in NT) is likely due to the animosity incurred by Felix over mismanagement in other affairs (see Johnson 419; Josephus *Ant.* 20:182). Thus, he left (κατέλιπεν, 3rd sg. aor. act. indic. of καταλείπω) Paul bound (δεδεμένον, acc. sg. masc. of pf. pass. ptc. of δέω). The measure is a political compromise, given the Sanhedrin appeared to want the death penalty.

HOMILETICAL SUGGESTIONS

Speaking the Truth against False Charges (24:10–21)

1. Deny false charges (vv. 10–13)
2. Confess Christ quickly (vv. 14–16)
3. Point out inconsistencies, legal or logical (vv. 17–21)

The Gospel, Past, Present, and Future (24:22–27)

1. Mankind's missing ingredient: righteousness (v. 25)
2. Mankind's missing discipline: self-control (v. 25)
3. Mankind's appointment with God: the coming judgment (v. 25)

3. Paul's Defense before Festus and His Appeal to Caesar (25:1–12)

The trial before Felix remained in a suspended state for two years. When Porcius Festus became procurator of Judea (c. AD 59, BASHH 130), he determined to complete it as (yet another) favor to the Judean leadership (25:9). Josephus described the state of Judea as a mess (implying the mismanagement of Felix for the Jews brought charges against him in Rome). Among the issues were robbers burning and plundering villages, the Sicarii were growing, a political imposter gathering a band in the wilderness, and internal strife over the temple (*Ant.* 20:185–88). Festus is pictured as "competent and engaged" (Bock 699) and as impartial as one could hope. He was appointed by Nero c. AD 59 only to die suddenly after three years of service (Witherington 717).

25:1 Ἐπιβάς (nom. sg. masc. of aor. act. ptc. of ἐπιβαίνω) with the dat. obj. ἐπαρχείᾳ (dat. sg. fem. of ἐπαρχεία, -ας, ἡ, "province") means "having set foot in the province" (see RSV, ESV), or it may be idiomatic for "he took his office" (Johnson 420, see NLT). He quickly (μετὰ τρεῖς ἡμέρας, "after three days") went up (ἀνέβη, 3rd sg. aor. act. indic. of ἀναβαίνω; see 3:1) to Jerusalem. Καισαρείας is the fem gen. sg. of Καισάρεια, -ας, ἡ, "Caesarea."

25:2 Ἐνεφάνισάν (3rd pl. aor. act. indic. of ἐμφανίζω, "disclose") takes a compound subj., the chief priest (by this time a certain "Ishmael," Johnson 420) and πρῶτοι. The term is used in several Gentile contexts referring to "leading men" (cf. 13:50; 17:4; 28:7); only here and in Luke 19:47 is it used in Jewish contexts. Κατὰ τοῦ Παύλου is "against Paul." Παρεκάλουν is the 3rd pl. impf. act. indic. of παρακαλέω.

25:3 Αἰτούμενοι is the nom. pl. masc. of pres. mid. ptc. of αἰτέω; attend. circum. The phrase χάριν (dat. sg. fem. of χάρις, -ιτος, ἡ) κατ' αὐτοῦ is lit. "a favor against him" (most EVV substitute "Paul" for the pron.). The manner of expression hints at nefarious intents. Ὅπως and the subjunc. (μεταπέμψηται, 3rd sg. aor. mid. subjunc. of μεταπέμπω, "summon") is normally a purp. clause but may be seen as an indir. command here. Robertson notes the cstr. is vague and still has purp. involved (R 1046). Previously the Sanhedrin was complicit in an attempt on Paul; here they hatched their own plot (Robertson, *Pictures*, 427). Ἐνέδραν is the acc. sg. fem. of ἐνέδρα, -ας, ἡ, "ambush"; see 23:16. Ποιοῦντες is the nom. pl. masc. of pres. act. ptc. of ποιέω; causal. Ἀνελεῖν is the aor. act. inf. of ἀναιρέω, "kill."

25:4 Μέν is part of a μὲν . . . δέ cstr. and not the disjunctive conj. of 1:6 (Barrett 2.1124). Τηρεῖσθαι is the pres. pass. inf. of τηρέω; indir. speech. Δέ introduces the contrasting clause. The refl. pron. (ἑαυτόν) normally could never be the subj.; however, in CGk. it often was interchangeable with αὐτός in inf. cstrs. as here (BDF §406), mng. "he himself" (as most EVV). Μέλλειν (pres. act. inf. of μέλλω; indir. speech) takes the compl. inf. ἐκπορεύεσθαι (pres. mid. inf. of ἐκπορεύομαι). Ἐν τάχει (dat. sg. neut. of τάχος, -ους, τό) is a temp. expression mng. "shortly" (BDAG 992c; cf. KJV, RSV, NASB, NRSV, ESV, NET).

25:5 Οἱ modifies the distant δυνατοί (BHGNT 474). Φησίν (3rd sg. aor. act. indic. of φημί, "he said" [on the word order, see 23:35]) transitions from indir. to dir. speech. The subj. δυνατοί (masc. nom. pl. of δυνατός, -η, -ον; subst. adj., subj. of the ptc.) is "the ones with authority." Συγκαταβάντες (nom. pl. masc. of aor. act. ptc. of συγκαταβαίνω) is "having come down with," assuming another person. Here it is an unexpressed "me," that is, as he goes back to Caesarea. The main part of the sentence is a first-class cond. (using εἴ, Wallace 694). The prot. is an impers. ἐστιν with the indef. pron. τί (in the neut. mng. "anything"; R 742) as the pred. nom. with ἄτοπον (acc. sg. neut. of ἄτοπος, -ον, "wrong"; appos.), mng. "if there is anything wrong." The vb. of the apod. κατηγορείτωσαν (3rd pl. pres. act. impv. of κατηγορέω, "accuse") takes a gen. obj. (αὐτοῦ).

25:6 Festus's stay (Διατρίψας, nom. sg. masc. of aor. act. ptc. of διατρίβω, "spend" [i.e., time]) is expressed in an approximation (ἡμέρας οὐ πλείους ὀκτὼ ἢ δέκα, "not more than eight or ten days"). Καταβάς is the masc acc. sg. of aor. act. ptc. of καταβαίνω; attend. circum. Festus took up Paul's case the very next day (τῇ ἐπαύριον; see 14:20). On βήματος (gen. sg. neut. of βῆμα, -ατος, τό; obj. of prep.), see 18:12. Ἐκέλευσεν is the 3rd sg. aor. act. indic. of κελεύω, "order." Ἀχθῆναι is the aor. pass. inf. of ἄγω, "bring"; indir. speech.

25:7 The main vb. in this sentence is flanked on both sides by a gen. abs. phrase referring to Paul (the second begins v. 8). Παραγενομένου is the gen. sg. masc. of aor. mid. ptc. of παραγίνομαι, gen. abs., temp., "having arrived." Περιέστησαν is the

3rd pl. aor. act. indic. of περιΐστημι, "stand around." Ἀπό Ἱεροσολύμων and the attrib. ptc. καταβεβηκότες (nom. pl. masc. of pf. act. ptc. of καταβαίνω) are in the attrib. position modifying Ἰουδαῖοι ("Jews"), together the subj. phrase. The phrase πολλὰ καὶ βαρέα (acc. pl. neut. of βαρύς, -εῖα, -ύ, "heavy") is lit. "many and serious" but is likely hendiadys, "many serious." Αἰτιώματα (acc. pl. neut. of αἰτίωμα, -ατος, τό, "charges"; NT hapax) is the obj. of the following ptc. and fronted for emphasis. Luke does not specify the charges but they are likely the same as 24:5–6 (Bock 701). He does note (using a rel. pron., ἅ) they were still unable (οὐκ ἴσχυον) to provide proof (ἀποδεῖξαι, aor. act. inf. of ἀποδείκνυμι, "prove"; compl. to ἴσχυον).

25:8 The second gen. abs. phrase completes the sentence. Ἀπολογουμένου is the gen. sg. masc. of pres. mid. ptc. of ἀπολογέομαι; gen. abs., temp. Ὅτι introduces dir. speech by Paul. He addressed the charges with a blanket denial in three parts (each joined by οὔτε εἰς, "neither/nor against"), saving the vb. till the end of the sentence for emphasis. The objs. reflect the charges; neither the law of Moses, nor the temple, nor something (τι) against Caesar (Καίσαρά, acc. sg. masc. of Καῖσαρ, -αρος, ὁ). The last was added because the Jews had previously hinted at sedition and that may have been part of the weighty charges (Bock 701). The main vb., ἥμαρτον (1st sg. aor. act. indic. of ἁμαρτάνω, "sin"), is tr. "offended" in most EVV.

25:9 Like Felix before him, Festus recognized the political advantage of granting a favor to the Jewish leadership (cf. 24:27). Θέλων (nom. sg. masc. of pres. act. ptc. of θέλω) is causal. Χάριν (acc. sg. fem. of χάρις, -ιτος, ἡ, "favor") is the obj. of καταθέσθαι (aor. mid. inf. of κατατίθημι, "grant"; compl.). Ἀποκριθείς is the nom. sg. masc. of aor. pass. ptc. of ἀποκρίνομαι; pleonastic, see 4:19. Εἶπεν is the 3rd sg. aor. act. indic. of λέγω. Festus asked if Paul was willing (θέλεις, 2nd sg. pres. act. indic. of θέλω) for a change of venue. Ἀναβάς is the nom. sg. masc. of aor. act. ptc. of ἀναβαίνω. Κριθῆναι is the aor. pass. inf. of κρίνω, "judge." The question seems odd, given that he has heard both the Jews' charges and Paul's defense (see Haenchen 669). Politically Festus is between a rock and a hard place. As Robertson noted, it would be unjust to condemn Paul but politically difficult to absolve him (Robertson, *Pictures,* 429). In some sense, it is accommodating the Jews, but not apart from Paul's consent (cf. 25:3; see Keener 4.3457–60).

25:10 Paul's response (εἶπεν, 3rd sg. aor. act. indic. of λέγω) is to put an end to the trial by demanding his rights. One suspects Festus's unusual response was a clue that the situation was not getting better for Paul (esp. since an ambush had been planned). The prep. phrase ἐπὶ τοῦ βήματος (gen. sg. neut. of βῆμα, -ατος, τό; obj. of prep.) Καίσαρος (gen. sg. masc. of Καῖσαρ, -αρος, ὁ), mng. "on Caesar's tribunal" (see 18:12), is fronted for emphasis. Ἑστώς (nom. sg. masc. of pf. act. ptc. of ἵστημι) εἰμι is a pf. periph. cstr. mng., as most EVV, "I am standing" (very emphatic, Barrett 2.1129). It is an appeal to be judged at Rome, the right of the Roman citizen. The rel. pron. phrase (οὗ) with δεῖ, with the compl. inf. κρίνεσθαι (pres. pass. inf. of κρίνω), has the sense of "where I ought to be tried" (cf. RSV, NLT, NASB, NIV). Ἠδίκησα is the 1st sg. aor. act. indic. of ἀδικέω, "wronged." Κάλλιον (comp. adv. of καλῶς) is used as an elative, "very well" (Bruce, *Acts of the Apostles,* 488). Ἐπιγινώσκεις (2nd sg. pres. act. indic. of ἐπιγινώσκω), "you know," is a way of saying the case is obvious.

25:11 Paul continued with a μὲν . . . δέ cstr., in which each part is a first-class cond. (using εἰ, Wallace 708). The first is a consent to the ruling of Caesar. The prot. clause features two vbs. The first, ἀδικῶ (1st sg. pres. act. indic. of ἀδικέω), in the pres. tense "sums" up the pfs. of the previous charges as a perfective pres. mng. "If I am a wrong-doer" (BDF §322; Barrett 2.1130). The second vb., πέπραχά (1st sg. pf. act. indic. of πράσσω) completes the cond. by referring to earning the death penalty (ἄξιον θανάτου). The apod. is a resignation to that penalty with a neg. παραιτοῦμαι (1st sg. pres. mid. indic. of παραιτέομαι). It is compl. by the aor. act. inf. ἀποθανεῖν, together mng. "I do not refuse to die." The contr. δέ clause proposes the alternate finding. Another first-class cond. (using εἰ) with an impers. ἐστιν taking a fronted οὐδέν ("nothing") as its pred. nom. Robertson locates ὧν (rel. pron.) as an attraction to an unstated antecedent (R 720). It is better understood as a gen. of ref. with κατηγοροῦσιν (3rd pl. pres. act. indic. of κατηγορέω), lit. "there is nothing in which they are charging me" (cf. RSV, ESV, MIT, CSB; see BHGNT 478). In the apod., με (obj. of inf.) is fronted for empha-sis. Δύναται (3rd sg. pres. act. indic. of δύναμαι) takes the compl. inf. χαρίσασθαι (aor. mid. inf. of χαρίζομαι); together mng. "no one is able to freely give me to them." The sense is "rightly give me up." The use of the specific vb. recalls Festus's desire to do a favor for the Jews (implying Paul's skepticism for a fair hearing). Καίσαρα (acc. sg. masc. of Καῖσαρ, -αρος, ὁ; fronted dir. obj.) ἐπικαλοῦμαι (1st sg. pres. mid. indic. of ἐπικαλέω, in the mid., "appeal to"; i.e., judicially; BDAG 373b) was the exercise of his rights as a Roman citizen. It is not an appeal of a verdict (as in the modern West) but an appeal to have Caesar hear the trial (Barrett 2.1131; BASHH 130; Keener 4.3465 notes it as irregular though).

25:12 Festus huddled with his advisors to respond. Συλλαλήσας is the nom. sg. masc. of aor. act. ptc. of συλλαλέω, "confer"; temp. The prep. obj. συμβουλίου (gen. sg. neut. of συμβούλιον, -ου, τό, "plan, council") refers to Festus's advisers. Thus, the art. is poss., "his council." The verdict is expressed in two brief clauses. First, Festus recognized Paul's appeal expressing Paul's request nearly verbatim, Καίσαρα ἐπικέκλησαι (2nd sg. pf. mid. indic. of ἐπικαλέω; see 25:11), "you have appealed to Caesar." Second, the granting of the appeal implies a change of venue to Rome, thus, in the same word order, ἐπὶ Καίσαρα πορεύσῃ (2nd sg. fut. mid. indic. of πορεύομαι), "unto Caesar you will go." All the costs of appeal (incl. travel and room and board) were to be paid by the one making it (Schnabel 992).

HOMILETICAL SUGGESTIONS

Turning Prosecution without Merit into a Platform for the Gospel (24:1–25:12)

1. Expect hostility (vv. 1–9)
2. Confess Christ openly (vv. 10–27)
3. Make wise use of civil law for the cause of Christ (vv. 1–12)

4. Paul before Agrippa: Charges Specified (25:13–26:32)

The first part of this section (25:13–22) is a fascinating peek into the perspective of the governor as he requested the aid of King Agrippa. While some suggest the event is wholly Luke's creation (for proponents, see Haenchen 673), a variety of sources would be available to Luke, incl. perhaps Festus's own preliminary statements at the hearing. The second part (25:23–27) is best considered preliminary announcements, explaining the interview. The section concludes with Paul's testimony (26:1–32) that is only superficially a criminal defense. It is primarily a gospel witness to the entire audience.

a. Festus and Agrippa (25:13–22)

The meeting with Agrippa (Herod Agrippa II, son of the Herod of 12:1ff; Herod the Great's grandson, the current Jewish client king; Barrett 2.1134; Bruce, *Acts of the Apostles*, 490) is a detailed introduction to Paul's final defense. The major question is why bring Agrippa into it? So far, Festus was in an uncomfortable position (due to Felix's inaction). He was under no real obligation to send Paul to Rome. His first option was to act locally. He could simply dismiss the charges (Schnabel 993). However, that puts him on difficult grounds with the Jerusalem leadership, something he clearly did not want. Or he could grant "the favor" to the Jewish leaders (who were intent on killing Paul). But ignoring the appeal would create a hazard for him with Rome (Johnson 428), or, at least, fodder for political enemies. Sherwin-White notes that to discount the appeal and act locally was not the action of a sensible man who desired eventual promotion (SW 65). On the other hand, he might send Paul on to Rome, but in doing so he had to send a letter explaining the charges. It could incur political damage to Festus's reputation back home if he wasted the time of the Roman courts with an obvious case (Witherington 726).

With Agrippa in town on a state visit, Festus had the opportunity not only to ingratiate himself with Agrippa, but to have political cover for sending Paul to Rome and to save face with the Jerusalem leadership (claiming the matter was out of his hands when Paul appealed [Johnson 428]). The hope seems to be that Agrippa would publicly agree with Festus that Paul is innocent of the charges and that the rest is a purely religious matter (Keener 4.3472). It was not a great risk, for even though Agrippa represented Jews, he was thoroughly Romanized (see Bruce, *Acts of the Apostles*, 490–91). **25:13** Ἡμερῶν δὲ διαγενομένων (gen. pl. fem. of aor. mid. ptc. of διαγίνομαι; gen. abs., temp.) τινῶν is an unspecific temp. expression mng. "after some days had passed." King Agrippa and his sister Bernice (on her, see Bruce, *Acts of the Apostles*, 491; BASHH 173) had arrived (κατήντησαν, 3rd pl. aor. act. indic. of καταντάω) on a "courtesy call." Ἀσπασάμενοι is the nom. pl. masc. of aor. mid. ptc. of ἀσπάζομαι. The exact syntax is debated since the aor. ptc. cannot express previous action here.

1. It might be attend. circum. expressing coincidental action. In this view, the coming down and "paying respects" is simultaneous (see Bruce, *Acts of the Apostles*, 491; Haenchen 672; R 1113; ZG §264). Robertson notes that such a thing is common in Luke's style.

2. Zerwick (ZG §265) also suggests the action of the aor. ptc. may be subsequent to going down. R (861–63), however, makes a compelling case for this not to be a category for aor. ptcs.

3. The aor. ptc. may, however, express purp. (so Wallace 637; cf. BDF §339[1]). While Robertson's grammar held to coincidental action, he wrote an article defending the use of the aor. ptc. for purp. (*JTS* 24 [1924]: 286–89, although he specifically cautioned against the use here [289]). However, because the ptc. expresses the outcome of the main vb., this use is compelling.

25:14 Ὡς is temp., "when." Διέτριβον is the 3rd pl. impf. act. indic. of διατρίβω, "spend time." Ἀνέθετο (3rd sg. aor. mid. indic. of ἀνατίθημι, "lay before") expresses the connotation of a request for a person's opinion regarding something (BDAG 74a). In this case it takes the art. τά (functions as a pron. nominalizing prep. phrase) κατὰ τὸν Παῦλον as the dir. obj. phrase ("the things against Paul"). Λέγων (nom. sg. masc. of pres. act. ptc. of λέγω) introduces dir. speech. The sg. subj. is fronted (ἀνήρ τίς "a certain man") for emphasis. The vb. is a periph. pf. cstr. with ἐστιν and καταλελειμμένος (nom. sg. masc. of pf. pass. ptc. of καταλείπω), mng. "having been left." The prep. phrase ὑπὸ Φήλικος (gen. sg. masc. of Φῆλιξ, -ικος, ὁ), "by Felix," has a hint of blame.

25:15 Γενομένου (gen. sg. masc. of aor. mid. ptc. of γίνομαι; gen. abs.) is the heart of the temp. expression "after I arrived in Jerusalem." Felix explained how he got into the case. Ἐνεφάνισαν is the 3rd pl. aor. act. indic. of ἐμφανίζω, "inform." Αἰτούμενοι is the nom. pl. masc. of pres. mid. ptc. of αἰτέω; attend. circum. Καταδίκην (acc. sg. fem. of καταδίκη, -ης, ἡ; obj. of the ptc.) is a sentence of condemnation, the death penalty.

25:16 Festus continued. Ἀπεκρίθην (1st sg. aor. pass. indic. of ἀποκρίνομαι) and ὅτι introduce indir. speech in an impers. pred. nom. cstr. with a neg. ἔστιν and ἔθος (nom. sg. neut. of ἔθος, -ους, τό) as the pred. nom. ("it is not the custom . . ."). Ῥωμαίοις (dat. pl. masc. of Ῥωμαῖος, -α, -ον) is a poss. dat. The inf. χαρίζεσθαί (aor. mid. inf. of χαρίζομαι) is likely the same use as 25:11 (recalling 25:2). However, one would expect a dat. recipient for "give up/deliver" ("as a favor" is inherent in the vb.). A number of textual vars. "correct" the issue. It is best to assume the indir. obj. as understood (Barrett 2.1137). Πρὶν ἤ and the opt. (ἔχοι and λάβοι below) is a CGk. (Ionic) temp. expression (instead of the Koinē subjunc.; here is the only place in the NT to do so; BDF §386; R 970) mng. "before" (cf. 7:2 with the inf., Luke 2:26 with the subjunc.). Barrett notes that Luke represents Festus with the vocabulary of an educated man, employing "suitably classical Greek" (Barrett 2.1137). Κατηγορούμενος (nom. sg. masc. of pres. pass. ptc. of κατηγορέω; subst., subj.) is "the one being accused." Κατὰ πρόσωπον is distributive "face to face." Ἔχοι (3rd sg. pres. act. opt. of ἔχω) is the first of two opt. vbs. completing the temp. expression. The phrase τόπον . . . ἀπολογίας (gen. sg. fem. of ἀπολογία, -ας, ἡ) λάβοι (the second opt., 3rd sg. aor. act. opt. of λαμβάνω) is to have an opportunity to defend himself (BDAG 1012a).

25:17 Συνελθόντων (gen. pl. masc. of aor. act. ptc. of συνέρχομαι; gen. abs. temp.) with ἐνθάδε is "after they came here" (referring to the Jerusalem accusers). The fronted dir. obj. phrase ἀναβολὴν (acc. sg. fem. of ἀναβολή, -ῆς, ἡ; NT hapax) μηδεμίαν and ποιησάμενος (nom. sg. masc. of aor. mid. ptc. of ποιέω) is "having made no delay." It is likely another criticism of Felix's handling of the situation. Τῇ ἑξῆς is a temp.

expression mng. "the next day." Καθίσας is the nom. sg. masc. of aor. act. ptc. of καθίζω; temp. Ἐκέλευσα is the 1st sg. aor. act. indic. of κελεύω, "order." Ἀχθῆναι is the aor. pass. inf. of ἄγω; indir. speech.

25:18 Festus claimed surprise at the charges. Σταθέντες (nom. pl. masc. of aor. pass. ptc. of ἵστημι; temp.) taking κατήγοροι (nom. pl. masc. of κατήγορος, -ου, ὁ) as subj. means "when the accusers stood up." Οὐδεμίαν αἰτίαν (acc. sg. fem. of αἰτία, -ας, ἡ, mng. "no charge") is the dir. obj. of ἔφερον (3rd pl. impf. act. indic. of φέρω). The rel. pron. (ὧν) is gen. by attraction to the subst. adj. πονηρῶν (R 718). Ὑπενόουν is the 1st sg. impf. act. indic. of ὑπονοέω, mng. "of the wicked things I was suspecting." It is possible that this represents the Latin legal formula *de quibus cognoscere volebam* ("of which I could take cognizance," BASHH 131).

25:19 What Festus did find (the developmental δέ is contrastive) were internal questions (ζητήματα [cf. 18:15] acc. pl. neut. of ζήτημα, -ατος, τό). The content (περί) of the questions was about τῆς ἰδίας δεισιδαιμονίας (gen. sg. fem. of δεισιδαιμονία, -ας, ἡ; NT hapax), "their own superstition" (KJV, RSV, MIT). Εἶχον is the 3rd pl. impf. indic. act. of ἔχω. Another περί adds more content ("about a certain Jesus"). Τεθνηκότος is the gen. sg. masc. of pf. act. ptc. of θνῄσκω, "die"; attrib. Ἔφασκεν is the 3rd sg. impf. act. indic. of φάσκω, "affirm." Ζῆν is the pres. act. inf. of ζάω; indir. speech. Clearly, Paul had presented the facts of Christianity to Festus.

25:20 Festus's excuse for sending Paul to Jerusalem is contrary to Luke's explanation (25:9). His was ignorance, ἀπορούμενος (nom. sg. masc. of pres. mid. ptc. of ἀπορέω; causal), "because I was at a loss." At best, it is only partially true. Τὴν . . . ζήτησιν (acc. sg. fem. of ζήτησις, -εως, ἡ) is an acc. of ref. with περὶ τούτων in the attrib. position, mng. "regarding the debate concerning these things" (cf. HCSB). Ἔλεγον is the 1st sg. impf. act. indic. of λέγω. Festus paraphrased the events of 25:9. Εἰ introduces an indir. question employing the delib. opt. βούλοιτο (3rd sg. pres. act. opt. of βούλομαι, see KMP 208). Πορεύεσθαι is the pres. mid. inf. of πορεύομαι. Κἀκεῖ is a crasis of καί ἐκεί, "and there." Κρίνεσθαι is the pres. pass. inf. of κρίνω; compl. to βούλοιτο.

25:21 Δέ is contrastive ("but"), yet the next important thing in the story. Ἐπικαλεσαμένου (gen. sg. masc. of aor. mid. ptc. of ἐπικαλέω; gen. abs., temp. or causal) takes the inf. τηρηθῆναι (aor. pass. inf. of τηρέω) as indir. speech. Σεβαστοῦ (gen. sg. masc. of σεβαστός, -ή, -όν; poss. gen. to διάγνωσιν [acc. sg. fem. of διάγνωσις, -εως, ἡ, "decision"]) is the Gk. form of the Latin *Augustus*, mng. "His Majesty the Emperor" (BDAG 917d). The use here, rather than Αὐγοῦστος (cf. Luke 2:1), is appropriate on the lips of a Roman official for it is the title, not the personal name (Bruce, *Acts of the Apostles*, 493; *TDNT* 7:174). Ἐκέλευσα is the 1st sg. aor. act. indic. of κελεύω, "order." Τηρεῖσθαι (pres. pass. inf. of τηρέω; indir. speech. The phrase ἕως ἀναπέμψω (1st sg. aor. act. subjunc. of ἀναπέμπω), is a potential statement mng. "until I could send." The destination was πρὸς Καίσαρα (acc. sg. masc. of Καῖσαρ, -αρος, ὁ), "to Caesar."

25:22 Agrippa's response was an affirmative. The impf. ἐβουλόμην (1st sg. impf. mid. indic. of βούλομαι) is a CGk. usage expressing an attainable desire (BDF §339[2]), mng. "I would like." Καί is adv., "also." Αὐτός is the intensive use of the pron., "I myself" (the subj. of ἐβουλόμην). The main vb. takes a compl. inf. ἀκοῦσαι (aor. act. inf. of ἀκούω). Festus's response (φησίν, 3rd sg. aor. act. indic. of φημί) was affirmative.

Ἀκούσῃ (2nd sg. fut. mid. indic. of ἀκούω) is the refl. mid., mng. "You will hear for yourself."

b. Preliminary Announcements (25:23–27)

25:23 On τῇ . . . ἐπαύριον, see 10:9. Much of the v. is an elaborate gen. abs. cstr. First, Agrippa (and Bernice) enter (ἐλθόντος, gen. sg. masc. of aor. act. ptc. of ἔρχομαι). The prep. phrase μετὰ πολλῆς φαντασίας (gen. sg. fem. of φαντασία, -ας, ἡ; NT hapax) is "with great pageantry." The ptc. switches to the pl. (εἰσελθόντων, gen. pl. masc. of aor. act. ptc. of εἰσέρχομαι), incl. the sister, who was an afterthought in the previous ref. The obj. of the ptc. ἀκροατήριον (acc. sg. neut. of ἀκροατήριον, -ου, τό, "audience hall") is not the official place of justice, but the audience hall of the procurator (this is an informal hearing; Barrett 2.1146). Included (in a τε . . . καί cstr., all dat. objs. of σύν) in the proceeding were tribunes (χιλιάρχοις, dat. pl. masc. of χιλίαρχος, -ου, ὁ; surely including C. Lysias, but there were at least five auxiliary cohorts in Caesarea, each with a tribune [Bruce, *Acts of the Apostles*, 493]) and the city elite (described with the art. τοῖς making an adj. out of the prep. phrase κατ' ἐξοχήν [acc. sg. fem. of ἐξοχή, -ῆς, ἡ; NT hapax], lit. "those according to prominence," modifying ἀνδράσιν). The main clause is introduced with a gen. abs., κελεύσαντος (gen. sg. masc. of aor. act. ptc. of κελεύω, "order") Φήστου (gen. sg. masc. of Φῆστος, -ου, ὁ), often tr. "at the command of Festus" (NASB, ESV). Paul is then brought forth (ἤχθη, 3rd sg. aor. pass. indic. of ἄγω).

25:24 Festus began with a summary of the situation as an address to Agrippa and those present (συμπαρόντες, nom. pl. masc. of pres. act. ptc. of συμπάρειμι; attrib., used as a voc., mng. "those present"). Θεωρεῖτε (2nd pl. pres. act. indic./impv. "you see" or "behold") takes τοῦτον ("this man") as the dir. obj. Ἅπαν τὸ πλῆθος τῶν Ἰουδαίων (part. gen.), lit. "all the multitude of the Jews," may ref. to the whole of the Jewish people (cf. RSV, NIV). If so, it is political hyperbole (Witherington 732). Johnson suggests that it ref. to the legal assembly, noting the resistance to the gospel was from the leadership (Johnson 427; see also Witherington 732). Ἐνέτυχόν is the 3rd pl. aor. act. indic. of ἐντυγχάνω, "entreat." The locations of Jerusalem and Caesarea (ἐνθάδε, "here") are joined by τε . . . καί. He described them with more hyperbole, indicated by βοῶντες (nom. pl. masc. of pres. act. ptc. of βοάω, "cry out"; attend. circum.). The neg. "must" cstr. with δεῖν (pres. act. inf. of δεῖ; indir. speech) takes the inf. ζῆν (pres. act. inf. of ζάω) and is tr. by most EVV as "ought not live. . . ." It is better, considering the repeated hyperbole, to tr. it "he must not live any longer" (KJV, RSV, NASB, NIV, NRSV, ESV, TNIV, NET).

25:25 Ἐγώ is emphatic by position and redundancy. Κατελαβόμην is the 1st sg. aor. mid. indic. of καταλαμβάνω, "perceive." The content is expressed by the inf. πεπραχέναι (pf. act. inf. of πράσσω; indir. speech). Μηδὲν ἄξιον (acc. sg. masc. of ἄξιος, -ια, -ον; modified by θανάτου) is the obj. of the inf. declaring Paul's innocence regarding the death penalty. Ἐπικαλεσαμένου (gen. sg. masc. of aor. mid. ptc. of ἐπικαλέω; gen. abs., causal) takes Σεβαστόν (acc. sg. masc. of σεβαστός, -ή, -όν; see 25:21) as the obj. of the ptc. Ἔκρινα is the 1st sg. aor. act. indic. of κρίνω. Πέμπειν is the pres. act. inf. of πέμπω; compl. Festus's declaration makes it clear that the judgment will be in Rome.

So, although he has political reasons for a consultation with Agrippa, this display is political theater.

25:26 Festus continued with the purp. of the meeting. Περί οὗ refers to Paul. Ἀσφαλές (acc. sg. neut. of ἀσφαλές, -ον) τι ("something definite") is the content of the epex. inf. γράψαι (aor. act. inf. of γράφω). Together it is the dir. obj. phrase of ἔχω. Προήγαγον is the 1st sg. aor. act. indic. of προάγω, "bring before." Ἐφ' ὑμῶν (lit. "upon you") has the sense of "before you." Ὅπως ("so that") and the subjunc. introduces a purp. clause. Ἀνακρίσεως (gen. sg. fem. of ἀνάκρισις, -εως, ἡ, "examination") is the subj. of the gen. abs. γενομένης (gen. sg. fem. of aor. mid. ptc. of γίνομαι; temp.), mng. "after our examination." Σχῶ (1st sg. aor. act. subjunc. of ἔχω) takes τί as its dir. obj. By form γράψω (1st sg. act. of γράφω) may be either fut. indic. or aor. subjunc. Since ὅπως clearly takes σχῶ without a copulative conj., it is best to understand γράψω as a fut., encroaching on the domain of the inf. (cf. BHGNT 487), "to write" (most EVV). Festus had to send a coherent report to Rome, thus he was defending the present hearing with Agrippa (Bruce, *Acts of the Apostles*, 494).

25:27 Festus concluded with his rationale (γάρ). The dir. obj. ἄλογον (acc. sg. masc. of ἄλογος, -ον, "absurd"; so NASB; "unreasonable," CSB, RSV, NIV, ESV, NET) is fronted for emphasis. Δοκεῖ is the 3rd sg. pres. act. indic. of δοκέω, "it seems." Scholars debate the syntax of πέμποντα (acc. sg. masc. of pres. act. ptc. of πέμπω).

1. Robertson (R 1039) felt it an example of a lack of assimilation between μοι and πέμποντα. Presumably this is why Barrett criticized Luke for not placing the ptc. in the dat. (Barrett 2.1148). Such a thing is possible in literary Gk. (cf. Heb 2:10). However, if other more standard grammar options are available, they should be preferred.
2. Culy and Parsons suggest it modifies ἄλογον (which is a pred. adj.) The ptc. is temp. modifying the inf. σημᾶναι (aor. act. inf. of σημαίνω, "signify"). The whole inf. phrase, then, is the subj. of the vb. δοκεῖ. They tr. it, "When sending a prisoner, not also to signify the charges seems ridiculous to me" (BHGNT 487). It is certainly possible, but not the simplest solution.
3. Another option significantly agrees with Culy and Parsons but takes the whole phrase as the obj. of an impers. δοκεῖ (see ZG 443). The tr., then, is "to me, it seems unreasonable, when sending a prisoner not to also signify the charges against him" (cf. RSV, ESV).

c. Paul's Testimony (26:1–32)

This speech is the last and most detailed speech by Paul in the book of Acts. While it is called an "apologia" (26:1, 2, 24) it provides nearly nothing that would be relevant in a Roman court (Witherington 735). Instead, it is a defense of the Christian faith with Paul not playing the defendant, but witness for the defense (Witherington 736). The audience is the most socially elevated in all of Acts (Keener 4.3491). So, in essence, it was Christianity's first defense to the sophisticated Gk. world (Johnson 440). Paul certainly seemed up to the rhetorical task. Most affirm he employs an elegant rhetoric. For example, he uses CGk. forms beyond Luke's normal expression (ἴσασιν, v. 4; ἀκριβεστάτην, v. 5; the pass. ἥγημαι, v. 2; ἕνεκα, ἐπειρῶντο, v. 21; παθητός, v. 23);

periodism (long sentences, cf. 9–11); an awareness of classical forensics (e.g., the lack of witnesses); paranomasia (puns, cf. ψῆφος, v. 10); hyperbole (v. 11); and a familiar Gk. proverb (v. 14) (for these and others, see Witherington 737; Keener 4.3496–533). It is important to note that, while utilizing the motifs, conventions, and literature of the Greco-Roman world, Paul does not transform Christianity into something palatable to Greco-Roman society. Jesus, instead, is the crucified and risen Messiah, and the legitimate heir of Judaism, each a stumbling block for educated Greeks to receive the gospel (Johnson 441).

26:1 Agrippa then addressed Paul (ἔφη, 3rd sg. aor. act. indic. of φημί, possibly impf., but less likely). Ἐπιτρέπεταί (3rd sg. pres. pass. indic. of ἐπιτρέπω) is impers., mng. "it is permitted." The dat. of advantage (σοι) and the refl. pron. in a prep. phrase (περὶ σεαυτου) has the sense of "for yourself." The vb. takes a compl. inf. λέγειν (pres. act. inf. of λέγω). Paul responds with the conventional hand motion of the rhetor (ἐκτείνας, nom. sg. masc. of aor. act. ptc. of ἐκτείνω, "gesture"; Witherington 738). Ἀπελογεῖτο (3rd sg. impf. mid. indic. of ἀπολογέομαι) is an inceptive impf., "he began to defend himself" (Bock 713; cf. NASB, "proceeded"; NIV, NET, MIT, NJB, CSB, "began").

26:2 Paul began his speech with an impressive introduction (*capatio benevolentiae*; Witherington 739; Robertson, *Pictures,* 442). He first acknowledged he was charged (ἐγκαλοῦμαι, 1st sg. pres. pass. indic. of ἐγκαλέω) by the Jews (perhaps implying no charges came from the Roman government). The essence of the speech would be a defense of his theological "crimes" rather than any civil crimes. The pf. ἥγημαι (1st sg. pf. mid. indic. of ἡγέομαι, "consider") has a pres. sense, a CGk. use. Barrett notes it is "a literary touch" (2:1149; BDF §341). It takes a double-acc. cstr. with the refl. pron. ἐμαυτόν as the obj. and, as the compl., μακάριον (most EVV rightly use "fortunate" rather than "happy/blessed"). Μέλλων (nom. sg. masc. of pres. act. ptc. of μέλλω) is causal and takes the compl. inf. ἀπολογεῖσθαι (pres. mid. inf. of ἀπολογέομαι), mng. "because I am going to make a defense."

26:3 Μάλιστα is a superl. adj. of μάλιστα used adv., mng. "especially." Γνώστην (acc. sg. masc. of γνώστης, -ου, ὁ, an "expert"; NT hapax) is the obj. of the ptc. The syntax of the ptc. ὄντα (acc. sg. masc. of pres. ptc. of εἰμί) is debated:

1. Culy and Parsons suggest that the acc. σε is the acc. subj. of the aor. act. inf. ἀκοῦσαι. The ptc. phrase, then, is an attrib. modifier of σε. The mng. would be "I ask you who are an expert . . ." (BHGNT 490). However, the presence of the conj. διό separates the clauses, making it esp. difficult.

2. Because it appears to be grammatically separated from the rest of the sentence, Robertson considers it the clearest case of the acc. abs. in the NT (R 490).

3. It is possible that it is an example of a lack of concord with σοῦ of v. 2 (ZG 433; see also Bruce, *Acts of the Apostles,* 497).

* 4. It is also possible that the phrase is in agreement with μακάριον and is a causal ptc. In this understanding Paul is esp. fortunate because Agrippa understands the issues well.

Διό has the sense of "consequently," making Paul's glad defense the basis of his request (δέομαι, 1st sg. pres. mid. indic. of δέομαι). The adv. μακροθύμως modifies ἀκοῦσαί (with the gen. obj. μου), mng. "patiently hear me."

26:4 Μὲν οὖν (see 1:6) signals Paul has moved to the defense proper. Paul begins with the fact that his life has been an open matter. Rhetorically he is calling his opponents as witness to his character; a highly effective strategy (Keener 4.3497). The dir. obj. βίωσίν (acc. sg. fem. of βίωσις, -εως, ἡ, "manner of life") and two adj. phrases are fronted for emphasis. The first (made an adj. by τήν) ἐκ νεότητος (gen. sg. fem. of νεότης, -τητος, ἡ), indicates his manner of life was from an early age. The second is an attrib. ptc. phrase (ἀπ᾽ ἀρχῆς γενομένην [acc. sg. fem. of aor. mid. ptc. of γίνομαι]) that defines his culture as among his people and (on τε, see 1:15) in Jerusalem. Ἴσασιν (3rd pl. pf. act. indic. of οἶδα; the CGk. form), "they have known," takes Ἰουδαῖοι ("Jews") as the subj.

26:5 Προγινώσκοντές (nom. pl. masc. of pres. act. ptc. of προγινώσκω, "know before-hand") is modified by ἄνωθεν (adv. "from the beginning"). Zerwick suggests, "having known for some time" (ZG 433). It is technically the apod. of a third-class cond. The prot. with θέλωσιν (3rd pl. pres. act. subjunc. of θέλω) and the compl. inf. μαρτυρεῖν (pres. act. inf. of μαρτυρέω), added much like an aside, is lit. "if they are willing to testify." Ὅτι completes the apod. by providing the content of προγινώσκοντές. Ἀκριβεστάτην (acc. sg. fem. of ἀκριβής, -ες; superl. adj.) αἵρεσιν (acc. sg. fem. of αἵρεσις, -έσεως, ἡ; obj. of prep.) is, in this context, "the strictest party." Ἔζησα (1st sg. aor. act. indic. of ζάω) is a constative aor., "I have lived." The nom. Φαρισαῖος is in appos. to the unexpressed subj. of the verb (BHGNT 491), and most EVV tr. it "as a Pharisee."

26:6 Paul has been consistent that the problem was his belief in the resurrection of the dead. He affirmed that in vv. 6–8 without actually mentioning it until v. 8. Since he connects it directly to Christ's resurrection, it will lead directly to his conversion by a resurrected Jesus. Καὶ νῦν refers to his pres. state, suggesting, however, a continuity with the former manner (Barrett 2.1152). Ἐπ᾽ with the dat. ἐλπίδι is referential with the sense of "regarding the hope." Εἰς τοὺς πατέρας ἡμῶν is in the attrib. position to τῆς . . . ἐπαγγελίας (gen. sg. fem. of ἐπαγγελία, -ας, ἡ), mng. "of the promise to our fathers" (gen. of content). Γενομένης (gen. sg. fem. of aor. mid. ptc. of γίνομαι; attrib.) has a pass. sense (BDAG 1036a), thus the agent is expressed by ὑπό. Ἔστηκα is the 1st sg. pf. act. indic. of ἵστημι, "stand." Κρινόμενος (nom. sg. masc. of pres. pass. ptc. of κρίνω) may be purp. But is likely attend. circum. (Rogers and Rogers 303; BHGNT 494; ZG [444] suggests the mng. "I stand trial").

26:7 The rel. pron. ἥν (obj. of prep.) has ἐλπίδι in v. 6 as the antecedent. Δωδεκάφυλον (nom. sg. neut. of δωδεκάφυλος, -ον; subst. adj., NT hapax), "the twelve tribes," is the subj. of the main vb. below. Ἐν ἐκτενείᾳ (dat. sg. fem. of ἐκτένεια, -ας, ἡ, "persever-ance, earnestness") describes the manner in which the tribes worshiped (most EVV, "earnestly"). The phrase νύκτα καὶ ἡμέραν λατρεῦον (nom. sg. neut. of pres. act. ptc. of λατρεύω) does not refer to a particular offering but means "continuously worshiping" (Barrett 2.1153). Ἐλπίζει (3rd sg. pres. act. indic. of ἐλπίζω) in the sg. presents the twelve tribes as a single unity. Καταντῆσαι is the aor. act. inf. of καταντάω, "arrive";

compl. The vb. and the inf. together express the tribe's effort was to attain resurrection. Paul reinforced the theological nature of the charge (Ἐγκαλοῦμαι, 1st sg. pres. pass. indic. of ἐγκαλέω) against him.

26:8 Because the charge was believing in the resurrection, Paul made a statement in the form of a rhetorical question that suggested opposition to the doctrine was absurd. Τί, "why," introduces the rhetorical question. The adj. ἄπιστον (here mng. "incredible") is technically a double-nom. subj./compl. cstr. (cf. BHGNT 493; Rogers and Rogers 303). The subj. is unexpressed ("it") with the adj. as its compl. It cannot be acc. because pass. vbs. (κρίνεται, 3rd sg. pres. pass. indic. of κρίνω) do not take a dir. obj. The vb. is used in a weakened sense, mng. "it is considered" (MM 360c). Εἰ introduces an indir. question and is virtually synonymous with ὅτι (Haenchen [684] "= 'if in fact'"; R 430, 1024; Z §404). Νεκρούς (acc. pl. masc. of νεκρός, -οῦ, ὁ) in the pl. is a general statement, "the dead," rather than a dir. ref. to Christ. Ἐγείρει is the 3rd sg. pres. act. indic. of ἐγείρω, "raise."

26:9 Paul transitioned to a new paragraph (on μὲν οὖν, see 1:6), elaborating on how he, too, held an unjustified position about Christianity. Ἔδοξα (1st sg. aor. act. indic. of δοκέω) with the ἐμαυτῷ (dat. of sphere) has the sense of a sincere conviction. The phrase τὸ ὄνομα Ἰησοῦ ref. to the Christian movement (Johnson 433; there is likely a conceptual link to Jesus referring to himself as the obj. of persecution). On Ναζωραῖος (nom. sg. masc. of Ναζωραῖος, -ου, ὁ, "Nazorean"), see 2:22. Δεῖν (pres. act. inf. of δεῖ; indir. speech) takes a compl. inf. with acc. obj. Here the obj. of the inf. is placed first (ἐναντία, acc. pl. neut. of ἐναντίος, -α, -ον, "hostile things"). Πρᾶξαι (aor. act. inf. of πράσσω) is the compl.

26:10 The neut. rel. pron. ὅ refers to the hostile things (ἐναντία) of v. 9 as a collective unity. Ἐποίησα is the 1st sg. aor. act. indic. of ποιέω. The τε . . . τε cstr. creates a close connection between clauses, "not only . . . but also" (BDAG 993c; cf. BHGNT 493). Κατέκλεισα is the 1st sg. aor. act. indic. of κατακλείω, "locked up." Λαβών (nom. sg. masc. of aor. act. ptc. of λαμβάνω) is a temp. ptc. taking ἐξουσίαν as an obj., mng. "after I received authority." In the attrib. position (made an adj. by τήν) παρὰ τῶν ἀρχιερέων expresses the source of the authority (the high priest). Ἀναιρουμένων (gen. pl. masc. of pres. pass. ptc. of ἀναιρέω, "put to death") is a gen. abs. taking αὐτῶν as the subj. Κατήνεγκα (1st sg. aor. act. indic. of καταφέρω) with ψῆφον (acc. sg. fem. of ψῆφος,- ου, ἡ, "voting-pebble") as the dir. obj. is lit. "I cast a pebble against them." It is best, "I cast my vote against them." It might be a lit. vote in lower-court settings (Paul was too young to be a member of the Sanhedrin at the time). It is more likely that the term is comprehensive of both attitudes and actions. Altogether, it was bad enough to do an assigned job, but Paul was wholeheartedly on board with the persecution.

26:11 Κατὰ πάσας τὰς συναγωγάς is distributive, mng. "in all the synagogues." Τιμωρῶν is the nom. sg. masc. of pres. act. ptc. of τιμωρέω, "punish"; attend. circum. Ἠνάγκαζον (1st sg. impf. act. indic. of ἀναγκάζω) is a habitual impf. with the sense of "I was attempting to force" (Z §273). As Turner stated, "One must not infer that his vicious onslaught achieved anything beyond the further spread of the new faith" (Turner, *Insights,* 87). It takes the compl. inf. βλασφημεῖν (pres. act. indic. of βλασφημέω). "Blaspheme" should be considered from Paul's present position. He was attempting to get them to renounce Christ. The adv. περισσῶς modifies ἐμμαινόμενος (nom. sg. masc. of pres. mid. ptc. of ἐμμαίνομαι, "be enraged"; NT hapax) and takes the dat. of disadvantage, αὐτοῖς. It describes an anger so violent it appears as insanity (BDAG 322b). Ἐδίωκον (1st sg. impf. act. indic. of διώκω; iter. impf.), because Paul names a destination (τὰς ἔξω πόλεις, "the outside cities"), is better tr. "I was pursuing" (cf. NLT, NASB, NRSV, NJB, CSB) rather than "I was persecuting" (cf. KJV, RSV, NIV, ESV, TNIV, NET).

26:12–13 V. 12 presents the background information to v. 13 (forming one sentence with the main vb. in v. 13). Ἐν οἷς is lit. "in these things," best rendered "in these circumstances" (cf. NASB, NIV, ESV, TNIV, CSB; Bruce, *Acts of the Apostles*, 500). It is not necessary to decide between temp. and circumstantial. The prep. ἐν still retains a temp. mng. (cf. BHGNT 494; Wallace 342; cf. Luke 12:1 [Thompson 199]; see Johnson [434], "while engaged in these things"). Πορευόμενος is the nom. sg. masc. of pres. mid. ptc. of πορεύομαι; temp. The prep. phrase μετ᾽ ἐξουσίας καὶ ἐπιτροπῆς (gen. sg. fem. of ἐπιτροπή, -ῆς, ἡ), "authority and commission," should be considered a unity. It is modified by τῆς τῶν ἀρχιερέων (Barrett 2.1158). The first art. makes the following gen. of source an adj. phrase (BHGNT 494), but most EVV simply tr. it "of/ from the high priests." Ἡμέρας μέσης is a gen. of time, "at midday" (gen. can be a point in time in HGk.; ZG 445; cf. BDF §186[2]). Εἶδον is the 1st sg. aor. act. indic. of ὁράω. The insertion of βασιλεῦ (voc. sg. masc. of βασιλεύς, -έως, ὁ) highlights the importance of what follows, getting the king's attention (and ours; Witherington 794). Two phrases precede the dir. obj. The first is a prep., ὑπέρ (with the acc. mng. "beyond" [seventeen times in NT]), that takes λαμπρότητα (acc. sg. fem. of λαμπρότης, -ητος, ἡ, "brightness"; NT hapax) as the prep. obj. It functions as a comp. mng. "brighter" (cf. BDF §230; RSV, NASB), taking the gen. of comp. ἡλίου ("than the sun"). The second phrase is ptc. (περιλάμψαν, acc. sg. neut. of aor. act. ptc. of περιλάμπω, "shine around"), functioning as a double-acc. cstr. (BHGNT 495) with the long-awaited dir. obj. φῶς. The ptc. takes a compound obj., με and the subst. ptc. phrase τοὺς σὺν ἐμοί πορευομένους (acc. pl. masc. of pres. mid. ptc. of πορεύομαι), "those traveling with me."

26:14 In Paul's testimony, there is some new information given. First, at the light, they all fell down (καταπεσόντων, gen. pl. masc. of aor. act. ptc. of καταπίπτω, "fall down"; gen. abs., temp.). Second, the voice Paul heard (ἤκουσα, 1st sg. aor. act. indic. of ἀκούω; with φωνήν as the dir. obj. [on the significance of the case, see 9:7]) has some added details. Λέγουσαν (acc. sg. fem. of pres. act. ptc. of λέγω) introduces dir. speech. Because he is speaking Gk., he notes it is in Heb./Aram. (τῇ Ἑβραΐδι διαλέκτῳ, see 21:40). What is more, a new phrase is added assuming an impers. ἐστίν with σκληρόν (nom. sg. neut. of σκληρόν, -ου, ὁ, "hard") as a pred. adj. Πρὸς κέντρα (acc. pl. neut. of κέντρον, -ου, τό, lit. an insect's stinger) refers to pointed sticks for driving livestock. The vb. is compl. by the inf. λακτίζειν (pres. act. inf. of λακτίζω, "kick"). The phrase is a common Gk. proverb referring to a reaction of an animal that causes a worse wound (Robertson, *Pictures*, 448; Keener [4.3515] suggests it is from Euripides).

26:15 This v. is a repetition of 9:5 except for a conversion to 1st sg. in the word εἶπα (1st sg. aor. act. indic. of λέγω; employing the alt. 1st aor. ending) and the addition of κύριος εἶπεν to introduce the Lord's response.

26:16 The commission itself is unique to Paul's speech at this place. Ἀλλ' expresses an implicit contr. that is clarified by the following commands. Instead of remaining where he is, Paul is to "get up" (ἀνάστηθι 2nd sg. aor. act. impv. of ἀνίστημι]). The second impv., στῆθι (2nd sg. aor. act. impv. of ἵστημι), with the prep. phrase ἐπὶ τοὺς πόδας σου, repeats Ezek 2:1 verbatim, recalling a prophetic commission (see Barrett 2.1160; Schnabel 1009). Εἰς τοῦτο is causal, mng. "for this reason." On ὤφθην (1st sg. aor. pass. indic. of ὁράω) in the pass., see 2:3. The inf. προχειρίσασθαί (aor. mid. inf. of προχειρίζομαι, "appoint"; purp.) takes a double acc. with σε as the obj. and a compound compl., ὑπηρέτην (acc. sg. masc. of ὑπηρέτης, -ου, ὁ, "servant") and μάρτυρα (acc. sg. masc. of μάρτυς, μάρτυρος, ὁ, "witness"). The gen. rel. pron. (ὧν) may be an attraction to an implied τουτῶν, but it is more likely a gen. of ref., "regarding the things" (cf. BHGNT 497; Robertson, *Pictures,* 448; the same is true of the next ὧν). The τε . . . τε cstr. is used for closely related sentences (BDAG 993c). Here it is best "both . . . and" (KJV) or "not only . . . but also" (NASB). Εἶδές is the 2nd sg. aor. act. indic. of ὁράω. Με (if orig.) is an acc. of ref. (Barrett 2.497). The vb. ὀφθήσομαί (1st sg. fut. pass. indic. of ὁράω) is an explicit promise of future revelation of Christ.

26:17 The ptc. ἐξαιρούμενός (nom. sg. masc. of pres. mid. ptc. of ἐξαιρέω) does not likely carry the CGk. mng. of "choose" (cf. Barrett 2.1160; Bruce, *Acts of the Apostles,* 502) but takes the HGk. sense of "rescuing" (ZG 445). The adv. ptc. is best a ptc. of means (BHGNT 497), unpacking the revelation of Christ to Paul. The promise is related to Paul's commission to the Gentiles expressed in the vb. ἀποστέλλω (1st sg. pres. act. indic. of ἀποστέλλω; likely progressive, "I am sending").

26:18 The purp. of the sending is expressed in three inf. cstrs. The first, ἀνοῖξαι (aor. act. inf. of ἀνοίγω), is an inf. of purp. The second and third infs. have a gen. sg. neut. art. (τοῦ) unpacking "to open their eyes" (cf. Rogers and Rogers 304), likely as a result (see Barrett 2.1162: " . . . so that"). Although this is the only instance in Acts, such a series of art. infs. following an anar. inf. is found elsewhere in Luke's Gospel (cf. Luke 1:77; Z §385). Ἐπιστρέψαι (aor. act. inf. of ἐπιστρέφω, "turn") takes two epex. phrases to complete it. "From (ἀπό) darkness unto (εἰς) light" is metaphorical of God versus Satan. The second does not employ a prep. but a gen. of source (ἐξουσίας). It is epex. of the previous phrase and makes the metaphor explicit. The inf. λαβεῖν (aor. act. inf. of λαμβάνω) might be subord. to the previous as a result of the previous purp. (ZG 444). It is more likely both art. infs. bear equal weight. The inf. takes a compound obj.: ἄφεσιν (acc. sg. fem. of ἄφεσις, -έσεως, ἡ, "forgiveness") and κλῆρον (acc. sg. masc. of κλῆρος, -ου, ὁ, "a portion"). Ἡγιασμένοις (dat. pl. masc. of pf. pass. ptc. of ἁγιάζω; subst., obj. of prep.) is lit. "the ones having been set apart." Πίστει (dat. sg. fem. of πίστις, -εως, ἡ) is a dat. of means, "by faith." The art. τῇ technically nominalizes the prep. phrase but functions like a rel. pron., mng. "which is in me" (cf. Vulg. *"quae est in me"*). The statement is sim. to Col 1:13–14. It strongly suggests the speech is based on an eyewitness account, likely Luke himself. Further, it suggests Paul never strayed far from the impact of the commission.

26:19 The voc. βασιλεῦ Ἀγρίππα again marks the statement as important (see 26:13). Paul was simply being obedient to Christ. Οὐκ ἐγενόμην (1st sg. aor. mid. indic. of γίνομαι) is an example of litotes (see 14:28). Ἀπειθής (nom. sg. masc. of ἀπειθής, -ές, "disobedient") takes a dat. to complete the mng. Οὐρανίῳ (dat. sg. fem. of οὐράνιος, -ον, "heavenly") modifies ὀπτασίᾳ (dat. sg. fem. of ὀπτασία, -ας, ἡ, "vision").

26:20 Ἀλλά continues the previous v. with a contr. Paul identified the objs. of his preaching in a series of dats., the first two employing the art. τοῖς as a pron. The sequence (indicated by πρῶτόν) is Damascus (Δαμασκῷ, dat. sg. fem. of Δαμασκός, -οῦ, ἡ), Jerusalem (Ἱεροσολύμοις), Judea (see below), and the Gentiles (ἔθνεσιν). Two issues occupy scholars regarding v. 20. First, the acc. πᾶσάν . . . τὴν χώραν τῆς Ἰουδαίας ("all the region of Judea") in a sea of dats. is problematic. This can be seen in textual vars. in the mss. and conjectural emendations offered (see Bruce, *Acts of the Apostles*, 503), none of which are necessary. It is also unnecessary to call them solecisms (contra Haenchen 687; ZG 445). Several legitimate grammatical options are available.

1. The phrase may indicate location (BHGNT 499).
2. Culy and Parsons suggest the indir. obj. has "advanced" to a dir. obj., thus, the accs. (BHGNT 499).
3. They may be accs. of extent, answering "how far?" With πᾶσάν, the suggestion would mean "throughout Judea" (see Robertson, *Pictures*, 450; BDF §161[1]).

The second problem is that Gal 1:22 states that the churches of Judea did not personally know him shortly after conversion. So, what did Paul ref.? The phrase is a summary of Paul's ministry and, notably, it somewhat mirrors Acts 1:8 in geographical sequence. It is not necessary to limit the phrase to Paul's early sequence that Galatians ref. Ἀπήγγελλον is the 1st sg. impf. act. indic. of ἀπαγγέλλω. The content of the message is given in indir. speech employing the infs. μετανοεῖν (pres. act. inf. of μετανόεω, "repent") and ἐπιστρέφειν (pres. act. inf. of ἐπιστρέφω, "turn"; with the obj. θεόν, it is a synonym for faith). Paul is careful to place righteous actions (ἄξια τῆς μετανοίας [gen. sg. fem. of μετάνοια,-ας, ἡ, "repentance"] ἔργα) after repentance and faith. Πράσσοντας (acc. pl. masc. of pres. act. ptc. of πράσσω; attend. circum.) is in agreement with the implied subj. of the infs. (BHGNT 499; Robertson [*Pictures*, 450] suggests αὐτοῦς).

26:21 Ἕνεκα (a CGk. form of ἕνεκεν, Barrett 2.1164) τούτων is lit. "for the sake of these," referring to the proclamation of the gospel. In this way, Paul exposes the real reason for his arrest. Συλλαβόμενοι is the nom. pl. masc. of aor. mid. ptc. of συλλαμβάνω, "arrest"; temp. Most EVV ignore ὄντα (acc. sg. masc. of pres. ptc. of εἰμί; temp.), mng. "when I was in the temple" (ZG 433). Ἐπειρῶντο (3rd pl. impf. mid. indic. of πειράομαι, "try, attempt"; NT hapax) is tendential, compl. by διαχειρίσασθαι (aor. mid. inf. of διαχειρίζω; describes seizing with a violent intent), mng. "they were trying to seize and kill me."

26:22 Ἐπικουρίας (gen. sg. fem. of ἐπικουρία, -ας, ἡ, "help"; NT hapax) is the gen. obj. of the causal ptc. τυχών (nom. sg. masc. of aor. act. ptc. of τυγχάνω), mng. "because I obtained help." Τῆς makes an adj. of the prep. phrase ἀπὸ τοῦ θεοῦ, functioning as a rel. pron. (cf. RSV, "that comes from God"). Ἕστηκα is the 1st sg. pf. act. indic. of ἵστημι. Μαρτυρόμενος (nom. sg. masc. of pres. mid. ptc. of μαρτύρομαι; manner) takes two dat. objs. (μικρῷ . . . μεγάλῳ) joined by τε . . . καί (both . . . and). The use of οὐδέν (the obj. of the ptc.) with the ptc. rather than μηδέν is a CGk. expression (Barrett 2.1165; a statement of fact). Ἐκτός is an adv. mng. "except." Λέγων is the nom. sg. masc. of pres.

act. ptc. of λέγω; attend. circum. The rel. pron. (ὧν) is equiv. to ἐκτὸς τούτων ἅ ("except these things which. . ."; R 720), together mng. "saying nothing except . . . ." The vb. of the rel. clause takes a compound subj. (προφῆται . . . Μωϋσῆς) joined by τε . . . καί. Μελλόντων (gen. pl. masc. of pres. act. ptc. of μέλλω) is gen. in agreement with the rel. pron. and takes the compl. inf. γίνεσθαι (pres. mid. inf. of γίνομαι), "would come to pass" (RSV, ESV) or "must come to pass" (BDAG 628b).

26:23 Εἰ (introducing the first two clauses) presents the content of Paul's gospel as a dir. question that is affirmed by the speaker but contested (see 26:8; BHGNT 501; ZG 446). The two clauses, then, are a compound prot. (see BHGNT 501; Johnson 439). Παθητός (nom. sg. masc. of παθητός, -ή, -όν; pred. adj.) is lit. "subject to suffer." Robertson prefers "can suffer" to "must suffer" (as in RSV, NRSV, ESV, CSB; Robertson, *Pictures,* 451). The second prot. affirms Christ's resurrection as the first (πρῶτος) of many, formally connecting his resurrection to the general resurrection (see 26:6–8). Neither clause expresses a vb., as a rhetorical device, heightening the urgency (BHGNT 501). The apod. begins with φῶς as the obj. of the compl. inf. belonging to μέλλει (3rd sg. pres. act. indic. of μέλλω). Καταγγέλλειν is the pres. act. inf. of καταγγέλλω, together mng. "he is going to proclaim light. . . ." The objs. (in the dat.) ref. to the people of Judea (τῷ . . . λαῷ) and the nations (τοῖς ἔθνεσιν) joined in a τε . . . καί cstr. ("both . . . and"). By framing the content in the form of a cond. statement, Paul both gives the content of his preaching and the rationale for the Gentile mission. It makes sense that since the suffering and resurrection of the Messiah is true, Christ would make provision to announce it. Paul is claiming obedience to Christ's calling to announce the good news.

26:24 Ταῦτα (acc. pl. neut.) is the obj. of ἀπολογουμένου (gen. sg. masc. of pres. mid. ptc. of ἀπολογέομαι; gen. abs., temp.), lit. "while he was defending these things." Festus blurted out (φησιν, 3rd sg. pres. act. indic. of φημί) a reproach against Paul. Μαίνῃ is the 2nd sg. pres. mid. indic. of μαίνομαι, "be mad." He further proposed a reason. Τὰ πολλά . . . γράμματα ("much learning") is a subj. phrase of the vb. (σε is the dir. obj.). Εἰς μανίαν (acc. sg. fem. of μανία, -ας, ἡ, "madness") is the "destination" inferred by περιτρέπει (3rd sg. pres. act. indic. of περιτρέπω, "turn").

26:25 Paul's response was a denial, οὐ μαίνομαι (1st sg. pres. mid. indic. of μαίνομαι), "I am not mad." It is made respectful by the voc. adj. κράτιστε (voc. sg. masc. of κράτιστος, -η, -ον, "most excellent"). The descriptive gens. ἀληθείας and σωφροσύνης (gen. sg. fem. of σωφροσύνη, -ης, ἡ, "reasonableness, rationality") affirm his words as true and wise. Ἀποφθέγγομαι is the 1st sg. pres. mid. indic. of ἀποφθέγγομαι, "declare." The contrast between μαίνομαι and σωφροσύνη is descriptive of the Gk. philosophical ideal (Johnson 439). Paul's expression should have resonated with his hearers.

26:26 Ἐπίσταται is the 3rd sg. pres. mid. indic. of ἐπίσταμαι, "understand." Γάρ indicates the grounds for Paul's assertion of sanity. Ὁ βασιλεύς refers to Agrippa, who Paul turned to address (πρὸς ὅν "to whom"). Καί is adv., "also." Παρρησιαζόμενος is the nom. sg. masc. of pres. mid. ptc. of παρρησιάζομαι, "speak openly"; manner. Λαλῶ is the 1st sg. pres. act. indic. of λαλέω, "speak." The reason for the turn (γάρ) was Agrippa's expertise. Λανθάνειν (pres. act. inf. of λανθάνω, "escape notice"; indir. speech) takes αὐτόν as the subj. and τι ("anything," if orig.) as the dir. obj. The inclusion of οὐθέν is best understood as a double neg. (Barrett 2.1169), strengthening Paul's assertion of confidence (πείθομαι, 1st sg. pres. pass. indic. of πείθω). Another γάρ gives the reason for confidence. The negated phrase ἐστιν (3rd sg. pres. indic. of εἰμί) πεπραγμένον (nom. sg. neut. of pf. pass. ptc. of πράσσω) is a periph. pf. mng. "has not been done." The prep. phrase ἐν γωνίᾳ (dat. sg. fem. of γωνία, -ας, ἡ), "in a corner," is used adv. and is a euphemism for "secretly."

26:27 Πιστεύεις (2nd sg. pres. act. indic. of πιστεύω) is a question, "Do you believe?" With a voc. (βασιλεῦ Ἀγρίππα), it is rather pointed. Προφήταις (dat. pl. masc. of προφήτης, -ου, ὁ) is the dir. obj. If the question was pointed, the following statement drives the goads deeper: οἶδα ὅτι expresses confidence and introduces the content of the knowledge, πιστεύεις (2nd sg. pres. act. indic. of πιστεύω). "I know that you believe" assumes "prophets" as the obj.

26:28 Agrippa's response has been understood in a variety of ways, and it may be the most disputed in all of Acts (Barrett 2.1169), normally revolving on the interpretation of the prep. phrase ἐν ὀλίγῳ (dat. sg. neut. of ὀλίγος, -η, -ον; subst. adj., prep. obj.). Three interpretations of the phrase are reflected in EVV.

1. The KJV and NKJV tr. it "almost." Robertson is right to call the rendering "impossible" (Robertson, *Pictures,* 453). Εἰς ὀλίγον or παρ᾽ ὀλίγου could carry this mng., but the pres. text cannot (Barrett 2.1170). Furthermore, Paul's response (ἐν ὀλίγῳ καὶ ἐν μεγάλῳ) does not fit with the sense of "almost."

2. The phrase may be a temp. adv. cstr. mng. "in a short time," that is, "quickly" (cf. RSV, NASB, NIV, NRSV, ESV, TNIV, NET; Bruce, *Acts of the Apostles,* 506; Schnabel 1017). The major issue here is whether or not ἐν μεγάλῳ can refer to time (time is at play whether a short time or speech is meant; Barrett 2.1170; Bock 723). Barrett (2:1170) and Robertson (*Pictures,* 453) strongly deny it.

3. Some have taken it to refer to extent. Robertson notes this is the choice of Tyndale and Crammer, who tr. it "somewhat" (Robertson, *Pictures,* 453). Johnson (431, 439) also takes it in this way.

4. Barrett (2:1170), Culy & Parsons (BHGNT 504), Robertson (*Pictures,* 453), and Turner (*Insights,* 99) suggest "effort" better fits both the setting and the lexical choices. See CSB, "so easily." Regarding Paul's response, BDF §195 renders it instr. "by easily, with difficulty" or "both small and great." They (like Bruce, *Acts of the Apostles,* 500) assume Paul was making a play on words so that v. 29 does not dictate the mng. in v. 28. While theoretically possible, there seems to be no compelling contextual reason for assuming such a play. "Easily or with difficulty" fits the context well.

If options 2 or 4 above are correct about ἐν ὀλίγῳ, πείθεις (2nd sg. pres. act. indic. of πείθω) is likely tendential, "you are trying to persuade" (BHGNT 502; KMP 262; MM 500d; Rogers and Rogers 305; T 63; Wallace 535; ZG 437). Χριστιανόν as the obj. of ποιῆσαι (aor. act. inf. of ποιέω) in this context seems odd. Bruce (*Acts of the Apostles,* 500) and Haenchen (689;"a technical term of the theater") suggest an idiomatic "to play the Christian" is the mng. Witherington is right to suggest a theater term does not fit the context as well as evangelism (Witherington 751; see also Barrett 2.1171;

BHGNT 504–5). Zerwick observed that if the obj. of an inf. is the same as the main vb., it may be left unexpressed (Z §395). Thus, the phrase may be rendered "make (me) a Christian" (Although not his main point, Zerwick's tr. ". . . that you made me a Christian" [Z §395; cf. CEB] is unlikely because it adds a time element unnecessary to the inf. and does not match Paul's response). The inf. then is likely purp. (BHGNT 505).

26:29 Εὐξαίμην (1st sg. aor. mid. opt. of εὔχομαι, "pray") with ἄν expresses an uncertain wish. On ἐν ὀλίγῳ καὶ ἐν μεγάλῳ, see above. On οὐ μόνον . . . ἀλλά, see 19:26. Ἀκούοντάς (acc. pl. masc. of pres. act. ptc. of ἀκούω; subst.) with σέ is the subj. of the inf. Γενέσθαι (aor. mid. inf. of γίνομαι) with the obj. τοιούτους ("such"; i.e., a Christian) is the purp. of Paul's prayer. Paul added a parenthetical comment in a pred. adj. cstr. with ὁποῖος (nom. sg. masc. of ὁποῖος, -οία, -οῖον, "of what sort") as the pred. adj. Καί is adv., "also." The prep. παρεκτός ("except"), found only three times in the NT and only here in Acts, takes a gen. obj. δεσμῶν (gen. pl. masc. of δεσμός, -οῦ, ὁ, "bond, fetter") τούτων ("these chains").

HOMILETICAL SUGGESTIONS

The Preacher and the Curious (25:13–26:29)

1. The curious seek information (25:13–27)
2. The witness gives his testimony (26:1–23)
   a. Paul's misguided commission (vv. 1–11)
   b. Jesus's redeeming commission (vv. 12–18)
   c. Paul, the gospel missionary (vv. 19–23)
3. The witness presses to evangelism (26:24–29)

26:30 The departure of the platform is expressed in a τε . . . καί cstr. that associates the nom. subjs. of "stood" (ἀνέστη, 3rd sg. aor. act indic. of ἀνίστημι, a collective sg.), Agrippa the king (βασιλεύς) and Festus the governor (ἡγεμών, masc. nom. sg. of ἡγεμών, - όνος, ὁ), then Bernice (Βερνίκη, nom. sg. fem. of Βερνίκη, -ης, ἡ) and the others sitting on the stage (συγκαθήμενοι, nom. pl. masc. of pres. mid. ptc. of συγκάθημαι, "sit with"). The latter is the term for the advisors on the stage (Haenchen 690).

26:31 Ἀναχωρήσαντες (nom. pl. masc. of aor. act. ptc. of ἀναχωρέω) is temp., "after withdrawing." Ἐλάλουν is the 3rd pl. impf. act. indic. of λαλέω. Λέγοντες (nom. pl. masc. of pres. act. ptc. of λέγω) ὅτι introduces dir. speech. The dir. obj. phrase οὐδὲν . . . ἄξιόν is fronted for emphasis. Ἄξιόν is modified by θανάτου ἢ δεσμῶν (gen. pl. masc. of δεσμός, -οῦ, ὁ, "bond, fetter"), mng. "worthy of death or imprisonment." If τι is orig. (as likely) the phrase means "in no way" (BHGNT 506). Πράσσει is the 3rd sg. pres. act. indic. of πράσσω. Because Paul was not present, ἄνθρωπος οὗτος ("this man"; masc. nom. sgs.; subj.) is not pejorative.

26:32 Ἔφη is the 3rd sg. aor or impf. act. indic. of φημί. The last word on the meeting belonged to Agrippa as a cond. sentence with the apod. first (BHGNT 507). Ἀπολελύσθαι (pf. pass. inf. of ἀπολύω) is compl. to ἐδύνατο (3rd sg. aor. mid. indic. of δύναμαι), mng. "to be released." Εἰ presents the apod. The neg. ἐπεκέκλητο (3rd sg.

plpf. mid. indic. of ἐπικαλέω, "appeal"), taking Καίσαρα (acc. sg. masc. of Καῖσαρ, -αρος, ὁ) as the obj., means "had not appealed to Caesar" (cf. CSB, RSV, NIV, NASB). Paul's earlier appeal has forced the hand of the governor; he should go to Rome. This is no surprise to Paul and the plan of Christ (see 23:11).

D. PAUL'S TRIP TO ROME (27:1–28:31)

The last section of Acts is presented in two parts. The first is the report of a sea voyage and shipwreck (27:1–28:16). It is presented in four scenes (27:1–8, 9–44; 28:1–6, 7–16) that brings the reader to the second section. It records Paul's arrival in Rome (28:17–31). The bulk of it is Paul's discussion with the Jewish leadership of Rome (28:17–29). The last two vv. (30–31) abruptly conclude the book.

1. Sea Voyage and Shipwreck (27:1–28:16)

The sailing narrative is both entertaining and difficult. Any reader would certainly enjoy the story. It is an exciting tale about disaster and survival on the high seas with more than a touch of divine intervention. It is, at the same time, perhaps the most difficult passage to tr. into Eng. It features Luke's style we have encountered before with a number of hapax legomena, otherwise common words that are surely nautical terminology in this context, and a few words we are sure are technical terms but scholars are not confident as to the exact mng. (see Barrett 2.1178; these will generally not be noted as NT hapax below). The details of sailing, weather, geography, etc., are so crisp, that denials of an eyewitness account seem rather hollow (cf. Haenchen's criticisms [709–11]).

For the present purposes, a greater issue is raised—why does Luke include the narrative, and how does it fit into the purposes of the Acts? Several themes are prominent that would edify the Christian reader (and perhaps testify to the unbeliever). The major purp. is that God's plans (for the gospel, see 1:8; for Paul, see 9:15; 19:21; 22:15; 23:11; and 26:16) are not thwarted by the violence of nature nor the actions of human beings. Second, the stature of Paul grows in the eyes of his fellow seafarers. He is shown to be more and more respected by the military and crew as the story progresses. His advice is ignored at the beginning (v. 11) but heeded later (vv. 21–26, 31, 33–34). More importantly, Paul is shown to have God's favor (as a witness) by surviving shipwreck and snakebite, receiving angelic visitations, and performing miracles. Third, Paul is God's messenger, not some sort of divine man, who commands nature (Johnson 458). Those who hear and receive God's message through Paul experience deliverance (Bock 728).

a. From Caesarea to Fair Havens (27:1–8)

27:1 Ὡς is temp., "when." Ἐκρίθη is the 3rd sg. aor. pass. indic. of κρίνω. The inf. ἀποπλεῖν (pres. act. inf. of ἀποπλέω, "sail away") is likely purp. due to the gen. art. The acc. pl. ἡμᾶς is the subj. of the inf. and continues the "we-section" phenomenon. The obj. of παρεδίδουν (3rd pl. impf. act. indic. of παραδίδωμι, "deliver"; referring to the government [Bruce, *Acts of the Apostles*, 511]) is compound: Παῦλον and τινας ἑτέρους δεσμώτας (acc. pl. masc. of δεσμώτης, -ου, ὁ; only twice in NT, here and 27:42); "certain other prisoners." Ἑκατοντάρχῃ is the dat. sg. masc. of ἑκατοντάρχης, -ου, ὁ, "centurion"; indir. obj. On ὀνόματι, see 5:1. Ἰουλίῳ (dat. sg. masc. of Ἰούλιος, -ου, ὁ, "Julius"; see v. 3) is most likely "a high ranking auxiliary soldier who also possessed citizenship" (BAFCS 3.270). The "Augustan Cohort," σπείρης (gen. sg. fem. of σπεῖρα,

-ης, ἡ) Σεβαστῆς (gen. sg. fem. of σεβαστός, -ή, -όν, see 25:21), cannot be identified with certainty but several legitimate options are available (see BASHH 132–33). Luke likely includes the name of the cohort for more than historical accuracy. Because the title is an honorific title (Bruce, *Acts of the Apostles*, 511), the implication is that it is not a run-of-the-mill military unit (see Keener 4.3572). All things considered, the transport is considered quite important.

27:2 Ἐπιβάντες (nom. pl. masc. of aor. act. ptc. of ἐπιβαίνω) is attend. circum. with the sense of "boarded" (ZG 447). The ship is identified by its origin, Ἀδραμυττηνῷ (dat. sg. masc., adj. of Ἀδραμυττηνός, -ή, -όν, "of Adramyttium," a city on the west coast of Asia Minor). Πλοίῳ takes an attrib. ptc. μέλλοντι (dat. sg. masc. of pres. act. ptc. of μέλλω) with the compl. inf. πλεῖν (pres. act. inf. of πλέω, "sail") expressing destination. The prep. phrase κατὰ τὴν Ἀσίαν (acc. sg. fem. of Ἀσία, -ας, ἡ) is in the attrib. position (functioning like a gen. phrase; BDAG 513d) to τοὺς . . . τόπους. It is lit. "the places along Asia," that is, Asian ports. The ship's itinerary was to skirt the coast of Asia Minor (thus, "a coasting vessel," Bruce, *Acts of the Apostles*, 512). Ἀνήχθημεν is the 1st pl. aor. pass. indic. of ἀνάγω, "put to sea." A further voluntary passenger with the team (σὺν ἡμῖν) is expressed with a gen. abs. phrase with ὄντος (gen. sg. masc. of pres. act. ptc. of εἰμί) and Ἀριστάρχου (gen. sg. masc. of Ἀρίσταρχος, -ου, ὁ, "Aristarchus"; subj. of ptc.), who is identified as a Macedonian (Μακεδόνος, gen. sg. masc. of Μακεδών, -όνος, ὁ) from Thessalonica (Θεσσαλονικέως, gen. sg. masc. of Θεσσαλονικεύς, -έως, ὁ, "Thessalonian").

27:3 On τῇ . . . ἑτέρᾳ, see 20:15. Κατήχθημεν (1st pl. aor. pass. indic. of κατάγω) in a nautical setting means "we put in" (cf. CSB, RSV, NASB; BHGNT 508). Εἰς Σιδῶνα (acc. sg. fem. of Σιδών, -ῶνος, ἡ, "Sidon") as the destination sets the limits on the first day's journey (about sixty-nine miles by sea; Barrett 2.1183). The adv. φιλανθρώπως modifies the ptc. χρησάμενος (nom. sg. masc. of aor. mid. ptc. of χράομαι; attend. circum.) that takes a dat. of pers. (Παύλῳ) mng. "having treated Paul kindly." Ἐπέτρεψεν is the 3rd sg. aor. act. indic. of ἐπιτρέπω, "allow" (i.e., Julius). Πορευθέντι (dat. sg. masc. of aor. pass. ptc. of πορεύομαι) is dat. by attraction to Παύλῳ (ZG 447). Ἐπιμελείας (gen. sg. fem. of ἐπιμέλεια, -ας, ἡ, "care, attention"; NT hapax) is the obj. of τυχεῖν (pres. act. inf. of τυγχάνω, "receive"). It is in the gen. rather than acc. because of conventions of the vb. (BDAG 1019b; BDF §410), together mng. "to get care." The ref. may be to medical needs (as in Luke 10:34) or supplies for his journey or perhaps both (see Keener 4.3578).

27:4 On κἀκεῖθεν, see 13:21. Ἀναχθέντες (nom. pl. masc. of aor. pass. ptc. of ἀνάγω; attend. circum.) in the pass. is "having put to sea." Ὑπεπλεύσαμεν (1st pl. aor. act. indic. of ὑποπλέω) with the dir. obj. Κύπρον (acc. sg. masc. of Κύπρος, -ου, ἡ) is lit. "we sailed under the protection ('the lee') of Cyprus," that is, protected from prevailing winds (BDAG 62a). Because the ship later (v. 5) goes through the Cilician and Pamphylian sea, most commentators understand the phrase to mean "north of Cyprus" (Barrett 2.1184; see Bruce, *Acts of the Apostles*, 512 [east and north]; BASHH 133). The reason for the itinerary is expressed in a prep. phrase that takes an art. inf. as the obj. (διὰ τὸ . . . εἶναι [pres. inf. of εἰμί]). Τοὺς ἀνέμους (acc. pl. masc. of ἄνεμος, -ου, ὁ, "wind") is the acc. subj. of the inf. The adj. ἐναντίους (acc. pl. masc. of ἐναντίος, -α,

-ον) is a pred. adj. Together it means "because the winds were hostile," that is, "against us" (cf. CSB, RSV, NIV, NRSV, ESV, TNIV, NET).

27:5 Τό . . . πέλαγος (acc. sg. neut. of πέλαγος, -ους, τό) is "open sea." Τό makes an adj. (modifying πέλαγος) of the prep. phrase κατὰ τὴν Κιλικίαν (acc. sg. fem. of Κιλικία, -ας, ἡ) καὶ Παμφυλίαν (see 27:4, BHGNT 509). The whole phrase is the obj. of the ptc. διαπλεύσαντες (nom. pl. masc. of aor. act. ptc. of διαπλέω, "sail through"; temp.). Κατήλθομεν is the 1st pl. aor. act. indic. of κατέρχομαι, "arrive, put in." The destination (εἰς) was Μύρα (indecl., "Myra") τῆς Λυκίας (gen. sg. fem. of Λυκία, -ας, ἡ), "Myra of Lycia," a city northwest of Cyprus.

27:6 On κἀκεῖ, see 14:7. Εὑρών (nom. sg. masc. of aor. act. ptc. of εὑρίσκω; temp.) takes πλοῖον Ἀλεξανδρῖνον (acc. sg. masc. of Ἀλεξανδρῖνος, -η, -ον), "an Alexandrian ship," as its obj. Πλέον is the acc. sg. neut. of pres. act. ptc. of πλέω, "sail"; attrib. to πλοῖον. Since Myra was the main site for Egyptian grain ships to port on the way to Italy (BASHH 134), it was likely the centurion's plan all along. Ἐνεβίβασεν is the 3rd sg. aor. act. indic. of ἐμβιβάζω, "put in" (referring to a ship).

27:7–8 These two vv. are one complicated sentence. Ἐν ἱκαναῖς (see 8:11) . . . ἡμέραις is a temp. expression mng. "for a number of days" (RSV, ESV). Βραδυπλοοῦντες (nom. pl. masc. of pres. act. ptc. of βραδυπλοέω, "sail slowly") expresses the speed. Haenchen suggests it was about 5 knots/6 mph (Haenchen 699). Μόλις (adv., see 14:18) γενόμενοι (nom. pl. masc. of aor. mid. ptc. of γίνομαι) has the sense of "barely reaching" (cf. ZG 448). Κατὰ τὴν Κνίδον (acc. sg. fem. of Κνίδος, -ου, ἡ) denotes an extent of space, "toward" or "up to" Cnidus, not a landing. The neg. ptc. προσεῶντος (gen. sg. masc. of pres. act. ptc. of προσεάω; gen. abs., causal) takes ἡμᾶς as its obj. and ἀνέμου (gen. sg. masc. of ἄνεμος, -ου, ὁ) as the subj. It gives the reason for the slow sailing, "because the wind was not permitting us" (see Barrett 2.1185; the sentence so far is the journey to Cnidus). On ὑπεπλεύσαμεν (1st pl. aor. act. indic. of ὑποπλέω), see v. 4. Κατὰ Σαλμώνην (acc. sg. fem. of Σαλμώνη, -ης, ἡ, "Salmone"; a cape on the eastern end of Crete) is the same mng. as 27:5. Here, it is on the southern side of Crete. On μόλις, see 14:18. On τε, see 1:15. With παραλεγόμενοι (nom. pl. masc. of pres. mid. ptc. of παραλέγομαι, only here and v. 13 in NT), the sense is "barely coasting along." Ἤλθομεν is the 1st pl. aor. act. indic. of ἔρχομαι. The place is named (καλούμενον, acc. sg. masc. of pres. pass. ptc. of καλέω; attrib.) καλοὺς λιμένας (acc. pl. masc. of Καλοὶ λιμένες, Καλῶν λιμένων, "Fair Havens"; a port still in existence; Barrett 2.1187). The rel. pron. ᾧ is the obj. of ἐγγύς ("near").

b. Storm and Shipwreck (27:9–44)

27:9 The sentence opens with a compound gen. abs. The gen. ἱκανοῦ . . . χρόνου (see 8:11) is the subj. of the ptc. διαγενομένου (gen. sg. masc. of aor. mid. ptc. of διαγίνομαι; causal), together mng. "because much time had been lost" (cf. RSV, NRSV). The second ptc. phrase (connected by καί) is also causal. Ὄντος is the gen. sg. masc. of pres. ptc. of εἰμί. Ἐπισφαλοῦς is the gen. sg. masc. of ἐπισφαλής, "dangerous"; pred. adj. of the ptc. Πλοός is the gen. sg. masc. of πλόος, -ος, ὁ, "voyage"; subj. of ptc. The causal prep. phrase διὰ τὸ . . . παρεληλυθέναι (pf. act. inf. of παρέρχομαι, "pass by"), with the acc. subj. νηστείαν (acc. sg. fem. of νηστεία, -ας, ἡ), means "because the fast had already passed." The ref. to the fast (Day of Atonement) is a synchronism setting the time after October 5 and before the 15th (Tishri 15, because the Feast is not mentioned; see BASHH 138). Ancient sailors considered the period from late September to mid-March to be unsafe to sail (Robertson, *Pictures*, 460). Παρῄνει is the 3rd sg. impf. act. indic. of παραινέω, "urge"; only here and 27:22. Zerwick (Z §272) suggests the impf. implies an unsuccessful attempt of asking or ordering.

27:10 The content of the warning is introduced by λέγων (nom. sg. masc. of pres. act. ptc. of λέγω). Θεωρῶ is the 1st sg. pres. act. indic. of θεωρέω, "perceive." Paul fronted the characterization of the trip. It is with injury (ὕβρεως, gen. sg. fem. of ὕβρις, -εως, ἡ) and much loss (ζημίας, gen. sg. fem. of ζημία, -ας, ἡ). On οὐ μόνον . . . ἀλλὰ καί cstr., see 19:26. Φορτίου (gen. sg. neut. of φορτίον, -ου, τό) καὶ τοῦ πλοίου (both are obj. gens.) is "the cargo and the ship." The escalation is their lives (ψυχῶν ἡμῶν, obj. gen.) as well. Μέλλειν (pres. act. inf. of μέλλω) is indir. speech giving the gist of Paul's perception. It takes the compl. inf. ἔσεσθαι (fut. mid. inf. of. εἰμί). Πλοῦν (acc. sg. masc. of πλόος, -ος, ὁ, "voyage") is the subj. of μέλλειν.

27:11 The warning went unheeded. The decision of the centurion (ἑκατοντάρχης, nom. sg. masc. of ἑκατοντάρχης, -ου, ὁ) is expressed by compound dats. in a contr. cstr. (employing μᾶλλον . . . ἤ, "rather than"). The first two masc. dat. sgs. (κυβερνήτῃ [of κυβερνήτης, -ου, ὁ, "captain/pilot"] and ναυκλήρῳ [of ναύκληρος, -ου, ὁ, "shipmaster/owner"], see MM 422–23a) contr. against the third rejected option (λεγομένοις, dat. pl. neut. of pres. pass. ptc. of λέγω; mng. "the things being said by Paul"). The dats. are either agency ("by") with ἐπείθετο (3rd sg. impf. pass. indic. of πείθω), "he was being persuaded"; or, more likely, compl. dats. with the vb. mng. "was paying more attention to" (BHGNT 512; see also BDAG 792b; Robertson, *Pictures*, 461). It is debated whether the centurion is at the top of the chain of command (so Bruce, *Acts of the Apostles*, 516; Robertson, *Pictures*, 461) or merely making a decision regarding passage on this ship (so Haenchen 700; Keener 4.3604). The point is that the centurion ignored Paul, "a mistake Julius will not repeat later in the narrative (27:31–32)" (Keener 4.3600).

27:12 Ἀνευθέτου (gen. sg. masc. of ἀνεύθετος, -ον, "unsuitable") is a pred. adj.; λιμένος (gen. sg. masc. of λιμήν, -ένος, ὁ, "harbor") is the subj. of the causal gen. abs. ὑπάρχοντος (gen. sg. masc. of pres. act. ptc. of ὑπάρχω). Πρός παραχειμασίαν (acc. sg. fem. of παραχειμασία, -ας, ἡ) is "for wintering." The unsuitability regards the safety of the ship for an extended stay. Apparently Fair Havens provided poor cover for the ship (and its cargo, see Keener 4.3605). Πλείονες (nom. pl. masc. of πολύς, πολλή, πολύ) as a comp. adj. means. "the majority" (i.e., the three mentioned above). Ἔθεντο (3rd pl. aor. mid. indic. of τίθημι) with βουλήν means "reached a decision" (BDAG 1003d). Ἀναχθῆναι is the aor. pass. inf. of ἀνάγω; indir. speech, "put to sea. Εἴ πως δύναιντο (3rd pl. pres. mid. opt. of δύναμαι) is the prot. of an incomplete fourth-class cond.; πως heightens the uncertainty (BHGNT 513l; KMP 208), together mng. "If somehow they could . . ." (cf. RSV "on the chance that somehow they could"; CSB "hoping somehow to . . ."). Καταντήσαντες (masc. nom. pl of aor. act. ptc. of καταντάω, "arrive"; temp.) is modified by the prep. phrase εἰς Φοίνικα (acc. sg. masc. of Φοῖνιξ, -ικος, ὁ, "Phoenix"), indicating destination. Παραχειμάσαι is the aor. act. inf. of παραχειμάζω, "winter";

compl. Λιμένα (acc. sg. masc. of λιμήν, -ένος, ὁ, "harbor") is in appos. to Φοίνικα, geographically about fifty miles west of Fair Havens (Barrett 2.1192). The majority's decision was likely considered safe due to the short distance. The harbor is described with the ptc. phrase βλέποντα (acc. sg. masc. of pres. act. ptc. of βλέπω; attrib.) κατὰ λίβα (acc. sg. masc. of λίψ, λιβός, ὁ, "southwest") καὶ κατὰ χῶρον (acc. sg. masc. of χῶρος, -οῦ, ὁ, "northwest"; a Latinism), together mng. "facing southwest and north-west" (cf. NASB, NRSV, TNIV, NET, MIT, NJB). Most likely it is the modern bay of Phineka that was a safer harbor in antiquity (Barrett 2.1193; BASHH 139; Bruce, *Acts of the Apostles*, 516–17; Keener 4.3605–06).

27:13 Ὑποπνεύσαντος (gen. sg. masc. of aor. act. ptc. of ὑποπνέω, "blow gently"; gen. abs., temp.) takes νότου (gen. sg. masc. of νότος, -ου, ὁ, "the south wind") as its subj. It is best tr. "after a gentle south wind began to blow" (cf. NIV, TNIV, NET, CSB). Δόξαντες is the nom. pl. masc. of aor. act. ptc. of δοκέω; causal. Προθέσεως gen. sg. fem. of πρόθεσις, , -εως, ἡ, "purpose") is compl. to κεκρατηκέναι (pf. act. inf. of κρατέω, "obtain"; indir. speech), with the sense of having the opportunity to carry out their plans since the southern wind was conducive to sailing west (Bruce, *Acts of the Apostles*, 518). The ptc. ἄραντες (nom. pl. masc. of aor. act. ptc. of αἴρω; attend. circum. or temp.) in a nautical setting is "having weighed anchor." The elative comp. adv. (BHGNT 514) ἆσσον ("nearer") with παρελέγοντο (3rd pl. impf. mid. indic. of παραλέγομαι) and the dir. obj. Κρήτην (acc. sg. fem. of Κρήτη, -ης, ἡ, "Crete") is best tr. "they were coasting Crete as close as possible."

27:14 Μετ' οὐ πολύ (lit. "after not much") is a temp. expression mng. "soon" (employ-ing litotes, see 14:28, BHGNT 514). Ἔβαλεν (3rd sg. aor. act. indic. of βάλλω) is intrans., best tr. with a vb. suitable to a violent wind in Eng. ("rushed" [NASB NRSV, CSB], "swept" [NIV, TNIV]). Κατ' αὐτῆς refers to Κρήτη in the previous v., mng. "down from her" (i.e., Crete; Johnson 447; R 606). Ἄνεμος τυφωνικός (nom. sg. masc. of τυφωνικός, -ή, -όν) is a "typhoon-like wind." Καλούμενος (nom. sg. masc. of pres. pass. ptc. of καλέω; attrib.) modifies εὐρακύλων (nom. sg. masc. of εὐρακύλων, -ωνος, ὁ, unattested elsewhere, most likely a combination of Εὖρος [southeast wind] and the Latin *Aquila* [northern wind], Barrett 2.1194), thus most EVV render it "northeaster."

27:15 This sentence opens with a compound gen. abs. cstr. describing the ship's inability to turn into the wind (a maneuver to reduce the profile against the wind to weather the storm at anchor [Haenchen 701]). Συναρπασθέντος is the gen. sg. neut. of aor. pass. ptc. of συναρπάζω, "catch"; gen abs., temp. The neg. δυναμένου (gen. sg. neut. of aor. mid. ptc. of. δύναμαι) takes the compl. inf. ἀντοφθαλμεῖν (pres. act. inf. of ἀντοφθαλμέω, "look directly at"), mng. "unable to face the wind." While ἀνέμῳ (masc. dat sg. of ἄνεμος, -ου, ὁ) modifies the inf., ἐπιδόντες (nom. pl. masc. of aor. act. ptc. of ἐπιδίδωμι, "yield"; attend. circum.) implies another assumed instance of the dat. noun (cf. Barrett 2.1140; BHGNT 516; Bruce, *Acts of the Apostles*, 519). Ἐφερόμεθα (1st pl. impf. pass. indic. of φέρω) has the sense of yielding to the wind, "we were letting ourselves be moved" (see NASB; cf. BDAG 1051d; ZG 449).

27:16 They next sought the brief protection of a small island that allowed the crew to make emergency preparations (Johnson 448). Νησίον (acc. sg. neut. of νησίον, -ου, τό, "small island") is the obj. of ὑποδραμόντες (nom. pl. masc. of aor. act. ptc. of ὑποτρέχω, "be under the protection of"; temp.) It is a synonym of ὑποπλέω (see v. 4) with the notion of speed (Barrett 2.1195). The island was named (καλούμενον, acc. sg. neut. of pres. pass. ptc. of καλέω) Καῦδα (indecl., "Cauda"; obj. of ptc.). Ἰσχύσαμεν (1st pl. aor. act. indic. of ἰσχύω), "we were able" (on μόλις, see 27:7), takes the compl. inf. γενέσθαι (aor. mid. inf. of γίνομαι). The inf. takes περικρατεῖς (masc. nom. or acc. pl. of περικρατής, -ές) as a pred. adj. mng. "to gain control" (ZG 449). The σκάφης (gen. sg. fem. of σκάφη, -ης, ἡ; obj. gen. modifying the pred. adj.) refers to the lifeboat/ utility boat. These were normally towed behind the ship, but the storm made it unsafe (Bruce, *Acts of the Apostles*, 519) or at jeopardy (Johnson 448). The difficulty was likely because the storm had swamped it (BASHH 143). Retrieving it was the first of three operations to secure their safety (Bruce, *Acts of the Apostles*, 519).

27:17 The rel. pron. phrase (with ἥν referring to σκάφης) expresses the completion of the first operation (ἄραντες, nom. pl. masc. of aor. act. ptc. of αἴρω). The next operation refers to bracing the hull of the ship with cables (βοηθείαις, dat. pl. fem. of βοήθεια, -ας, ἡ, lit. "helps"; in a nautical setting the term refers to cables [Bruce, *Acts of the Apostles*, 519]). Ἐχρῶντο is the 3rd pl. impf. mid. indic. of χράομαι, "use." Ὑποζωννύντες is the nom. pl. masc. of pres. act. ptc. of ὑποζώννυμι, "undergird." The third operation was done for a specific fear. Φοβούμενοί (nom. pl. masc. of pres. mid. ptc. of φοβέομαι) is causal. Μὴ . . . ἐκπέσωσιν is the 3rd pl. aor. act. subjunc. of ἐκπίπτω, a nautical term; cf. BDAG 308a. Together they mean "lest they drift off course," with the destination (εἰς) of the Σύρτιν (acc. sg. fem. of Σύρτις, -εως, ἡ; an extensive zone of sandbars and quicksand greatly feared by sailors [BASHH 144]). The action was (likely) dropping drift anchors to keep them off the Syrtis. Χαλάσαντες (nom. pl. masc. of aor. act. ptc. of χαλάω, "let down"; attend. circum.) with the obj. σκεῦος (acc. sg. neut. of σκεῦος, -ου, τό) is a nautical term mng. "having lowered the gear" (Bruce, *Acts of the Apostles*, 520). Although not abs. clear, it might refer to anchors (Barrett 2.1197; BHGNT 517). The phrase οὕτως ἐφέροντο (3rd pl. impf. pass. indic. of φέρω) describes drifting in this state for a while.

27:18 Σφοδρῶς (adv. "violently") χειμαζομένων (gen. sg. masc. of pres. act. ptc. of χειμάζω, "toss in a storm"; gen. abs., causal [cf. ESV]) mng. "because we were being severely storm tossed." On τῇ ἑξῆς, see 21:1; 25:17. The main clause, ἐκβολήν (acc. sg. fem. of ἐκβολή, -ῆς, ἡ) ἐποιοῦντο (3rd pl. impf. mid. indic. of ποιέω), is lit. "they were doing/making a jettisoning" (cf. Jonah 1:5). It refers to the crew lightening the ship by throwing objects overboard. If the mng. is the cargo, it was not all the cargo (Bock 736; see v. 38). Things indeed were desperate.

27:19 Τῇ τρίτῃ means "on the third day." Αὐτόχειρες is the nom. pl. masc. of αὐτόχειρ, -ρος, ὁ, "with their own hands." Σκευήν (acc. sg. fem. of σκευή, -ῆς, ἡ) τοῦ πλοίου is, if the mng. is the same as v. 17, a ref. to the anchors or simply the spare tack (BASHH 144). Ἔρριψαν is the 3rd pl. aor. act. indic. of ῥίπτω, "cast out." Whatever the exact ref., Luke is showing escalating measures to protect their lives.

27:20 The sentence begins with another compound gen. abs. phrase. Ἡλίου . . . ἄστρων (gen. pl. masc. of ἀστήρ, -έρος, ὁ, "star"; the entire phrase is the subj. of the first gen. abs.) are in a neither . . . nor cstr. (μήτε . . . μήτε), implying day and night buffeting. Ἐπιφαινόντων is the gen. pl. masc. of pres. act. ptc. of ἐπιφαίνω, "appear"; gen. abs.

Ἐπὶ πλείονας ἡμέρας is a temp. phrase expressing extent, mng. "for many days." The second gen. abs. phrase makes it explicit. Χειμῶνός (gen. sg. masc. of χειμών, -ῶνος, ὁ, "storm"; subj. of gen. abs.) modified by οὐκ ὀλίγου (litotes, see 14:28) means "no small storm." Ἐπικειμένου is the gen. sg. masc. of pres. mid. ptc. of ἐπίκειμαι, "lay upon." Both gen. abs. are causal. Περιῃρεῖτο is the 3rd sg. impf. pass. indic. of περιαιρέω, "cast off." Ἐλπὶς πᾶσα (fem. nom. sgs., "all hope") is the sub. of the epex. inf. τοῦ σώζεσθαι, identifying their hope (BHGNT 518; Rogers and Rogers 308).

27:21 Πολλῆς . . . ἀσιτίας (gen. sg. fem. of ἀσιτία, -ας, ἡ), lit. "much abstinence," is the gen. subj. of ὑπαρχούσης (gen. sg. fem. of pres. act. ptc. of ὑπάρχω; gen. abs., temp.) with the sense of "after a long time without food" (cf. RSV, NASB, NIV, ESV, CSB) either due to nausea or anxiety (Bock 737). Σταθείς is the nom. sg. masc. of aor. pass. ptc. of ἵστημι; attend. circum. Εἶπεν (3rd sg. aor. act. indic. of λέγω) introduces dir. speech. Ἔδει (3rd sg. impf. act. indic. of δεῖ) will take two compl. infs. On μέν *solitarium*, see 1:1. Πειθαρχήσαντάς (acc. pl. masc. of aor. act. ptc. of πειθαρχέω; attend. circum.) means "having obeyed [authority]," modifying the first (neg.) inf. ἀνάγεσθαι (pres. pass. inf. of ἀνάγω) mng. "not to put to sea." The second compl. inf. κερδῆσαί (aor. act. inf. of κερδαίνω, "gain") is purposefully ironic (Bruce, *Acts of the Apostles*, 521), pointing out that their intent to gain a benefit has gained ὕβριν (acc. sg. fem. of ὕβρις, -εως, ἡ, "injury") and ζημίαν (acc. sg. fem. of ζημία, -ας, ἡ, "loss") recalling Paul's warning of v. 10.

27:22 On καὶ τὰ νῦν, see 4:29. Παραινῶ (1st sg. pres. act. indic. of παραινέω) takes the compl. inf. εὐθυμεῖν (pres. act. inf. of εὐθυμέω), mng. "I urge you to take heart." The grounds (γάρ) is presented with a fronted ἀποβολή (nom. sg. fem. of ἀποβολή, -ῆς, ἡ, "loss"), neg. by οὐδεμία (mng. "no" [BDAG 735b]) as a pred. adj. of an impers. ἔσται (3rd sg. fut. mid. indic. of εἰμί), "there will be no loss of life." The ship, however (πλήν, "except"), was doomed.

27:23 The grounds (γάρ) for Paul's confidence was a visitation of an angel. Παρέστη (3rd sg. aor. act. indic. of παρίστημι) with the dat. μοι has the connotation "he approached me" (BDAG 778c). Ταύτῃ τῇ νυκτί has the sense of "last night" (Bruce, *Acts of the Apostles*, 521). Θεοῦ modifies ἄγγελος at the end of the sentence. The rel. clause, οὗ εἰμι [ἐγώ], denotes ownership. Another rel. clause phrase, ᾧ καί (adv. "also") λατρεύω (1st sg. pres. act. indic., "I serve/worship"), represents Paul as a faithful servant (Barrett 2.1201).

27:24 Λέγων (nom. sg. masc. of pres. act. ptc. of λέγω) introduces the dir. speech of the angel. Μὴ φοβοῦ (2nd sg. pres. pass. impv. of φοβέομαι) is always on the lips of Jesus or angels in Luke-Acts. Καίσαρί (dat. sg. masc. of Καῖσαρ, -αρος, ὁ) is a dat. of place ("before Caesar," likely a euphemism for the Roman government [Keener 4.3632]) and fronted for emphasis. Σε is the acc. subj. of the inf. (required by δεῖ, a subtle ref. to God's plan) παραστῆναι (aor. act. inf. of παρίστημι, "stand before"; compl.). On καὶ ἰδού, see 1:10. Κεχάρισταί (3rd sg. pf. mid. indic. of χαρίζομαι, "grant [as a gift]," i.e., God) takes σοι as the indir. obj. and τοὺς πλέοντας (acc. pl. masc. of pres. act. ptc. of πλέω, "sail"; subst.) as the dir. obj. The phrase is best understood as an answer to prayer (Barrett 2.1201).

27:25 Paul repeated his encouragement with an affirmation of his confidence in the vision. Εὐθυμεῖτε (2nd pl. pres. act. impv. of εὐθυμέω) is repeated from v. 22. Paul's faith (πιστεύω, 1st sg. pres. act. indic.) in God was the grounds (γάρ) for the encouragement. Ὅτι introduces the content of his faith. Οὕτως with καθ᾽ ὃν τρόπον ("in the same way"; BDAG 1017a) is redundant and therefore emphatic (cf. NASB, NRSV, "exactly as"). Ἔσται (3rd sg. fut. mid. indic. of εἰμί) is impers., "it will be." Λελάληταί is the 3rd sg. pf. pass. indic. of λαλέω.

27:26 Paul went on to clarify their fate that should have been comforting in that it implies they would not lose the ship in the open ocean. Εἰς νῆσον (acc. sg. masc. of νῆσος, -ου, ὁ) . . . τινα, "on a certain island," is fronted for emphasis. Δεῖ (see above) takes the compl. inf. ἐκπεσεῖν (aor. act. inf. of ἐκπίπτω, "run aground") indicating that grounding the ship was also part of God's plan.

27:27 Ὡς is temp., "when." Τεσσαρεσκαιδεκάτη (nom. sg. fem. of τεσσαρεσκαιδέκατος, -η, -ον) νύξ is "the fourteenth night," the subj. of ἐγένετο (3rd sg. aor. mid. indic. of γίνομαι). Διαφερομένων (gen. pl. masc. of pres. pass. ptc. of διαφέρω; gen. abs., temp.), when used in a nautical setting in the pass., means "as we were drifting." Ἐν τῷ Ἀδρίᾳ (dat. sg. fem. of Ἀδρια, -ας, ἡ) employs the monadic art. to ref. "the Adriatic Sea." Κατὰ μέσον τῆς νυκτός is an approximate temp. expression mng. "about midnight" (BDAG 512b). Ὑπενόουν is the 3rd pl. impf. act. indic. of ὑπονοέω, "suspect." Προσάγειν (pres. act. inf. of προσάγω, "approach") is indir. speech taking τινὰ . . . χώραν ("some land") as the subj.

27:28 Βολίσαντες (nom. pl. masc. of aor. act. ptc. of βολίζω, "sound"; attend. circum.) refers to a process where depth is ascertained by dropping a line with a lead weight (Bock 739). Εὗρον is the 3rd pl. aor. act. indic. of εὑρίσκω. The depth of "twenty fathoms" (ὀργυιὰς [acc. pl. fem. of ὀργυιά, -ᾶς, ἡ] εἴκοσι) was about 121 feet (a fathom was the length of a sailor's outstretched arms [about 6 feet; 1.85 meters; BDAG 721c]). The phrase βραχύ (adv., lit. "short") . . . διαστήσαντες (nom. pl. masc. of aor. act. ptc. of διΐστημι; temp.) is "having gone a little farther." This time the sounding (βολίσαντες, see above) is fifteen (δεκαπέντε) fathoms (ὀργυιάς, see above). The ship was moving closer to shore.

27:29 Φοβούμενοί (nom. pl. masc. of pres. mid. ptc. of φόβεομαι) is causal, "because they were fearing." The phrase που κατὰ τραχεῖς (acc. pl. masc. of τραχύς, -εῖα, -ύ, "rough, uneven") τόπους (lit. "somewhere against uneven places") ἐκπέσωμεν (1st pl. aor. act. subjunc. of ἐκπίπτω) is best rendered "run aground on the rocks." Πρύμνης (gen. sg. fem. of πρύμνα, -ης, ἡ; obj. of prep.) is the stern of the ship. Throwing out (ῥίψαντες, nom. pl. masc. of aor. act. ptc. of ῥίπτω, "throw out"; temp.) four anchors (ἀγκύρας, acc. pl. fem. of ἄγκυρα, -ας, ἡ) was the correct procedure under the circumstances (i.e., not an act of extreme desperation, though an exceptional action; BASHH 147). The mng. of ηὔχοντο (3rd pl. impf. mid. indic. of εὔχομαι) is debated:

1. It might represent a generic "were wishing" (KJV, NASB, NET, MIT; BDAG 417b).
2. The other option is that it expresses "were praying" (RSV, NLT, NIV, ESV, TNIV, NJB, HCSB; cf. BHGNT 524). Given the circumstances, prayer for

daybreak (ἡμέραν) to happen (γενέσθαι, aor. mid. inf. of γίνομαι; indir. speech) seems appropriate.

27:30 This v. introduces at least some of the sailors' (ναυτῶν, gen. pl. masc. of ναύτης, -ου, ὁ; subj. of ptc.) attempt to leave the ship, in a compound gen. abs. cstr. (to be completed in the next v.). Keener observes that a ship of this size would need about a dozen sailors (Keener 4.3638) so it could have been all of them. Ζητούντων is the gen. pl. masc. of pres. act. ptc. of ζητέω; gen. abs., temp. Φυγεῖν is the aor. act. inf. of φεύγω, "flee"; compl. The second gen. abs. employs χαλασάντων (gen. sg. masc. of aor. act. ptc. of χαλάω, "let down" [each instance in the NT involves ropes]; temp.). On σκάφην (acc. sg. fem. of σκάφη, -ης, ἡ), see v. 16. The combination of προφάσει (dat. sg. fem. of πρόφασις, -εως, ἡ, "pretense"; instr. dat.), ὡς, and the ptc. μελλόντων (nom. sg. masc. of pres. act. ptc. of μέλλω) is best rendered "on the pretext they were going to . . ." (Bruce, *Acts of the Apostles*, 524; see also BHGNT 524; cf. NJB). Ἐκτείνειν is the aor. act. inf. of ἐκτείνω, "stretch out"; compl. The procedure to set the anchors at the bow (πρώρης, gen. sg. fem. of πρῷρα, -ης, ἡ) of the ship from the smaller boat was a standard procedure designed to lock the ship in a single orientation (in this case into the wind; Barrett 2.1205). Because of this, Luke's interpretation has been called into question (see Haenchen 706). It was, however, the legitimacy of the maneuver that made a panicky attempt at flight possible (BASHH 148). But since the maneuver really only needed one man in the boat, a skiff full of sailors would naturally look suspicious (Keener 4.3638).

27:31 As the attempt was underway, Paul spoke (εἶπεν, 3rd sg. aor. act. indic. of λέγω) to the centurion (ἑκατοντάρχῃ, dat. sg. masc. of ἑκατοντάρχης, -ου, ὁ) and the soldiers (στρατιώταις, dat. pl. masc. of στρατιώτης, -ου, ὁ). The ἐὰν μή cstr. introduces a third-class cond. mng. "except" (Robertson, *Pictures,* 471). Οὗτοι μείνωσιν (3rd pl. aor. act. subjunc. of μένω) completes the prot. with an emphatic cstr. (redundant pron., Wallace 322). The pron. ὑμεῖς is also emphatic in the apod., suggesting the sailors' skills were necessary to keep them all alive. Σωθῆναι (aor. pass. inf. of σῴζω) is the compl. to a negated δύνασθε (2nd pl. pres. mid. indic. of δύναμαι), "you are not able." Paul's warning should not be seen as contradicting the vision reported in vv. 23–24 for two reasons. First, prophecy is often conditional. Second, the warning may simply be wise observation of their need for the sailors.

27:32 At Paul's alert, the soldiers took action and cut the skiff from the ship. Ἀπέκοψαν is the 3rd pl. aor. act. indic. of ἀποκόπτω, "cut off." The σχοινία (acc. pl. neut. of σχοινίον, -ου, τό; used here and John 2:15 in the NT) refers to the cords lashing the bow (σκάφης, gen. sg. fem. of σκάφη, -ης, ἡ) to the ship. Εἴασαν is the 3rd pl. aor. act. indic. of ἐάω, "allow." Ἐκπεσεῖν is the aor. act. inf. of ἐκπίπτω, "fall away"; compl. Both passengers and crew were now, lit., all in the same boat.

27:33 On ἄχρι . . . οὗ, see 7:18. Ἡμέρα ἤμελλεν (3rd sg. impf. act. indic. of μέλλω) γίνεσθαι (pres. mid. inf. of γίνομαι; compl.), lit. "day was about to be," is best, with the prep. phrase "as day was about to dawn" (RSV, NET). Παρεκάλει is the 3rd sg. impf. act. indic. of παρακαλέω. Μεταλαβεῖν (aor. act. inf. of μεταλαμβάνω, "partake"; indir. speech) takes a gen. obj., τροφῆς (gen. sg. fem. of τροφή, -ῆς, ἡ, "food"; a part. gen.). Λέγων (nom. sg. masc. of pres. act. ptc. of λέγω) introduces dir. speech. BDF (§161[3]) identifies the phrase τεσσαρεσκαιδεκάτην σήμερον ἡμέραν as a "special idiom" under the acc. of extent, mng. " . . . now already fourteen days." However, it is more likely "this is the fourteenth day that . . ." (Bruce, *Acts of the Apostles*, 524), given that v. 27 identified the previous night as the fourteenth (counting a twenty-four-hour period to begin with the night; see Barrett 2.1207). Προσδοκῶντες (nom. pl. masc. of pres. act. ptc. of προσδοκάω; attend. circum.) refers to expectation (either in dread, hope, or neutral, as supplied by context; BDAG 877c). Used abs., the obj. must be supplied. Here, the context suggests anxiety. Therefore, some EVV rightly tr. it "continued in suspense" (cf. RSV, NIV, NRSV, ESV, TNIV, NET, NJB), suggesting anxiety (cf. ZG 451). Ἄσιτοι (nom. pl. masc. of ἄσιτος, -η, -ον) is technically a subst. pred. adj. of διατελεῖτε (2nd pl. pres. act. indic. of διατελέω, "continue"; a durative pres.; KMP 257) with the sense of "having gone without food" (cf. RSV, NASB, NIV, TNIV, NET, CSB). A neg. προσλαβόμενοι (nom. pl. masc. of aor. mid. ptc. of προσλαμβάνω; attend. circum.) likely refers to taking only bits of food and not a meal (Robertson, *Pictures*, 472).

27:34 Paul suggested a meal. Παρακαλῶ is the 1st sg. pres. act. indic. of παρακαλέω. On μεταλαβεῖν τροφῆς, see v. 33. The reason given (γάρ) is for their health. Σωτηρίας (gen. sg. fem. of σωτηρία, -ας, ἡ) is the obj. of πρός, the only time it takes a gen. in the NT. It means "in the interest of" ("literary language" [BDF §240]; cf. BHGNT 526; R [623]: "a classical idiom"). Ὑπάρχει (3rd sg. pres. act. indic. of ὑπάρχω) is used as a being vb. here. The second γάρ is explanatory. The argument is from lesser to greater. No hair (θρίξ, nom. sg. fem. of θρίξ, τριχός, ἡ) will be lost (ἀπολεῖται, 3rd sg. fut. mid. indic. of ἀπόλλυμι).

27:35 Εἴπας is the nom. sg. masc. of aor. act. ptc. of λέγω; temp. Several items could suggest a ref. to the Lord's Supper. These begin with the phrase λαβών (nom. sg. masc. of aor. act. ptc. of λαμβάνω; temp. or attend. circum.) ἄρτον ("bread"). See also εὐχαρίστησεν (3rd sg. aor. act. indic. of εὐχαριστέω) and κλάσας (nom. sg. masc. of aor. act. ptc. of κλάω, "break"; temp. or attend. circum.). However, while Luke has presented Paul as echoing Christ in other places in Acts, these are normal words for eating (see Haenchen 707). Ἤρξατο (3rd sg. aor. mid. indic. of ἄρχομαι) ἐσθίειν (pres. act. inf. of ἐσθίω; compl.) is "he began to eat."

27:36 Εὔθυμοι (nom. pl. masc. of εὔθυμος, -η, -ον, "cheerful") is the pred. adj. of γενόμενοι (nom. pl. masc. of aor. mid. ptc. of γίνομαι; attend. circum.) with the sense "they were encouraged." Προσελάβοντο (3rd pl. aor. mid. indic. of προσλαμβάνω, "received") takes "food" (τροφῆς, gen. sg. fem. of τροφή, -ῆς, ἡ; part. gen.) as a dir. obj. The whole phrase describes the response to Paul's example that encouraged them to eat.

27:37 Ἤμεθα (1st pl. impf. mid. indic. of εἰμί) takes αἱ πᾶσαι ψυχαί as the subj. It is lit. "all we souls were . . . ." Incl. the prep. phrase, it is smoother to render it "there were . . . of us on board." Διακόσιαι ἑβδομήκοντα ἕξ is a pred. adj. giving the number of people on board ("276"). The number of passengers is not particularly high for one of these ships. Josephus (*Vita* 15:3) recounts a shipwreck with 600 passengers.

27:38 Κορεσθέντες is the nom. pl. masc. of aor. pass. ptc. of κορέννυμι, "satisfy." The vb., ἐκούφιζον (3rd pl. impf. act. indic. of κουφίζω), is likely an inceptive impf. mng.

"they began to lighten" (cf. NASB, CSB). This is in the hopes of beaching closer to shore. Ἐκβαλλόμενοι (nom. pl. masc. of pres. mid. ptc. of ἐκβάλλω; means) with the obj. σῖτον (acc. sg. masc. of σῖτος, -ου, ὁ) means "by throwing out the wheat."

27:39 After the sun came up (ἐγένετο, 3rd sg. aor. mid. indic. of γίνομαι), they turned their attention to landing. While the major port at Malta would be known (Robertson, *Pictures,* 473), they did not recognize (ἐπεγίνωσκον, 3rd pl. impf. act. indic. of ἐπιγινώσκω) the coastline (τὴν γῆν). Κόλπον (acc. sg. masc. of κόλπος, -ου, ὁ) τινα as a nautical term is "a certain bay." The force of the impf. κατενόουν (3rd pl. impf act. indic. of κατανοέω, "notice") has been much debated.

1. Barrett suggests that Luke chose a tense that was not very suitable (Barrett 2.1211). This is unnecessary.
2. Every EVV tr. it an aor., essentially treating it like a historical pres.
3. Moulton suggests it is iter., "noticed one after another" (Moulton 117).
4. Robertson (*Pictures,* 473) suggests it means "gradually perceived after some effort." This is an interpretation of the progressive impf. Culy and Parsons have a similar take (BHGNT 528).

The adj. ptc. phrase, ἔχοντα (acc. sg. masc. of pres. act. ptc. of ἔχω; attrib.) αἰγιαλόν (acc. sg. masc. of αἰγιαλός, -οῦ, ὁ), is "having a beach," modifying "bay." Ἐβουλεύοντο (3rd pl. impf. mid. indic. of βουλεύω) in the impf. here suggests deliberation, "they were deciding" (most EVV tr. it like an aor.). Εἰ δύναιντο (3rd pl. pres. mid. opt. of δύναμαι) means "if possible" (an implied indir. question; R 1021). Ἐξῶσαι (aor. act. inf. of ἐξωθέω, "push out"; compl.) takes as its obj. πλοῖον; in nautical terms, it is "to beach the ship."

27:40 To beach the ship, the crew takes three actions. First, they cut the anchors (ἀγκύρας, acc. pl. fem. of ἄγκυρα, -ας, ἡ), lit. "having cast off" (περιελόντες, nom. pl. masc. of aor. act. ptc. of περιαιρέω; temp.), and allowed (εἴων, 3rd pl impf. act. indic. of ἐάω) them to drop into the sea. At the same time (ἅμα) they loosed (ἀνέντες, nom. pl. masc. of aor. act. ptc. of ἀνίημι; temp.) the straps (ζευκτηρίας, acc. pl. fem. of ζευκτηρία, -ας, ἡ, "ropes/bands"). This may possibly be the crossbar connecting two rudders (Barrett 2.1212). These rudders are not to be confused with modern rudders (Bruce, *Acts of the Apostles,* 527). The πηδαλίων (gen. pl. neut. of πηδάλιον, -ου, -τό) are "steering paddles" that descended from the bow of the ship (normally two on a Greek ship [Barrett 2.1212]) and were controlled by the helmsman using a long tiller (Keener 4.3651). The action would ostensibly be done to let the wind steer. Finally, they hoisted (ἐπάραντες, nom. pl. masc. of aor. act. ptc. of ἐπαίρω; temp.) the foresail (ἀρτέμωνα, acc. sg. masc. of ἀρτέμων, -ωνος, ὁ) into the breeze (πνεούσῃ, dat. sg. fem. of pres. act. ptc. of πνέω; subst., dat. indicates direction, lit. "to the thing blowing"). Then they headed (κατεῖχον, 3rd pl. impf. act. indic. of κατέχω; as a nautical term, "they were holding course") toward the beach.

27:41 Luke vividly describes the fate of the ship becoming fixed and being ripped apart by the sea. Περιπεσόντες is the nom. pl. masc. of aor. act. ptc. of περιπίπτω, "strike, fall upon"; temp. Διθάλασσον (acc. sg. masc. of διθάλασσος, -ον, "a point"; lit. "of two seas") refers to either an exposed reef or visible sandbank (with water on both sides; Keener 4.3652). Ἐπέκειλαν is the 3rd pl. aor. act. indic. of ἐπικέλλω, "run aground."

The destruction of the ship is expressed in a μὲν . . . δέ cstr. The prow (πρῷρα, nom. sg. fem. of πρῷρα, -ης, ἡ,) stuck fast (the mng. of the phrase ἐρείσασα [nom. sg. fem. of aor. act. ptc. of ἐρείδω, "become fixed"; see ZG 452] ἔμεινεν [3rd sg. aor. act. indic. of μένω] ἀσάλευτος (nom. sg. fem. of ἀσάλευτος, -ον, "immoveable"; pred. adj.]). The stern (πρύμνα, nom. sg. fem. of πρύμνα, -ης, ἡ) lit. "was being loosed" (ἐλύετο, 3rd sg. impf. pass. indic. of λύω). The impf. is interpreted three ways:

1. Ingressive, "was beginning to break up" (Bruce, *Acts of the Apostles*, 527; BDF §326 [possible]; BHGNT 528; Robertson, *Pictures*, 475; ZG 452; cf. CSB, NLT, NASB, NJB).
2. Progressive, "was being broken apart" (perhaps durative). In this case, Luke was describing the ship being broken up bit by bit (Barrett 2.1213; BDF §326; Schnabel 1048; ESV, NET, MIT).
3. Some EVV (e.g., RSV, NIV, TNIV) tr. it as an aor. ("was broken").

Given that λύω suggests reducing to component parts and is used elsewhere of dismantling a ship (BDAG 607b) and the deliberation to the end of the ch., it does not seem likely that the breakup was immediate. It was, however, clearly about to happen. Either 1 or 2 fits the context well. The agent is expressed by the prep. phrase ὑπὸ τῆς βίας (gen. sg. fem. of βία, -ας, ἡ, "force") κυμάτων (gen. pl. neut. of κῦμα, -ατος, τό; subj. gen.), mng. "by the force of the waves."

27:42 Commonly in such disasters, prisoners were executed rather than risk their escape (which would put the soldiers at risk for punitive actions; BASHH 152; Keener 4.3654; Schnabel 1048; cf. 12:19, 16:27). The choice of τῶν . . . στρατιωτῶν βουλή (nom. sg. fem. of βουλή, -ῆς, ἡ, "plan") indicates more than a mere suggestion. It is expressed with ἐγένετο (3rd sg. aor. mid. indic. of γίνομαι) and a ἵνα clause (expressing purp.) functioning as the pred. nom (see BHGNT 530; Wallace 678). Ἀποκτείνωσιν is the 3rd pl. aor. act. subjunc. of ἀποκτείνω, "kill." The neg. adv. μή is best "lest." Ἐκκολυμβήσας is the nom. sg. masc. of aor. act. ptc. of ἐκκολυμβάω, "swim out." Διαφύγῃ (3rd sg. aor. act. subjunc. of διαφεύγω, "escape") is still controlled by ἵνα.

27:43 The causal ptc. βουλόμενος (nom. sg. masc. of pres. mid. ptc. of βούλομαι) is compl. by the inf. διασῶσαι (aor. act. inf. of διασώζω, "bring safely through"). Ἐκώλυσεν (3rd sg. aor. act. indic. of κωλύω, "forbid") with the obj. αὐτούς and the gen. of separaton (BDF §180) βουλήματος (gen. sg. neut. of βούλημα, -ατος, τό, "intention") is best rendered "kept them from carrying out their plan" (NIV, NRSV, ESV, TNIV, CSB). The new plan was announced as an order, ἐκέλευσέν (3rd sg. aor. act. indic. of κελεύω), introducing indir. speech. Δυναμένους (acc. pl. masc. of pres. mid. ptc. of δύναμαι; subst., dir. obj.) takes the compl. inf. κολυμβᾶν (pres. act. inf. of κολυμβάω), mng. "those who could swim" (cf. CSB, RSV, NASB, NIV). Ἀπορίψαντας is the acc. pl. masc. of aor. act. ptc. of ἀπορίπτω, "jumped overboard"; attend. circum. Ἐπὶ τὴν γῆν modifies ἐξιέναι (pres. act. inf. of ἔξειμι, "go out"; purp.) and means "to get to shore."

27:44 Τοὺς λοιπούς (acc. pl. masc. of λοιπός, -ή, -όν, "the rest") is another dir. obj. of ἐκώλυσεν, that is, those who cannot swim. It is divided into two groups by the rel. prons. οὕς in a μὲν . . . δέ cstr. The first group could use planks (σανίσιν, dat. pl. fem. of σανίς, -ίδος, ἡ). The second would use some wood from the ship (ξύλον is implied by the neuts. τινων "some" and τῶν, a nominalizer for the prep. phrase ἀπὸ τοῦ πλοίου;

BHGNT 531). Ἐγένετο is the 3rd sg. aor. mid. indic. of γίνομαι. Not only Paul, but all the passengers were saved (διασωθῆναι, aor. pass. inf. of διασῴζω; cf. v 43). Paul's vision (27:22) was thus validated.

c. Provision and Ministry on Malta (28:1–9)

28:1 Διασωθέντες is the nom. pl. masc. of aor. pass. ptc. of διασῴζω,"rescue"; temp. (see vv. 43, 44). Ἐπέγνωμεν is the 1st pl. aor. act. indic. of ἐπιγινώσκω, "recognize." Ὅτι introduces the content of the knowledge. Rather than the objs. being in double-acc. cstr., here the subjs. are (see BHGNT 532; in the pass. vbs. transpose the objs. to the subj.). Μελίτη (nom. sg. fem. of Μελίτη, -ης, ἡ, "Malta," south of Sicily) is the compl., and νῆσος (nom. sg. fem. of νῆσος, -ου, ἡ, "island") is the subj. of καλεῖται (3rd sg. pres. pass. indic. of καλέω).

28:2 Βάρβαροι (nom. pl. masc. of βάρβαρος, -ου, ὁ, "barbarians") is variously tr. "natives" (RSV, NASB, NRSV, ESV ["native peoples"]), "islanders" (NIV, TNIV), "inhabitants" (NET, NJB), "local people" (CSB), and "aborigines" (MIT). This is an effort not to carry the dismissive baggage the word has in Eng. today. It referred to non-Gk.-speaking people. It need not imply an inferior status (Barrett 2.1220). Παρεῖχον is the 3rd pl. impf. act. indic. of παρέχω, "offer." Luke again employs litotes (with οὐ, see 14:28). Τὴν τυχοῦσαν (on the mng. here, see 19:11) φιλανθρωπίαν (acc. sg. fem. of φιλανθρωπία, -ας, ἡ) means "unusual kindness" (RSV, NIV, NRSV, ESV, TNIV, NJB) or "extraordinary kindness" (NASB, NET, CSB). Ἅψαντες (nom. pl. masc. of aor. act. ptc. of ἅπτω, "light"; attend. circum.) takes πυράν (acc. sg. fem. of πυρά, -ᾶς, ἡ, "fire") as its obj. Προσελάβοντο (3rd pl. aor. mid. indic. of προσλαμβάνω, "receive") refers to both prisoner and soldier alike (πάντας ἡμᾶς, "us all"). The reason for the fire was two-fold (both acc. objs. of διά, "because"). First, rain (ὑετόν, acc. sg. masc. of ὑετός, -οῦ, ὁ) had begun (ἐφεστῶτα, acc. sg. masc. of pf. act. ptc. of ἐφίστημι; attrib.). The second reason was the cold (ψῦχος, acc. sg. neut. of ψῦχος, -ους, τό).

28:3 The v. is introduced with a compund gen. abs. phrase about Paul gathering fire-wood. Συστρέψαντος (gen. sg. masc. of aor. act. ptc. of συστρέφω, "gather"; gen. abs., temp.). The obj. phrase of the ptc., φρυγάνων (gen. pl. neut. of φρύγανον, -ου, τό, "brushwood") τι πλῆθος, lit. "a certain multitude of brushwood," is best tr. (as most EVV) "a bundle of sticks." Ἐπιθέντος is the gen. sg. masc. aor. act. ptc. of ἐπιτίθημι; gen. abs., temp. A viper (ἔχιδνα, nom. sg. fem. of ἔχιδνα, -ης, ἡ; subj.) was apparently in the bundle, for it came out (ἐξελθοῦσα, nom. sg. fem. of aor. act. ptc. of ἐξέρχομαι; attend. circum.) because of the heat (θέρμης, gen. sg. fem. of θερμός, -ή, -όν, "warm"; subst., obj. of prep.) from the fire. Καθῆψεν (3rd sg. aor. act. indic. of καθάπτω, "seize") takes a gen. obj. (χειρός, gen. sg. fem. of χείρ, χειρός, ἡ), mng. "fastened on his hand."

28:4 The sight of a poisonous snake dangling from Paul's hand led the natives to draw a conclusion about the nature of his crime, knowing he was a prisoner. Ὡς is temp., "when." Εἶδον (3rd pl aor. act. indic. of ὁράω) takes a double-acc. cstr. with a compl. ptc. (κρεμάμενον, acc. sg. neut. of pres. mid. ptc. of κρεμάννυμι, "hang") and θηρίον (acc. sg. neut. of θηρίον, -ου, τό), best tr. as "creature" (cf. RSV, NASB, ESV, NET). Ἔλεγον (3rd pl. impf. act. indic. of λέγω) is progressive, suggesting what follows is indir. speech. The adv. πάντως here means "no doubt" (cf. RSV, NLT, ESV, NET,

CSB). Φονεύς (nom. sg. masc. of φονεύς, -έως, ὁ) is a pred. nom. with ἐστιν and ὁ ἄνθρωπος οὗτος ("this man") as the subj. phrase. Διασωθέντα (acc. sg. masc. of aor. pass. ptc. of διασῴζω, "rescue"; attrib.) with the rel. pron. is a dir. obj. phrase, "him who escaped the sea" (BHGNT 533; Rogers and Rogers 311). Δίκη (fem. nom sg. of δίκη, -ης, ἡ) may be a personified justice or the name of a local deity (Barrett 2.1222; Bruce, *Acts of the Apostles*, 532). Ζῆν (pres. act. inf. of ζάω) is a compl. to εἴασεν (3rd sg. aor. act. indic. of ἐάω, "allow"), together mng. "Justice has not allowed . . . to live."

28:5 On μὲν οὖν, see 1:6. Ἀποτινάξας is the nom. sg. masc. of aor. act. ptc. of ἀποτινάσσω, "shake"; temp., only here and Luke 9:5. Ἔπαθεν (3rd sg. aor. act. indic. of πάσχω, "suffer") takes οὐδὲν κακόν ("no harm") as the dir. obj. phrase.

28:6 The art. οἱ functions as the pron. subj. of προσεδόκων (3rd pl. impf. act. indic. of προσδοκάω), mng. "they were waiting." The vb. takes an acc. and an inf. (BDAG 877c). In this case, the pres. act. inf. μέλλειν (of μέλλω) also takes a compl. inf. πίμπρασθαι (pres. pass. inf. of πίμπρημι, either "burn with fever" or "swell up"), mng. " . . . for him to begin to swell." An alternative expectation (still under the control of προσδοκάω) would be to fall down (καταπίπτειν, pres. act. inf. of καταπίπτω) suddenly (ἄφνω) dead. Luke uses a compound gen. abs. phrase to describe the natives' observation of Paul. Ἐπὶ πολύ is a temp. expression denoting a long time span (BDAG 367b; ZG 453). It modifies προσδοκώντων (gen. pl. masc. of pres. act. ptc. of προσδοκάω; gen. abs., temp.), mng. "waiting for a long time." Θεωρούντων is the gen. pl. masc. of pres. act. ptc. of θεωρέω; gen. abs., temp. Μηδὲν ἄτοπον (acc. sg. masc. of ἄτοπος, -ον) means "nothing unusual." Γινόμενον is the acc. sg. neut. of pres. mid. ptc. of γίνομαι; compl. At this point we should expect the subj. to change due to the previous gen. abs. That it does not may be one of those rare cases where one does not find a change. It may be, however, the shift is from all the islanders to merely some (BHGNT 535). Μεταβαλόμενοι is the nom. pl. masc. of aor. mid. ptc. of μεταβάλλω, "change one's way of thinking"; attend. circum.; NT hapax. Ἔλεγον (3rd pl. impf. act. indic. of λέγω) is inceptive, mng. "they began saying." Εἶναι is the pres. inf. of εἰμί; indir. speech. Θεόν is the acc. sg. masc. of θεός, -οῦ, ὁ, "a god"; obj. of inf. Their estimation of Paul went from bad to unprecedented; the deification of justice and then Paul demonstrates a society bathed in idolatry.

28:7 The prep. ἐν has an unusual obj. The art. τοῖς nominalizes another prep. phrase, περὶ τὸν τόπον ἐκεῖνον, to be the obj., mng. "in the regions around that place." Ὑπῆρχεν (3rd sg. impf. act. indic. of ὑπάρχω) is impers., taking χωρία (nom. pl. neut. of χωρίον, -ου, τό; pred. nom.), "there were lands." The poss. dat. τῷ πρώτῳ ("first man") is a title known to be current on Malta (BASHH 153) and either refers to the highest Roman official on the island (Schnabel 1052) or the leading benefactor of the area. That he has land and is hospitable leads Johnson to think the latter (Johnson 462). On ὀνόματι, see 5:1. Ποπλίῳ (dat. sg. masc. of Πόπλιος, -ου, ὁ) is a Roman praenomen, normally tr. "Publius." Ἀναδεξάμενος is the nom. sg. masc. of aor. mid. ptc. of ἀναδέχομαι, "receive"; attend. circum. The "us" (ἡμᾶς) does not have to include all 276 passengers. It might refer to Paul's group alone; esp. if Publius was a Roman official, it would make sense. Φιλοφρόνως ἐξένισεν (3rd sg. aor. act. indic. of ξενίζω) means "hospitably hosted."

28:8 On ἐγένετο δέ, see 4:5. Πατέρα is the subj. of the inf. below. Πυρετοῖς (dat. pl. masc. of πυρετός, -ου, ὁ, "fever") and δυσεντερίῳ (dat. sg. neut. of δυσεντέριον, -ου, τό, "dysentery") are the objs. of συνεχόμενον (acc. sg. masc. of pres. pass. ptc. of συνέχω), likely causal, "because he was seized with a fever and dysentery." Κατακεῖσθαι (pres. mid. inf. of κατάκειμαι, "lie down") is best tr. "bedridden." The healing at the hands of Paul is in the simplest of terms. Three attend. circum. ptcs. provide the background to Paul's action: εἰσελθών (nom. sg. masc. of aor. act. ptc. of εἰσέρχομαι); προσευξάμενος (nom. sg. masc. of aor. mid. ptc. of προσεύχομαι); and ἐπιθείς (nom. sg. masc. of aor. act. ptc. ἐπιτίθημι), "put [hands] upon." The result was a miraculous recovery (Ἰάσατο, 3rd sg. aor. mid. indic. of ἰάομαι, "heal").

28:9 The news apparently got out quickly. Τούτου . . . γενομένου (gen. sg. masc. of aor. mid. ptc. of γίνομαι; gen. abs.) is a temp. expression mng. "after this." The subj. of the vb. (λοιποί) is modified by a subst. ptc. that is modified by a prep. phrase. Ἐν τῇ νήσῳ (dat. sg. fem. of νῆσος, -ου, ἡ, "island") is in the attrib. position to ἔχοντες (nom. pl. masc. of pres. act. ptc. of ἔχω; attrib.) and takes the obj. ἀσθενείας (acc. pl. fem. of ἀσθένεια, -ας, ἡ), "sicknesses." Προσήρχοντο is the 3rd pl. impf. mid. indic. of προσέρχομαι, "approach." The impf. ἐθεραπεύοντο (3rd pl. impf. pass. indic. of θεραπεύω) is iterative.

d. Journey to Rome (28:10–16)

28:10 The rel. pron. οἵ takes the healed islanders as the antecedent. Luke employs a cognate cstr.; τιμαῖς (instr.) ἐτίμησαν (3rd pl. aor. act. indic. of τιμάω) may refer to "fees" or "honors." In the past, scholars connected it to medical fees (see Bruce, *Acts of the Apostles*, 533; Robertson, *Pictures*, 481) for the noun always refers to money in Acts (cf. 4:34; 5:2, 3). The vb. often merely means "honor" (see Luke 18:20). Whatever the honors were, it is unlikely to have been merely abstract praise (Keener 4.3693). If it is "pay" rather than "honor" it is an example of God's providence, for the team will need resources when they get to Rome (see 28:16; note the Philippians gave to Paul's need while in Rome [see Phil 4:10–14]). Ἀναγομένοις (dat. pl. masc. of pres. pass. ptc. of ἀνάγω) is temp.; the dat. ptc. is used in lieu of a fut. ptc. (ZG 454; cf. BDF §339[2]); that is, it looks forward to a later time (see v. 11); most EVV tr. it "when we sailed." Ἐπέθεντο is the 3rd pl. aor. mid. indic. of ἐπιτίθημι, "put upon." Τά nominalizes πρὸς τὰς χρείας (lit. "the things toward the needs") and is best rendered "all the supplies we needed" (NET) or "what we needed" (CSB; ZG 454).

28:11 Three months (τρεῖς μῆνας) would indicate an early February departure (ἀνήχθημεν, 1st pl. aor. pass. indic. of ἀνάγω, "we put to sea") at the latest. This is quite early in the season but not unheard-of (BASHH 153). Both the ptc. παρακεχειμακότι (dat. sg. neut. of pf. act. ptc. of παραχειμάζω, "winter") and Ἀλεξανδρίνῳ (dat. sg. neut. of Ἀλεξανδρῖνος, -η, -ον, "Alexandrian") are attrib. to πλοίῳ. Two matters entangle the dat. παρασήμῳ (dat. sg. neut. of παράσημος, -ον; NT hapax). First, it may refer to either an insignia/emblem (KJV) or a figurehead (most EVV). The mng. changes little either way. Second, the dat. case is disputed.

1. According to BDF (§198[7]) the dat. may be an abs. cstr. mng. "with . . . as the ship's emblem." Turner (*Style*, 243) admits the category is merely possible.

2. BDF prefers the idea that it was "a mechanical declension of a registry— like . . . 'a ship, insignia the Dioscuri'" (BDF §198[7]). Under this interpretation it is something like the ship's name (Bruce, *Acts of the Apostles*, 534; Barrett 2.1228; Haenchen 717). Only this explanation readily explains why Luke included the ref. at all.

3. Zerwick takes it as a dat. of means, "*distinguished* by the sign of . . ." (ZG 452). Blass thinks this option is hardly the mng. (BDF §198[7]).

Διοσκούροις (dat. pl. masc. of Διόσκουροι, -ων, οἱ, "Dioscori"; a Latin loanword; lit. "sons of Zeus") refers to Castor and Pollux, considered the helpers of seafarers (see Schnabel 1054).

28:12 The first stop (καταχθέντες, nom. pl. masc. of aor. pass. ptc. of κατάγω, "put in") was Syracuse (Συρακούσας, acc. pl. fem. of Συράκουσαι, -ῶν, αἱ), a city on the island of Sicily. They waited (ἐπεμείναμεν, 1st pl. aor. act indic. of ἐπιμένω, "stay") three days, likely due to weather (BASHH 154).

28:13 EVV are split between the rdg. περιελόντες (nom. pl. masc. of aor act. ptc. of περιαιρέω, "cast loose," perhaps implying "weighed anchors" [cf. 27:40], NRSV, NET, MIT) and περιελθόντες (nom. pl. masc. of aor. act. ptc. of περιερχομαι, often tr. "we made a circuit," implying skirting along the coast, RSV, NASB, ESV, NJB). Given the minute difference (a θ that could easily be unintentional), being somewhat better attested and older, and geographically well distributed, the latter rdg. seems best (see BHGNT 538; for the opposite opinion see Metzger 443). Κατηντήσαμεν is the 1st pl. aor. act. indic. of καταντάω, "arrive." Ῥήγιον (acc. sg. neut. of Ῥήγιον, -ου, τό, "Rhegium"; dir. obj.) was the closest port on the Italian mainland. After a day's wait they received (ἐπιγενομένου, gen. sg. masc. of aor. mid. ptc. of ἐπιγίνομαι, "become"; gen. abs., temp.) a favorable wind from the south (νότου, gen. sg. masc. of νότος, -ου, ὁ; subj. of gen. abs.). Δευτεραῖοι (nom. pl. masc. of δευτεραῖος, -αία, -ον) is a CGk. idiom (R 550); with ἤλθομεν (1st pl. aor. act. indic. of ἔρχομαι), it is lit. "We came as second-day men" (Barrett 2.1229; Robertson, *Pictures*, 483). It means a day later they arrived at Puteoli on the bay of Naples (Haenchen 718).

28:14 On οὗ, see 1:13. At Puteoli, they found (εὑρόντες, nom. pl. masc. of aor. act. ptc. of εὑρίσκω; attend. circum.) the hospitality of other Christians (ἀδελφούς). Apparently, Christianity had spread to Italy apart from Paul (cf. Rom 1:13). Although there is a lack of archaeological evidence in the area (see Barrett 2.1230; BASHH 155) there is no reason to doubt the report; Puteoli was a cosmopolitan area. Παρεκλήθημεν (1st pl. aor. pass. indic. of παρακαλέω, "invite") takes an inf. of indir. speech ἐπιμεῖναι (aor. act. inf. of ἐπιμένω, "stay"). Εἰς τὴν Ῥώμην ("unto Rome") is fronted for emphasis, likely indicating the momentous occasion as part of the fulfillment of the vision at 27:24 (perhaps Ananias's vision at 9:15; and to some extent 1:8). Since they don't actually enter the city until v. 16, οὕτως likely indicates "this is how we made our way toward Rome" (Barrett 2.1230; Schnabel 1055) Ἤλθαμεν is the 1st pl. aor. act. indic. of ἔρχομαι (on the spelling, see Z §489).

FOR FURTHER STUDY

33. Ancient Sailing Practices

Cadbury, H. J. "Ὑποζώματα." In *Beginnings* 5, 345–53.
Hemer, C. "First Person Narration in Acts 27–28." *TynBul* 36 (1985): 75–109.
Lake, K., and H. Cadbury. "The Winds." In *Beginnings* 5, 338–44.
Rapske, B. "Acts, Travel, and Shipwreck." In BAFCS 2, 1–48.
———. *DNTB*, 1245–50.
Smith, J. *The Voyage and Shipwreck of St. Paul: with Dissertations on the Life and Writings of St. Luke, and the Ships and Navigation of the Ancients.* 4th ed. Revised by W. E. Smith. London: Longmans, Green, 1880.

28:15 The Christians in Rome (κἀκεῖθεν, crasis for καὶ ἐκεῖθεν, "from there") got news of Paul's arrival (ἀκούσαντες, acc. pl. masc. of aor. act. ptc. of ἀκούω; temp.). Ἦλθαν is the 3rd pl. aor. act. indic. of ἔρχομαι; on the ending, see v. 14. The prep. phrase εἰς ἀπάντησιν (acc. sg. fem. of ἀπάντησις, -εως, ἡ, "meeting") functions like an inf. of purp. mng. "to meet," fulfilling the hospitality customs of greeting and escorting arriving dignitaries to your city (see Bruce [*Acts of the Apostles*, 536] who notes 1 Thess 4:17). Ἀππίου (gen. sg. masc. of Ἀππίος, -ου, ὁ) φόρου (φόρον, -ου, τό) with the prep. is "as far as the Appian Market." It was a way station along the *Via Appia* (about forty miles southeast of Rome; Keener 4.3712; see BASHH 156). The other way station mentioned (likely indicating a second delegation, Schnabel 1056), Τριῶν ταβερνῶν (gen. pl. masc. of ταβέρναι, -ῶν, αἱ), "Three Taverns," was about nine miles closer to Rome. Ἰδών is the nom. sg. masc. of aor. act. ptc. of ὁράω; temp. Εὐχαριστήσας is the acc. sg. masc. of aor. act. ptc. of εὐχαριστέω; attend. circum. The phrase ἔλαβεν (3rd sg. aor. act. indic. of λαμβάνω) θάρσος (acc. sg. neut. of θάρσος, -ους, τό, "courage"; dir. obj.) is best tr. "he was encouraged" (NLT, NIV, TNIV). It was not that he was discouraged, but their presence was an emotional lift.

28:16 The entrance to Rome (εἰσήλθομεν, 1st pl. aor. act. indic. of εἰσέρχομαι) first notes Paul's custody conditions. Notably it is the last "we" ref. in the book (Bruce, *Acts of the Apostles*, 537). The phrase ἐπετράπη (3rd sg. aor. pass. indic. of ἐπιτρέπω) μένειν (pres. act. inf. of μένω; compl.), mng. "he was permitted to stay," is modified by καθ' ἑαυτόν (spatial, "by himself"). The ptc. φυλάσσοντι (dat. sg. masc. of pres. act. ptc. of φυλάσσω) takes αὐτόν as its obj. and is attrib. to στρατιώτῃ (dat. sg. masc. of στρατιώτης, -ου, ὁ, "soldier"; obj. of prep.); together, "with the soldier guarding him." The arrangements of a rented place, single soldier, and a single chain (28:20) represent the lightest form of custody in the Empire (*custodia liberior*) and demonstrates the respect Paul had earned as well as the threat level anticipated from him (Keener 4.3725–26).

HOMILETICAL SUGGESTIONS

Storms, Threats, and the Mission of God (27:1–44)

God works patiently to demonstrate his providence and fulfill his purposes

1. God often gives us warning signs that trouble lies ahead (vv. 1–8)
2. God will give us sound advice that is foolish to ignore (vv. 9–20)
3. God will grant us grace when we do start listening to him (vv. 21–44)

All work in concert to fulfill his purposes

God's Providence and Mission in the Meantime (28:1–16)

1. God's providence supplies a platform for the gospel (vv. 1–6)
2. God's providence supplies ministry and provision (vv. 7–10)
3. God's providence supplies safe route and housing at the destination (vv. 11–16)

2. Paul Preaches the Gospel Openly in Rome (28:17–31)

a. Meeting with the Jewish Leaders of Rome (28:17–29)

The penultimate scene in Acts is Paul's meeting with the Jewish leadership of Rome. It features the Jewish scuttlebutt regarding Christianity and arranging a meeting (vv. 17–22); the meeting itself (vv. 23–25); and a long quote from Isaiah 6 (vv. 26–28). Some have suggested that the citation indicates that the mission to Israel is over. The text does not suggest such a conclusion. Throughout the book, Luke has consistently maintained that the gospel is the fulfillment of OT promises and that it is for Israel. Paul stated both premises in this text (see vv. 20 and 23). It is likely that the orig. context as an initial call to Israel and a warning about judgment is applicable in the present position. Thus, the current status of ethnic Israel is that they are, by and large, rejecting the gospel although having a continual witness. The final statement about the Gentiles' reception of the gospel is expressed with an adv. καί, indicating not the rejection of ethnic Israel's opportunity but the sure inclusion of the Gentiles. It is most likely that Paul cited (and Luke included) the passage for a literary/theological statement regarding ethnic Israel and the gospel. As such, the call to continue preaching in the face of resistance is in the foreground. Furthermore, this status recalls Acts 1:6 and the question regarding the restoration of Israel. It appears the answer is still "be my witnesses."

28:17 On ἐγένετο δέ, see 4:5. Within his first week, Paul called a meeting (συγκαλέσασθαι, aor. mid. inf. of συγκαλέω). Αὐτόν is the subj. of the inf. The ptc. phrase that follows may be understood in three ways:

1. The ptc. ὄντας (acc. pl. masc. of pres. ptc. of εἰμί) τῶν Ἰουδαίων (part. gen., "of the Jews") is attrib. and means "the local Jews" (cf. 5:17). In this rdg. τοὺς . . . πρώτους is a subst. adj., the obj. of the inf. (Bruce, *Acts of the Apostles*, 538; RSV, NLT, NIV, NRSV, ESV, TNIV, NET).
2. Τούς may modify the ptc., making it subst., the acc. obj. of the inf. It would further take πρώτους as a pred. adj. mng. "the ones who were leading men among the Jews" (BHGNT 541; Schnabel 1066; KJV, NASB).

3. The ptc. of εἰμί may indicate some sort of technical naming convention: "those who bore the title . . ." (Barrett 2.1237). There is little to commend this understanding.

Συνελθόντων is the gen. sg. masc. of aor. act. ptc. of συνέρχομαι, "gather"; gen. abs., temp. The vb. ἔλεγεν (3rd sg. impf. act. indic. of λέγω) introduces dir. speech. It may either be a progressive or an inceptive impf. He first declares his innocence with the concessive ptc. ποιήσας (nom. sg. masc. of aor. act. ptc. of ποιέω), mng. "although I did nothing." It is modified by two dats. of disadvantage, λαῷ ("against the people") and ἔθεσιν (dat. pl. neut. of ἔθος, -ους, τό), with the poss. dat. πατρῴοις, mng. "the customs of our fathers." Παρεδόθην is the 1st sg. aor. pass. indic. of παραδίδωμι, "delivered." Εἰς τὰς χεῖρας τῶν Ῥωμαίων (gen. pl. masc. of Ῥωμαῖος, -α, -ον, "Roman") expresses the arrest as a destination, "unto the hands of the Romans."

28:18 On οἵτινες, see 7:53. Ἀνακρίναντές is the nom. pl. masc. of aor. act. ptc. of ἀνακρίνω, "examine"; temp. Ἐβούλοντο (3rd pl. impf. mid. indic. of βούλομαι) is compl. by ἀπολῦσαι (aor. act. inf. of ἀπολύω, "release"). The causal διά takes a neg. inf. ὑπάρχειν (pres. act. inf. of ὑπάρχω) that functions like an impers. vb., "because there was no. . . ." Αἰτίαν (acc. sg. fem. of αἰτία, -ας, ἡ, "cause") is the obj. of the inf.

28:19 The pres. tense of ἀντιλεγόντων (gen. pl. masc. of pres. act. ptc. of ἀντιλέγω, "speak against"; gen. abs., temp.) suggests repeated insistence by the Jews for Paul to remain in custody (Schnabel 1068). Thus, Paul felt compelled (ἠναγκάσθην, 1st sg. aor. pass. indic. of ἀναγκάζω, "compel, force") to appeal higher. Ἐπικαλέσασθαι (aor. mid. inf. of ἐπικαλέω, "appeal"; compl.) takes Καίσαρα (acc. sg. masc. of Καῖσαρ, -αρος, ὁ, "Caesar") as its obj. Paul was quick to point out he was not accusing his nation of anything. Ὡς with the ptc. ἔχων (nom. sg. masc. of pres. act. ptc. of ἔχω) gives the reason for an action (BDAG 1105a). Οὐχ ὡς is idiomatic functioning concessively, "not as if" (see BDF 430[3]). Κατηγορεῖν (pres. act. inf. of κατηγορέω, "charge") is epex. of τι.

28:20 The causal prep. διά is anaphoric (BHGNT 542). Παρεκάλεσα is the 1st sg. aor. act. indic. of παρακαλέω, "invite." Both ἰδεῖν (aor. act. inf. of ὁράω) and προσλαλῆσαι (aor. act. inf. of προσλαλέω, "address") are indir. speech. Ἐλπίδος τοῦ Ἰσραήλ (gen. obj. of prep.) is best understood to ref. the resurrection (see 24:15; 26:6–8; Keener 4.3744). Ἅλυσιν (acc. sg. fem. of ἅλυσις, -εως, ἡ, "chain, imprisonment"; dir. obj.) is fronted for emphasis. The phrase, with περίκειμαι (1st sg. pres. mid. indic. of περίκειμαι, "wear, have on"), is best tr. "I am wearing this chain" (NASB, ESV, NJB ["wear"]).

28:21 Οἱ functions as a pron., the subj. of εἶπαν (3rd pl. aor. act. indic. of λέγω). The response from the Roman Jews is in an οὔτε . . . οὔτε ("neither . . . nor") cstr. Ἡμεῖς" ("we") and γράμματα (acc. pl. neut. of γράμμα, -ατος, τό, "letters"; dir. obj.) are fronted for emphasis. Ἐδεξάμεθα is the 1st pl. aor. mid. indic. of δέχομαι. Τῆς Ἰουδαίας (gen. obj. of prep.) refers to the Judean leadership (cf. the usage in the Gospel of John). Nor had they heard oral reports. Παραγενόμενός (nom. sg. masc. of aor. mid. ptc. of παραγίνομαι, "arrive, be present"; attrib.) takes τις τῶν ἀδελφῶν (part. gen.) as the subj. It is best tr. "some of the brothers who came" (cf. KJV, NLT, NIV, TNIV). The difference between ἀπήγγειλεν (3rd sg. aor. act. indic. of ἀπαγγέλλω) and ἐλάλησέν (3rd sg. aor. act. indic. of λαλέω) is the difference between "official" and "unofficial" reports (Bruce, *Acts of the Apostles*, 539).

28:22 Ἀξιοῦμεν (1st pl. pres. act. indic. of ἀξιόω) is lit. "we deem it worthy"; most EVV tr. it idiomatically "we want to" or "we would like to." Ἀκοῦσαι is the aor. act. inf. of ἀκούω; compl. The rel. pron. phrase ἃ φρονεῖς (2nd sg. pres. act. indic. of φρονέω, "think") is the obj. of the inf. On μέν, see 1:1. Γνωστόν (nom. sg. neut. of γνωστός, -ή, -όν) is the pred. adj. of an impers. ἐστιν, best tr. "it is known to us" (= γινώσκομεν). Ὅτι indicates the content of the knowledge. Πανταχοῦ ἀντιλέγεται (3rd sg. pres. pass. indic. of ἀντιλέγω) is best "denounced everywhere" (NLT).

28:23 Ταξάμενοι is the nom. pl. masc. of aor. mid. ptc. of τάσσω, "appoint"; temp. Αὐτῷ is a dat. of advantage, "for him." The obj. of the prep., ξενίαν (acc. sg. fem. of ξενία, -ας, ἡ), is lit. "hospitality" but best understood to be a place of lodging (Johnson 470; Witherington 801; ZG 455; cf. Phlm 22). Πλείονες (nom. pl. masc. comp. of πολύς, πολλή, πολύ) ref. to more than the previous meeting (ZG 455; possibly ela- tive mng. "in great numbers," so Barrett 2.1243). The rel. pron. οἷς (the antecedent is πλείονες) is the indir. obj. of ἐξετίθετο (3rd sg. impf. indic. act. of ἐκτίθημι, "explain"). Διαμαρτυρόμενος (nom. sg. masc. of pres. mid. ptc. of διαμαρτύρομαι) is likely means, "by testifying" (possibly attend. circum.; BHGNT 545). The same goes for πείθων (nom. sg. masc. of pres. act. ptc. of πείθω). On τε, see 1:15. The objs. βασιλείαν and Ἰησοῦ specify the content as "the gospel" and "the Messiah" (Schnabel 1071). The source is specified by a τε . . . καί cstr. "the Law" and "the Prophets." That the time was ἀπὸ πρωΐ (temp. adv., "early in the morning") ἕως ἑσπέρας (gen. sg. fem. of ἑσπέρα, -ας, ἡ, "evening"), together, "from early morning to evening," with the pres. ptc. suggests a progressive event.

28:24 The response is expressed with a μέν . . . δέ cstr., each part with a nom. pl. masc. art. (οἱ) functioning as a pron. subj. mng. "some" (a CGk. cstr., Barrett 2.1244). Ἐπείθοντο is the 3rd pl. impf. indic. pass. of πείθω, "some were being persuaded." Λεγομένοις is the dat. pl. neut. of pres. pass. ptc. of λέγω; means. Ἠπίστουν is the 3rd pl. impf. act. indic. of ἀπιστέω, "they were unbelieving." The contrast between persuaded and unbelief suggests the former became disciples (Barrett 2.1244; Keener 4.3750; Schnabel 1071), although some disagree (Bruce, *Acts of the Apostles*, 540; Haenchen 724).

28:25 Ἀσύμφωνοι (nom. pl. masc. of ἀσύμφωνος, -ον, "in disagreement"; subst.; NT hapax) is the pred. adj. of ὄντες (nom. pl. masc. of pres. ptc. of εἰμί; most likely causal), together with πρὸς ἀλλήλους, mng. "because they disagreed with each other." Ἀπελύοντο (3rd pl. impf. mid. indic. of ἀπολύω), an inceptive impf. in the mid., is "they began to leave" (cf. CSB, NASB, NIV, NET). The next ptc. phrase is often described as the impetus for the departure as a temp. ptc. (Barrett 2.1244) or as a ptc. of result, the last word as they were filing out (Bruce, *Acts of the Apostles*, 540). Since the stated reason for breaking up was the disagreement, it is more likely the latter. However, it should not be considered as a classic "Parthian shot" because that is more vitriolic than this situation suggests. It is more like a sad commentary on the spiritual state of Israel. Εἰπόντος (gen. sg. masc. of aor. act. ptc. of λέγω; gen. abs.) is likely result, "so Paul spoke one word." The aor. here would not need to represent action before the main vb. (BHGNT 545), but since the departure is in progress, it is not necessarily after they are gone either. Ὅτι introduces dir. speech. The adv. καλῶς here has the connotation of "correctly" (Haenchen 724). That it was the Holy Spirit who speaks demonstrates Paul's belief in the inspiration of Scripture, for it is the voice of Yahweh speaking in Isa 6:9–10 (Barrett 2.1244).

28:26 Λέγων (nom. sg. masc. of pres. act. ptc. of λέγω) introduces a dir. quote from the LXX, Isa 6:9–10. Πορεύθητι is the 2nd sg. aor. pass. impv. of πορεύομαι, "go." Εἰπόν is the 2nd sg. aor. act. impv. of λέγω. The expression employing a cognate dat. and a fut. (ἀκοῇ ἀκούσετε [2nd pl. fut. act. indic. of ἀκούω]) is a rather literal tr. of the Heb. qal inf. cstr. mng. "you will surely hear." Here and at 13:41 (both OT quotes) are the only appearances of the emphatic neg. οὐ μή in Acts. Συνῆτε is the 2nd pl. aor. act. subjunc. of συνίημι, "understand." The same Heb. cstr. is repeated with βλέποντες (nom. pl. masc. of pres. act. ptc.) βλέψετε (2nd pl. fut. act. indic.) and ἴδητε (2nd pl. aor. act. subjunc. of ὁράω). In spite of intently hearing and seeing, the people will neither understand nor perceive.

28:27 Γάρ indicates the grounds for their blindness. The state of the heart, ears, and eyes is balanced by the result of that state in a chiastic str. The heart "has grown dull" (ἐπαχύνθη, 3rd sg. aor. pass. indic. of παχύνω). The other organs of perception are various objs. of vbs. The ears (ὠσίν, dat. pl. neut. of οὖς, -ωτός, τό; dat. of means) and βαρέως ἤκουσαν (3rd pl aor. act. indic. of ἀκούω) means "they hardly hear with their ears." The eyes (ὀφθαλμούς, acc. pl. masc. of ὀφθαλμός, -οῦ, ὁ) and ἐκάμμυσαν (3rd pl. aor. act. indic. of καμμύω) means "they closed their eyes." The result (μήποτε, "lest") is expressed with 3rd pl. aor. act. subjuncs. and dats. of means: ἴδωσιν (of ὁράω), ὀφθαλμοῖς (masc. pl. of ὀφθαλμός, -οῦ, ὁ); ὠσίν (neut pl. of οὖς, -ωτός, τό; fronted), ἀκούσωσιν (of ἀκούω); καρδίᾳ; συνῶσιν (of συνίημι, "understand, comprehend"). The ultimate result they avert is conversion (ἐπιστρέψωσιν, 3rd pl. aor. act. subjunc. of ἐπιστρέφω) and healing (ἰάσομαι, 1st sg. fut. mid. indic. of ἰάομαι). The chilling reality is that God brings judgment "upon people who go on too long and too far in rejecting his message to them" (Beale and Carson 601).

28:28 Γνωστόν (nom. sg. neut. of γνωστός, -ή, -όν) is a pred. adj. to Ἔστω (3rd sg. pres. impv. of εἰμί), "let it be known," announcing a solemn statement. Ὅτι introduces the content of the announcement. Paul's proclamation has been interpreted in the past as a renunciation and shutting off of Israel (see Bock 756 for details). The Gentiles (ἔθνεσιν, dat. pl. neut. of ἔθνος, -ους, τό; indir. obj., fronted for emphasis) are included as objects of the gospel, not replacing Israel. Ἀπεστάλη is the 3rd sg. aor. pass. indic. of ἀποστέλλω. This salvation (τοῦτο τὸ σωτήριον) is modified by τοῦ θεοῦ. It is either poss. (cf. NIV) or source (cf. NET); both suggest Paul has not created it. Although some EVV make καί copulative (cf. NIV), or ignore it (most EVV), by position, it must be adv., "also." (cf. NASB). In this case, it strengthens the vb. ἀκούσονται (3rd pl. fut. mid. indic. of ἀκούω). It is rather prophetic, promising a positive response. This is the third such statement in Acts (see 13:46–47 and 18:6; Schnabel 1075). In neither previous text did the gospel ever stop being preached to the Jews. In fact, individual Jews repented and came to Christ, while the nation largely rejected him as Messiah. There is no reason to suggest Paul's statements here should not be taken in the same light. The gospel is for everybody, Jews included.

28:29 The v. in the *byz.* seems to be a Western expansion of the text (although several Western txts. omit it (e.g., it^e it^ro it^s). Although the inclusion is geographically widely distributed, these mss. are later. Furthermore, since it is easier to explain its existence as an improvement to an abruptly ended scene than its removal, it is best to assume it was an addition (see Metzger 444).

b. Conclusion: Paul's Extended Imprisonment (28:30–31)

28:30 Luke's final statements wrap up the narrative. Ἐνέμεινεν is the 3rd sg. aor. act. indic. of ἐμμένω, "remain." Διετίαν (acc. sg. fem. of διετία, -ας, ἡ, "two years") ὅλην, "two whole years," expresses complete years and not inclusive parts of a year. Ἰδίῳ μισθώματι (dat. sg. neut. of μίσθωμα, -ατος, τό, "a rented house"; obj. of prep.) refers to personally rented quarters (cf. vv. 16 and 23). It is likely he is still chained to a soldier, but guests are permitted freely. These he received gladly (ἀπεδέχετο, 3rd sg. impf. mid. indic. of ἀποδέχομαι). Εἰσπορευομένους (acc. pl. masc. of pres. mid. ptc. of εἰσπορεύομαι; subst., dir. obj.) πρὸς αὐτόν is "those who came to him."

28:31 Luke's abbreviation of the message to the Jews in v. 23 is repeated. Paul preaches (κηρύσσων, nom. sg. masc. of pres. act. ptc. of κηρύσσω; manner [modifying ἐνέμεινεν in v. 30]) the kingdom of God (i.e., the gospel). And he teaches (διδάσκων, nom. sg. masc. of pres. act. ptc. of διδάσκω; manner) the nature of the Messiah. Both are characterized by παρρησίας ("boldness"). The last word of the book is an adv. that makes Luke's point. The gospel is preached and taught boldly and without hindrance (ἀκωλύτως). Throughout the book the message of Christ has traveled through opposition and hardship, under the direction and provision of the risen Christ, to the uttermost parts of the earth. Furthermore, it continued to be so.

FOR FURTHER STUDY

34. The Ending of Acts (28:30–31)

Davies, P. "The Ending of Acts." *ExpTim* 94 (1983): 334–35.
Mealand, D. L. "The Close of Acts and Its Hellenistic Greek Vocabulary." *NTS* 36 (1990): 583–97.
Troftgruben, T. M. *A Conclusion Unhindered: A Study of the Ending of Acts within Its Literary Environment.* WUNT 2/280. Tübingen: Mohr Siebeck, 2010.
Winters, G. P. "With a Whimper or a Bang? Acts 28 and the Ending of Acts." *RTR* 74 (2015): 1–14.

HOMILETICAL SUGGESTIONS

The Hope for Humanity (28:17–31)

1. The gospel is the fulfillment of the OT: the hope for Israel (vv. 17–22)
2. The gospel is also the only hope for Gentiles (vv. 23–28)
3. The Christian should proclaim it openly to all (vv. 30–31)

Exegetical Outline

I. Foundations for the Church and Her Mission (1:1–2:47)

   A. Preliminary Steps (1:1–14)

      1. Review of Jesus's Ministry and Instructions (1:1–5)
      2. The Ascension of Jesus (1:6–14)

   B. The Replacement of Judas (1:15–26)
   C. Pentecost: The Church Is Born (2:1–47)

      1. The Event: The Exalted Jesus Sends the Spirit (2:1–4)
      2. The Evidence of the Spirit's Coming: Foreign Languages (2:5–13)
      3. The Explanation: Peter's Message (2:14–40)

         a. Peter Identifies the Event (2:14–21)
         b. Peter Proclaims the Resurrection of Jesus (2:22–24)
         c. Scriptural Support for the Resurrection of the Messiah (2:25–32)
         d. The Implications (2:33–36)
         e. The Response of the Hearers (2:37–40)

      4. The Expansion: The Growth of the Early Church (2:41–47)

II. The Early Church in Jerusalem (3:1–6:7)

   A. A Miracle and Its Aftermath (3:1–4:31)

      1. The Miracle (3:1–10)
      2. Peter's Temple Sermon (3:11–26)
      3. The Aftermath: Peter and John's Arrest and Bold Witness (4:1–31)

   B. Trouble Within and Without (4:32–6:7)

      1. The Sharing of Property in the Early Church: A Good Example (4:32–37)
      2. The Sharing of Property in the Early Church: A Bad Example (5:1–11)
      3. Further Growth in Numbers and Geographical Extension (5:12–16)

A. First Missionary Journey (12:25–14:28)

   1. Syrian Antioch: Sent Out (12:25–13:3)
   2. Cyprus: Proconsul Sergius Paulus Believes (13:4–12)
   3. Pisidian Antioch: Gentiles Believe despite Jewish Opposition (13:13–52)

      a. In the Synagogue (13:13–16)
      b. Paul's Sermon (13:17–41)

         1) Israel until David's Greater Son (13:17–25)
         2) The Gospel (13:26–37)
         3) Paul's Appeal (13:38–41)

      c. The Response (13:42–52)

   4. South Galatia: Iconium, Derbe, Lystra (14:1–23)

      a. Iconium (14:1–7)
      b. Lystra and Derbe (14:8–23)

   5. Return to Syrian Antioch (14:24–28)

B. Jerusalem Council (15:1–35)

   1. Setting (15:1–5)
   2. The Formal Council: Dispute and Testimony (15:6–12)
   3. James's Response on Behalf of the Jerusalem Church (15:13–21)
   4. The Letter Sent to the Gentile Churches (15:22–29)
   5. Return to Syrian Antioch (15:30–35)

C. Second Missionary Journey Begins (15:36–16:5)

   1. Paul and Barnabas Separate (15:36–41)
   2. Paul and Silas Deliver Decisions of Jerusalem Council, Take Timothy (16:1–5)

VI. The Gentile Mission: Part 2, Greece (16:6–19:20)

A. Continuing the Second Missionary Journey (16:6–18:23)

   1. Ministry in Philippi (16:6–40)

      a. Paul's Vision of the Macedonian (16:6–10)
      b. The First Converts in Europe (16:11–15)
      c. Disturbance in Philippi (16:16–24)
      d. Deliverance in Custody (16:25–34)
      e. Final Adjudication (16:35–40)

   2. Ministry in Thessalonica (17:1–9)
   3. Ministry in Berea (17:10–15)
   4. Ministry in Athens (17:16–34)

      a. Paul's Arrival (17:16–21)
      b. Paul's Speech on the Areopagus (17:22–34)

D. Paul's Trip to Rome (27:1–28:31)

   1. Sea Voyage and Shipwreck (27:1–28:16)

      a.   From Caesarea to Fair Havens (27:1–8)
      b.   Storm and Shipwreck (27:9–44)
      c.   Provision and Ministry on Malta (28:1–9)
      d.   Journey to Rome (28:10–16)

   2. Paul Preaches the Gospel Openly in Rome (28:17–31)

      a.   Meeting with the Jewish Leaders of Rome (28:17–29)
      b.   Conclusion: Paul's Extended Imprisonment (28:30–31)

Grammar Index

Scripture Index